The Country Life Book of the

Living History of Britain

The *Country Life Book of the*

Living History of Britain

Consultant Editor: Professor Emeritus W.G.V. Balchin

BOOK CLUB ASSOCIATES
LONDON

This edition published 1981 by
Book Club Associates.
By arrangement with Country Life Books,
The Hamlyn Publishing Group Limited
London . New York . Sydney . Toronto

Printed in Spain
by Printer industria gráfica sa
Sant Vicenç dels Horts   Barcelona   D.L.B. 18208-1981

Created by
Stan Morse,
Midsummer Books Limited

Editor
Trisha Palmer

Designer
Rod Teasdale

Editorial assistance
Penny Holmes
Valerie Noel-Finch
Aubrey Lawrence

Consultant editor
Professor Emeritus W.G.V. Balchin MA (Cantab),
    PhD (London), FRGS, FRMetS

Authors
John Beavis BA
Chris Bushell
Chris Chant MA (Oxon)
Christopher Coleman MA (Cantab)
John Creasey MA
Martin Daunton MA, PhD
Brian Golding MA, DPhil
David Hall BA (Hons), DipEd
John Hall BSc
Negley Harte BSc (Econ), FRHistS
Brenda Innes BA (OU) Hons
John Lowerson MA
N. J. Mayhew MA and C. E. King DPhil
Pat Morris BSc, PhD
John Myerscough BA
Edward W. Paget-Tomlinson MA
Ron Pigram MCIT
Richard Reece BSc, DPhil, FSA
Richard Roberts BA
John Rule MA, PhD
Geoffrey Tyack MA, MLitt
Gillian M. Tyler BA, PhD
Adrian Vinson BA
Sadie Ward BA, PhD
Martin Welch MA, DPhil
Nigel Yates MA, FRHistS

Typesetting
SX Composing Ltd

Colour reproduction
Process Colour Scanning Ltd
Culvergraphics Ltd
Bantam Litho Ltd
J. T. Graphics Ltd

Film work
Precise Litho Ltd

Monotone reproduction
Tenreck Ltd

Artists
Dave Etchell
John Ridyard
Helen Senior
Falcon Hildred
Keith Fretwell
Rachel Birkett/The Garden Studio
Michael Fisher/The Garden Studio
John Marshall/Temple Art
Dave Richardson
John Burrell
Roy Castle
Peter North
Colin Barker
Clive Spong
Fred Anderson/The Garden Studio
Owain Bell/The Garden Studio
E. Scott Jones(The Garden Studio
Angus Grey-Burbage/The Garden Studio

Contents

———◆———

This book is dedicated to
W. G. Hoskins CBE
whose pioneering work
THE MAKING OF THE ENGLISH LANDSCAPE
provided the inspiration for this volume

Foreword

Britain possesses one of the richest and most fascinating histories of all countries on Earth. It is a history of early Man first visiting and then settling in a group of islands on the north western edge of the European Continent. It is the story of their creativity, invention and enterprise. And it is the story of a landscape crafted over generations to fit exactly the civilisation it supported.

That history has provided the basis of our society; we are as much a product of it as it is of us. It is the foundation of our pride and self-confidence which has stood us in good stead in troubled times past. It is a living history.

But history can be destroyed more quickly than it is made. Early Man came to these islands and found them mostly thickly wooded or covered by marsh and fen. That has all but gone. He grazed his stock on the cleared downlands and for five thousand years created a classic landscape rich in wild flowers and insects. Modern agricultural practice has seen that virtually destroyed in one generation. Britain's present heritage was largely created in the towns and farmlands of the Industrial and Agricultural Revolutions of the 18th and 19th centuries. The buildings which bore witness to those revolutions now mostly lie in ruins, and with them the special crafts and cultures that bound their communities together.

While few regret the passing of the poverty and injustices of those times, there is much spiritual value in the fabric that remains. Our museums do a fine job in preserving the objects and paraphernalia of the past, and the new 'living museums' greatly extend their scope. But should our contact with our history be reduced to visiting it in museums while our real environmental heritage, the towns and countryside of our grandparents and their forefathers, is in danger of being demolished, lost and forgotten? There will always be an argument for demolishing a Victorian warehouse in favour of a car park, a town centre for a shopping precinct, a thatched barn for an asbestos shed, a street of artisans' cottages for a high rise estate. But what will we have when it has all gone? What pride can our future citizens have in their world if we show little regard for ours?

The maintenance of our environmental past is clearly a worthwhile objective. The remedy is undoubtedly costly, for it is not easy for an advancing society to maintain buildings erected in previous eras or to readopt farming practices of the past. But the driving force is understanding, knowledge and care.

We hope that this book contributes to that cause and that future generations will be able to enjoy and receive fulfilment from the heritage that we leave them in this wonderful country of ours.

May 1981   W. G. V. Balchin

42

The Birth of Britain

*The emergence of the British Isles is a very recent
geological event in the 4,600 million years of Earth's history. Before Man's
arrival there had been tremendous geological activity with the land
that was to become Britain being submerged under the ocean, raised to Himalayan heights,
buried by molten lava, torn apart by earthquakes and frozen under sheet
ice before emerging as the islands of today.*

The entire history of Man is merely the tip of an historical iceberg; this dominant, destructive bipedal mammal is an evolutionary upstart. Man and his ape-like forebears have existed for a mere two million years, and despite all the changes he has wrought during his stay, especially during the last few hundred years, we should not forget that the earth existed for over 4,600 million years without him. So where should we begin the history of Britain? The life and landscape of this country still owe their basic character to natural processes; human intervention is only a cosmetic for the countryside, changing and reshaping the surface of what was already there.

The geological foundations of this country were laid nearly 3,000 million years ago when the rocks of the Hebrides and western Highlands were formed from volcanic eruptions. But the land we call Britain has not always been the same size, shape or structure as it is today; its history has been one of continuous change, parts of it at different times being invaded by swampy forests, gouged by glaciers, buried under mud, baked in the sun, rent by earthquakes and smothered in molten lava. For long periods our section of the earth's surface was not land at all, but sea bed.

At various times there have been major upheavals in the surface of the earth, raising the sea bed to form dry land or even folding layers of rock over each other like crumpled bedclothes. At other times, the sea level rose to inundate land which had been formed millions of years earlier under a quite different sea. None of these changes was very abrupt, and relatively constant conditions, often very different from today's, may have persisted for millions of years. These long periods of different characteristic conditions are called the geological epochs, and each has left us a legacy of particular rock types formed at that time, often as a result of reforming the land that already existed.

Past climatic changes wiped out many forms of life which could not cope with the new circumstances, and also provided fresh opportunities for the advancement of new and different types. A record of the extinct species was sometimes preserved in the form of fossils which now help us to interpret the nature of past environments. For example, probably the whole of England and Wales was covered by sea in Silurian times (400–450 million years ago) leaving as evidence fossil marine animals like corals and sea lilies preserved in the sediments formed on the sea bed at that time, whereas fossils from the Carboniferous period (270–350 million years ago) are more characteristic of warm swamps and include giant dragonflies and many ferns. In both examples the muds and silts in which the dead animals and plants lay were later compressed and hardened into the rocks we see today.

So the essence of Britain's geological history is change, each new set of circumstances giving rise to different rocks and geological features which are the major determining factors of our scenery, wildlife, towns, farms and industries today. Few places in the world contain so much geological history compressed into so small an area, hence the diversity

Planet Earth
The Earth is part of a solar family of nine major planets that revolve continuously around the Sun in elliptical orbits. Planet Earth is nearly 8,000 miles in diameter, a distance of some 93,000,000 miles from the Sun, and travels at 18.5 miles per second.

Additionally, the Earth rotates on an axis which is tilted relative to its elliptical orbit: the rotation produces night and day, and the tilt of the axis the seasons. The Earth is the only part of the solar system with known life upon it.

Britain from space (left). Part of the British Isles seen from an orbiting satellite in space. The immediate foreground covers the counties of Devon, Cornwall and South Wales, with the English Channel to the right and the Bristol Channel to the left. Altostratus cloud covers much of the North Sea.

of our landscapes; a day's car journey can pass through forest, rolling hills, along sandy and rocky coasts, past rivers and lakes and end up by a rushing stream on open moorland. Most of these places will have been radically altered by man during the last 10,000 years to provide a kaleidoscope of scenery, itself a major stimulus to the rich diversification of plants and animals that share this country with us.

The geological inheritance

The physical and chemical properties of rock dictate the shape of the land, the soil that covers it and the types of farming that may be pursued in different places. These are essential aspects of our living landscape today. The general pattern has been for each subsequent epoch to leave behind a contribution to our geology, with the deposits becoming progressively more recent towards the south and east (though locally there are many small areas of recent deposits elsewhere). The oldest rocks tend to be hardest; if they were

not they would have been eroded away long ago. Consequently, the scenery to the north and west, dating from the pre-Cambrian period over 600 million years ago, consists of hard erosion-resistant rocks which not only produce a rather angular landscape, but profoundly affect practically every form of life occurring in these regions. Conversely, the softer rocks (like chalk and limestone) weather readily and form low, rounded, rolling hills. Limestone is hard enough to use for stone walling, a characteristic feature in appropriate areas; but chalk is younger and too soft for this and hedgerows or fences dominate its landscape.

The most recent geological deposits are those like sand, gravel and clay which are often still being formed today along rivers and in estuaries. These are sediments that sink from flowing water, the coarser particles (gravel) settling first while the water movement is still brisk and the finest particles (mud) settling out last when the water is almost stationary in lakes and estuaries. Sedimentation leaves

BRITAIN BEFORE MAN

Britain as we know it is of recent age compared with the 4,600 million years of Earth history. The molten mass which had become detached from the Sun had first to cool and a crust had then to form. This was followed by the development of an atmosphere and the oceans before the essential geological agents which were to fashion the Earth's history could begin to operate. Throughout geological time we find a continuous interplay between volcanic eruptions, the creation of sedimentary rocks from eroded igneous rocks, mountain building episodes and marine incursions, all shaping and reshaping the continents and oceans. Modern theory favours the idea of crustal plates continually growing by the addition of new volcanic material at their edges in mid ocean, by a process known as sea floor spreading. The movement of these tectonic plates neatly explains past and

present locations of most mountain zones, volcanoes and continental masses.

Before the British Isles began to emerge, however, the area had first to experience several major periods of mountain building with intervening periods of prolonged erosion.

Britain 250 million years ago was part of a super-continent which was destined to split into Eurasia, the Americas, Africa, Australia and Antarctica. Areas of rifting and subsidence were to widen into oceans as the continents drifted apart. The tensions and compressions of ocean floor spreading and mountain building created an ever-changing geography of land, rivers, lakes and seas in which igneous and volcanic intrusive rocks were mixed with sedimentary clays, sandstones, limestones and chalk to form the basis of the present day geological formations.

An artist's impression of the surface of the Earth as the molten mass began to crust over some 4,000 million years ago.

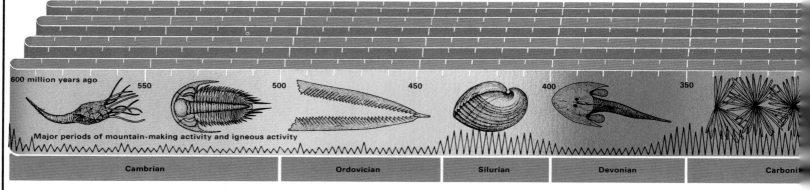

600 million years ago   550   500   450   400   350

Major periods of mountain-making activity and igneous activity

| Cambrian | Ordovician | Silurian | Devonian | Carboni |

Permian Britain 250 million years ago. Arid deserts, wind-blown sand and deltaic flats dominate the landscape.

Jurassic
A seascape of about 170 million years ago, showing reptilian ichthyosaurs (rear), plesiosaur (pursuing cuttlefish, centre) and bat-winged pterosaurs, together with shark (left). Clays and limestones were laid down in the Jurassic seas and these deposits, subsequently tilted in the Alpine mountain building movements, now form the scarp and dip slopes of the Cotswolds. Blooms of plankton also produced oil shales in the North Sea area.

Cretaceous
A landscape of sub-tropical vegetation of conifers and cycads, with the reptile Iguanodon and pterosaurs (flying reptiles) — a typical scene in the Wealden area about 100 million years ago. Later in this period, Britain was blanketed in chalk mud which was subsequently consolidated and elevated by the Alpine mountain building movement to form the chalk Downs of south east England.

material in horizontal layers, so land thus created is rather flat and ideal for building on, especially near rivers. Hence the siting of many of our cities.

Lowlands tend to accumulate useful minerals and organic material washed down by the rain from higher ground, so their soils tend to be richer and, being flat, are prime sites for arable farming. The old uplands tend to have poor, shallow soils because rain washes away nutrients and particles from the steep slopes. Flatter upland ground is often waterlogged because hard, old rocks are dense and relatively impermeable and so impede drainage. Consequently our uplands are unsuitable for extensive arable farming (the climate is frequently too severe anyway) and grazing is the normal form of agriculture there today. Grazing generally earns less money than arable farming, so the uplands are often poor and the farmers may need subsidies to help them remain there. Depopulation of the uplands (and the Scottish islands, which suffer from similar geological limitations) is thus an economic

inevitability and has resulted in many social and economic problems. Hence the efforts made by the Forestry Commission to transform huge areas of unproductive uplands into forests to provide potential wealth and jobs in these geologically disadvantaged areas, but afforestation programmes profoundly change the scenery and wildlife of a region. Upland areas, because of their open character, tend to be regarded as 'scenic' and 'natural', and it is no coincidence that most of our National Parks are sited in such places.

Different types of rock are of interest, not only to the geologist and naturalist but to the historian too; generations of builders have constructed the houses, churches and walls of Britain from the products of our geological epochs. The physical properties of rocks allow some to be elegantly sculpted and others to support massive loads or resist weathering and damage. Individual rock types can be recognised as coming from particular quarries or regions, shedding some light on past patterns of trade and transport.

Pre-Cambrian
A scene about 3,800 million years ago. The beginning of an oceanic area is visible with early traces of sedimentary and volcanic rocks. In Britain, much of the Lewisian gneiss of Scotland originates in this period but was subsequently buried to great depths and altered (metamorphosed) by repeated deformation and recrystallisation.

Ordovician
By the Ordovician period, some 450–500 million years ago, the foundations of the Britain we know today were being laid. Muds and sandstones destined to become shales were being deposited in shallow seas trapping early fossils known as brachiopods, trilobites and graptolites. Volcanic activity was also a feature of this period.

The Evolution of Life
The planet Earth first came into existence 4,600 million years ago, but for nearly 90 per cent of this time it was barren and supported no life.

Carboniferous Britain some 300 million years ago. Swamps and tropical forest covered the land between successive marine incursions, eventually to form coal seams.

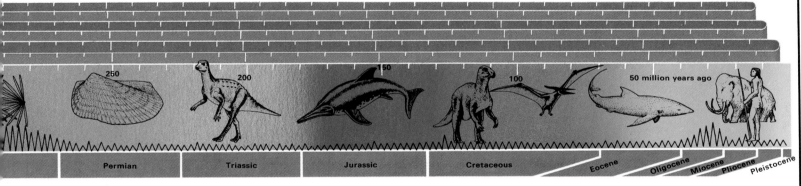

| 250 | 200 | 150 | 100 | 50 million years ago |

| Permian | Triassic | Jurassic | Cretaceous | Eocene | Oligocene | Miocene | Pliocene | Pleistocene |

Late Cretaceous. An impression of the sea floor on which fragmented hard parts of planktonic algae (coccoliths) were laid to form the chalk.

Pleistocene interglacial period
The million years of Pleistocene time were marked by several successive advances and retreats of vast ice sheets from the Polar areas: glacial and interglacial periods respectively. This diorama illustrates an interglacial landscape associated with Swanscombe Man – the earliest human fossil remains found in Britain, and dating from the late Hoxnian Interglacial about 250,000 years ago.

Pleistocene glacial period
A glacial landscape about 200,000 years ago when most of Britain north of the Thames was covered with ice and the woolly mammoth roamed southern England. Many of our present landscape features are the result of Pleistocene ice erosion, for example: U-shaped valleys, fjords, overflow channels, corries and lakes; or deposition, such as erratics, glacial gravels, boulder clay and fluvioglacial deposits. Highland Britain, in particular, has been subject to glaciation.

Volcanic material welling up from deep in the earth's crust is of interest to the historian because it often contains high concentrations of metallic oxides and sulphides which intrude into cracks in other rocks and solidify to form the rich lodes eagerly sought by miners in the past and on which whole industries have been based since the Bronze Age. Similarly the humid stinking swamps of the Carboniferous epoch which covered the north east of England, the Midlands and South Wales millions of years ago have also shaped our recent human history by providing in those places the coal on which cities and industries have flourished and from which stem major social advances and evils. The proximity of many different geological riches to each other, so characteristic of this country, was a major reason for the growth of industrial cities based on them and the Industrial Revolution which Britain began and exported to the world.

The Ice Ages

The basic framework of our land was gradually built up over millions of years and each of the major epochs made its contribution to Britain's geological richness. Then, between one and two million years ago the geological 'finishing touches' were added by the Pleistocene Ice Ages, remodelling the land and setting up the familiar shape and form of Britain for Man to take over. Colloquially we often speak of *the* Ice Age, but in fact there were at least four of them. During these glacial periods the polar ice cap advanced to cover most of Britain and northern Europe for thousands of years. In between times, during the long interglacials, our climate was often warm and humid (much like parts of Africa today).

When ice, in the form of glaciers, creeps across the landscape it obliterates all life in its path. It flattens and smoothes, grinds and gouges, thus modifying the underlying rock in characteristic ways to form round bottomed valleys and cirques (corries) in the mountains. Moving ice carries boulders with it, scraping characteristic grooves in the bedrock. The boulders are ground together and reduced to stones and mud, a mass of which is left behind as a moraine when the ice recedes. Some of these moraines form prominent hills and ridges today. Melting glaciers caused large rivers to spread extensive deposits of muds and gravel over their flood plains, and later the same rivers, reduced in size, would cut new courses through the material they laid down earlier, leaving flat 'terraces' on their banks. These are very obvious in the Thames Valley and London is built on a series of old river terraces.

The advance of Arctic conditions caused the extinction of most of our plants and animals each time it happened. During the most severe glaciation, ice extended as far south as the Thames and the periglacial climate was so severe that few things could survive even in the unglaciated areas. The board was wiped clean, ready for new plants and animals to colonise the land when the ice finally melted due to a warming of the climate.

The last glaciation was less severe than some of its predecessors and it is likely that some of our hardier plants and animals lived through it; if Britain had always been an island these are probably the only native species we would have here today. However, during the whole of Pleistocene times, we were still a part of the European land mass, so that when warmer conditions returned during the interglacials, it was possible for land animals to spread into this country from the south. Plants too could extend their range northwards, bit by bit each year, and thus colonise Britain from the Continent.

THE GEOLOGY OF BRITAIN

The geology of Britain is dominated by a major dividing line running from the Exe to the Tees estuaries. North west of this line is Highland Britain, a mountainous zone where the rocks are old, hard, metamorphosed and Palaeozoic in age: south east of the line is lowland Britain, with a scarp and dip slope topography of younger, softer sedimentary rocks of Mesozoic and Cenozoic age. Except for an area south of a line from the Severn to the Thames estuaries the whole country has been further subject to the more recent Pleistocene glaciation.

In the Highland zone intrusive igneous and volcanic rocks, mainly granites, gabbros, basalts, rhyolites and tuffs, often form the basement complex and are frequently exposed. These are succeeded by metamorphic Precambrian gneisses some 2000 million years old.

The main sequence of Palaeozoic rocks then follows with ages between 600–230 million years: Cambrian slates and sandstones, Ordovician shales and mudstones, Silurian greywackes and limestones, Devonian sandstones and conglomerates, Carboniferous limestones and coal seams, Permian marls and magnesian limestones all mark distinctive Palaeozoic accumulation phases and provide the basis for modern rugged mountainous scenes.

In the Lowland zone the Mesozoic rocks are all sedimentary in origin and have been formed within the last 230 million years. Triassic marls and sandstones, Jurassic limestones and clays, Cretaceous chalks and clays were eroded in the Cenozoic era to form a scarp and dip topography which has been further modified by Pliocene marine action and Pleistocene glaciation.

Magheramorne Quarry, Co. Antrim, Northern Ireland. Tertiary basalt lavas (top of picture) resting upon chalk of Upper Cretaceous age (bottom). A magnificent example of an unconformity marking a major break in the geological sequence.

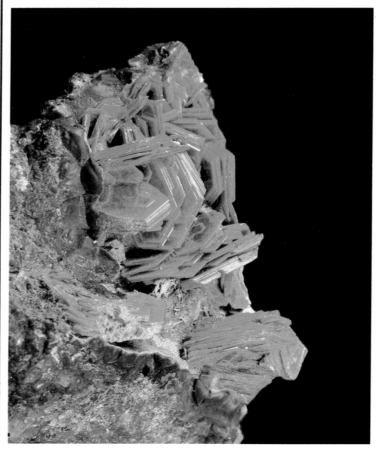

Chalcophyllite, Cornwall. Crystals may result from evaporation of a solution or the cooling of a melt; if the conditions of growth allow, they will be bounded by naturally formed plane faces. This leaf-like crystallisation is impregnated with copper.

Key

SEDIMENTARY ROCKS

CENOZOIC

Tertiary and marine Pleistocene
Mainly clays and sands
Pleistocene glacial drift not
shown   up to 65

MESOZOIC

Cretaceous Mainly chalk, clays
and sands   65–140

Jurassic Mainly limestones and
clays   140–195

Triassic Marls, sandstones and
conglomerates   195–230

PALAEOZOIC

Permian Mainly magnesian
limestones, marls and
sandstones   230–280

Carboniferous Limestones,
sandstones, shales and coal
seams   280–345

Devonian Sandstones, shales,
conglomerates (Old Red
Sandstone); slates and
limestones   345–395

Silurian Shales, mudstones,
greywacke; some limestones
                                    395–445

Ordovician Mainly shales and
mudstones; limestone in
Scotland   445–510

Cambrian Mainly shales, slate
and sandstones; limestone in
Scotland   510–570

UPPER PROTEROZOIC

Late Precambrian Mainly
sandstones, conglomerates and
siltstones   600–1000

METAMORPHIC ROCKS

**Lower Palaeozoic and
Proterozoic** Mainly schists and
gneisses   500–1000

Early Precambrian (Lewisian)
Mainly gneisses   1500 to 3000

IGNEOUS ROCKS

Intrusive: Mainly granite,
granodiorite, gabbro and dolerite

Volcanic: Mainly basalt, rhyolite,
andesite and tuffs

**Figures at end of captions denote
millions of years**

0   50   100 mile

Fluorite, Weardale, Durham. A common mineral composed of calcium fluoride that crystallises as well formed cubes. They may be transparent, yellow, green, blue or violet.

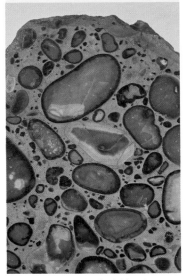

Pudding stone, Hertfordshire. A conglomerate consisting of wave-rounded pebbles from the Eocene age about 45 million years ago.

Brimham Rocks, near Harrogate, Yorkshire. Great bare scarps of Millstone grit appear as near vertical cliffs where the rocks have broken away on joint planes. Subsequent weathering may carve the rocks into peculiar shapes: chimneys, stacks, rocking stones and arches may result from the action of wind, frost or water.

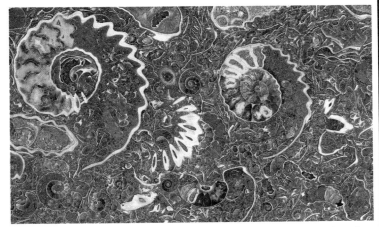

Ammonites — coiled mollusc shells with successive chambers — were dominant in the Mesozoic period. This polished surface is from the Lower Lias, Somerset.

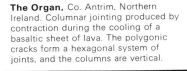

The Organ, Co. Antrim, Northern Ireland. Columnar jointing produced by contraction during the cooling of a basaltic sheet of lava. The polygonic cracks form a hexagonal system of joints, and the columns are vertical.

Cheddar Gorge, Somerset. Cut in Carboniferous limestone on the southern edge of the Mendips, Cheddar Gorge has been left dry by the river which cut it going underground. The dip of the rock determines the cliff shapes.

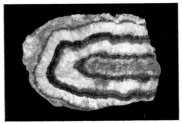

Blue John Fluorspar, Derbyshire. The Carboniferous rocks of the Pennines are well endowed with minerals.

Compressional earth forces have folded Middle Purbeck clays and limestones at Lulworth, Dorset.

This process followed the retreat of the last glaciers 10–20,000 years ago, but not for long. Gradual sinking of the land in the south east finally resulted in permanent flooding by the sea; and, about 7,000 years ago, Britain became an island. The sinking continues, hence the recent need to erect expensive flood defences to protect London from the sea. Today, North Sea fishermen sometimes trawl up bits of giant deer and hyenas from the Dogger Bank; reminders not only of a warmer climate, but also of the time that Britain and Europe were physically joined.

The first species to re-invade post-glacial Britain would have been the hardiest. They spread furthest and even today often have the widest distribution. Many that were not able to move in until the climate had substantially improved (e.g. moles that need dry, unfrozen ground and snakes that need plenty of sunshine) failed to spread throughout Britain before changes in sea level cut off Ireland from the mainland. Thus, even today, there are no snakes or moles in Ireland. The stoat, well adapted to cold conditions and thus widespread soon after the last glaciation is common in Ireland; the weasel is absent; similarly the frog is present but the more temperature-sensitive toad is not.

For the past 7,000 years the sea has been a barrier to many successful Continental invaders, preventing the colonisation of Britain by white toothed shrews, midwife toads and tree frogs. None came nearer than the French coast, all for the same reason that was to later keep out Napoleon and Hitler.

Once Britain was surrounded by the sea, the climate became markedly milder and wetter, encouraging a rapid and luxuriant development of forest over the whole country. A rich blanket of deciduous trees clothed the land everywhere except perhaps for some upland areas. After millions of years of upheaval and change, Britain had achieved its present general shape and was inhabited by species of plants and animals familiar to us today. The scene was set for the emergence of Man.

The advent of Man

In fact Man as a species evolved elsewhere, probably in what is now Africa, and first arrived in Britain among the immigrant fauna several thousand years before the last glaciation. These creatures were hardly Man in the modern historical sense. They lived in small groups and initially had little more effect on their environment than did any other species of animal. Their crude stone tools are evidence of greater intelligence than in any other British animal, but for thousands of years their impact was negligible. However, unlike the animals Man could learn and communicate his knowledge, and groups and families could help each other with tasks too big for a single person. Each new generation could be told or shown what their parents had learnt much more quickly than by finding out for themselves, and so the pace of human advancement began to speed up and Man emerged from among the animals to become an increasingly significant part of the British scene, ultimately to dominate it totally. Stone tools were improved to the point where they were able to fell large trees and make clearings in the woods; fire was also used to clear the ground and begin the process of subjugating nature. However, it was not until much later that the planting of crops began the process of Man's manipulation of his habitat and later still that the keeping of domestic animals began to reshape nature by preventing forest regeneration and fostering grassland development. The process of turning the Garden of Eden into the Garden of Man had begun.

THE NATURAL LANDSCAPES OF BRITAIN

Whilst the foundations of Britain's landscapes were being laid by the mountain building and denudation of Palaeozoic and Mesozoic time the details of the Highland and Lowland zones relate to the erosion, uplift and tilting of Tertiary time, especially the Mio-Pliocene marine transgressions coupled with the effects of the Pleistocene ice ages.

The Highland zone of Scotland, Ireland, northern England and Wales have a common identity of ancient structures in metamorphic or volcanic rocks which, although cut by upland erosion surfaces, have been heavily glaciated, thus giving rise to rugged mountainous country. Fault zones and less resistant rocks often guide erosion and explain river and valley patterns. Individual rock types such as Lewisian gneiss, Torridon sandstone and Devonian Old Red sandstone correlate with distinctive landscape types but glacial patterns of fluvio-glacial deposits, drumlins, eskers and moraines often mask the underlying rocks whilst pyramidal peaks, arêtes, corries and U-shaped valleys frequently sharpen the already rugged scenery.

The contrasting Mesozoic sedimentary rocks of the Midlands and south east England consist of limestones, chalks, clays and sandstones only gently tilted or folded. The more resistant limestones and chalk stand up as escarpments and dip slopes such as the North and South Downs, whilst the softer clays are eroded into broad vales such as Holmesdale and Oxford. There is a close correlation of landscape type with rock type in the south east, especially in those areas which were not glaciated.

Landscape types, however, are dependent upon present as well as past climatic conditions. The interaction of the climate with the geology contributes to the production of distinctive soil types, which in turn determines the resulting vegetation. The latter may range from forest, woodland and scrub to moorland, grassland and peat bog. The immense range of rock types combined with climatic variation has given Britain a great variety of landscape types which change rapidly over short distances.

Additionally, the interaction of the sea with the land has produced a wide variety of coastal features ranging from cliffs (as in the Hebrides) to cuspate forelands (Dungeness), shingle spits (Orfordness) offshore bars (Scolt Head) and salt marshes (Essex). Changes in sea level particularly related to the Pleistocene glaciation have produced features such as fjords (western Scotland), drowned valleys and rias (south west England), raised beaches (South Wales) and submerged forests (west Wales).

The final touches to the landscape of Britain are however of human origin. Most of the natural forest has been cleared, the fenland and marshland has been drained and the moorland reclaimed. A chequer-board pattern of fields with landscaped woods now covers much of the land, and the natural wildscape is restricted to the inhospitable parts of the Highland zone.

Beachy Head, Sussex. Chalk cliffs up to 500 ft in height dominate much of the coastline of south east England. Fractured by vertical joint planes, the chalk coastline is slowly retreating as a result of marine erosion.

St Ann's Head, Pembroke. Part of the coastal plateaux of Wales and Cornwall cut in Palaeozoic rocks.

The Fal Estuary, Cornwall. A coast of drowned river valleys (rias) transecting the Palaeozoic coastal plateaux.

Snowdonia, Wales. Glaciated mountain scenery resulting from igneous intrusions, volcanic rocks and lavas which were subjected to ice erosion during the Pleistocene period. Characteristic glacier-eroded ridges (arêtes) and ribbon lakes can be seen in the picture.

Pewsey Down, Wiltshire. Typical chalk landscape of south west England with smooth, rounded slopes and dry valleys. The topography is dependent on the dip of the rocks: little or no dip produces flat areas, such as Salisbury Plain, whilst a steep dip results in escarpments, as in the North and South Downs.

Lands End, Cornwall. Castellated cliffs, 400 ft high, produced by marine erosion on strongly jointed granite rock.

Bishop's Dyke, New Forest, Hampshire. Heathland scenery typical of the Tertiary sands and gravels of southern England.

West of Ireland, Cos. Clare and Galway. Carboniferous limestone pavements and drumlins are common.

Gordale Scar, Yorkshire. Carboniferous limestone country with vertical scarps, screes and pavements.

Orfordness and Havergate Island, Suffolk. Marine erosion in some parts of eastern England is counterbalanced by deposition in other areas. Orfordness is a large shingle spit built by wave action from eroded material drifting south.

Strathglass, Scotland. Typical glaciated highland scenery showing an infilled U-shaped valley with a modern meandering river and fertile flood plain. Wild, open heathland still dominates the glaciated upland area.

The First Settlers

*The Britain of today is a
synthesis of the labours of little more than 100 generations of men
working ant-like upon the natural landscape. Flint
tools of Palaeolithic Man have been found, but he left few marks upon the
landscape. The first people who permanently altered their natural
surroundings were those of the Neolithic, Bronze Age and Iron Age periods between
4,000 and 2,000 years ago. They began clearing the natural woodlands and
also left a legacy of stone circles, henges, tumuli, barrows, hill forts,
field boundaries and settlement sites. Although thinly and
unevenly scattered, they are a tribute to a remarkable
achievement by a tiny population.*

Small groups of 'primitive' Palaeolithic people visited Britain intermittently during the last 200,000 years of the Pleistocene period. They wandered into north west Europe mostly during the warmer interglacial phases, hunting temperate forest animals and gathering plant food. Their principal tool was the hand axe, shaped from a lump of flint.

Eventually *Homo sapiens sapiens* evolved, who was able to survive the tundra conditions of southern Britain during the last full glaciation. His ability to cope with such a harsh environment was probably related to the evolution of more complex systems of social interaction, perhaps supported by a sophisticated language, which enabled him to solve the problems of providing warmth and shelter (he lived in caves and on open sites; needles for sewing skin clothing have been found), and also to specialise in the hunting of large herds of migratory tundra animals (e.g. the reindeer) as his main food resource. His tool kit, based on sharp blades of flint, contained many tools for working bone, antler and leather, and reflects clearly his inventiveness and dexterity. Much art work survives from this period on the continent, but is barely represented in Britain.

By 10,000 years ago temperatures were increasing steadily; the last ice age was over. Great environmental changes were taking place such as the adjustments in land and sea levels which resulted in the formation of the English Channel and the North Sea by 6,500 BC, and, even more important, the increasingly dense and spreading cover of forest in which the hunting strategies of late Palaeolithic man would no longer be appropriate. Man's adaptation to this changing environment coincided with new patterns of tools and behaviour known as Mesolithic.

Mesolithic man sought an alternative to the abundant meat supply of the disappearing tundra herds in a diversity of foods: small woodland animals, fish, birds and plants. The exploitation of these demanded seasonally variable behaviour, and large areas in which small groups of people could migrate and gain access to several habitats. This seems to imply that hunting groups would have varied in size during the year, and that occupation sites would often have been temporary, and perhaps specialised for a particular phase in the hunting pattern.

Archaeologically, these implications are only faintly recognised, but Mesolithic adaptations are well shown in the tools found. There is a variety of flint scraping and engraving tools for working bone, leather and wood. Many are minute 'microliths' of flint used to tip and barb projectile points. The bow was an important weapon, and arrows were specialised for various tasks. Small hafted axes were used in woodworking. Dug-out boats were made, which were important in transport and for access to aquatic resources; shell-fish were collected and fish were caught with hooks, nets and traps. They were also speared with antler or bone harpoons, weapons which were used to kill terrestrial mammals too.

Whilst Mesolithic man can be seen to have responded dynamically to his changing environment, he was not entirely at its mercy. There is growing evidence to suggest that he might have cleared small areas of woodland, perhaps to attract some of the animals he hunted, and these clearings may occasionally, when soil and climatic conditions were appropriate, have remained free of trees to the present day.

Farming, comprising the cultivation of primitive wheats, barleys and the keeping of domesticated cattle, sheep and

The Uffington White Horse, Oxfordshire, is situated close to an Iron Age hill fort and thought to be associated with it, although the date of its cutting is still disputed. However, it is certainly the oldest of the several white horses cut into the southern downlands. Overlooking a hill where, in legend, St George slew the dragon, the horse obviously held special significance for the Celtic people and became the emblem of Iron Age coins.

The Mesolithic people who intermittently occupied a lake-side camp at Star Carr, Yorkshire, about 7600 BC may have worn these modified elk antlers as ritual headgear, or perhaps to decoy the large mammals they hunted.

pigs, was brought to Britain from the Continent in the mid 5th millenium BC. Some of the earliest evidence, from Ireland and the Lake District, suggests that small patches of forest were cleared, probably by felling and burning, and crops sown. When crop yields fell, these areas were grazed, and eventually reverted to forest when the Neolithic farmers moved on to clear new areas. Elsewhere, such as on the Wessex Chalklands, similar land use seems to have led to permanent clearances that began to shape the vegetation patterns seen today.

Once farming was sufficiently established to support people in other work, the early Neolithic inhabitants of Britain began prospecting and mining for flint and other rocks for the large-scale production of polished axes, and they started to build impressive monuments, requiring many thousands of man-hours of effort. Two kinds are particularly important: burial mounds and causewayed enclosures.

Earthen long barrows, the earliest burial mounds, are sometimes grouped around causewayed enclosures. The latter consist of one or more roughly circular discontinuous ditches which provided material for concentric internal banks. From pottery, animal bones, stone axes and other objects apparently buried deliberately in their ditches, they appear to have been visited intermittently by people from a large surrounding area. A popular interpretation sees them as seasonal gathering places for the dispersed but tribally related farmers, at which tribal business was transacted, goods exchanged, and ceremony and feasting took place. Evidence of ordinary domestic settlements is rare throughout the Neolithic period.

It is possible to consider some causewayed enclosures in Wessex and their surrounding earthen long barrows as a record of early Neolithic territorial groupings, and this view may be reinforced by the fact that in several of these 'territories' a major henge monument was constructed in the late Neolithic (about 2500 BC) not far from a causewayed enclosure which had probably gone out of use. The major henges are huge enclosures (up to 35 acres) formed by a deep circular ditch and massive outer bank, the construction of which involved hundreds of thousands of man hours. Some contained enormous circular timber settings, probably roofed buildings. There are several reasons for suggesting a non-domestic function for these sites, and if, indeed, they took over from causewayed enclosures as tribal foci, perhaps their buildings may be seen as 'council chambers'.

Sometimes people who lived during the early Bronze Age replaced these timber buildings with circles and settings of large stones, features which are common within the 80 or so minor henges scattered throughout the British Isles. In some cases their dates are similar to those of the major henges, but many seem to have been used well into the Bronze Age, after 2000 BC. They are generally thought to relate to ritual aspects in the lives of late Neolithic and early Bronze Age people, and ritual purposes almost certainly lay behind the construction, probably in the late Neolithic, of the extraordinary, narrow, parallel-sided enclosures (the longest over 6 miles) called cursus.

The Bronze Age

Not long after the building of the major henges, immigrants called Beaker people came to Britain from the Continent. Traditionally the Bronze Age begins with their arrival as they used copper and bronze, but it should not be thought that the late Neolithic way of life suddenly ended.

The Beaker people influenced Neolithic burial practices,

THE NEOLITHIC AGE

The Neolithic period began with the arrival of the first farmers in Britain about 3500 BC. By that time, 5000 years had passed since the end of the last Ice Age and deciduous woodland clothed all but the highest and least hospitable land. The immigrants must have encountered small groups of Mesolithic people who moved from place to place in their seasonal quest for animal and plant food from the forest, and for fish from river, lake and the sea. Farming was to bring to an end a hunting/gathering way of life which had evolved through a multitude of forms, against a background of changing environmental conditions ranging from tundra to temperate woodland, and had supported the human species in Britain for a quarter of a million years. Farming was also to have a profound effect on the landscape.

This came about largely as a result of the clearance of woodland for the cultivation of primitive wheat and barley, and the grazing of cattle, sheep and pigs. In some areas the Neolithic clearances were small and shortlived; elsewhere, such as on the chalk lands of Wessex, the clearances were large scale and permanent.

Once farming was established and the population had grown, Neolithic people began to build impressive earthworks which still survive today. Amongst the earliest of these were the long, narrow, burial mounds called earthen long barrows, and the related megalithic tombs. The two types are similar in that they usually contain multiple disarticulated burials, but differ in the possession of wooden structures, and stone chambers, respectively, to contain the bones. Their geographical distribution also differs. Almost certainly 'special' people were buried in this way, and the barrows may have served a socio-religious purpose beyond that of the simple disposal of dead. As their construction involved several thousand man-hours of work, they may have been constructed by social units larger than the family. Long barrows were not often built after about 2500 BC.

Whilst long barrows were being constructed, the Neolithic people in the south east of the country were also building causewayed enclosures. There are far fewer of these than barrows, and the labour input was much greater. They typically consist of one or more rough circles of discontinuous quarry ditches

and adjacent internal banks, enclosing ten or so acres of hilltop. Little evidence of permanent occupation is found within them, and examination of the ditch contents, sometimes deliberately buried deposits, leads to the impression that seasonal occupation and ritual activities played an important part in their use. Gathering of dispersed tribal groups to transact social business and perform religious ceremonies probably took place at some causewayed enclosures, whilst others may have been used in the exposure and disposal of corpses. Domestic settlements of Neolithic farmers are rare, particularly in the early part of the period, but clustering of earthen long barrows about some causewayed enclosures in Wessex may reflect territorial groupings of the inhabitants of that area. It is likely that social organisation was well developed throughout the Neolithic, as specialised activities such as the quarrying of stone and mining of flint for polished axes were supported, and large labour forces for earthwork building were co-ordinated.

In the later Neolithic, about 2500 BC, a different type of enclosure called a major henge sometimes seems to have replaced causewayed enclosures as a tribal focus. The major henges of Wessex are particularly impressive as the labour invested in them approaches a million man-hours. Essentially they consist of a massive circular quarry ditch which provided material for a bank constructed outside it, the bank and ditch being interrupted by two or more entrances. Within three of these enclosures, which may be up to 35 acres in area, excavations have revealed the presence of concentric circular arrangements of huge post holes, which have been interpreted as roofed buildings, 30 m or so in diameter. It may be (if these sites were not for domestic occupation) that these buildings are analogous to council chambers. The major henge at Avebury contains settings of stones.

Several hundred minor henges were also constructed in the late Neolithic and early Bronze Age. They are superficially similar to those already described, but are much more widely distributed, and contain settings of posts, stones, pits and burials.

The construction of stone circles also began at this time, but their development is better considered in the context of the early Bronze Age.

Windmill Hill, Wiltshire, is one of several Neolithic causewayed enclosures. While some were seasonal meeting places, others were associated with burial rituals.

Skara Brae, Orkney. Settlement sites in Neolithic Britain are rare and this stone-built village is not typical. All the houses were very similar and inter-connected by passages.

The stone house fittings at Skara Brae provide a unique example of late Neolithic furniture. Most houses contained a 'dresser', and two beds.

Decorated Neolithic pottery succeeded the early plain pots.

The Neolithic period is marked by a diffusion of cultural ideas by means of western seaways along the Atlantic coasts. Migrants from the Mediterranean travelling from promontory to promontory brought with them stone fashioned implements, a knowledge of farming and an ability to make pottery. Although Ireland was probably more important in this period than Britain, Grimes Graves in East Anglia was, however, the centre of a flourishing flint industry with a trade in axes and other tools finished in wood or antler remains. Later in the Neolithic, megalith builders introduced stone built tombs, gallery graves and passage graves which are common in the Scilly Isles and Ireland (e.g. New Grange). The first part of Stonehenge (the circular earthwork) and the Aubrey Holes date from this period.

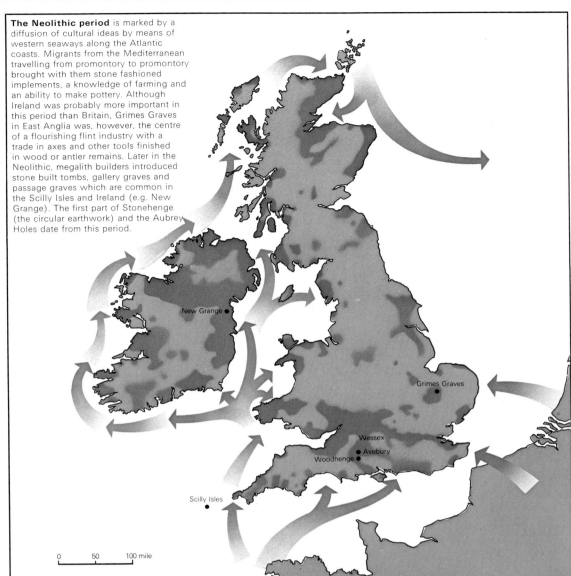

Waylands Smithy, Oxfordshire, is a megalithic tomb built on an earlier Neolithic earthen long barrow. This covered a mortuary containing the bones of 14 individuals.

The Grimes Graves' goddess, a chalk figurine, was found together with a chalk phallus, a cup and seven antler picks, at the base of a shaft in one of the Graves flint mines. The miners' work seems to have been unproductive on this occasion.

Flint implements, Easton Down, Wilts. Neolithic flint tools include scrapers and awls for preparing skins and shaping wood, engraving tools, knives, and arrow and spear heads.

Neolithic axes, shaped at quarries, were polished at 'finishing sites'.

Silbury Hill, Wessex, is a unique monument whose purpose remains unexplained.

West Kennet long barrow stone chamber showing galleries to side chambers.

Avebury, Wiltshire. Part of the outer ring of sarsen megaliths.

Avebury, Wiltshire, the most impressive of the henge monuments, covers 28 acres.

favouring single contracted interments of complete corpses accompanied by grave goods such as knives, flint arrow heads, archer's wrist guards and pottery beakers, all covered by a round mound.

Although evidence of their dwellings is rare (Beaker people probably practised mixed farming in many parts of the British Isles) they were concerned with the development of certain non-domestic sites which had originated in the late Neolithic. Their involvement with henge monuments was noted above, but they were also associated with the construction of stone rings in western Britain. It seems that, in some areas, accurate standards of length may have been used in the construction of these. Many rings are distorted circles, the distortion apparently being based on constructions involving perfect Pythagorean triangles. Other rings and their associated standing stones seem to record observations of solar and lunar rising and setting positions at the horizon, with an accuracy capable of providing data for eclipse prediction, or, at least, very accurate calendars.

Bronze Age burial

In the centuries following 2000 BC burial beneath round barrows became the major funerary rite and cremation became more popular. Round barrows were usually clustered in groups, and still often form prominent land marks on the crests of hills.

Beneath some rather distinctive forms of round barrows in central southern England are the so called Wessex Culture burials. These are accompanied by exotic grave goods which include bronze daggers, and jewellery made from amber, faience (an artificial blue-glazed material) and gold, and which seem to imply that the dead belonged to an aristocratic group in the Bronze Age society of that region. Furthermore, some of the grave goods may have come from central Europe, and may reveal the distant exchange contacts of these people. Despite the ostentatious burials little is known of their domestic life or their farming practices – this is also a problem outside the Wessex region, occupation sites being rare throughout the British Isles – though soils buried beneath some round barrows on what is now heathland show that such areas may have been cleared of forest by early Bronze Age farmers.

In the two or three centuries before 1000 BC permanent ditch and bank enclosed farmyards containing a few small round houses, and surrounded by groups of fields, became established. These are particularly well known in parts of southern Britain. Mixed farming was practised by largely self-sufficient groups probably comprising a few families, and a single acre used for prolonged cross ploughing was responsible for the small squarish 'Celtic' fields. It is not known to what extent climatic factors influenced these developments of agriculture, although late Bronze Age farms on Dartmoor, for example, were being deserted soon after 1000 BC, probably because of soil deterioration, and there is evidence of windblown soil erosion in Wessex somewhat earlier than this. It is clear, however, that to sustain this form of permanent farming a knowledge of methods of maintaining soil fertility must have been acquired.

By the later Bronze Age, patterns of large scale landscape organisation appeared. Celtic fields were often laid out in blocks; groups of these did not grow haphazardly. Linear ditch systems (ranch boundaries in Wessex) or walls (neaves on Dartmoor) began to divide up large tracts of land, and sometimes occupation sites seem to have acquired importance at the foci of these. The origins of the hillforts which

THE BRONZE AGE

The Bronze Age in Britain is usually taken to begin with the appearance of artefacts (which may include bronzes) characteristic of the Beaker people, a name deriving from the pottery beaker found with their burials, on their rare occupation sites, and sometimes in association with sites built by Neolithic people. Beaker burials differ from those in long barrows, as they are usually single, articulated, crouched inhumations, accompanied by grave goods, and covered by a round mound. The grave goods, besides the beaker, may include flint barbed and tanged arrow heads, archer's wristguards of stone and simple copper or bronze knives. Beaker people were undoubtedly involved in the first exploitation of copper and tin ores in Britain, but were also farmers, and appear to have been connected with the development of ritual sites, particularly stone circles.

There are many hundreds of stone circles, mainly in the Highland zone, which have been interpreted, traditionally, as the religious sites of the early Bronze Age. Careful study of these in recent years has also suggested that in many cases the builders were competent surveyors, apparently concerned to incorporate a limited number of important geometrical principles in their work and to record sophisticated astronomical observations relating to the apparent movement of sun and moon. Stonehenge is the most outstanding stone circle in Britain and illustrates these concepts well. It also demonstrates a striking continuity over several centuries of development, beginning with its origins as a late Neolithic henge monument, passing through a possibly Beaker-inspired stone phase using rocks brought from South Wales, and progressing to a series of phases using enormous local sarsen stones as well, assembled, dressed and shaped and erected possibly under the patronage of Wessex culture chieftains.

The Wessex culture is represented by a group of cremation and inhumation burials, mostly beneath specialised round barrows confined largely to central southern England, and to the earliest part of the Bronze Age. Burials were usually accompanied by a range of exotic grave goods including bronze daggers and pins, battle axes, necklaces of amber, jet and faience beads, and various ornamental objects decorated with sheet gold. Some of these objects suggest a form of contact with contemporary cultures in Europe, and

the apparent extravagance of the burials suggests that they belong to an aristocratic element in society.

Little may be said of the domestic aspects of the Wessex culture, and little evidence exists for the type of farming practised during the first half of the second millenium BC. In Wessex, transhumant pastoralism has been suggested, partly to account for the rarity of 'permanent' farmsteads, but in several areas of Wessex, at least, wind blown sediments deposited towards the end of the early Bronze Age suggest over grazing, or possibly over cropping. There is also evidence to suggest that many of the country's heathland areas had their origins in forest clearance at this time.

After about 1200 BC there is evidence of permanent, mixed farming in several parts of the country. Again the best known sites are in the south, and here, in the Lowland zone, a typical small farm would have consisted of a ditched and banked, or palisaded, enclosure containing the farmyard and a few small round houses with wattle and daub walls, and conical thatched roofs. Villages of stone walled houses existed at this time on the moors of the South West. Groups of fields (called 'Celtic' fields because they were once thought to be of Iron Age origin) would have been associated with these farms. They were characteristically small and squarish, and etched lightly into the landscape by prolonged cross-ploughing with a primitive plough called an ard.

In the later Bronze Age some fortified hilltop settlements were also constructed, and these represent the beginnings of a settlement form which was to develop into the dominating and numerous hillforts of the Iron Age.

There is also evidence of large scale land control in some areas of Britain in the later Bronze Age. This takes the form of large areas of Celtic fields laid out as 'blocks' regardless of topography, and linear ditch systems or stone walls which seems to have served as land boundaries, or to control grazing animals.

The development of bronze artefacts – flat and socketed axes, palstaves, daggers, rapiers, swords, spearheads and so on – is an important complement to the domestic and social topics mentioned above. Their study can provide chronological frameworks for the period, and can demonstrate an ever growing competence in the technical aspects of metal working.

Stonehenge, Wiltshire, was a site of unique importance in the late Neolithic and early Bronze Age of southern Britain. Enormous effort was put into its construction over several centuries from about 2200 to 1200 BC; it began as a rather unusual henge monument with a ditch and inner bank surrounding 56 pits filled with chalk rubble and some cremation burials, and the present form emerged only through a series of alterations and additions, including the building of the banked and ditched avenue from the site to the River Avon by the Beaker People. Stonehenge, along with other less spectacular rings, suggests that the builders adhered to geometrical principles during construction, and the sites may also have been associated with the observation of astronomical phenomena.

Collared urns were among the vessels used to contain cremated human bones.

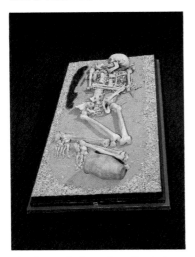

The Barnack Grave from Cambridge-shire. In contrast to Neolithic burials, Beaker people were often buried individually accompanied by grave goods such as vessels and weapons.

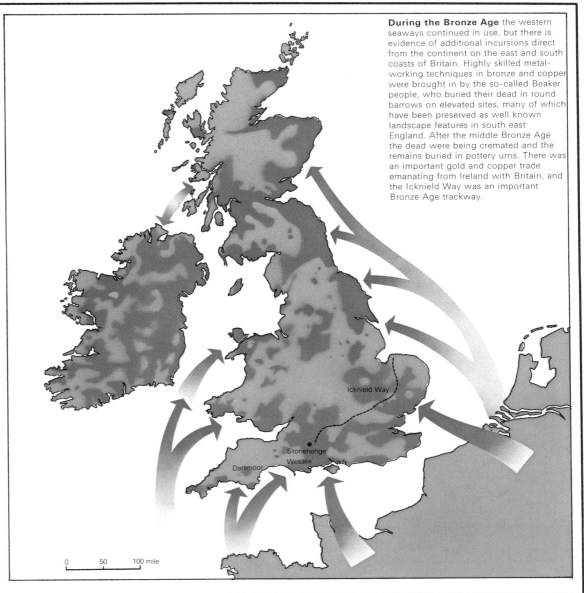

During the Bronze Age the western seaways continued in use, but there is evidence of additional incursions direct from the continent on the east and south coasts of Britain. Highly skilled metal-working techniques in bronze and copper were brought in by the so-called Beaker people, who buried their dead in round barrows on elevated sites, many of which have been preserved as well known landscape features in south east England. After the middle Bronze Age the dead were being cremated and the remains buried in pottery urns. There was an important gold and copper trade emanating from Ireland with Britain, and the Icknield Way was an important Bronze Age trackway.

Icknield Way

Stonehenge
Wessex
Dartmoor

0   50   100 mile

Pygmy cups sometimes accompanied larger urns in round barrow burials. Other distinctive miniature vessels were sometimes placed with beads, daggers and gold objects in the aristocratic "Wessex culture" burials of southern Britain.

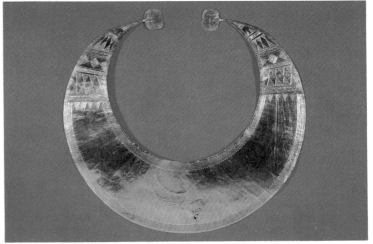

The Mongerton lunula is an example of the group of beaten sheet gold collars, many of which were made in Ireland and which represent the most important use of gold during the Early Bronze Age.

The Caergwrle Bowl from Clwyd is unique and controversial. It is probably late Bronze Age in date, and its shape and gold leaf decoration have been interpreted as a model boat with oars and round shields resting on the gunwale.

A beaker of the Beaker People. The various distinctive styles found suggest that there were regional groups of people originating from continental immigrations during the early Bronze Age.

Gold disc from Kilmuckridge, Co Wexford, one of a group of thin discs with impressed cruciform decoration found in Ireland, and thought to be early examples of Beaker craftsmanship.

were to dominate the Iron Age landscape may be sought in these developments.

The Iron Age

Despite the introduction of iron working and the proliferation of iron tools from the seventh century BC, many changes in agricultural practice and settlement patterns developed only gradually from those of the late Bronze Age.

There was an increasing tendency towards pastoralism in the Highland Zone, and in the Lowland Zone mixed farming became more efficient. New crops were introduced and the horse became an important domestic animal. A variety of settlement types emerged. In the Lowland Zone small late Bronze Age style farms remained, but there were some much larger farming settlements, surrounded by palisades or banks and ditches, and sometimes associated with the systems of ranch boundaries of the Bronze Age, which were developed further in the Iron Age. These enclosures often contained a very large round house with a porch, walls of wattle and daub, and a thatched roof. Perhaps an extended family with animals and stores occupied such a dwelling. The social unit would have been largely self-sufficient, working leather, wood and iron, weaving cloth on an upright loom, grinding corn on a rotary quern, baking food in a domed clay oven, and using good quality pottery which, by the end of the period, might have been wheel turned. The farmyard would have contained large pits for the storage of grain and other produce, and perhaps sheds raised on rectangular settings of posts for similar purposes.

Another settlement form dominant in many places was the hillfort. Hillforts show regional variations, but basically they defended a piece of high ground and began often in the Bronze Age as simple circuits of palisades, fronted by a ditch and broken by a simple gateway. It is not entirely clear why hillforts were so strongly defended. A few seem to have been damaged by burning but warfare may not have affected many directly. The sling was favoured for hillfort defence and rampart design may have been influenced by its use.

Other types of settlement include the raths of south west Wales, the wetland villages of Somerset, artificial islands (crannogs) of Scotland and Ireland, some stone built villages in the north and south of the Highland Zone, and the spectacular stone towers (brochs) of the late Iron Age in west and north Scotland.

Celtic burials are rather rare, but notable are the early Iron Age Arras burials of Yorkshire which were inhumations grouped in cemeteries, with grave goods including food offerings and occasionally even with the chariot of the dead person, and some later burials which include males with swords, females with mirrors and some very richly furnished cremations from south east England.

In the Celtic mind, no doubt, concepts of death and burial were part of a general spiritual awareness. A little is known of this. Celtic gods inhabited natural places: hilltops, groves of trees, springs, streams and marshes. Votive offerings to them can sometimes be inferred from concentrations of metalwork in bogs and rivers.

By the end of the Iron Age period, distinctive characteristics and territories of tribal groups had become apparent. Social structure within tribes is much more obscure, but a popular generalisation might include a feasting, wine drinking aristocracy able to gain prestige in its sponsorship of skilled craftsmen, its boastfulness in warfare, in the strength and size of its fortifications, and the size of subject population and agricultural wealth it controlled.

THE IRON AGE

Although there is no clear-cut transition from the Bronze Age to the Iron Age, the beginning of the latter is usually taken to be about 600 BC. Settled farming systems established during the later Bronze Age do not change dramatically, but some farms built in the early Iron Age are larger, more strongly fortified, and contain more impressive round houses. These (and houses on less pretentious sites) would have contained a hearth, oven, loom, quern for grinding corn, cooking and storage pots, and leather and woodworking tools of flint, bone, bronze and, most significantly, iron; all essential to a largely self-sufficient existence. Characteristic features of an Iron Age farmyard were large pits for the storage of grain and other produce, and structures supported on groups of, usually, four posts, that may have been raised granaries. Cattle were the most important farm animals and along with these, sheep and pigs were kept; horses were also managed, probably for traction.

Iron Age arable fields contained cereal crops similar to those grown in the later Bronze Age, but there were now varieties of wheat and barley which could withstand autumn sowing; Celtic beans were also grown. Some farmsteads were connected to systems of linear earthworks, 'ranch boundaries', probably involved in the control of animals.

Such farms formed a vital part of an Iron Age settlement pattern which was dominated by the hillforts, the fossilised remains of which are often dominant features in the present day landscape. Hillforts were built in many parts of the country and display important regional variations. Essentially they range from 'hamlet' to 'town' sized settlements built on hill tops and surrounded by a strong defensive system. The fortifications, regardless of size, may contain a densely packed settlement of buildings and storage pits along rudimentary streets; or they may consist of an open space free of buildings which might have been used for keeping stock.

Depending on the hillfort's location and its date of construction the settlement might have been fortified by a wooden palisade, stone wall, earth bank rampart, or a combination of these. Gates, weak points in any defensive system, were often strengthened by guard chambers, or overlapping ramparts of complex design.

In some cases a hillfort seems to have assumed an importance which led to its continued development over several centuries, at the expense of others which were abandoned relatively early. Such development may have included an increase in the area of the site, a gradual strengthening of the fortification through the provision of multiple ramparts and ditches, and an increase in the strength, complexity and impressiveness of the gateways. To what extent this phenomenon reflects the appearance of tribal capitals, or expresses the prestige of particular Celtic chieftains, is not clear. Almost certainly, because of their small size, the latter is the case with the Scottish brochs which display particularly impressive architectural and masonry skills. By the time of the Roman Conquest of Britain, which may be taken as the end of the prehistoric Iron Age, the names and approximate territories of Celtic tribes are known.

A little is also known about the organisation of Celtic society, and the Celtic mind, from classical writers. A useful character sketch portrays the Celtic aristocrat as boastful, gluttonous, but essentially cowardly, relying for prestige on the display of wealth. The subject population is less clearly seen and the extent of its exploitation or autonomy difficult to estimate. Some aristocratic burials are found in very richly furnished graves. The most outstanding are those of warriors containing the chariot of the deceased. Most people do not seem to have received inhumation burial during the Iron Age, however.

The Celts had a complex spiritual existence, populating the natural world of hill tops, springs, and tree-groves with gods. Their Druidic priesthood placated these spirits with ritual that was considered intolerably barbaric by the Romans who encountered it, and makes a rather curious contrast to the artistic quality of some of the Celtic metal work which appears to have been offered votively to the same gods.

Maiden Castle, Dorset, is one of Britain's most impressive hillforts. Iron Age occupation began about 350 BC when a fort was built at the eastern end of the hill; it was enlarged about 100 years later, and after another century the defences were strengthened and additional ramparts constructed. It was probably quite densely occupied by huts. The site fell at the Roman conquest.

Jarlshof, Shetland. In the early Iron Age the site of a late Bronze Age stone built village was reoccupied.

Stone hut, Jarlshof, from the Bronze Age village. The Iron Age settlers added stone built houses, and a strongly fortified broch was built later.

Bronze helmet dredged from the Thames. This was probably made by a smith under aristocratic patronage.

During the Iron Age invasion directly from the adjacent continental area predominated; from 500 BC successive waves of Celts arrived from the Rhineland and Saxony. They brought a knowledge of iron working and improved methods of agriculture including the use of the plough. Two important waves were the Hallstatt and La Tène peoples, now known as Iron Age A and Iron Age B. The Belgae followed towards the end of the Iron Age in about 100 BC, and western Britain also experienced incursions from Ireland.

Hill of Tara

Limit of Iron Age A and Belgae.

Maiden Castle

Limit of Iron Age B

0   50   100 mile

Gold torc, or neck ring, from Snettisham, Norfolk. Almost certainly worn by Celtic chieftains, the torcs are amongst the richest items of Iron Age metal work.

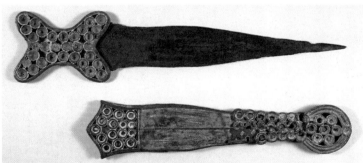

Iron dagger from the Thames at Cookham, Berks. Iron's great impact came, however, through its use in the manufacture of simple, effective tools.

Reconstructed buildings at Butser Hill, Hants, based as closely as possible on archaeological information about Iron Age buildings and part of a detailed simulation of Celtic activities.

Grave goods from a late Iron Age cremation burial at Welwyn Garden City, Herts. Although not a typical Iron Age burial, it does convey something of the wealth and interests of an important Celt with its silver vessels and gaming board.

Roman Britain

*Four centuries of Roman rule laid down a pattern
of settlement sites and roads which are clearly traceable today,
nearly 2,000 years later. Thousands of miles of roads
were built in arrow-straight lines connecting military forts and towns carefully sited in
strategic and economic positions. Towns still occupy the same sites today
and many modern roads follow the lines of the Roman
ones, which could not be bettered. In the country large farming estates
surrounded comfortable Roman villas.*

Textbooks about Roman Britain paint a picture drawn from the historical sources and analogy with the well documented Mediterranean civilisation of the first two centuries AD. By 700 or 800 AD Britain was firmly medieval. The transitional period must have been fascinating, but it is one about which we still have much to learn.

Several problems exist in trying to make a detailed study of a cross-section of society in 'Roman Britain'. Many of the historical sources have little to say to the person inquiring into the pattern of life on a Roman farm, or a windswept settlement north of Hadrian's Wall, or in a Cornish village known as a Round. Archaeology, on the other hand, may one day be able to give us a complete view, but at present insufficient artefacts have been found for us to piece the puzzle together.

However, we can dispel some myths. The mosaic pavement, a prime archaeological exhibit, and very attractive to look at, is something which only a tiny minority of the inhabitants of Roman Britain could ever have seen. Most people lived not in four-square mortared stone buildings but in far less obvious huts of wood, clay and dry-stone walling. The floors of these buildings were not firm hard stone or mortar, but simply trampled earth. The sites are very hard to find and rather uninteresting to look at, and therefore simply do not attract sufficient attention either from archaeologists or historians.

It would be a mistake to assume that the towns and villas were typical of Roman Britain. For example, some equally prosperous farming and commercial settlements in Wales do not belong to either category; and in the north of England we know much about the army at the frontier, but nothing of the natives who were pacified or from whom the army derived its food. Our information on 'Roman Ireland' is even more patchy, as we know only about possible army raids from Britain, barbarian raids to Britain and trade, such as dogs and gold, between the two. In truth, there is not a Roman period as such in Ireland; its late Iron Age archaeological society continued at least until the time of St Patrick in the 5th century, when prehistory turned into medieval Christianity without much interference from Rome.

If we apply the same sort of reasoning to Britain as a whole the results can be interesting. One of the great problems about Roman Britain is what became of it. The textbook answer is that it was destroyed by the invading Anglo-Saxons, but this is not supported by any concrete evidence.

The language changed from British to a Germanic dialect, and some burial customs changed – but not all. The Roman pottery industry had stopped before the Anglo-Saxons arrived, but the metal workers carried on. Obviously, most of rural England remained unchanged, notwithstanding the presence of the foreigners.

The Roman invasions

The arrival of the Romans in Britain can be taken as marking the end of prehistory and the beginning of recorded history. One of the major points vital to the study of Roman Britain is the connection between recorded history and archaeology, our sole source of reliable information up to that time. The two subjects are very different, for the history of Roman Britain was written almost completely by educated Italians, Greeks, Spaniards and Africans, many of whom had never seen the islands, whereas the archaeology of Roman Britain is, of course, based on the solid material remains which survive, or have been dug up and studied. To give a series of pegs on which to hang the more general information, it is useful to start with the history.

Roman Britain is still very much with us. This aerial view (left) of the Roman town of Verulamium clearly shows the remains of the walls, the theatre and the general plan of the town.

When the towns and forts of Roman Britain can no longer be seen above ground, there is still an enormous amount of material buried out of sight. This is an army parade helmet from Ribchester, Lancashire, where a fort once stood.

Julius Caesar spent much of his career at the head of part of the Roman army in Gaul. Britain was to him something of a nuisance, a set of islands from which help was given to the rebellious Gauls against the Romans, and a haven to which troublemaking Gauls could escape. He crossed the Channel in 55 and 54 BC and, according to his own account, subdued the British and bound them in a general way to Roman way of life. Although his actual 'invasions' may have had very little practical effect on the way of life in Britain – even in the south east corner where most of his activities took place – the general unsettling of Gaul made this a period of great change both in North Gaul and in Britain itself. The links across the channel which Caesar's wars had forged meant that the people nearest the south coast came quickly up to date in continental methods, such as using a wheel on which to make pottery, and using a heavy metal plough instead of the traditional lighter one, which probably could not cope with clay soils. Through contact, such changes must inevitably have brought the Britons closer to Roman habits, though there may have been no political control from Rome.

By the middle of the 1st century AD the country was ripe for annexation, and the Emperor Claudius took the credit for a great campaign involving four legions and other troops by which a new province was won for the Roman Empire. In 43 AD Britain became a Roman province with all the legal and administrative machinery that this involved. The conquest itself seems to have gone smoothly at first, but there were teething troubles in the country, and at the death of one of the client kings (rulers who were tolerated by Rome in the hope of taking over their administrations at their deaths), Roman mismanagement and British independence flared up in a savage rebellion. This episode was led by the widowed queen Boudicca in 60–61 AD to such effect that Londinium (London), an undefended straggle of commercial settlements, Camulodunum (Colchester) and Verulamium (St Albans) were severely damaged in the fighting.

Roman policy became more sensitive after this disaster, and British thoughts unknown from this time, for they never again produced any effective action deemed worthy of record by the foreign historians.

The spread of Romanisation

Military advances went on: Scotland was the scene of long marches and some fierce fighting in the 70s and 80s AD; Wales had been policed a little earlier; Ireland was left to itself for the moment. The time never came for a full Roman conquest, though trade in goods continued from the west coast of Wales, and the Irish seem to have started to emulate the Romans in the goods which they imported and in their methods of agriculture. The Emperor Hadrian visited Britain, perhaps in 122 AD, and he has always been credited with the decision that Scotland was too inhospitable for the Roman administration, hence the drawing of a line, the establishment of a frontier, and the building soon after his visit of Hadrian's Wall. For a time in the 140s and 150s his successor, Antoninus Pius, tried to push the frontier northwards, and the turf wall which he had built still stretches roughly between Glasgow and Edinburgh, and is known as the Antonine Wall. A final attempt on Scotland was made by the Emperor Septimius Severus from 208 to 211, when he campaigned with his two sons right up the east coast of the country. He died between campaigns at Eburacum (York), and his attempts to subjugate the Picts were the last to be recorded in detail.

TOWN AND COUNTRY

Towns were brought to Britain by the Romans as a means of exacting taxes and obedience from the natives, and ensuring that they lived according to the new law. This is of course an oversimplification, and there is disagreement between prehistorians and specialists on Roman Britain over the use of the word 'town'. Some of the settlements in pre-Roman Britain were quite large, were defended, had planned rows of houses, and fulfilled many of the functions which we require of a town; briefly, they acted as central points in the locality to which tribute might be sent and from which services might be gained. But to the Roman specialist, reared on the classical and Mediterranean idea of the city state, these enhutments just do not come up to the Roman ideal of towns.

So far as we can judge from the material remains that we can date, it took some time, perhaps almost a century, before the idea of town life caught on in Britain. Even when the walled cities, one major centre to each tribal area, showed a rash of new stone houses, there was still an element of Mediterranean city life missing. Each house seems to have been set in its own garden, with plenty of land, yet the cities of the Mediterranean were much more crowded; apartment blocks were the rule, open spaces were rare, and the density of people per acre was high. To this extent Roman towns in Britain could never have made the sailor from Italy or Asia Minor feel at home. There were other differences too; the amphitheatre was a good copy of Italian or French models, but the theatre and the temple went their own way. Thus most of the temples of Roman Britain are not classical temples such as you would see in Italy, or in Nimes and Vienne in France; they were Romano-Celtic temples with a special ground plan and, presumably, a special use. The theatre at St Albans is not the same as the great theatres which survive in France, Italy and the East, for instead of being a semicircle with its great back-wall along the diameter, it is more than half the circle, almost a cross between the oval of the amphitheatre and the semicircle of the classical theatre. Again, a peculiarity of the north west of the Empire.

Towns had walls, either very costly status symbols to keep up with the continental towns, or practical defences, though we do not know of any particular threats to town life at the time when the walls were built. Through the walls were pierced the gateways with dual carriageways and two pedestrian walkways on each; one arch of such a gateway still stands at Lincoln. In the centre of each tribal capital was a large rectangular complex of law courts, administrative offices and stalls – this was the forum. The town was usually planned in regular chess board pattern on the central forum, and in some towns stone-built sewers ran under the streets – such as at York and Lincoln – to carry away the waste from public baths and lavatories.

We know far more about the Romanised countryside than the native countryside. You can visit today the remains of the Roman villas – stately homes and farms combined – at Chedworth in Gloucestershire or Bignor in Sussex. You can even visit the remains of a village at Kingscote near Tetbury in Gloucestershire, but you cannot see anywhere the remains of a native farmstead of the Roman period laid out for inspection. There is a good reason for this bias: at the villas and the village you can see good stone-built houses still standing up to one or two feet high, mosaic pavements, and museums with many interesting finds. If a native farmstead were to be displayed all you would see would be small holes in the ground where the wooden posts of the building had stood, a few rubbish pits emptied of their poor contents, and a display made up of bits of pottery, a few animal bones and very little else. To the casual visitor, such a site would be uninspiring; yet it is the real basis of Roman Britain, for the farms and villages of the countryside produced the food to feed the administrators and the specialists in the towns, and the armies on the frontiers.

Although very little detailed information survives, we do however have a good general impression of the countryside in Roman Britain; we know that there were good flocks of sheep and that their wool was of high quality, for woollen cloaks and rugs from Britain were expensive items on a list of maximum prices set up in markets around the year 300 AD. We know of the existence of one Imperial weaving mill, but, like the flocks of sheep, it cannot be placed in detail. Corn must have been a major crop, and the major source of food, but again we do not know which were the richest arable areas. Finally, the remains of leather and the debris of food bones tell us that cattle were reared on a large scale.

The country villas are dotted around the more fruitful parts of the countryside, and in between are villages and single farmsteads which range from solid stone buildings with all Roman amenities to wooden shacks with none. As yet we know little about the division of land, though it is just possible that in some cases the medieval manor or parish boundaries may derive from relics of the late Roman estates.

Hinton St Mary, Dorset. The central roundel from the mosaic found at this villa is clear evidence for Christianity in the countryside.

The Jewry Wall at Leicester is part of a Roman municipal bath building and is a rare survivor.

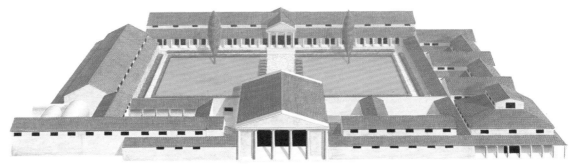

The Roman Palace at Fishbourne on the coast of Sussex was built about AD 75 and flourished for over 100 years. By the year 300 it was deserted and the ruins were being ransacked for tiles and building stone. When it was first decorated, workmen were called in from across the Channel to lay intricately designed mosaics and place marble inlay on the walls.

The Gorgon head, Bath. The classical Gorgon was female; this head may combine Roman and British ideas.

The Great Bath at Bath, a famous spa town and centre of Roman religious healing.

Forrestier's reconstruction of London in AD 400. Much of the picture is now known to be wrong, but it is the general atmosphere which counts, and the densely built up area seems fairly accurate. The capital city was the most Romanised place in the province, and the largest town. To compare it with the modern city, Ludgate Circus would be west of the bridge.

Tombstone of a Roman soldier from Chester. Many tombstones belonged to wealthy merchants.

Chichester, West Sussex. Much overlaid by medieval, Georgian and later building, the site had been settled even before the Roman invasion. The centre of the town still clearly shows the pattern laid down by the Romans with the four main streets meeting at right angles. At the outer end of each street was a gate in the wall which then surrounded the town.

Meanwhile, Romanisation seems to have moved swiftly. The Roman army had passed through most of present day England to settle in Wales and on the northern border, and left behind a fully populated province which already had a fully developed trade structure and social life; it is virtually certain that to a very large extent the British way of life continued unchanged. The countryside had already been well developed so that farms and villages were already properly distributed and organised; in turn, the existence of farms and villages would seem to imply the existence of a network of communications and markets, well developed before the Roman invasion. A new concept was the concentrated, stone built town, with a regular street grid, and the lowland and southern part of Britain saw a network of towns develop in the century from 50 to 150 AD. In practice, each tribe had one town, with a distance of about 60 miles separating them. Historians have suggested reasons for the building of these towns, how they functioned, and what went on in them, but it is simply not known how densely populated they were, who lived in them and why, what services were available from them, whether they acted as markets, why they were positioned where they were, and what happened to them through the four centuries of Roman rule.

Most towns were provided with defences, and it is reasonably certain that the original programme of wall-building was not the result of one historical cause, as the dates of construction of the walls of different towns were widely spaced out. In most cases walls replaced earth banks and, in the 4th century, towers were added to the outside of walls. Although this would make them more effective for offensive warfare, rather than simply as stone curtains to shelter behind, there is no direct evidence to suggest that any town wall in Roman Britain was ever used for defence.

Town walls were a feature of the third century, when the government and the Emperor were hard pressed by attack from outside the Empire. Britain seems to have been relatively free from these attacks and to have flourished. Certainly this was a time when many farms became more Romanised with good mosaic pavements, or at least solid stone built structures to replace earlier smaller farm buildings.

Around the south coast and the east up to the Wash a series of forts was built, known as the forts of the Saxon Shore. Again, the problems of mixing history and archaeology become apparent, for documentation on these forts belongs to the late 4th century, whereas most of them were built before 300 AD. So, although we know what they were called after a century of life, we do not know their original name or the exact purpose for which they were built. Since they are all built on the shore it can be assumed that they may have something to do with trouble coming from the sea, but even so obvious an assumption is questionable, for none of them seems to have had garrisons of any naval type, and evidence of harbours is associated with only two of them.

A succession of emperors

From 259 to 273 AD Britain was a separate, but definitely not separatist, part of the Roman Empire directed from Cologne. Then, in 286, the admiral who had been given the command of the Channel declared himself Emperor, and until 293 reigned in Britain as the emperor Carausius. He was then killed by his assistant, Allectus, who succeeded him. Allectus died in his turn when Constantius Chlorus, the father of Constantine the Great, recaptured Britain for the central Empire. At this time Wales was suffering attacks from

ROADS AND LANDSCAPE

Before the coming of the Romans, the landscape of Britain was uncivilised and unco-ordinated; there were settlements but very little communication, and only the Romans and their roadbuilding provided some sort of link and civilisation between the towns they established.

Romanisation, however, spread only through today's England as far as the most obvious remains are concerned. It stopped short of the far west of Cornwall, Wales and Ireland, and to the north there was a quite definite line, still visible between Carlisle and Newcastle, at which Hadrian's Wall brought Roman civilisation to an end, except for a brief period around 150 AD when Roman influence extended up to a second line, the Antonine Wall, now visible as a bank and ditch of impressive dimensions between Glasgow and Edinburgh.

The most obvious clue to the spread of the Roman way of life is in the appearance of the Roman road, a major feature of the landscape even today. The basic characteristic, which was unique in Britain until the turnpike roads of the 18th century, was a series of straight alignments ignoring all but the most awkward natural obstacles. What now survives, apart from many alignments in modern roads, are a few surfaces of good metalling, and a number of green tracks, footpaths and bridleways which cut through the countryside in remarkably straight lines. The road network ran evenly over the whole Empire, connecting the major cities to one another, and providing a solid basis for the movement of troops to maintain order and supplies to maintain the troops. Along the main roads a posting system was spread with rest-houses, and changes of post horses at regular intervals. Such amenities were allowed only to officials on Imperial business; even the governor of a province, the direct representative of the Emperor himself, asks permission in a letter that has survived for his wife to go by Imperial post in a family emergency.

Where there were no towns to visit in order to collect taxes and administer justice, where there were no soldiers to keep order and protect the local population from raids by sea or land, there were no roads on the Roman

model. A satellite picture of Roman Britain would have shown a simple straight road system spreading out from London, much like our old system of main roads, the A1 to the A6, several of which are on top of their Roman predecessors. And the way in which the roads are seen to die out to the far west, and to stop firmly where the last outpost fort to the north would have been reached, gives a good idea of the spread of Romanisation throughout these islands.

In the non-Roman areas of Britain, round buildings are common. In Cornwall the settlement of this period is known as a 'round'; inside a stone limit there are separate houses or dwellings, sometimes free-standing, sometimes built together. In Ireland there are the ring-forts, rounded defences inside which buildings of different plans and purposes cluster. In the west and north of Scotland the broch (a high round tower) and the wheel-house continue this emphasis on rounded forms. The Romans, however, went in for square buildings; they were skilful enough to prepare and use the well cut stone and heavy blocks or, in timber building, the stout posts which would be needed to cope with the stress on the corners inherent in a square structure, whereas the round buildings of the rest of relatively uncivilised Britain needed no specially dressed or heavy material.

The shape of the arable fields of the period, however, was determined by the plough. They were the length of a convenient furrow and the width of several furrows, and their remains have never been obliterated by later agriculture. Known as Celtic fields — a term applied to small, squarish fields — they appear too irregular to be Roman, and yet seem to be of the right date.

A very obvious feature of the landscape is the dyke system of the fens of East Anglia. These have always been recognised as partly Roman works and used to be quoted as examples of inland waterways — Roman canals — but when looked at in detail this just will not work, for they sometimes run uphill and are sometimes crossed by the course of Roman roads. They are probably the best attempt at draining the fens until the late 19th century.

King Street, which starts near modern Peterborough and runs to Bourne in Lincolnshire, was originally a Roman road. It is a notable landscape feature, travelling from point to point in a series of straight lines seldom deflected by natural obstacles.

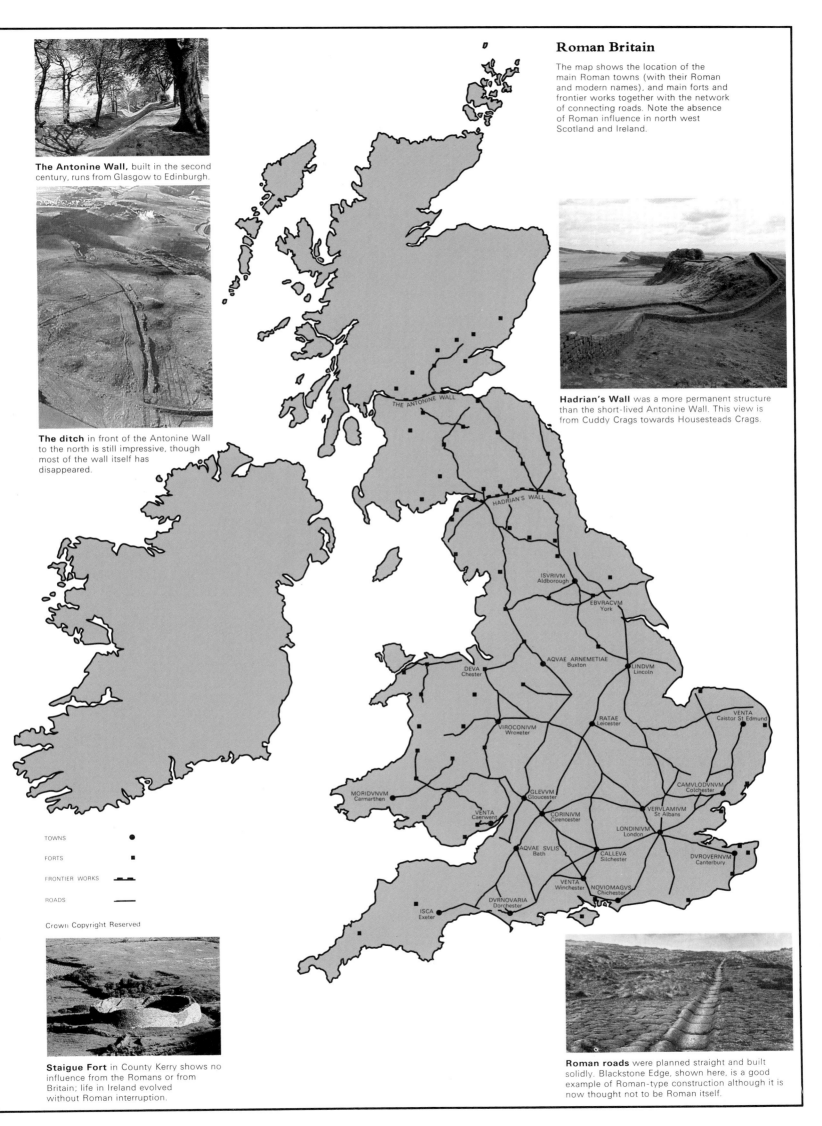

Roman Britain

The map shows the location of the main Roman towns (with their Roman and modern names), and main forts and frontier works together with the network of connecting roads. Note the absence of Roman influence in north west Scotland and Ireland.

The Antonine Wall, built in the second century, runs from Glasgow to Edinburgh.

The ditch in front of the Antonine Wall to the north is still impressive, though most of the wall itself has disappeared.

Hadrian's Wall was a more permanent structure than the short-lived Antonine Wall. This view is from Cuddy Crags towards Housesteads Crags.

Staigue Fort in County Kerry shows no influence from the Romans or from Britain; life in Ireland evolved without Roman interruption.

Roman roads were planned straight and built solidly. Blackstone Edge, shown here, is a good example of Roman-type construction although it is now thought not to be Roman itself.

Crown Copyright Reserved

TOWNS

FORTS

FRONTIER WORKS

ROADS

THE ANTONINE WALL

HADRIAN'S WALL

ISVRIVM
Aldborough

EBVRACVM
York

AQVAE ARNEMETIAE
Buxton

LINDVM
Lincoln

DEVA
Chester

VENTA
Caistor St Edmund

RATAE
Leicester

VIROCONIVM
Wroxeter

MORIDVNVM
Carmarthen

CAMVLODVNVM
Colchester

GLEVVM
Gloucester

VERVLAMIVM
St Albans

VENTA
Caerwent

CORINIVM
Cirencester

LONDINIVM
London

AQVAE SVLIS
Bath

CALLEVA
Silchester

DVROVERNVM
Canterbury

VENTA
Winchester

NOVIOMAGVS
Chichester

DVRNOVARIA
Dorchester

ISCA
Exeter

31

the Scotti raiders from Ireland, and the northern frontier was being pressed by the Picts. Constantius and his son started a military campaign but, just like Septimius Severus 100 years before, Constantius died at York in 306 and was succeeded by his son Constantine.

After a quiet period in the middle of the century there was more trouble from the north, the west and possibly from across the North Sea in 367, which needed help from the continent. In 383 another British general, Magnus Maximus, declared himself Emperor. Finally, in 410 historical sources tell us that the Emperor Honorius wrote to the cities of Britain telling them they must henceforward look after themselves. No doubt the Empire had more than enough to do looking after its important parts such as Italy and North Africa; Britain was expendable.

The Roman legacy

We have the material remains of Roman Britain: the town walls, the theatres – at Venta Silurum (Caerwent) and Verulamium (St Albans) – and amphitheatres, as at Isca (Caerleon); and in the countryside, the long straight roads, rural villas like Chedworth (now open to the public), and the great series of drainage dykes in the Fens. Each person probably wants something different from a period of history; if a clear, simple story is required, then confine yourself to the recorded history where the sources are limited, can easily be made to agree with one another, and the whole period made to tie in with the great events that happened thousands of miles away in Rome or Constantinople. But archaeology – our real legacy – is so much more attractive, and fortunately is growing in importance because of the unexplained mysteries that it still presents, which must eventually provide the answers to the questions that people today are still asking.

COINS

Roman coins first came to Britain in significant numbers after the invasion by Claudius in 43 AD, although some earlier pieces did precede them. The earliest Roman bronze coins, possibly used to pay the troops, were very commonly imitated, particularly asses of Claudius with the Minerva reverse. The quality of the copies varies considerably.

contained only one to three per cent of silver. These coins and their fourth century successors are found in abundance on British sites and indeed throughout the Roman empire. They are also commonly copied.

Counterfeiting 'epidemics' occurred in the later third century AD when Britain was under the domination of the Gallic emperors (c. 260–274), and in the fourth century, during the 330s under Constantine and again in the 350s under his sons.

This period marks perhaps the first time that coins of low value were in sufficient supply for almost everyone to have had at least a few and used them.

For a few years at the end of the third and beginning of the fourth centuries Britain had its own mint producing Roman coins. It was first opened by Carausius (286–294), a usurper, who was succeeded by his chief financial official Allectus.

A mint of London flourished especially from c. 298 up till 325 when it was closed permanently except for a brief issue of precious metal coins later in the century.

Portrait coins of Carausius and Allectus.

The number of Roman bronzes reaching Britain in the late first and second centuries AD was relatively small, but there was an upsurge of their number in Domitian's reign which is presumably related to Agricola's campaigns, and another under Antoninus Pius in 142–3 AD when the Roman wall from the Forth to the Clyde was constructed. It was under Antoninus that a special series of coins were struck commemorating the provinces; the one for Britain was the prototype for the Britannia featured on the modern English copper.

A severe economic and military crisis in the mid third century led to wholesale debasement and the production of extremely large issues of so-called 'silver' coinage, which by the late 260s

Minerva As with good and poor copies

DOMESTIC LIFE

Much of the work of the Roman craftsman has disappeared, and so we know little about some aspects of their work. It is almost certain, however, that the majority of the population were clothed in woollen and linen garments; spinning and weaving were therefore major industries, even if much was made at home, yet the cloth which survives from Roman Britain is not enough, particularly enough to make one decent cloak. The work of the joiner and carpenter has mostly gone the same way. Decorated leatherwork for clothes or equipment is, apart from in shoes, very rare, and of the food industries we know practically nothing.

At the other end of the scale pottery and brick are virtually indestructible, so that most of the pottery made in Roman Britain, except for the little that was exported, still remains – it is a continual problem to the archaeologist who excavates Roman sites, for it turns up literally by the ton. Where they have not been disturbed, Roman tesselated (plain) and mosaic (decorated) pavements survive and, because they are still so obvious and, even to modern taste, attractive, their discovery is almost always noted. The work of the blacksmith also survives, though much Roman ironwork is rusted beyond either recall or recognition. But materials such as iron, bronze and glass were not thrown away like pottery when broken because they could be re-used: iron could be reforged, bronze, lead and copper could be recast, and glass, even when completely shattered, was saved as raw material for later reworking.

Because the jobs to be done around the farm or the house were much the same as they have always been, the tools that were used in Roman Britain look very much like tools of the recent past. We do not have many examples of the woodworker's ability, but from the few tools we have found we can see that his skills and the requirements of his clients must also have been very similar to those of today.

Turning from the domestic to the spectacular, the achievements of the Roman engineers were, by any standards, remarkable. The remains of aqueducts in England are not like the great monuments of France and Spain, but they are still triumphs of engineering skill. The exact levelling required at Dorchester and Lincoln to bring water to the town from springs miles away is obvious; but the other half of the job lies in selecting materials to be watertight, and to withstand the great pressure of water propelled by an inverted syphon.

The work of Roman jewellers and goldsmiths is rarely found in Britain, but this is for the very obvious reason that it was seldom lost, although the drain of the great bath at Bath revealed some items of Roman jewellery, particularly engraved gems, and these miniature masterpieces of engraving turn up every so often on excavations. We know that Britain was probably self-supporting in its production of silver from the silver-lead mines in Somerset, the Peak district and Flint; the same may be true of gold, for there is certainly one Roman gold mine – at Dolaucothi in Wales – and more gold may have been brought over from Ireland.

Tin had been mined for many years before the Romans arrived in Cornwall, and this continued during the Roman period. The other main metal in everyday use, apart from lead, was copper; all our evidence for Roman exploitation of copper ores comes from Anglesey and north Wales.

Although much Roman technology was advanced there are some gaps which are still surprising today. All implements and tools made of iron had to be forged and hammered because the Roman iron-worker never mastered the production of steady temperatures high enough for casting. All tools therefore had to be forged, and the process of

iron smelting meant that this was done not to pure iron, but something approaching steel. The actual mining of iron ores and smelting them to get the metal happened all over Britain, because the Romans would apparently use ores that today are judged uneconomic. Most of our evidence of iron extraction is on the Sussex Weald, the Forest of Dean, and Northamptonshire.

Money in the Roman world, and Britain was no exception, was produced by the state to pay its own bills. There was a mint in Britain only for a short time from 286 AD to 326 AD; at all other times coins had to be imported, first from Rome, and then from Trier and Lyon. Gold and silver coins were in constant use by the state and its servants whether in the civil service or the army, but such coins were not often lost, and we therefore have very little idea how much they were used by the civilians of the town and countryside. Bronze and copper coins, of lower value, were lost more commonly, and they tell us that use of these coins spread quite widely through the community.

Mosaic pavements may be thought of primarily as decorations, but they can also be used to provide information on trade and culture. In the fourth century AD there were several schools, or firms, of mosaicists, each with their specialities. Around modern Cirencester are many mosaics with circular patterns, especially using the motif of Orpheus and the birds and beasts. The Dorchester (Dorset) firm seems to have had Christian connections, and was better at human figures than the other firms. The firm centred on Water Newton (Cambridgeshire) specialised in patterns, and perhaps the kindest thing to say about the Brough on Humber firm is that it was the least Roman in its designs.

The production of pottery was perhaps the nearest thing Roman Britain had to an industry. At first much pottery was imported from the continent; the heavy grinding bowls were unknown to Britain, and it took a little time for British potters to start to manufacture them. The red gloss pottery known as Samian was never copied successfully in Britain and was imported from Gaul and Germany so long as it was manufactured there. In the fourth century Britain supplied all its own needs in pottery and two of the main production centres were in the New Forest and the Thames Valley around modern Oxford; further north, the Nene valley near modern Peterborough continued a production begun many years before, perhaps under the stimulus of the army stationed temporarily nearby, and kilns in Derbyshire and Yorkshire started up to supply the northern frontier. So far as we know, Roman pottery production ceased in Britain at the beginning of the fifth century AD; we know the rough date, but not the reason. It seems to be too early for the Anglo-Saxons to be blamed, and it is therefore not surprising that Anglo-Saxon pottery starts off in a fashion totally different from that of the vanished Roman industries.

Pewter plates from Verulamium Museum, St Albans. For the majority table vessels were of pottery; the upper classes used silver, while pewter and bronze came in between.

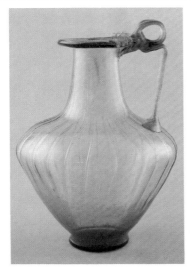

The glass industry began in the final years BC. When the Romans came, vessels like this were known but a luxury.

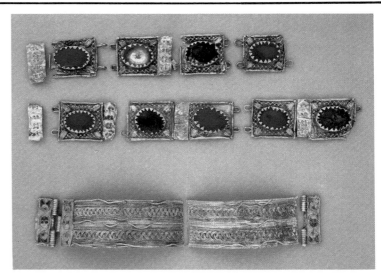

Roman jewellery followed the fashions of the Greek world. Gemstones were polished, but never cut to sparkle, and gold work was of a high standard. These examples are part of the British Museum's fine collection of Roman artefacts.

Statue of Hercules from Hadrian's Wall. Roman religion was far more organised than that of the Britons, whose gods were often unnamed and ill-defined.

These glass bottles were probably used as containers for goods on sale. Bottles were often also used as urns for the ashes of the cremated dead.

The earliest Roman glass, like this pillar-moulded bowl, was highly coloured. Clear and colourless glass took some time to develop.

A bronze helmet which may have been imported, although Britain had a good standard of metalworking before the Romans arrived.

Roman medical care was of a high practical standard, but lacked inspiration and did not develop. Surgical and toilet implements, such as these from Verulamium Museum, were often not improved upon until the 20th century.

THE MILDENHALL TREASURE

The great silver treasure from Mildenhall in Suffolk compares favourably with silver ware found anywhere in the Roman Empire. We do not know where it was made. Many of the pieces are highly decorated and show no signs of cuts or scratches, so they were probably for show rather than for everyday use. They belong to the fourth century but do not resemble the prevailing style of late Roman art; it seems as if silver workers were more conservative than the sculptors and painters of the time. The spoons have Christian markings while the style of decoration is completely pagan, but this is not an uncommon combination.

This bronze head from Suffolk, now in the British Museum, is often said to be of the Emperor Claudius. It probably belongs to his period, but does not closely resemble his coin portrait.

Lead was one of the metals mined extensively in Britain. It was used for a variety of containers, from hot water boilers to small canisters such as this, now in the British Museum.

Wine goblets

A strainer, possibly for serving wine

A large scalloped dish, decorative but impractical

A small platter, brilliantly worked

A large ornamental dish

The Dark Ages

*The withdrawal of the Romans in
AD 410 left Britain vulnerable to invaders from the continent, who
descended upon its shores and moved inland to lay down
much of the present day rural settlement pattern. Historically a confused and chaotic
time, with many warring kingdoms and little recorded data, this period
has become known as the Dark Ages. But despite the troubled nature of the times, clearance
of the woodland continued apace and well over 14,000 self-sufficient
village communities were founded, although no trace of buildings
remains save for stone churches and fortifications. Around the
villages were great open fields divided into strips, individually owned to ensure
fair shares of the land, and although the open fields
have long since disappeared, evidence of these strips remains
in field boundaries and ridge and furrow patterns.*

The six hundred years which separate Roman Britain from the Norman Conquest are commonly referred to as the Dark Ages. Originally so called because of a general disregard by pre-19th century historians of everything that was achieved between the fall of the classical (Roman) empire and the Renaissance, the name has achieved a more recent significance because of the paucity of historical information about the period. Yet these were the formative years in which new elements and new patterns emerged that were to shape medieval and modern Britain. The many gaps in the written record for this period can be filled to some extent by turning to forms of evidence other than historical documents, whether in the form of placenames or the archaeological record, which enable us to reconstruct the way of life of its peoples. Certainly the Dark Ages are less obscure than they used to be.

The spread of Christianity

Rome had never succeeded in conquering the Picts in Scotland, or the Irish, but the Emperor Constantine's acceptance of Christianity in 312 AD was to have important consequences. Roman Britain was at least partially christianised before Imperial rule came to an end in 410. Ireland was converted by Roman missionaries in the fifth century, and Irish monks later played a leading role in converting the Picts and the Anglo-Saxons in Britain.

Major migrations to Britain from north Germany and Scandinavia occurred in two waves. Both peoples spoke Germanic languages, in contrast to the Celtic tongue which predominated among the British and Irish. In the fifth and sixth centuries the Anglo-Saxons arrived and settled, bringing their ancestral version of our English language. They came initially as mercenaries hired by the British, but soon overthrew their masters and founded their own states. Over the centuries various Anglo-Saxon kingdoms developed into major political and military powers levying taxes from their neighbours. By the end of the seventh century there were

three major kingdoms: Northumbria in north east England and southern Scotland, Mercia in the Midlands, and Wessex in the south and south west. Their progress in annexing western Britain was slow and uncertain, for Cornwall was not incorporated into Wessex until the ninth century and Wales was never subdued. It was during the ninth century that a second wave of Scandinavian invaders, the Vikings of Denmark and Norway, settled in eastern England, Scotland and Ireland. They had come initially in the late eighth cen-

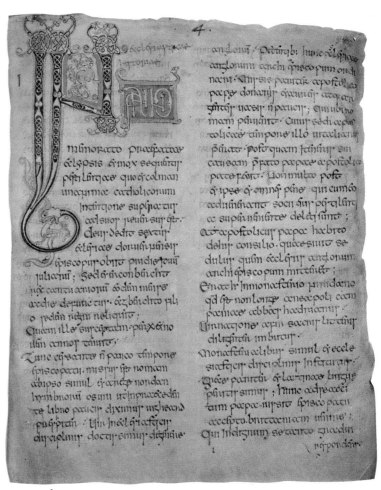

Bede, a Northumbrian monk, completed his Ecclesiastical History, shown above, in 731. It chronicled the conversion of the Anglo-Saxons to Christianity.

Offa's Dyke, the great earthwork constructed in the eighth century, separates the Midlands from Wales and bears the name of the greatest king to rule Mercia. Its almost continuous ditch and bank still form an impressive monument, but there are no traces of forts and the manner in which it functioned is far from clear.

tury as raiders seeking silver and slaves, but from the mid-ninth century they wintered in the territories they systematically ravaged, safe inside fortifications on islands in Kent: in 850 they were based on Thanet and in 854 they wintered on Sheppey. Although their armies destroyed the English kingdoms of East Anglia, Northumbria and Mercia, they failed to conquer Wessex. The West Saxon kings counter-attacked in the 10th century and briefly created a kingdom of England; this passed into the hands of a Danish king, Cnut, in 1016, but after 1042 was again ruled by a West Saxon king, Edward the Confessor. He presided over a state still divided into regions based on the old kingdoms and ruled by powerful earls. Only a year after Edward's death, England had been seized by a new ruler, the French duke of Normandy. Meanwhile from the ninth century an Irish dynasty from western Scotland was creating the new kingdom of the Scots to replace the kingdoms of the Picts, and Viking power in Ireland had been finally crushed by the Irish at the battle of Clontarf in 1014.

The first migrations

Roman Britain was apparently in a state of economic collapse by the beginning of the fifth century, its towns in decline and its larger industries, notably pottery production, no longer functioning. Its provinces were threatened on three fronts: from the west by Irish raiders, some of whom settled permanently on its coast, from the north by the Picts of northern Scotland raiding along the east coast, and

from the east by the Saxons of north west Germany attacking Britain's south east. St Patrick, the fifth century missionary bishop of Ireland, had been captured and enslaved as a boy during a raid by the Irish on South Wales, but after the conversion of the Irish to Christianity, their threat to Britain seems to have diminished. Late Roman coastal forts have been recognised in the west, notably at Lancaster and Cardiff, but there was no chain of forts to compare with the defences in south east Britain. These stretched from the Wash to the Isle of Wight and were described as the 'Saxon Shore' in a late Roman military list.

In 406 the greater part of the Roman army left Britain to campaign in Gaul, presumably leaving only a few garrison troops, and in 410 the Emperor Honorius told the British that Roman military aid was no longer available and they would have to defend themselves. Apparently the British successfully repelled the barbarian attacks for a time; we are told that they were ruled by tyrants – local emperors – one of whom, Vortigern, recruited Saxons as mercenaries against the threat of a Pictish invasion in the 430s or 440s. The Picts never again appeared as invaders, so his policy succeeded, but another problem arose as the Saxons did not go home. Instead they rebelled and seized territories on the south and east coasts. The British fought them resolutely, but even the legendary Arthur was unable to drive them out. By the seventh century, Britain was divided into a multitude of kingdoms and principalities, ruled in the west by Celtic-speaking British and in the east by English-speaking Saxons.

MIGRATION AND SETTLEMENT

Open rowing boats of overlapping planks based on a keel – the clinker construction – brought the Anglo-Saxon invaders and settlers to Britain from the northern Netherlands, north west Germany, Denmark and southern Norway in the fifth and sixth centuries.

From archaeological evidence we know them to have been tall, well built people, with both men and women very close to modern average heights. Although their diet was good, their life expectancy was much shorter than ours, most dying before they reached their 20s. Women often died in childbirth, while men met violent ends; but if they survived into their 20s then they might have expected quite a long life. They spoke an ancestral version of English, belonging to the Germanic group and related to modern Flemish, German and the Scandinavian languages. In Britain they met Celtic and a few Latin speakers among the natives.

At first the Anglo-Saxons came by British invitation as mercenaries, but soon came to seize land for themselves in eastern and southern Britain in a migration which involved several generations. At the expense of their British neighbours their kingdoms gradually expanded westwards to create England. This process was largely completed in the eighth century with the construction of Offa's Dyke which marked the Welsh frontier, and in the ninth century with the conquest of Cornwall.

The English migration was not the only movement of its kind, for in the fifth and sixth centuries many British people crossed the Channel to Armorica and there created Brittany. This has been interpreted as a reaction to overpopulation in western Britain caused by refugees from the regions conquered by the Anglo-Saxons. It seems probable, however, that much of the British population had stayed and was absorbed by its conquerors. A more powerful motive for the migration may have been the wish to escape the political and military strife of the British kingdoms and come closer to the Christian life in a new land.

The Irish too had been settling

overseas towards the end of the Roman period. Apparently they colonised much of the western coastlands of Britain from Scotland to Cornwall, but often the archaeological evidence for this is tantalisingly slight. The Scotti of Dalriada, who settled in the Argyll region, were of major importance, however, for through them Christianity was transmitted to the Picts and the northern Anglo-Saxon kingdoms. Later in the ninth century a Scots dynasty was chosen to rule the Picts and the creation of the kingdom of Scotland (still incomplete in the 11th century) had begun. By contrast, Ireland remained divided into a multitude of small kingdoms throughout the Dark Ages, inviting the intervention of foreigners – first the Vikings of Scandinavia and later the Normans of South Wales.

Anglo-Saxon Migration
After the Roman departure from Britain in AD 410, renewed invasions of south and east Britain took place from the continent. Angles, Saxons and Jutes from Friesland, Saxony and Denmark pushed inland along the waterways and settled in the lowlands until halted by Romano-British tribes and Celts. Ireland had in the Roman period become a centre of Celtic Christianity and responded to the pagan invasions by sending missionaries to western Britain during the 'Age of the Saints'. The Scotti of Ulster invaded Argyll and were eventually to unite with the Picts to form the base of medieval Scotland.

Pictland

Iona

Lindisfarne

Mercia

East Anglia

Friesland

Offa's Dyke

Wessex

0   50   100 mile

FARMSTEADS, VILLAGES AND BUILDINGS

Many of our English village names appear to be of Anglo-Saxon origin and a few can be traced back in documents to the Anglo-Saxon period. Linguists have attempted to isolate the earliest English placenames and use these to map the initial Anglo-Saxon settlement. Until quite recently, it was believed that one of the earliest placenemes was composed of a person's name combined with the ending -ingas; for example, Heastingas (Hastings). -ingas implies ownership by an individual or family, and was thought to represent a land taking. However, scholars have since changed their minds, because the distribution of places with -ingas — or indeed related endings, such as -ham and -tun — bears little relationship to that of the excavated early Anglo-Saxon cemeteries and settlements.

It seems more likely that placenames constructed in this way represent a phase of consolidation of settlement, when families had become firmly established in their localities and could then give their names to their farmsteads. The dates of this phase are uncertain, but in much of England it had certainly begun by the seventh century and continued for some centuries thereafter.

Just as it is difficult to accurately date a settlement from its name, so it is becoming increasingly unreliable to assume that our modern village plans, whether laid around a central green or spread along a street, are creations of the Anglo-Saxon period. Modern research indicates that such village plans are creations of the 11th century and many of them must have developed later in the Middle Ages.

Archaeological excavations have made us more aware of the tendency of settlements to shift within a parish, while possibly retaining the same name. As the evidence from sites accumulates we will be able to construct a more accurate picture of the changes in rural settlements throughout the period.

Archaeology also provides us with a more reliable, though as yet very incomplete, portrait of actual settlements in the Anglo-Saxon period. It at least enables us to compare villages in England with those abandoned by the Anglo-Saxons when they migrated to Britain from Germany and Scandinavia during the fifth century.

A number of villages have been excavated in Lower Saxony, notably at Feddersen Wierde and Flögeln. At Feddersen Wierde the waterlogged conditions have preserved its wooden buildings in a remarkable manner. The basic house structure was a long rectangle with a living area for the family at one end and the greater part of the building usually taken up with cattle stalls, in which livestock could be kept over the severe winters. At Flögeln, ground plans for similar farmhouses enclosed in a farm stockade are associated with small square or rectangular fields, the so-called Celtic fields, that are also found in prehistoric and Roman Britain, thus enabling us to dispel the myth that the Anglo-Saxon immigrants introduced new methods of agriculture based on large, open fields divided into long strips.

Of the settlements excavated in England, Chalton (Hampshire) is perhaps the most complete. It was occupied in the seventh century and apparently consisted of a series of adjacent farmsteads forming a hamlet. Like the settlements of Lower Saxony, the houses were built of wood and were rectangular in shape. But additionally they were surrounded by a square or rectangular fenced enclosure, possibly with a farmyard attached to one end. Within the enclosure were two or three other rectangular buildings. The buildings are all smaller than those in Lower Saxony and none has an attached byre for animals, possibly due to England's milder climate and perhaps a greater reliance on sheep rather than cattle.

Similar settlements with buildings set in fenced enclosures can be found at Basingstoke (Hampshire) and Catholme (Staffordshire). At West Stow (Suffolk) the rectangular wooden house is a rarity and the so-called sunken hut predominates. Typically this type of structure had a minimum of two upright wooden posts carrying a ridge pole over a rectangular hollow, around which a simple roof could be constructed. In Germany and elsewhere such buildings appear to be used as workshops, particularly for weaving cloth. The same may be true in England, but there is controversy at West Stow whether the hollow formed a floor surface or was planked over. In any case, the clustering of these huts around each of the rectangular buildings suggests that they were subsidiary structures; each cluster, then, may again represent a family farm unit, as at Chalton. In such hamlets the farm unit appears to be self-contained. Isolated farmsteads surrounded by their own fields may have looked very similar to these village components.

It is probable that the single farm was an important element in the early Anglo-Saxon landscape, as it certainly was in Celtic Britain and Ireland. The large nucleated village, accompanied by open fields worked in strips with a heavy plough pulled by oxen, is a relatively late feature in Anglo-Saxon England. A fine example founded in the late Saxon period and occupied until the 15th century occurs at Goltho (Lincolnshire). In many parts of England the open field never established itself at all, and smaller enclosed fields remained.

Early Anglo-Saxon sunken huts are being experimentally reconstructed at West Stow (Suffolk). These make use of the original hollows and postholes discovered in the excavations. Evidence for the planked walls and for the type of wooden flooring were provided by a hut which had burnt down, while the thatched roof is set at the same roof-angle traditionally used in thatched cottages in Suffolk.

Writing in about 730, the English historian Bede describes his ancestors as consisting of

the Saxons, the Angles and the Jutes. The people of Kent and the inhabitants of the Isle of Wight are of Jutish origin, and also those opposite the Isle of Wight . . . From the Saxon country, that is, the district now known as Old Saxony, came the East Saxons, the South Saxons and the West Saxons. Besides this from the country of the Angles, that is the land between the kingdoms of the Jutes and the Saxons which is called Angulus, came the East Angles, the Middle Angles, the Mercians, and all the Northumbrian race.

These territories can be identified today: Jutland is the peninsula of Denmark, while at its southern end in Schleswig-Holstein is the district of Angeln. Old Saxony is Lower Saxony (Niedersachsen today), while in England Essex is the territory of the East Saxons, East Anglia that of the East Anglians, and so on. Peoples from the entire coastline between the Netherlands and Norway crossed the sea to Britain in the fifth and sixth centuries.

Similarities in the styles of pottery and jewellery found in both settlements and cemeteries in Britain and in Europe show that Bede's groupings have some justification. East Kent and Jutland show links, while in the sixth century the Isle of Wight may have been a colony belonging to Kent. The Saxon areas in Britain, the south west Midlands, Thames valley and south of the Thames, show connections with Lower Saxony, particularly in female jewellery. There are close links between relics found in the British Anglian areas, the north east Midlands, East Anglia, Lincolnshire, Yorkshire and Northumberland, and those in west and south Scandinavia, particularly Schleswig-Holstein.

Although in the confusion of migration Saxon and Anglian relics can be found in the same cemeteries, suggesting an amalgamation of peoples, the division of England into three main regions as described by Bede is reflected in the dress and burial fashions of the sixth century. Cremation interment, in which burnt bones from the corpse were placed in a vessel (usually a pot) and then buried, was more fashionable in the Anglian area than in the Saxon or Kentish regions. The Anglo-Saxon inhumation rite, where an unburnt, fully dressed body was laid out in the grave,

Three Pictish cross-slabs combine a Christian cross with pictorial scenes of human and animal figures; some represent hunting scenes and others are of Biblical stories. These examples are on view at the National Museum of Antiquities of Scotland in Edinburgh.

CHURCHES

After the Saxon settlement, Christianity was restored to southern England by Augustine's mission to King Ethelbert of Kent in 597. Thence it spread to Northumbria in 627, but on the death of the Northumbrian King Edwin (632) the north reverted to paganism. The following year, however, Celtic monks from Iona came to Northumbria. They settled on Lindisfarne (Holy Island) and during the abbacy of Aidan much of the north was converted.

In those parts of sub-Roman Britain which had not fallen to the pagan Saxons Christianity had survived. Since they had long been cut off from the mainstream of western Christianity their churches were organised along different lines and followed different customs from those introduced by Augustine; Roman christianity was organised upon diocesan, episcopal and hieratic lines while Celtic christianity was much more loosely organised and tended to consist of itinerant missions and monks based on monasteries. These differences were resolved in England at the Synod of Whitby in 664. This resulted in a total victory for the Roman faction which determined the basic structure and organisation of the church in Britain to the present day. Its most important achievement was to establish a 'national' church before the country was unified politically.

The conversion was however largely an aristocratic one, and while 'official' paganism was fairly rapidly eradicated pagan customs continued amongst the peasantry for generations.

The Danish invasions of the ninth century dealt a severe blow to the churches. Many monasteries, unprotected and wealthy, were plundered and burnt as were, for example, Lindisfarne and Peterborough. The recovery of Anglo-Saxon England under Alfred and his successors provided a favourable atmosphere for a monastic and general ecclesiastical revival.

Anglo-Saxon churches were divided into three main types: the headminsters, minsters and thegns' churches. The first category consisted of the great churches of Anglo-Saxon England, the diocesan centres and great abbeys such as the Old and New Minsters of

Church of St Lawrence, Bradford-on-Avon, Wilts. A church was established here by St Aldhelm in the early eighth century, but the present structure, rediscovered in 1856 after use as a school, is a Late Saxon rebuilding. It is the first small Anglo-Saxon church in southern England. Remarkably high in proportion to its width, it demonstrates many typical features of Anglo-Saxon ecclesiastical architecture such as pilaster strips and blank arches on the exterior and small round-headed windows and arches. The church contains sculptures of two angels that are amongst the finest surviving examples of Anglo-Saxon sculpture.

Church of St Peter-ad-Murum, Bradwell-juxta-Mare, Essex. Built by St Cedd in about 660 on the site of an old Roman fort called Ythancester, this church originally possessed an apse which has now vanished.

Church of St John, Escomb, Co Durham. The late seventh or early eighth century church is one of the most impressive of the Northumbrian churches. Typically, it is a rectangular building, narrow and comparatively high.

Winchester, Hexham and Ripon. The minsters were mother churches. They were often the earliest church founded in a district, they received tithes and other offerings from a large number of surrounding settlements and were most suited to a country which was still thinly settled and where the process of conversion was not yet complete. By the Norman Conquest they were declining in importance. Their role was diminished by the creation of parishes and the building of a large number of small village churches, and they gradually declined to the status of well-endowed parish churches themselves. The thegns' churches were proprietary churches founded on a lord's estate to serve its spiritual needs. The priest acted as the lord's chaplain and the lord took the tithes of the church.

Many Saxon churches were built of wood: only one survives, much restored, at Greensted-juxta-Ongar (Essex). Churches built of stone tended to be the wealthier and more prestigious churches and those that survive may not therefore be a representative sample. A large number of churches, however, still retain Saxon work, especially

towers. A few churches do remain more or less intact from the seventh century. They include Brixworth (Northamptonshire), Jarrow (Durham) and Bradwell-juxta-Mare (Essex). The crypts of Wilfrid's churches of Ripon (Yorkshire) and Hexham (Northumberland) also remain. Perhaps the finest of all small early Saxon churches is Escomb (Durham), dating from the eighth century. Though many great churches were built following the Danish invasions fewer survive more or less complete than from the pre-Danish period. Amongst the more notable are Wing (Buckinghamshire) and Worth (Sussex). The Norman Conquest, though it did not make a complete architectural break with the past, ensured that future churches would be built, and most old churches rebuilt, in a style drawing heavily on northern French models. It is one of the greatest ironies of medieval history that Harold Godwinson, the last Anglo-Saxon king, should have employed Norman masons to build his abbey church of Waltham (Essex) in 1065.

Odda's Chapel, Deerhurst, Glos (above and below right). Built by earl Odda and consecrated in 1056, this is a rare survival of an Anglo-Saxon private estate chapel and lies close to the better known Saxon monastic church of Deerhurst.

Church of All Saints, Earls Barton, Northants. The Saxon tower, built c. 1100, reveals many features of Anglo-Saxon architecture including the baluster shafts of its windows and the pilaster strips attached to the building.

Church of All Saints, Brixworth, Northants. The finest of the early Saxon churches, Brixworth was founded in the last quarter of the seventh century by monks of Peterborough. Its builders made use of Roman bricks. Later additions were made at the end of the tenth century when the west porch was made into a tower and a circular turret stair added. The interior remains substantially as built; Roman bricks can be seen around the small windows and tall, narrow chantry area.

Church of St Andrew, Greensted-juxta-Ongar, Essex. This church, though much restored, is the sole surviving example of a Saxon wooden church in Britain. It traditionally sheltered the body of King Edmund of East Anglia after his murder by Danes.

provides us with evidence of sixth century regional fashions in female dress. Brooches lie in the positions in which they were worn and corrosion can preserve impressions of textiles to which they had been fastened. The British, Picts and Irish lacked such an informative burial rite and we know little of how their ring brooches and dress pins were worn. After their seventh century conversion to Christianity, the Anglo-Saxons also gradually abandoned the practice of depositing their dead richly dressed (in the case of women) or accompanied by weapons (in the case of men) and began to bury more simply in Christian graveyards.

In recent years archaeologists have been turning their attention from the early Anglo-Saxon cemeteries to their settlements. A number of villages have been excavated in Lower Saxony – notably at Feddersen Wierde and Flögeln – all apparently abandoned by the Saxons in the fifth century when they sailed to England; and quite a few early Anglo-Saxon settlements have also been excavated in England. Examples of well preserved settlements can be found at Chalton and Basingstoke in Hampshire and at Catholme (Staffordshire). At West Stow (Suffolk) the typical rectangular wooden house is largely replaced with a more primitive design, the Saxon sunken hut, which was basically a roof over a hollow in the ground.

The greater part of the population worked on the land throughout the period, as the Domesday Survey of 1086 makes clear. The most prosperous English shires were those which engaged in sheep farming for wool, much of which

may have been exported either raw or as cloth. Around the year 1000, Aelfric, the greatest prose writer of Anglo-Saxon times, describes the tasks of the ploughman: a slave who must complete at least an acre a day. Slavery was an important element in the economy, though in 1086 there were many more slaves in the west and south west of England than in the Scandinavian-settled Danelaw in the east and north east, where many of the descendants of Danish and Anglo-Saxon farmers possessed varying degrees of freedom.

Although portrayed in the contemporary literature as a time of heroic battles when warrior virtues were praised beyond all others, the real nature of Dark Age aristocratic society was quite different. It was a world of intrigue, bloody battles and often senseless killing, kept in check only by the imposition of *wergilds,* or fines, that were paid to the kinsmen of the injured or dead, and whose value depended on the social status of the injured party.

In order to be successful the kings needed wealth, and this they could obtain by attacking their neighbours and extracting tribute from them, which in time could become regular taxation. They also required luxury items and a trading community to supply them. The trading and manufacturing settlement at present under excavation in the suburb of St Mary's, Southampton, may have fulfilled this function for the kings of Wessex between the last years of the seventh and the early decades of the ninth century.

Viking raids on Britain for loot and slaves began in the last decades of the eighth century, and the monks, who were the

TRADE AND TOWNS

Most of the towns of Roman Britain were already in economic decline before the Anglo-Saxon invasions, and those that were not, did not survive the onslaught. Early Anglo-Saxon buildings have been found in some towns, for example at Canterbury, but these seem to indicate no more than rural farmsteads within the old stone walls of the town. Christian missionaries from Rome at the end of the sixth century revived some towns as centres of church administration. Each newly converted Anglo-Saxon kingdom had a bishop appointed and wherever feasible a Roman town was chosen as his seat, for example Canterbury, York and Winchester.

Exchanges of gifts between kings and princes was one mechanism by which exotic objects from the Mediterranean world might reach Anglo-Saxon England, but traders also journeyed to obtain rare and precious things. The concentration in Kentish graves of such objects as bronze bowls from Egypt, and

fine jewellery of gold and silver, implies that Kent played an important role in cross-Channel trade until the seventh century. Indeed, we may suspect a monopoly situation in which all goods traded between England and the Frankish kingdoms passed through Kent. Gold and silver coinage was first minted in Kent in the seventh century, modelled on contemporary Frankish coinage. Coins provided standard units of precious metal for exchange with other goods and at the same time made it easier for a king to collect taxation.

The trading centre at St Mary's, Southampton, which operated between the end of the seventh and early ninth centuries, marks the breakdown of Kent's prominence in cross-Channel trade. This important site, which is still being excavated, is located halfway between a Roman fort at Bitterne (Clausentum) and the 10th century walled town of Southampton. Judging by the many coins and large quantities of foreign pottery discovered there,

much of which consists of tableware from France, it was probably the residence of foreign merchants and native craftsmen who provided the kings of Wessex with the luxury goods they demanded. It was unfortified and its abandonment coincides with an intensification of the Viking raids on the British and French coasts, which had begun in the later eighth century.

There was fairly free movement of trade to and from England at this time — not always honest — and a letter from the Frankish emperor Charlemagne to Offa, King of Mercia in 796 tells of the French ruler's problems with English pilgrims who were also acting as traders and avoiding paying tolls, of Offa's request for millstones to be sent to England, and of the export of woollen cloaks from England. The lava quernstones from the Rhineland found in the excavation of an eighth century watermill at Tamworth (Staffordshire) may be the 'black stones' sent by Charlemagne. Other imports to England included eastern silks, glass and sword blades from the Rhineland, wine, dried fish and furs. Apart from the cloaks, the

English exported raw wool, hides, lead, butter, cheese, honey and human slaves. Pope Gregory's encounter with the fair-headed pagan slaves in Rome prompted him to plan a mission in the sixth century to convert the Anglo-Saxons, but the slave trade continued long after their conversion.

The West Saxon kings built a chain of towns and forts in the ninth and early 10th centuries to ring their kingdom for its defence. Sometimes they reused old Roman town or fort walls, but many of these *burhs* were on new sites. Some of them developed into major towns after the threat of Viking attack diminished and the number of moneyers striking coins at each *burh* provides some idea of the prosperity of these communities. Others failed to develop and were eventually abandoned altogether.

The Vikings, however, were not merely destructive raiders, but also traders and craftsmen. Their colonisation of northern and eastern England, the Danelaw, was centred on towns such as York, and some of the crafts practised here have been revealed in the well-preserved workshops at Coppergate.

Two bronze bowls from Christian Coptic Egypt were found in Anglo-Saxon graves in south east England. They probably reached England via northern Italy and the Rhine Valley.

Seventh century gold and garnet brooch and cross, found in Kent and Suffolk.

Jewellery from Berinsfield, Oxfordshire, typically worn by richer women of the time.

HEROES AND KINGS

We know very little about the personalities and lives of the kings, bishops and abbots — the leading figures of Dark Age society. The literature of the time — dominated by a theme of hero worship in both secular poetry and clerical biography — often gives a false impression because of its preoccupation with heroic victories and warrior virtues, and it is often difficult to separate fact from fiction.

The Anglo-Saxon, British and Irish poetry concentrates on praising the virtues of its warrior lords. Battles are described as a series of individual combats where men preferred to die as heroes rather than desert their lord in war. One famous example is the eighth century poem *Beowulf*, which commemorates the exploits of a Swedish prince of the Geats, who fights monsters and dragons as well as men, and who is honoured by all after his heroic death. The poem also provides a picture of an ideal society where the kings were generous, rewarding their noble warriors with treasure and fine weapons, and in which the troops would share a communal life with their kings, feasting in their halls during peacetime and fighting bravely for them in war.

The Battle of Catraeth, on the other hand, describes a raid by British horsemen on the Anglo-Saxons which ends in disastrous defeat. Such poetry served several functions, providing entertainment, commemorating the great men of the past and acting as a means of describing the virtues of manly conduct to which all men should aspire. Life in these societies was often violent and frequently brief, with seasonal warfare endemic, and quarrels, sordid assassinations, feuds and vendettas commonplace.

We owe much of our definite historical knowledge to writers like the Venerable Bede, whose detailed records of the lives of missionaries and clergymen give considerable insight. Bede's *Life of St Cuthbert* provides a picture of a man who, as a result of seeing a vision of God, rose from his life as a humble shepherd to become the bishop of Northumbria. Some of the relics from his late seventh century shrine are still preserved in Durham Cathedral Library including his gold cross. Many of the gifts to the shrine made by later kings had been removed before the 19th century, probably by Henry VIII's commissioners in 1539.

Another seventh century Bishop of Northumbria, Wilfrid, represents a very different type of cleric. Born a nobleman, he had political ambitions which placed him in frequent conflict with kings and saw him exiled several times. Bede distrusted the grandeur and pomp of Wilfrid and his large retinue, but as the Church was a major landowner, it is not surprising that bishops and abbots often appeared to be worldly men.

Bede himself was a remarkable cleric and although he spent virtually all his life in two monasteries in the Tyne valley, he was fluent in Latin and Greek and was the first great scholar of Germanic origin in Europe. His *Ecclesiastical History of the English People*, completed in 731, was a textbook for the eighth century English missionaries, who repaid their debt to Pope Gregory for their conversion by preaching to the Frisians and Saxons in north Germany.

We know very little about the early pagan Anglo-Saxon kings, but Bede provides us with a series of anecdotes which bring to life the great seventh century kings of Northumbria, notably Edwin (whose palace at Yeavering has been excavated) and Oswold. Everyone has heard of Alfred the Great, however, the ninth century King of Wessex, and this is not surprising for there is a contemporary biography of him by Asser, and the *Anglo-Saxon Chronicle* is a major product of his court. In the introduction to his own translation from Latin to English of St Gregory's *Pastoral Care*, Alfred explains his active campaign to revive the monasteries and churches of his kingdom after the Viking wars. Alfred was clearly an able propagandist, and knowledge of his work has survived because the kings who followed him were so successful.

We know much less about Offa, the eighth century King of Mercia, for Wessex had broken Mercian supremacy in 825. Offa must have been a great man, the effective ruler of all the English except the Northumbrians and the builder of the great dyke, by which he separated the Midlands from Wales. From a few surviving letters, we know that he regarded himself the equal of the Frankish emperor Charlemagne, refusing to allow his daughter to marry Charlemagne's son, unless his own son could have a similar wedding. During a disagreement with the Pope in Rome, Offa apparently suggested to Charlemagne that they could depose the Pope just as they dismissed their own bishops, and replace him with a Frank. It is not surprising, therefore, to learn that Offa was not loved by the Church.

The penultimate English king, Edward the Confessor, on the other hand, was revered after his death as the pious founder of Westminster Abbey. Yet he had been educated as a warrior noble of the royal house in England and northern France, not as a cleric, and emerged as an opportunist embittered by long exile in France before he achieved the throne.

Beowulf, the epic poem, describes the life and heroic death of a Scandinavian prince. Its descriptions of royal buildings have been borne out by excavations such as those at Yeavering in Northumberland.

The Alfred and Minster Lovell Jewels. The larger bears an inscription meaning "Alfred had me made" and may have belonged to Alfred the Great.

The Bayeux Tapestry is an important source for the history of the mid 11th century, and here shows Edward the Confessor addressing Earl Harold of Wessex, who was to be elected his successor yet lost the decisive battle of Hastings in 1066.

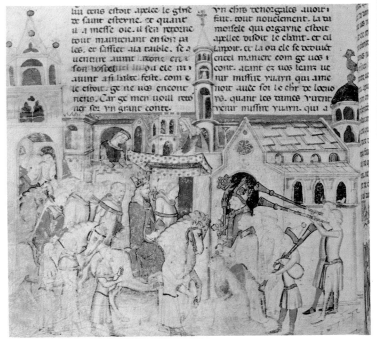

Arthur enters Camelot. King Arthur is a literary invention of the 12th century though there may have been a military leader of that name in the late 5th century.

literate class of Anglo-Saxon society, have provided us with a full and vivid record of atrocities caused by the seamen in their clinker-built longships. Raiding continued until the middle of the ninth century when the Vikings turned to invasion with a view to settlement. The only English Kingdom which successfully resisted them was Wessex under Alfred. As well as organising a highly successful army, Alfred had built a chain of fortifications, called *burhs*, along the coast and land frontiers to protect inland areas from surprise raids and to provide a refuge for the local population and its livestock. Some of these re-used old Roman town walls, as at Chichester and Winchester; others were constructed on new sites, as at Wallingford and Wareham. By no means all of these *burhs* developed into towns, but many of them acquired a mint to produce coinage in the 10th century. Some of them are still important towns today, for example Oxford, while others, such as Wallingford, where a large section of the ditch and bank defences still survives, suffered a decline later in their history.

The Scandinavian seamen were also traders, whose territory ranged from Russia and the Black Sea to Arabic Spain and the Mediterranean. Their major settlements in the British Isles were the towns of Dublin, York and the 'five boroughs' of Stamford, Lincoln, Derby, Leicester and Nottingham. In recent years major excavations have been taking place in Dublin, revealing an extensive waterfront area of the Viking town, and at York demonstrating its well-preserved timber houses and workshops at Coppergate, the street of the coopers.

The Vikings also settled in the countryside as farmers and landlords, but there is still controversy about the numbers of land-hungry Scandinavians who actually settled in Britain. The surviving evidence can be given many interpretations and the presence of Scandinavian personal names in eastern England in the later 11th century may reflect widespread English adoption of the Scandinavian names of their lords, just as northern French names became popular in the generation after the Norman Conquest.

THE VIKINGS

The Scandinavian invaders of the 9th to the 11th centuries are usually referred to as Vikings, from the Old Norse word for pirates, and they first appear off the coasts of Britain in the eighth century as marauding raiders. These Danish and Norwegian seamen used their streamlined shallow-draught longships powered by sail and oars, to raid far upstream. They also rode horses, either captured locally or transported on board ship, to give them equal mobility on land. They had no scruples about attacking defenceless monasteries for their gold and silver vessels, vestments and fine books, and the large accumulations of precious metal found buried in hoards in Scandinavia bear witness to their success. In all cases, surprise and speed were their weapons, and if cornered by superior forces, they were prepared to avoid battle, sheltering behind fortifications until the enemy had exhausted its supplies and dispersed.

After the middle of the ninth century, however, the Scandinavians turned their attention to conquest and settlement. The Danes conquered much of England, and the only kingdom which successfully resisted them was Wessex under Alfred. He built a fleet to meet the Vikings at sea, organised an army which could be called up in sections enabling him to fight long sustained campaigns, and built a chain of fortifications known as *burhs* around his borders. Having successfully worn the Vikings down, a treaty was drawn up that made Watling Street a frontier between Alfred and the Danes.

The region to the east was under Danelaw and that to the west under the laws of the West Saxons and the Mercians. Norwegians concentrated their settlements on the Shetland and Orkney islands, north west Scotland, the Isle of Man, the coast of north west England, Anglesey, the coast of South Wales and Ireland. These settlers were based principally in towns in England and Ireland and acted there as traders and craftsmen. Excavations at York and Dublin have revealed many of their activities. In the countryside around these towns, modern village names record Scandinavian settlement in England, notably those names ending in -*by* and -*thorp*. Evidence from placenames seems to imply that the Scandinavians settled initially in areas not occupied by the Anglo-Saxon population. A Scandinavian placename need not imply a large Viking population, however, for a village might well be renamed after its new Scandinavian lord yet not incur any substantial change in the population.

Alfred's successors conquered Danelaw in the 10th century and ruled a united Anglo-Scandinavian kingdom. Their triumph was short-lived, however, for well organised raids from Scandinavia began again before the end of that century, culminating in the offer of the English throne to a Danish king, Cnut, in 1016. Edward the Confessor, a descendent of Alfred, became king in 1042, but the Scandinavian threat remained. A Norwegian invasion in 1066 was defeated by Harold at Stamford Bridge, but William the Conqueror had to maintain a paid army in England long after the Norman Conquest to guard against the possible threat of a Danish invasion.

King Cnut is shown with his queen Aelfgyfu or Emma in a drawing of about 1020, presenting a gold cross for an altar at the New Minster in Winchester. Cnut seized the English kingdom by force in 1016 and ruled it until his death in 1035.

COINS

The earliest Dark Age coinage used in Britain was imported from Merovingian France. By the middle of the century, however, England was producing her own gold coinage based on the Merovingian denomination, the third of a solidus, and these coins are found together with imported pieces in the Crondall hoard from Hampshire. These are the earliest Anglo-Saxon coins, and they seem to have been restricted to south east England.

Soon, however, the gold coinage was replaced by silver coins known today as *Sceattas*, from the Anglo-Saxon word for treasure.

Around 770 two Kentish kings named Heaberht and Ecgberht struck the first English pennies. However, the power of these small Kentish kings was soon overshadowed by that of Offa of Mercia, one of the great Anglo-Saxon kings, who ordered the production of a coinage of considerable size and great variety.

From this time the quantity of coins made is also important. Since England produced only a very little domestically mined silver, almost all the precious metal used in her coinage had to be earned from abroad. A large and flourishing silver coinage in England was usually a sign of a flourishing export trade bringing in hard cash.

The most famous of all Anglo-Saxon kings, Alfred, owes his place in history chiefly to his courageous struggle against the invading Danes. Some of his coin designs illustrate this; for example, the London monogram was first used to celebrate Alfred's occupation of London in 886.

The Scandinavian invasions left their mark on the coinage in a number of ways. Firstly, the Vikings struck their own coinage, often in close imitation of the English coins. They also took vast quantities of English coins back to Scandinavia.

Coin portrait of Offa, king of Mercia.

English penny of Ethelred the Unready.

The end-slab of a stone tomb from the churchyard of St Paul's Cathedral in London. It is ornamented with a 'great beast' with tendrils on its body and a lesser creature around its front legs. Traces of the original paint survive, indicating that the 'beast' had a blue-black body with white spots. It is presumed to have been carved by a Scandinavian mason in London.

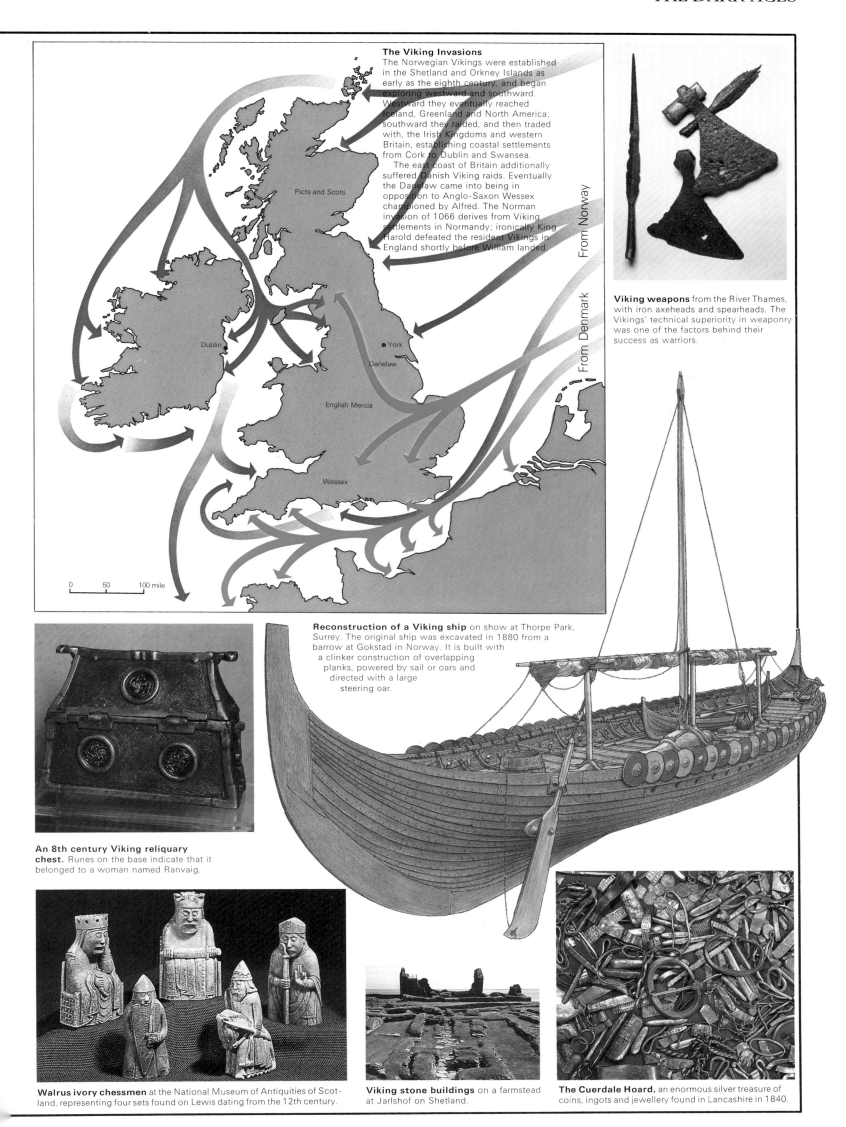

The Viking Invasions
The Norwegian Vikings were established in the Shetland and Orkney Islands as early as the eighth century, and began exploring westward and southward. Westward they eventually reached Iceland, Greenland and North America; southward they raided, and then traded with, the Irish Kingdoms and western Britain, establishing coastal settlements from Cork to Dublin and Swansea.

The east coast of Britain additionally suffered Danish Viking raids. Eventually the Danelaw came into being in opposition to Anglo-Saxon Wessex championed by Alfred. The Norman invasion of 1066 derives from Viking settlements in Normandy; ironically King Harold defeated the resident Vikings in England shortly before William landed.

From Norway

From Denmark

Picts and Scots

Dublin

York

Danelaw

English Mercia

Wessex

0   50   100 mile

Viking weapons from the River Thames, with iron axeheads and spearheads. The Vikings' technical superiority in weaponry was one of the factors behind their success as warriors.

Reconstruction of a Viking ship on show at Thorpe Park, Surrey. The original ship was excavated in 1880 from a barrow at Gokstad in Norway. It is built with a clinker construction of overlapping planks, powered by sail or oars and directed with a large steering oar.

An 8th century Viking reliquary chest. Runes on the base indicate that it belonged to a woman named Ranvaig.

Walrus ivory chessmen at the National Museum of Antiquities of Scotland, representing four sets found on Lewis dating from the 12th century.

Viking stone buildings on a farmstead at Jarlshof on Shetland.

The Cuerdale Hoard, an enormous silver treasure of coins, ingots and jewellery found in Lancashire in 1840.

The Later Middle Ages

*The Norman conquest of 1066
unified England once more. In the following 400 years stone castles, cathedrals
and churches were built, trade began to flourish and
many new communities were established. But in 1348 the Black Death almost halved the
population and caused the abandonment of many villages.*

Contemporary writers divided medieval society into three components: those who worked, those who fought and those who prayed; that is, the peasant agricultural labourers, the knights and the clergy. Each of these orders had a divinely appointed role and all contributed to the well being of the community. Not surprisingly, moralists and chroniclers condemned any attempts to disturb this order by violence; all writers therefore denounced the Peasants' Revolt of 1381. Normally they also attacked other confusion of the orders such as, for example, the carrying of arms by the clergy. Nevertheless these orders were not totally sealed from each other. It was possible for an ambitious peasant's son to rise into the ranks of the knights or to achieve spectacular success as a cleric, as did William de Wykeham, the son of an unfree peasant of a Hampshire village who became the most powerful churchman and politician in the land during the latter years of Edward III's reign. He was the founder of Winchester College and New College, Oxford and the rebuilder of the cathedral at Winchester. Professional men, especially lawyers, could join the gentry and purchase landed estates, as did the famous Norfolk family of Paston in the late 14th century.

We know less about the conditions of the medieval peasantry than of any other class. They left no written records and all documentary evidence concerning them derives from their lords. Moreover, very few of their dwellings survive from periods earlier than the 15th century. Their houses were usually built of materials less durable than stone and such houses as do survive have usually been rebuilt and altered almost beyond recognition. The plans of villagers' houses can, however, often be made out on the sites of deserted medieval villages where they appear as slightly raised plots lying along the village street, often surrounded by a small enclosed garden, the close, and having rear access to the open fields. Although open fields, great fields cultivated communally in strips held by individual peasants, survive today only in a very few places (most notably at Laxton, Nottinghamshire) the form of the strips, an elongated S-bend, can still be seen over wide areas of England, especially in the Midlands and southern England. Elsewhere in the country, in the Highland Zone and in the Celtic areas, social customs and agricultural methods differed. Pastoral farming predominated and arable fields were small and enclosed in total contrast to the great fields.

Much more is known of the way of life of the warrior aristocracy. They were the heroes of much contemporary literature and their exploits were a commonplace of medieval chronicles. Though comparatively few were literate at least until the end of the middle ages, they were able to employ scribes and clerks to whom letters could be dictated and who could keep their accounts and other records, such as the court rolls preserving the details of the manorial courts held for their tenants. From surviving account rolls it is possible to establish the income lords were receiving from their estates at a given time and the type of agriculture they were producing. Finally, the survival, if only in a ruined state, of many of their homes (usually castles) demonstrates how these men and their lands dominated the landscape. They also allow a much more detailed picture of the daily life of the aristocracy to be drawn than is possible in the case of the peasants.

Within the ranks of those who prayed there were great

Corfe Castle, Dorset (left) was begun by William the Conqueror and stands on a small hill at the end of the limestone ridge of the Isle of Purbeck, dominating the local landscape and the small town of Corfe.

Sir Geoffrey Luttrell is shown here as an idealised early 14th century warrior on the opening page of the Luttrell Psalter, being armed by his wife and daughter. Only after the 14th century were actual physical likenesses attempted.

social and economic distinctions. At the lowest level, the unbeneficed clergy and those who only possessed small parishes were little, if at all, better off than the neighbouring peasantry. Poor parish priests often cultivated their glebe (land belonging to the parish church) amongst the strips of the laity. Where the glebe land had been enclosed it was often still of small extent. Above the parish clergy stood the dignitaries of the church, the lesser, such as the rural deans, having limited power but the most important, the bishops, being men of considerable wealth, often related to the lay aristocracy and with responsibility over wide areas. Their prestige and social positions reflected in their houses, often fortified, many of which survive today such as Lambeth Palace (London home of the Archbishops of Canterbury), Wolvesey Palace (belonging to the bishop of Winchester) and Old Sherborne Castle (a residence of the bishop of Salisbury).

Besides these secular clergy there were the regular clergy, the monks and friars, who were forbidden by their rule from having individual income but whose communities often disposed of considerable landed wealth. Again, however, there were wide fluctuations in wealth between the great and often long established Benedictine abbeys on the one hand and small communities that were poorly endowed and comprised only a few monks.

Though the four centuries between the coming of the Normans and the establishment of the Tudor dynasty saw many changes both in the English landscape and in English society, in two fundamental areas there was little or no change. First, the population of Tudor England was little different from what it was in the mid 11th century. Then it probably stood at a little below two million; at the end of the 15th century it was probably a little above two million. The population reached its peak at the end of the 13th century, when it has been estimated at around 6.5 millions. Thereafter famine and disease (especially the recurrent outbreaks of plague) brought about a considerable reduction. Secondly, this population was almost entirely rural; over 90 per cent of the people lived in the countryside. No town, with the exception of London, could compare in size, prestige and power with the contemporary towns of Flanders or northern Italy. Such towns as did exist tended to be concentrated in the south and west of England, and in Wales, Scotland and Ireland the urban economy was even less developed than in England. Throughout the medieval period, therefore, there was a predominantly peasant population, the great majority of whom, especially during the 13th century, lived at near

subsistence level on small holdings cultivated by individual families.

In 1066 much of the country was uncolonised. Large areas were still given over to woodland – much of which was shortly to be protected from agricultural encroachment by the creation of royal forests – undrained marsh or fen. The high moorlands were scarcely populated and the population was concentrated in East Anglia and the eastern Midlands. Towns were small and little differentiated from the surrounding countryside. Nearly all of them served only a limited regional area. There was, however, some trade with the Continent, especially with Flanders and the Low Countries, whose merchants had been active in south east England since the ninth century, if not earlier. The only industry producing for a wide market was that of cloth, which exported materials of high quality to northern Europe. The lack of harnessed energy prevented production to capacity, though both water and windmills were common.

The Norman Conquest

The Norman Conquest coincided with a boom in economic activity throughout Europe. The reasons for this expansion are still unclear but the decline of barbarian raids, whether Viking, Magyar or Saracen, certainly played a considerable part in producing favourable conditions for economic growth. There was a general increase in population, expansion of urban life, commerce and industry, and a growing concern, stimulated by population pressure, to develop and exploit the land more effectively. In Britain the effect of the Norman Conquest upon the society and economy has been much debated: many changes effected during the late 11th and 12th centuries may well have been no more than coincidental with the Conquest rather than a direct result of it. It is certain that the economy grew faster during these years than at any time since the departure of the Romans. In the country such expansion is demonstrated by the rapid colonisation of many waste regions by individuals or communities, whether villages or ecclesiastical, such as the great Benedictine abbeys of the southern counties. At the same time towns expanded; old towns developed suburbs, while new towns were created to serve both as centres of administration and political power and as regional or national markets.

While the peasants continued more or less unaffected by the Conquest, continuing to cultivate their own holdings and to provide service upon their lord's *demesne* as they had for many generations, the new aristocracy established them-

The field on which the Battle of Hastings was fought remains little altered today. This view is taken from the ridge occupied by Harold's army, looking across rough pasture to the hilltop from which the Normans launched their attack.

Dover Castle, Kent, on one of the most important strategic sites in England, was built by William I. Its keep was begun in 1168 and it is surrounded by a curtain wall which was extended in the 13th century.

THE NORMAN INVASION

The victory of Duke William of Normandy over Harold II, king of England on a hillside a few miles to the north of Hastings (Sussex) on 14 October 1066 was perhaps the most momentous victory in English history. The Norman settlement that followed replaced within one generation the native English aristocracy in positions of secular and ecclesiastical authority. A new form of society based upon the mounted aristocratic warrior, the knight, and upon his home, the castle, was introduced into England. The English church, moribund and archaic, was reformed in accordance with the practices of Normandy. This reform was symbolised by the replacement of the small Saxon churches and cathedrals by new buildings in the Romanesque style and in the grand manner, as happened for example, at St Albans (Hertfordshire) or Winchester (Hampshire). Latin replaced English as the language of administration, and French became the language of the aristocracy. Though the institutions of government remained virtually unaltered, the personnel of both local and central government were changed. In the most important change of all, the cultural and political outlook of England was now towards France rather than towards Scandinavia.

In a sense the Norman invasion began many years before 1066. Edward the Confessor had spent much of his early life as an exile at the Norman court, and as king he favoured a Norman faction whom he introduced to England. He settled some lands in the Welsh marches and even appointed a Norman, Robert of Jumièges, as archbishop of Canterbury in 1051. Robert was soon expelled in the anti-Norman reaction led by earl Godwine of Wessex, which was largely successful in reducing Norman influence. Nevertheless the childless Edward nominated Duke William as his successor. In 1064 Earl Harold, the son of Godwine, journeyed to Normandy, probably to confirm the nomination. This action and the succeeding history of Anglo-Norman relations until the battle are graphically displayed on the Bayeux Tapestry, which was probably commissioned by Odo, bishop of Bayeux and Duke William's half-brother. Both this and other sources describe how Harold swore homage to William

and promised to support him in his claim to the throne, yet how on Edward's death in January 1066 Harold was elected king. In September Harold successfully defeated an invasion of Northumbria led jointly by Harold's brother Tostig and Harald Hardraada, king of Norway. While on this expedition Harold heard of William's invasion of England at Pevensey (Sussex); he hurried south and was shortly afterwards defeated and killed.

William rapidly established control over southern England and was crowned at Westminster abbey on Christmas Day 1066. Northern England proved more recalcitrant and Norman rule was only effective there after 1070 when William ruthlessly put down a major rebellion against his authority.

For much of our knowledge about the history and geography of England in the 11th century we are dependent on the Domesday Book. Although a great deal of evidence can be gleaned from a variety of agricultural documents, from charters of various kinds and the Anglo-Saxon Chronicles, the bulk of the information available is derived from the Great Survey itself and from its ancillary books.

The origin of the survey dates from the Gloucester meeting of Christmas 1085 where the king 'had deep speech with his witan . . . He then sent his men over all England into every shire' to collect the information which was collated in the manuscript volume which became known as the Domesday Book. 'So very narrowly did he cause the Survey to be made', records the Anglo-Saxon Chronicle, 'that there was not a single hide nor a rood of land, nor was there an ox, or a cow, or a pig passed by, that was not set down in the accounts, and then all these writings were brought to him'.

Domesday reveals that the Norman conquest had relatively little effect on the lower levels of society. Some actually improved their status, for slavery, a common phenomenon in Anglo-Saxon England, was abolished by the Normans. At a higher level the thegns suffered greatly. Those who had not been killed during the 1066 campaigns or who had not fled to Scotland, Scandinavia or Byzantium (where some joined the Varangian

guard) were largely replaced by Norman or French knights. By 1086 only 8 per cent of all land held directly of the king was in the hands of the native aristocracy. A similar pattern was seen in the church. By the time of William's death only one English bishop, Oswald of Worcester (himself educated on the continent) remained. The rest had been deposed or replaced on their death by foreigners such as Lanfranc of Canterbury, a Lombard canon lawyer and abbot of the Norman monastery of Bec. At the parish level English priests survived, preached in the vernacular and served in churches that continued to be built by native craftsmen. The larger churches, abbeys and cathedrals, however, were rebuilt in Norman Romanesque style and were almost exclusively staffed by foreign clergy.

The great stone keeps of the Norman castles and the grandiose Romanesque churches of the late 11th century stand together as the most impressive memorials to the Norman invasion. They symbolise, and were meant to symbolise, the introduction of an alien aristocracy and its assumption of power. The invaders, predominantly but not exclusively Norman, were to dominate English society and politics for many generations. Though intermarriage with the native population soon occurred, assimilation of the races was not achieved for many generations. Only in the 14th century, when Edward III declared war on France, did his nobility discover the political virtues of the English language. French remained the language of polite society, however, for many generations more to come.

The Bayeux Tapestry, probably commissioned by Bishop Odo of Bayeux (though the embroidery was probably worked by English seamstresses) towards the end of the 11th century, provides a graphic account of events leading to the Battle of Hastings from a Norman viewpoint. Here the death of Harold is portrayed; it is thought he may be the soldier on the horse rather than the famous figure with the arrow in his eye.

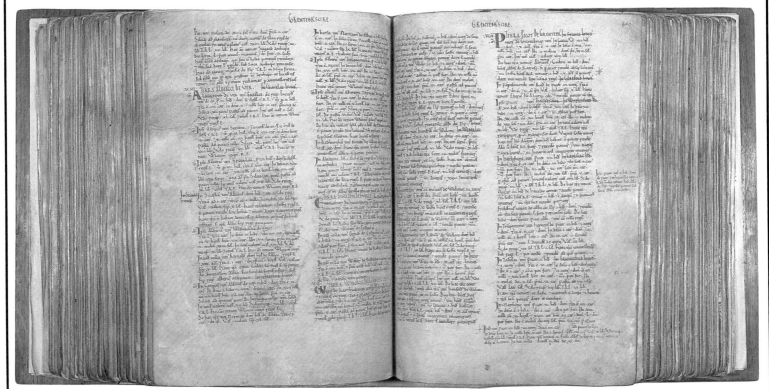

The Domesday Book was a survey ordered in 1085 by the government in order to determine the extent and value of all lands held by the King and his tenants-in-chief. Though it was never completed and omits the northern counties, London and Winchester, it is an invaluable guide to late 11th century England. These folios describe some of the lands in Cambridgeshire.

selves upon their newly acquired lands, and the wealthy constructed stone castles as residences and defensive places against possible unrest. The new lords founded new monasteries. At first they tended to endow favoured Norman abbeys with English lands but within one or two generations monasteries were founded on English soil and replaced the Norman abbeys in the affections of the aristocracy. During the 12th century Cistercian abbeys, established in great number across Britain but especially in northern England, Wales and the Scottish Borders, were greatly favoured. Their energetic farming contributed to the changing landscape, for their spiritual and economic life demanded that they settle in remote places, and where this was not possible they attempted to farm their lands as separate entities rather than in the traditional open fields. Thus, on the one hand Cistercian abbeys encouraged the reclamation of underpopulated and waste areas, and on the other their practice of enclosing lands foreshadowed the enclosure that was to be so common a feature of late medieval and early modern England.

The expansion of the economy continued into the 13th century, and a still increasing population put growing pressure on the land. Land values rose dramatically and reclamation began to be made of marginal land of limited agricultural potential. The population, however, increased faster than did the reclaimed land; as a result the size of peasant holdings decreased and many peasants were pushed close to starvation level. In many areas the population was as high as it was to be at any time before the mid 19th century. A few peasant families, though, were able to prosper. By investing in land some, especially free peasants, were able to join the ranks of the gentry or knightly class. The majority, however, possessed holdings of only a few acres or were entirely landless, forming a pool of un- or under-employed labour on which the wealthier peasants or lords could draw for seasonal employment. It is not surprising that by the end of the century the population was beginning to decline. In many areas reclamation of land stopped and some land even reverted to waste. A series of bad harvests and cattle and sheep plagues, combined with frequent and extensive flooding in many areas, during the early years of the 14th century exacerbated the situation. The climate of western Europe was worsening: summers were wetter, winters colder. The outlook for the early 14th century peasant was grim.

Economic instability

During the 13th century too many of the knightly class were falling into difficulties. In the first quarter of the century unprecedented inflation rates made it increasingly difficult for a knight to maintain his status and economic condition. The cost of military equipment, more and more sophisticated, was rising. Land and agricultural prices were high so that the great landholders benefited more than did the lesser knights, whose estates were of only a few hundred acres. Those who produced food for the market could take advantage of high prices: those who relied on rents for their income suffered as rents, long fixed by custom, lost their real value. Not surprisingly, many lords fell into the hands of money lenders and were forced to sell their lands to survive.

Economic instability made the knights politically unstable also. Discontent at the high handed activities and heavy taxation imposed by King John and King Henry III led to the rebellion of many. The ultimate failure of these rebellions in 1217 and 1266 meant that many knights were heavily fined or had their lands confiscated, thereby adding to their

CASTLES

Castles were the most dominant buildings in the medieval landscape; today their remains stand as the most evocative symbols of medieval society At once fortress and home, the castle fulfilled many functions. It was a residence for the king or lord and his retinue, an administrative centre and a meeting place for councils and an advertisement of the wealth and status of its owner. As a fortified place the castle could form part of a system of royal defences protecting frontier country, as did the Anglo-Norman castles of the south coast such as Portchester (Hampshire), Pevensey (Sussex) and Dover (Kent), or it could stand as an outpost in an hostile environment as did the Edwardian castles of north Wales or magnatial castles such as Caerphilly (Glamorgan) More often, however, the castle's defensive role was confined to the immediate locality; castles protected or controlled bridgeheads, fords, important roads or mountain passes. In towns they often served to protect markets that developed at their feet (as happened at Newcastle) and they were often, as at Oxford and Caernarvon (Gwynedd) attached to a system of urban defences. Above all, the castle was a symbol of

authority, at first representing Norman domination over a native population and then more generally signifying the power of the landed aristocracy.

The English castle was a Norman innovation. Earlier fortresses, such as the Anglo-Saxon *burhs*, had formed part of a coherent, national and royal defensive system: the castle as fortified residence of the military aristocracy was unknown until the first motte and bailey castles were built in Herefordshire by Normans whom Edward the Confessor had brought to the court. After 1066 castles rapidly proliferated, especially during periods of civil strife such as Stephen's reign (1135–54). They took many forms, from the simple motte and bailey (of which there are about 750 known examples) or ring-work (an earth-banked enclosure) to the great stone keeps exemplified by the royal castles of the White Tower (Tower of London) and Colchester (Essex) or by baronial fortresses such as Castle Rising (Norfolk). Only the very wealthy magnates could afford such fortresses, and the majority of castles were of much simpler design. Though comparatively few castles were built after 1200 their design reached a high

Bamburgh Castle, Northumberland, was largely built in the 12th century and consists of a keep and three baileys on a superb natural site.

point of military and architectural sophistication during the 13th and 14th centuries. Additions to the royal castle of Corfe (Dorset) at the beginning of the 13th century and Henry III's work at Windsor (Berkshire) in the mid century demonstrate the growing luxury of the castle. The Welsh campaigns of Edward I resulted in the building of a number of fortresses such as Conwy (Gwynedd) in which new emphasis is placed upon the gatehouse and concentric curtain walls rather than the keep. While Edward's castles owed much to continental models, his foremost engineer being the Savoyard James of St George, other royal and baronial castles in turn borrowed much from the Welsh Edwardian types.

Thereafter castle building declined, although large ones were built on a lavish scale until the end of the 15th century and beyond. Bolton Castle (Yorkshire), Tattershall (Lincolnshire), Kirkby (Leicestershire) and Thornbury (Gloucestershire) all testify to the magnates' (and especially the parvenus') desire to proclaim their wealth by building castles. Fortified manor houses on a much smaller scale were, however, more common. There were a number of reasons for this decline. The military role of the castle became of less importance, and only in the frontier regions of northern England did the tradition of building primarily defensive residences continue. Wales had been subdued, and only one castle, Queenborough (Kent; now destroyed), was newly built against the French threat during the Hundred Years War.

In general, though lawlessness and civil disorder were perhaps increasing, the castle's military importance declined as greater emphasis was placed upon its residential function. Military design made increasing concessions to luxury and comfort. Many 15th century castles were built in new fashioned brick rather than in traditional stone. At the same time sieges became less common, and the pitched battle more frequent, in warfare. Castles played a comparatively minor role in the Wars of the Roses. Moreover they were costly to build and maintain, and they were especially a financial burden to the impecunious late medieval kings. The 'new' aristocracy and the rising merchant class had no military tradition. In their world castles were anachronistic; their residences tended to be in the towns or in more or less country houses. Even if the military function of the castle was not quite dead by the beginning of the Tudor period, it was dying. The decline of the castle was both a symptom and a sign of the end of the middle ages.

The White Tower of the Tower of London served as royal headquarters for the city's administration and is the largest and most impressive of the great Anglo-Norman keeps.

Caerphilly Castle, Glamorgan, was a stronghold of the Marcher Earl of Gloucester. Begun in 1268, it covers a wide area and is notable for the sophistication of its design and the elaborate use of water defences. It is the finest example of an English baronial castle in Wales.

distress. Many knightly families did, of course, survive; by royal service as administrators or soldiers or by astute estate management it was possible for knights to prosper and even to enter the ranks of the peerage. These were, however, a minority; for most it was a difficult and testing time.

The great magnates, both lay and ecclesiastical, gained most during the 13th century. They increased their own estates at the expense of the gentry class, and because they produced for the market profited from high prices. Books of estate management were written for them and were widely disseminated. It was the age of the great 'improving' ecclesiastical landlords such as prior Henry of Eastry of Christ Church, Canterbury. Such men rationalised their estates, specialised their farming, reclaimed land and increased the productivity of older lands by the greater use of fertilisers. Moreover, they were able to take advantage of the land scarcity and abundance of peasant labour to increase rents and to increase the number of labour services required from the peasants on their land. Thus they further added to the peasants' distress. With the proceeds of their expanded rent rolls and agricultural profits the magnates were able to invest in more land and to demonstrate their own wealth in more luxuriously appointed castles or in the rebuilding of old cathedrals or abbey churches in new, more lavish style.

The growth of towns

At the same time town life flourished. New towns continued to be founded throughout the century. Many asserted civic pride by the building of elaborate urban defences: most developed their own institutions of government and obtained, for a price, considerable independance from royal officials. Trade was increasingly controlled by monopolistic craft guilds and their influence over all aspects of urban life was to be a feature of urban society until the end of the middle ages. Most towns still served only as regional markets but a few, especially the ports of the south and east such as Southampton or King's Lynn, developed a flourishing international trade. The chief export was wool, taken to the Flemish towns for finishing into cloth. Wool was produced by both lay and ecclesiastical growers but it was a commodity especially suited for production on open moorland, and Cistercian producers who held much of the uplands of the north played a considerable part in wool production. Wool made the fortunes of the producers; it also made those of the wool merchants who rose to pre-eminence in the towns, and

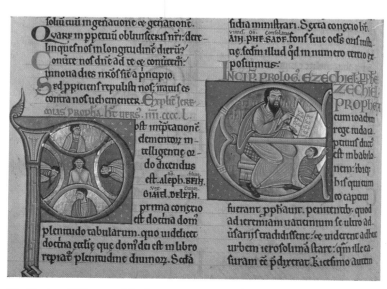

The Durham Bible, one of the finest surviving English Romanesque manuscripts, was donated to Durham Priory Library by Bishop Hugh de Puiset of Durham (1153–95).

CHURCHES AND CATHEDRALS

Churches, from small parish churches to great cathedrals, are the most commonly surviving structures of medieval Britain. Throughout the medieval period they fulfilled many functions: as centres of community worship, as foci for pious benefactions from both individuals and groups, as meeting places and centres for commercial transactions and as stages for the performance of sacred dramas. The larger churches, particularly the cathedrals, dominated the religious life of their region and their presence stimulated the growth of the towns around them. Other churches fulfilled more specialist functions: some were, for example, centres of local or national cults with shrines attracting large numbers; some, especially in the towns, belonged to local guilds; others served as mausolea for local magnates and gentry.

By 1066 the parish system was already well developed and there were already many parish churches in existence. Many more parishes and churches were founded during the 12th century, partly as a response to the increasing population. Most of these churches were small, their priests tended to be English and of little higher status than the peasantry they served. They were often married, though by the late 12th century bishops were making strenuous efforts to enforce celibacy, as well as attempting to improve their education and material state. Many churches previously owned by lay lords who appointed the parish priest at will, paid him and in return received all tithes and offerings to the church, were being handed over to monasteries who retained similar rights over the churches and who often paid their clerks very poorly. To counter this, reforming bishops such as Hugh of Wells and Grosseteste, bishop of Lincoln, instituted vicarages stipulating that such priests should be provided with a house and a regular, fixed income. Though these rulings did much to alleviate the problem, the majority of resident priests remained relatively poor throughout the period.

Meanwhile, a great number of parish churches were rebuilt during the 12th century and were both enlarged and modernised. This pattern continued in the 13th century, regarded by some as representing the apogee of English medieval architecture. The growing wealth of some areas of the country, such as East Anglia, is reflected in the high quality of churches built there such as West Walton and Great Yarmouth (Norfolk), the largest non-monastic church in the country. Clearly every church depended for its growth (or decline) on a number of local factors, of which the most important was the economic position of its region. In general the prosperity of the 13th century is reflected in its churches; thereafter the economic recession limited, though it by no means prevented, the building or reconstruction

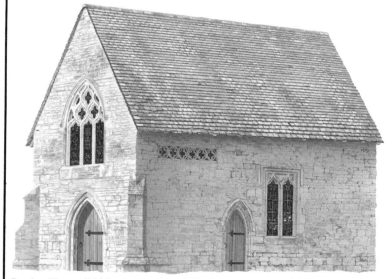

Bradwell's small 14th century chapel, Bucks, was never a parish church but a cult chapel housing relics of the Virgin, administered by the adjacent priory.

Church of St Mary and St David, Kilpeck, Herefordshire has elaborate exterior sculpture but is otherwise a typical small Norman parish church.

Church of St Mary, Fairford, Gloucestershire, is one of the finest late medieval churches. Its Great West Window depicts the Last Judgement.

of churches. Indeed the decline in lay support of monasteries during the late-medieval period led to greater attention being focused upon the local church. A great number of church rebuildings at this time can be directly attributed to the piety of individual parishioners eager to insure their souls by such good works, but some church building was inspired as much by rivalry as by piety. The churches of the neighbouring Devon towns of Cullompton and Tiverton provide a clear example of ostentatious emulation. Such rivalry could be both individual or communal; in the latter case the wool and cloth producing communities took the lead. Churches such as Cirencester, Fairford and Northleach (Gloucestershire) demonstrate the growing wealth and pride of the Cotswold wool producers, while in East Anglia the neighbouring churches of Long Melford and Lavenham (Suffolk) illustrate similar tendencies among the cloth producers, especially the Cloptons of Long Melford and Springs of Lavenham, both of which families founded chantries and were buried in the churches they endowed. Other churches could be founded as the centres of small religious and charitable complexes. At Ewelme (Oxfordshire) the parvenu de la Poles, earls of Suffolk, greatly enlarged the church and founded an adjacent almshouse and school: at Tattershall (Lincolnshire) Ralph, Lord Cromwell built a rich church and endowed a college of clerks to serve there and say masses for his soul within the shadow of his new castle.

If parish churches provided the infrastructure of ecclesiastical organisation and were the centres of local piety, the cathedrals acted as religious and ceremonial centres for the whole region. They were served either by monks, as at Ely and Canterbury, or by canons as at Salisbury and Exeter. Though they were often endowed with lands by local people they played a much less important part in the spiritual lives of the majority of the population than did the parish church. Perhaps the most important role of the cathedrals for the laity was as cult centres. Most cathedrals housed important shrines. Some were of international fame such as that of Thomas Becket at Canterbury, others such as those of St Hugh and 'Little' St Hugh at Lincoln and St Thomas Cantilupe at Hereford were of more local importance. All, however, brought valuable income to the cathedrals and cemented the lay and spiritual community together.

Building work was carried out at most cathedrals throughout the medieval period, continual additions and 'improvements' being made to the fabric. The most famous example of such 'improvement' is the encasing of the Norman pillars of the nave of Winchester in the Perpendicular style by bishop William de Wykeham at the end of the 14th century. Only one cathedral, Salisbury, was built in its entirety in a unified continuous building programme, and this took over a hundred years to complete. It was a special case as the diocesan centre was moved from Old Sarum (Wiltshire) in 1220 because of a poor water supply and cramped conditions to the water meadows of the Avon where the new cathedral and city were built.

Church of St Mary, Warwick. Warwick Castle was the chief residence of the Beauchamps, earls of Warwick; the parish church served as their burial place. In the mid 15th century a chantry chapel was constructed as the burial place of Richard, earl of Warwick, in which masses would be said for the repose of his soul.

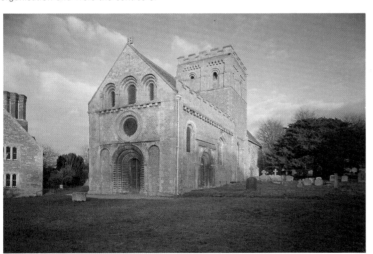

Iffley Church, Oxfordshire, an outstanding example of an English Romanesque village church. Lavishly decorated both inside and out, the richness of its carving is remarkable.

Lincoln Cathedral became the see of Dorchester-on-Thames after the Norman Conquest, and during the middle ages the diocese extended over a vast area stretching from the Humber to Oxford. The cathedral was both the mother church of this region and an important cult centre. It was begun between 1072 and 1075, but of Norman work only the west end survives. Rebuilding commenced in 1192 and was substantially complete by the end of the 13th century.

The nave vault of Lincoln Cathedral (above) dates from the second quarter of the 13th century. It is of tierceron form based on that of the choir, which is the first known example of such a vault. The nave pillars are of Lincoln stone and Purbeck marble.

Church of St Andrew, Cullompton, Devon (left). The splendour of this 15th century church testifies both to the wealth of late medieval Devon and to the significance of the parish church. It is particularly notable for its lavishly carved and coloured rood screen and roof.

who demonstrated their new wealth in lavish building projects as did Lawrence of Ludlow, who built Stokesay castle at the end of the century.

By 1300, however, it was already clear that the economy was in decline. Unprofitable land was falling out of cultivation; high taxation to finance the French, Welsh and Scottish campaigns of Edward I affected merchants, especially in wool; the French wars disrupted Anglo-Flemish trade; towns began to contract and very few new towns were now being founded. Agricultural prices began to fall and, though some lords continued to farm their lands directly, relying on peasant labour, many began to farm out their lands once more and to live off rents rather than agricultural profits. The wages of the peasantry began to rise, though slowly, and it is clear that even without the outbreak of the plague in 1348 a recession was likely.

The plague of 1348–9 killed around 40 per cent of the population. Though the famines of the early years of the century had led to widespread starvation and the reduction of resistance to disease, the Black Death mortality was unprecedented. Furthermore, later outbreaks of plague continued to harass the population for the remainder of the medieval

UNIVERSITIES

The President's Gallery of Queen's College, Cambridge, was built largely in wood in about 1540 and is one of the most picturesque surviving medieval college buildings.

Universities were an outcome of the intellectual revival in Europe during the 12th and 13th centuries. In some respects monastic in form, a *universitas* was a guild or corporation, and the two earliest British universities, Oxford and Cambridge, were developed on the model of Paris — a *universitas magistrorum*. Oxford appears to have been established in the reign of Henry II, largely as a result of a migration of foreign born scholars from Paris in 1167 to the already existing monastic centre at Oxford. Cambridge may be deemed to begin about 1209 when, following upon disturbances between townspeople and the students at Oxford, a number of scholars migrated to Cambridge.

It was the latter part of the 13th century, however, that saw the emergence of a distinctive British contribution to the *universitas* concept in the shape of the collegiate system. This first began at Oxford with University College (1249), Balliol College (1263–68) and Merton College

(1264). The system spread to Cambridge with the founding of Peterhouse College (1284) and the pattern of future development for many centuries was thus determined. Nine more colleges followed at Oxford and Cambridge in the 14th century, seven more in the 15th century and 12 more in the 16th century.

During this period we also see the emergence of universities in Scotland — at St Andrews (1411), Glasgow (1451), Aberdeen (1494) followed by Edinburgh (1583) — all much influenced by the collegiate models of Oxford and Cambridge.

Instruction was in the form of lectures by licensed teachers. To the seven liberal arts of the medieval schools (the *trivium* — grammar, logic and rhetoric, and the *quadrivium* — arithmetic, geometry, music and astronomy) were added the three higher 'faculties' of theology, law and medicine to provide preparation for the learned professions.

MONASTERIES

Monasticism was central to the religious life of medieval Britain. In England alone there appear to have been somewhere between 500 and 600 monasteries, and there were also a large number in Wales, Scotland and Ireland. For much of the period they provided a focus for lay piety and served as regional spiritual centres. Some had schools attached to them, for example Dunstable (Bedfordshire); others were famous for their literary productions, as was St Albans (Hertfordshire), home of the chronicler Matthew Paris in the 13th century. Matthew was also a scribe, and several monasteries had famous *scriptoria* for the production of illuminated manuscripts, notably Canterbury and Bury St Edmunds (Suffolk) in the 12th century and St Albans in the 12th and 13th centuries.

Many leading ecclesiastical dignitaries were drawn from monastic ranks; other monks served as royal councillors and confessors. The friars catered especially, but not exclusively, for the specific spiritual needs of the town while other religious houses served as hospitals, such as St Bartholomew's in London. Other monks served as priests in parish churches. Though perhaps the spirituality of many monasteries declined during the late middle ages, some retained a reputation for piety and devotion until their dissolution. The small Carthusian priories and Bridgetine foundations of the 15th century were especially famed for piety. As great landholders the monasteries had a profound effect upon the economic and social life of wide areas, and their combined income was considerably in excess of that of the king himself.

In 1066 there were some 30 monastic foundations in Britain. All followed the Benedictine rule and most had been founded prior to the Danish invasions. They included Westminster, the two great abbeys of Winchester, Bury St Edmunds, Peterborough and Evesham (Worcestershire). Their fortunes were temporarily eclipsed at the Conquest; many of their abbots were replaced by Normans, the duty to perform military service was imposed upon them, attempts were made to bring their liturgy and rule more into line with continental (especially Norman) practices, and the new knights and magnates tended to grant lands to Norman, not English, monasteries. The great monasteries, however, soon recovered and played an ever increasing role in spiritual and economic life during the 12th and 13th centuries. All these monasteries were concentrated in the south; the Danish invasions had affected northern houses, such as Lindisfarne (Northumberland) to a much greater degree than elsewhere. Recovery did not come until the last years of the 11th century when some old monasteries were refounded, and early in the following century Cistercian abbeys such as Fountains and Rievaulx (Yorkshire) and Melrose across the Scottish border were founded in great numbers in the north.

The 'new' monastic orders like the Cistercians, Premonstratensians and Gilbertines (founded by the Englishman Gilbert of Sempingham) represented a new spiritual movement away from the old established Benedictine monasteries which many reformers believed to be too intermeshed with secular society. Drawing much of their inspiration from the ideals of Eastern monasticism and contemporary eremitical behaviour the Cistercians established themselves in remote, sparsely populated areas such as were readily found in the north and in Wales. Here large Cistercian estates, often concentrating upon pastoral farming, were created. Initially the Cistercians were extremely popular throughout Britain but their appeal was relatively short-lived. Satirists were criticising the order by the end of the 12th century and by 1200 the new orders had virtually reached the limits of their expansion.

With the exception of the Augustinian canons the new orders did not cater for the needs of the towns. The coming of the friars, especially the Dominicans (Black Friars) and Franciscans (Grey Friars), in the early 13th century was a powerful stimulus to urban piety. Rapidly establishing themselves in most British towns the friars concentrated on preaching and provided some of the greatest theologians of the middle ages. The friars lacked ostentation and appealed both to urban poor and patriciate, and though they were increasingly criticised by the secular clergy, who rightly saw them as threats to their own influence, in general the friars remained popular with the laity until the Reformation.

Other monasteries during the late middle ages were not so fortunate. Most suffered in some measure from the economic recession of the late 14th and 15th centuries, though many were able to diversify their resources and to maintain their material standards because their endowments were so large. Many abbeys embarked upon ambitious building projects intended either to increase the comforts of the monks' living quarters or to expand or modernise their churches. At the same time recruitment was declining heavily and though only a few small houses actually had to disband all suffered from the fall in numbers. The fall in recruitment is one indication of the declining appeal of the monasteries; another is the decline in endowments. The more individualistic piety of the late middle ages was directed at new expressions of devotion such as the endowment of charities rather than the support of great monastic corporations. And though some monasteries, notably those of the Carthusians, continued to be founded and endowed in the late middle ages, they were exceptional. By the end of the 15th century the great age of the monasteries was over. Neither outstandingly pious nor notoriously immoral, the majority of monks lived a comfortable life of mediocrity, conservative in their living and spirituality and for the most part out of touch with the spiritual aspirations of the laity.

Fountains Abbey, North Yorkshire. Founded in 1332, this was the richest Cistercian abbey in England. The picture shows the cellarium.

Great Coxwell tithe barn, Berkshire, is one of the finest surviving examples and belonged to the Cistercian abbey of Beaulieu (Hampshire). Such barns were used to store agricultural produce from monastic estates, together with the proceeds of tithes, a levy of one-tenth of the parish's produce.

Rievaulx Abbey, Yorkshire, was founded by Walter Espec, lord of Helmsby, in 1131. Its exceptionally well preserved and beautiful ruins provide one of the best examples of Cistercian architecture in England. The nave of the church dates from 1135–40 and its choir from the 13th century.

period and beyond. Recovery was slow; not until the early 16th century did the population begin to increase again and it is possible that for much of the 15th century it was still actually declining rather than holding level. The sudden shift from an over-populated to an under-populated land is the single most important factor in the explanation of the changing social and economic conditions of the later middle ages.

For the peasants who survived the outbreaks of plague, the changes were almost exclusively beneficial. For the first time in centuries there was abundant land to spare, and as a result all peasants were able to increase their holdings. The wealthier peasants could now be scarcely differentiated from the lesser gentry, but those who benefited most were the landless poor. The ranks of the smallholders and landless were greatly depleted as they moved into the class of peasants above, who each farmed from 20 to 40 acres of land. Moreover, so long as the peasants continued to cultivate their land themselves rather than to rely upon hired labour (and it would seem that most did so) then they would not suffer from having to pay higher wages.

The corollary to labour shortage was higher wages.

This brass in Exeter Cathedral is of Sir Peter Courtenay, a representative of the noted Devon family, who died in 1409. It is one of the finest surviving brasses commemorating a knightly figure and is surrounded by heraldic shields.

TOWNS AND BUILDINGS

The period 1066 to c.1250 saw an hitherto unparalleled growth of towns in Britain. While it remains true that at no time during the middle ages did more than 10 per cent of the population live in towns, for the first time since the end of Roman Britain towns began to play an important role in the country's economy. Old towns expanded and many new ones were created by kings and lords eager to take advantage of the profits available from possession of urban lordships. The 11th century saw a rapid growth of towns and urban institutions throughout western Europe as the threat of barbarian invasions receded and as international trade and commerce flourished as never before. Eleventh century England was relatively wealthy, with a well-developed administration and a burgeoning money economy. Though the Norman Conquest brought temporary setbacks to some towns, such as Lincoln or York where many houses were demolished to create space for new castles, the creation of closer ties with France and western Europe acted as a catalyst to urban growth, especially in the south. Jewish communities were established in major towns for the first time and the growth in credit facilities provided by their advent was a powerful stimulus to the growth of trade. The Jews continued to play an important role in the urban economy until their expulsion from England by Edward I in 1290.

Thereafter towns continued to expand everywhere. The possession of a town was recognised as a valuable source of seigneurial revenue, which was obtained from tolls, market dues and from the purchase of constitutional and economic privileges by the burgesses. As regional and international trade grew, so did the need for markets, and by the mid 13th century most of the population lived within 15 miles of a market town. Though no English town boasted international fairs to rival those of northern France or Italy, those of Boston (Lincolnshire), St Ives (Huntingdonshire) and Winchester (Hampshire) attracted foreign merchants. Trade across the North Sea and English Channel stimulated the growth of eastern ports, and old established river ports such as York, Lincoln and Norwich also benefited from long-distance trade. Bristol grew as trade with Ireland, Gascony and Spain expanded; its great churches, notably St Mary Redcliffe, testify to its continuing importance throughout the medieval period. Most towns, especially inland, were more humble and served a smaller hinterland. All were small and only London could compete in size with contemporary European cities.

Nevertheless a growing civic pride is revealed by the magnificent churches of many English towns during this period and by the building of impressive town walls such as at Southampton, both for defence and as an expression of urban dignity. Burgesses were granted considerable privileges by their lords and were, for the most part, free men without the liability to perform servile dues. The clearest example of urban growth was the creation of new towns, that is, towns laid out and planned on rural sites. There were some 170 new towns during this period, most being created between 1170 and 1250. They ranged in importance from Newcastle and Salisbury (which replaced Old Sarum as the cathedral city in 1220) to small market towns like New Romney (Kent) and Baldock (Hertfordshire). Many of the country's most important ports in medieval and modern times began as new towns such as Boston (Lincolnshire), Hull (Yorkshire), King's Lynn (Norfolk), Liverpool (Lancashire) and Portsmouth (Hampshire). Other towns were founded with a defensive purpose and were often linked with a castle. They include many towns in Wales such as Caernarvon and Conwy

in the north and Caerdydd and Caerphilly in the south. Other medieval new towns of local importance include Stratford-upon-Avon (Warwickshire), Windsor (Berkshire) and Leeds (Yorkshire).

After 1300 very few new towns were created and some towns failed altogether, as did Newtown (Isle of Wight) and Ravenserodd (Yorkshire). By this date there were too many towns in proportion to the population necessary to support them, and no room for further expansion. In some cases geographical changes caused the silting up of harbours, as at Chester, the withdrawal of the sea, as at Winchelsea (Sussex) and Harlech (Merionydd) or, conversely, the advance of the sea as at Dunwich (Suffolk).

Towns suffered more heavily than the countryside in the Black Death, and it was long before many towns recovered their pre-1348 population levels. Moreover, the general slackening of economic demand further affected urban fortunes. The Hundred Years' War disrupted international trade and many towns, especially in the south, were raided. Southampton, heavily attacked in 1338, did not recover until the early 15th century. Prolonged war brought high taxation, especially on wool for export. As a result the wool trade and wool exporting ports such as Boston declined in importance while the growth in the cloth trade led to the rise of new centres such as Lavenham (Suffolk), the thirteenth most wealthy town in 1515. By the 16th century the southern counties dominated the economy of England and the wealthiest towns were found there, especially in the south west and East Anglia. Even though these towns also suffered from the mid-15th century recession in the cloth trade, they proved resilient and survived to flourish into the early modern period.

This late Anglo-Saxon drawing (about 1000) of a walled town provides an idealised picture of a Saxon *burh*, a fortified residential and commercial centre. King Alfred built a chain of *burhs* along the coast and land frontiers of Wessex as a means of defending his lands against Viking invaders. Some were built on existing Roman town walls, while others used new sites, and some, such as Oxford, survived as important towns to the present day.

Boothby Pagnell manor house, Lincolnshire, was built around 1200 and is the finest example of only a few surviving small Norman manor houses. Unfortified and defended only by a moat, such houses were residences of lesser knightly and gentry families.

This house at Weobley, Herefordshire, is a good example of a cruck-framed dwelling, in which large, curved beams at both ends of the structure support the walls and roof.

Caernarvon was developed by Edward I as part of the English colonisation of north Wales after his successful campaigns. This aerial view demonstrates how the town, town walls and castle form a single settlement unit.

The hall of Berkeley Castle, Gloucestershire, is typical of mid 14th century design, with the dining area separated from the service area by a richly carved screen.

The Jew's House, Lincoln, is a superb and rare example of a stone-built, late 12th century merchant's house with a hall upon the first floor.

Lords were obliged to increase wages in order to keep their tenants on the land, and at the same time they had to accept lower rents if their land was to be cultivated at all. The position of the peasant was therefore doubly improved. The lords did attempt to recoup their losses by the Ordinance and Statute of Labourers in 1349 and 1351, measures designed to hold wages and rents at pre-Black Death levels and to restrict labour mobility, but these measures proved unpopular and difficult to implement. Some lords attempted to maintain their position by rigorously enforcing labour services upon their tenants, but such moves were at best temporary expedients and produced much bitterness that finally exploded in the Peasants' Revolt of 1381. Though the rising was put down and the peasant leaders executed, most of their demands were eventually met. Economic pressures rather than violence gradually led to the withering away of serfdom and the legal and social disabilities that went with unfreedom, and the late 14th and 15th centuries witnessed a period of unrivalled prosperity for the English peasantry.

Lesser lords who farmed out little of their land and who consumed much of their produce were in an analogous position to the peasants. Many of these men were later to become great magnates in the early modern period, and it was in the 15th century that their fortunes began to be made. Though some had always formed part of the 'squirearchy' their ranks were reinforced by successful lawyers and merchants eager to proclaim their new status and wealth by the purchase of country estates. Moreover, political and military opportunities were considerable. Some served in the Hundred Years War against France. If they were successful, and this was more likely in the early years rather than in the 1430s or 1440s, and were able to acquire a wealthy French ransom such men could rapidly rise to positions of rank. The most famous example of a successful soldier is Sir John Fastolf who was able to establish himself in East Anglian society, to build himself Caister Castle (Norfolk) and to invest his war profits in the expanding cloth industry on his manor of Castle Combe (Wiltshire). Other families took advantage of the political unrest of the 15th century and by astute manoeuvring gained considerable landed rewards by their support of noble factions. Such behaviour was dangerous and could be disastrous to both individuals and

Charters began to be used as written evidence for land transactions in the Anglo-Saxon period. Few survive from before the Norman Conquest, but many thousands of charters are preserved dating from the late middle ages. By this time they were used not only as evidence for the possession of land but to record the grant of privileges to individuals or corporations by kings and lords. This example, dated at Westminster 1484 and bearing the Great Seal of England, records Richard III's grant of incorporation to the Wax Chandlers' Guild of London.

THE IMPROVEMENT OF THE WASTELAND

Between the 11th and the end of the 13th centuries the population of Britain (and western Europe in general) increased dramatically. An immediate effect of this population growth was the need for more land for agricultural production and the period was marked by the clearing of forests and waste land, the draining of fens and marshes and by a general extension of the frontiers of arable land to, and in some cases beyond, the margin of cultivable soil. In some cases villages were expanded, in others new hamlets were created within the boundaries of pre-existent parishes and at times entirely new parishes were established on reclaimed land. Reclamation and colonisation could be carried out by individuals or by communities. Peasants were often offered reclaimed land at low rents by their lord in order to stimulate agrarian expansion, and frequently the lead in colonisation was taken by local monasteries which usually possessed more capital than other landholders to invest in such programmes.

Perhaps the most dramatic of all medieval colonisation was the drainage of the marshes. In such enterprises monasteries took the lead. Glastonbury was largely responsible for the drainage

of the Somerset levels, Christ Church Canterbury for the reclamation of Romney Marsh (Kent), particularly during the priorate of the energetic Henry of Eastry (1285–1331), and Peterborough and the other Fenland abbeys played a great part in the drainage of the fens. Peterborough, for example, was responsible for the creation of Market Deeping (Norfolk), a new settlement developed from the older village of Deeping St James but given its own identity, symbolised by the creation of a new parish, by the abbey. Some drainage in these areas had been carried out during the Anglo-Saxon period, but the process was a long one and required corporate rather than individual effort. For this reason and also because the reclaimed marsh was, at least initially, more suited to pastoral than arable farming, reclamation tended to be the work of great local monasteries, though there is also considerable evidence that village communities were also advancing into the fen, each villager taking responsibility for a certain area of fen in proportion to the amount of arable land he held. Local communities were also made responsible for the upkeep of dikes and sea walls.

As important in the colonisation of

The ancient custom of pannaging involved the raising of pigs on a staple diet of acorns. On the left, the November illustration for a calendar of around 1280 shows pigs feeding, while the photograph on the right of pigs beside the road in the New Forest shows that the custom has survived to the present day.

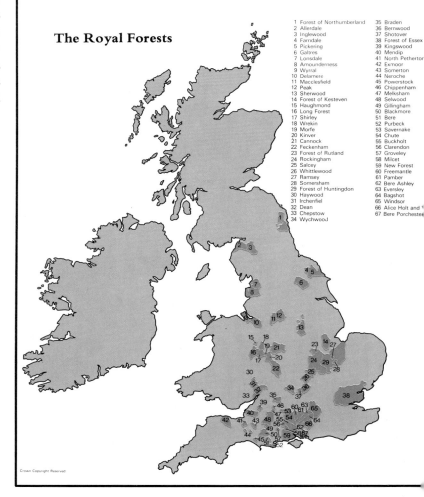

The Royal Forests

1	Forest of Northumberland	35 Braden
2	Allerdale	36 Bernwood
3	Inglewood	37 Shotover
4	Farndale	38 Forest of Essex
5	Pickering	39 Kingswood
6	Galtres	40 Mendip
7	Lonsdale	41 North Petherton
8	Amounderness	42 Exmoor
9	Wyrral	43 Somerton
10	Delamere	44 Neroche
11	Macclesfield	45 Powerstock
12	Peak	46 Chippenham
13	Sherwood	47 Melksham
14	Forest of Kesteven	48 Selwood
15	Haughmond	49 Gillingham
16	Long Forest	50 Blackmore
17	Shirley	51 Bere
18	Wrekin	52 Purbeck
19	Morfe	53 Savernake
20	Kinver	54 Chute
21	Cannock	55 Buckholt
22	Feckenham	56 Clarendon
23	Forest of Rutland	57 Groveley
24	Rockingham	58 Milcet
25	Salcey	59 New Forest
26	Whittlewood	60 Freemantle
27	Ramsey	61 Pamber
28	Somersham	62 Bere Ashley
29	Forest of Huntingdon	63 Eversley
30	Haywood	64 Bagshot
31	Irchenfiel	65 Windsor
32	Dean	66 Alice Holt and
33	Chepstow	67 Bere Porchester
34	Wychwood	

Crown Copyright Reserved

medieval Britain were the clearances of woodland and forests. Much of England remained covered with woods until the early modern period, but during the middle ages woodland areas were substantially reduced. Assarting (the clearing of woodland) was common over all England, and even proceeded in the royal forests where the king was prepared to allow land clearance in return for money payments. In 1204, for example, King John agreed to the deforestation of the whole of Devon with the exception of Dartmoor and Exmoor, in return for 5,000 marks (£3,333). The wide extent of assarting is well evidenced from place names relating either to the clearances themselves or to the new settlements created. This is particularly the case in the Midlands, such as in the Forest of Arden. Elsewhere place names with 'end' or 'green' as their second element testify to the creation of settlements on cleared land subordinate to the main village.

The usual pattern in such clearances was for individuals to make small piecemeal clearances of woodland within the parish, often acting with the encouragement of the lord. Many enterprising peasants took advantage of such opportunities during the 12th and 13th centuries to carve out small estates for themselves, where they lived relatively free from oppression, and it has recently been suggested that many of the moated farmsteads, common in the comparatively recently settled

regions of the Midlands, represent the dwellings of such peasants who began to aspire to gentility during the 13th century.

Less spectacular, but no less important, colonisation occurred on moorland and other upland areas. Until there was a growing realisation of the potential of the uplands for pastoral farming in the 12th and 13th centuries the Highland Zone was thinly settled. Small hamlets and single farms were established at comparatively high altitudes. A large number of such farms were monastic, belonging to the Cistercian and other orders. Though these farms concentrated on pastoral farming, arable farming was not unknown in the uplands. Peasants were as active in such colonisation as they were in forest clearance and the typical settlement of a hamlet containing three or four houses was often the result of community activity by local peasants. The fact that such holdings were established on very unproductive, and often acid, soils in areas where the climate was unfavourable for corn and other food production as it was, for example, on Dartmoor or the high Yorkshire dales, is an indication of the pressure on land exerted by the rising population. When the population began to fall in the 14th century it is not surprising that these settlements were amongst the first to be abandoned, leaving the moor to revert to open, rough sheep pastorage.

Ely, Cambridgeshire. The topography of the fens has changed considerably since the drainage carried out in medieval and early modern times. Ely, built on a raised area, stood as an island above the marshes before drainage.

The Queen's Bower in the New Forest, one of the few surviving Norman Royal forests, is popularly believed to have been the favourite walk of Queen Eleanor.

Ploughing with oxen is depicted in this marginal illumination from the Luttrell Psalter, one of the best sources of contemporary agricultural illustrations.

The Hardwick Tapestry, once in Hardwick Hall (Derbyshire) and now at the Victoria and Albert Museum, depicts falconry, one of the many forms of hunting. The tapestry is an extremely fine and rare example dating from the early 15th century and was probably manufactured in Flanders.

families, but if successful the dividends were high, as families such as the Hungerfords, who established themselves at Farleigh Hungerford (Somerset) by their political support of the Lancastrians, proved. Such men were especially fortunate if they were wool producers. Though wool was by now superseded by cloth as England's most important export commodity, sheep farming was as important as it had ever been. One possible solution to falling rent rolls and a declining labour supply was to turn from arable to less labour intensive pastoral farming. The extent to which late medieval lords actively depopulated villages by creating vast sheep enclosures has certainly been exaggerated. Rather, lords took advantage of population decline and village desertion to develop their pastoral activities. By such production many lords were able to weather the late medieval recession.

The great magnates faced greater problems. Though many lords survived the immediate post-Black Death years their troubles increased in the 15th century; the severe recession that affected all aspects of the economy hit them hard. Agricultural incomes fell heavily and those lords who relied predominantly on rents and money payments suffered especially as land values fell. Those who did not possess land for pastoral farming or who were too slow to adapt also suffered.

In the 13th century the Benedictine abbeys had been in the forefront of agricultural reform; now, however, they appear to have become lax. They persisted for the most part in producing grain for the market at a time when grain prices were extremely low, and they had also to pay high wages to their labourers. This did not prevent many abbeys and cathedrals from embarking on ambitious building projects, as happened at Winchester under bishop William de Wykeham in the late 14th century, or at Christ Church Canterbury under prior Chillenden a few years later. Though some lords were able to augment their incomes by revenue derived from feudal sources such as wardships or reliefs, this did not offset their other losses. For the great lords, as for the lesser in the 13th century, the only real opportunities were to be found in royal service. They were, however, limited. Losses in France and final defeat in the Hundred Years War meant a decline in the profits of war and of political office in France. The political situation at home was too unstable for any but a few of the magnates to maintain their income by royal service at Westminster or in the provinces. For every magnate who did survive there were others who lost lands or life during the Wars of the Roses.

Early cloth industry

The towns felt the late medieval recession too. The Black Death had especially affected them with their high population density, and it had particularly struck the labour intensive trades. In the 15th century wool and cloth exports fell as did exports of other goods, and imports of wine declined. The older towns in particular fell on hard times, and only the great regional centres such as London, Newcastle or Coventry held their own.

By the mid 14th century cloth had superseded wool as England's premier export commodity. Export wool had been heavily taxed and its supply to the Flemish markets so frequently interrupted in the French wars, when English kings used their control of the wool trade to influence the political and military activities of the Flemish towns, that English producers now manufactured their own wool into cloth for export. This shift to cloth production provided a catalyst for the growth of many northern and western towns, where proximity to high quality wool was combined with the presence of fast flowing rivers to provide energy for cloth manufacture. The decline in cloth exports during the 15th

St George's Chapel, Windsor Castle, Berkshire. Begun in 1475, this is the spiritual centre of the Knights of the Garter, whose flags hang in its chancel. The existing chapel replaced one built in 1348 by Edward III, who founded the Order of the Garter. In architecture and furniture, the chapel is one of the glories of the English perpendicular style.

THE BLACK DEATH AND LOST VILLAGES

By the end of the 13th century the population of medieval England had reached its peak. In many areas food yields were falling as poor soils, reclaimed over the past two centuries, became exhausted. Many peasants were at, or below, subsistence level and lived on small holdings of only one or two acres. This situation was exacerbated by disasters in the early years of the 14th century; the climate deteriorated, becoming both colder and much wetter, and harvests frequently failed, particularly between 1315 and 1322. At the same time a series of sheep and cattle plagues affected pastoral production. By 1348 some settlements, particularly those made recently in unproductive or upland areas, were already being abandoned.

The effects of the Black Death in the British Isles between 1348 and 1350 have been much debated. It seems clear, however, that the mortality rate was between 33 and 50 per cent and that the towns suffered particularly heavy losses; moreover, the plague returned at various times throughout the late middle ages and early modern period, the plagues of 1361 and 1368–9 being particularly virulent. The mortality varied from region to region and from village to village, but there were many villages like Cuxham (Oxfordshire) where all the peasant tenants died within the year. Though some lords weathered the storm and were able to fill vacant holdings with comparative ease, nearly all suffered from a considerable decline in income. In many cases lords were obliged to cut their losses by leasing out their estates to tenant farmers.

Industrial and agricultural production was affected. Labour was now comparatively scarce, and, in spite of government attempts to limit wages by the Statute of Labourers (1351), labour costs were rising. Since land was now freely available rents fell and men were no longer obliged to cultivate poor land. In an attempt to maintain production lords tried to enforce the performance of labour services upon their unfree tenants. This inevitably led to tensions which combined with discontent at government mismanagement and the imposition of an unprecedentedly high Poll Tax to explode in the Peasants' Revolt (1381).

The earthworks and ruins of deserted villages remain as witnesses to changes in the economy and declining population during the late middle ages. Many hundreds of deserted villages have been identified; others continue to be revealed, often with the aid of aerial photography. It is debatable how far village desertion was a result of forcible eviction by lords eager to enclose their land for pastoral farming, and how far the desertion and the subsequent use of arable fields for pasture was a response to the declining population. Certainly by the end of the 15th century complaints were being voiced in parliament and elsewhere at the enclosure of lands and the depopulation of villages, and certainly too there was an unprecedented number of village desertions during the late 14th and 15th centuries, the greater part of the more than 2,000 known deserted villages declining at this time. This figure should be seen in the context of some 15,000 settlements in existence at the end of the 13th century.

Though very marginal settlements such as Hound Tor on Dartmoor were disappearing by 1300, depopulation elsewhere was a later phenomenon. Particularly vulnerable were the clayland villages of the Midlands, since land here could easily be turned over to sheep farming. The majority of villages deserted in the 15th century are to be found in the midland areas. It is difficult, however, to generalise concerning the reasons for village desertion: each desertion was the result of a combination of a number of individual, and often very local, factors. Small villages tended to be forsaken more readily than large ones, but much also depended on the social structure of the village, the relative number of free and unfree peasants, the economic potential of the site and the extent of lordship exercised over the village. Some villages were not wholly abandoned but shrank to contain only one or two farmsteads.

Except in cases where the lord himself took direct action to remove a village, desertion took time. It normally extended over several generations and was not inevitably an irreversible process. Peasants who remained upon the land were able to consolidate and expand their holdings; taking advantage of high wages and low prices and rents they could prosper as never before. For those fortunate enough to survive, the 15th century was indeed the golden age of the English peasantry. Deserted villages indicate a falling population and changing economic times, but they do not suggest that the peasants themselves were in decline.

Hound Tor, near Moretonhampstead in Devon, was a small agricultural settlement colonised on high Dartmoor. It is probable that the village never prospered, being one of the first to be deserted at the end of the 13th century. Its excavation has revealed a variety of 12th century stone-walled buildings and traces of large kilns which were probably used for drying corn.

century, as foreign importers either turned to new suppliers or developed their own industries, affected towns which had concentrated on luxury cloth exports. Some cloth-producing communities, sometimes in industrial villages, such as Castle Combe, did survive. This was achieved by the production of lesser quality cloth for the mass home market. As a result a number of small villages developed rapidly into prosperous towns, such as Totnes and Cullompton (Devon) in the south west, and Sudbury (Suffolk) and Coggeshall (Essex) in East Anglia. By the beginning of the 16th century urban wealth was concentrated in southern England, especially in the Home Counties, East Anglia and the south west. The northern and midland towns had, for the most part, correspondingly declined.

Recession and growth

In some respects the late medieval economy presents a paradox. On the one hand there is clear evidence that there was contraction and recession; many towns were declining and some merchants falling upon hard times. In the countryside yields were falling, as were the incomes of the magnates. On the other hand, the peasants enjoyed a higher standard of living than ever before, many of the gentry were prospering and there is no indication that the economic contraction was in any way hindering building projects or setting limits on conspicuous expenditure. This paradox can still be sensed in the landscape today. Deserted or shrunken villages bear witness to a declining population, as do churches which contracted in size by blocking up or demolishing aisles. In the towns there is archaeological evidence that urban settlement did not greatly expand outside the bounds set by town walls built during the 13th century. Towns that failed through lack of trade, the rivalry of neighbouring centres or by natural causes can still be seen. At the same time there is clear evidence that individual persons and communities were flourishing; the evident comfort of 15th century 'yeoman' homes points to the well being of the upper ranks of the peasantry, and the country houses and semi-fortified castles of magnates and gentry show that some at least of the nobility flourished. The rebuilding of many abbeys or cathedrals such as Canterbury and Winchester suggest that these communities still had money to spend on large scale projects, even during a time of recession.

COINS

William wisely retained much that was good in the Anglo-Saxon monetary tradition after the conquest. He was naturally keen to keep the English tradition of supreme royal authority over the coinage; in Europe the kings had gradually granted away the right to strike coin to the aristocracy and the Church, but in England this process was held in check. This had also helped the Anglo-Saxon kings to maintain a coinage of good weight and silver fineness, and William continued this.

During the 13th century millions of silver pennies were struck in England – a fact which illustrates the prosperity of the wool trade and which may have contributed to rising prices.

The plentiful pennies of Henry II, Richard, John and Henry III, all have the legend Henricus Rex. The Short Cross penny reading Henricus was so plentiful and well known that neither Richard nor John wanted to change such a successful formula. Henry III made a slight modification halfway through his reign, extending the arms of the cross on the reverse to the edge of

the coin in an attempt to stop people clipping off the edges of the coins. Nevertheless clipping remained a problem, as did forgery. The English penny was so popular at this time that copies were made in Europe as well as England.

In the 14th and 15th centuries silver became scarcer in England; the shortage was, however, partly offset by the introduction of gold.

A gold noble of Edward III (1327–77), showing a stylised portrait of the king above a medieval ship.

William the Conqueror (1066–87).

1066   The defeat of Harold Godwinson at Hastings on 14 October establishes **William of Normandy** as the king of England
1069–70   Opposition to Norman rule leads to the ruthless Harrying of the North by William I
1070–89   Lanfranc, archbishop of Canterbury, achieves considerable reforms of ecclesiastical life and organisation
1086   All great landholders swear overriding loyalty and homage to William I by the Oath of Salisbury. Shortly afterwards, William orders the Domesday Inquest
1087–1100   **William II** effectively curbs baronial rebels and establishes control over Scotland, Wales and Normandy
1093–1109   The rule of Anselm, archbishop of Canterbury, is marked by a vigorous stand for church liberties and reform
1100–1135   **Henry I** maintains control over England and Normandy. The reign sees the introduction of far-reaching administrative reforms
1106   Henry I's defeat of his brother Robert at Tinchebrai ensures his rule over the duchy of Normandy
1121   The drowning of Henry's only heir in the White Ship Disaster leads to the succession dispute of Stephen's reign
1135–54   **Stephen**'s reign is disputed in bitter civil war by his cousin Matilda and her son Henry of Anjou
1154–89   The reign of **Henry II**, king and duke of Anjou, Normandy and Aquitaine, extends royal control over church and baronage
1155   The papal bull Laudabiliter sanctions royal intervention in Ireland, paving the way for English colonisation
1164   Henry's attempts to formalise royal control over the church by the Constitutions of Clarendon provoke conflict with Becket, archbishop of Canterbury
1166   The Assize of Clarendon formalises the jury system and expands the competence of criminal law
1170   The murder of Becket creates the most important English pilgrimage cult
1173–4   A great baronial revolt, aided by the French and Scots king against Angevin rule, foreshadows the Magna Carta crisis
1189–99   **Richard I**'s rule is marked by internal unrest and increasing French hostility during his long absence on Crusade
1199–1216   The attempts of **John** to extend control over the church and magnates ultimately lead to civil war
1204   The loss of Normandy to the French proves a turning point in John's reign

1206   John's opposition to the election of Stephen Langton, archbishop of Canterbury, lead to the Interdict and John's excommunication
1214   The crushing defeat of John's allies by the French at Bouvines ends all hope of English recovery of Normandy

Edward I (1272–1307) presiding over Parliament, shown in a manuscript now at Windsor Castle. He was an unpopular king during whose reign both the Welsh and Scots rebelled.

1215   Baronial opposition to John culminates in the Magna Carta, curbing royal arbitrary rule
1216–72   The rule of **Henry III** was marked by factional strife and constitutional reform
1221   The first English Dominicans settle at Oxford, followed by Franciscans at Canterbury, London and Oxford (1224)
1235–53   Grossetete, bishop of Lincoln, attacks abuses at Rome and secular interference in ecclesiastical affairs
1258   The Provisions of Oxford for administrative reform and government are forced on Henry III by a baronial council
1264   Simon de Montfort wins a convincing victory over Henry III at Lewes, prince Edward becoming his hostage
1265   In the Parliament, burgesses join knights of the shire for the first time
1265   At Evesham, prince Edward kills de Montfort and re-establishes royal control of government
1272–1307   **Edward I** wins great victories in Wales and Scotland, introduces notable legal reforms but is increasingly unpopular for his autocracy
1282   The Welsh revolt under Llywelyn ap Grufydd is crushed by Edward I
1290   The English Jews, established by the Normans, are expelled
1292   John Balliol, the English nominee, is crowned king of Scotland
1297   Robert Bruce leads a Scots revolt which lasts until 1303, resuming three years later in 1306 when he becomes Scottish king
1307–1327   **Edward II**'s reign is marked by growing hostility between magnates and royal councillors and favourites
1314   At Bannockburn, Bruce leads a notable Scots victory against the English
1320   Royalist forces defeat a magnatical rebellion led by Thomas of Lancaster at Boroughbridge
1327   Edward II is dethroned by a baronial *coup d'etat* led by his wife Isabella and her lover Mortimer.
Edward III becomes king (1327–77)

Henry V (1413–22) who renewed the war with France on his succession.

culminating in the outbreak of the Wars of the Roses in 1455
1429 Joan of Arc relieves the siege of Orleans, a turning point in the Hundred Years' War
1445 Henry VI marries Margaret of Anjou as part of an Anglo-French peace treaty
1450 Growing political violence leads to the murder of the Duke of Suffolk and the Bishop of Salisbury, and Jack Cade, a member of the Kentish gentry, leads a revolt against corrupt officials and magnates
1453 The French defeat of an English force at Castillon effectively ends the Hundred Years' War
1455 The opening battle of the Wars of the Roses at St Albans sees the defeat of the Duke of Somerset by Yorkist forces
1459 At the Coventry Parliament Yorkist lords are attainted and their property confiscated
1460 Richard, Duke of York, claims the throne but is defeated and killed at Wakefield
1461 Henry VI is deposed and York's son becomes **Edward IV**, decisively defeating the Lancastrians at Towton. He reigns until 1483
1467 Edward IV marries Elizabeth Woodville

At Agincourt Henry V inflicts a heavy defeat on French forces
1420 The Treaty of Troyes makes Henry V heir to the French kingdom
1422–71 **Henry VI**'s reign sees rapidly growing magnatical violence,

Henry VI (1422–71) came to the throne when still an infant. His two brothers acted as regents.

Edward IV (1461–83) acceded to the throne after over 30 years of the 'Wars of the Roses'.

Richard II, 1377–99. Son of the Black Prince and successor to Edward III, he acceded to the throne at the age of 10.

1337 The Wool Stable is established, giving a syndicate royal monopoly in wool exports
1337 The Hundred Years' War breaks out when Edward III, confronted by a Franco-Scottish alliance, claims the French throne
1339 Parliament establishes that consent of the Commons is necessary for all taxation
1340 The crippling defeat of the French fleet of Sluys gives Edward control over the channel
1346 Edward III's defeat of Philip III at Crecy leads to major English advances in France
1348–9 The Black Death, a pandemic of bubonic plague, destroys between 33 and 50 per cent of the British population
1351 The much-resented Statute of Labourers attempts to curb wages at a time of labour shortage
1356 In Edward III's overwhelming victory at Poitiers, king John of France is captured
1359 The Treaty of Bretigny ratifies Edward III's gains in France
1376 The Good Parliament uses impeachment for the first time against allegedly corrupt royal councillors and merchants
1377–99 **Richard II**, grandson of Edward III and son of the Black Prince,

accedes as a minor. His court was one of the most cultured in medieval England
1380 John Wyclif's teachings are condemned as heretical
Towards the end of the century, William Langland's great allegorical poem *Piers Plowman* and Geoffrey Chaucer's *Canterbury Tales* mark high points of medieval poetry
1381 The Peasants' Revolt is the only major peasant rising of medieval England
1388 In the Merciless Parliament five lords accused Richard II's favourites of treason. Most of the favourites were executed
1399–1413 Henry Bolingbroke deposes Richard and seizes the throne, becoming **Henry IV**.
1401 The Statute *de heretico comburendo* attempts to extirpate Lollardy, providing for the burning of obdurate heretics
1403 A rising of northern barons who had aided Bolingbroke is crushed at Shrewsbury
1413–22 **Henry V**'s reign is largely dominated by the renewed French war
1414 An abortive Lollard rising led by John Oldcastle is quickly suppressed
1415 A plot led by the Earl of Cambridge to assassinate Henry V at Southampton is betrayed and the conspirators executed

Richard III was once popularly believed to have ordered the deaths of the 'Princes in the Tower'. Edward V (to whom he had been Regent) and his brother.

The Tudors and Stuarts

*The intellectual Renaissance and religious Reformation
caused dramatic changes throughout Britain. A continual struggle between state and
individual for power characterised the dissolution of the monasteries,
the Civil War, the Puritan Protectorate and the restoration of the monarchy.
Meanwhile, scientific learning flourished, great country houses and parks were
created, much of rural Britain was rebuilt and agricultural
techniques were greatly improved. Abroad, the Great Age of Discovery set
the stage for the emergence of the First British Empire.*

The kingdom ruled by Henry VII, the first of the Tudors, was strikingly different from that ruled by Anne, the last of the Stuarts. In the late 15th century, England was a poor, backward, sparsely populated and, by the standards of foreign observers, unbelievably rural country. Nine-tenths of its inhabitants were agricultural labourers who subsisted on a meagre and monotonous diet, wore coarse, ill-fitting clothes, lived in hovels, and worked in small – and shrinking – enclaves of cultivation in a predominantly natural landscape. Its urban population was minuscule. London, where some 33,000 people lived, was worthy of comparison with all but the greatest cities of Italy and south Germany, but the towns of the provinces were, by continental standards, little more than large villages. Only 20 had more than 3,000 inhabitants, and only four – Bristol, York, Norwich, and Coventry – more than 4,000.

There were signs everywhere of over a hundred years of population decline: decaying buildings in the towns, abandoned villages in the country (over 90 in Warwickshire alone), and sheep-walks where formerly cereals had been cultivated. Overseas trade, though flourishing, had acquired potentially dangerous features: it was alarmingly subject to the control of Hansards and other aliens, most of them Italian; it was serviced by a negligible mercantile marine; it was over-dependent on one market – Antwerp; and, most importantly, it was dominated by the foreign demand for a single commodity, cloth, which alone accounted for about 70 per cent of all exports. There were no signs that a period of chronic political instability and sporadic civil war was at an end, and there was nothing to suggest to a monarch as hard-headed as Henry VII that there was any chance of making good the territorial losses of the Hundred Years' War.

By contrast, in the early 18th century England was one of the wealthiest nations in the world and the possessor of a flourishing and diverse economy, the largest mercantile marine in Europe (about 450,000 tons by 1750), and huge markets in Asia, North America and the West Indies. About 17 per cent of the population lived in towns with more than 10,000 inhabitants, and London, with a population of about 500,000 in 1700, was not only the biggest city in western Europe, but also the principal centre for the transatlantic and Africa trades, and the rival of Antwerp as the banking and credit capital of the world. In spite of a near tripling of the population between 1450 and 1750, there was a consistent grain surplus which permitted, for the first time ever, the export of massive quantities of cereals – over 900,000 quarters a year by the 1740s. Nothing illustrates better the transformation that had taken place than the fact that the England, which had been able to send only 6,000 men to Agincourt, was now able to challenge, successfully, the France of Louis XIV for the hegemony of Europe.

Although Henry VII did not know it when he ascended the throne in 1485, an important era in social and economic history was coming to an end. Between 1086, when the Domesday survey was undertaken, and the beginning of the 14th century, the population of England rose, virtually

Gold medallion of Elizabeth I. The victory of the Spanish Armada in 1588 raised Elizabeth to a pinnacle of prestige and popularity, and gave rise to a spate of celebratory portraits.

The Sun, Saffron Walden, Essex. Symbolic of the unprecedented prosperity and relatively settled conditions of the late 17th century, the building was refurbished and decorated in 1676 with a variety of plaster enrichments.

without check, from approximately 2,000,000 to something between 4,500,000 and 6,000,000. Agricultural output failed to keep pace with this growth because productivity was low (it took the labour of two men to feed three); substantial areas were, for a variety of reasons, uncultivatable; and one-third of all arable land was kept fallow each year. By 1300, there was insufficient food, even when harvests were good, to provide an adequate diet for the whole population. This meant that malnutrition was widespread, and that, for many, the fear of starvation was an ever-present feature of life. In short, the country was ripe for the demographic catastrophe which followed. In the second decade of the century, torrential rains destroyed the harvests of three consecutive summers and produced a famine of almost unimaginable severity, which, it was said, the poor of London only survived by eating dogs, cats, the dung of doves, and their own children. Consequently, the Black Death of 1348–9, the Grey Death of 1361–2, and the great plagues of 1369 and 1375 fell upon a people whose capacity to resist epidemic disease had been undermined by chronic undernourishment. The resulting mortality rate was frightful. It is impossible to discover how many people actually died – there were no parish registers in those days – but between 1348 and the end of the century, the population as a whole declined by something like two-fifths, and 15 more national or extra-regional epidemics in the 15th century prevented a recovery.

By 1485, when the battle of Bosworth was fought, the inhabitants of England were about as few as they had been in 1086, but they were far better off than their 14th century predecessors. For one thing, there was now a favourable balance between food supplies and population, which meant that there was a much reduced danger of famine. In fact, there was an excess of capacity over demand, so that in the long term agricultural prices had fallen. There was also a shortage of labour, and so wage-rates had risen. Most significantly, though, there was a shortage of tenantry, thus entry fines and rents had declined. Exceptional opportunities had arisen for landowners to convert arable land to pasture and pursue the increasing profits of the cloth trade, for the richer peasants to improve their holdings, and for many of the labouring poor to secure holdings of their own. Cumulatively, these developments had transformed both tenurial relationships and the social structure – by discouraging customary land tenure and serfdom – and had produced a level of real wages for craftsmen and labourers which was not to be exceeded until the end of the 19th century. In a material sense, then, the 15th century was something of a golden age, but the prosperity of the majority was dependent less on economic and social progress than the continuation of a long period of population decline which, as it happened, was about to end.

In the 1470s and 1480s, disquieting signs began to appear that the trend of the preceding 150 years or so was going into reverse. The frontiers of cultivation began to stabilise; the demand for land quickened; rents started to rise; and complaints against the socially damaging effects of enclosure were brought to the attention of parliament. As we can tell now from the study of wills and inquisitions *post mortem*, there was also a tendency for the number of sons surviving their fathers to increase. Clearly, a resumption of population growth was in the offing.

The plague of 1485 – a strange disease known as the 'English Sweat' – probably delayed the start of the process, but the final years of the century were, relatively speaking,

AGRICULTURE

In the late 15th century, as indeed in the earlier medieval period, agriculture not only dominated the economy of England but also shaped the lives of the majority of its inhabitants. Roughly 90 per cent of a population of about two million lived in the small towns, villages, hamlets and isolated farms of an essentially rural landscape, and worked, in familial or other units of five or six individuals, upon the land. Life was both hard and precarious at a time when the only sources of power were wind, water and the muscles of men and animals, and when, thanks to low productivity, the existence of extensive wastelands and a shortage of fertiliser, agricultural output was barely equal to the demands made upon it.

The harvest was for most men the most important event of the year: a good one meant freedom from anxiety about the staple diet of bread and beer for another 12 months, and a bad one the misery of hunger and the possibility of death by starvation. Since the yield of the harvest was to a considerable extent determined by the weather, whose vagaries it was impossible to control or predict, the fear of famine can rarely have receded far from men's minds.

By 1714, however, when the last of the Stuarts died, the situation was very much changed for the better. In spite of an increase of about 150 per cent in the size of the population, and, as a result of the growth of the towns and developments in industry, a decrease in the proportion of the population involved in agriculture, there was a sufficiently large grain surplus to permit a flourishing export trade. Exactly how, and when, this transformation had taken place is still very much a matter of debate. Certainly, there had been some reorganisation of farms. In many places, and in particular in the Midland Plain, the scattered strips of the old open field system had been consolidated into compact holding and enclosed (that is to say, fenced or hedged), and many small farms had been engrossed (or amalgamated) to form larger, more coherent units. Cultivation had been extended into hitherto unproductive areas – either through the introduction of convertible or 'up and down' husbandry (which involved the alternate use of a field for grazing and tillage)

into wood-pasture districts and regions of permanent grass such as the Vale of Evesham, or through the drainage of fens, marshes, and saltings lying along lengths of the English coastline, estuaries, and inland rivers.

Productivity had been increased both by the adoption of new techniques, such as the floating of water meadows (which meant flooding fields to protect them from frost and enrich them with silt deposits), and by the introduction of new field crops such as carrots, turnips, sainfoin, ryegrass, clover, trefoil and lucerne, which, either directly or indirectly, improved the fertility of light soils. But the relative contribution of each of these developments to the overall process of change is impossible to establish precisely, as also is the rate of progress in the period as a whole. The one thing that can be said with some certainty is that by the late 1670s, the spectre of famine which had haunted the Middle Ages had been banished from the country.

Our knowledge of the landscape of Britain during this period owes much to a succession of topographical writers, county surveyors and map makers. Leland (1506–1552) seems to have initiated the fashion for direct enquiry and observation followed by subsequent recording, and his *Itinerary* gives us quite a good picture of Tudor England. He distinguishes between 'champaign' (open and unenclosed) country, enclosed, and 'metely wooded' country, and he notes whether areas are rich, moderate or scant of corn. The areas of pasture and meadow are recorded along with those of subsistence agriculture and surplus production. The importance of climate and soil were noted, and some of our present day patterns of agriculture are clearly discernable. Wheat was noticeably scanty on the sandy soils of the Triassic Midlands and in Northern England where oats dominated. The importance of sheep in the upland and mountainous areas emerges; the grass country for fattening cattle in east Leicestershire and Northamptonshire was already famous. Warwickshire was an important source of wheat, and beans were a special feature of the Vale of Aylesbury and the plain of Somerset.

Leland is followed by Camden (1561–1623), who adopted the same

THE
English Farrier,
OR,
Country-mans Treasure.

Shewing approved Remedies to cure all Diseases, hurts, maymes, maladies and griefes, in Horses: and how to know the severall Diseases that breed in them, with a description of every Veine, how and when to let them blood, according to the nature of their Diseases.

With directions to know the severall Ages of them.

Faithfully set forth according to Art and approved experiment, for the benefit of Gentlemen, Farmers, Inholders, Husbandmen, and generally for all.

At London printed by *John Beale,* and *Robert Bird.* 1636.

The English Farrier, 1636, a treatise on the care of horses. The 17th century saw an increasingly rationalistic and systematic approach to agriculture, as witnessed by the demand for this type of practical handbook.

pattern of topographic description — although in Latin — in his *Britannia*. In Herefordshire, for example, he writes of the Golden Vale of Dore: 'The hills that incompass it on both sides, are cloathed with woods; under the woods lie cornfields on each hand; and under these fields lovely and fruitful meadows. In the middle between them glides a clear and crystal river'.

At the end of the 17th century Gregory King provides us with another pen picture of the country which reveals that about half of England and Wales was under cultivation as arable, pasture or meadow. He also thought that there were about three million acres of woods and coppices and another three million acres of forests, parks and commons, and at least 10 million acres of heaths, moors, mountains and barren land.

Defoe spans the latter part of the 17th century and early part of the 18th century (1659–1731) and is also known for a famous *Tour of Britain*. The way in which both attitudes and conditions change is well illustrated by his account of Bagshot Heath in Surrey: 'Here is a vast tract of land, some of it within seventeen or eighteen miles of the capital city; which is not only poor, but even quite sterile, given up to barrenness, horrid and frightful to look on, not only good for little, but good for nothing; much of it is sandy desert, and one may frequently be put in mind here of Arabia Deserta, where the winds raise the sands, so as to overwhelm whole caravans of travellers, cattle and people together; for in passing this heath in a windy day, I was so far in danger of smothering with the clouds of sand, which were raised by the storm, that I could neither keep it out of my mouth, nose or eyes; and when the wind was over, the sand appear'd to spread over the adjacent fields of the forest some miles distant, so as that it ruins the very soil.'

John Stow's *Survey of London and Westminster* (1598), Richard Carew's *Survey of Cornwall* (1602) and the *Journey of Celia Fiennes* are further sources of valuable information, whilst accompanying these descriptive accounts we have the work of the estate and county surveyors and map makers which include such names as Lily, Lhuyd, Saxton, Norden, Molyneux, Speed, Ogilby and Seller.

Cilewent Farmhouse (above), now at the Welsh Folk Museum, St Fagans. Many medieval farmhouses were 'long houses' similar to the 18th century farmhouse shown above. One building, divided into two by a through passage, housed both the farmer and his cattle the former in the heated living accommodation to the right of the door, the latter in the unheated byre to the left.

Y Garrag Fawr (left), a husbandman's farmhouse now at the Welsh Folk Museum. This sturdy building, of a type common in north Wales between about 1550 and 1750, was built around 1570 for a husbandman and his family in Waunfawr village, Gwynedd. Of slate and granite construction, it provided five rooms on two floors, heated by fires at each end of the house.

Granary from Temple Broughton, Worcs (right). In parallel with other developments in agriculture, new types of farm building were introduced in the 17th and 18th centuries, among them granaries of the kind illustrated here. Constructed around an elm frame on brick piers, and with an external, detached stair, it provided rat-free storage for grain, a shelter for carts or ploughs and kennels for dogs.

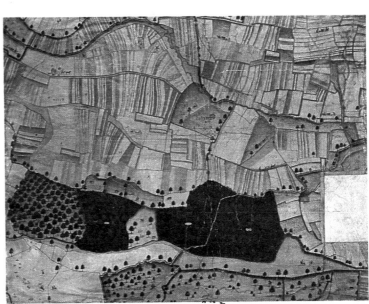

Laxton Fields, Notts. Of the old open field system, only this village survives; three fields totalling 483 acres are worked in 165 strips. The extent to which private ownership has transformed the landscape, even here, can be gauged by comparison of the aerial photograph, taken from the west, with Mark Pierce's map of 1635.

healthy ones, so the delay was only temporary. From the 1490s onwards, the population expanded rapidly, until in the 1640s it nearly reached the level at which it had stood on the eve of the Black Death. It did not, of course, grow consistently. There were occasional remissions for plague or famine, notably in the late 1550s, the 1590s, and the 1630s, but none was sufficient to halt for more than a few years the inexorable upward drive. The consequences were entirely predictable. Since a great deal of land had been allowed to go out of cultivation in the 15th century – through neglect or the conversion of arable to pasture – and since no great increase in agricultural efficiency had been achieved, it once again proved impossible to expand the food supply fast enough to satisfy the rapidly increasing demand. As a result, many of the less happy features of medieval life reappeared.

Hard times for the poor

Cultivation was, with difficulty and incommensurate reward, extended into the unproductive or inaccessible lands which had previously been allowed to go to waste. Intense competition for holdings drove up the rents of those who were successful, and forced those who were not to take on labouring jobs in their own villages, or, worse still, leave home and search for work.

High profits in the cloth trade (in the first half of the 16th century at least) and in agriculture from about 1515 onwards encouraged enclosure and so gave rise to widespread social unrest, since the movement was seen – not altogether justly – as the prime cause of scarcity, land shortage, and, in some areas, continuing depopulation. Inevitably, prices soared. The rise was not a consistent one as wide variations in harvest-yield produced violent short-term fluctuations, and other forces were at work in different ways at different times, notably the inflationary effects of the Great Debasement of 1544–51, heavy government expenditure on the French and Scottish wars of the 1540s and the Spanish war of 1585–1603, and the influx of foreign bullion from the 1590s onwards. But between 1515 and 1650 there was only one period of deflation, namely in the 1560s, after an influenza epidemic had temporarily cut back the population. Over the

The Battle of Malplaquet was fought on September 11, 1709 between the forces of the Duke of Marlborough and Marshal Villars. After inconclusive fighting on both wings, the French were driven from the field by a cavalry attack on their centre. Marlborough had received many honours because of his victories early in the campaign, but went on to offend Queen Anne with his arrogant demands and was finally dismissed from his official positions. The roots of the long-standing conflict with France lay in the former monarch William of Orange's determination to remove the French threat to his homeland, the Netherlands.

RECLAMATION IN EASTERN ENGLAND

Coastal reclamation has vied with coastal recession in eastern England during the whole of historic time. Today it is the reclamation that is the most obvious and most dramatic, for no trace now remains of a coastal strip up to two miles in width that has, in places, been lost since Roman times; nor of villages such as Wilsthorp, Hartburn, Hyde, Old Aldeburgh, Ravenspur, Shipden, Snitterley, Overstand, Eidesthorp, Whimpwell and Old Dunwich, long since consigned to the waves.

But what the sea has taken away in some areas it has replaced in others: for much of the coast, especially in Lincolnshire and Norfolk, is fringed with mud flats which, aided by deposition, tend to evolve naturally through salt marsh into fresh water marsh and eventually grassland. Nature has a cycle of up to 100 years for this transformation to take place, but by embanking man can accelerate the cycle to less than half the normal time.

Around the Wash place names such as Bicker Haven, Surfleet, Seas End, Fleet Haven, Seadyke, Holbeach, Moulton Seas End and others now up to 15 miles inland tell their own story, quite apart from the succession of dykes and embankments which mark successive enclosures. The Roman part of this story remains enigmatic and the Roman contribution, such as it was, must have fallen into disuse after the fifth century. There is clear evidence, however, of Anglo-Saxon and Danish defensive settlement sites on the silt islands in the Fenland and along the coast, and of the way in which the inhabitants of these villages gradually began to reclaim land as their numbers increased.

Written evidence becomes more common in the later Middle Ages; near Boston, for example, we hear of Saturday Dike in 1160, Hassock Dike in 1190 and Common Dike in 1241 where advances were being made into the adjacent Fen. Conversely the men of Holbeach and Whaplode south of the Wash were building sea dykes in 1286. Whilst the process was continuous through the centuries some of the major advances came with the 16th and 17th centuries when there was a twofold movement, inland and on the coast.

On the one hand major reclamation was achieved around the coast of the Wash, more especially east of the road which now joins Boston and Wainflete, and north of the road from Whaplode to Holbeach. Secondly, a major attack was made on the draining of the inland Fen area between Wisbech, Peterborough and Cambridge. Here some 1300 square miles had by 1600 become ripe for a

'greate designe' of reclamation. James I himself showed a lively interest in the various schemes proposed, but it was eventually left to the 4th Earl of Bedford, who owned 20,000 acres near Thorney and Whittlesey, to initiate with 13 Co-Adventurers between 1630 and 1634 a scheme which involved the Dutch engineer Vermuyden.

Improvements in the drainage were based upon extensive new cuts, drains and sluices, the most spectacular being the Old Bedford River, some 70 feet wide and 21 miles in length. The Civil War interrupted the drainage work but a resumption was made in 1651 when the New Bedford River or Hundred Foot River was cut, along with the Forty Foot Drain, Twenty Foot River and Sixteen Foot Drain.

At first the drainage produced entirely successful results, but the engineers had not realised that the drying out of the peat soils would lead to shrinkage and also to wastage as a result of bacterial and wind action. Gradually the peat level dropped and before long the river cuts and drains were flowing above the level of the surrounding countryside, which could only be drained by the introduction of wind operated pumps.

Towards the end of the 18th century drainage problems again became acute as the level of the peat continued to drop and differences of up to 10 feet became common. The situation was saved by the introduction of the steam pump at the beginning of the 19th century and the electric pump in the 20th century.

The reclamation of marsh and fen has brought hundreds of square miles of land into productive use, but the methods employed have produced two distinctive landscapes; the small scale individual-type reclamation has given us an irregular patch pattern of ditches, banks, fields and roads with dispersed settlement, whilst the large scale corporate reclamation provides in contrast long, dead straight drainage canals and dykes, wide open rectangular fields, straight roads and nucleated settlement. These patterns are very clear both on the ground and on the Ordnance Survey maps.

Medieval man, like the sea, was also consuming as well as reclaiming the land. We now know from records in Ely Cathedral that the Broads of Norfolk (for a long time thought to be natural features) are in fact man made. They were produced by medieval peat cutters and at one time were much more extensive than the present series; natural vegetation is gradually filling the remains and threatening a very prosperous 20th century recreational industry.

Wicken Fen, Cambs, now a nature reserve. The landscape of much of eastern England would have resembled this fen in early historic time.

Denver Sluice drainage system, Norfolk, looking south; a flat, low-lying area dominated by dykes, ditches and canals. The top right drainage line is the Old Bedford River and parallel to it is the New Bedford River. In the foreground is the Great Ouse, and Denver Sluice is at the junction in the middle distance.

Salthouse, Norfolk. The one time coastal village is now half a mile from the modern beach as a result of marine deposition and salt marsh growth. The beach grades into the famous Blakeney Spit. In the background is the Cromer moraine.

The Norfolk Broads. Once thought to be natural landscape features, the Broads are now known to be the result of medieval peat cutting. They are a valuable recreational resource nowadays but are gradually disappearing due to vegetation.

Cley Mill, Norfolk. Wind operated pumps were the main means of solving the land drainage problems in the 18th century and a few examples have survived to the present day. Most were replaced by steam pumps in the 19th century and by electric pumps in the 20th. Fenland and coastal marshland were treated alike.

whole period, the price of the cereals on which the population was crucially dependent for nourishment rose sevenfold, but wage-rates, in a time of labour surplus, rose only three-fold, as did the price of industrial products, which was kept down by the low cost of labour. As a result, real wages fell steadily until, in 1650, they reached a level 60 per cent below that which had prevailed in the first decade of the 16th century. In fact, the level enjoyed at the accession of Henry VIII was not reached again until 1880, and in the exceptionally difficult year of 1597 – when, interestingly enough, that great piece of escapist literature, Shakespeare's *A Midsummer Night's Dream* was written – wage rates fell temporarily to the lowest point in history.

Just what effect these developments had on the population at large is extremely difficult to say. The evidence from which our knowledge of prices and wage-rates derives is thoroughly unsatisfactory; the statistics which have been compiled are, in spite of considerable research, incomplete, narrow in range, and unrepresentative of the country as a whole. It is also impossible to discover how far people were insulated from the effects of the price rise by what we know were well-established features of social and economic life; for example, what proportion of the population were subsistence farmers who, in normal circumstances, would not need to purchase foodstuffs in significant quantities; how many labourers were paid in kind, with food, drink and accommodation, for their services; how far were the wages of the individual supplemented by the earnings of other members of his family; how prevalent was the practice of barter not only north of the Trent, where there was always a shortage of coin, but also in the more prosperous south of England. There are no certain answers to these fundamental questions, and only general, rather tentative conclusions can be reached.

Prosperity for the gentry

As far as the small number of substantial landowners – the yeomen, the gentry and the great magnates – were concerned, the period was a highly prosperous one, and one which presented splendid opportunities for enrichment. As possessors of a valuable commodity in increasingly short supply they were able to choose between two equally attractive courses of action. They could either farm their lands themselves with a view to producing a marketable surplus – in which case they would benefit from the falling cost of labour and booming food prices – or they could let them out to others and so benefit, through increasing entry fines and rents, from cut-throat competition for holdings. In either case, high profits would enable them to make the most of the relative fall in the price of manufactured goods, to improve their estates – for instance, by converting pasture to arable land as the profits of the cloth trade fell – or to extend them by the purchase of the highly attractive land liberated by the Dissolution of the Monasteries. Those tenant farmers who were fortunate enough to hold their lands by leases which guaranteed them security of tenure were similarly placed, but, as a consequence of having smaller holdings and therefore smaller surpluses, were incapable of equalling the profits of their social superiors and were vulnerable to misfortunes such as harvest failure. For manufacturers, the position was an equivocal one. On the one hand, an abundant supply of cheap labour enabled them to hold down their costs and therefore to market their goods at increasingly competitive prices: on the other, the rapid fall in real wages diminished the demand for their products, as more and more

THE REBUILDING OF RURAL ENGLAND

In the early part of the 16th century, most people were living in the rather poor and cramped dwellings of their forefathers. Most often these were two-roomed houses built as timber frames with cob walls and rubble foundations. There were no glazed windows, only one fireplace and no ceilings. By the middle of the century wealthier yeomen had begun to build themselves larger and better houses, and from 1560 to at least 1650 a great surge of rebuilding swept through the country leading to a complete transformation of housing conditions.

In most cases the old houses were pulled down and rebuilding took place in free stone where it was available. Before the end of the century the fashion for rebuilding had spread down from the yeomen to the husbandmen (the lesser farmers) and to the cottagers.

The wave of rebuilding in the countryside was particularly marked in the first 20 years of the 17th century, and by 1620 whole villages in the limestone belt across central England had been rebuilt. Similarly, in the Yorkshire Dales, there arose solid stone built farmsteads with mullioned windows and date plaques over their front door lintels. Many of the houses and farmsteads rebuilt in this period still survive today, and some villages and even towns, especially in the south and east of England, remain almost unaltered.

The appearance of these houses depends to a great degree on the materials employed in building. In the Middle Ages most houses were constructed of wood or of cob (clay and straw). As long as wood remained reasonably plentiful, it remained a popular material; in areas such as the West Midlands and East Anglia it continued to be used well into the 17th century. A timber building consisted of an oak frame with walls of wattle and daub. The whole building, including the timbers, was usually covered with plaster, which might be elaborately patterned, although in some places the intricate carving of the wood suggests that it was left exposed.

In many parts of the country, however, the builders abandoned timber in favour of stone, and there are now very few timber buildings to be seen in the Cotswolds, much of the south west, Wales, Scotland and the north of England. Where there was no good stone locally available, as in much of south east England, brick began to replace timber in the 17th century; in Devon cob continued to be used, and some villages there are built almost entirely of this material. Most houses were roofed with thatch, but this too began to be replaced by stone slates or brick tiles in the 16th century. Glazed windows were also becoming more common, at least in more prosperous houses, and fireplaces were replacing the medieval open hearths. At the end of the 16th century William Harrison, rector of Radwinter in Essex, referred to the 'multitude of chimneys lately erected' in his village.

Changes of this sort were slower to reach the more backward north: in 1698 Celia Fiennes described houses on the Scottish border as looking 'just like the booths at a fair . . . they have no chimneys, their smoke comes out all over the house and there are great holes in the sides of their houses which let out the smoke when they have been well smoked in it'. Similar conditions were noticed by Dr Johnson when he visited the Highlands of Scotland in 1773.

Houses varied greatly according to the social status of their occupants. Most people still lived in the country and depended on the land for their living. Many were extremely poor, the population was rising, and an increasing number of people had to rely mainly on their wages for subsistence. Rural labourers' houses were often small, primitive and badly built, with only one or two rooms almost empty of possessions; relatively few of these houses survive today. Farmhouses were larger, but not necessarily much more sophisticated architecturally, and they varied greatly from one region to another.

The highland zone (including most of Scotland and Wales) still supported a predominantly pastoral economy with a small scattered population and few towns. Here the standard pattern of settlement was the isolated farm, in which animals and human beings often lived under one roof in a 'long house'.

Uppark, Sussex, was built in the 1680s to the designs of William Talman and exhibits all the features of formality and regularity that became common in post-Restoration country houses. The symmetrical brick facade is surmounted by a hipped roof and wooden cornice; the servants were relegated to the basement.

In the more economically advanced 'lowland' areas (which included most of southern and eastern England), farmhouses were more commonly grouped into villages or hamlets, and the animals housed separately, away from the main house.

The basic living requirements within any farmhouse were for a hall where meals were cooked and eaten, bedrooms and some storage space. With the advent of chimneys, halls were no longer open to the roof but had rooms above; the number of other rooms depended on the wealth of the farmer. Most farmers were 'husbandmen' who farmed only a few acres, and their houses were small and plain. The better-off 'yeomen', or capitalist farmers, could, however, in the words of one contemporary, 'keep good houses and travail to get riches . . . and with much grazing, frequenting of markets, and keeping of servants . . . come to great riches'. Their houses were quite large, with a parlour or private living room in addition to the hall, and accommodation for farm-servants or living-in labourers. Externally, yeomen's houses increasingly imitated the houses of the gentry and aristocracy in a growing concern for compactness and symmetry.

Urban housing has always differed greatly from that of rural areas. Because less space was available in towns than in villages, the tendency was to expand upwards rather than outwards. With the exception of the very largest houses in London and some other cities, which were built around courtyards, town houses had narrow frontages with long plots stretching back from the street. The main rooms, including the hall, were placed on the first floor, the ground floor often being given over to the 'shop' (meaning a place for manufacture rather than retailing), and the second floor to bedrooms. Most of the main towns in 'lowland' Britain were still built almost entirely of timber, the upper floors of the houses projecting outwards over the street with the gables elaborately ornamented; frontages of the important houses often contained two or more of these gables. Behind the main frontage, smaller houses were built in courts — the forerunners of the notorious slums of the Industrial Revolution — and these, together with the 'suburbs' beyond the old city boundaries, became the homes of the poor, whose living conditions may well have worsened in this period as the population grew.

The Market Cross, Wymondham, Norfolk, is a timber-framed, octagonal structure, built in 1617. Left open for market stalls, a staircase leads to the market hall above.

The Guildhall, Lavenham, Suffolk, showing the elaborate carving with which early Tudor craftsmen adorned their more important buildings. The hall was built by the guild of Corpus Christi in the 1520s.

The Feathers Inn, Ludlow, Shropshire. Inns were prominent features of all market towns, and many were rebuilt in the 16th and 17th centuries. Dating from 1603, The Feathers exhibits a wealth of rich carving on its three-gabled facade.

Townend Farm, Troutbeck, Cumbria. A typical 17th century yeoman's farmhouse from the 'highland zone', it is built of rubble stone and whitewashed.

Little Moreton Hall, Cheshire, is a 15th century hall house of timber, to which the gabled bay windows, characteristic of the 16th century, were added in 1559.

The state bedroom at Powis Castle, Welshpool, the culminating point in the 'state apartment', seems to have been remodelled for a visit by Charles II in the 1660s. The bed is placed, like a shrine, in an alcove and is railed off from the body of the room, where the king received visitors and dined privately.

The Old Hall, Gainsborough, Lincolnshire, was built at the end of the 15th century on the typical medieval courtyard plan. The kitchen, with its huge brick fireplace, calls to mind the vast households kept by the early Tudor nobility and the lavish hospitality exercised in their houses.

men were obliged to spend a larger and larger proportion of their earnings on the basic necessities of life – food and drink. Successful exploitation of the market by the individual was by no means an impossibility, but it depended to a much greater extent than in the case of the landowners and tenant farmers on energy, intelligence, resources, and good luck. But for the great majority of the population the period must have been at best a frightening and uncomfortable one, at worst, an unspeakably horrible experience, especially for the urban labourer who was rarely paid in kind and was unable to produce any of his own food, and in addition was obliged to put up with the dangers and discomforts that were part of town life. The small-holder was unable either to resist the pressure of enclosers or to meet the increasing costs of entry fines and rents, and was therefore commonly evicted from his holding. If he failed to find employment in the locality, he often had no alternative but to go into the towns where, by the end of the 16th century, over half the inhabitants were already living in the direst poverty and squalor, on the

verge of destitution and starvation. It is not really surprising, therefore, that from the 1540s onwards, there were hordes of vagabonds and thieves on the roads, innumerable grain riots and incidents of hedge-breaking and rick-burning, and, as the landed classes were only too well aware, there was an ever-present danger of the sort of peasant revolt which in fact erupted in 1549: what is, perhaps, surprising is the success with which the Tudors were able to deal with the majority of the problems with which they were faced, and to contribute, not always intentionally, to the accelerating process of national unification.

Government by the Crown

In the 15th century, responsibility for the government of England was vested in the Crown. Its possessor was endowed with considerable theoretical powers, but not, as it happened, with the means to exploit them fully. The revenues the monarch was entitled to receive were sufficient to pay for a moderately impressive court and what may loosely be

COUNTRY HOUSES AND PARKS

As a high level of internal security was achieved in England under the early Tudor kings, castle building ceased and was replaced, in the early 16th century, by the construction of country houses. In Scotland, however, feudal warlords were still inadequately controlled by the central authority, and there was widespread disorder, particularly in the Borders where the way of life resembled that of the 'Wild West' with blood feuds, cattle raids and a great deal of violence. So here the great houses continued to be planned for defence, with forbidding turreted exteriors and the main rooms on the upper floors.

The country houses of England were very different: basically medieval in arrangement, they contained a ground floor hall – used mainly on formal occasions and, increasingly, as the servants' dining room – a suite of rooms on the first floor for formal entertaining, another downstairs for private use, and 'lodgings' for guests. At first the larger country houses were planned around one or more courtyards, with each range one room deep; the courtyard was entered through an impressive gatehouse which evoked the fortified houses of the recent past. Many of these houses, especially in south east England, were built of brick, although timber and stone were also used.

The courtyard plan, though it might have been appropriate for gigantic households like that of Cardinal Wolsey at Hampton Court (who is said to have

had 180 indoor servants), was in many respects wasteful and inefficient. By the end of the 16th century, therefore, it had been superseded by a more compact plan based on a central hall block with two cross-wings, one of which contained the kitchen and service rooms and the other the main living quarters. This plan first emerged during the Middle Ages in the houses of the smaller gentry and yeoman farmers, but was used by some courtiers under the early Tudors, and spread to the rest of the landed gentry during Elizabeth I's reign. Not only was the 'H' or 'half-H' plan compact, it also gave the builders an opportunity to construct a symmetrical façade, and so paved the way for the more widespread adoption of Renaissance architectural ideas.

The gentry and aristocracy benefited from the price inflation of the late 16th and early 17th centuries, and replaced their timber-framed houses with new ones of brick or stone in which they could display their increasing possessions – furniture, tapestries, plate and pictures. The most active builders were courtiers, often relatively 'new men', who had recently acquired or augmented their estates with the spoils of the dissolved monasteries, and saw their houses as massive status symbols.

To encompass such grandiose aims, a new architectural language emerged, a strange and imaginative mixture of medieval and Renaissance ideas, often evoking a romanticised vision of the past. Windows were large, and

ornament profuse. The Elizabethans and Jacobeans admired detail and intricacy, and these characteristics appeared also in gardens and garden buildings, where the fancies of their owners could be indulged unchecked. These gardens have long since been destroyed, but we can appreciate them through contemporary descriptions such as that of the garden of the poet Sir Fulke Greville at Warwick Castle, which a writer in 1634 described as 'a second Eden . . . adorn'd with all kind of delightful and shady walks, and arbours, pleasant groves and wildernesses, fruitful trees, delicious bowers, odoriferous herbs, fragrant flowers . . . and many rare and curious fish ponds'.

Although the great houses of Elizabethan and Jacobean England contained much Renaissance decorative detail, it was not until the second decade of the 17th century that houses began more than superficially to resemble those of Renaissance Italy. According to the rules of classical architecture houses had to be strictly symmetrical within and without and their elevation arranged according to a rigid system of proportions. The new taste was first cultivated in the courts of James I and Charles I, but was not at that time widely accepted among the gentry, mainly because the economy fell into recession in the 1620s and the later political upheavals were not conducive to large scale building.

However, many new houses were built after the Restoration as the

landowners entered a period of greater economic and political security which culminated in the Glorious Revolution. Architecturally these houses reflected a formal, hierarchical view of the world with the centre strongly emphasised, often with a classical pediment. With the spread of Baroque ideas from Europe at the end of the century, the main block in the larger houses was often flanked by lower pavilions, a dramatic arrangement frequently enhanced by the lavish use of sculpture. Gardens were also arranged formally with alleys and paths radiating from the house in strict symmetry. In the words of Pope:

'Grove nods grove, each alley has a brother
And half the platform just reflects the other'.

Unfortunately, few of these gardens survived the later craze for landscaping.

Houses were equally formal inside, their arrangement owing much to the France of Louis XIV. The grandest houses were in many respects like hotels, with lavish suites of rooms for family and guests, culminating in the rarely used 'great apartment', whose climax was the state bedroom with the bed (on which vast sums of money were spent) arranged like a shrine in an alcove behind rails. These rooms were situated upstairs, with the everyday living rooms downstairs, and the servants banished to the basement from which they would emerge when required via the back stairs.

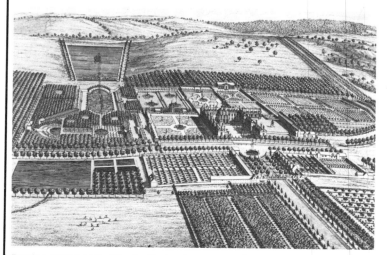

Bretby, Derbyshire. After the Restoration many gardens were remodelled in the formal manner pioneered in France and Holland and immortalised in the bird's-eye views of Kip and Knyff (1707–1715). Bretby, which belonged to the earls of Chesterfield, was one of the most famous gardens, with fine avenues and fountains.

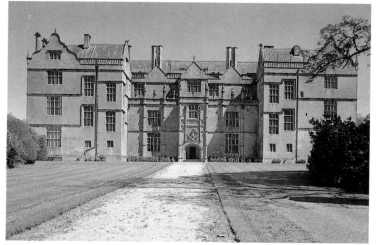

Montacute House, Yeovil, Somerset. It was started in about 1588 by Sir Edward Phelips, who intended it to be the most magnificent house of its time. Of a 16th century formal garden only the boundary walks, pavilions and balustrades remain, but there is a fine 19th century layout.

termed a small civil service, but for precious little else besides. Additional revenues could be raised, but only by negotiating loans on the foreign or domestic money markets, selling land, or taxing the movable property or income of subjects. The first and second of these options were, in the long term, counterproductive; raising taxes was not, but it was conditional on the consent of a parliament whose members were prepared to contribute only to the extra-ordinary expenses of government – for example, the cost of a war with Scotland or of rebuilding the fortress at Berwick. As a result, the Crown was incapable of maintaining a standing army, police force, or effective civil service, or of securing the means to do so. It was unable, therefore, to acquire the coercive powers it in fact needed to govern effectively.

For a variety of reasons, some legal, some traditional, some merely accidental, there were areas of the realm over which the King had very little control; for example, most of Ireland outside the Pale; most of the 130-odd Welsh

The hall was the focal point of all medieval houses. The 15th century example at Gainsborough Old Hall, Lincolnshire, is built of timber with a fine arch-braced roof. The outer doorways at the end of the hall led into the buttery and pantry, where food and drink were served, while in the centre a passage gave access to the kitchen.

Compton Wynyates, Warwickshire. Since the house was first built at the end of the 15th century, the surroundings have been altered extensively. The open parkland and ponds to the left of the house are medieval, while the lawn in front marks the site of a courtyard which contained stables and subsidiary buildings. The formal garden on the right was created in the 19th century.

marcher lordships outside the Principality; the east, middle, and west marches on the Scottish border; the palatinate of Durham; and innumerable manors and liberties such as Tyndale and Ripon. He had just as little authority over the 'over-mighty' subjects who ruled the localities, in some cases with quasi-regal powers; some borough corporations; and, most importantly, the Church. On the eve of the Reformation, the latter was probably the richest and most powerful organisation in the Kingdom and, in effect, a state within a state. It was ruled by, and paid taxes to, a foreign master, the Pope, whose authority extended beyond spiritual and judicial matters to the appointment even of its prelates. It was endowed with a very substantial proportion of the landed wealth of England – perhaps as much as a third. It was represented, since there were about 50 bishops and abbots, by a permanent majority in the House of Lords; and it possessed its own courts, in which legislation independent of royal control was enforced.

The King's position was, therefore, a far from enviable one. He was supposed, among other things, to secure the peace, prosperity and stability of his kingdom, to protect the property and rights of all his subjects, and to enforce obedience to the law: but he was, in effect, denied the means to perform these duties himself. This meant, inevitably, that he had to get others to perform them for him, namely the men who, by virtue of their wealth, social status and prestige, enjoyed real authority in the localities. Since his ability to coerce was limited his success in securing the co-operation of what is often called the 'political nation' depended essentially on the pursuit of popular, or at least acceptable, policies, and the exploitation to the full of his rather limited capacity to reward loyal servants. He had, in other words, to be a skilful politician as well as an energetic and efficient administrator.

As it happened, the personal qualities of the men and women who ruled England between 1485 and 1603 – the

CHURCHES AND CHAPELS

The 16th and 17th centuries were not a very active period of church building. Much of the period was dominated by the Reformation and its after-effects, which meant that there was little building at all between 1530 and 1670. Before 1530 the Perpendicular form of Gothic reached its climax in such buildings as Bath Abbey, the chapel at King's College, Cambridge, and King Henry VII's chapel at Westminster Abbey; after 1670 most of the best buildings were in the revived Classical style, the most notable being St Paul's Cathedral and the other city churches in London built by Sir Christopher Wren to replace those destroyed in the Great Fire of 1666.

Although Classical architecture came to dominate church design by the end of the 17th century, Gothic never really died. The few churches built between the completion of the English Reformation in 1560 and the beginning of the Civil War in 1640 were designed in a form of Gothic which was a logical continuation of the Perpendicular architecture of the early 16th century, and even in the 1690s the nave of St Mary's, Warwick, was rebuilt after a fire in an unmistakably Gothic style.

The Reformation was a rather less savage affair in England and Wales than it was in Scotland. The main changes were in doctrine and in the services which were celebrated for the first time in English instead of Latin. But some ceremonial was retained, and in the cathedrals and larger churches the clergy still wore copes, had candles lit upon the altar and even sweetened the atmosphere with incense. The administration of the church continued much as before, the power being concentrated in the hands of the bishops, though now they were responsible to the King and not to the Pope. All this was highly objectionable to those known as Puritans, who wanted a more radical Reformation and the abolition of all ceremonies and bishops. During the 1630s the bishops, under Archbishop Laud, responded by increasing their power with the active support of King Charles I, ordering an improvement in the standards of ceremonial and the care of churches. Churches which had turned their altars into simple communion tables set up in the middle of the chancel, with the congregation sitting or standing around them, were ordered to replace these against the east wall, to adorn them with frontals,

and to fence them in with altar rails, many of which have survived.

The differences between the Puritans and the Laudians can be seen in the architecture of two neighbouring Yorkshire churches. Bramhope Chapel, built in 1649, is a simple oblong building with box-pews and three-decker pulpit. St John's, Leeds, completed in 1634, has elaborate carved pews, canopied pulpit and screens in the best Laudian tradition. Another significant Laudian building is the church of Staunton Harold in Leicestershire, completed in 1665, and similar elaborate woodcarving can be found in several churches in County Durham furnished during the episcopate of Bishop John Cosin (1660–1672).

In Scotland the Reformation was extremely violent and a full Presbyterian system of church administration was set up in the 1560s. After the union of the Scottish and English crowns in 1603, strong efforts were made to impose bishops and English practices on the Scottish church, and this can be seen in the arrangement of some late 17th century churches, such as that of the Canongate in Edinburgh. But in most Scottish churches the interiors were divided so that some of the larger medieval buildings were turned into as many as three separate preaching houses, arranged so that the pulpit was dominant. Usually the communion table was placed before the pulpit with seats for the elders around it. Attempts to Anglicise the Scottish church were finally defeated in the 1690s, and the established church has been without bishops since then. In England, bishops were briefly abolished during the Commonwealth, but restored in 1660. Those Puritans who could not accept this left to become dissenters.

Throughout Britain, except in Ireland, the Reformation had broken the link with the western Catholic Church under the Pope, and very few people retained an allegiance to Rome. Because of the political implications of being a Roman Catholic, those who remained what were termed recusants were subject to harsh penalties, although the laws against them were generally only enforced with full rigour after the discovery of a plot to overthrow the monarch or at times of national anti-Papal hysteria. It did, however, mean that Roman Catholics were completely unable to contribute to the church architecture of the 17th century.

Bolton Abbey, Yorkshire. The Augustinian priory was suppressed in 1539, only 19 years after the church had been completed. However, the nave was retained for use as a parish church and only the eastern parts of the church were allowed to fall into ruin. The rectory, to the south of the church, incorporates substantial parts of Bolton Hall, and other masonry from the former priory buildings was used in its construction. This adoption of parochial and secular uses was common throughout England.

Bath Abbey, Avon. This handsome Perpendicular building, begun in 1499, was incomplete at the dissolution when it became a parish church. The fan vault of the chancel is 16th century, but the nave (right) was roofless until a century later and only vaulted at the 19th century restoration.

Bramhope Chapel, Leeds (above and below) is dated 1649 and contains contemporary fittings.

St Stephen's, Walbrook, City of London. The first of Wren's city churches, with a large central dome, was begun in 1672 and completed in 1679.

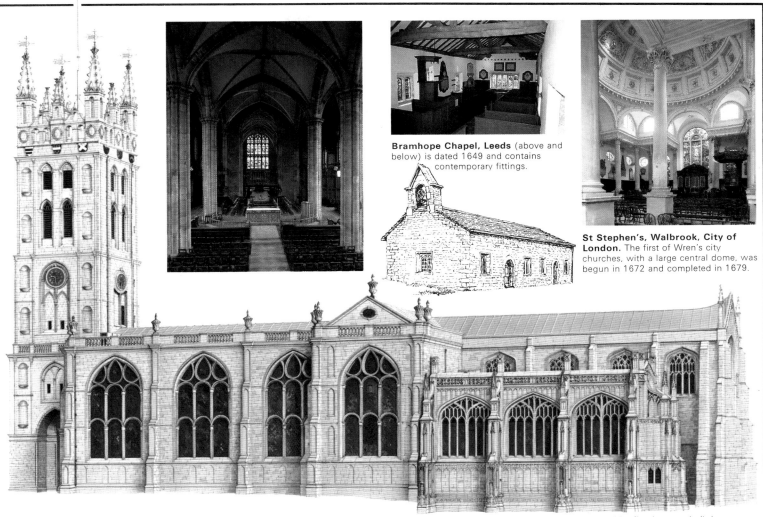

St Mary's, Warwick (above) and interior (top). In 1694 the tower, nave, aisles and transepts of this large collegiate church were destroyed by fire. It was rebuilt between 1698 and 1704 in a style which was still substantially Gothic and with a vault of stone and plaster, copying the hall churches of the late 15th century.

Canongate Kirk, Edinburgh (above, left and right). A typical late 17th century Presbyterian exterior ranged inside to imitate a 17th century Anglican interior.

St Paul's Cathedral, City of London. The most significant classical church in Britain, designed by Sir Christopher Wren to replace its predecessor which was partially destroyed in the Great Fire of 1666. Rebuilding began in 1675.

The organ case of St Stephen's, Old Radnor, Powys, which dates from the 17th century, is claimed to be the oldest in Britain.

Maesyronnen Chapel, Powys (above and below). A typical early Welsh nonconformist chapel.

St John's, Briggate, Leeds. Built in 1632–4 it is a logical development of 16th century perpendicular, retaining its elaborate pews, pulpit and screens (left).

Tudors – were of a very high order. Henry VII (1485–1509) was an intelligent, hard-working and practical man with a flair for financial administration. Henry VIII (1509–47) proved to be one of the most extraordinary figures in English history: a handsome, clever man with a powerful personality that enabled him to charm or terrify at will, and a horrifying but useful capacity for cold-blooded, calculated cruelty, as Richard Empson and Edmund Dudley discovered to their cost in the first year of his reign. There is little doubt that it was his determination to divorce his first wife, Catherine of Aragon, in the face of all odds, that brought about the English Reformation, since it provoked the dispute with the papacy between 1527 and 1533 which began the train of events. Edward VI (1547–53) was a gifted scholar, with an intellectual passion for Protestant theology. Mary (1553–8) was, in spite of her unhappy reputation, a highly principled and courageous woman who endured a miserable life with great fortitude, and who, somewhat unusually in her family, was by nature gentle, merciful and generous. Elizabeth I (1558–1603) was as brave as her sister, but, unlike her, a shrewd, tolerant, practical woman with a flair for handling men (both individually and collectively) and for successful self-advertisement. All five maintained splendid courts in which elaborate ceremonies and sumptuous furnishings and costumes combined to enhance their dignity and authority; and all but Edward (who was too young even at the time of his death to demonstrate genuine independence of judgement) and Mary (whose freedom of choice was limited by her religious convictions) showed uncanny skill in the selection of ministers. As a result, the dynasty was served by a succession of brilliant men, amongst whom Cardinal

Wolsey, Thomas More, Thomas Cromwell, Thomas Cranmer, William Cecil, Francis Walsingham, and Robert Cecil were probably the most distinguished.

Not surprisingly, this conjunction of talents had beneficial consequences. Though the Tudors were by no means invariably successful in dealing with the problems with which they were faced – for instance, they were never able to provide effective government for Ireland or to devise a really efficient method of taxing the wealth of the nation – they presided, nevertheless, over a period of striking achievement, four aspects of which are worthy of examination. Firstly, in the course of a long and sometimes painful struggle, the 'over-mighty subjects' who had plagued Lancastrians and Yorkists alike were brought to heel. Rivals and potential rivals were put to death, often on the flimsiest of pretexts, among them the Earl of Warwick in 1499, the Duke of Buckingham in 1521, and, notoriously, Mary Queen of Scots in 1587; magnates such as the Cliffords, Dacres, and Percys of the North were deprived of, or denied, their hereditary military commands, excluded from the Council, obliged to undertake ruinous bonds for good behaviour, and more significantly, subjected to legal harassment, for instance by conciliar enforcement of the 1504 Statute of Liveries. The gentry were won over by the skilful distribution of rewards and punishments, the adoption of policies of which the majority usually approved, and the provision of an increasingly important role for them in administration and government.

Secondly, as the powers of the subject declined, so those of the Crown were enhanced. 'Ordinary' revenues were substantially increased by the expansion of the royal estates

Tudor London as shown in Braun and Hogenberg's map, published in 1574. Palaces and inns along the Strand to Charing Cross have linked the original City of London with the Court of Westminster, while the wards of Farringdon, Bishopsgate, Cripplegate and Aldersgate have spilled over outside the city walls.

SCHOOLS AND UNIVERSITIES

*And then the shining schoolboy,
   with his satchel,
And shining morning face, creeping
   like snail
Unwillingly to school.*

Schoolboy nature appears to have altered little and, although the school of Shakespeare's day bears almost no resemblance to a modern comprehensive, it too was a result of social changes and an increasing population. What remained of the monastic grammar and song schools and the small schools sometimes attached to chantries was swept away, along with the monasteries and chantries, in the reigns of Henry VIII and Edward VI. Their purpose had been the training of priests and they taught little but Latin grammar and music. The grammar schools that replaced them still taught in Latin, but the emphasis was less on learning by heart and more on the use of Latin as the key to an understanding of the literature, theology and science of the classical civilisations which were considered to be the fount of all learning.

The change from rote learning to analysis was aided by the growth of printing, which not only made cheaper books available (to the schoolmaster if not to the boys), but also encouraged paper manufacture, enabling schoolboys to keep 'common place books': carefully indexed notebooks in which extracts from the books studied were written, a practice recommended by humanist educational reformers such as Colet, Erasmus and Vives. In time this was to add a new interest and direction to the process of learning.

Like the medieval schools before them and modern schools today, the new secular grammar schools trained boys for the careers currently open to educated men. The country, once administered largely by the Church, was by later Tudor and Stuart times a secular administration in which the House of Commons came to have increasing importance. Not only did a knowledge of Latin enable statesmen and merchants to correspond with their counterparts in Europe, but in classical literature Tudor and Stuart schoolmasters found for their pupils a training for political life and a grounding in such diverse

subjects as mathematics, medicine and the law. Nevertheless, the use of the English language in many areas of administration and business was increasing, encouraged by Henry VIII's decrees, intended to consolidate his position as head of the English church, that services were to be held in English and an English bible was to be accessible in every parish church.

Throughout the country there are grammar schools called King's or Queen's schools, or more specifically named for Henry VIII, Edward VI, Elizabeth or (more rarely) Mary. These schools were not always founded in the reign indicated and were even more rarely donated by the monarch named. Many, including most of the cathedral schools were re-foundations of monastery and chantry schools. Sometimes funds were allocated from the original foundation with the Royal authorisation for the school, but frequently citizens subscribed to them or one prominent merchant provided the money to re-start a town's school.

In addition to these schools for Latin grammar, of which we have comparatively extensive knowledge, there were doubtless numerous one-teacher schools of which no record remains. All teachers were supposed to be regulated by the Crown through the established Church, but small 'ABC' schools, teaching only reading and writing in English, were probably ignored as presenting no threat to orthodoxy.

If the fact that education was not compulsory and not even considered necessary for girls or the sons of manual workers by any except the most advanced humanist reformers is accepted, it appears that Tudor and Stuart schools, provided by the established church and private philanthropy, were adequate for contemporary needs. Indeed schooling was not radically re-organised until the end of the 19th century, during which period the country had become a leading world power.

After the Reformation a further burst of interest in university education led to the foundation of additional colleges in Oxford and Cambridge, and in Scotland. This did not last, however, for despite a demand for education of a more secular type, Oxford and Cambridge became stereotyped as Anglican institutions, largely as a result of the Acts of Uniformity of 1559 and 1662.

This led, in fact, to a relative decline of the English universities: few new colleges were founded and all the new medical colleges appeared in London. Teaching at Oxford and Cambridge

became mainly traditional and formal, and life in College was more social than academic. As a result the more able academics, together with both Protestant and Roman Catholic dissenters, turned elsewhere for their education – to Scotland, to the continent and to the Dissenting Academies which began to appear throughout the country. In particular the Scottish universities flourished because of their more serious approach, and a new university foundation appeared in Trinity College, Dublin.

During the greater part of this period, in which the population gradually grew to reach around $5\frac{1}{2}$ million by 1700, the British Isles mustered seven major university foundations, four in Scotland, two in England and one in Ireland. Although many factors contributed to their respective foundations it is not without significance that their distribution pattern largely coincided with the areas of dense and prosperous population. All attempts to found a *universitas* in the poorer thinly populated Principality of Wales (notably by Owen Glendower) had failed.

Blundell's School, Tiverton, Devon, was founded by a wealthy local merchant. In an age of expanding business, many such left money to provide schools.

The Old Grammar School, Market Harborough, Leicestershire, was founded by Robert Smyth, a poor boy from the district who made a fortune as a merchant in Elizabethan London.

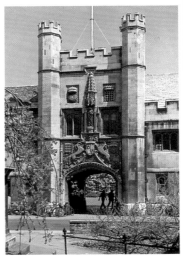

Christ's College, Cambridge, founded in 1505 by Lady Margaret Beaufort. The ornate gateway bears the Beaufort Arms.

Tom Tower and Quadrangle, Christ Church College, Oxford.

through the processes of attainder, escheat and forfeiture, and, most significantly, through the seizure of monastic property between 1536 and 1540; 'extraordinary' revenues were augmented by the introduction of a form of income tax (the subsidy), the extension of taxation to the clergy, and the clever management of parliament. Under Thomas Cromwell and men who were associated with him but were lucky enough to survive his fall, the central administration was completely reorganised between the 1530s and the 1560s, and, after much trial and error, brought to a new peak of efficiency in the 1570s and 1580s. The King's authority in the localities was enlarged by, amongst other things, the elimination of franchises by the Act of 1536, the creation of powerful councils in the north and the Welsh marches, and the employment of powerful royal commissions, especially the commission of the peace, about justice and government business; and his coercive powers were extended by increasingly severe legislation (for instance, on the subject of treason), and heavy, and often quite well-directed expenditure on fortifications, the navy, and, in Elizabeth's reign, the army.

Thirdly, in spite of the efforts of Mary to reverse the process in the abortive Catholic counter-reformation of 1553–8, the Church was turned into an adjunct of the state, a national Church under the authority of the monarch, in which the latter, not the Pope, was responsible for its law, courts, appointments, revenues, and doctrine. The transformation had many important consequences. It exalted the status of the monarch; it improved the standing of parliament, whose co-operation had been essential to Thomas Cromwell's legislative programme; it radically altered the composition of the House of Lords, since the expulsion of 31 abbots changed a spiritual into a temporal majority; it undermined the authority of the surviving prelates, since it made them dependent for their sees on royal favour (Elizabeth dismissed all but one of Mary's bishops); and ultimately it brought about the establishment, in 1559, of a unique Anglican episcopal church and the reversal of the centuries-old domination of the laity by the clergy; but nothing, surely, can have impressed contemporaries more than the Dissolution of the Monasteries (1536–40), which transferred, first to the Crown, later to any who could afford to buy, all the lands and goods of all monasteries, friaries, nunneries, and commanderies of the Knights of St John of Jerusalem, dispossessed the unfortunate inhabitants, and brought a

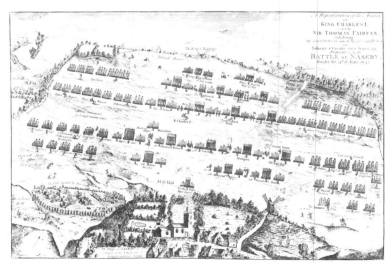

The Battle of Naseby. This decisive battle of the English Civil War was fought in north west Northamptonshire, on June 14, 1645. It began well for Charles I, but Prince Rupert's success on the right wing (top left in the picture) was offset by the crushing defeat of Langdale on the left wing (top right) by Cromwell. Only the royal cavalry escaped the rout.

THE CLOTH INDUSTRY

Before the great mill towns of Yorkshire grew up in the 19th century the manufacture and export of a great variety of wool cloths had formed the major industry of England for more than 400 years, and considerable evidence of the old, unmechanised industry and the wealth it produced remains in our present day towns, villages and landscape.

In the 14th century Edward III commanded that the most important man in the House of Lords – the Lord Chancellor – should sit on a sack of wool (which he still does) as a reminder of the importance of the wool trade. Edward knew that the great monasteries and abbeys of England were largely 'built on wool', the practical monks having made good use of tracts of dry, infertile land, unsuitable for arable farming, by using it for sheep runs which produced a surplus of wool to sell in Europe. He envisaged greater prosperity for England (and himself!) if, instead of exporting wool, we were able to produce really good cloth to sell; accordingly he encouraged expert weavers from Flanders to settle here.

In medieval towns such as Bristol and Norwich each craftsman worked at home, owning both tools and materials. In wool cloth manufacture the weaver wove yarn bought from the spinner, sold cloth to the fuller, and so on until the finished cloth was in the hands of the merchant tailors. This independence was tempered by compulsory craft guilds which imposed standards and laid down working methods. Like the modern trade unions they resembled, guilds often proved restrictive to enterprise and innovation and by the Tudor period entrepreneurs called clothiers were producing wool cloth outside the incorporated towns, which lost trade as a consequence. Clothiers were capitalists who bought wool from the farmer (often travelling widely to obtain the requisite quality or type of

wool), put it out to the spinners and then to the weaver, fulling, dyeing and finishing usually being done on their own premises. Spinning was often done by farm women and the weaving by the men when farm work was slack, but people (especially 'spinsters') totally dependent upon this work were underpaid and vulnerable to unemployment. John Aubrey, a Wiltshire landowner who disliked the clothiers, described them as 'keeping their spinners but just alive'. Thus workers suffered poverty and capitalists became very rich long before the Industrial Revolution.

Tudor and Stuart clothiers, like Victorian industrialists, married their children into the aristocracy; one Trowbridge clothier's daughter became the great grandmother of two Queens of England, Mary II and Ann. Unlike the medieval merchant who amassed wealth, the successful clothier had no guild on which to lavish money for religious ceremony or charity. Nevertheless, some of them contributed to church building and helped to meet other needs, formerly the responsibility of guilds and religious houses, such as the provision of almshouses and schools. Successful clothiers usually built themselves impressive houses: like modern stockbrokers they needed to demonstrate their prosperity. Although at first they settled in villages, these sometimes developed into 'clothier towns' such as Trowbridge in Wiltshire.

There were also clothiers in Yorkshire, but here the name had a different meaning. Unfinished (or 'white') cloth was made by clothiers and their families in their small hillside farms. It was carried (often many miles over the moors and by the weaver himself) to markets for sale to merchants who dyed and finished the cloth. These clothiers rarely became wealthy but the industry grew, wrested the worsted trade from Norfolk, and formed the basis of the huge 19th century industry.

The Shepherd's Great Calendar, printed at the end of the 15th century, shows the importance of sheep rearing for wool to supply the flourishing cloth industry.

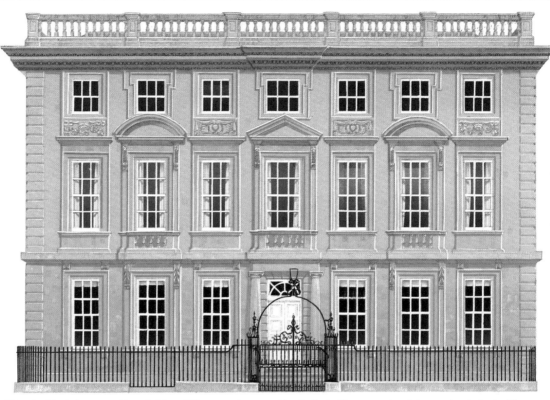

A wool coat with silver embroidery of lighter weave, which became fashionable after the Reformation.

This clothier's house at Trowbridge, Wilts, now houses a Lloyd's Bank. The prosperity of the wool trade in the West Country is shown in the 18th century classical grandeur of the clothiers' homes, although most had dye shops and warehouses at the back.

Interior of a weaver's cottage reconstructed at the Castle Museum, York. The looms were in use on the top floors of the houses where rows of large windows gave a good light for working.

The market house at Chipping Camden, one of the many fine buildings indicating the wealth of this medieval wool town. Wool was graded for sale in the Woolstapler's Hall in the High Street.

The Guildhall, Lavenham, Suffolk. In many towns the wool trade was organised under guilds which controlled the wages, prices and work standards of the local tradesmen. The Lavenham guildhall was built as a business and social centre, but after the decline in the industry it became a town hall and then a gaol.

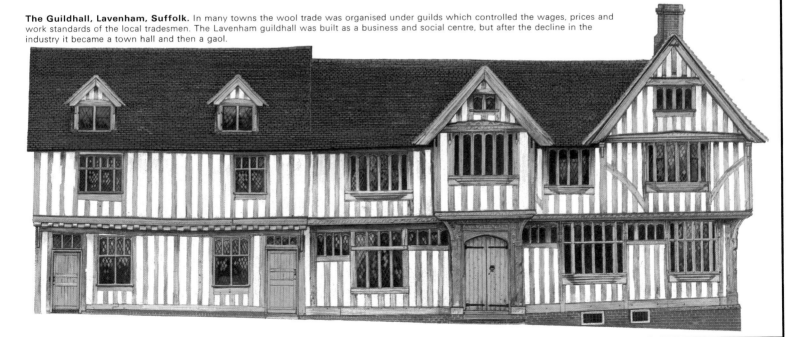

whole way of religious life to a close.

Fourthly, partly by luck (good and bad), partly by sensible initiatives and hard work, the problems caused by the turbulent frontier areas of the kingdom were, to a large extent, solved. Wales was reduced to order by the acquisition by the Crown of large numbers of marcher lordships, effective service by the Council of the marches, and important legislation in 1536 and 1543, which merged the Principality and the marches, created 12 Welsh shires, and enabled the ordinary local administration of the English county to be extended to those regions. Ireland was conquered, after much ferocious campaigning, in 1603. The Scottish border was pacified (relatively speaking) as a result of well-timed support for the revolt of 1559 which brought about the expulsion of the French from Scotland and the establishment of a protestant government headed, after 1567, by a man destined to be king of England. The north was taken firmly in hand by an energetic council after the suppression of the

1569 Rebellion of the Northern Earls. Calais, the last of England's once-great possessions in France, succumbed to siege in 1558 and was never subsequently recovered.

To sum up, the Tudors succeeded in establishing a strong and respected – indeed reverenced – monarchy which was responsible for the abolition of private wars between subjects, the defeat of all direct challenges to the dynasty (Wyatt's Rebellion of 1554 was the last), the suppression of the last peasants' revolt (in 1549) and the last feudal revolt (in 1569), the defeat of the Spanish Armada in 1588, and the prevention of a civil war of religion. By 1603, when Elizabeth died, England was a politically unified, well-governed, and internally peaceful country, with a flourishing educational system, good communications, well-integrated towns, and an enviable freedom from internal tariff barriers. Since it was also endowed with cheap labour, an abundance of natural resources, and, given the discovery of the New World, a strategically convenient geographical position, it

THE EVOLUTION OF THE WARSHIP

Until the 16th century ships operating out of British ports were small, the largest not more than 80 feet long on the keel. They were descendants from the longships of the Norsemen, although to carry cargo they had become wider in proportion to their length. They relied entirely on sail (although the Norsemen had used oars for their war vessels). But there was no such thing as a medieval English warship. When the king needed a navy he simply commandeered merchant ships, which acted as transports for men and horses, and which, in the event of a naval engagement, would act as platforms for a land-type battle with the ships locked together.

The introduction of the gun altered all this. The warship became a specialised vessel, a gun platform engaging the enemy at a distance and endeavouring to overcome her through superior fire power. By the reign of Henry VIII guns were being mounted low in the hull – because the ship's stability had to be maintained – and were fired through ports cut in the side. As the century progressed naval ships became progressively bigger (well over 100 feet long) and carried up to 46 guns of various calibres. They were also elaborately rigged, with three or four

masts which gave them a considerable sail area and so more speed and, because of improved sail design, better handling qualities. The well known galleon of Elizabeth I's reign owed her success to her stout north European hull modelled, with considerable modifications, on the carack, the major type of 16th-century merchant ship, and to the use of a combined square and fore and aft rig which enabled her to sail much closer to the wind.

Merchant ships lagged behind warships in size, but not in design of hull or rigging, since they were dependent on both for their living. By the 16th century they, like the warships, were equipped with three masts which gave them a balanced sail plan. At first the original middle or main mast remained vastly bigger than the other two, but gradually proportions were evened out, so that by the 17th century the seagoing merchant ship was a three-master with square sails on the first two, a lower sail and a topsail on each, and on the third mast the Mediterranean style lateen (Latin) fore and aft sail. The Pilgrim Fathers' *Mayflower* had a rig of this type. She also had a centrally hung rudder, invented as early as the 13th century,

but not wheel steering, which did not appear until the 1700s. Instead seafarers handled the helm through a cumbrous arrangement of levers which did not allow much rudder movement. Radical alterations of course were achieved by trimming the sails.

During the 17th century warship design became more standardised, hulls losing the towering effect of the galleon with her piled-up aftercastle. The largest warships mounted guns on three decks; 86 in the *Naseby* of 1655 and 100 in the *Prince* of 1670, her largest being 42 pounders. This was the century of rich ship decoration, with

the painted geometric patterns of the Tudors giving place to lavish carved work, particularly aft, wreaths round each gun port and massive figureheads, often of equestrian figures. In spite of the wealth of exterior display, conditions aboard must have been appalling in these ships which carried a complement of over 700, two-thirds of whom were expected to die in action or from disease, leaving the remaining 230 as entirely adequate to work and fight the ship. Merchant ships were far more modestly manned, with 30 to 40 men at the most.

The ornate 17th century warship Sovereign of the Seas was built at Woolwich to the design of Commissioner Phineas Pett, whose portrait appears here with his ship. She was launched in 1637 with three gun decks and a total armament of 102 brass guns. She took part in all the Dutch Wars and in two actions against the French, but she was accidentally burned in 1696.

Van de Velde the Younger (1673–1707) and his father (1610–93) were the leading marine artists of their day. Although Dutch, they worked much in England and Charles II appointed them official artists. One of the Younger's finest works is of the third rate *H.M.S. Resolution* in a gale. The *Resolution* was built at Harwich in 1667 and carried 66 guns and 400 men.

was well equipped for economic expansion.

However, disappointingly little progress was made in the first half of the 17th century. Exports of 'new draperies' (either worsteds or mixtures of woollen and worsted yarns) nearly doubled, but the textile trade as a whole declined as exports of traditional cloths fell. English settlement in Ireland (as a result of the Plantation of Ulster, 1610), the West Indies, Virginia, Maryland and New England was extended substantially between 1610 and 1640, but it took time for a significant net increase in the size of the overseas market to develop. The rate of coal production increased rapidly, but only because the output of the coalfields at the end of the Tudor period was very small: even in the 1640s, Newcastle was shipping less than 400,000 tons a year. The yield of cereals was improved, but only because of expansion of the areas under cultivation and the increase of regional specialisation, not the introduction of new techniques. The mercantile marine grew in size from, very

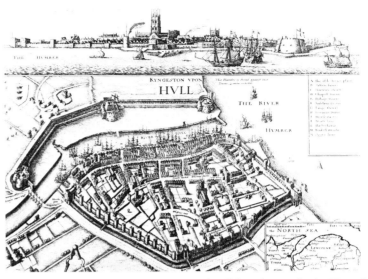

This early 17th century map and panorama of Hull from the Humber by Wenceslas Hollar shows the Old Harbour (the River Hull itself) crammed with shipping.

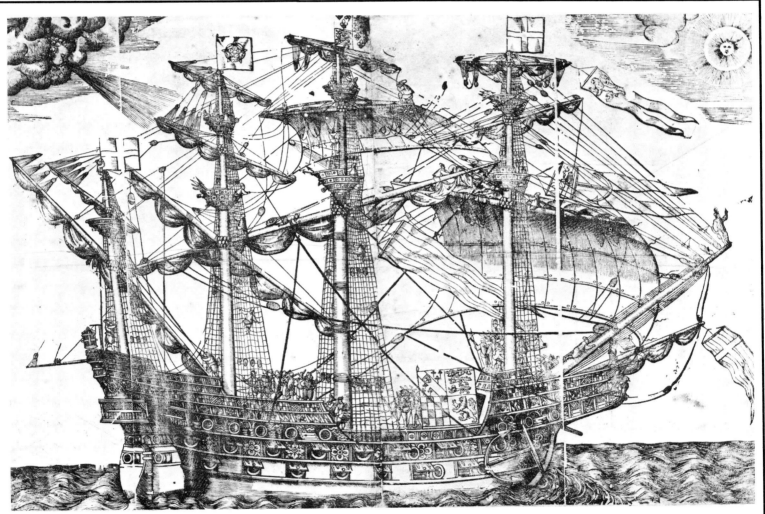

One of Queen Elizabeth I's larger warships, the Ark Royal, was built as the *Ark Raleigh* in 1587. Lord Howard of Effingham chose her as his flagship against the Spanish Armada and she was present throughout the engagement in July and August of 1588. She became the *Anne Royal* in James I's reign.

Fragments of Ancient English Shipwrightry, preserved in the Pepys Library at Magdalene College, Cambridge, is thought to be the work of a late 16th century master shipwright, Matthew Baker. Note the famous cod's head and mackerel tail representation of the lines of one of these ships.

approximately, 50,000 tons in the 1560s, to 115,000 tons in the late 1620s, and to 150,000 tons in 1640, but the success of the carrying trade, to which this development related, was insecurely based on the continuing neutrality of England during a period of almost continuous war in Europe. For the majority of the population, therefore, there was no indication that the long years of rising prices and falling wages were about to come to an end: rather, the conjunction, in the 1640s, of bad weather, appalling harvests, rocketing food prices, and chronic social and political problems, must have convinced many that things were changing inexorably for the worse.

As it happens, neither the incompetence of the first two Stuart kings, James I (1603–25) and Charles I (1625–49), nor their legendary inability to manage their parliaments, nor the great Civil War of 1642–5, can be blamed for the state of the economy at this time. James was an exceptionally kindly, intelligent and humane man, whose habitual commitment to peaceful policies was undoubtedly beneficial. Charles, for all the faults of his extraordinarily complex character, made great efforts during the 'Eleven Years' Tyranny' of 1629–40 to expand trade, encourage new developments in industry, suppress piracy and privateering, and maintain good relations between the Crown and the great businessmen of the City of London. Dramatic though the fighting was between royal and parliamentary forces, and significant the result in terms of English constitutional history, it had remarkably little effect on the basic characteristics of the pre-industrial economy. Indeed, the economy was to a great extent dependent upon circumstances over which individuals – even kings – had little or no control, and it was to changes in these characteristics that the prosperity of the second half of the century was due.

Under the impact of epidemic disease (there were serious outbreaks of plague in 1603, 1625, and 1665–6, the latter famous as the Great Plague of London); famine (the harvest failed in 1629–30, 1636–7, and 1647–9); and, perhaps, successful attempts at contraception, the long period of population growth ended. Between the late 1640s and 1695 (for which year good figures are available), the population steadied at a level of about five million. Pressure on the food supply eased and the surplus of labour disappeared. Wages rose, and prices (particularly those of foodstuffs) began a long slow fall which lasted, with of course many short-term fluctuations, until the middle of the 18th century. As a result, tl_e standard of living improved significantly. In addition, notable advances began in agriculture; fruit, vegetables and hops were grown in ever greater quantities, and production

The Great Fire of London, 1666. It started in a bakery in Pudding Lane and spread rapidly, causing immense devastation. The buildings of the time were predominantly of wood and were crowded closely together, prohibiting any effective fire-fighting. The new city was built mostly in stone with wider streets.

THE GREAT AGE OF DISCOVERY

Add the terror of sailing into completely unknown seas and climates to the uncomfortable and unhealthy conditions that existed on board ship, and it is not surprising that long sea voyages were rarely undertaken, and that until the end of the 15th century Europeans knew only of two continents apart from their own. Trading vessels hugged the coast and kept land in sight by sailing from island to island. What is perhaps surprising is that the changes which took place at this time could provide sufficient incentive for the many voyages into the unknown that labelled the 16th century the Great Age of Discovery.

The change in attitudes that occurred was typical of Renaissance thought: people began to study the world around them and to apply their observations to subjects previously shrouded in mists of ignorance and religious taboo. This quest for knowledge and understanding produced advances in astronomy and mathematics and new ideas about geography. However, it is doubtful whether any voyages would have been undertaken solely for discovery had the prospect of trade and profit not tempted merchants and princes to put up money for the expensive outfitting of ships. At this time the most lucrative trade of all – in spices and other luxuries from the East – that had provided the wealth of mercantile cities like Venice, Genoa and Florence was being strangled as the tentacles of the Moslem empire grasped the caravan routes across the Sahara desert from the Red Sea and the North African ports from which these goods were shipped to Europe.

The development of astronomy and the spread of the new knowledge by means of printed books meant that by the end of the 15th century most merchants and sea captains were convinced that the world was spherical. It was therefore logical that if established routes to the treasures of India, China and the Spice Islands were barred, 'Cathay' could be reached from other directions. Part of one route – around the south of the African continent – was the long-term result of the work of Portugal's Prince Henry, who in the first half of the century had encouraged the development of ships and navigational skills for voyages further and further south down the west coast of the continent, earning himself the name of 'Henry the Navigator'. From one of the trading bases established earlier in the century, Bartolomeu Dias actually rounded the Cape of Good Hope (which he would have preferred to call 'Cape of Storms') in 1488, before being forced back by the state of the men on his two ships. The way was open and 10 years later Vasco de Gama sailed all round the African coast to Mombasa, then crossed the Indian Ocean to Calicut.

But before Vasco de Gama set off, the most famous voyage of discovery of all had already taken place: in seeking a direct western route to Cathay Columbus had in 1492 discovered America. As he persisted in the claim that he had reached India, the islands where he landed became known as the West Indies; the new continent, however, received the first name of Amerigo Vespucci, a Florentine who, also sailing west in search of Cathay in 1499, travelled so far along the coast of South America without finding the cities described by Marco Polo, that he concluded he had found 'a new world'.

In 1494, in order to avoid conflict between two Catholic states, Spain and Portugal signed the Treaty of Tordesillas which gave Portugal the freedom of the African coast, while allowing Spain to exploit America. The gold described by

Columbus drew Spaniards across the Atlantic in increasing numbers to pillage the ancient civilizations of the Aztecs, Mayas and Incas. One of these military expeditions, that of Nunez de Balboa in 1513, first sighted the Pacific Ocean from the isthmus that joins North and South America. In 1519 Hernando Cortes conquered the Aztecs of Mexico and in 1533 Francisco Pizarro conquered the Incas of Peru. Shortly thereafter, in 1541, Francisco de Orellana discovered the Amazon headwaters and descended the river to the Atlantic.

The Tordesillas Treaty meant that seamen who wanted to undertake voyages of discovery in the South Atlantic had to gain the support of the appropriate crown, and when the Portuguese Magellan set out in 1519 to find the passage to Cathay going south of the new continent he sailed with seven ships provided by Spain. Magellan was killed by natives in the Philippines – probably with justification as the early explorers treated the indigenous people savagely – but one ship from his expedition, the *Victoria*, returned to Seville under Sebastian del Cano: the first recorded circumnavigation of the world.

The first European to make a recorded landing on the North American continent sailed from Britain: John Cabot, Genoese by birth, but with sailing experience gained as a Venetian subject, found his financial support from Bristol merchants anxious to acquire some of the gold Columbus had reported on the other side of the Atlantic. In 1497 Cabot sailed in a very small ship carrying letters patent from Henry VII, tactfully worded: 'for the discoveries of new and unknown lands' in order not to offend Spain or Portugal. But he discovered no rich trading cities, only the cold misty landfall of Newfoundland where the only riches were the infinite quantities of fish on the Newfoundland Banks. Cabot concluded he had found an uninhabited part of Cathay, and in 1498 returned with his son Sebastian to follow the coastline northward – the first exploration in the direction of a north west passage – but they were beaten back by the cold. Exploration of North America was then taken up by the French, Jacques Cartier ascending the St Lawrence in 1535, Samuel de Champlain reaching the Great Lakes in 1613–15 whilst later still La Salle, in 1681, was to sail down the Illinois and Mississippi to the Gulf of Mexico.

Sebastian Cabot helped to found the Muscovy Company, which in 1553 mounted an expedition to seek a north east route to Cathay; the leader, courtier Sir Hugh Willoughby, died with his whole ship's crew in the rigours of an arctic winter when their ship had to be beached near what is now Murmansk. A second ship also disappeared but the third, under (Sir) Richard Chancellor, eventually reached the White Sea of Muscovie and despatched a party overland to Moscow. The search for the North East Passage was subsequently taken up by the Dutch, with most notable contribution arising from the three voyages of William Barents in 1594, 1595 and 1596.

The search for the North West Passage was spearheaded by the three voyages of (Sir) Martin Frobisher in 1576, 1577 and 1578. These were followed by the three voyages of John Davis in 1585, 1586 and 1587, and continued with three more voyages of Henry Hudson in 1607, 1608 and 1609. But all these voyages were blocked by ice. The north east passage was not navigated until 1878–9 (by A. E. Nordenskjöld) and the north west until 1903–5 (Amundsen), and owing to their rigorous climate both were useless as shipping routes.

In the Pacific and Indian Oceans (Sir) Francis Drake had been active in 1578, Tasman had established the insularity of Australia and discovered Tasmania by 1642 and William Dampier was active on the north west coast of Australia between 1683 and 1698. Further north the Dutch had reached Japan in 1598 with the aid of the British pilot William Adams, who was rediscovered by John Saris of the East India Company in 1611 happily absorbed into Japanese life!

English efforts to explore the New World, other than its inhospitable northern parts, were met with French, Portuguese, and more especially, Spanish hostility.

The voyages of Raleigh, Drake, Frobisher, and other Elizabethan seamen pursued a fascinating mixture of trade, discovery, war and sheer piracy, but none of them was made without the burning curiosity that drives the true explorer. Both Drake and Raleigh carried artists on their expeditions to make records of the landscape, people and the wild life of the new lands they encountered. Raleigh's complement also included mathematicians and metallurgists, making them in some

ways the forerunners of modern scientific exploration and discovery two centuries before Cook.

The purpose of Spanish and Portuguese exploration was exploitation: settlements were fortified trading bases and depots for military expeditions. English exploration began in a similar way, but the religious schisms of the Stuart period produced the first effective colonisers of the newly discovered lands: groups of people who wished to follow their own precepts in peace. Their first concern was the religious life and survival of their colonies which were mainly agricultural. As land was plentiful and they had no cause to compete with the Red Indians to increase their territories, there was little exploration of the interior of the American continent for more than a century. The new routes to Cathay had been found, trading groups such as the English and Dutch East India companies concentrated on building up their suppliers and did not press on with exploration, and the hectic spate of exploration of the late 15th and 16th centuries was over until the late 18th century.

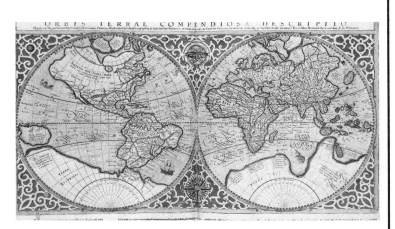

Rumold Mercator's map of the world. After nearly a century of exploration the coasts of Africa, India and the east and west of the Americas were known. 'Terra Australis Incognita' was not fully explored until two centuries later.

Map of the world by Henricus Martellus, about 1489. Despite the absence of the Americas, it is remarkably recognisable considering the scanty information available at the time. The Portuguese voyages encouraged by Henry the Navigator are reflected in the detailed representation of the west coast of Africa.

The Golden Hind was the flagship of Francis Drake, the first Englishman to circumnavigate the globe. Having set out to find a south west route to Asia he sailed through the Magellan Strait and passed the west coast of America, continuing around the world and arriving home in 1580 after three years.

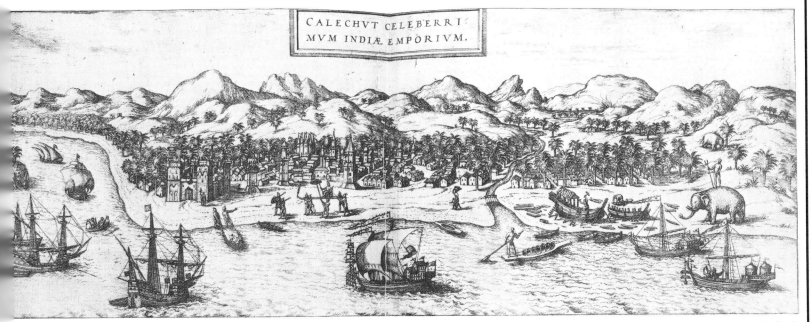

William Barents, a Dutchman, made three attempts in the 1590s to find the north east passage to India. Pictures of the ship's crew hunting polar bears and walrus for food form part of the remarkable observations made when the expedition was caught by the ice. They were the first Europeans to survive a winter above the Arctic Circle, but Barents and many of his crew died at Novaya Zemlya where their winter quarters and part of his journal were discovered in the 1870s.

of industrial crops such as hemp, flax, madder, woad and saffron was expanded. Greater attention was devoted to forestry. Turnips and grasses were found to have useful roles in crop rotation, and the cultivation of sainfoin and clover was introduced. Increasing use was made of floating water meadows.

The consequential improved supply of feed for beasts had a great effect on cereal cultivation: the increasing number of better-fed beasts produced more dung, and this permitted the improvement of yields – in fact, a large marketable surplus was produced at a time when a huge fall in cereal exports from eastern Europe was creating substantial demand on the continent. The decline of the Iberian powers (Spain and Portugal) made possible the acquisition of a new commercial empire in sugar, tobacco, slaves, Asiatic spices and textiles, and the carrying trade; and a powerful, confident, and aggressive republican government, headed by Oliver Cromwell, was quite prepared to inaugurate, with the first Navigation Act and the Dutch War of 1651, what eventually amounted to 100 years or so of largely successful wars for the advancement of trade.

Together, these developments transformed the economic environment, and permitted an expansion of trade, agriculture, and industry which would have been unimaginable at the beginning of the century. Overseas trade trebled in size between 1650 and 1750. Internal trade was stimulated by the improvement of rivers, harbours, roads and carrier services. Grain exports, which were negligible in the 1660s, were increased from 300,000 quarters a year in the late 1670s to 900,000 in the 1740s. In the same period, the mercantile marine was expanded from 340,000 to 450,000 tons, and London, substantially rebuilt after the Great Fire of 1666, displaced Antwerp as the commercial capital of the world. For the first time, the Midlands and north began to rival the wealth of the south as the textile industry of Yorkshire and Lancashire flourished. Hull, Liverpool and Newcastle benefited from the success of North Sea trade, Irish and American commerce, and the coal industry respectively. The population at large was relieved of the threat of famine and introduced to 'luxuries' such as sugar, tea, wheaten bread, tobacco, alcohol, and cotton fabrics. In short, the later Stuart period was, for Englishmen, a time of extraordinary material progress, and for England, an era of unprecedented prosperity and strength, as the Duke of Marlborough demonstrated on the battlefields of Europe.

COINS

Spanish New World silver coin, of which a huge amount came to Britain.

Coin of Elizabeth I with a good likeness rather than a stylised portrait.

On the Henry VIII gold medal, the king claims in Latin, Greek and Hebrew that he is supreme head of the Church in England. This medal, one of the earliest struck in England, neatly illustrates the Protestant Reformation and the flowering of culture and art of the Renaissance.

The influx of bullion to Europe from the Americas contributed to rising prices, as did debasement. Henry VIII and

Edward VI sought quick profits by reducing the silver content of the coinage. The people noted the slightly redder copper tinge of the debased coins, and said that they b ushed for shame.

The Tudor coinage is notable for the introduction of proper royal portraits, giving a true likeness of the monarch. A coinage for Cromwell was prepared, but never officially issued.

EVENTS AND PERSONALITIES

Henry VII, whose great achievement was the reform of the country's corrupt and clumsy legal system.

1485–1509 Henry Tudor defeats Richard III at Bosworth and ascends the throne as **Henry VII**
1487 Henry VII defeats Lambert Simnel at Stoke, in the last battle of the Wars of the Roses
1492 Christopher Columbus discovers the New World
1494 Poynings Law makes Irish legislature dependent on England
1497 Henry VII suppresses the Cornish rebellion
1498 Erasmus teaches at Oxford
1504 The Statute of Liveries is passed
1505 John Colet is appointed Dean of St Paul's
1509–47 Henry VIII succeeds Henry VII and marries Catherine of Aragon
1510 Colet founds St Paul's School

1513 The French are defeated at the Battle of the Spurs, the Scots at Flodden
1514 Thomas Wolsey becomes Henry VIII's principal minister
1515 Sir Thomas More's *Utopia* appears
1517 Martin Luther's *Ninety-Five Theses* begins the Reformation in Germany
1521 Henry VIII opposes Luther in *The Assertion of the Seven Sacraments*
1526 Henry VIII begins his quest for divorce
1529 Wolsey is dismissed and More succeeds him as Lord Chancellor
1531 Henry VIII is recognised as Supreme Head of the Church in England
1532 The Submission of the Clergy begins the political Reformation
   More resigns as Lord Chancellor
   Thomas Cromwell becomes Henry VIII's principal minister
1533 Archbishop Cranmer declares Henry VIII's marriage to Catherine void, his marriage to Anne Boleyn lawful
   Princess Elizabeth is born
1534 The Act of Supremacy transfers the Pope's judicial and political powers to Henry VIII
1535 John Fisher, Bishop of Rochester, and Sir Thomas More are executed
1536 The dissolution of the lesser monasteries begins
   Anne Boleyn is executed: Henry VIII marries Jane Seymour
1536–7 Rebellions in Lincolnshire and the north (the Pilgrimage of Grace) are suppressed
1537 Prince Edward is born and Jane Seymour dies
1539 The dissolution of the greater monasteries begins
   Cranmer's Great Bible is issued
1540 Thomas Cromwell is executed
1542 The Scots are defeated at Solway Moss
   The Tudor conquest of Ireland is completed

Henry VIII succeeded his father Henry VII in 1509. He married his brother Arthur's widow Catherine of Aragon – the first of the famous six wives.

1547–53 **Edward VI** succeeds Henry VIII
1548 The first prayer book of the Church of England is authorised by the Act of Uniformity
1549 Rebellions in Norfolk and the west are suppressed
John Dudley (later Duke of Northumberland) overthrows Protector Somerset
1552 Cranmer's second prayer book, a new Act of Uniformity, and the Forty-Two Articles render the Church officially Protestant
1553 Edward VI dies and **Mary I** succeeds to the throne
Northumberland's plot on behalf of Lady Jane Grey fails: he is executed
Mary begins a Catholic Counter-Reformation
1554 Wyatt's Rebellion is suppressed
Mary marries Philip of Spain
Parliament re-establishes Catholicism
1555 Bishops Hooper, Ridley and Latimer are burnt
1556 Archbishop Cranmer is burnt
1557 Burnings of Protestants at Smithfield discredit Catholicism
1558 Calais is captured by the French
1558–1603 **Elizabeth I** succeeds Mary
Sir William Cecil (later Lord Burghley) becomes Principal Secretary
1559 The Elizabethan Settlement establishes the Protestant Church of England
1560 The Treaty of Edinburgh ends French influence in Scotland and ensures a Scottish Reformation
1562 The Thirty-Nine Articles are promulgated
1568 Mary Queen of Scots flees to England
1569 The Rebellion of the Northern Earls is suppressed
1572 Burghley becomes Lord Treasurer
1577–80 Francis Drake circumnavigates the world
1585 War with Spain begins with the Earl of Leicester's expedition to the Netherlands
1587 Mary Queen of Scots is executed
Drake sacks Cadiz
1588 The Spanish Armada is defeated
1590 Sir Philip Sidney's *Arcadia* and Edmund Spencer's *Faerie Queene* appear

1590–1 William Shakespeare begins writing: *Henry VI* and *Titus Andronicus* are published
1593 Christopher Marlowe dies, aged 29
1596 Lord Howard of Effingham and the Earl of Essex sack Cadiz
1598 Burghley and Philip II die
1599 Essex mismanages the war in Ireland and is replaced by Lord Mountjoy
1601 The Essex Revolt is crushed and the Earl executed
1603–25 James VI of Scotland succeeds Elizabeth I as **James I** of England
Mountjoy completes the conquest of Ireland
1604 England and Spain make peace
Marlowe's *Dr Faustus* is published posthumously
1605 The Gunpowder Plot is uncovered
1610 The Plantation of Ulster
Robert Cecil's 'Great Contract' fails
1611 *The Authorised Version of the Holy Bible* appears

James VI of Scotland became James I of England in 1603. The famous Gunpowder Plot of 1605 came about due to James's strong anti-Catholicism.

William and Mary (daughter of James II) were proclaimed King and Queen after Parliament had asked the Protestant William for help against Catholic James.

1612 Shakespeare's last play, *The Tempest*, is published
1614 Sir Walter Raleigh's *History of the World* is published
1617 George Villiers is created Duke of Buckingham
1618 Bacon is created Lord Chancellor
Raleigh is executed
1619 William Harvey discovers the circulation of the blood
1620 The Pilgrim Fathers sail to Massachusetts
1624 Lord Treasurer Cranfield is impeached
1625–49 **Charles I** succeeds James I
Conflicts with Parliament intensify
1626 Buckingham is impeached
1627 The Crown wins the Five Knights Case
1628 Charles I accepts the Petition of Right
Buckingham is assassinated
1629 Charles I's 'personal rule' begins
1633 Thomas Wentworth (later Earl of Strafford) becomes Deputy of Ireland
William Laud becomes Archbishop of Canterbury
1640 Charles I summons the Long Parliament
Strafford, Laud, and Lord Keeper Finch are impeached
1641 Charles I accepts the Triennial Bill

Charles I, whose rein was marked by the Civil War. He was beheaded in 1649.

Strafford is executed
Catholic rebellion breaks out in Ireland
The Grand Remonstrance is passed
1642 Pym, Hampden, Haselrig, Holles and Strode escape arrest in Parliament
The royal family flees from London
Civil War begins
The battle of Edgehill is fought
1644 Oliver Cromwell defeats Prince Rupert at Marston Moor
1645 Laud is executed
The Self-Denying Ordinance is passed
The New Model Army is created
Cromwell defeats the Royalists at Naseby
The Civil War ends
1646 Charles I surrenders to the Scots
1647 Cornet Joyce seizes Charles I for the army

Charles I wins Scottish support
1648 The Scots begin the Second Civil War: Cromwell defeats them at Preston
1649 Charles I is executed
England is declared a Commonwealth
Cromwell crushes the Irish rebels
1650 Cromwell defeats the Scots at Dunbar
1651 Cromwell defeats Charles (II) at Worcester
1652 The Act of Settlement for Ireland is passed
1653 Cromwell is appointed Lord Protector
1655 Government by Major-Generals is tried
1657 Cromwell rejects the Crown
1658 Cromwell dies: his son, Richard, becomes Lord Protector
1659 Richard Cromwell resigns and the Commonwealth is re-established
1660–85 The Restoration of **Charles II** takes place
1661 Charles II assents to the Corporation Act
1664 The Triennial Act is repealed
1665 The Great Plague of London breaks out
The Five Mile Act is passed
1666 The Great Fire of London virtually destroys the City
1667 John Milton's *Paradise Lost* is published
1671 John Milton's *Paradise Regained* and *Samson Agonistes* appear
1673 The Test Act receives royal assent
1675 Sir Christopher Wren begins St Paul's
1678 The Popish Plot is uncovered
John Bunyan's *The Pilgrim's Progress* appears
1679 Whig and Tory parties form
1685–88 **James II**, a Catholic, succeeds Charles II
Monmouth's Rebellion is crushed
1687 Isaac Newton publishes his *Principia Mathematica*
1688 William of Orange overthrows James II in the Glorious Revolution
The War of the League of Augsburg begins
1689–1702 **William and Mary** are proclaimed King and Queen
The Bill of Rights is enacted
1690 William III wins the Battle of the Boyne
1693 The National Debt is established
1694 Mary II dies
1701 The War of Spanish Succession begins
1702–14 **Queen Anne** succeeds William III
1704 Sir George Rooke captures Gibraltar
The Duke of Marlborough defeats the French at Blenheim
Isaac Newton's *Opticks* is published
1706 Marlborough defeats the French at Ramillies
1707 England and Scotland are united
1708 Marlborough defeats the French at Oudenarde
1709 Marlborough defeats the French at Malplaquet
1711 Marlborough is dismissed
1713 The Peace of Utrecht ends the war
1714–27 **George I** succeeds Anne

Elizabeth I succeeded her sister Mary in 1558. More than any previous monarch, she set out to win the love and loyalty of the people.

The Industrial Revolution

*Steam displaced wind and water power,
and with a host of other inventions transformed industry
and transport. Economic activity shifted to the
coalfields. Population rose and industrial towns developed; agriculture was
changing too, and today's chequerboard field pattern was created.
Ireland joined the United Kingdom, and Scotland's union with England was
accepted after the suppression of the two
Jacobite rebellions. The American colonies were lost but
Australia and New Zealand were acquired.*

When Queen Anne died without surviving children in 1714, the exclusion of the Catholic line of the exiled James II meant that the Elector of the German state of Hanover became George I of Britain. There was still an air of uncertainty, however; it could by no means be assumed that James, son of the deposed James II, could not command support in England as well as in the Catholic areas of Scotland.

Jacobites, as the supporters of the exiled Stuart line were known, included several ministers who were close to the late Queen, and there were general misgivings about the direction of popular loyalties. The death of the Queen produced no attempted Jacobite coup in England, although the Duke of Ormonde, a leading Tory, fled to France after he was discovered to be planning an uprising. There were popular demonstrations of Jacobite support too in London and Oxford, but it was from Scotland that the serious threat came. There the Earl of Mar had been planning a rising in the summer of 1715: calling the clans of the Highlands to the Stuart standard with Colonel John Hay he took several of the Scottish towns. Difficulties with the French, upon whose support he counted, delayed the arrival of James (the Old Pretender) and by the time he reached Scotland the impetus of the revolt was already on the wane. The government forces under the Duke of Argyll took control and by February 1716 James had fled once more to France.

Although another futile attempt with Spanish help was put down at Glenshiel in 1719, for the most part a long period of prosperity reduced English Jacobitism to a mere sentiment, while the lowland Scots were finding expanding commerce to their liking. Nevertheless, so long as the French were interested in helping, the prospect of a Jacobite rising remained. A French invasion was being actively planned in 1744–5 and Charles Edward Stuart, the 24-year-old son of James, was in Paris. Known to history as the 'Young Pretender', he is more familiar in song and romance as 'Bonnie Prince Charlie'. When in 1745 French enthusiasm for an

invasion began to wane he decided to go it alone. Arriving on the Hebridean island of Eriskay with one 44-gun frigate he set out to conquer a kingdom. Once on the mainland with the support of the influential Highland chief Donald Cameron of Lochiel he marched and took Edinburgh, and by defeating the government forces at Prestonpans on September 21st became master of Scotland. Now began the march into England.

He got no further than Derby. The English had shown little enthusiasm for his cause and his Highlanders, disliking fighting so far from home, had begun to desert. Against the inclinations of some of his generals and not telling his men until they were actually on the march, he retreated to Scotland, where after enjoying a brief triumph at Falkirk, his forces were massacred by those of the Duke of Cumberland on the terrible field of Culloden. The royal 'butcher' allowed the killing of captives and the wounded and unleashed an orgy of murder and looting. The Government determined to destroy the reservoir of men that formed a Jacobite army, and set out to destroy the clan system of the Highlands. The powers of the great chieftains were removed and the keeping of arms, the wearing of the kilts and the

Coalbrookdale's place in history was assured when Abraham Darby bought the local iron works in 1708, and discovered how to extract iron using coke instead of charcoal. The foundry originally produced cast iron cooking pots but later parts for the first iron bridge and the first locomotive were cast there.

Landscape of the new Britain: Dudley in the heart of the coal and iron region of the 'black country' displays mines, smoking chimneys and crowded buildings. Canals were the arteries of the Industrial Revolution: by moving raw materials they permitted the concentration of industry before the advent of the railway.

playing of the bagpipes forbidden. Charles Edward fled once more into exile.

The Jacobite risings were two major alarms which punctuated an otherwise long period of political stability. George I could not speak English and had little interest in English affairs, but it was from this unpromising position that the great office of Prime Minister evolved. George was happy to leave effective government to a man who showed himself capable of preserving stability and maintaining the revenues. Such a man was Sir Robert Walpole, generally regarded as the first British Prime Minister. A Norfolk squire, he came to political prominence with the Whigs as the Tory ministers of Anne, tainted with Jacobitism, re-treated. Within his own party he took over the leadership largely because he was one of the few ministers to escape entanglement in the 'South Sea Bubble', when the South Sea company crashed in 1720 after one of the most spurious and speculative share flotations in British financial history. Walpole's aims were simple: stability at home and peace abroad. To this end he built up with the aid of two adept party managers, Henry Pelham and his brother-in-law the Duke of Newcastle, the Whig oligarchy, a political system of influence, patronage and reward which dominated 18th century politics. All vacant offices were filled with nominees, and the crown's patronage was used for party and private interest (for Walpole and his friends made, indeed expected to make, great profit from public office). It was however a stable, if corrupt, administration in which the spoils of office were elevated above principle and vision. Walpole had his periods of unpopularity, such as his attempt to introduce the excise tax in 1733, but he was adroit enough to withdraw the bill when the extent of public hostility became manifest. Making himself just as indispensable to George II when he succeeded his father in 1727, he held secure office until 1742.

It was popular feeling in support of war which suddenly put Walpole out of step with the times, and brought William Pitt, later Earl of Chatham, eventually to power. Britain was entering its great age of expansion, and even Walpole's 'man', the Duke of Newcastle, was convinced by 1741 that the drive for commercial supremacy made war with Spain necessary. 'It is your war', Walpole told him, 'and I wish you joy of it'. Half-heartedly he continued in office for a year with the war going badly, and in 1742 resigned, dying three years later. Under Henry Pelham, with Newcastle still running the political machine, the war dragged on without bringing great glory, while William Pitt, due to the king's intense dislike, waited in the sidelines. The outbreak of the Seven Years' War in 1756 meant his talent and energy could no longer be ignored. Henry Pelham had died in 1754, and while Newcastle continued to manage the government system, William Pitt took direction of the war. He was not unduly concerned that he had joined that very Whig oligarchy whose 'corruption' he had so strongly con-demned as an opposition politician.

Pitt was a man of ambition with a strong sense of Britain's destiny in dominating world trade. To this end he spoke for the merchants of London, and the support of the City was always assured him. Suffering from poor physical and mental health (today he would be described as a manic depressive) he put his driving egotism to work in the direction of his country's expansion, and more than any other man brought Britain the origins of her great empire, especially in India and North America. Until 1761 he dominated the scene and enjoyed success in all the main theatres of the war. Britain

AGRICULTURE

The term 'agrarian revolution' was originally employed to describe the changes in agriculture in the British Isles believed to parallel those of the Industrial Revolution. The concept envisaged a relatively rapid trans-formation of British, and especially English, agriculture during the 100 years from about 1750 to 1850. Parliamentary enclosure, the introduction of a Norfolk four-course rotation incorporating new crops such as the turnip and cultivated grasses, and the improvement of livestock breeds, were held to be the key developments of this period. A particular emphasis was placed on the part played by the great innovators of the 18th century, including Jethro Tull, the advocate of seed-drilling and horse-hoeing between the rows; 'Turnip' Townshend, the 'father of Norfolk husbandry'; Robert Bakewell and the livestock breeders who followed him; the publicist Arthur Young and the great aristocratic landowners like Coke of Holkham and the Duke of Bedford, who initiated advanced farming methods.

Recent research has re-examined many of these traditional concepts. In particular, the period of the agrarian revolution has been extended both backwards to the end of the 16th century and forwards to the beginning of the 20th. It has also been suggested that many of the most revolutionary changes in farming techniques have taken place entirely since 1880; among these are the use of the internal combustion engine tractor, of electricity and the chemical control of disease.

It is now realised that what the average farmer did was more important than what an exceptional 'improver' advised or practised. Consequently increasing attention is being paid to the analysis of the farmer's business records, including the account books of farms and estates as well as the inventories which listed a farm's crops and stock. The expansion of the total arable acreage after 1750, much of it into previously uncultivated land, was of equal if not greater significance in the raising of agricultural output than mechanical or even biological innovation. New rotations and crops appeared in many open fields before enclosure (and it should be remembered that the latter process affected only half of the arable land of England in the first half of the 18th century). Perhaps more important than the rationalisation of holdings and the abolition of communal management of cropping and grazing was the provision of new farm buildings, roads, hedges and fences which normally accompanied enclosure. The traditional view of agricultural improvement has tended to over-emphasise developments in southern arable farming and has neglected events in northern and western parts of the country, for example, the role of the Scottish lowland farmers as practitioners of the most advanced methods of husbandry.

British agriculture largely supplied the food needs of a population which trebled between 1700 and 1850, for it was still about 80 per cent self-sufficient in grain by the latter date. The growing English conurbations did, however, depend upon substantial imports of livestock and dairy produce from Scotland and Ireland.

The concept of an agrarian revolution in Britain has suffered, first by being too closely linked to certain personalities and improved techniques, a view that is no longer tenable, and more recently by having become little more than a convenient title for textbooks on the history of agriculture during the early modern period and the Industrial Revolution. None the less, during the 400 years of this 'agrarian revolution' a number of crucial developments did occur. Among the more important was the transfer of land from small inefficient producers farming scattered holdings into the hands of large commercially minded tenant farmers with capital and expertise. Also significant was the extension of the market economy and the rational application of scientific principles to all operations of agriculture. Many of the greatest biological and technological advances have, nevertheless, been made only in this century and perhaps the history of agriculture from 1600 should be regarded less as a revolutionary than as an evolutionary process.

This four Wheel Drill Plow, with a Seed and a Manure Hopper was first Invented in the Year 1745 and is now in Use with Mr Ellis at Little Gaddesden near Hempstead in Hertfordshire, where any person may View the same. It is so light that a Man may Draw it but Generally drawn by a pony or little Horse.

William Ellis' drill plough (top), based on a 17th century model, was found to be ineffective. A more successful implement was Crosskill's clodcrusher (above), an improved type of roller.

The cowhouse provided winter shelter and milking accommodation for cattle, with hay stored in the loft. Adjoining it is a wagon shed and wagoner's cottage.

19th century slate-pillared hayshed with cattle shelter from a Gwynedd estate, re-erected at the Welsh Folk Museum, St Fagans, Cardiff.

Farm worker's cottage from Rhostryfan, Gwynedd, re-erected at the Welsh Folk Museum. It was built in 1762 of glacial boulders and roofed with slate.

Fattened hog, killed 1797, showing the impact of the imported eastern strains crossed with the native Berkshire pig. It was fashionable to commission portraits of such proud beasts.

Longhorn cattle, now a conserved rare breed, were 'improved' for beef, instead of dairy, qualities by Webster and Bakewell. Their popularity subsequently declined against that of the Shorthorn.

Threshing barn, Kildwick, Yorkshire. Harvested corn was stored here until hand threshing, when the draught between the doors was used to winnow it.

took Guadeloupe in the West Indies; Dakar in Africa, with its gum and control of the slave trade; Canada, where success was assured by the brilliant victory of James Wolfe at Quebec; and India where Eyre Coot and the even more outstanding Robert Clive won victory after victory. His failure to capture Mauritius was a blow, but more than compensated for by the taking of Manila and the control of the China tea trade.

Success unknown since the heady days of the Duke of Marlborough was being enjoyed. At sea the French were destroyed. Admiral Boscawen smashed half of the French fleet at Toulon in 1759, the same year in which Admiral Howe routed the rest of it at Brest. However, war was expensive, and there were fears that this very success might lead to the rest of Europe combining against Britain, therefore support for a consolidating peace was growing – a movement fiercely resisted by Pitt. Circumstances changed, however, when George III came to the throne in 1760. George hated the Whigs, whom he regarded as having exercised undue power over his grandfather George I. Nothing was more certain than that he would try to rid himself of the incumbent government as soon as he could, and opposition to that government was best manifested by concluding a peace. When peace was made in 1763 much was given back to the French including the captured West Indian islands, Dakar and the right to fish off Newfoundland. Pitt was disgusted and bitter, but in fact his two greatest gains, Canada and India, remained intact.

The intentions of George III have been disputed, but at the very least he aimed to destroy the power of the Pelham/Newcastle system. His chosen instrument, however, was a poor one. The royal favourite, the Earl of Bute, was handi-capped by more than his Scottish birth, for he was overbearing and incompetent. The Pelhamites were routed from office, but it was many years before George III could find a stable alternative. Bitterly accepting that Bute could not do it, he tried ministry after ministry until, after ten years, Lord North provided relative cohesion and stability.

George found himself faced with a rising tide of popular hostility. John Wilkes, *nouveau riche* and a member of the notoriously depraved Hellfire Club, had become in middle life a London alderman and journal publisher. In an issue of the *North Briton* (a satirical publication whose title was deliberately aimed at the Scottish Lord Bute) he attacked the King's speech to parliament in 1763. Although an MP and supposedly privileged he was imprisoned in the Tower. He was arrested under a general warrant, i.e. one in which individuals were not named, and in a vigorous campaign succeeded not only in getting his release, but in getting the illegality of general warrants established and the ruling that 'state necessity' was not acceptable as justification for arbitrary action under English law. To the cry of 'Wilkes and Liberty', London crowds made him a popular hero. The government continued to persecute him, however, and were able to use his authorship of an obscene poem as a weapon. Recuperating in France after being wounded in a duel, he thought it wise to remain there. In his absence he was outlawed. In 1768 he thought the time right to return, and during the election that year he stood as candidate for Middlesex, one of the few constituencies with a broad electorate. The government imprisoned him for two years and excluded him from Parliament, but at each re-election the voters of Middlesex returned him yet again.

Wilkes was no thorough-going reformer, but he had

THE GREAT ESTATES

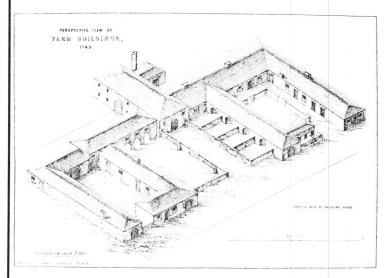

PERSPECTIVE VIEW OF FARM BUILDINGS, 1849

In the late 18th century estate farming was profitable and improvement fashionable: the best architects were employed to make country houses more splendid and to design extravagant farmerys. Coke of Holkham, for instance, claimed to have lavished £¼m on new buildings alone. Spending dropped during the post-Napoleonic recession, but another expansionary phase began in the mid century. Victorian farm buildings, however, tended to be more functional in style and arrangement than their predecessors. Thomas Sturgess noted in 1849:

The essential buildings of a farmstead are those which will enable the farmer to house and thresh his corn, convenience for the storing of the straw, preservation of the manure, shelter for fat cattle, milching cows, farm-houses, and other livestock kept upon the farm; also convenience for the housing and preparing of the various descriptions of food which they consume, shelter for waggons, carts and other agricultural implements used.

The fact that landlords remained responsible for capital outlay on tenant farms reinforces the view that for much of the century the relationship worked mainly to the benefit of tenants.

At the end of the 18th century England was a country in which the landed aristocracy was pre-eminent. The peerage led the government, set the 'tone' for fashionable society and commanded enormous wealth, yet it consisted of a comparatively small group of about 300 families, many of whom enjoyed an income of at least £10,000 a year and possessed an estate of over 10,000 acres.

Some great dukes and earls could trace their ancestral lands to grants made at the time of the Norman Conquest, but much of the feudal nobility had been destroyed or impoverished during the Wars of the Roses and the remnant were dependent for their survival on the powerful Tudor monarchy. During the hundred years that preceded the Civil War many families entered the ranks of the gentry, and by various means – including royal patronage, successful business undertakings, careful land management and judicious marriage – built up considerable land holdings.

After the Restoration, however, the great landowners gradually re-asserted their position. A number of factors contributed to this. Firstly, the size of the electorate increased as a result of the growth in population and monetary inflation – which devalued the existing property qualification and expanded the numbers of those eligible to vote. Eventually only the aristocracy and greater gentry could afford the enormous cost of elections and in this way gradually re-established control over Parliament and government policy.

Secondly, certain trends within agriculture itself favoured the growth of estates. Depression in the first half of the 18th century contributed to a fall in rents and hence in estate incomes. The larger landowners with more substantial revenues – which were often augmented by fortunes made from trade with the East Indies and sugar colonies – were better able to absorb losses than the lesser gentry and were well placed to buy up small estates coming on to the market. On the other hand, rising rents after 1750, associated with the growing demand for food and rising agricultural output, also benefited large landowners.

Lastly, although it was always possible to dissipate a landed fortune, there were strong bonds tending to keep estates intact. The English custom of primogeniture ensured that on the death of the owner the estate passed to the eldest son – unlike the continental practice, whereby a holding was often divided between all the male heirs. The effect of primogeniture was reinforced by the legal device of strict family settlement, which gave the owner a life interest only in the estate and severely curtailed the possibility of its alienation away from the designated heirs.

The trend towards an ever greater concentration of land ownership continued until well into the 19th century. As late as 1874 Lord Derby's Return on the Owners of Land (the so-called New Domesday Survey) reported that 525 members of the nobility owned one fifth of all the land in the United Kingdom, while some 7,000 persons owned as much as four fifths. However, by this time the landowners, unable to resist the aggressive demands of, first, the middle classes and then the working classes, had lost their monopoly of political power. They also suffered a loss of economic power as rental incomes fell substantially during the late 19th century agricultural depression. This, combined with the introduction of death duties in 1894 and the threat of further discriminatory legislation after 1906, set in motion the sale of estates, which was to become a flood after the First World War. Thereafter, although the social prestige of the aristocracy and greater gentry remained high, they no longer possessed a decisive say in national or even local affairs.

THE ENCLOSURE ACTS AND FIELD & VILLAGE PATTERNS

The enclosure of open fields, commons, meadows and wastes, concentrated between 1760 and 1830, was one of the more notable developments in English agrarian history in modern times. In some areas it created a new rural landscape, while generally it formed part of a complex of processes which re-ordered the pattern of social and economic life in the countryside. Enclosure had been continuous since the end of the medieval period, but at the beginning of the 18th century perhaps as much as half the existing arable land still lay in open fields. The classic area for the survival of the open field system was the Midlands and central southern England. The distinctive feature of enclosure in the second half of the 18th century was that it was increasingly effected by Act of Parliament rather than by agreement between interested parties; in spite of its higher cost, Parliamentary enclosure was preferred as it enabled large areas of land to be redistributed in one block and allowed the owners of the greater part of the land in a village to force an enclosure on the remainder. Between 1760 and 1844 there were more than 2,500 Acts dealing with more than four

million acres of open field, and between 1760 and the end of the 19th century another 1,800 Acts enclosing nearly two million acres of commons and waste.

The reasons for enclosure are complex and still controversial. An advantage to the open field system was that under abnormal weather conditions some strips would produce a crop while others did not, thereby reducing the risk of total harvest failure. By the 18th century, however, the benefits to be derived from enclosure outweighed those of open field husbandry; the productivity of an enclosed farm could be significantly greater, although this varied from parish to parish and it is impossible to quantify the increase. The main advantages, however, were that enclosure made a farm easier to work and rotation increased the yield of the land, and that former common or waste land could be used as crop or grazing land.

What still has to be explained is the heightening of enclosure activity in two periods — the 1760s and 1770s and between 1793 and 1815, the Napoleonic War years. It may well be that rising prices and reduced costs (the fixed price of enclosure in terms of legal,

Parliamentary and other fees tended to fall over a period of time) combined to make Parliamentary enclosure particularly attractive during the Napoleonic period. The initiative was usually taken by landlords, who used the opportunity to raise rents; unenclosed tenancies were often under-rented, although the trend towards shorter leases after 1750 allowed landlords to review rents more frequently on such land. On enclosed land, however, rents were easier to arrange — since the landlord had only to bargain with one farmer and not several, and on average rents perhaps doubled.

Large landowners undoubtedly benefited from enclosure. So also did the larger tenant farmers, as the greater productiveness of an enclosed farm was usually more than sufficient to meet the increase in rent. The classes most often said to have suffered as a result of enclosure were the small farmer, cottager and squatter, who often relied on access to the commons or waste for their livelihood. Such access might allow a cow, or more likely pigs or geese, to be kept and peat, firewood or fruit to be gathered. The enclosure commissioners are frequently accused of swindling the poor out of their rights, but allotments and cow-pastures were often set aside for the use of labourers, irrespective of whether or not their recipients possessed legal rights of common and were properly entitled to compensation. There were, of course, abuses and sometimes even where an allotment was allocated

it might be too small or too far from a dwelling to be useful.

There was no mass migration of unemployed rural labour to the cities during the height of the enclosure movement; indeed it has been argued that enclosure created work — in fencing, erecting new buildings, making roads and in providing more productive employment. As a result of the population explosion after 1750, however, poverty began to increase within the countryside and the post Napoleonic period was one of acute misery for the poorer rural classes. It was not until the 1830s, when the growth of industrial employment began slowly to draw off the rural labour surplus, that the situation improved.

In conclusion, it may be said that the enclosure movement had an obvious and lasting effect upon the physical landscape. Vast open fields of perhaps several hundred acres were replaced by a chequerboard pattern of small, squarish and hedged fields; this pattern is still predominant, although it is inevitably being modified to meet the needs of modern mechanised farming. As an historical process, however, it is important to see the enclosure movement as part of a wider framework of events, contributing to the triumph of large scale farming and to the creation of the most technically advanced and productive agriculture in 19th century Europe.

An enclosure map of 1770 produced by the commissioners at Ashbury, Berkshire, where nearly 3,000 acres were enclosed by Private Act.

Dufton, Westmorland. Here fertile soils have been enclosed but the hilltop areas give way to unenclosed grazing.

In upland Britain dry stone walls often form field boundaries. They are sometimes of prehistoric origin, but more regular patterns indicate a later enclosure.

Open field strips at Southam, Warwickshire, showing the 'ridge and furrow' pattern superimposed by the hedges of the enclosures.

won important liberties and increased the disrepute in which the political system was held. Organised public opinion began to disturb the serenity of George and his ministers at the very time when difficulties with the American colonies were about to bring them to the brink of disaster. There were many issues behind growing American disaffection: unpopular duties and taxes and inhibitions on expansion, but in general they amounted to a feeling that government was being exercised without representation, and potential prosperity prevented by an imposed economic servitude to the mother country. The final breach came after several preliminary incidents, such as the famous Boston Tea Party of 1773. After George Washington had been appointed commander-in-chief of the American forces, the Congress declared the independence of the colonies on 4th July 1776. The war went badly for Britain. Despite the well known defeats of Gage at Bunker's Hill and Burgoyne at Saratoga in 1777, the British commanders were by no means as incompetent as they are sometimes represented. They lacked proper naval support and in the end the issue was largely settled by the involvement of Britain's European rivals; while Washington was creating a formidable army, Benjamin Franklin was in Paris securing first French gold, and then their active military support. France came into the war in 1778 and Spain joined in 1779. By 1781, with Cornwallis surrendering at Yorktown, the British cause was lost. James Cook's discovery of Botany Bay was some consolation, for it solved the problem of where to dispose of unwanted convicts.

Radicalism at home gained strength from the success of the American revolution and developed a stronger core than that offered by the flashy Wilkes. Within Parliament the Whig group associated with Lord Rockingham, to which Edmund Burke was attached, was attacking corruption while remaining uncommitted to extension of the franchise. In 1780 Parliament passed the 'Dunning Resolution' proclaiming that the influence of the crown was increasing and ought to be diminished. By 1782 not even the stubbornness of the King could keep Lord North in office, and the Rockingham Whigs came to power. Allowing William Pitt the Younger to introduce a bill for an inquiry into the representation system, even though the motion was defeated, helped create the quiet expectation that when Pitt himself came to the highest office in the land in 1784 at the age of only 24 Parliament would begin to put its own house in order.

The French Revolution

What shattered this serene expectation and obliterated the programme for gradual reform for a generation was a great event outside Britain: the French Revolution of 1789. Fearful of the 'Swinish multitude', in Burke's phrase, the middle class moderates fled into the arms of the Establishment and democracy was shelved. Artisan reformers (the 'Jacobins', as they were called, after the French revolutionaries) strove to produce a vigorous low-class radicalism in the 1790s, but were harassed and repressed by the government: Habeas Corpus was suspended in 1790 and again in 1794. New Treason and Sedition Acts were passed in 1795 and 1799, and a general statute to make trade unionism illegal in 1799. All this took place in the context of war with France from 1793, which lasted with only a brief interlude until the defeat of Napoleon in 1815. That war produced its two great English heroes: Horatio Nelson brought naval supremacy with his victories at the Nile and in 1805 at

WATER POWER

The power provided by falling water has been used in many countries for centuries and is of increasing interest now as part of the 'alternative technology'. Its importance in the Industrial Revolution was that it provided the power for the first real factories, and the skills developed by millwrights and engineers in taking power from a water wheel were useful in devising machinery to use the force generated by the new steam engines.

First brought to Britain by the Romans for grinding corn, and widely used for this purpose (the Domesday book records 5,624 mills in operation in 1086) various designs of water wheel later came to be used for a variety of additional operations: fulling of cloth had been water-powered since the 12th century, and a similar power take-off was in use to operate forging hammers. In the Weald the main clues to the existence of vanished iron smelting and forging works are the furnace and hammer ponds. The former were created to power bellows that would maintain a constant blast of air, and so provide oxygen to increase the fire's heat sufficiently to extract iron from the ore; the hammer ponds were then used to provide power for the operation of tilt or trip hammers to work the extracted iron.

It is generally agreed that the first true factory built in England was a silk mill, constructed for John and Thomas Lombe at Derby between 1718 and 1722. Based on the design of those in use in Italy, the mill was five or six storeys high, employed 300 men and was driven by water power from the river Derwent.

Within 50 years, there were several silk factories each employing between 400 and 800 men, but it was the use of water power in the cotton industry in the 1770s that really sparked off the factory *system*. This owed a great deal to Matthew Boulton, who opened his Soho Manufactory outside Birmingham in 1762. An engineering works dependent on water power, the factory was surrounded by the workers' houses (all workers had to walk to work in those days), and so set the pattern of the subsequent industrial town.

In 1769, Richard Arkwright, an ex-barber and wig-maker of Bolton, patented the first spinning machine driven by a horse. He set up a spinning mill in Nottingham based upon this device, but followed it in 1771 with a second mill at Cromford on the Derwent, based on water power.

The water power phase in the cotton industry produced many small hamlets and villages clustered around one or more mills. In the area around Ashton-under-Lyne, for example, there were nearly 100 cotton mills within a 10-mile radius, all on the river Tame and its tributaries.

Throughout the 1770s Arkwright invented or adapted (or filched!) a number of devices so that by the 1780s the mill at Cromford was a true factory operating a sequence of carding and spinning processes, and producing a superior yarn suitable for weft or warp or for frame knitting. In spite of constant involvement in law suits and disputes about his patents, Arkwright prospered and built more cotton spinning mills; others imitated him and a pattern was set for large textile factories before steam engines were adapted to perform the necessary rotative motion. Arkwright and his son who succeeded him had difficulties with the water supply at Cromford, which could not meet their increasing demands and was actually being reduced by the closing of lead mines whose drainage formed a large part of the supply. Other water mills built by Arkwright and the early cotton spinners were better sited and planned and, in areas where coal for steam engines was not cheaply available, continued in use until the 20th century. Some mills were operated by both steam and water, the fuel-expensive steam engine being used only when a water shortage would have meant a shut down. However, the fact that a textile mill is sited on a stream does not necessarily mean that it was once water powered: the large steam engines also needed considerable amounts of water.

The ultimate development of the mill wheel is the water turbine, but, although a number of designs were produced in the first part of the 19th century, it was not until the end of the century that the search for fast rotative power to operate electricity generators led to its application in hydroelectric schemes. Water wheels, however, did inspire one more form of water power application: in 1836 William Armstrong (then a solicitor, but later to become Sir William Armstrong, the armaments millionaire), while travelling in the Craven district of Yorkshire, observed how much of the potential power of a waterfall was not being utilised by an overshot water wheel. Armstrong devised equipment that would make more use of the force of descending water and tried it out using the Gateshead water supply, where its descent from high collection areas to the town provided the required pressure to force the water through pipes to the users. Armstrong recognised that the steady hydraulic force could be useful in lifting heavy weights and next designed a crane. It was erected on Newcastle quay, where the skilful workman who demonstrated it (who went by the name of 'hydraulic Jack'!) convinced the engineer Jesse Hartley that hydraulic cranes were essential for the new Albert Docks the latter was designing in Liverpool. Use of hydraulic equipment in docks (including dock gates) spread rapidly and, when taken up by Isambard Kingdom Brunel, became standard for railway sidings and goods yards. But after 1849, when Armstrong began to employ steam power to obtain the hydraulic pressure, the development of this form of power, like the later growth of textile mills, becomes part of the story of the steam engine.

Breastshot water wheels at Cheddleton flint mills, near Leek, Staffs, driven by water pumped up by a beam engine. They in turn drove heavy stones inside the mills which ground the flint, used in pottery making.

Driveshafts at Quarry Bank Mill.
Power from the water wheel travelled via these shafts to numerous leather belts, which turned 4000 spindles.

Melin Bompren overshot wheel, now reconstructed in the Welsh Folk Museum, Cardiff, once powered a corn mill. The wheel is so geared that the launder above has only to drop a small amount of water onto the top of the wheel to turn it rapidly.

Lady Isabella wheel, Laxey, Isle of Man, the largest waterwheel ever built in Britain. Water poured onto the top of the wheel, where its weight in the buckets turned the wheel backwards.

Tide mills, Bow, London. Water was impounded in a pond behind the mill by closing a lock at high tide, then fed through sluices as the tide ebbed to turn five broad wheels backwards by pressure on the lower paddles.

WIND POWER

Until the Industrial Revolution, water and wind were the main sources of power additional to horse and hand power. The Romans used the water wheel for grinding corn and the watermill appeared in England in the 8th century. Towards the end of the 12th century the fulling mill was used in the preparation of cloth and windmills were introduced for grinding corn in the reign of Richard I. They were also used for drainage pumping in the fens. Surveys of Essex, Kent and Sussex immediately before industrialisation reveal as many as 212, 78 and 66 windmills respectively in each county, the majority of which have long since ceased to operate and most have been demolished. A few have been preserved and converted to dwelling houses or, like Wimbledon windmill illustrated below, have become museums.

Wimbledon Windmill, a hollow post flour mill built by Charles March in 1817. The fan tail ensures that the sails are always facing into the wind.

Trafalgar, while the 'Iron' Duke of Wellington dealt the final blow to Bonaparte's ambitions at Waterloo. But there were naval mutinies at Spithead and the Nore in 1797, food riots were widespread in 1795–6, 1800–1 and in 1812, while the machine-breaking activities of the Luddites tied up more troops in holding the peace in the East Midlands, Lancashire and the West Riding of Yorkshire than were used in Sir John Moore's famous campaign in the Iberian peninsula.

William Pitt had died at the age of 46 in 1806 and there was no one of comparable stature to take the reins. If George III is remembered for anything other than losing the American colonies it is for going mad, and this he permanently did in 1811, giving way to the Regency of his son, the worthless and disreputable dandy who later became George IV. The low regard in which he was generally held lowered the standing of the monarchy even further than had the

incompetence and unfortunate illness of his father.

At the end of the war in 1815, the incumbent prime minister was Lord Liverpool, whose uncertainty in facing growing problems of discontent and disturbance was responsible for a period of notable reaction and repression. Political parties were still led by the nobility, and in the country districts the rural squirearchy ruled as justices over daily affairs. However, the growth of manufacturing had sharply emphasised the unsatisfactory nature of the electoral system: decaying pocket boroughs with a handful of houses were represented, while dynamic Manchester was not. Only in London, Westminster and Bristol was there anything approaching a popular vote. Elsewhere votes were the 'property' of the borough-mongers or cast automatically to the wishes of landed patrons and employers.

The Tory party had by now become a union of all who

COAL—THE NEW POWER BASE

Together with iron, the steam engine, and an increasing population creating demand, coal was one of the vital factors that generated the Industrial Revolution in Britain. Without abundant supplies of coal, iron could not have been produced in quantities sufficient for large machines and structures, and steam power would not have been available for factories and transport. Coal had been mined for local domestic and industrial use from early times and where it could be transported by water was used in areas distant from coalfields.

Output rose dramatically as the Industrial Revolution got under way: 21 million tons were produced in 1826, in 1854 the figure was 64.5 million and by 1880 it had reached a staggering 154 million tons.

'Coals from Newcastle' were shipped coastwise to London as early as the reign of the first Elizabeth and the City began its love/hate relationship with 'sea coal': the heat was appreciated, but the smoke deplored. Ironically, Wren's pristine Portland stone churches were largely paid for out of a tax on coal, but soon lost their beauty as the result of the smoke and sulphuric acid released.

Coal was taken from shallow bell pits or drift mines in most of the areas where it is mined today (except the Kent coalfield, which does not outcrop), but by the 18th century it was being followed deeper into the ground, below the water table, necessitating mechanical pumping equipment – a need which gave impetus to the development of the steam engine, which in turn increased considerably the demand for coal.

In addition to fuelling and encouraging

the development of the steam engine, coal mining was responsible for the first canals and railways. The canal widely held to be the forerunner of the canal boom of the 18th century was built by the Duke of Bridgewater in order to transport his coal cheaply to Manchester; while, before the first passengers were carried, railways had a history of more than a century entirely involved with the under- and overground movement of coal. Of the pioneer locomotive designers, Trevithick ran the first successful locomotive on the coal truck plateway at Pen-y-Darren, South Wales in 1804 while George Stephenson was a colliery engine wright who went to work on the public railway of a colliery owner and Quaker, Edward Pease of Darlington.

Many early miners worked only some of their time underground and remained part of the local farming community, but as mining became deeper and more specialised greater capital was needed and the landowners – dukes and earls as well as lesser gentry – began to take an interest in the profit that could be made from the exploitation of this apparently mundane mineral asset. Sometimes impoverished younger sons of the gentry engaged in the actual supervision of mining, but usually the viewers, underviewers, overmen, deputies, corporals, doggys and charter masters (to list some of the regional names for the various mine officials) were employed by the landowners to run mines their owners hardly ever saw.

As other forms of manual labour became mechanised in the 19th century men drifted into mining (in which only since nationalisation has hand hewing been replaced by machinery) and when

new mines opened alien miners settled around them. Isolated mining villages developed and it is not surprising that the men – either blackened with coal dust or unnaturally white, perhaps with blue weals where the coal had discoloured scars – should become objects of suspicion to ordinary people. In Durham, in particular, the mining villages were very isolated and intermarriage produced almost a separate race of people. These men were tough – they had to be for the work they did – and had a reputation for political belligerence. Their fight to obtain even reasonable pay and conditions for work that could never be anything but difficult and dangerous and the community spirit that had to develop between fellow workers (marras in Durham) at the coal face to make the job endurable, led very early to strong trade unionism with which to combat their natural enemies, the coal owners and their agents.

These agents were not always dishonest and often developed considerable mining and engineering expertise, and in the 19th century contributed their skill to groups such as the North of England Institution of Mechanical and Mining Engineers (founded 1852) and the Royal School of Mines which promoted ideas from safety lighting to coal cutting machines to improve mining throughout the country, with the result that coal mining became a major industry and the steam-powered headstocks and coal spoil heaps became a familiar part of the landscape of the North and in South Wales. The tips are now being landscaped and it has only just been realised that if steps were not taken the headstocks and engine houses would soon be just a memory; consequently one or two have been scheduled for preservation.

The coal of the Tyne and Wear valleys had formed the basis of industry for more than two centuries when this water colour of Wearmouth colliery was painted in 1879.

Above: Cross section diagram of the pithead engine house at Beamish open air museum.

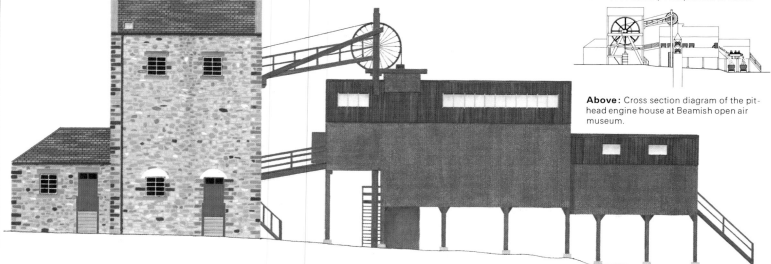

Pithead buildings at Beamish open air museum. The stone building houses the steam engine and winding drum, and the wheels (headstocks) guide the ropes from the winding engine onto the 'cages' which carry coal tubs up and down the shaft below. The coal was sorted in the 'screens' building on the right, then loaded into railway trucks beneath.

feared radicalism and opposed political reform. Now it was recognisable radicals rather than the Whigs who set the pace. Societies were formed all over the country and the movement was headed by experienced campaigners like Sir Francis Burdett, Major John Cartwright and 'Orator' Hunt. Their efforts were backed by a group of journalists and pamphleteers: Thomas Wooler of the *Black Dwarf*, Richard Carlile of the *Republican* and, the greatest of all, William Cobbett of the *Political Register*. In 1819 came the infamous 'Peterloo Massacre' when mounted yeomanry sent in by the magistrates rode into a crowded reform meeting near Manchester, killing 11 people and wounding 400 more. The incident became a symbol of oppression as the Government responded to the growing radical tide with the 'Six Acts' designed to prevent public meetings and control the radical press. Political reform did not come until the Reform Act of 1832, and even then it was secured only with difficulty and stopped far short of what even moderate reformers sought. The bill had been carried by the Whig leaders Lord John Russell and Earl Grey only because of the timely concession of Tories like Wellington and the threat of the king to swamp the lords with new peers if the diehards resisted any longer.

The middle class had secured the vote, but it was to be a further 35 years before the urban working class did the same and 20 beyond that before the farm labourer was enfranchised. Women had to wait until the 20th century. Two years after 1832, Parliament showed how harsh a face it could still present to the labouring poor by passing the New Poor Law Act in 1834. On the principle of 'less eligibility', this tried to end out-relief and put the poor into the workhouses wherein Darby and Joan were separated when their only crimes had been old age, infirmity and poverty.

A pitman's cottage of the 1890s reconstructed at Beamish Museum on the Durham coalfield. Note the foldaway bed in the kitchen – the warmest place to sleep in winter!

Rhondda valley, South Wales. Long rows of miners' cottages follow the hill contours within easy reach of the coal mines and works in the valley.

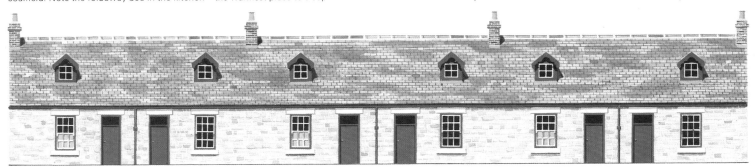

Pit cottages, Durham coalfield, preserved at the Beamish Museum. Elsewhere, the once familiar rows of pit cottages are rapidly disappearing. They were close built, and primitive with regard to sanitation and lighting, but were warm with free coal and good kitchen ranges.

Miners' lamps, Beamish Museum, Durham. As mines went deeper, researchers battled to replace the naked candle with a lamp which would not ignite the gas.

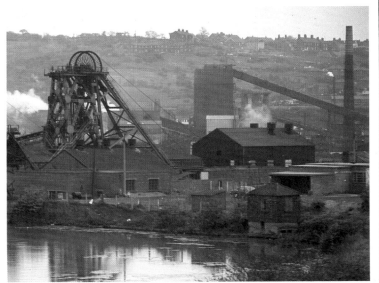

The 2 metre thick coal seam at Barnsley, Yorkshire, supplied half the coal in the region in the 18th century, and supported a thriving textile and metal working industry.

The Industrial Revolution

The term 'Industrial Revolution' was first popularised by the English historian Arnold Toynbee in 1884. Conventionally regarded as referring to the years between about 1760 and 1850, it is the shorthand and instantly recognisable way of describing those fundamental changes which took place in Britain and set the pattern for the development of the world as we know it. Only the development of agriculture in Neolithic times could rival its far-reaching effects.

It was the pivotal historical experience by which men in the western world (and later further afield) escaped from the constraints on growth and material achievement imposed by ancient and medieval handicraft technology. Compared with what had been known before, or even with what would have been conceived possible, the process of industrialisation and the accompanying technological innovation unbound Prometheus to release unprecedented material prosperity. In a wide sense the Industrial Revolution was an international experience gone through at different times by all of those countries which we now designate 'developed', from 19th century America to Stalin's Russia. It is also an experience to which the less developed aspire, for they see it as the only historically proven path to prosperity and power. However, used with capital letters the phrase has a more specific meaning. It describes a unique period in British history: Britain was the first industrial nation, her experience was a blueprint for others, but for more than a generation the process of industrialisation was the unique experience of this country alone, and Britain became the 'Workshop of the World'.

The process of growth through industrialisation began in the 18th century, during which population grew by a remarkable two thirds and output by an unprecedented 250 per cent. Over most of the 19th century the British economy grew at around two to three per cent a year in per capita terms. Modest as this might at first sight seem, its implications are tremendous, for that rate of growth doubles the volume of goods and services produced per head in rather less than a generation. At the heart of the process lie two related factors: the substitution of power-driven machinery for human muscle and the rationalisation of methods of production. The factory embraces both of these aspects. It also reflects the growing role of investment as the amount of fixed capital increased in relation to labour. To Edward Baines, the contemporary historian of the cotton industry, the factory was, 'the most striking example of the dominion obtained by human science over the powers of nature which modern times can boast' (1835). But there was another side: William Wordsworth saw the factory as a temple, where was 'offered up to Gain . . . perpetual sacrifice'. The unforgettable images of the factory children, hungry, tattered and deformed, stay in our minds even when we properly admire immense achievements in material production and marvels of engineering.

The industrialisation of Britain did not come about as the result of any state programme: there was no perceived end, no plan for growth. It happened 'naturally' as manufacturers responded to increasing market opportunities not only by intensifying their output, but also by innovating new methods of production. These involved both a more rational organisation of the labour force, for example by bringing workers together to work under supervision in factories rather than putting out materials for them to work up at home, and the substitution of power-driven machinery for

STEAM POWER

The atmospheric engine and its successor the steam engine were the first 'man-made' sources of power and, during the century and a half that saw the Industrial Revolution, were the motive force that replaced most applications of wind, water and muscle power and the main technological development responsible for industrialisation. Although the principles governing the operation of atmospheric or steam engines were understood by the 17th century and the subject was widely discussed in scientific circles in Britain and on the Continent, it was not until the second decade of the 18th century that the first commercially effective engines appeared.

Thomas Newcomen was a manufacturing ironmonger and his 'Fire Engine' (now usually described as an atmospheric engine) was designed with a thorough knowledge of the materials and skills available: supported by a brick or stone and wood building and with the engine beam of wood (before cheap iron was available), the bulk of the structure called only for masons' or millwrights' work. The boiler did not have to stand high pressures, the piston was simply sealed with leather and the seal made good with water. Only the cylinder was costly as it had to be made of brass and hand finished, but as ironmasters Darby and Wilkinson developed the manufacture of good cast iron cylinders the cost was greatly reduced. Although Newcomen engines represented exceptional capital expenditure for their period, they were the only means by which many mines could be de-watered and by 1775 there were about 100 on the coal mines of the Tyne alone and 60 on the Cornish metal mines.

The first economy came about as a result of a trained instrument maker at Glasgow University being given a model Newcomen engine to repair. James Watt was not impressed by the efficiency of the model when he had repaired it and, concluding that the cylinder was not the best place for the condensation of the steam to take place, designed a separate condenser so that the cylinder itself would not have to be cooled down for each stroke. Insulation of the cylinder to keep it hot and a separate condenser resulted in much lower consumption of steam and therefore saved coal. His improvement impressed the Birmingham manufacturer Matthew Boulton and in 1775 the famous partnership was formed, in which Boulton paid and encouraged Watt to concentrate his skill on steam engines. Of the many improvements Watt then made, the most important in the development of the steam engine was his adaptation to rotative motion

which extended its use from mere pumping to all the grinding and rolling operations and the powering of textile machinery carried out by water wheels. So economical were Boulton & Watt engines that their royalty payments were based upon the amount of fuel saved against using a Newcomen engine for the same work.

An engineer with no doubts about using steam at high pressure was the swashbuckling Captain Dick Trevithick (captain of a Cornish tin mine, not a ship) whose life reads like a boys' adventure story. Trevithick devised the strong Cornish boiler which, instead of operating like a kettle with a fire underneath it, was a long horizontal cylinder with the fire box running through the centre completely surrounded by the boiler. Watt had devised a double-acting closed cylinder in which the piston was forced both up and down by steam pressure, but as he declined to use steam at pressures much higher than the atmosphere the effect was similar to that obtained in the Newcomen engine using atmospheric pressure for the working stroke. Trevithick, using high pressure steam in a double-acting cylinder was able to give the Cornish mines a most economical engine which soon replaced the Boulton & Watt engines, leaving as a legacy the remains of sturdy engine houses that are now almost the badge of the Duchy.

Trevithick's innovations also made possible a steam engine light enough to propel a vehicle. His first attempt to operate one was on a road near Camborne after which he decided the future of the steam vehicle was on rails, but although he built successful locomotives, the cast iron rails were not adequate. He did, however, make one last contribution to putting the steam engine on wheels: he knew George Stephenson and his son Robert, and they are likely to have examined his Newcastle locomotive of 1805 which was used as a stationary engine by the coal owners before they began the series of engines which started with the colliery engine 'Blucher' and culminated in the 'Rocket', a machine that at last convinced some influential people that railways had a future.

Although many Boulton & Watt low pressure engines — even Newcomen engines — continued in use all over the country until the end of the 19th century and beyond, the development of high pressure, compound and triple expansion steam engines in all their many forms really took off in the reign of Victoria, powering large ocean-going ships such as the *Great Britain*, lake paddle steamers, railways right across the world and vast industrial towns.

A Boulton & Watt beam engine of 1777 which pumped water for the Birmingham Canal until the late 1890s, when this photograph was taken during demolition.

Cornish winding engine house and drum. This example at East Pool, built in 1887, was operated until 1949 and is now preserved by the National Trust. It and many others now derelict were used to raise men and ore from the mines.

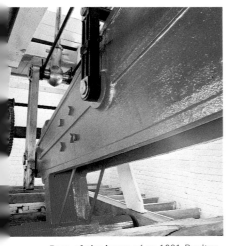

Part of the beam of an 1801 Boulton & Watt engine used to pump water up into the Kennet & Avon Canal at Crofton.

Over two million gallons of water per day were pumped by this engine in the Brighton and Hove Engineerium. It was built in the 1870s. By then the efficiency of steam engines had been vastly increased by 'compounding' – two cylinders were used; high pressure steam entered the first and then gave up more of its energy in a larger, low pressure cylinder.

Steam for fun. Steam engines were not only used for serious industrial purposes. This one at Thursford Museum, Norfolk, used to drive a merry-go-round.

Pumping engines at Ryhope, near Sunderland. Here the twin cylinders of compound engines can be seen, the smaller high pressure cylinders being at the back.

human energy. The willingness to innovate in response to expanding market possibilities offering higher profits is the key to understanding the Industrial Revolution. Innovation rather than pure invention is what matters; the real dynamic force was provided not by the inventors, but by the entrepreneurs. The old school textbook idea of change coming about as the result of 'Great Inventors' producing 'Great Inventions' puts the cart before the horse; there would have been no Industrial Revolution, whatever the state of technology, unless there had been a reason to develop methods of large scale production. Expanding markets provided such a reason.

The Industrial Revolution was to an extent preceded and accompanied by four other 'revolutions' in economic and social life – the Demographic, the Commercial, the Agricultural and the Transport – and it is necessary to examine these in order to understand the reason for Britain's rapidly expanding market. However, although it is possible to establish their main characteristics they interacted with each other in a way which sometimes makes the separation of cause and effect difficult.

The Agrarian Revolution

Only a progressive and productive agriculture could have supported such a shift within the economy towards industry and still have fed a rapidly growing population. The improvements which took place in British agriculture during the 18th century were so impressive that historians traditionally write of an 'agrarian revolution'. The basic achievement was a simple but essential one. British farmers not only increased their output of both crops and animal products, but did so while employing a decreasing proportion of the total occupied population.

This came about in part from new forms of land-holding and in part from new techniques in farming. The old idea of a dynamic enclosure movement, ending quickly and abruptly the centuries-old medieval method of cultivating open fields where individual holdings were held in the form of separated strips, is somewhat exaggerated. In most districts agriculture by the beginning of the 18th century had already moved considerably forward from the Middle Ages in terms of methods used, crops grown and the forms of tenure under which land was held. Enclosure of open fields and the common pasture and waste lands was already increasing and new crops, particularly from Holland, were already being popularised by such works as Sir Richard Weston's *Discourse on the Husbandrie used in Brabant and Flanders,* published in 1645. The idea of treating farming as a business, with the emphasis on efficient production, had taken firm hold. Throughout the 18th century, while landowners in France were asserting their feudal claims on the labour of a subject peasantry, the English landowners were displaying a growing realisation that their incomes could be better increased from the higher rents which efficient tenant farmers using improved methods would be able to pay. The self-sufficient peasantry which so long determined the agrarian structures of continental Europe was being replaced by the triad of landlord, tenant and labourer. It was a shift which had long been taking place, but which in England was substantially completed (although not so in Scotland, parts of Wales or Ireland) by the increasing pace of the enclosure movement in the latter half of the 18th and the early years of the 19th centuries.

Traditional rural society had been stratified from landlords at the top who leased to tenants, through freeholders

IRON—THE NEW CONSTRUCTION MATERIAL

The first step towards the production of the quantities of iron and steel needed for the machines, buildings and railways of the Industrial Revolution could be said to have been taken as far back as 1543 when the first iron casting in Britain was made. The cannon cast at Buxted, Sussex was important, not so much as an advance in the technique of war, although the subsequent development of the industry in the Weald was largely based upon armaments, but because it introduced an entirely new way of making iron. Instead of the ancient, low-temperature method which produced 'blooms' – small lumps of slaggy iron – which had to be skilfully worked to produce wrought iron, the high temperature of the new 'blast' furnace actually melted the iron, enabling it to be cast directly as finished objects. If a springier iron was required the cast iron could be run into 'pigs' which were re-heated in a 'finery' – a hearth with a current of air playing upon it – to burn out some of the carbon and so convert it into wrought iron. As well as facilitating the production of two varieties of iron with different qualities, the blast furnace could be built far larger than a bloomery and greater quantities of iron could be produced as a continuous process, ore and charcoal being added at the top of the furnace and the molten iron tapped from the bottom.

A smelting technique having been established, there remained two limitations to the manufacture of iron: reliance on water power for both blowing processes and for heavy tilt hammers meant that works had to be established on streams with a good fall, often a long way from any market for the product; and using charcoal as fuel meant there must be a considerable acreage of woodland available locally as even if the charcoal was made from the twigs produced by coppicing (cutting back trees to induce them to shoot from the base), they could only be harvested about every 15 years.

Demand for iron goods was nevertheless increasing by the end of the 17th century, and although the obvious solution was to use coal instead of charcoal ironmasters knew that coal produced iron that was 'red-short': brittle and useless. However, Abraham Darby I, a man who had experience in a number of manufacturing trades, applied the inquiring and unfettered mind of a Quaker to the problem and around 1709 produced the first acceptable iron using coal. It will probably never be known how much of Darby's success was due to foresight and how much to luck, but at Coalbrookdale he had all the necessary factors: coal, iron ore, limestone (to act as a flux), water for power and a route to wide markets along the navigable Severn. Not only did coal and iron outcrop together in Coalbrookdale, but the ore was the right type for making cast iron (which was Darby's object) and the coal was of a type that would coke, which was the method Darby had hit upon for removing the coal gases that produced 'red short'.

Abraham Darby's original coke fired furnace was found in the 1950s under many feet of debris from later iron making in Coalbrookdale. It was successively enlarged – as proved by the dated cast iron lintels – to cope with larger orders for iron.

Although Darby took no steps to patent or conceal his discovery the idea did not spread rapidly even among neighbouring ironmasters, perhaps because his product did not convert into such good wrought iron as charcoal iron. However his company prospered on the sale of inexpensive cast pots and kettles as well as cylinders for Newcomen engines, and in 1779 Darby's grandson produced the largest iron structure the world had ever seen: the first iron bridge in the world.

At this time developments were already taking place that were to remove the last obstacle to the bulk manufacture of iron. As early as 1742 the Coalbrookdale Company had installed a Newcomen engine to pump water back into the mill pond so that production did not have to stop during a drought, but in 1774 the bucolic John Wilkinson — a neighbouring ironmaster of the Darbys who had little in common with them except enthusiasm for iron — devised an improved machine for boring cannon. James Watt was at this time developing his steam engine, the cylinders of which also required accurate boring. Wilkinson produced the cylinders, and the second Boulton & Watt steam engine made was built for Wilkinson's foundry, adapted to provide the air blast in place of a waterwheel.

Steel could not be produced in large-scale engineering quantities until the Bessemer converter came into use in the 1860s, but in the 18th century developments were taking place in the production of steel that contributed to the Industrial Revolution as a material from which tough machine tools could be made. Steel for the Sheffield cutlery industry was originally made by a process called cementation: bars of good wrought iron (that from Sweden was preferred) surrounded by powdered charcoal were heated for up to ten days hermetically sealed in a clay or

sandstone container, but the 'blister steel' bars produced only had carbon diffused into the surface and needed repeated breaking up and forge welding to produce a more homogeneous steel. It occurred to Benjamin Huntsman, a clockmaker who found this metal inadequate for his clock springs, that if the blister steel were re-melted in a crucible any slag could be skimmed off and a thoroughly homogeneous steel would result. In 1740 he succeeded in producing a really hard steel which was to have particular value for tools to cut softer metals.

Wrought iron, like steel before Huntsman's process developed, could only be produced in small quantities by slow, elaborate, hand processes using charcoal. The greater tensile strength of wrought iron made it particularly valuable for moving parts of engines and a number of ironfounders were looking for a direct means of producing this material. The first workable process was devised by Henry Cort in 1784, who adapted the reverberatory furnace for non-ferrous metals to melt pig iron and burn out the excess carbon to convert the cast iron to wrought iron. Since in a reverberatory furnace (so called because the heat reverberates from the roof of the furnace onto the metal) fuel and metal are in separate containers, coal would not contaminate the iron and could be used in place of the more expensive charcoal. The puddling process, as it came to be called, still involved heavy hard work — the puddlers stirred and tested the molten metal until they judged it to have reached the correct consistency — but large quantities of an homogeneous material could be produced and wrought iron became the engineering material that enabled the railways to develop, being used not only for rails, wheels and moving parts of the engines, but also for bridges of entirely new forms.

Cast iron 'missionary' pots, from Abraham Darby's Coalbrookdale works, were mass produced for domestic and industrial use. They were Darby's first iron products and formed the basis of his manufacturing and financial success.

Blists Hill blast furnaces, near Ironbridge, Salop. The three furnaces produced molten iron from ore which was then run into channels ('pigs') in the three casting shops in front, re-melted and cast into artefacts or worked into wrought iron.

Barrow Iron and Steel Works, in 1871 from a water colour by George Henry Andrews. The Furness area produced non-phosphoric haematite ore which enabled the Bessemer steel making process to be successfully pioneered here.

The first iron bridge in the world at Ironbridge, Salop, was designed by Thomas Pritchard and built in the 1770s to connect two thriving industrial areas and to replace a dangerous ferry on the unpredictable River Severn.

Cast iron plate rails were popular on small horse or man drawn works railways, but cast iron was not strong enough to bear the weight of locomotives, whose development had to wait for the introduction of wrought iron.

owning and farming small units, large tenant farmers employing labour and small rent-paying farmers without labour, to groups like smallholders, cottagers and squatters who had no legal title to land but possessed certain customary rights to make use of common and waste ground. Farming for the profitable market led to the transformation of English agriculture by squeezing out the small independent farmers and the rural poor without legal title. Enclosure and the consolidation of holdings into more efficient units had long been taking place by private agreement. Perhaps 50 per cent of English acreage had already been enclosed by 1750 and in some areas, especially in the north and west, the open field strip system had never been known. The near unanimity needed for enclosure by private agreement could not be guaranteed, but a second method of enclosure by private act of parliament allowed the resistance of a minority of less than one fifth of the commoners to be overridden with the consent of the lord of the manor and of the tithe owner. The effect of this ability to enclose by act of parliament was cumulative rather than cataclysmic, but the pace certainly quickened after 1760 with 1500 acts being passed in the last four decades of the 18th century, and a further 1000 in the first 40 years of the 19th. Low corn prices in the first half of the 18th century did little to encourage expensive improvements, but the higher prices of the latter half of the century and the very high ones of the years of the French Wars (1793–1815) most certainly did. The General Enclosure Act of 1801 completed the encouragement by simplifying and cheapening the process and so making it profitable for even small acreage to be enclosed.

Enclosure alone was not a sufficient condition for progressive farming. Investment, application and a willingness to try new methods were important, but enclosure was the necessary step before improved methods could be used. The standard of livestock breeding could hardly have been improved beyond recognition if the promiscuous mixing of stock on common pasture had remained the norm; the thin cattle and scraggy sheep of the pre-enclosure era could never have been transformed into those marvellous, majestic and mammoth beasts painted in such loving detail alongside their proud owners by George Stubbs. The consolidation of holdings allowed the development of new crops and, through the use of rotation farming, the ending of the need to leave land fallow every third year to recover its fertility. In itself this must have added considerably to the total acreage under cultivation in any given year, just as did the enclosure of common and waste land. Not only did rotation systems dispense with the fallow, but the introduction of courses of fodder crops, especially turnips, allowed better winter feeding of livestock, lessening the traditional Michaelmas slaughter of beasts for winter salting. The sowing of lucerne and clover offered superior feeding to the unimproved natural grass of the traditional common pasture. In short, enclosure permitted the application of scientific knowledge and experimental methods to an industry which had for centuries been regulated by tradition, communal practice and rule of thumb.

These features of constant tillage, new crop rotations and a closer association of crops with stock were advancing on a fairly broad front, but several of the innovations which together make up the agrarian revolution are usually attributed to a group of individual pioneers. Jethro Tull (1674–1741) who published his famous *Horse-hoeing Husbandry* in 1733 certainly showed awareness of the value of machinery, even if the seed drill which he invented was not wide-

TIN, LEAD AND COPPER

Three non-ferrous metals mined in Britain — copper, tin and lead — all had widespread and important industrial uses. All three had long histories of exploitation; bronze, an alloy of copper and tin, was the first metal made use of by man, while lead was very widely used by the Romans. In the period of the Industrial Revolution, however, the demand for, and use of, all three considerably increased. Copper, with much smaller amounts of either tin or zinc, was the base of the most widely used and important of all alloys, brass. As such it was fundamental to the extensive hardware manufacturers of Birmingham, to the developing engineering trade as well as in a purer form for coinage and to sheathe the bottoms of ships. Tin, as well as having widespread uses on its own, was the basic component of pewter; this was usually made at around 20 parts tin to three of lead and one of brass — any larger use of lead would have introduced the possibility of poisoning.

The uses of lead were manifold. In building it was used for roofs and for pipes, it was essential for the manufacture of glass and paint, in typefounding for the printing trade and for glazing in the potteries. In many of these trades workers suffered badly from the effects of lead poisoning.

During the mid 1750s England's lead output was ahead of that of copper and tin. The Romans had for the most part mined in the Mendip hills and that area remained important to the end of the 17th century, when it was joined by other centres; the North Pennines around Alston Moor on the borders of Cumberland was a major mining area, as were Durham, Northumberland and the Peak district of Derbyshire. There were many other less important but not insignificant districts; compared with the large copper and tin mines, lead mining operations were often small in scale with the total output being made up from a great number of mines. As late as 1872 there were in Derbyshire 200 separate mining concerns, 138 of which produced less than five tons of ore a year.

By 1854 lead output had been passed by that of copper. Tin was not mined outside of Cornwall where it had been a major industry since medieval times; copper was also mined in Cumberland and Ireland, but except for the 1780s when easily-worked deposits in Anglesey had been rapidly and dramatically worked out, Cornwall dominated production throughout the 18th and early 19th centuries. It was joined in the mid 19th century by mines just across the border in Devon where the Devon Great Consols mine was for a time the most important copper mine in the world.

The mid 19th century was a period of investment boom in the mines of the west country. Often it was of a speculative kind: mine swindles form the plots both of Trollope's novel *The*

Three Clerks (1858) and of R. M. Ballantyne's *Deep Down* (1869).

In 1838 a listing was made of 160 mines in Cornwall which gave employment to 27,208 people. They varied greatly in size, but five mines employed more than a thousand with the largest, Consols and United Mines (Gwennap) employing more than 3,000. A further five mines each employed more than 500. These figures include women and children, for the mining of lead, copper and tin all involved considerable surface labour forces in sorting, washing and breaking ores. By 1851 one in every four Cornish males over the age of 20 was employed in the mines and the total labour force was 30,284 males and 5,922 females. All of the latter worked above ground, for unlike some of the coal mining districts no females worked underground in Cornwall.

The mining industry was of great strategic importance for the Industrial Revolution. It was the cradle of the steam engine; copper mining could only have expanded to the extent that it did because James Watt's steam engine made the pumping of deep levels economically possible; previous engines had been too costly in terms of coal consumption. Cornish engineers improved on Watt's design once his jealously guarded patent expired, and the Cornish Beam Engine became a sophisticated, efficient and widespread feature of mining.

Miners were hard-working and short-lived men; bad air and dust destroyed their health. One Cornish miner told a parliamentary inquiry in 1864 'You cannot expect miners to live as long as other men', and a mine captain agreed that a man of 50 or 60 was 'very old' for a miner. Perhaps this was one of the reasons why John Wesley had such a remarkable success in mining districts all over England. The Methodists chapels to this day remain alongside the ruined enginehouses to remind the interested observer of one strong influence on the lives of the men who laboured underground.

The great days of British metal mining were over by the third quarter of the 19th century as cheaper, more easily worked sources of supply were discovered overseas. Large numbers of Cornish miners went overseas to work in the mines of North America, Australia and South Africa, and Cornish communities became a feature of all the world's major hard-rock mining regions. They carried with them the skill and knowledge acquired during a period when a remote corner of south west England had been the most important non-ferrous metal mining area of the world. Copper and lead mining are now effectively dead; tin mining lingers on in Cornwall and now and again as world metal prices soar there is talk of revival. But Cornish mines are deep and wet, and their future can only be described as precarious.

Surface workers at Dolcoath in 1900. Breaking and washing copper ores employed large numbers of surface workers. 'Bal maidens' with their white aprons and weather-shielding hats were a familiar sight.

Underground meal break, with traditional Cornish pasties. Candles fixed to helmets by lumps of clay were still in use at the end of the century. Metal mines did not produce explosive gases, so the safety lamp was not needed.

A typical engine house for the steam powered beam engines, which pumped the mines. The desolated countryside is partly explained by the herbicidal effects of burning arsenic which was associated with the tin and copper ores.

Odin Kein, near Castleton. Lead mining in the Peak District of Derbyshire went back to Roman times. By the beginning of the 18th century most of the miners were working underground. Defoe describes miners as working at 75 fathoms. The discovery of rich ores in Australia in 1885 ended the best days of lead mining in Britain.

Botallack mine, Lands End. With its engine house dramatically poised on the wild Atlantic cliffs, Botallack was a must for 19th century visitors, and some of the workings can still be seen. In its day the mine was very rich.

Killhope lead mine, Durham. The northern Pennines were the most important lead-mining district. Lead ore was separated from waste rock by washing; the heavy lead sank to the bottom. Before washing, ores were crushed using water power.

Dolcoath man-engine, 1892. In larger mines the beam engine was used to raise and lower the miners. They stepped on and off the rod from platforms, timing the up-and-down movement and being conveyed in a series of steps.

spread in its use. It should not be overlooked either that he was stressing the use of the horse rather than the ox as a traditional draught animal. Rotherham's triangular plough of 1730 similarly permitted a more rapid and effective turning of the soil by a team of two horse and one man, instead of the slow, rectangular plough driven by four, six or eight oxen which needed both an ox-driver and a plough-man. It did not, however, come into general use until the 1830s. Robert Bakewell (1725–95) was the best-known of the stock improvers. His New Leicester sheep were actually bred to provide meat as well as wool and dung, and were so heavy that they were said to 'quake with tallow'. He followed the principles of the race-horse improvers who had been the real pioneers of stock improvement. Beginning with Lincoln stock he bred in to produce animals that fattened rapidly and had a high proportion of flesh to bone. He

also played a role in the development of the modern shire horse, but was less successful with cattle: his New Longhorns quickly put on weight but gave less milk and offered less fecundity than the original stock. Later came the crossing of his New Leicester sheep with Lincoln improved stock to produce a less fat mutton. The Colling brothers, who farmed near Darlington, developed the Durham Shorthorn cattle which quickly displaced the long horn varieties favoured by Bakewell, and soon after came Tomkin's Herefords and Lord Leicester's Devons.

Such men were only the best known of large numbers of stock-improving farmers whose efforts can be seen in the increase in weight of beasts sold at Smithfield between 1710 and 1795. Beef cattle increased from an average of 370 lbs to 800 lbs, while sheep improved from 28 lbs to 80 lbs – a far cry from the old ram described by the agricultural writer

THE TEXTILE INDUSTRY

The rise of the textile industry is undoubtedly one of the most dramatic parts of the story of the Industrial Revolution. Foremost in this development was cotton, which in the course of a few decades passed from being a luxury fabric available only to the rich to a standard fabric for the poor. The change was brought about by a combination of new sources of power and increased invention, which increased productivity to hitherto unknown heights. The industry grew in size until eventually it became the biggest employer of labour in Britain.

Foremost among the inventions was Kay's flying shuttle, patented in 1733 but not effectively employed until the 1760s. This was followed by Hargreaves' spinning jenny, but the real breakthrough came with Arkwright's roller spinning in the 1770s. Although initially this was horsepowered it was quickly adapted to water power and then to steam power. Crompton's mule followed in 1779,

combining the principles of both the jenny and the roller: it was not patented and its use quickly spread.

The early machine age can be divided into two periods. From 1770–1790 there was an emphasis on adequate supplies of yarn, the evolution of the factory system and the introduction of water driven machinery. The second period from 1790–1800 saw the introduction of Watt's steam engine, the development of which had been in progress since 1782.

Weaving, however, was still lagging behind spinning as Cartwright's power loom of 1785 had not proved successful and the industry had to await the improvements of Radcliffe in 1804 and Horrocks in 1806. Other important inventions included carding machines, drawing machines, and methods of bleaching and printing. By the beginning of the 19th century all the essential ingredients were present for the massive expansion of a mechanised

factory-based, coal-driven cotton industry which was to dominate the world market for many decades.

The industry's location in Lancashire can be explained by the fact that the environment was capable of dealing with each new development as it occurred. With the arrival of machinery, water power was available. With the transfer to steam power, coal was present underground. The method of manufacture required large quantities of water which were readily obtained from the Pennines. Bleaching required large amounts of salt, again accessible in the adjacent Cheshire salt field. The import of the raw cotton from America and the export of manufactured goods were facilitated by the easy construction of canals and railways on the Lancashire plain. Even an inland port at Manchester was eventually constructed.

The adaptation of the mechanical inventions to the woollen industry came later as wool was more difficult to

manipulate. Gradually, however, the new ideas crossed the Pennines via Huddersfield and Halifax into the Yorkshire woollen district around Bradford. Although we now find many mills located adjacent to the rivers the water power in the woollen industry was used for a much shorter period than in cotton manufacture and in some cases mills started up with steam power. The growth of the West Riding woollen industry also took place against the relative decline of the traditional woollen manufacturing areas in East Anglia and the West country.

Accompanying these changes were great social upheavals as the domestic cottage industries were replaced by the organised labour of the factories. Great scandals were involved in the employment of cheap child labour and considerable problems arose as labour needs fell with progressively increasing mechanisation. Society had yet to learn how to cope with redundancy.

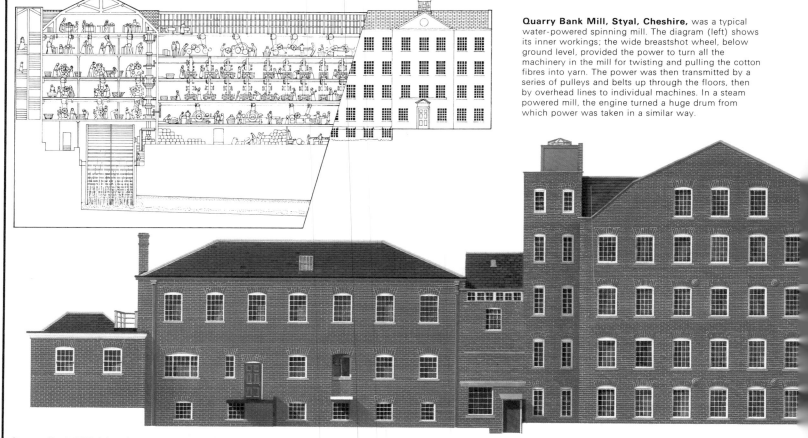

Quarry Bank Mill, Styal, Cheshire, was a typical water-powered spinning mill. The diagram (left) shows its inner workings; the wide breastshot wheel, below ground level, provided the power to turn all the machinery in the mill for twisting and pulling the cotton fibres into yarn. The power was then transmitted by a series of pulleys and belts up through the floors, then by overhead lines to individual machines. In a steam powered mill, the engine turned a huge drum from which power was taken in a similar way.

Quarry Bank Mill (above) preserves on one site an outline history of textile manufacture. Built as a water powered mill by Samuel Greg in 1784, it was adapted under successive generations of Gregs to operate with a water turbine, then by steam power (not the chimney on the right), and later power looms were added. To work the mill Greg had to build a whole industrial community alongside, including an apprentice house, owner's house and workers' cottages. Presented with its records to the National Trust in 1939, it is now a museum exhibiting the history of cotton manufacture.

William Marshall: 'His frame large and loose, his bones heavy; his legs long and thick; his chine, as well as his rump, as sharp as a hatchet; his skin rattling on his ribs like a skeleton covered with parchment.'

Particularly associated with the development of crop rotation and the introduction of new crops was Lord 'Turnip' Townshend (1674–1738) who did not originate new methods but employed them to much-publicised effect on his Norfolk farm of light, sandy soil where, before he began his improvements, 'two rabbits fought for every blade of grass'. He improved its potential by liberal use of marl (clay) and cultivation on the Norfolk four-course rotation with its use of roots and clovers in alternation with cereals. Thomas Coke was another Norfolk pioneer of note. He did not introduce the main features of Norfolk farming – the large farms, long leases, rotation of crops and marling – but he successfully employed and popularised them, especially through insisting on improving clauses in the leases of his estate tenants. It is clear that we can no longer accept the 'heroic' view of Lord Ernle in his classic *English Farming Past and Present*, first published in 1912, that an agricultural revolution sprang from the originality and enterprise of one or two great pioneers: agricultural progress in the 18th century came on a broader front and from deeper origins.

The efforts of propagators were as important in many respects as those of farmers, for they played an essential role in the dissemination of ideas. Arthur Young (1741–1820) was the best known and the most prolific. The periodical which he edited, *Annals of Agriculture*, informed parts of the country of developments in other regions of which they could not otherwise have learned. So too did the regional reports of William Marshall, which provided a valuable

The Dinner Hour, Wigan, Eyre Crowe, 1878. By the late 1800s working conditions in the cotton mills had improved considerably, with a 10 hour day and meal break.

Mill girls at work had to contend with continuous noise from the grating of metal gears and overhead line shafting. Like their predecessors in the 18th century, these early 20th century workers were provided with cheap cotton dresses and overalls by their employers, suitable for the warm damp conditions in the mills.

Cromford Hill cottages, built by Arkwright for his mill workers (left). Originally the top storey was continuous across all the houses, being intended as a workroom where his employees' families could make cotton stockings on knitting frames. Arkwright also provided his 'town' with a school, chapel, corn mill, inn and a market.

Gardner and Bazley's Dean cotton mill, on the moors between Bolton and Manchester, was famous for its excellent working conditions.

critique of those *County Reports* published by the Board of Agriculture after its formation in 1793. Young became Secretary to the Board, and if not the most accurate of guides to late 18th century farming practices he represents in his enthusiastic and tireless advocacy of change the pioneering spirit of the agriculture of his day. Even George III ran a model farm at Windsor, and was not ashamed of the nickname 'Farmer George'.

Revolutions in economic life do not often have the suddenness of *coups d'état*; the pace of agricultural advance was steady rather than speedy. The cumulative effect was, however, impressive, and agriculture met the challenge of feeding Britain's increasing population while employing a declining share of the working population. In so doing it kept within the domestic economy purchasing power that would otherwise have gone to foreign markets. Increased incomes in agriculture enabled increased purchases to be made from the manufacturing sector and helped create a solid home market base, which made large scale production methods profitable by reducing the risk of dependence on the volatile overseas outlets. It is no longer accepted that the enclosure movement drove the peasants from the land to become the first factory proletariat; the process was much more complicated and drawn out than is conveyed by the use of such terms as the 'expropriation of the peasantry'. Nevertheless, if it did not bring about as rapid a rural depopulation as has sometimes been suggested, by converting tied into mobile labour it did make possible a structural change in employment within the national economy away from agriculture and towards industry. Historians now recognise that agricultural profits played a not insignificant part in the capital formation of industrialisation. Landlords put very considerable resources into activities like coal-mining or iron manufacture, while the cotton manufacturing family of Peel which produced the famous prime minister came from a farming background.

The rural labourer in the south, although not in the north where factory competition kept wages up, would not perhaps have seen the long-term benefits and essential nature of the fundamental changes which were taking place in the economy and to which the transformation of agriculture was central. The growth in population and the effects of enclosure created a supply of landless labourers in excess of the constant demand for farm work. Farmers tended to employ workers weekly, daily or just for a particular job, and when work was slack the labourer fell back on the degrading poor relief.

So low did agricultural wages in the south become by the end of the 18th century that the famous Speenhamland system of poor relief, developed in Berkshire in 1795, became widespread and in effect fixed a minimum standard of subsistence by topping up wages by reference to the size of a labourer's family and a scale tied to the price of bread. Although frequently taking the form of resentful attacks on threshing machines, the rural labourers' revolt which convulsed the southern counties in 1830 was the product of years of poverty and degradation. Even after the suppression of the 'Swing' riots (so-called because the name of the mythical leader, 'Captain Swing', was frequently signed at the bottom of threatening letters), rick-burning, poaching and sheep stealing were persistent reminders of the sullen resentment of the rural labourer at some of the features of the capitalisation of English agriculture.

In Ireland such protest activities and some more extreme had long been part of the 'war' of the peasants against the

THE POTTERIES

It is hard to imagine living without the numerous pottery objects we use today, but before the 16th century the poor used mainly wooden platters and bowls (treen) and horn or leather drinking vessels, while wealthier people preferred pewter or silver. Much of the pottery found on medieval archaeological sites came from the Continent, but by the beginning of the 17th century vigorous and attractive, if unsophisticated, pottery was being made all over the country. It was produced in small family potteries using local clays and glazing materials, once-fired at fairly low temperatures, and comprising mainly useful domestic wares for local sale. However, there were incentives to decorate the wares: local customers wanted commemorative plates and mugs, while packmen who carried them to markets and fairs wanted pieces that would attract the impulse buyer or the innkeeper.

When tea, coffee and chocolate drinking were introduced to Europe fine cups were needed to complete the pleasure of the ritual: metal coffee or tea pots were suitable for hot drinks, but metal cups were not. With the tea from China (tea was only later introduced into India by the British) came ceramic tea pots, cups and saucers and all over Europe potters tried to imitate the fine Chinese 'china'. Continental rulers set up prestigious Royal potteries and it was from the Continent that many new ceramic processes came to Britain. By the 18th century potteries were established on the Thames close to London and near many large towns, but a concentration of small firms was growing up in a part of Staffordshire which was later to have so large a share of ceramic manufacture that it became known as the Potteries. There were plentiful supplies of clay in the area, together with coal for fuel, and from about the 14th century onwards the clay and later the coal had been used to make coarse earthenware as a sideline to subsistence

China clay pits near St Austell, Cornwall. Britain's white spoil heaps are the residues from china clay extraction, originally for ceramics, now mainly for paper manufacture. William Cookworthy, a Quaker chemist, recognised in Cornwall the same type of clay as was used to make the Chinese porcelain that came from the Kaolin Hills. He set up china works at Bristol and Plymouth and soon Staffordshire potters began to use 'Cornwall' clay and ball clay from Devon to improve their white earthenwares and, combined with calcined bones, to make bone china.

Josiah Wedgwood, a ceramic portrait painted by George Stubbs in 1780. Wedgwood's scientific skill made such a sophisticated product possible, while his business acumen in both select and mass markets enabled him to pay the finest artists such as Stubbs and the sculptor Flaxman to design for him.

Wedgwood jug. Although best known today for his jasper ware decorated with classical figures, one of Wedgwood's greatest contributions to ceramics was his development of a fine cream earthenware which, although sufficiently elegant to be used by Queen Caroline, was the forerunner of our cheap white tableware.

farming. By the early 18th century the village of Burslem had become a noted centre.

The local clays, however, contained iron impurities which were unsuitable for the white tableware that rapidly replaced the unsophisticated brown pottery, and the area had no road or water communication with London or other large markets. However, it did have vigorous and inventive families of potters who were quick to adopt new ideas and devise improvements. Foremost among them were the Wedgwoods, and Josiah Wedgwood, born in 1730, was destined to lead the industry into the new age of mechanisation.

Wedgwood rose rapidly from being a small potter working alongside his few employees to a wealthy industrialist/landowner employing hundreds of workers. He owed his initial success to recognising the high value that 18th century aristocratic society would set on pottery made in imitation of the antique classical pieces being uncovered at that time at Herculaneum in Italy, and he

scientifically set about supplying this lucrative market. Wedgwood's continuing expansion and his contribution to the industrialisation of pottery manufacture was due to his realisation that, while there were limits to the number of classical medallions and copies of the Portland Vase that could be sold to the wealthy, demand for tableware by the expanding middle classes was almost limitless and could be profitably met by the manufacturer able to adapt pottery-making processes to mass production using steam power. Wedgwood also realised that to supply this mass market from his Staffordshire works better communications were essential. This led to his leadership of various turnpike trusts and later canal-building companies. By the coming of the railways the Potteries had effective canal links, not only with the coal supplies in the area, but also with Liverpool for coastwise shipment of clays from Cornwall and Dorset, flint from the eastern part of England, and connection with the markets of London and the Midlands; railways were

therefore somewhat slow to develop in the area.

The position of leading potter in the country, held by Wedgwood in the 18th century, passed in the 19th to a Londoner. Like Wedgwood, Henry Doulton came of a family of potters: his father, born and apprenticed at Fulham, had set up a successful pottery at Vauxhall. When he was 17 Henry could throw on a wheel the 20-gallon chemical jars that were one of Doulton's specialities and by the 1850s Doultons were the leading potters in Lambeth. When, at this time, it was finally decided that an efficient drainage scheme was imperative for London, Henry Doulton saw and grasped the opportunity for his firm to make the enormous quantities of stoneware drainpipes and other sanitary fittings required. Like Wedgwood also, Henry was inventive: he claimed to have built the first steam-driven pottery wheel for throwing his exceptionally large wares and, in order to mass produce drain pipes, devised mechanical means of shaping them.

Having made a fortune from the production of useful wares, Doulton decided to go in for decorated ceramics and was drawn, as most other potters were in the late 19th century, to the Burslem area where he could find suppliers of all the clays, glazes and pigments, together with experienced workers. The concentration of the pottery industry in North Staffordshire produced a landscape whose grim and unique character has only recently disappeared as a result of the introduction of the last piece of mechanisation in the production of pottery: the tall, smoke-belching, bottle ovens have given way to modern, continuous firing, tunnel kilns through which the ware is slowly conveyed on a moving floor. However, pot banks are preserved as museums at the Gladstone Pottery in Longton and at Coalport near Ironbridge, and the atmosphere is captured in Arnold Bennett's novels set in the 'Five Towns'. Actually there are six: Burslem (the oldest), Fenton, Hanley, Langton, Tunstall and Stoke-on-Trent (the largest).

A Wedgwood lead-glazed earthenware teapot from Staffordshire, dated about 1765 and now part of the Fitzwilliam Museum's collection.

Rough conditions in an 1890s casting shop, where items were formed by pouring liquid clay or 'slip' into plaster moulds. Here it would have been cold and damp, while other workers, notably those involved with the firing of pottery, were exposed to the extremes of heat and dryness.

A small potbank of the 1890s. Work in these small potteries was hard, unhealthy and for the girls in particular, of very low social standing.

A coal fired bottle kiln preserved at the Gladstone Museum, Stoke on Trent. Iron bands round the kilns helped to support the brickwork under the enormous stresses of heating and cooling.

Stoke on Trent, 1948 (left). The smoke pall that used to hide the whole area was considerably reduced in the 20th century as many potteries had gas fired kilns. Semi-detached houses were replacing the terraced workers' cottages and the hundreds of bottle kilns had all but disappeared by the end of the 1950s, although most of the pottery made in Britain is still manufactured there. Today the Potteries of Bennett's novels are indistinguishable from other industrial towns.

hated absentee landlords. There the problem of land reform, inseparable from that of nationalism, was to persist well beyond the period of the agrarian revolution. Many of the improvements reached into lowland Scotland, but in the highland areas the difficulty of the land kept the crofter in being, although the 'clearances' by which the great land-owners leased their lands to lowland sheep farmers and dispossessed the crofters go back further in origin than is always assumed. Equally a problem for the crofter was an increase in population, especially after the introduction of the potato as an intensive food crop. These two factors produced a hunger in and an emigration from north west Scotland which would have attracted the attention of historians to a greater extent if it had not been overshadowed by the 'Great Hunger' in Ireland of the 1840s, when more than a million Irish died in five years of starvation and of the diseases associated with malnutrition, and almost a further million emigrated to North America. The dis-possessed highlander of Scotland, however, could turn his bitterness not just towards England, but nearer home to the lowlands where not only prosperous agriculture but expand-ing industry meant that Scotland was economically 'two nations'.

The Demographic Revolution

The modern industrial economy as it emerged in the 18th and 19th centuries was distinguished from its predecessors in the long line of economic development in that it demon-strated sustained long term growth in *both* population and output. The mechanics of the modern rise in population are still only imperfectly understood by historians; final answers are probably impossible given the deficiency of pre-Census demographic statistics (the first British census was not taken until 1801), and the area of inference and speculation remains large. Broadly speaking, in a traditional peasant society crude birth rates (i.e. live births per thousand of the popula-tion) generally range between 35 and 50. Death rates also tend to be high but *normally* lower between 30 and 40 per thousand. This implies a 'natural' growth rate of between 0.5 and 1 per cent per annum. What prevented this natural tendency to increase being sustained over a long period of time? The explanation lies in periodic mortality peaks, crises caused by harvest failure, famines or epidemic fevers, or indeed, commonly by famine and fever reinforcing each other, which checked the population when it began to press too heavily on the means of its subsistence. This sequence of growth and check is sometimes called the 'Malthusian trap' after the Rev. Thomas Malthus (1766–1834), the English economist who in his famous *Essay on the Principles of Population,* first published in 1798, made a blunt identification of the ultimate demographic choice: restraint or starvation. To Malthus the underlying and unavoidable certainty was that while food production could increase only arithmeti-cally, population increased in *geometric* progression.

For our purposes we need to explain why the population of Britain was able to escape the 'Malthusian trap' and rise continuously from about 1740. We should rather say the population of Great Britain, for Ireland as evidenced by the dreadful famine of the 1840s most certainly did not escape. The population of England and Wales in 1700 was around 5.8 million and it remained rather static through the first half of the century, reaching 5.9 million in 1740. Thereafter growth became sustained: by 1770 it was more than 7 million, by 1790 8.25 million and at the first census of 1801 it had passed the 9 million mark. Scottish population grew

FACTORIES AND UNIONS

The organisation of labour under factory conditions was largely pioneered by Matthew Boulton who opened his Soho Manufactory outside Birmingham with several hundred workers in 1762. Initially an engineering works dependent on water power and surrounded by the workers' houses – all having to walk to work – it was to provide the pattern for the factory system of the cotton industry and hence the industrial town of the 19th century.

For the workers the major impact of the factory was to change the nature of work from its conduction at an individual pace in homes and small workshops, where the master supervised his men or was simply assisted by his wife and children, to the more specialised and monotonous work dictated by the speed of water or steam driven machinery. Employees also became wage earners and factory hands instead of inde-pendent workers. They were expected to work long hours in the absence of shift systems, had few holidays, and with the extensive employment of women and children, received low wages.

Conditions were clearly ripe for the growth of Unions – another aspect of the Industrial Revolution. Unions were of course already in existence, especially among the skilled workers, in the 18th century, but the hostility of the law meant that most were secret despite their ancestry in the medieval guilds and companies. The legal difficulty revolved around the concept of 'conspiracy' and the movement had first to be freed from this stigma before any public advance could be made.

The French Revolution of 1789 was at first an inspiration to English reformers but as it developed became a nightmare, because it set all respectable England against reform. The 1790s were marked by a series of repressive acts against unlawful societies, treasonable practices and seditious meetings. However, the close juxtaposition of several hundred workers in one factory encouraged the formation of 'benefit clubs', such as appeared among the Oldham operatives as early as 1792, and during the next 30 years a network of spinners' societies spread throughout Lancashire. They

were followed from 1805 by the framework knitters who took action over frame rents and low wages. From individual groups and societies there came the union of a number of trades (hence trades unionism). The formation of these unions, notably among the building trades, became a distinctive feature of the period 1829–34. The Operative Stone Masons, based on local masons' lodges, were especially strong although they only mustered about 10 per cent of the total work force.

Between 1840 and 1870 organised labour was to some extent diverted from unionism because of alternative activities and political causes that led to the formation of such associations as the Ten Hour Movement, the Anti-Corn Law League and the repression of Truck and Chartism. However, 1851 saw the emergence of the New Model Unionism which was typified by the Amalgamated Society of Engineers where the emphasis was on friendly benefits, sick pay, unemployment pay and pensions, and where peaceable negotiating methods rather than strikes were employed. Many other national craft unions – carpenters, joiners, bricklayers, iron workers, boot and shoe operatives – were later to follow this pattern. These, with the help of the London Trades Council of 1860, were to fight the battle for legal recognition between 1871–75.

Concurrent with the workers' efforts to improve their lot were the campaigns carried out by the middle and upper class reformers largely motivated by the appalling conditions experienced by pauper and orphan children in the factories and mines. Until 1833 a working day of 14 hours was quite common, even for six and seven year olds. It is not surprising, therefore, that these conditions were also under attack in the period which led up to the abolition of slavery in 1833. Factory Acts followed in 1833, 1847, 1864, 1867 and 1878 each progressively reducing the hours of work and improving conditions first for women and children and eventually for men. The seventh Earl of Shaftesbury and Lord Althorp were the most active instigators of these reforms.

A banner carried by a trade union in the 1832 Reform Bill procession in Edinburgh and now in the Huntly House Museum. 'Christopher North' was the *nom de plume* of a Tory anti-reformer, Professor John Wilson. Flags and banners have throughout history provided a focus for social groups; from the first, trade unions and political campaigners used them as rallying points at open air meetings. Their subjects vary from the satirical, as here, to portraits of leaders, pictures of mine disaster memorials and, most commonly, of united workmen clasping hands.

Soho manufactory. By the mid 18th century Birmingham was a centre for the manufacture of small metal goods in domestic workshops, but 'Brummagem' wares did not have a good name. In 1762 Matthew Boulton moved out from the crowded centre of the town and established this works at Soho where all stages of manufacture took place under one roof. The works used water power at first but were later powered by a steam engine designed by James Watt.

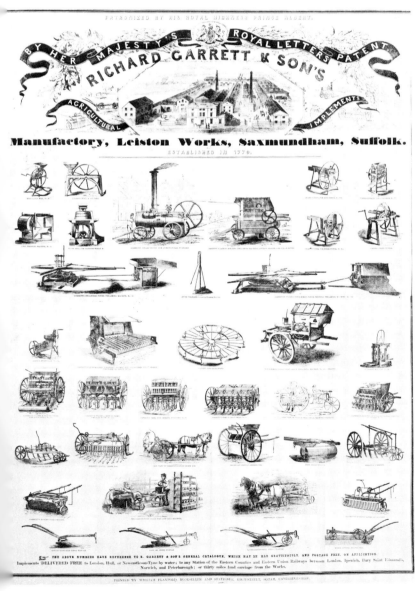

The site of the original Soho manufactory pictured above; once elegant, now transformed into the dreadful jumble of Smethwick's industrial landscape.

Machines make machines. Factories making a standard range of agricultural machinery spread the industrial revolution to the countryside, and incidentally created the need for this innovation, the catalogue.

New Lanark, Strathclyde. Under Robert Owen, the cotton mills of New Lanark became a famous example of humanitarian management that made a profit. Workers' housing was good and there was full time schooling for children under 10.

more slowly in the 18th century, from a little more than 1 million in 1700 to 1.5 million by 1790. The Irish population, however, was already beginning to show clear signs of the growth which was eventually to produce the crisis of the mid 19th century and make that small country such a large exporter of people: her 1700 population was more than 2.5 million and by the end of the century she had passed the 5 million mark.

Growth continued through the 1800s: in a century the population of Great Britain had more than trebled. Many people must have seen the population double in their own lifetimes. Ireland presents a different picture. In 1841 her population reached a peak of more than 8 million, but famine and emigration reduced the population to 6.51 million by 1851, a fall of more than 20 per cent in a decade, and by 1901 it had declined remorselessly to a level of 4.45 million. In a country where there was no significant shift in the economy away from peasant agriculture, demographic growth had outpaced economic growth and the Malthusian check had operated.

Explanations of why the population of England and Wales began its sustained increase around 1740 differ. Some demographers stress the importance of falling mortality rates. It has been argued that improvements in medical knowledge, especially the development of a viable smallpox inoculation, reduced mortality. Particularly significant was a fall in infant mortality which meant that more people survived to bear children. With the effects of smallpox reduced, the check of epidemic fever was further lessened by the disappearance of the dreaded Bubonic plague. The great cycle of 'black death' seemed to end its gruesome course in Britain after the last great visitation of the 1660s; we do not fully understand why. Possibly the ascendency of the 'foreign' brown rat over the native English black rat, which had not only been a favoured host of the plague-bearing flea but had lived close to humans, had something to do with it. Whatever the reason, had the plague returned after the 1660s with anything like its usual virulence, then Britain's economic and social history must have been very different.

If the check of pestilence was so much lessened, so too was that of its accomplice, famine. A run of good harvests in the first half of the century produced a base from which the great achievements of the agricultural revolution expanded food supply ahead of population growth.

Other demographers have suggested that a rising birth rate was more important. They argue that medical improvements were not so effective as has been supposed, and that part at least of the explanation lies in an increase in family size. The childbearing potential of a marriage is basically determined by the number of years between marriage and the ending of the wife's fertile period. It follows that the most obvious variable in determining family size, if we do not presume any practice of family planning (and admittedly that is a rather large presumption), is the age of the woman at marriage. In peasant societies the age of marriage tended to be high, in the mid twenties for women and the late twenties for men. This is because the setting up of a fresh household depended upon the availability of land, and marriage was postponed until economic independence became possible. Manufacturing employment offers an earlier opportunity for economic independence and hence permits a lowering of the age of marriage. The effect that this had on family size is further enhanced by the opportunities which manufacturing afforded for the employment

ROADS

'More like a retreat of wild beasts and reptiles, than the footsteps of man' was one of the mildest descriptions of the state of English roads in the early 18th century. The maintenance of roads was clearly inadequate for the needs of increasing traffic. A statute of 1552 had made each parish responsible for repairing its own roads, each parishioner being obliged to spend four (later six) days a year on the task, under the supervision of a surveyor usually appointed for one year by the churchwardens. The system did not make for efficiency; the surveyors, unpaid amateurs acting under compulsion, were as reluctant, and as ignorant, as their enforced labour. Work was undertaken spasmodically, without knowledge of the most effective techniques, and with little chance of a coherent and uniform network of roads crossing the boundaries between parishes, let alone between counties and regions. Strains were bound to develop when the needs of long distance through traffic were added to merely local traffic within the parish.

The solution was the replacement of statute labour by turnpike trusts. In return for repairing the roads, the trusts were to erect toll barriers in order to charge the road users for the service. The first turnpike act was passed in 1663, in response to the great repair demands made on parishes along part of the Great North Road by the increased volume of through traffic. At first, the intention was to assist the parishes, but the trusts of the 18th century came to replace rather than supplement statute labour and the work of the parishes. The turnpikes were promoted by the merchants, farmers and landowners in the locality who were interested in improved communications, and in the early stages were opposed by the road users – the drovers, stage coach proprietors, carriers – who resented the transfer of the cost of road works from the parishioners to themselves. However, during the 18th century resistance became less severe and effective as the benefits of the improved roads became clear and as continued growth of traffic strained the resources of parishes to the limit. Meanwhile a quite different solution was being tried in Scotland where, after the 1745 Jacobite rebellion, the Government built a system of military roads under the direction of General Wade. The attacks launched by farmers of west Wales disguised in women's clothing upon toll gates in the Rebecca riots of 1839 and 1842–3 were a late bizarre revival of hostility to trusts, viewing them and their tolls as visible symbols of the changes disrupting the local economy.

One of the major incentives for turnpiking roads was the burgeoning demand of London for provisions. By about 1750 most routes into London had been turnpiked, reflecting, as Daniel Defoe had noted, 'the general dependence of the whole country upon the city of London, as well for the consumption of its produce as the circulation of its trade'. But the general development of the economy also led to turnpikes in areas away from London, serving the growing provincial towns and industries. In the 'Turnpike Mania' of 1751–72, 389 new trusts were established to lay the basis for a coherent road network. Whilst continued economic growth did lead to more trusts in the late 18th and early 19th centuries, the next manias were to be in the construction of canals and railways. By the 1830s, the country had over 1,000 trusts and 20,000 miles of turnpikes, collecting £1½ million a year.

The development of an adequate repair technology was a product of the

Clifton Suspension Bridge over the Avon Gorge at Bristol, designed by Isambard Kingdom Brunel, an outstanding achievement both in terms of engineering and aesthetics. It was not built until after his death due to lack of funds.

Turnpike at Hyde Park Corner, with St George's Hospital on the right. The turnpike acts transferred responsibility for the upkeep of roads from the local parishes to newly created turnpike trusts, who were empowered to charge tolls.

early 19th century, associated with the innovations of John Metcalfe (1717–1810, known as Blind Jack of Knaresborough as he was blind from the age of six), Thomas Telford (1757–1834, a Scotsman who also built bridges and lighthouses), and John Loudon McAdam (1756–1836, also a Scottish engineer). During the 18th century the main concern had been to control the vehicles in order to protect the roads rather than to improve surfaces. The weight of vehicles was limited, while the Broad Wheel Act of 1753 required wagons drawn by more than five horses to have nine-inch wide wheels. Although techniques were conservative, repairs were at least more systematic, and the improvement in the roads did offset the increased cost of the tolls to the carriers and coach proprietors. The facilities for road transport were transformed. Wagons pulled by six or eight horses replaced packhorses for the carriage of goods. Specialist firms of carriers established regular services of stage wagons and warehouses along the principal routes; the most famous firm was Pickfords. Similarly, for passenger travel a national network of stage coaches developed in the 1780s and 1790s, reaching a peak in the first third of the 19th century. By 1818, York, for example, had 38 regular coach services leaving daily, whilst the speed increased to 10 miles an hour and above. A journey from London to Bath in 1752 took from 2 am on one day to 7 pm the next, but in 1791 could be done in 15 hours. The fastest coaches were those run by the Post Office after 1784 for the carriage of mail, but generally the business was in the hands of the proprietors of coaching inns who established inns and teams of horses along the route. The largest London firm was Chaplin and Co, which in 1834 had 64 coaches, 1,300 to 1,500 horses, and inns throughout the country.

The coming of the canals took away much of the long distance freight from the roads, whilst the railways took away the long distance passenger traffic. Roads were relegated to feeders to the nearest station, and from the 1840s the turnpike trusts became largely redundant. Road transport by the 1840s was less a matter of stage coaches from London to Bath than of cabs to Paddington, less a matter of stage wagons linking towns as of vans taking parcels to the station or of carts delivering coal from railway sidings. By the middle of the century it was clear that the inter-city turnpikes had had their day. Between 1865 and 1895 the whole system was gradually wound up and the care and maintenance of the roads reverted to the newly emergent local and county councils.

The promoters of railways claimed that they would replace a million horses, and that since each horse took the food of eight men, this would free enough land to feed 8 million people. But in fact the number of horses continued to rise. In London alone in 1840, 2,000 cabs required 4,000 horses, 620 buses required 700 horses, whilst the railway companies had perhaps 500 horses at each terminus to collect and distribute goods. In the early 19th century, commercial vehicles required at least 250,000 horses. Economic growth had at first led to an improvement in the roads for long distance trade, creating the new institution of the turnpike trust, but further growth created the canals and railways, the demise of the trusts, stage wagons and stage coaches. But at the same time, there was the development of a more dense, short distance, horse-drawn road transport. Attention in the future turned to an improved urban road system. The age of the stage coach might have ended, but the age of the horse omnibus and railway company parcel van had arrived.

A 'Continental' chaise of the mid 18th century. Road improvement led to the development of lighter, faster vehicles which could be driven as a sport.

The hansom cab became a familiar sight in Victorian town streets and was nicknamed 'the gondola of London' by Disraeli. This scene is at the Castle Museum, York.

Telford Bridge and toll house at Conway, North Wales, designed by Thomas Telford. The road to Holyhead was a vital link with Ireland, and was rebuilt by the Holyhead Road Commission after 1815 with Telford as surveyor.

North Country mail coaches at The Peacock, Islington, London. At the end of the 18th century a coaching inn would provide teams of horses to take the mail coaches on their first stage out of London.

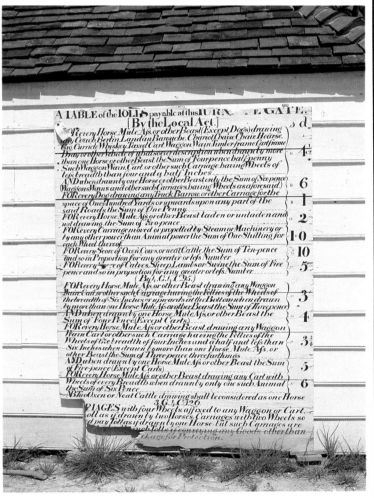

A list of tolls displayed on the Beeding Toll Cottage, now preserved at the Weald & Downland Museum near Chichester. The turnpike trusts laid down in great detail the maximum tolls which could be levied on each class of traffic.

of children; this had tended to happen, even before the Industrial Revolution got properly under way, in industrial villages like those of the East Midlands where framework knitting of stockings offered plentiful opportunities for home employment. In time this was reinforced by the vigorous demand for labour in the early stages of the Industrial Revolution.

The relationship of the demographic to the industrial revolution was one both of cause and effect. It seems reasonable to suppose that the rise in output after 1740 postponed the Malthusian trap, but it is just as probable that the labour needs of an expanding industrial sector could not have been met without the population increase. The expanding population was an essential element in the rising demand to which the manufacturers responded, and in responding they expanded employment opportunities, which in turn encouraged people to marry and produce families earlier than they had done in the past. In short, only an industrial society could have supported a population of the size of that of 19th century Great Britain – the tragedy of Ireland shows this – and only an expanding population could have stimulated the emergence of that industrial society.

The Commercial Revolution

The great expansion of English overseas trade in the latter half of the 17th and the early part of the 18th centuries is sometimes described as a 'Commercial Revolution'. By making supplies of raw materials available and by offering overseas outlets for British-made goods it is seen as an essential precondition for the coming of the Industrial Revolution. Such an expansion of trade encouraged the development of commercial and financial institutions in areas like banking, credit and insurance ahead of the development of the industrial sector, and earnings from trade increased the national income of the country so that it could much better bear the investment needs of the new industrial era than could a simple, agrarian society. The importance of all this is evident, but perhaps the idea of a 'commercial revolution' should also be extended to cover a remarkable expansion in *inland* trade, for the home market too had a sustaining role to play in the Industrial Revolution.

Britain gained much from the great wars which preoccupied 18th-century Europe. Not so directly involved in the struggle for territory and power on the continent itself, she had, largely at the expense of France, secured the true

This engraving commemorates the opening of the Paddington Canal in 1801. It extended the former Grand Junction Canal (which ran from Birmingham to Brentford) to London. Bulk cargoes were carried by fleets of boats and Paddington became a commercial centre. At this time farmland surrounded Paddington and places along the new canal, such as Willesden, Greenford and Southall.

THE AGE OF CANALS

Between the 1750s and the 1820s came the age of canals. There was a quickening rate of investment in making rivers navigable, and many inland towns were linked together via the coasting trade in the only European country to have the advantage of being surrounded by water. Transport costs, especially for bulky goods, were thus lowered, and increased commercial and industrial opportunities were opened up in a way that was crucial for Britain's take-off into economic growth.

The first proper canal of the new age was built between 1755 and 1761 alongside (but quite separate from) the Sankey Brook between the river Mersey and St Helens in Lancashire. Before it was opened, work was begun on a second and more famous canal, that linking the Duke of Bridgewater's coalfields at Worsley with the growing industrial centre of Manchester. As a result, the price of coal in Manchester was halved. In building this canal, the Duke of Bridgewater had the assistance of James Brindley, who came to be known as 'the father of English canals'. He was a working mill-wright with no theoretical education, but with a brilliant practical grasp; it is said that he used to create his designs for complex canal lines and locks by cutting them out of Cheshire cheese.

With Bridgewater and Brindley in the 1760s, water and coal were linked to provide an important basis for the industrial revolution. Brindley worked on canals to serve Leeds, Birmingham, Derby, Salisbury and Glasgow and he began what he called the 'Grand Trunk' which would connect the Mersey with the Trent and ultimately the Severn with the Thames, though he himself did not live to see the completion of this major artery in a nationwide canal system.

The canal-building enthusiasm of the 1760s became the mania of the 1790s. In 1793 alone, twenty new canal routes were authorised by Parliament, involving a total capital outlay of nearly £3 million. The thousands of 'navigators' employed in the construction of the canals left a permanent linguistic tribute: they were the original 'navvies'.

Not all the canals planned in the 1790s were actually realised, but over 4,000 miles of navigable waterways were brought into existence by 1830, when the opening of the Liverpool and Manchester Railway began a new era in transport. Canals lost their monopoly, but by being forced to lower their prices they held their own against railways for another generation, and then went into decline. A few are still in commercial use, and several more can still be navigated by pleasure craft. In many parts of the country, canals in various stages of preservation remain, with their associated distinguished architecture, as an enduring monument to the era of early industrialisation.

Thomas Telford, one of this country's greatest civil engineers, was born in Scotland in 1757 and died in 1834. He was associated with many canal projects, chiefly the Ellesmere, Caledonian and Shropshire Union main line.

James Brindley, a Staffordshire millwright, became the pioneering engineer of British inland navigation. Born 1716, he masterminded many canal schemes, but only the Bridgewater and Trent & Mersey were completed before his death in 1772.

John Rennie (1761–1821) was a Scots farmer's son. He designed road bridges like Southwark over the Thames, docks at Hull and Chatham, and the Plymouth breakwater. His main canals were the Lancaster and the Kennet & Avon.

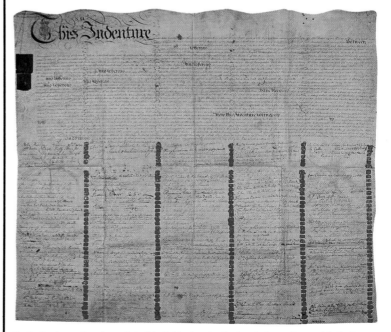

An indenture showing a list of individuals who took out shares to provide further capital for the construction of the Warwick and Birmingham Canal.

Traditional narrow boats of the canals fit a lock 7' by 70'. Engines replaced horses in the 19th century and it became common for a motor boat to tow a 'butty' (unpowered craft). The butty cabin is shown here: living quarters for a family in a confined space. Most Number Ones (who owned their boats) decorated their cabins with bright paintwork. Notice the cast iron cooking range, hand crochet work and 'lace' plates.

The Napton flight of locks on the Oxford Canal (opened 1790), looking southwards from Napton-on-the-Hill. The absence of any hint of urban or industrial development in the photograph typifies this stretch of the canal.

Few original canal boatmen and women remain (left). Younger people have taken to the water to preserve the tradition of coal-carrying by narrow boat. These are moored at Stoke Bruerne on the Grand Union Canal near Northampton, next to the Waterways Museum.

This handsome snake bridge near Congleton in Cheshire spans the Macclesfield Canal (opened 1831). It carries the towing path, which here changes sides of the canal. When the waterway was built, boats were towed by horses, donkeys or mules. The serpentine form allows the towing animal to cross without being unhitched from the boat.

The Leeds & Liverpool Canal (opened 1816) crosses the Pennines, with much of the route over moorland made famous by Charlotte Bronte. One of its most impressive features is the Five Rise of locks at Bingley, Yorkshire, designed by Joseph Bottomley. He used this method to overcome a 60' high gradient. The five locks are all joined together in a 'staircase'.

The demise of the canal brings with it the ruin of its associated buildings. Built with elegant functional craftsmanship, many unique structures are now unwanted, unmaintained and at risk. The warehouse (below) is next to the former Chester Canal Company's headquarters near Northgate Locks; the Chester Canal was one of the early waterways and the first stage, from Chester to Nantwich, was opened in 1779.

Narrow boat folk, wearing their Sunday best, celebrate a canal christening in 1915. When most canals were privately owned, the companies halted all boats on Bank Holidays to carry out maintenance and repairs to the canals and the boat people had a rare, enforced day off. This was during such a 'stoppage' at Buckby Locks near Northampton on the Grand Union Canal.

colonial plums: she had secured control over the resources of Canada, India and, until the American Revolution, the American colonies. Here were raw materials in abundance and markets to be supplied. The value of such overseas possessions is clear. The cotton manufacture of Lancashire was the pioneer of the factory economy; it depended on a foreign-grown raw material, and it exported a high percentage of its output. By the mid 19th century, when a quarter of the world's trade passed through British ports and a third of world industrial output came from British mines, mills and workshops, two thirds of the annual value of exports came from textiles and a half from Lancashire alone. Raw cotton imports rose prodigiously from under 5 million lbs per annum in 1778–9 to more than 800 million by 1860.

In the crucial formative years 1750 to 1780, however, it seems likely that the growth of the home market was the significant factor. Income per head was rising, and was, relatively speaking, more evenly distributed in Britain than in her continental rivals. However great by today's standards might seem to have been the gap between the rich and the poor of the 18th century, by the standards of France or Germany, let alone Russia, it was narrow. On the continent a self-sufficient peasantry living on the edge of subsistence exerted little purchasing power for manufactured goods, while the rich sought only luxuries. In Britain not only did a large range of middle class people separate the rich from the poor, but even the latter, if we include among them small working tradesmen, exerted a formidable aggregate purchasing power, so that a demand for mass consumer goods became the driving force behind the factory system at a time when continental craftsmen were still concentrating on luxury goods.

Contemporaries frequently commented on the growing consumer demands of the lower orders as they aspired to imitate their betters. Foreigners were astonished at the style of dress and pretensions of the middle and lower classes. Henry Fielding remarked in 1751 that aping one's betters had permeated to the very dregs of society, while a writer in the *British Magazine* in 1763 remarked:

The present rage of imitating the manners of high-life hath spread itself so far among the gentlefolks of lower life, that in a few years we shall probably have no common people at all.

Exaggeration was widespread among such commentators, but complaints that it was becoming impossible to tell masters from their servants were too frequently forthcoming to have been entirely illusory. Even at the lowest levels of society commodities like soap, earthenware utensils, watches and clothes were being regularly purchased, while the paupers outraged their betters by insisting on consuming such luxuries as tea and white bread!

The course and nature of the Industrial Revolution

Having established the reasons for the increased demand for British manufactured goods, we can consider how the manufacturers responded to it. Government attitudes and prevailing ideologies during the period of the Industrial Revolution were favourable to profit-seeking entrepreneurs. Adam Smith in his famous *Wealth of Nations* in 1776 was giving intellectual force to ideas and assumptions which had long been established among manufacturers and merchants. The laws of the market and the dangers of governmental interference with those laws had been constantly

THE IMPACT OF THE RAILWAY

Ancestors of the modern railway can be traced at least as far back as the early 16th century, when wagons running on parallel wooden planks were used in coal mines. Later extended down to nearby rivers, these wagonways had become quite extensive in mining districts by the end of the 18th century. Iron rails had replaced the wooden planks; the basic principle of the railway – flanged iron wheels running on iron rails – had become established.

Horse power was the order of the day on the first public railway, the Surrey Iron Railway of 1803, and on the Oystermouth Railway at Swansea, opened in 1807, which was the first to carry passengers. In 1804, Richard Trevithick had successfully demonstrated a steam locomotive on the Pen-y-Darren Tramway in South Wales, though it was some time before problems of adhesion could be overcome. Blenkinsop's rack system achieved this on the Middleton Railway at Leeds in 1812, but a year later Hedley's *Puffing Billy* proved that sufficient natural adhesion could be obtained between wheel and rail to dispense with the cumbersome rack.

Wylam, near Newcastle, scene of *Puffing Billy*'s triumph, was by coincidence the birthplace of George Stephenson, the colliery engineman who foresaw the potential of the railway as a countrywide transport system for goods and passengers. It was Stephenson who engineered the Stockton & Darlington Railway of 1825, enshrined in history as the world's first public steam railway.

The S & D was a great commercial success but, while the cost advantage of the embryonic steam locomotive was soon realised, poor reliability caused most trains to remain horse-drawn. It was with the Liverpool & Manchester line of 1830 that the railway age really began. Here, Stephenson combined for the first time all the ingredients of the modern railway – lavish engineering works to achieve a favourable route; steam traction for goods and passenger trains; timetabled services; a double-track route with rudimentary signalling. Above all, the line was built by entrepreneurs with the specific intention of undercutting the waterways whose monopoly was strangling growth of the two great northern towns.

Conclusive proof of steam's superiority was provided once and for all at the Rainhill Trials of 1829, when the directors of the L & M offered a £500 prize to the steam locomotive whose performance matched a set of most stringent criteria. Other entrants were soundly beaten by George Stephenson's *Rocket*, dispelling all thought that L & M trains might be rope-hauled by stationary steam engines.

Widespread interest in the Stockton & Darlington experiment crystallised with the runaway success of the Liverpool & Manchester. Before long, cities and towns up and down the country were clamouring for their own railway connections, though some others were equally fervent in their opposition to the 'iron road'. By the end of the decade, 1,500 miles of route had been laid, with London already linked to the major industrial towns of the west Midlands and the north west.

The mid 1840s saw a dramatic rise in the number of schemes proposed, as the country became gripped by a 'railway mania'. Everyone wanted a share in the high profits of the early lines, and more than 4,500 miles of route were approved by Parliament in 1846 alone. Most spectacular of those who won and lost fortunes in the rush was George Hudson, creator of the Midland Railway, and known as the 'Railway King'. The financial crash of 1847 ended much of the speculation, but not before Hudson, and other less than scrupulous promotors, had helped lay the foundations of the main lines and the great companies of the railway age.

The railways provided the vital catalyst that fused together all other elements of the Industrial Revolution. Swift, efficient and cheap transport meant that raw materials and finished goods could be moved around the country at will, feeding new industries and serving new markets. The canals had begun the process, but only the railways could carry it through.

Puffing Billy. A problem with the very early steam locomotives was their inability to provide sufficient adhesion between wheel and rail; although they could haul themselves along, they were unable to shift loads. William Hedley, manager of the colliery at Wylam near Newcastle, made extensive experiments and as a result built *Puffing Billy* in 1813. Despite the complexity of the drive between cylinders and wheels, the locomotive was a success, proving that sufficient adhesion could be obtained to pull a train on all but the steepest gradients.

Steam-hauled goods, 1830s style! The technical advance of railways owes much to Stephenson, whose ideas were put into practice on the Liverpool & Manchester Railway.

The Liverpool & Manchester railway abounded in substantial engineering works, including the 70 ft deep Olive Mount Cutting outside Liverpool with its Moorish arch. It is depicted on this commemorative jug.

Stephenson's Rocket, winner of the Rainhill Trials, confirmed the superiority of steam over horse traction and laid the foundations for Victorian locomotive practice.

Construction of a railway cutting. There was a ready made workforce in the labourers who had been involved in canal construction — the navvies. Civil engineering techniques developed rapidly with railway construction.

2-2-2 locomotive Columbine, built by the London & North Western Railway at Crewe in 1845. Designed by Alexander Allan, the Crewe-type locomotive with its outside cylinders influenced locomotive design for over 40 years.

London Bridge station was opened in 1844 by the South Eastern, London & Brighton and London & Greenwich railways, but was demolished in 1849.

Derby joint station, designed by Francis Thompson and built in 1839–41, had a three-span light iron roof which originally covered only a single platform.

stressed in opposition to any lingering tendency to control prices, prevent the use of labour-displacing machinery or insist on preserving statutory apprenticeship to hinder the employment of cheaper, unskilled labour. *Laissez-faire* was triumphant, and in England a landowning class, itself busily engaged in farming for the market and rationalising agricultural methods, was hardly likely to offer the entrenched resistance to bourgeois values shown by continental aristocracies.

At first increasing demand was met by intensifying existing methods of production. Capitalist entrepreneurs put out work to increasing numbers of hand workers; weavers, framework knitters and metalworkers expanded as output increased. As a second stage machinery was substituted for hand labour, the factory for the home. Supervision and quality control, even a concern to limit the

amount of embezzlement of materials by home workers, were early motivations for establishing factories, but the opportunity to use power-driven machinery made their advance irreversible. Textiles led the way. A series of inventions came in rapid succession, transforming first the cotton manufacture and then that of woollen and worsted. First Lancashire and then the West Riding of Yorkshire witnessed the birth and spread of the factory town and the industrial proletariat.

The first inventions did not presuppose the need for the factory. John Kay's Flying Shuttle of 1733 was intended to speed the pace of handloom weaving. James Hargreaves' Spinning Jenny of 1770 replaced the wheel, but until it increased in size and spindlage it was used in the home. Things changed with Richard Arkwright's water frame for roller spinning, which led to the establishment of the first

SHIPPING AND PORTS

One of the key distinguishing features of the 18th century was an upsurge of a sense of expansion – most visibly in terms of commerce and trade. The quickening pace of industrial production at home led to increased demand both for more raw materials from abroad and constantly expanding markets in which to sell finished goods. As the century advanced, the speed by which trade expanded increased rapidly: many more factories were built, more and deeper canals were cut, and a network of railways was appearing.

The wars of the 18th century against France were essentially struggles for territorial expansion coupled with an obsession to acquire the sources of required raw materials: sugar, cotton, dyes, spices, tobacco. On balance, England emerged the stronger from these military confrontations, but the loss of the American possessions was an unparalleled disaster.

Naval activity during this period was intense, with fleets operating in the Mediterranean, Indian Ocean, the West Indies, St Lawrence and in home waters. The ships themselves abandoned their ponderous, over-decorated configurations in favour of hulls of more utilitarian proportions; the sizes of warships were standardised and precise classes of fighting vessel appeared. The rates, a term applied in the previous century, were now rigidly

adhered to. Frigates with one gun deck and their smaller sisters, sloops and corvettes, were built in large numbers for patrol and blockade work and to act as the eyes of the battle fleet, while the role of the most useful ships in the battle fleet, the 74s – the third rates with two gun decks – was enhanced.

Both warships and merchant ships benefited from considerable technical advances, maritime manifestations of the innovative impact and confidence of newly-industrialised Britain. Most important was copper sheathing of the hull, necessary to resist the ravages of the shipworm, whose boring activities, particularly in the tropics, if left unchecked would reduce a vessel to a waterlogged hulk in a matter of weeks. Tremendous strides were also made in the science of navigation with the introduction of the reflecting quadrant and, later in the 18th century, of the chronometer. Hitherto, ships had relied on inaccurate, altitude-finding instruments to ascertain their latitude and on dead reckoning for their longitude. The Hadley quadrant, introduced in 1731, was an accurate observing instrument, while the chronometer perfected by 1762 and used by Cook on his second Pacific voyage kept the time on the meridian of Greenwich, the difference between Greenwich time and ship's time allowing for the accurate

calculation of longitude.

It was no accident that Cook's exploring voyages were undertaken in merchant colliers impressed into naval service. Cook was brought up in the east coast coal trade and he was fully acquainted with the maritime qualities of the Newcastle, Shields and Whitby brigs and barks. By the 18th century merchant ships were becoming more specialised, designed more carefully for their ocean-traversing work. At the top of the scale were the elegant, well-built East Indiamen, up to 1,200 tons burden by 1800. They were run on naval lines and, indeed, carried a considerable armament. From Glasgow, Liverpool and Bristol came the smaller West Indiamen and Guineamen, some in the slave trade. All were three-masted, full-rigged ships as they came to be called, but behind them appeared a host of smaller vessels, brigs, brigantines, schooners, cutters, spritsail barges, herring luggers. Whereas the square sail provided the necessary driving power for the larger ships, the fore and aft gave increased manoeuvrability. When combined with the square sail, this produced a highly adaptable vessel of peculiarly British and Irish design, the topsail schooner.

Building the ships needed to handle and protect the trade and marine traffic of industrial Britain put a great strain on the country's timber resources; between 3,000 and 4,000 oak trees were needed to build Nelson's *Victory*, just one first-rate ship-of-the-line. By the early decades of the 19th century the forests

were becoming denuded and more reliance came to be placed on iron fittings and fastenings, a prelude in fact to the development of the iron ship.

Most of the shipyards of the period had changed little through the centuries; they were mostly small local enterprises sited up rivers and creeks, anywhere where there was space to lay a slip, stack timber for seasoning and dig a sawpit. The Royal Dockyards were, however, on a considerable scale with their ropewalks, sail lofts and, later, block making machinery, representing an early example of the marine production line.

Along with increased shipbuilding activity went port development to deal with both bigger ships and bigger cargoes. Enclosed docks were needed which would maintain a constant water level and so speed cargo handling. They could be entered through gates at high water or through a lock which would allow ships to come and go at any state of the tide. They could be designed to provide as many berths as were required, and enlarged if the traffic demanded. Equipped with warehouses and cranes and fed by the new canals, turnpike roads and eventually railways, the new ports, like Liverpool and Hull, handled ever larger tonnages. Thus they were forced to build more and more docks, Liverpool ending with a seven-mile system. But this took more than a century to complete and the bulk of it was designed for the steamship.

The Customs House, Poole, Dorset, is a fine example of 18th century architecture. Any port receiving overseas trade was required to have a customs house, and Poole's was built at a time when the port handled a considerable trade with Newfoundland. Today, it continues as the office of H.M. Customs and Excise.

Steamships quickly captured the coastal passenger trade since they provided an infinitely more comfortable and reliable means of travel than the road coach. Between 1810 and 1840 the British Isles were served by a wealth of competing steam packet companies, many of which also operated in continental trades.

spinning mill at Cromford in 1771. Samuel Crompton's Spinning Mule of 1779 was a combination of the jenny and the water frame that produced a smoother and finer yarn, and could easily be adapted to steam power.

In the 1790s the cotton spinning mill became commonplace, and by 1812 one factory spinner could produce as much in a given time as 200 domestic spinners could have done before the invention of the jenny. The modernisation of weaving lagged behind, and the handloom weavers considerably increased to convert the factory yarn into saleable cloth. The handloom weavers are often presented as the archetypal victims of the Industrial Revolution, but it should be remembered that they were first of all its creation in that they multiplied in response to the growth of the spinning mills. Edmund Cartwright invented a power loom in 1787, but it remained experimental until after the Napo-

leonic Wars and only began to be introduced on a considerable scale in the 1820s, 30s and 40s. Worker resistance and 'luddism' played a part in its slow introduction. Manchester was the major centre of production, and with other towns like Bolton, Preston, Oldham and Blackburn worked at an industry which from its origins to the present day remained firmly located in Lancashire, although with a base in Scotland, in Lanarkshire, where the socialist Robert Owen ran his famous factory.

The transformation of cotton manufacture had taken less than three decades, but progress in the woollen and worsted industries, the staple manufactures of pre-industrial England, was comparatively less rapid. Partly this reflected entrenched working habits in a centuries-old manufacture, but also the fact that wool as a fibre is more difficult to work by machinery than cotton. After a slow start there was rapid progress,

An elaborate trade union banner awarded to a Sunderland member of the United Society of Boilermakers and Iron and Steel Shipbuilders.

Hull's dock system was opened in 1778. It was entered from the River Hull by a pair of tidal gates. This dock was desperately needed because there was no space in the tidal Old Harbour to handle the increasing number of ships coming into Hull.

A dry compass card: the magnetic needles were inserted underneath.

Harrison's No. 4 marine clock (right), the first to keep Greenwich time at sea.

THE SOUTH WEST PROSPECT OF LIVERPOOLE, IN THE COUNTY PALATINE OF LANCASTER.

Liverpool's first dock, completed in 1715, can be seen in this engraving by the brothers Sebastian and Nathaniel Buck, whose prints provide an accurate guide to our cities in the early 18th century. Extensions were soon needed and two more docks were completed in 1753 and 1771, the start of Liverpool's great system.

however, for by 1850 the horsepower capacity of woollen and worsted machinery had doubled by comparison with 1835. Before the Industrial Revolution there had been several major centres of the industry of which the West Riding towns of Leeds, Halifax, Bradford and Wakefield had been only one. The other major regions had been the light-worsted cloth production centred on Norwich and surrounding East Anglian towns and villages; the long established broad woollen cloth region of the west country centred on Wiltshire, Gloucestershire and parts of Somerset and involving towns like Devizes, Chippenham, Trowbridge, Warminster, Gloucester, Minchinhampton, Frome and Bradford-on-Avon; while further west still was the old serge manufacture of the Exe valley, centred on Exeter and carried on in towns like Tiverton, Bradninch and Taunton. With the coming of the factory all regions other than the West Riding went into decline, as Yorkshire took advantage of its coal and the stimulation of being adjacent to the technologically advanced cotton manufacture.

The machine production of textiles would not have been possible without advances in coal mining, iron making and engineering. There was then, as now, no lack of coal reserves in Britain; the main problem was to find an efficient method of pumping out the water as deeper levels were worked. Here steam power provided the solution. The mining industry rather than the mill or the locomotive was the initial stimulus to the development of steam technology. Thomas Savery had invented a form of steam driven engine in 1698, but the modern development begins with the coal-fed engine of Thomas Newcomen in 1712. Until the improvements of James Watt, these engines proved vital to the extension not just of coal mining, but also of the expanding tin and copper mines of Cornwall. This region, being situated far from coal supplies, found the Newcomen engine increasingly expensive to use as mines went ever deeper, and so the Cornish mine owners became natural customers for the engines of James Watt when his patenting of the separate condenser in 1769 dramatically lowered fuel costs.

Machine construction demands a constant supply of quality iron. At the beginning of the 18th century the British iron industry was in crisis as the timber it needed to produce the charcoal for smelting became increasingly scarce and expensive, and old centres like the Sussex Weald could no longer maintain adequate levels of output. The solution was produced by the Shropshire ironmaster Abraham Darby, who discovered how to produce good iron by smelting with coke at his famous Coalbrookdale works between 1709 and 1714. Now the iron industry moved to the coalfields, not only to Shropshire but also to the north east where the famous Crawley works were among Europe's largest in the 18th century, and to South Wales. Darby's method was a breakthrough, but it had limitations: the use of coke in the forge, that is in the conversion of pig iron into bar iron, introduced impurities which lessened the reliability of the finished product. At Coalbrookdale the use of a reverbatory furnace intermediate between founding and forging overcame this, but the added cost narrowed the advantage of using coke instead of charcoal. In 1784 Henry Cort patented a puddling and rolling process which overcame the problem of coke impurities at a price which effectively finished the use of charcoal for other than quality steel production. Cort's process was taken up most rapidly in South Wales where Richard Crawshay had been quick to introduce the method. Nielson's subsequent discovery of

ARCHITECTURE AND BUILDINGS

The population of Great Britain rose from less than seven million in 1700 to over 26 million in 1850. The country's economy was meanwhile being transformed by the Industrial and Agricultural Revolutions, and these developments created an unprecedented demand for buildings of all kinds, especially for houses.

Most people still lived in the country. In an age when the economically fittest were best equipped to survive, the old rural peasant farming class gradually died away. In England the peasant farmers were slowly absorbed into the large and growing class of landless labourers; in the highlands of Scotland, however, the process was more abrupt, as vast areas were cleared for sheep-farming, and those who did not emigrate were re-housed in new villages closer to the coast where they could engage in what were judged to be more economically rewarding activities. Many villages in the north of Scotland are a witness to this process. The growing number of English farm labourers were housed either in the existing villages or in new (or enlarged) hamlet settlements which had often grown up on the edges of commons. Farm labourers' cottages were built by small speculative builders, either in rows or haphazardly in ones or twos wherever patches of land were available. They rarely contained more than two or three rooms, and were often cramped and insanitary. Sometimes, when a village belonged to one man, it

was completely rebuilt by the landlord, often on a new site, and to a rather high standard. The designs of these planned villages reflect the architectural changes which were taking place in the country houses of their owners; for much of the 18th century they were simple and restrained, but at the end of the century formality gave way to 'picturesque' groupings, and restrained simplicity to the rural never-never land evoked by the *cottage orné*. Agricultural change, meanwhile, improved the status of the better-off farmers and they rebuilt their houses, often in the middle of newly-enclosed farms, leaving the old village farmhouses to be divided up as labourers' cottages.

The rural population continued to expand throughout this period, but it was in the towns that the most spectacular rise in population took place. Urban housing developments were influenced at first by formal Renaissance ideas of design. Covent Garden in London, built as early as the 1630s, was the first place in Britain to introduce the principle of the square with houses arranged in an orderly fashion around an open space, and a church at one end; this form (with variations in the form of the circle and the crescent) remained popular until the middle of the 19th century. Estates like this were planned by developers, who leased the land from the landowner, built the houses and then sold the leases.

Internal design changed remarkably

Cumberland Terrace, overlooking Regent's Park, London, was designed by John Nash in 1826. The stucco-faced façades evoke a mood of classical magnificence.

The Circus at Bath (1754–8), reflecting the plan of a Roman amphitheatre, was part of an elaborate scheme prepared by John Wood and his son to expand the town.

little; a narrow street frontage, behind which were service rooms at the bottom and pairs of rooms one behind the other going up through several stories. The facades were always of brick or stone (in London timber was outlawed after the Great Fire of 1666), but from the end of the 18th century it became common to cover the brickwork in new houses with stucco, and to introduce cast-iron balconies which can be seen in large numbers in towns like Cheltenham. It was only at the beginning of the 19th century that semi-detached houses began to be built, and estates laid out on more irregular lines. The most impressive housing developments were in the larger towns, but many of the smaller country towns flourished too; improvements in road and river communications led to a need for larger inns and hotels, and as wealth increased the more wealthy inhabitants rebuilt their houses, often adding a brick or stone facade to an earlier timber-framed building.

Middle-class housing developments, impressive though they were, affected only a minority of the urban population. Disparities in wealth became increasingly apparent, when the French writer Alexis de Tocqueville visited Manchester in 1835 he wrote:

On the watery land, which water and art has contributed to keep damp, are scattered palaces and hovels . . . Amid this noisome labyrinth, this great sombre stretch of brick, from time to time one is astonished at the sight of fine stone buildings with Corinthian columns. It might be a mediaeval town with the marvels of the 19th century in the middle of it.

The great expansion of wealth in 19th-century England, like the concentration of large numbers of people in overcrowded manufacturing cities, was the result of industrialisation. In the early stages of the Industrial Revolution some stages of textile manufacture were still carried out on the 'domestic system', and throughout the 19th century a large proportion of the industrial working class (for instance coal miners) lived in industrial villages rather than cities. Once steam-power was applied to manufacturing, however, factories could be concentrated in towns where speculators could be relied upon to construct cheap housing for the workers. At worst working-class housing was shockingly bad — cellars and greatly overcrowded 'courts' lacking even the most elementary sanitary provision — and by the middle of the 19th century the existence of these slums was beginning to be recognised as an important social problem, though little was actually done about it for a long time. Industrial towns were products of *laissez-faire*, and it is therefore not surprising that their centres should remain for a long time unplanned. As civic pride began to burgeon, however, they began to be provided with buildings commensurate with the wealth of the towns. These buildings — town halls, literary and scientific institutions, banks and later on railway stations — were at first almost always classical in inspiration, either Grecian or Italianate. Taken together they could, despite the grime with which they were very soon covered, stand as an apt symbol of the wealth and confidence of the 'captains of industry who created the world's first industrial society.

Church Row, Hampstead. This house, built in the 1720s, follows the fashion pioneered in London in the 17th century and modified by the Building Acts of 1707 and 1709, which greatly limited the use of external woodwork. Most London houses of the 18th century were built of brick; here contrasting shades of brick are used.

Woburn Walk, London, was built by Thomas Cubitt in 1822 to serve the expanding residential area of Bloomsbury. The panes of glass in the shop windows are small, since plate glass was not yet being manufactured.

Peckover House, Cambs, was built in about 1722 on the bank of the Nene at Wisbech, a prosperous inland port.

No. 10 Downing Street, London. The entrance was remodelled in 1766.

Working class houses, like these in Leeds, were built in vast numbers in the industrial towns of the Midlands and north of England in the early 19th century. Building controls were virtually non-existent, and houses crowded into the most exiguous spaces. Leeds became notorious for its 'blind back' and 'back to back' houses; here there are separate dwellings on each floor, and those on the upper floor do not appear to have consisted of more than one or two rooms apiece.

Roupell Street, London. Artisan cottages were built in large numbers in the expanding towns of early 19th century England. With two rooms on each floor, they provided cramped but more comfortable accommodation than the cellar dwellings and 'rookeries' of the poor. The doors and windows reflect those of contemporary grander houses.

the advantages of a hot air blast in lowering coke consumption was particularly valuable for Scotland, where the black-band ironstone had been unusable before the hot blast method arrived and where there was plentiful coal but of poor coking quality.

The Midlands ironmaster John Wilkinson invented in 1775 a cylinder-boring machine which may be regarded as the first machine tool and brought new standards of accuracy to the making of machinery. In their famous Soho works in Birmingham, Matthew Boulton, the industrialist, and James Watt, the inventor, brought nearer throughout their long partnership the era of mass-produced efficient machinery, step by step, process by process. One major advance however still lay in the future. Until Henry Bessemer patented his converter in 1856, steel of a consistent quality could only be produced by traditional charcoal methods. The Industrial Revolution in Britain may have been an age of iron; it was not yet one of steel.

The material achievement of industrial Britain by the mid 19th century was truly impressive. The index of all industrial production excluding building rose dramatically, yet many important areas of manufacture had not changed very strikingly in their methods of production. Small workshops continued to dominate the greatest centre of British hardware manufacture, Birmingham, a town which on its own produced three million muskets for the British forces in the French Wars. It was the major centre for the production of all kinds of brass, copper and enamel ware. At Wolverhampton locks were still made by locksmiths working on their own premises, while the famous cutlery trade of Sheffield was similarly carried on by craftsmen at small forges. Josiah Wedgwood had transformed the Staffordshire pottery manufacture, but the organisation of labour, not the application of power, was the rationale of his famous factory Etruria: 'I must make', he boasted, 'such machines of men as cannot err'. These industries and many more, including the factories of Lancashire and Yorkshire, the coal mines, the copper and tin mines, the iron forges and the largest single employer of all, farming, contributed to the astonishing fact that over the century ending in the 1850s the national

Wedgwood's Etruria manufactory was built in 1769 for the production of mass-market pottery. Leading 18th century industrialists like Wedgwood demanded efficiency which meant that the large factories usually offered better working conditions, but imposed stricter discipline than the unruly small potbanks.

CHURCHES AND CHAPELS

The 18th century Church of England has had a bad press, mostly undeserved. The church had lost members in the 1660s when many Puritans became dissenters, and again in the 1690s when some bishops and clergy felt unable to take the oath of allegiance to King William III. The two secessions had greatly weakened the church, and caused its later Victorian critics to regard it as decadent and lethargic. But recent research has shown this to be far from true. Many examples of Georgian Anglican churches have survived, and they fall into three distinct categories.

Firstly, there are the churches constructed in the principal expanding towns. Most of these were built by private subscription and the minister paid by those who rented the pews. The architecture was usually classical, with high box-pews, commanding pulpits, and elaborate altar-pieces containing representations of the Ten Commandments and portraits of Moses and Aaron. Virtually every large town has at least one such church although, in recent years, many of those situated in areas no longer residential in character have become redundant.

Secondly, there are the churches built on country estates by the nobility and gentry which, though technically parish churches, were treated as — and still look like — private chapels. Some of these were in the classical style, but from the late 18th century a number were built in a romantic version of Gothic. The best example of this sort of 'Gothick' church is Shobdon in Hereford and Worcester, with delightful carpeted and cushioned pews, and elaborate plastered ceilings, painted in pink, white and blue, giving a sugary wedding-cake effect. Many of the family pews in these chapels were provided with fireplaces for greater comfort. They needed them, for the morning service of Mattins, Litany and Ante-Communion, with Holy Communion once a quarter or even once a month could last anything up to three hours.

Thirdly, there are the churches that were enlarged or altered in the 18th century and have been left intact since; usually a jumble of box-pews and galleries constructed by a local carpenter. Most of these unrestored churches are to be found in the country — Launcells in Cornwall, Molland and Parracombe in Devon, Inglesham and Old Dilton in Wiltshire, Minstead in Hampshire — but there are a few in the towns such as St Mary's, Whitby, and Holy Trinity, Goodramgate, York.

The weak state of the Church of England led to a rise in nonconformity and there are several Independent and Unitarian chapels dating from the 18th century. Later on there arose the movement known as Methodism, which began its existence within the Church of England and eventually seceded from it. Methodism was particularly strong in Cornwall and Yorkshire. In Wales various groups of nonconformists, Independents, Baptists and Calvinistic Methodists, flourished to become in effect, though not in law, the religious establishment of the country, and their simple chapels dominate the Welsh landscape. Most have altered over the years, but a few of the early ones have survived intact. By the 18th century the Roman Catholics were also being permitted to build their own churches, though most of those that survive were private chapels built by Roman Catholic landed families such as the Welds. They built chapels attached to their houses at Lulworth in Dorset and Wardour Castle in Wiltshire.

In Scotland, with Presbyterianism firmly established, the 18th century was a period of considerable religious building and many earlier churches were pulled down and rebuilt. There was little challenge to Presbyterianism. The surviving Episcopalians, those loyal to the Scottish bishops imposed on the Scottish church in the 17th century, were a small and impoverished body. And it was not until the 19th century that serious splits developed in the Church of Scotland on a scale equivalent to Methodism within the Church of England.

Parish Church of St Mary, Whitby, Yorkshire. This medieval church — begun in 1100 — underwent a series of alterations right up to the late 18th century, when it was extended to cater for a growing seaport town. The exterior view (above), with Caedmon's Cross in the foreground, shows the jumble of medieval and Georgian work. The interior (below) is, however, almost entirely Georgian with its handsome three-decker pulpit and box pews.

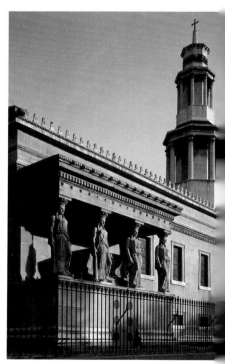

New Parish Church of St Pancras, London (above and right), is the first Greek Revival church in Britain, built between 1819 and 1822 to the designs of H. W. and W. Inwood. At the west end is a portico with six fluted Ionic columns, whilst at the east end there are additions on both sides with decidedly pagan sculptured maidens by Rossi.

Church of Scotland Parish Church, Carrington, Lothian. A typical early 18th century Scottish exterior, in a style of architecture which combines the traditional shape of a medieval church with the austerity of a non conformist chapel.

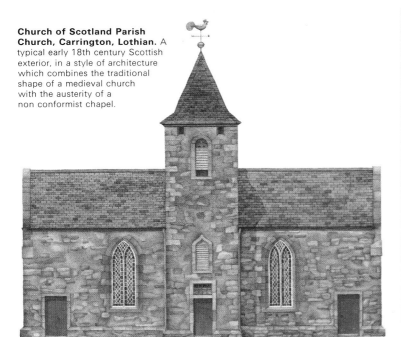

Wesley's New Room, Bristol (above and below). The earliest Methodist church in Britain, it was opened in 1739. The exterior is plain and set well back from the street. Inside is a contemporary galleries and pulpit arrangement.

Chapel of St Mary, East Lulworth, Dorset (above and below). One of the few surviving pre-Victorian Roman Catholic churches was built as a private chapel for Thomas Weld in 1786–7. To avoid controversy the exterior was designed not to look like a church, but rather like one of the large garden temples then fashionable. The interior has four apses, three with galleries supported by Tuscan columns, the fourth containing the altar space. There are fine collections of contemporary plate and vestments.

Octagon Unitarian Chapel, Norwich, Norfolk (above and right). Very much grander than Wesley's New Room though only a little later, the interior has galleries supported on eight giant Corinthian columns. The fittings are mostly contemporary though the pulpit and organ composition was altered in 1889. The chapel has an octagonal pyramid roof with dormers, hence its name.

Parish Church of St John, Shobdon, Hereford and Worcester (above and below). The church was rebuilt in a delightful 'Gothick' style. The interior is painted in pale blue, pink and white. Note the tripartite pendant ogee arches.

Parish Church of St Mary, Molland, Devon. A typical pre-Victorian west country church interior with box pews, low three-decker pulpit and solid tympanum over the rood screen.

product of Britain increased almost two and a half times.

After union with Scotland in 1707 Great Britain formed the largest free trade area in Europe, with no internal tariff barriers or prohibitions to perpetuate regional economies. Effective realisation of the potential this afforded depended upon the development of an adequate transport system, not only to enable finished goods to reach their markets but, even more importantly, to carry heavy raw materials, especially coal, to the centres of production. Other countries, especially those like the United States or Russia with vast continental interiors, awaited the arrival of the railway before their industrialisation could effectively get under way. Britain, however, had been moving towards an industrial economy for 70 years before the railway played any significant role.

Her long coastline and good harbours favoured the development of an important coasting trade. Collier vessels had brought the coal from the Tyne and Wear down the east coast to London since Tudor times – Shakespeare's 'sea coal' – and its importance increased through the 18th century. Other coastal routes developed: for example, coal from South Wales was shipped to Cornwall where it was needed to fuel the Watt steam engines which drained the booming copper mines. The copper ore was then carried back to South Wales to be smelted at Neath and Swansea. Timber was more efficiently and cheaply carried in coastal vessels than by overland methods.

The canals

The most striking development in water borne transport in the 18th century – and indeed the most important innovation before the railway – lay in the improvement and construction of inland waterways: the second half of the century can be called 'the Canal Age'. The peak was reached in the last decade with no less than 81 Acts for canal construction being obtained in the 'canal mania' of 1790–94. The early Industrial Revolution needed a high capacity, low cost system and the canals provided this; transport by water was as low as 1d per ton-mile, while by land it cost 6d or more, hence the vital role of canals in moving heavy bulk goods like coal. In that they required a very large capital outlay in the expectation of returns over a long period, they also symbolised the growing role of capital investment.

Not always, but often enough, canals paid good dividends to their financiers. The Oxford Canal paid 30 per cent for more than 30 years, while the shares of the old Birmingham canal originally worth £140 were fetching £900 in 1792. In 1825 the average dividend of the ten most successful canals was 27.6 per cent.

The length of navigable waterway was first extended by improving rivers. From around 700 miles in the early 17th century they had reached 1160 miles by 1725, by which time they had reached the industrial north; for example, the Aire and Calder Navigation linked Wakefield and Leeds by the 1720s. Thirty-ton vessels towed by a single horse or hauled by gangs of men developed trade up and down this extended river system. The Weaver, a tributary of the Mersey, was made navigable in 1732 and by doubling salt shipments forced attention on fuel supply to the salt-works. There was no available river, so the Sankey brook, little more than a stream, was formed into an eight-mile-long canal which rose through nine locks and was opened in 1757. This was followed by the building of the first section of the Bridgewater Canal, which was the first true 'dead water' canal, from the coalmines at Worsley to Stretford on the turnpike

COUNTRY HOUSES AND THE LANDSCAPE GARDENERS

The 18th century and early 19th century were in many respects the halcyon days of the British aristocracy. Their political power was matched by increasing revenue from their 'improved' estates, and their social prestige endowed them with the sense of effortless superiority reflected in the portraits of Reynolds, Gainsborough and Lawrence. The 'leaders of society' in the 18th century saw themselves as inheritors of the traditions of ancient Rome, and their veneration for classical antiquity goes a long way towards accounting for the architectural style of their houses, as well as for that most English of art forms, the landscape garden. The poet Alexander Pope exhorted Lord Burlington, a munificent patron and amateur architect of great talent to

'Erect new wonders and the old repair;
Jones and Palladio to themselves restore,
And be whate'er Vitruvius was before.'

Houses like Burlington's villa at Chiswick with their crisp, clean outlines and rich internal arrangements demonstrate the results of this successful attempt to purge British architecture of the accretions of the Baroque.

The landscaped gardens which surround the Palladian houses of the 18th century do not seem at first to be so overtly classical in inspiration until we remember that contemporaries believed the ancients to have followed nature in their gardens, rather than imposing an artificial pattern on it. As early as 1711 Lord Shaftesbury, an influential writer on aesthetics, had declared: 'I shall no longer resist the passion in me for things of a natural kind'. The landscaped garden as evolved by Bridgeman, Kent and 'Capability' Brown presented nature on an idealised form; as Horace Walpole said, 'every journey is made through a succession of pictures'. Gardens were carefully planned, so that a series of contrasting views, often containing temples and similar buildings, would present itself to the viewer. At the same time the invention of the ha-ha, or concealed fence, enabled the gardener to 'call in the distant view', and extend the illusion of ownership as far as the eye could see, very often over a landscape which had also been transformed by the enclosure of open fields and commons. The view from the house, however, did not always include the homes of its dependants who were sometimes removed to 'model villages' out of sight on the fringes of the estate.

The country house was the focal point of the estate. It was still a self-sufficient economic unit with its own brewhouse, bakehouse and laundry, which were often arranged with the stables around a courtyard adjoining the house. Its main function was hospitality, and there was an increasing stress on comfort, but

Cronkhill, Salop, was designed by John Nash in 1802. With its irregular elevations, and asymmetrical plan, it embodies many of the principles of the Picturesque.

Harlaxton Manor, Lincolnshire, designed by Anthony Salvin and built in 1831, is perhaps the most spectacular of all the country houses built in the 'Elizabethan' revival style by the squires and aristocrats of Regency and Victorian England.

owners were also very eager to display their possessions. Guests conversed among works of art, often acquired on Grand Tours, and many houses took on something of the character of museums to be visited by seekers after culture, or after a glimpse of the great, just as they are today — Horace Walpole even printed admission tickets for Strawberry Hill. The house itself was in many respects a work of art, with specially designed furniture, and the walls and ceilings planned to evoke the emotions appropriate to each particular room. As the century progressed and archaeological discoveries revealed more about the internal arrangements of the houses of ancient Rome, the decoration of these rooms became more delicate and refined. The Adam brothers wrote in 1778 about 'a remarkable improvement which had recently taken place in 'the form, convenience, arrangement, and relief of apartments; a greater movement and variety in the outside composition, and in the inside, an almost total change', for which they took considerable credit themselves.

The archaeological interests which led to new discoveries about the ancient world also evoked a new interest in English architecture of the past. Gothic revival houses were being built as early as the 1750s, although they bore little resemblance to anything that had been built in the Middle Ages. Old English houses appealed to people of the late 18th century partly because of their romantic associations in an age when 'sensibility' was coming into vogue. They were also admired because they seemed to fit well into the landscape. As a new generation of writers and travellers went in search of 'the picturesque' in areas like the Wye Valley

and the Lake District, they endeavoured to make their gardens less bland and smooth, more wooded and natural. Houses were increasingly designed to fit into this type of landscape. Irregularity became highly prized, and stylistic correctness or consistency ceased to be important; visual effect was all. Castles, abbeys, Elizabethan manor houses and Italianate villas were produced to order, and the restraint practised by earlier generations vanished. Architectural style became a matter of consumer choice. Picturesque irregularity became the hallmark of interiors as well as exteriors; furniture, instead of being arranged around the walls, was scattered about the room, and the attempt to create a stylistic unity was abandoned.

The picturesque movement in architecture and gardening became popular during the Napoleonic Wars, when there was a great increase in country-house building occasioned by high agricultural prices. These houses were built against a background of great social distress and widening class-divisions. This is reflected in the increasingly rigid segregation of servants from the family within the house, which reached its climax in the vast houses of the mid-Victorian period. Servants' rooms in new houses were placed in a block attached to the main house, where main rooms were now on the ground floor. Both the main house and the service block became increasingly subdivided, as if in imitation of Adam Smith's principle of the division of labour. It was this type of house which continued to be built until the agricultural depression of the last third of the 19th century.

The gardens at Stourhead, Wiltshire, were created by Henry Hoare, grandson of a prominent London banker, over a period of 40 years, starting in the 1740s. The landscape evokes an image of arcadian perfection in which woods and water blend harmoniously with classical buildings such as the temple.

The entrance hall at Heveningham Hall, Suffolk, designed by James Wyatt, is an outstanding example of the refined interior decoration of the later 18th century.

Chiswick House, London, was designed in neo-Palladian style by Lord Burlington as a villa in which he could house his extensive library and art collection.

Penrhyn Castle, Gwynedd, was built in 1827 for the owner of one of the largest slate quarries in north Wales. The choice of the castle style reflects an increasing interest in English medieval architecture with all its romantic overtones.

Blenheim Palace, Oxon, was begun in 1705 as a gift by a grateful nation to the Duke of Marlborough and designed by Sir John Vanbrugh as a national monument. The landscaped gardens by Capability Brown replaced the original formal layout.

road to Manchester. This canal was financed by the Duke of Bridgewater, the 'Canal Duke', and designed and built by James Brindley. These two men, the financier and the engineer, were the greatest names of the 'Canal Age'. Brindley a poorly-educated millwright, stressed the importance of avoiding rivers with their variable water flow and flood risk, and constructing instead 'dead water' systems with locks. The canals he built were among the engineering marvels of the time; his great tunnel at Hare Castle was no less than 2880 yards long. The first stretch of the Bridgewater canal to Manchester was followed by a branch to Runcorn. Reaching Runcorn had taken five years and it took a further nine to link up with the Mersey and the sea, costing the Duke more than £200,000.

His success sparked the first burst of canal building in the 1760s and early 1770s before activity slowed during the American war years, after which it peaked in the late century 'mania'. Carriage of coal was far and away the single most important motivation; more than half of the Acts passed between 1758 and 1802 for setting up canal companies were for this purpose. The first great achievement was the construction of the Grand Trunk Canal from Runcorn through the salt and pottery districts to join the great navigable riverway of the Trent at Wilden Ferry: 139 miles of canal. Josiah Wedgwood, the transformer of the pottery manufacture, was one of its chief promoters and cut the first sod – as well indeed he might have, for the benefit to his business was immense. Potters used vast quantities of heavy materials, clay, lime and coal, and the goods they made were both brittle and bulky. The opening of the Grand Trunk Canal in 1777 reduced the old carriage rates to a quarter of their previous level.

THE DEVELOPMENT OF TOWNS

The growth of towns is part of the process of industrialisation, and is likewise dependent upon the development of transport. Before the industrial revolution towns tended to be only a walk or horse-ride apart, and small because produce could only be brought in to feed the townspeople from a limited area. London, well-sited on a navigable river system which also gave access to coastal trade, had no curb to its growth and was, when Daniel Defoe travelled round Britain describing how each area contributed its produce to the Capital, already by far the largest town in the country. When Defoe and Celia Fiennes toured England in the 17th and early 18th centuries the lack of good roads made horseback the best way to travel and navigable rivers the most efficient means of transport for merchandise, but in the 18th century development of engineered roads under local turnpike trusts and carriages to travel upon them made possible the expansion of some market towns (with the stagnation of others) and encouraged travel for pleasure.

At the same time the improvement of river navigations, such as the Severn where tow paths enabled barges to be drawn by horses instead of men, and the cutting of canals gave manufacturing towns access to new markets and supplies of raw materials which enabled them to grow. Turnpikes were designed to link existing towns but canals, which were dictated by such natural circumstances as land contour, water supply and minerals which were to form the basis of their trade, sometimes created new towns at transshipment points.

In pre-industrial towns the chief citizens had their houses in the centre, often round a square or market place, with their warehouses or workshops, even their poor employees, nearby. London was the first town that became so unpleasant as a result of its trades and industries that wealthier people moved out to the west – the direction of the prevailing wind and therefore out of its smoke and smells – and the Duke of Bedford built the Piazza on his land at Covent Garden, beginning the process of joining up the Westminster of the Court with the commercial City of London and giving London its first planned square: a design innovation of classical architects on the Continent.

With paved roads leading out of the Capital it became practicable for citizens to ride or walk out to the surrounding villages on holidays and, finding higher places such as Hampstead and Blackheath pleasant and healthy, families that could afford it made their homes there and the men who travelled in every day to manage their City businesses became London's first commuters. These City men needed carriages to get from home to place of business and as it was probably more difficult to 'park' horse and vehicle for the day than it is to park a car today, the development of a public urban transport system began, first with carriages that could be hired, until in 1829 Mr Shillibeer put the first omnibus on the streets of London.

At the beginning of the 19th century the industrial towns of the Midlands and North began to expand and although, undeniably, there had been slums in the pre-industrial towns (usually where a large house was felt to be old-fashioned or otherwise displeasing to its owners and was turned over to multiple occupancy), the first 'built slums' appeared in these rapidly growing industrial towns. Working people, even if well paid, could not live far from their work as there was, until the horse was replaced, no really cheap form of transport. The art of getting the greatest number of houses into the centre of a town was therefore practised to obviate the need for operatives to walk long distances to work. The speculative builder, with no building regulations to guide or control him, also felt the need to put up houses at the minimum cost to himself. These needs brought forth the 'back-to-back' – houses in double rows which meant that each house required only one outside wall – and economies in space and materials could also be made by infilling the gardens and back-yards of existing houses with courts and alleys of tenements. Combined with inefficient or non-existent sanitation these forms of housing in towns led to situations that involved later Victorian writers in heated arguments as to which was the most horrible town.

The industry created that the horrors of Bradford, Sheffield, Manchester and other towns where workpeople and smoky factories were closely packed together also created wealth and a class of people – bitterly denounced by journalist William Cobbett – who could make their money work for them. It is to these people and their desire to get away from the industrial towns that we owe most of the towns and suburbs we admire today. Spas such as Bath, Leamington and Buxton, also seaside towns such as Brighton, Weymouth and Scarborough were developed originally as places to which people resorted for their health and which slightly later in the Georgian period developed into fully residential towns for the gentleman and retired industrialist. These towns and new suburbs such as Nash's Regents Park, Edinburgh's new town and Edgbaston, Birmingham were built with considerable taste on high and healthy ground and every effort made to keep them pleasant and exclusive – a bitter contrast to contemporary building of workers' housing in the industrial areas.

Demand for town centre housing and landlords' opportunism caused the infilling of yards and gardens of existing houses with slums like these: airless courts, bad sanitation and dreadful overcrowding.

By contrast, speculative building in Bath produced a town of extreme elegance. Richer clients could buy more space: John Wood I's circus (background) has 33 houses and his son's Royal Crescent has just 30.

The next few years saw the system reaching Birmingham and beyond to London and the south. The Birmingham canal was authorised in 1768 and provided a link with Liverpool, Bristol and Hull. The connection between the Thames and the Severn was completed by 1783, and by 1789 was passing 30 ton barges into the Thames just above Lechlade. The most important undertaking after the Grand Trunk was the Grand Junction Canal which, finished in 1805, redressed the deficiencies of the existing Thames Navigation by a direct cut from Brentford and the Northern stretch of the Oxford Canal at Braunston 93 miles away. This completed an efficient link between the capital and the industrial midlands and north and the construction of a branch to Paddington (1795–1801) and the Regent's Canal (1812–20) took the system right into the city's heart. Further west there was less activity, but the Kennet and Avon Canal (1794–1810) served as a barge link between London and the west, and was fed by the prosperous Somersetshire Coal Canal. The Gloucestershire and Berkeley Ship Canal provided an alternative to the difficult reaches of the Severn for ships of up to 600 tons, but the waterways of southern England probably carried less than a fifth of the country's total water traffic.

By the time the railways came, Britain had some 4,000 miles of navigable waterways providing a system which linked most of the producing areas of the country to each other and to the coast. The coming of the railway, with its greater speed and flexibility, pushed the canal system into its long decline; there were still, however, achievements to come. Between 1886 and 1894 the Manchester Ship Canal was constructed at a cost of £14 million, taking ships of up to 12,500 tons direct to Manchester. The importance of the

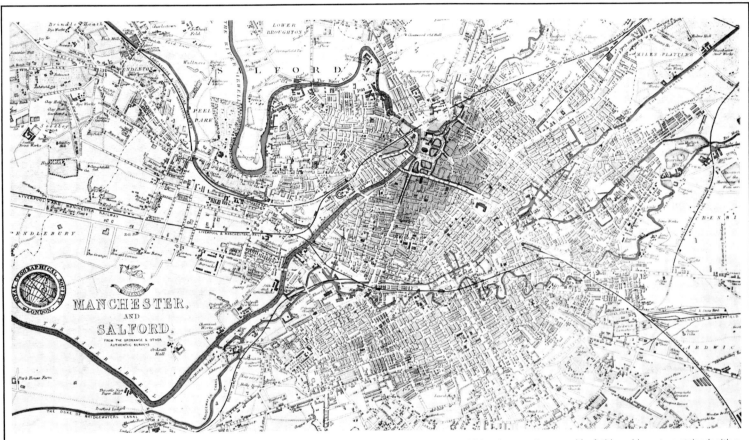

Manchester started as a small village by the bridge connecting it with Salford on the west side of the River Irwell, near its junction with the River Irk. By 1670 it was spreading along the main thoroughfares of Market Street and Deansgate but building was still limited to the road frontages (red lines on map); behind the houses were fields, like many villages today. These areas had been filled in by 1750 (pink area on map). The extent of the town was still only ½ mile each way but explosive growth was imminent.

The Bridgewater Canal of 1759 brought cheap coal to Manchester. In 1776 it was extended to Runcorn, so raw cotton could be brought in. Cotton mills multiplied. By 1805 more canals connected the town to Bolton, Bury, Oldham and Rochdale which grew as spinning and weaving towns. Thus Manchester became a merchant city as well as a manufacturing one. Its pre-eminence was confirmed by the opening of the Liverpool and Manchester railway in 1830 and the other lines which followed. Its commercial growth attracted a vast increase in population. In 1801 it was 90,000, in 1831 195,000 and in 1861 (the time of this map) it was 355,000.

In the 18th century factories lined the rivers which powered them; and with the coming of steam, waterside sites were still needed for coal delivery, transport of materials and goods, and for waste disposal. In 1835 a French visitor wrote 'the fetid muddy waters, stained with a thousand colours by the factories they pass, wander slowly round this refuge of poverty'. The workers fitted in where they could. Without transport they had to live near their work, and high density slums were the result. Later the railways provided another magnet for factories, warehouses and slums alike.

Such was the typical pattern of the growth of industrial towns in the first half of the 19th century.

Unfettered industry in Leeds. In such towns older features such as churches were dwarfed by chimneys and blackened by smoke. Town houses were abandoned and became tenements, while waste land was covered with rows of mean houses. The wealth created by industry was usually spent miles away.

Canal Age can hardly be overestimated. A writer in the 1790s put the significance of canals very clearly: they could be considered as 'so many roads of a certain kind, on which one horse will draw as much as thirty horses do on the ordinary turn-pike roads'. They alone could have coped with the coal-carrying demands of the industrialising economy, and their building not only gave experience in raising and managing large amounts of investment capital, but also trained a generation of engineers and workers, the 'navvies', whose experience contributed markedly to the early phases of railway construction.

The roads

Road transport developed more slowly. A significant step was the emergence of the turnpike trusts, which took the responsibility for provision and maintenance of key routes away from the parishes and placed it in the hands of trusts who derived their income from tolls. It should not be supposed that all turnpike roads were good roads.

Road engineers developed improved techniques. John Metcalf's basic system was a solid foundation of stone blocks covered with rammed-down chippings with a slight camber for drainage. Basically this was the old Roman system, and the 18th-century methods were variations on it. Thomas Telford used two layers of three-inch stones before laying seven inches of brocken stones and an inch of gravel. John McAdam (1756–1836) employed a less expensive method, using several layers of broken stones instead of large blocks. He finished with several layers of small chips which settled to form a smooth hard surface, and emphasised good drainage as being just as important as solid foundations. His ideas were perpetuated to modern times: 'macadam' and, later, 'tarmacadam' were the bases of British road construction right up to the concrete and asphalt era.

English roads still left much to be desired even in the last third of the 18th century; Arthur Young wrote of ruts four feet deep on the turnpike between Preston and Wigan, and of 30 or 40 horses being needed to pull wagons from the Essex mire. Nevertheless, they were probably more effective than the roads kept up by statute labour in the old way, and by shifting the cost of upkeep to the user the turnpike method was an important administrative step. The first Turnpike Act was passed in 1663, but the system did not become established until around 1700. By 1750 13 main roads out of London had been turnpiked along almost their entire lengths to places as distant as Bristol, Hereford, Chester, Manchester and Berwick. Carriers' wagons and carts had already developed a sizeable network of services by 1700 with inns serving as collection and dispatch points, and the famous firm of Pickfords was engaged in road transport from Manchester and London by the mid 18th century. Against the horror stories of delayed and stuck travellers must be set statistics which firmly point to a steady and cumulative improvement in road transport; coaching speeds improved through cutting out night stops and using relay horses. The journey from London to Manchester was reduced from four and a half days in 1754 to three days in 1760 and 28 hours by 1778. The coaches were limited in their carrying capacity, carrying four to six passengers inside and ten to 12 outside. Fares were high; a single journey of four and a half hours between Liverpool and Manchester just before the opening of the railway in 1830 was 12s inside and 7s outside, very high indeed in proportion to wages of the day.

The volume of traffic increased as well as speed. In 1756 only one coach a day ran regularly from London to Brighton;

BUILDING MATERIALS

Building, except of the most expensive kind, was until the 20th century considerably influenced by geology. The exceptions were cathedrals, very large country houses and important civic architecture: buildings where no expense was spared and materials could therefore be brought in from a distance. Ignoring these exceptions, a broad pattern can be discerned among older buildings whereby west of a line drawn from Portland to the Wash stone predominates, while east of this line local traditional or vernacular building uses wood and plaster, brick and tile. There are, of course, many buildings that do not fit this pattern, among them the cob cottages of Devon, Cheshire's black and white timber and plaster houses in the west and isolated areas of stone building in the eastern section, such as around Horsham in Sussex. Building of the humblest sort – flimsy cottages and outbuildings made of small pieces of wood, thatch and earth – have disappeared and we can only guess at their appearance. Nevertheless all these building types had connections with local geology – the wood produced by the deep soils of the east, or local clays and limes.

As well as the effects of geology the influence of fashion is apparent on even quite modest buildings: from the more obvious classical or Gothic style and details to subtle nuances such as a preference for a particular material or even a certain shade of brick. The combined effects of availability and fashion can be observed in unspoiled villages like National Trust-owned Lacock in Wiltshire. Lacock can boast a cruck cottage – an example of a very early type of timber construction – in the same street as a stone house with classical capitals, which dates from a later period when stone was being quarried nearby, and a house of 1778 built when local stone was evidently despised, for its front elevation is of brick and only the sides and back of roughly dressed stone. The joke 'Queen Anne front and Mary-Ann behind' is an accurate description of much 18th century building where very little attention was paid to the rear elevation.

Although a good many of the early mills and factories were built of stone and sometimes roofed with stone tiles, even in towns with good local stone, such as Bradford, Leeds or Rochdale, stone building eventually gave way to brick, usually with slate roofs, particularly for workers' houses as these materials were cheaper to produce and easier to use. Industrial towns in areas where no suitable stone was available, such as London, had brick and slate or tile clad houses from the 17th century onwards. Welsh slate became the ubiquitous roofing material of Victorian Britain as, although it had sometimes to be carried long distances, slate was light in weight, easy to use and economies could be made in the timber of the roof structure as compared with that needed for other, heavier, fire-proof roofing materials such as stone or tiles. Unlike slate, brickearth could be found all over the country and variations in the clays produced regional brick types that can still be recognised among the older buildings. The yellow London stock brick is pale because it contains chalk: it was often made from the clay on the actual building site, fired in simple clamps. In the Norwich area another pale yellow brick, known as a 'Cossey White' was produced. But red is the most common colour as iron is found in nearly all the clays and sands from which bricks are made. Red brick goes in and out of fashion: many Georgians hated it, late Victorians loved it, recent architectural writers rail against it, but even Accrington Bloods – the fieriest of the bricks from the northern coal measure shales – must have been preferable to blackened millstone grit, being almost totally impervious and retaining their colour in the smoky atmosphere of Victorian towns. There is today a trend back to the use of hard red bricks – perhaps a revulsion against concrete stained by polluted rainwater. As well as being possible to trace the distribution of bricks from particular clays, one can recognise the fancy products of Victorian brick and tile works: an enormous range of decorative motifs, ridge tiles and finials, chimney pots, keystones and other terracotta items were made and many can still be seen on houses in the vicinity of these works.

Despite the greatly increased use of brick the improved transport of the Industrial Revolution did not bring about the closure of stone quarries; rather it increased the area over which a stone could economically be sold, which was especially to the advantage of stones with particular uses like slate, York stone (valuable for paving) and granite. Slate, being light, was sold everywhere, while the heavier York paving and granite curbs and setts tend to be commonest in towns to which the stone could be brought direct from the quarries by water.

The Industrial Revolution brought many changes in building materials and distributed some very widely, but it did not extinguish local styles or materials: that was left for 20th century lorry transport to do.

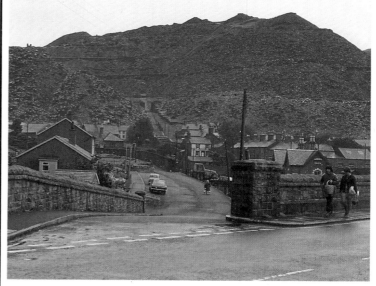

Blaenau Ffestiniog in North Wales, a town created by the slate industry and dominated by its quarries and spoil heaps. Concrete tiles have now replaced roofing slates generally, so most of the quarries have ceased production.

Granite quarry near Aberdeen. Huge blocks like this were for buildings and monuments, but much of the output paved the streets of Victorian towns.

THE GEOGRAPHY OF BUILDING MATERIALS

Aberdeen, 'Granite City', supplied the material for dock and lighthouses around Britain.

Craigleith. Much of old Edinburgh was fashioned in this sandstone.

Cookstown, source of a white freestone used extensively in Belfast.

Lake District, famous for its green slates.

Yorkshire. York Minster is built from the wonderful limestone of the district.

Pennines. The hard sandstones were ideal for the building of the smoky industrial towns of the north.

Connemara, source of a black serpentine polished and worked as marble.

Ffestiniog, centre of the North Wales slate industry.

Mountsorrel. Hard wearing granite.

Stamford displays some of the famous limestone of this area.

Carlow flags. A sandstone much used in Dublin.

Corbally, the Ffestiniog of Ireland in the 19th century.

Welsh Border Counties, famous for pink or red sandstone.

Fletton, an enormous brick production centre.

Box. Limestone quarries from this area produced Bath.

Caerphilly. Numerous surrounding sandstone quarries were used to build the town.

Northfleet, home of the Portland cement industry based on local chalk and clay.

Martock, noted for its rich gold Ham Hill stone from which Montacute House was built.

Brighton. Many of the buildings in this area are built using local flints and pebbles.

Delabole, largest of the West Country slate quarries and worked since the reign of Elizabeth I.

Purbeck, suppliers of specialised limestones and marble for early ecclesiastical buildings.

Haytor. Granite quarrying produced the material for Nelson's Column and the Thames Embankment.

Portland. Extensive quarries shipped their white limestone by barge to build many public buildings in London, e.g. Whitehall.

Penmaenmawr granite quarries. The shape of the mountain can be seen; terrace by terrace it is being nibbled away. The type of granite extracted here, in the form of small stones rather than blocks, is particularly suitable for roadmaking: originally for McAdam's turnpikes and recently as aggregate in motorway concrete.

Brickworks at Fletton, near Peterborough. From the 1860s mass production entered the brick industry.

An early 19th century stone 'railway' on which 18 horses pulled trains of 12 wagons laden with granite from Dartmoor.

Sheer-legs for loading Portland stone. Being near the sea, it could be shipped to London for building.

Capstan in limestone quarry, Purbeck, used with a donkey to haul stone up inclined mine shafts.

Expansion of the Portland quarries took place at the end of the 19th century to satisfy the demand from expanding cities, where the stone was much favoured for grandiose commercial buildings in 'Wrenaissance' style.

by 1811 28 made the journey. In 1820 it was remarked that a person had 1500 opportunities in 24 hours of leaving London by coach for one destination or another. The faster carrier vans were capable of reaching five miles an hour on a well kept road like that between London and Birmingham, but most travelled more slowly than that. Stage wagons took 24 hours to accomplish the 45 miles between Manchester and Leeds, and 40 hours to link Sheffield and Manchester, while as late as 1829 wagons between Newcastle and Carlisle averaged less than 20 miles a day.

The most spectacular achievements of road vehicles were clearly, then, in the field of passenger carriage. Here the canal barges were not likely to offer any competition. Where bulky freight was concerned it was a different story; it is hardly surprising that the Duke of Bridgewater's canal halved the cost of coal in Manchester when it opened in 1759, when the alternative method was in panniers on horses with a usual load per animal of 280 lbs. Without the canals in Britain too, industrialisation would have had to await the arrival of railway.

Railways were of limited significance until the late 1840s. Their origins, however, are firmly rooted in the period of the Industrial Revolution; 'wagonways' were already well known as a means of moving coal in the larger collieries in the 18th century, and by the early 19th iron rails were replacing wooden ones. The vital change in locomotion came with the introduction of steam which came to the Stockton and Darlington mineral line in 1825. The Liverpool–Manchester Railway, the world's first modern railway, opened in 1830 and rapidly halved the passenger fares between the two towns compared with the road coaches. Development was slow. The 2000 mile mark was not reached until 1843 by which time 5 million tonnes of freight, of which four million was coal, was carried annually. The economic and social effects of the railway were important and wide ranging, but they were felt during the boom years of the mid-Victorian economy when Britain was the 'workshop of the world'.

The human experience of industrialisation

No one can dispute that the affluent western world, as well as Japan, owes its prosperity to the process of industrialisation. The standards of living enjoyed in the modern developed world are a sharp contrast with the widespread poverty of pre-industrial society and with that of the underdeveloped, non-industrialised world of the present day. There is less agreement, however, among historians as to the impact of the Industrial Revolution on the lives of those who lived through it.

The 18th century was a good age for the landowning classes. Their control of the National government was unchallenged, and as county officers and justices they dominated the localities. The building of their great Palladian country houses and their lavish gardens testify to the security of their position. Some of them under whose lands ran rich seams of coal or minerals had their fortunes greatly enhanced from their exploitation. Many more of them saw their rent yields increase through the new profitability of agriculture. A commercial and merchant middle class had long been aspiring to power and status as its wealth increased; now it was joined by the manufacturing middle class. Many of its members still aimed to convert their gains into landed estates to guarantee the standing of their heirs, but there was a

growing self confidence in their own worth as they came to regard themselves as the backbone of the nation. With their securing of the vote in 1832 the shifting of the balance of political influence had begun, although it was far from complete. The new industrial and urban society in itself vastly expanded the professional recruits to the middle class, not only through the demand for new skills like engineering and management but through the expansion of the civil service and the banking, insurance, legal and, later, teaching professions. Below them the new lower middle class of the clerks was expanding, separated very little from many skilled workers in income but proud of its 'white-collar' status. A distinctive way of life was emerging in the suburban villas where even the lower ranks of the middle class could emphasise their standing by keeping a servant. The number of servants increased faster than the population, from 600,000 in 1801 to 1,300,000 in 1851, as the daughters of the working class sold their labour to lesser as well as greater households.

But what of the bulk of the population, the working classes? We have already seen that the southern farm labourer's experience of these years was one of poverty and degradation, but the working people did not form a homogeneous group all sharing for good or ill the same experiences. There was a 'labour aristocracy' largely made up of craftsmen, printers, joiners, cutlers and others who in the old society were not easily separable from the middle class tradesmen. Many formerly skilled trades were overtaken by machinery, such as calico-printing and woolcombing, as well as lower ranked occupations like handloom weaving. However, a number of new skilled trades like the iron puddlers, the fine mule spinners, and later the engine drivers rose into their places. Such men were paid from 50 to 100 per cent above labourers and in general managed to increase the margin of their spending power over that of the average worker. Below them came the factory workers, like the male mule spinners who enjoyed an improved standard of living.

They were, however, the second stage in the evolution of the factory labour force. The first stage had been that of the exploitation of the cheap and available labour of women and children, many of the latter being pauper apprentices and consequently an unfree form of labour. Miners and transport workers probably at least maintained their standards. All these were considerably outnumbered by those below them among whom must be included many obvious victims of the Industrial Revolution like the handloom weavers and the framework knitters whose skills, already tending to be in over-supply, were made redundant by the factory. Such groups were representative of a vast number of displaced domestic workers who filled the urban slums alongside the unskilled and casual labourers, the street traders, the beggars and the criminals. For them there was no benefit from industrialism. Poverty remained their usual condition until the Welfare State and the general rise in unskilled wages of the 20th century improved their lot.

Apart from changes in the basic standard of living of the lower classes, certain kinds of freedom are lost when a labourer leaves the home or small workshop for the factory. A folk song from late 18th century Sheffield, *The Jovial Cutlers,* well captures the weekly pace of the out-working cutler: given a certain number of knives to make at piece rates for his master, he did not have to work regular hours equally spread over the week. Instead he extended his weekend into Monday, and worked long and briskly on a Friday to finish his stint. The practice of keeping 'St Monday' was

THE SCIENTIFIC REVOLUTION

One of the most important legacies of the Industrial Revolution that has been handed down to the present generation was the flowering of science and culture, expressed initially by like minded individuals being drawn together and forming societies. These societies and institutes often constituted the base from which the great development of 19th century universities took place.

The activities of men such as Watt, Boulton, Crompton, Banks and Wedgwood in the 18th century and Darwin, Fitzroy, Young, Davy, Faraday, Tyndall, Dewar, Lyell, Wheatstone and Birkbeck in the 19th century were instrumental in promoting and sustaining a succession of scientific and learned societies that emerged in quick succession from 1750 onwards and now enshrine the basic framework of British culture.

From 1750 onwards there emerged in quick succession:

1754 Royal Society of Arts
1759 Royal Botanic Gardens Kew
1768 Royal Academy of Arts
1774 Royal Humane Society
1791 Ordnance Survey
1795 Hydrographic Dept of the Admiralty
1799 Royal Institution of Great Britain
1800 Royal College of Surgeons
1804 Royal Horticultural Society
1818 Royal Observatory Edinburgh
1820 Royal Astronomical Society
1822 Royal Academy of Music
1830 Royal Geographical Society
1831 British Association for the Advancement of Science
1837 Royal College of Art
1838 Royal Agricultural Society
1844 Royal College of Veterinary Surgeons

1855 Meteorological Office
1868 Royal Colonial Institute (now Royal Commonwealth Society)

The transformation of the university scene began half way through the great burst of intellectual and scientific activity associated with the Industrial Revolution. Oxford and Cambridge had become stereotyped as Anglican institutions and this had led to their decline as teaching had become mainly traditional and formal, and life in College was for the majority more social than academic. No lecture was delivered by any Regius Professor of Modern History at Cambridge between 1725 and 1773!

That the first serious move to break out of this straitjacket should come from London is not surprising in view of its pre-eminence in the cultural life of the country. Here, out of the discussions of men such as Campbell, Brougham and Birkbeck, there crystallised the concept of a London University which would be open to all with no theological tests and no residential qualifications.

The 'university' began in 1826, but even before it opened its doors action had been taken to found a rival and orthodox institution. King's College London, deliberately Anglican and Tory, was the answer and this appeared in 1829. But neither foundation could grant degrees, a point of great concern to the medical schools founded in association with the two colleges. The problem was resolved in 1836 by the establishment of the new 'University of London' which emerged as an examination body with the power to grant degrees to the two colleges, which became constituent parts of the new university.

Meanwhile the Anglican element, aghast at the London events, had taken action in two areas which were remote from existing university facilities. In Wales, St David's College Lampeter was established (as a result of moves made as early as 1822) for the training of clergy for the established church; whilst in the north of England a University of Durham was established in 1832 under the auspices of, and with the financial assistance of, the wealthy Bishop and Dean and Chapter of Durham Cathedral.

Elsewhere in the country, and especially in the major urban areas, the needs of higher education were increasingly being met by the development of voluntary societies such as Royal Institutes, Literary and Philosophical Societies, Atheneums, Mechanics' Institutes and Medical Schools.

Concurrent with much of this surge of intellectual activity was a growth in medical science and in hospital facilities. If the 17th century was an age of Faith, the 18th century could be said to have been an age of Philanthropy. County hospitals for all kinds of patients were set up and lying-in hospitals were started in all the principal towns. In London between 1720 and 1760 Guy's, Westminster, St George's, London and Middlesex hospitals were all founded and improvements were made at the already existing St Thomas's and Bart's hospitals. In the course of the 125 years after 1700 no less than 154 new hospitals were established in Britain.

Compound microscope by William Cary, a celebrated scientific instrument maker until his death in 1825. He was a member of the Astronomical Society.

'An Experiment on a Bird in the Air Pump' painted in 1768 by Joseph Wright of Derby, showing the demonstration of an experiment first performed a century earlier by Robert Boyle. The bird is in a glass vessel from which most of the air has been removed; it is distressed and on the point of death, proving that air is essential for animal life. Air was not then known to be a mixture but by 1775 Joseph Priestley had isolated oxygen and proved it to be the life-support element.

Map of Kent produced in 1801 by the Board of Ordnance of the British Army, later the Ordnance Survey. The reason for the survey was the threat of invasion from France, but accurate maps proved invaluable to civilians as well as to the army.

The Royal Botanic Gardens, Kew: famous for the scientific development of botany since foundation in 1759.

Royal Observatory building, Greenwich, now a museum. The observatory moved to Sussex after the last war.

widespread among home workers, in small workshops and in the mines. For all the uncertainty of work under the domestic system, the worker was not yet subject to the routine and monotony of factory employment. The factory clock was as much a symbol of the new society as the smoking chimney.

If trade was brisk and rates of pay high so that the worker could earn in four days what in normal times took him five or six, then frequently he worked only the four days, preferring leisure to earnings. The factory masters needed to eradicate such irregular working habits, and absenteeism was a real problem during the period of adjustment to factory routines and new work disciplines. The campaign of factory workers for the Ten Hour Day is significant in that it marks a point of acceptance that work time should be sharply divided from leisure time.

The Industrial Revolution brought not only a new working environment but brought many people into a new living environment: the factory town. In 1801 25 per cent of the population lived in towns with more than 10,000 inhabitants. By 1831 the same percentage lived in towns with more than 20,000 inhabitants, and by 1851 half the population did. The factory towns with their rows of hurriedly built, often back-to-back houses, crowded into smoke-filled air, were bleak and dismal indeed. There were few recreational or cultural facilities other, perhaps, than those associated with the pub or the chapel. Damp and ill-ventilated dwellings combined with poor sanitation to encourage the spread of sickness and disease. Two famous parliamentary 'blue books' exposed the appalling state of health in the towns: the *Report on the Sanitary Condition of the Labouring Population* produced by Edwin Chadwick in 1842, and the less well known but equally revealing *Report on the Health of Towns* of 1840. Chadwick thought that even prison conditions were superior to those of the bottom ranks of urban society:

> *amongst the cellar population of the working people of Liverpool, Manchester or Leeds, and in large portions of the metropolis . . . At Edinburgh, there were instances of poor persons in a state of disease committed from motives of humanity to the prison, that they might be taken care of and cured.*

Typhoid and cholera were commonplace, and it was only when major outbreaks like that of cholera in 1831, which killed thousands in urban Britain, that the authorities began to face up to the problem. The Public Health Act of 1848 was the first step towards national control. The expectation of life in urban Britain was much lower than that in the rural districts; in 1842 a labourer's average life expectancy was 38 in Rutlandshire and 28 in Truro, while for Manchester it was 17, Bethnal Green 16 and Liverpool 15. A Halifax doctor in the same year calculated the average age at death as 'gentry, Manufacturers and their families at 55: shopkeepers, 24: operatives, 22'.

There were two types of child labourer in the early mills – apprentice pauper labour and 'free' labour. Pauper apprenticeship provided the main source of machine-minding labour in the early Industrial Revolution. Hungry for workers which their immediate localities could not fully supply, the factory masters drew labour from the poor law authorities, often from far away in the south. At the age of seven orphans and other destitute children were transported to factories where they worked, in some mills, a 15-hour day for six days a week. A series of parliamentary investigations exposed the conditions of these factory children beginning

CITY INSTITUTIONS

By 1700 London had become the largest city in the world, with the possible exception only of Constantinople. London's population fully doubled in the first half of the 17th century, reaching some 400,000 by 1650, and it increased further to nearly 600,000 in 1700. At that time just over one-tenth of the entire English population lived in the hugely expanded metropolis, which gave London a uniquely important role in the life of the nation. The feeding of so many people exerted a powerful influence on agriculture. London was a vast consumer's market, the focus for all the fashion trades, as well as many others. It was also the country's largest manufacturing centre and, as the port, handled three-quarters of England's overseas trade.

The City of London was becoming merely a part of the new metropolis. The old medieval city, still largely contained within the walls first built by the Romans, was substantially destroyed in the Great Fire of 1666. It was speedily rebuilt, with stone largely replacing the old timber and plaster buildings, from which time the phrase 'the City' came increasingly to mean the commercial and financial interests concentrated there. The fashionable world moved more and more into the developing 'West End'; government and administration were concentrated on Westminster and Whitehall; the City became the business centre first for Britain and much of western Europe, and then for much of the whole world.

The Royal Exchange, founded originally by Sir Thomas Gresham in 1567, was magnificently rebuilt after the Fire, and its interior courtyard was constantly thronged with merchants and shoppers, tourists and job-seekers, hawkers and pick-pockets. The first coffee house opened in 1652 and others quickly followed, many of them concentrated around the area near the Royal Exchange. Coffee houses provided venues for business meetings, for the exchange of news and gossip and for the new habit of newspaper-reading (the first daily newspaper appeared in 1702). Lloyd's Coffee House became the acknowledged centre of marine insurance, first issuing Lloyd's famous list of ships in 1734, and the Stock Exchange originated in the Stock Exchange Coffee House opened in 1773.

In the generation following the Great Fire, fire insurance and life assurance schemes were just two of the developments in the City. The period also saw great strides in banking, with the setting up of the large private banks – Child's, Hoare's and Mocatta and Goldsmid were all operating by the 1690s – and the Bank of England, the government's bank, founded in 1694, which was the main institution in a 'financial revolution' centred on the new London of the late 17th and early 18th centuries.

This was the time when London also developed its commodity markets, trading taking place either directly or by sample in the complete range of foodstuffs, raw materials and goods from all over the world. Additionally there were the offices of city government – the Guildhall, originally built in 1425–45, and the Mansion House, designed in the mid 18th century by George Dance – along with the headquarters of several score of guilds and livery companies which were the successors of the religious and social fraternities of the 11th century. The law was represented by the Royal Courts of Justice, rebuilt in the mid 19th century to a Gothic design of G. E. Street, whilst just outside the city proper were the Inns of Court housing the legal fraternity: the Middle Temple, Inner Temple, Lincoln's Inn and Grays Inn, which were all rebuilt in the 18th century.

Liberally sprinkled throughout this complex were the rebuilt Wren churches surmounted by the crowning glory of St Paul's Cathedral, at the time one of the largest buildings in the world.

Today much of the architectural heritage of this period has disappeared, for the City was to suffer a second Great Fire during the blitz on London in the Second World War. Much of the area was laid waste or badly damaged; only three of over 80 livery companies, for example, survived intact. Substantial rebuilding or repair work has been necessary for historic buildings such as St Paul's Cathedral, The Guildhall, The Bank of England, the Stock Exchange and nearly all the livery companies. But a new 20th century city, typified by the Barbican scheme, has risen Phoenix-like from the wartime ashes and the Roman square mile still continues to play a major role in the life of Britain and the rest of the world.

The Corn Exchange, Leeds. The growth of the railway system meant that corn could be traded beyond the nearest market and, with grain imported from America, it became a commodity to be dealt and speculated in by brokers. In large towns throughout the country corn exchanges grew up and were often fine architectural examples; this one was designed by Cuthbert Brodrick. The enormous skylights facilitated examination of the grain.

A caricature of the Coffee Room at Lloyd's in 1798. The first Coffee House in London opened in 1652, and 50 years later there were 450 such institutions providing refreshment, conversation, newspapers and places to conduct business.

Lloyd's Subscription Room in the Royal Exchange. Lloyd's original Coffee House had opened in the 1680s and in the 18th century became the meeting place for arranging marine insurance. After 1774 the business moved to the Royal Exchange.

The Bank of England was built by Sir John Soane in the late 18th and early 19th centuries.

Ship auctions were held frequently at Lloyd's; bidding continued until a small candle flickered out.

The Royal Exchange was designed in the 1670s by Edward Jerman, and provided the main meeting place for the City. The building was burnt down in 1838, and replaced in the 1840s by the present classical building in Cornhill.

Traditions preserved. Thames swans belong to the Queen and the Vintners' and Dyers' companies. At swan-upping in July cygnets are marked to show their owners.

The Stock Exchange, now a major institution of the City providing vital financial services to the whole world, developed from a Coffee House in the 1770s.

A fire insurance mark was displayed on many buildings in 18th century London. The Sun Fire Office was the earliest of the fire insurance companies; it was founded in 1710, though there had been short-lived friendly societies for the same purpose from the 1680s. The Westminster (1717) and the Hand-in-Hand (1719) soon followed, as did general insurance companies operating in the same field. Marks such as these from various companies are still to be found on many 18th century buildings.

Brokers' medals were issued by the City of London in the 19th century to show that the holder had been sworn as a licensed broker. This one, bearing the City's 14th century shield and its 17th century motto, was issued to Andrew Duncan, a member of the Baltic Exchange between 1860 and 1883. The Baltic Exchange also has its origins in an 18th century Coffee House where trade in tallow was concentrated. Now it is the main centre for cargo arrangement for shipping.

with Sir Robert Peel's Act of 1802, which restricted the hours of apprentices in textile mills to 12, banned night work and improved lodging conditions. Loudly the mill-owners complained that such 'interference' would price Britain out of export markets, and enforcement of the act was weak and haphazard. It covered only pauper apprentices and these were being increasingly replaced by 'free' local children. Their lot was little different except that they lived at home, and were bound not by indenture but by their parents' poverty. John Fielden, a humane owner, calculated that in attending the spinning machinery a child walked 20 miles a day, and only the strictness (and sometimes brutality) of the overseers could keep such tired infants awake and attentive.

In 1816 Peel moved the establishment of a committee to investigate fully factory conditions, but the resulting bill, after passing the Commons, was thrown out by the Lords. A new committee gathered evidence which carried through the Cotton Factory Regulation Act of 1819, setting limits to the hours worked by children between nine and 16 and forbidding altogether employment of those under nine. However, lack of factory inspection weakened the effect of the act. The Factory Act of 1833 introduced by Lord Shaftesbury followed the massive exposure of conditions by Michael Sadler's committee, and limited the working hours of children between nine and 13 to eight hours a day, and also tried to force the employers to make provision for elementary education. Importantly, a factory inspectorate was established to enforce the Act. The Ten Hours Act for all women and children under 16 not covered by the act of 1833 was passed in 1847.

Conditions in the coal mines were investigated in 1840. This famous 'blue book' was the first to be illustrated and its line drawings of half-naked children working like beasts shocked many (including some who were more shocked by the near-nakedness than by the labour). Many children began work underground at the age of seven. Some worked as trappers, sitting all day in darkness to open ventilation doors to allow the coal trucks to pass through. Others, sometimes on all fours, dragged the loaded trucks along passages barely two feet high. The report led to the passing in 1842 of Lord Shaftesbury's Mines Act which prohibited the employment underground of females and of boys under the age of ten.

Popular views of the Industrial Revolution owe as much, probably more, to the haunting images of novelists and poets of the time than to contemporary radical criticisms. The Fabian socialist husband and wife team J.L. and Barbara Hammond published a trilogy of books, *The Village Labourer, The Town Labourer* and *The Skilled Labourer* in the

Children working in a brickworks, 1871. Some industries managed to slip through the net of the early Factory Acts for many years.

THE FORMATION OF THE EMPIRE

In the period 1750–1850 Britain changed from a largely agricultural country into the first industrial nation the world had ever seen; at the same time a unique empire, usually regarded as its Second, began to accrue overseas, and provided both raw materials and markets for the expanding industry. From the start this second British Empire had great variety, not only of race but also of origin and organisation, which called for different types of government. Some areas, such as India, already had sophisticated settlement with towns, while others were sparsely populated by primitive people.

Britain came comparatively late into empire building: by the 16th century Spain and Portugal already possessed territories many times their size, while in the 17th century British trading companies, anxious to establish contact with regions such as India and China, whose products were coveted in Europe, found themselves in competition with similar Dutch and French companies.

British settlements in North America were also competing with the Dutch and French. Here the colonists inhabited an undeveloped land and were mainly subsistence farmers with little to offer in the way of exports or as a market for industrial products. The acquisition of Canada from France in 1763 was regarded more as a liability than an asset except by those who appreciated the potential of the fur trade, and even the loss of the 13 colonies to American independence in 1776 was more of a blow to British prestige than to trade.

At the time that the American states were breaking away from British control a brilliant naval explorer, James Cook, was staking claim to Australia and New Zealand, lands which later came to replace America as colonies for Britain's surplus population. Many American settlers still loyal to Britain emigrated to Canada after 1776 to mix, not very amicably, with the French already settled there. Australia, described by Cook as an attractive and fertile land, was considered suitable for the re-settlement of these loyalists, but in the event convicts occupied the first settlement in Australia. The convicts were perhaps lucky: as a replacement for America unhealthy sites on the west coast of Africa had been suggested as a place to which felons could be transported. However, if the convict was sturdy enough to survive confinement on the dreadful hulks in England and the long voyage (usually well over six months) chained together in pairs, he had a chance of making good in Australia. Because of the unlikelihood of escape, the penal settlement was run more like an open prison. Many convicts stayed on after they were pardoned to found families in the colony: their children taller and fitter and showing no more predisposition to crime than the 'pure bred merinos' or free settlers. One enterprising widow, shipped out for stealing a horse when she was 13 in 1792, was able to describe herself in the 1828 census as having arrived 'Free on the *Mariner* in 1821', as she had been on a visit to England with her daughters.

New Zealand had a far larger native population than Australia, and as the Maoris were hunters rather than farmers they needed wide territories. This led in the 19th century to conflict with English settlers, massacres and wars, but ultimately a truly integrated society emerged with a welfare state many years ahead of that in Britain.

India was completely different: it was never a settlement colony, but a land already heavily populated; the British were attracted to India as a source of luxury products including fine cotton and silk cloth. (Ironically, when cotton production became mechanised in

Britain in the mid 19th century it killed India's hand loom industry.) Small trading posts were set up by the East India Company in the 17th and early 18th centuries as a concession allowed by the powerful rulers of highly civilised states. These 'factories' grew into forts, such as Fort St George and Fort William, which later became Madras and Calcutta respectively. Bombay, the best harbour in India, was acquired from Britain's trade rivals, the Portuguese, as part of the dowry of Catharine of Braganza when she married Charles II. With only a precarious footing on the coast at first, the men of 'John Company' gained power as the Mogul Empire, to which the lesser states of India paid allegiance, disintegrated in the 18th century.

Warren Hastings began the process of binding India together by means of alliances between the Princes and Britain, a process which resulted in his lengthy trial for corruption (1788–1795). During this trial, however, both Hastings and his accusers began to voice new ideals of responsibility towards the governed populations; ideals that were very much in accord with the campaign for the abolition of the slave trade which was gaining adherents at that time. By the time of the Mutiny in 1857 practically the whole of India was under Company rule. But this rule was ended in the subsequent reorganisation which brought India directly under British Government control; Victoria became Empress of India in 1877.

From the start trade with the subcontinent had been so valued that foreign policy was directed at securing the routes to India. During the Napoleonic Wars, Cape Colony was taken over from the Dutch who had established it as a calling point for their East India Company ships in 1652. This take-over sowed the seeds of many of today's problems in South Africa: it produced conflict which led in the 1830s to the Great Trek of the Boer farmers inland to territory where they could be free of British rule and to the Boer War in 1900. When a much shorter route to India was developed in 1840 with an overland journey by camel from Alexandria to the Red Sea, and further shortened in 1869 with the cutting of the Suez Canal, Britain took a strategic interest in Egypt.

Although China was as aloof in the 18th and early 19th centuries as she has been in the 20th, nevertheless after the Opium Wars of the 1840s Hong Kong was ceded to Britain, Kowloon was added in 1860, and in 1898 the New Territories were leased for 99 years.

Britain emerged from the Napoleonic Wars with world naval dominance and a need for bases for her fleet and merchant ships. One excellent site was chosen by Sir Stamford Raffles. Born in the colonies the son of an unsuccessful ship's master in Jamaica, he had risen by ability in the service of the East India Company in Java and Sumatra, eventually to be knighted by the Prince Regent. In 1819 he founded the free port of Singapore at the focus of trade routes between China, India, Japan, Australasia and the Pacific. Raffles was typical of the men who built the British Empire – brilliant, impetuous and with a real respect for Eastern culture; quite unlike the Victorian administrators that followed, who, although having a genuine desire to help the natives, felt that their culture was superior and theirs the only true religion.

Australian emigration. This government offer is aimed at the Scottish labour surplus caused by the Highland clearances, when farmers were evicted to make way for large sheepwalks. No provision was made for elderly dependants.

An emigrant ship about to leave port for the other side of the world and, for some, a better life. In the 19th century thousands of people — the majority Scots and Irish — were driven by famine or unemployment to seek work in the colonies. They were indeed sought by the developers of the countries themselves, labour there being scarce and vital.

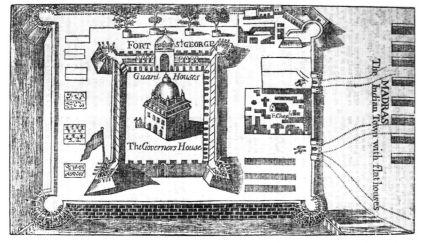

Fort St George belonged to the East India Company which had a statutory monopoly of British trade with India and also assumed government powers.

Comfort for the wealthy (right) is offered; but steerage passengers were badly overcrowded. In 1846 two ships to Canada had 308 dead out of 896.

Captain James Cook (above), the greatest explorer in the history of the British Empire, was murdered by Hawaiian natives in 1779. A labourer's son, his achievements included the surveying of New Zealand and Australia's east coast.

Acquiring slaves in Africa (right). Much of Britain's 18th century trade and empire depended on slave labour and her economy thrived on the 'triangular trade': cotton goods to Africa, slaves to the West Indies and sugar back to Britain. The slave trade was abolished in 1807.

first quarter of the 20th century. They sold in amazing numbers (indeed, they continue to do so) and propagated widely the 'human disaster' view of the Industrial and Agrarian Revolutions. Their books continued to sell long after critics, notably Sir John Clapham in the 1920s, vigorously combatted their view. Nevertheless, more persistent even than their literate and readable history are William Blake's unforgettable 'Dark Satanic Mills' and Charles Dickens' bleak evocation of a factory town and its stern master, Mr Gradgrind, in *Hard Times*.

There are indeed two aspects of the Industrial Revolution. It was a triumph; its achievements in transforming first the British economy and then the economies of the rest of the developed world brought previously undreamed-of increases in output of goods, and indirectly of services. But it also brought desperate hardship to many who lived through it and a deterioration to the environment. John Stuart Mill, in the 1848 edition of his famous *Principles of Political Economy*, clearly saw that the benefits of the Industrial Revolution would not be reaped by the experiencing generation, but rather by those who were to follow:

Hitherto it is questionable if all the mechanical inventions yet made have lightened the day's toil of any human being. They have enabled a greater proportion to live the same life of drudgery and imprisonment and an increased number of manufacturers and others to make fortunes. They have increased the comforts of the middle classes. But they have not yet begun to effect those great changes in human destiny, which it is in their nature and their futurity to accomplish.

Perhaps two generations were sacrificed to the creation of an industrial base which was completed by the beginning of the mid-Victorian boom in 1850. Thereafter the people of Great Britain, but not those of Ireland, were lifted, for the first time in history, over the bare subsistence level. At the same time hours of work were cut, and protective legislation began to influence working conditions for the good. In part at least improvement was obtained through working people's own organised action, through their trade unions and radical political parties, for the Industrial Revolution also brought about the emergence of modern stratified class society and its related class politics.

COINS

From the 17th century, the lack of an adequate supply of small change was a growing problem. Individual traders and corporations began to issue their own token coinages in an attempt to meet this need. Sporadic attempts were made to issue official halfpennies and farthings, but in the late 18th century the issue of unofficial tokens reached its zenith, producing a huge and varied output illustrating almost every facet of life in this revolutionary period. The industrial revolution — in the form of machines, bridges, canals and ironworks — is well illustrated.

A 1797 token showing a Free School. Tokens in many communities showed municipal buildings.

Not only do these tokens illustrate the industrial revolution; the coins themselves are often products of it. The copper coinage of 1797 was struck on steam-powered machinery at the Boulton and Watt works at Soho, Birmingham.

Agriculture is also represented. New buildings — often symbols of civic pride — were also depicted, as were whole series of churches. Tokens were also used as a means of political expression, the issues of Thomas Spence representing the radical view being particularly famous.

A token of 1793, one of many issued depicting industrial machinery and trades; here a metal worker is shown.

EVENTS AND PERSONALITIES

George II came to the throne in 1727.

1715 The first Jacobite revolt in Scotland under Lord Mar fails to put James Stuart, son of James II (The Old Pretender) on the throne
1720 The South Sea Bubble: the collapse of the South Sea Company produces Britain's most infamous financial scandal
1721 Sir Robert Walpole becomes the first Prime Minister. An astute politician, he provided stable if corrupt government for 20 years
1727–60 **George II** succeeds his father George I
1729 Wars with Austria and Spain are ended by the Treaty of Seville
1733 Walpole's proposal to introduce an unpopular excise tax produces the most serious political crisis of his period of office
John Kay's invention of the 'Flying Shuttle' speeds the pace of handloom weaving
Jethro Tull's *Horse-hoeing Husbandry* is published
1739 John Wesley joins George Whitefield to begin open-air preaching near Bristol. The effective start of Methodism, although Wesley later split with Whitefield
1739–40 Wars with Spain, the 'War of Jenkin's Ear', and the War of Austrian Succession, upset Walpole's policy of minimal intervention in continental affairs
1742 Resignation of Walpole, ostensibly over a domestic issue
1743 Battle of Dettingen, the last in which a British monarch took the field. George II had already established a reputation as a soldier in the War of Spanish Succession

1745 Second Jacobite rising as the Highland clans rally to the cause of Charles Edward Stuart ('Bonnie Prince Charlie'), the 'Young Pretender'. His army reached Derby, but retreated again to Scotland. The French invasion he had hoped would assist him did not materialise, and anticipated support in England was lacking
1746 In the Battle of Culloden, one of the bloodiest ever fought on English soil, the 'Butcher' Duke of Cumberland, brother of the king, destroys the Jacobite forces. Charles Edward Stuart flees back to exile and the Highland clan system is destroyed in the brutal aftermath
1755 Outbreak of the Seven Years' War. William Pitt the elder (Earl of Chatham) was in charge of the war in the new ministry of the Duke of Newcastle, who had succeeded to the leadership of the Whig interest built up by Henry Pelham
1757 Robert Clive's victory at Plassey wins Bengal and ensures British domination of India
1759 James Wolfe defeats the French at Quebec; he and the French general Montcalm were both killed
1760–1820 **George III** succeeds his grandfather George II. Best known for losing the American colonies and for going mad in later life, he came to the throne determined to break the Whig monopoly of power exercised since Walpole, and to end the Seven Years' War.
1761 His 'favourite' Lord Bute becomes Prime Minister
1763 Important questions of freedom and liberty are raised when John Wilkes attacks Bute in his paper the *North Briton* and is imprisoned
1764 James Hargreaves invents the Spinning Jenny. Able to produce yarn much faster than the wheel, it was still used in the home rather than the factory
1765 James Watt's invention of the separate condenser by improving both efficiency and fuel economy provided the most significant step in the development of power technology
1767 James Brindley's canal joins Manchester to the Mersey
1768 The return of John Wilkes from abroad and his repeated election by the Middlesex voters despite his exclusion by Parliament renews the Wilkite issues of freedom and liberty
1771 Richard Arkwright uses water power to drive his spinning frame in his factory at Cromford. The age of the cotton-mill had begun
1773 Boston Tea riots begin the period of skirmishing, introducing the American War of Independence
1775 The British are defeated by George Washington at Bunker's Hill
1776 On 4 July the American Colonies declare Independence. Washington is appointed their Commander-in-Chief

The Battle of Culloden, 1746. The army of the Young Pretender, exhausted and low in morale, was cornered near Inverness on its retreat from England.

George III came to the throne in 1760, an unpopular king. Many overseas colonies – including America – were lost during his reign.

Adam Smith's *Wealth of Nations*, the founding text of modern economics, is published

1779 Samuel Crompton invents the Spinning Mule; its real significance was that it could be adapted for steam power

1780 In an effort to prevent Catholic emancipation, Lord George Gordon leads a massive demonstration of the Protestant Association – the Gordon riots

1781 James Cook's landing at Botany Bay begins British development of Australia, initially as a penal colony

Defeat of General Cornwallis at Yorktown ensures American independence. By this time both Spain and France had entered the war on the side of the colonists. The Prime Minister, Lord North, much blamed for poor conduct of the war, resigned in 1782. American independence was effectively recognised in the following year

1782 The reforming ministry of Lord Rockingham includes William Pitt the Younger's first bill for parliamentary reform and Edmund Burke's for economical reform

1783 William Pitt becomes Britain's youngest ever Prime Minister at the age of 24. A second proposal for parliamentary reform by him was rejected in 1785

1786 A commercial treaty with France marks the beginning of the movement towards free trade

Impeachment of Warren Hastings. A major political trial of the man who had become the first Governor General of India in 1773

1787 Edmund Cartwright invents the power loom, but it was not used on a wide scale in cotton before the 1820s and in wool a decade or so later

1793 War with Revolutionary France begins; it was to last with only brief intermission until 1815

1794 Increasing radical sympathy at home with the French Jacobins leads to suspension of the Habeas Corpus Act and other acts of repression. Fears intensify with widespread rioting over high bread prices in 1795–6 and again in 1800–01

1797 Naval mutinies at Spithead and the Nore alarm the government by showing that radical sentiments had spread to the sailors

1798 The Irish Rising is crushed at Vinegar Hill. The Irish had not received the expected French help

Admiral Horatio Nelson destroys the French Fleet at the Battle of the Nile and a period of amazing hero-worship by the British public begins

Thomas Malthus publishes his *Essay on the Principles of Population*, the founding text of demography with its famous 'trap' of population growth outstripping food supply, and very influential on social policy

1799 and 1800 The Combination Acts to prevent the growth of trade unions are passed

1800 The Act of Union with Ireland is passed. Ireland is to be represented at Westminster

The surrender of Malta to the English fleet continued the great run of naval victories

1801 The personal determination of George III prevents Pitt's plan for Catholic emancipation from being passed. Pitt had hoped to enfranchise both the Irish and the Catholics of Great Britain

1802 The Peace of Amiens provides a brief interlude in the long period of war, but only until the declaration of war against Napoleon in 1803

Robert Peel's act to restrict the hours of work of young apprentices in cotton mills marks the beginning of factory legislation

1805 On 21 October at the Battle of Trafalgar, Lord Nelson is killed on the *Victory* during his most famous and decisive victory over the French and Spanish fleets

1806 The death of the still young Pitt brings in the ministry of Lord Grenville

1807 The slave trade is abolished following the efforts of the campaign led by William Wilberforce

1808 The Peninsular War begins; the British are successful in preserving Portugal's independence after the French Invasion of Spain

1809 Famous duel between two leading cabinet ministers, George Canning and Lord Castlereagh, who was wounded in the thigh. Canning briefly became Prime Minister before his death in 1827

1811 The growing mental instability of George III leads to the appointment of Prince of Wales as Regent

Beginning of the 'Luddite' disturbances of machine-breaking in the east Midlands and later in Lancashire and the West Riding

1812 Prime Minister Spencer Percevel is assassinated and the ministry of Lord Liverpool begins

America declares war on Britain

1814 The British are defeated at New Orleans by General Jackson

Napoleon Bonaparte is defeated and is exiled to Elba. The Bourbon dynasty is restored by the victorious allies

1815 Napoleon leaves Elba and returns to France, and is finally defeated by the Duke of Wellington and his Prussian allies at Waterloo. The long war is brought to an end by the Treaty of Vienna

The Corn Laws, by prohibiting imports of cheap grain, attempt to preserve the high prices to which the landed interest had become accustomed in the war years

George IV, after nine years as Regent, became king in 1820.

1819 Growing radicalism and government reaction to it leads to the Six Acts suppressing basic freedoms. At Peterloo, near Manchester, 11 persons peacefully attending a reform meeting were killed when the Yeoman Cavalry charged the crowd with drawn weapons

1820–30 **George IV** succeeds his father after many years as Regent

1821 Although the personal hostility of George III has gone, the House of Lords rejects a bill for Catholic relief

1824 Repeal of the Combination Laws following the successful agitation led by Francis Place allows the open growth of trade unions

1825 George Stephenson's Stockton and Darlington Railway is opened: the first steam hauled public line

1828 The Duke of Wellington becomes Prime Minister

Nonconformists gain political rights

1829 The struggle for Catholic emancipation ends

Sir Robert Peel, Home Secretary, establishes the Metropolitan Police Force

1830 Low wages and unemployment among farm labourers in the southern counties lead to the 'Swing Riots' with attacks on threshing machines and burning of ricks. Special Commissions hand out severe sentences to the rioters

The Liverpool and Manchester Railway opens

1830–37 **William IV** succeeds his brother and is prepared to accept the reforms of the electoral system proposed by the Liberal ministry of Lord Grey

1832 The First Reform Act extends the franchise to the middle classes and removes representation from the 'rotten' boroughs. Passage is secured through the House of Lords by a threat to create new peers in favour of reform

William IV, nicknamed 'Sailor Billy'.

1832–37 Robert Peel continues the reform of the criminal law pioneered by Samuel Romilly and James Mackintosh by abolishing capital punishment for horse, sheep and cattle stealing, coining, and rick-burning

1833 A quarter of a century after the abolition of the slave trade, the keeping of slaves is forbidden in British possessions

John Keble leads the Tractarian (Oxford) Movement to reform the Anglican church along Catholic lines with a greater insistence on ritual

The Factory Act introduced by Lord Shaftesbury is passed following the campaign led by Michael Sadler and Richard Oastler

1834 The New Poor Law is introduced to much popular hostility. On the principle of 'less eligibility' it intended the limitation of relief at home in favour of forcing the poor into the workhouses.

Sir Robert Peel becomes Prime Minister for a short time (he was to head a ministry again in 1841). He is regarded as the first modern Conservative Prime Minister

The Tolpuddle Martyrs: six Dorset farm labourers are transported for administering a secret oath in the formation of a trade union

The Grand National Consolidated Trades Union is formed under the influence of Robert Owen. Important as a pioneering attempt at general unionism, it had in fact collapsed by the end of the year

1836 The 'Great Trek' of the Dutch settlers from British Cape Colony takes place to form the independent Boer Republics of the Transvaal and the Orange Free State

The Victorian Era

*In the years of Victoria's reign Britain became
the first industrial society and the workshop of the world. The creation of
a dense railway network revolutionised transport, resulting
in increased productivity and new wealth, and the growing urban population and a sense of
pride and civic responsibility led to the creation of public utilities
and services. After the desperate years of potato famine Ireland re-emerged as a
political problem at home, while overseas the Second
British Empire reached its zenith, providing the raw materials and export
markets for Britain's thriving industry.*

The Victorians were the first generation of our ancestors to be photographed; but while their visual image has been preserved, it is hard to understand these people who stare back at us with their unsmiling faces and formal poses. What was life like for them?

The first point an historian would make is that there were more people in Britain then ever before, as the population doubled between the time Queen Victoria came to the throne in 1837 and her death 64 years later. This created many problems, not least of which was how these people were to be fed. We know now that changes in agricultural methods and the increased production from industrialisation meant that there were more food and jobs to meet the new demands, but not quite enough. The result was that the Victorian poor lived and died in wretched conditions at a time when manufacturers were making England the richest country in the world.

An economic historian would stress that to understand the Victorian experience it is first necessary to look at the revolutionary changes of industrialisation. These changes meant that more people began working in manufacturing, commercial and service activities, rather than in agriculture as they had done previously. The scale of production increased and the factory replaced the household as the place of work.

The social historian, however, would argue that to really know the Victorians we must examine how their society was ordered and how the various groups in that society behaved towards one another. What makes this interesting is that during Victoria's reign social relations underwent many changes. When the Queen was born in 1819, England was basically an agricultural country with most of its people living in villages rather than towns. The existence of the poor was taken for granted, but by tradition they were dependent on their 'betters' for the 'right to work' and the 'right to eat'. In practice this was not always the way things worked out, but there was the comforting feeling that the rich should behave in a charitable, if paternalistic, fashion towards the poor, and the poor should respond by being hard-working and deferential. The small size of the village encouraged a sense of community, and the distress of the needy was visible to their neighbours. As countrymen moved into the cities in search of higher wages and a more varied

lifestyle, a new relationship developed between rich and poor. The businessmen who were building factories felt no special responsibility to look after the poor who could not care for themselves. Their sympathies lay with other men who were striving to make the most of unprecedented business opportunities. They began calling themselves the middle class, as they saw their interests being different from the privileged aristocracy above them and from the poor below.

These new attitudes were intensified as the industrial towns and cities grew. Like the population increase, the growth of towns and cities at this time was spectacular. By 1851, for the first time in history there were more people living in the towns of Britain than in the countryside. The social strain of altering the basis of national life from farming to industry and from country to town was tremendous, and if we are to understand the experiences of our great-grandparents, they must be pictured against this background.

If there was one subject that preoccupied the Victorians it was the question of social and economic differences between the classes. Dudley Baxter, whose book on *National Income* (1868) attempted to provide a statistical analysis of Victorian society, described that society as being like the Atlantic island of Tenerife, 'with its long low base of labouring population, with its uplands of middle classes and with its

Ford Madox Brown's painting 'Work' depicts a theme cherished by the Victorians. The excavation in the centre of the picture represents physical work, while the two gentlemen on the right are Carlyle and F. D. Maurice, whose seeming idleness is really the organising force behind the work of others.

The Bluebell Line (left) is a preserved steam railway, open to the public. The growth of the rail network in Victorian times radically altered the lifestyles of ordinary people, many of whom had never been more than a few miles from home.

towering peaks and summits of those princely incomes'. The view of society based on economic differences was beginning to be widely held and the terms 'upper', 'middle' and 'lower' class entered the language at this time. Class divisions were of the greatest importance and many looked on social and economic inequality as the law of nature. Class distinctions pervaded every aspect of Victorian life: railway trains were segregated into three types of accommodation; public houses were divided into public and saloon bars; and even churches and chapels isolated the poor into separate pews. The divisions between the classes remained immense, but it was the jostling for position within a class that was of the most importance to an individual. Subtle degrees of status, such as where one lived, who one's relatives were, or how many servants or carriages one kept were all essential in determining on which rung of the social ladder an individual was to be placed, and how a family was to maintain or improve its social standing.

Social status was not only important to the prosperous; the poor had equally rigid categories for ranking individuals based on their jobs, behaviour and possessions. On the social ladder of the working classes tradesmen and artisans came first, followed by the semi-skilled in regular employment, and by then by the various trades of unskilled workers. Nevertheless, the character of a person, suggested by such phrases as 'he was poor but honest' designated a social standing that was assigned regardless of occupation.

Why were the Victorians so fascinated by these distinctions? Part of the answer lies in the pressures of social change that were taking place. Many Victorians, especially those in the middle classes, were proud and excited by the signs of progress they saw around them. By the mid 19th century Britain had obtained an unchallenged ascendancy over other nations in commerce and manufacturing, but for individual men and women the chance to elevate themselves socially was even more important. Ideally, there was nothing to prevent an individual, fired with ambition, from rising as high as his talents would allow. In practice, however, he was more likely to improve his standing within his own social group. Impressive leaps between classes would take a couple of generations, ability and good luck; they were possible for only a very few fortunate families. The rise of the original W. H. Smith from an ordinary London newsvendor to a wealthy nationwide wholesaler, partly through acquiring the franchise for those still familiar station book stalls, formed the basis of his son's political career (the son rose to lead the Conservative Party in the House of Commons). Women could always improve their social position

Britain was the first urbanised, industrial nation, but to many Victorians the countryside remained an ideal in contrast to widespread urban poverty.

AGRICULTURE

The first half of the 19th century saw the completion of the transformation of the open fields, commons and much of the waste land into a pattern of enclosed fields and compact farms. The cultivation of the land by freeholders and 'customary' tenants disappeared in favour of tenant farmers on small farms.

The farming community was far from happy during the early years of the century, partly owing to high taxation and partly to tithe difficulties, but mainly due to the agitation over the Corn Laws. The tithe burden was eased in 1837, however, when tithes were commuted into a fixed grain rent. The re-imposition of income tax in 1842 (it had been abolished in 1816) established once more a fairer balance between rural and urban societies.

It was the Corn Laws, however, which gave rise to the greatest difficulties. The Corn Laws gave to the farmer a bounty on wheat exports in normal years which was then suspended in years of scarcity. It was thought that this method would prevent grain from being either so dear that the poor could not afford it or so cheap that the farmer could not make ends meet. This traditional method of adjustment, however, could not cope with climatic variations combined with the rapid growth of the industrial urban population. During the 18th century Britain had exported as much foodstuff as she imported, large quantities of wheat being exchanged for oats and sugar. The need towards the end of the Industrial Revolution was for the free import of large quantities of wheat to feed the growing population; this was achieved by Sir Robert Peel with the abolition of the Corn Laws in 1846.

Between 1800 and 1850 the main source of foreign wheat had been Russia and north-west Europe. Thereafter North America was to play an important role, with the USA and, eventually, Canada becoming the main source of imported wheat. These supplies were supplemented after the opening of the Suez Canal in 1869 with imports from India and Australia.

Despite many gloomy prognostications, agriculture survived the abolition of the Corn Laws largely as a result of the fortunate juxtaposition of a new set of factors. It can even be said to have prospered over the next 30 years. The reasons were several; in the first place, farmers turned from arable to pasture and began to concentrate on meat and dairy products for which there was a ready market. Secondly there was a new scientific approach to farming as a result of the founding by Lawes in 1843 of the Rothamsted Experimental Station and of the work of the German scientist Liebig. Liebig showed the relation between plant nutrition and the composition of the soil, and inspired the chemists to analyse the manures into the two great groups of the nitrogenous life-givers and the non-nitrogenous body builders. This paved the way for business firms to manufacture fertilisers, and vast quantities of Peruvian guano poured into the country in the 1850s.

Accompanying the fertiliser revolution was a great spurt in land drainage promoted by the Scottish engineer James Smith of Perthshire. These two factors combined meant increased productivity in many marginal areas, and by 1875 farming was in good heart throughout much of Britain.

Shortly thereafter, however, a depression set in which was to continue until the end of the century with the worst phases during the early 1880s and 1890s. The causes were again multiple and were not readily recognised. There were some exceptionally bad harvests (especially 1879), Canadian wheat began to pour in large quantities into the country, and there was a steady growth of meat imports from Argentina, Australia and New Zealand as a result of the introduction of refrigeration n the 1880s.

By 1900 the industrial-urban population was in the ascendant so far as the struggle for cheap food was concerned and many agricultural-rural communities were in a state of decay.

The story in Ireland was to follow a somewhat different course of events. It also had been subject to a great increase in population, but there had been no industrialisation and urban development to absorb the increase. The population had risen to over eight million, at least half of which existed almost wholly on potatoes: much of the grain production was still being exported to Britain. It was a precarious state of affairs that no government was prepared to tackle in advance of the disaster which overwhelmed the country.

Portents of what might happen were realised with the partial failure of the potato crop in the autumn of 1845. A more or less complete failure in 1846 and 1847 followed, but a partial recovery occurred in 1848. During these four years Ireland lost, either by death or emigration, over a million people. In the spring of 1847 over three million people were destitute and being supported by public funds. Wholesale evictions took place and a massive emigration programme was instituted with the result that the population of Ireland dropped to six and a half million in 1851 and five and a half million by 1871.

The decline in numbers permitted consolidation of holdings but it was not until the end of the century that the population reached a level which Ireland's agricultural economy could safely support. The famine and its after effects dominated Anglo-Irish relations for the rest of the century, produced the Home Rule Movement, the Land League, established a huge Irish population in the USA with a grievance against Britain, and it also revealed the gap between Ulster and the rest of Ireland.

Ulster was less dependent on the potato and was in fact benefiting from the offshoots of the industrial revolution. It suffered much less severely from the 'black forty-seven', which hardly figures in its current folklore. The distinctive character of the north-eastern counties which has dominated 20th-century Irish politics was beginning to emerge.

Harvesting in early Victorian days. Hand cutting of corn with scythes was common, and local labour was supplemented with Irish labourers who followed the harvest.

A Welsh farmwife making butter in a plunger churn. Victorian farms were largely self-sufficient.

For the Victorian farm worker, relaxation centred on the village inn. Male workers commonly wore smocks.

A Victorian farm worker's cottage, cramped and poor. The farmhand and his family endured appalling conditions. Work was seldom regular and never well paid. Whole families laboured long days in the fields to maintain their meagre existence.

Farm worker and family evicted in Milton Abbas, c. 1874. His offence was membership of the National Agricultural Labourers' Union, founded in 1872. In the 1870s strikes were ineffective, and a ruthless landlord could do as he liked.

A two-horse team drawing a Norfolk plough. Ploughs hauled by stationary steam engines were being used experimentally in the early 19th century, but horse drawn ploughs remained the most common method.

The Blackhouse, Highland Folk Museum, Kingussie, Scotland. Even in the 19th century, primitive turf-roofed stone walled dwellings without windows or built chimneys, often doorless, were common in remote parts of Scotland, Ireland and Wales.

Hand threshing of corn could often be seen in the remoter parts of the country; farming remained labour intensive throughout much of the Victorian period.

Treading corn using horses was an alternative to hand threshing. Today in rural Yorkshire the horse and corn have been replaced by the tractor and sheep.

through marriage. Robert Roberts, author of *The Classic Slum*, described how his aunts in the 1860s attended a Wesleyan chapel on the edge of a middle class suburb. They were only the daughters of a skilled artisan, but they were attractive and intelligent and each married well above her station: one a journalist, another a traveller in sugar and the third a police inspector.

While in reality social advancement was modest, the idea of a spectacular rise remained appealing, as can be seen from the fact that Samuel Smiles' book *Self Help*, chronicling the careers of self-made industrialists, sold 20,000 copies in the first year of publication. It was, however, because such limited social mobility was possible that distinctions between classes and divisions of status within classes became so important. Industrialists who owed their positions to individual initiative, and workers who sought to improve their positions, needed to know exactly where they stood in the social ranking and where to place others. On the personal level, this was important because in times of rapid change people needed some way of assessing their surroundings. It was also important on the group level as a way of establishing solidarity and acted as a springboard for political action.

The aristocracy and gentry likewise became eager to define the limits of their social group. The sense of belonging to a community with obligations and responsibilities to those above and below them began to break down and tensions between the classes heightened. The 20 years between the era of the Napoleonic Wars and Victoria's accession to the throne were anxious times for all. The aristocracy were frightened by the example of the French Revolution and disturbed by middle class demands to limit their privilege. The middle classes wanted to share in governing the country, and both groups were afraid of the lower orders. The Chartist agitations of the 1830s and 1840s, reflecting the economic distress of the times, seemed to confirm the worst upper and middle class suspicions. It is perhaps no coincidence that when Karl Marx and his associate Frederick Engels observed the conditions of the labourers in England, the tensions between the buyers and sellers of labour were such that they predicted the eventual collapse of capitalist society.

Karl Marx (1818–83), father of modern Socialism and author with Engels of the Communist Manifesto. From 1849 he lived in London where he wrote 'Das Kapital', in which he argued that capitalism was inherently unstable and would be succeeded by the dictatorship of the proletariat and then the classless society.

AGRICULTURAL ENGINEERING

Between 1801 and 1851 the population of England and Wales doubled, rising from nearly 9 to nearly 18 million. This surge, which began in the mid-18th century, greatly increased the demand for food. Imports grew rapidly after 1815, but less rapidly than consumption, giving British farmers an even larger share of the home market than formerly. Yet the growth in demand did not stimulate technical innovation, and increases in output occurred chiefly as a result of biological experimentation with new crops and rotations and with chemical fertilisers — as long as labour remained cheap and plentiful there was little incentive to mechanise. Before 1850 the traditional husbandry practices survived with scant modification; the main advance was in threshing where water- and horse-powered machines were introduced by farmers to enable them to cope with rising corn output, and from the 1840s threshing by steam gradually replaced all other methods.

Despite limited technical improvement this period witnessed the birth of the agricultural engineering industry. Already by the end of the 18th century a few entrepreneurs had established small implement manufactories, serving a more than local community. Such businesses benefited from the generally favourable conditions for agriculture during the Napoleonic Wars, and having survived the post-war depression by diversifying into general engineering, entered a phase of rapid expansion after 1835. In the case of some firms, like Ransomes of Ipswich, this was particularly associated with the taking on of railway work.

The mid to late Victorian period is characterised by the mechanisation of agriculture. Of crucial importance in explaining this process was the long term migration of people off the land into urban areas. The rural population fell steadily from the mid-century, creating a shortage of agricultural labour in some districts. This revealed itself first during the harvest and often left farmers no choice but to mechanise. The horse drawn reaper was adopted widely in the 1860s and the reaper-binder appeared in the following decade. The old hand methods — using sickle, reap-hook or scythe — were still employed occasionally, but by 1914 almost all the corn harvest was cut mechanically. The same degree of progress was not evident in the dairy and livestock sectors. The farm dairy was often small and run by the farmer's wife. The equipment was simple and cheap, and the increased emphasis on liquid milk production after 1880 offered little inducement to replace the existing butter and cheese making appliances. One notable invention, however, was the Lawrence refrigerator (first used in the brewing trade) which cooled milk so that it could be carried fresh by rail to the cities, whose demand for milk, meat and vegetables had scarcely begun to be satisfied.

Any breakthrough to raise work output in agriculture was dependent on a new prime mover. The second half of the 19th century saw much experimentation with steam power. A few early and improbable machines were used as a substitute for the horse in direct cultivation, but more commonly steam engines stationed at the headlands hauled tillage implements over and back across the field by means of cables. Although many of the technical problems in steam cultivation were resolved, it was rarely an economic proposition, and it was chiefly in respect of threshing and barn work, where cheaper, single cylinder machines could be utilised for a variety of tasks, that steam was successful. The development of the internal combustion engine provided another and more enduring solution. The first tractors were made in the United States, but a surprising number of British firms had produced a tractor by 1914. Many, however, were only prototypes and were never sold commercially. The widespread adoption of the tractor in British farming, like that of the oil engine, lay in the future.

The agricultural engineering industry entered a period of decline in the last quarter of the 19th century. It was in one sense the victim of its own success: the earlier phase of expansion had brought a large number of firms into existence, manufacturing high quality, long lasting products, but by the 1870s the market for many machines was reaching saturation point, while the contraction in demand was aggravated by the arable depression of the 1880s and 1890s. Some firms failed completely and others only survived by concentrating on the export side of their business, but even in this area they faced increasing competition from the United States. In the period immediately before the First World War, it was the firms that moved into new lines, such as electrical plant and oil powered machinery, that had the brightest prospects.

A 'blue' Hereford wagon, characterised by its large body, plank sides, heavy undercarriage and broad wheels. There were perhaps 100 regional designs, but factory-made products slowly ousted traditional forms.

AGRICULTURAL MACHINERY MANUFACTURED BY **RANSOMES & SIMS**

Ransomes & Sims, a well known farm machinery firm, had by the 1840s expanded into general engineering, but after 1870 overseas demand for agricultural equipment was the chief factor in their progress.

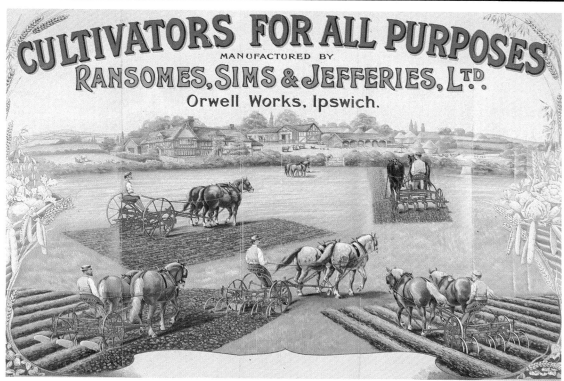

CULTIVATORS FOR ALL PURPOSES
MANUFACTURED BY
RANSOMES, SIMS & JEFFERIES, LTD.
Orwell Works, Ipswich.

Cultivating machinery. The second half of the 19th century saw improvements in existing horse-powered machines — for instance, lighter, all-metal implements, which were not surpassed until the development of tractor-drawn equipment.

Threshing on a Norfolk farm. Rising demand for corn during the Napoleonic period stimulated the mechanisation of threshing. Early machines were driven by water, hand or horse power, but the breakthrough came with the development of the portable steam engine in the 1840s.

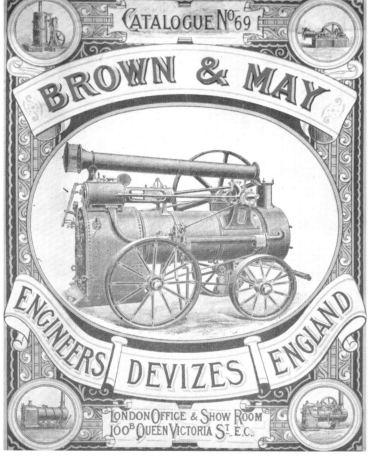

CATALOGUE Nº 69
BROWN & MAY
ENGINEERS DEVIZES ENGLAND
LONDON OFFICE & SHOW ROOM
100ᴮ QUEEN VICTORIA Sᵀ. E.C.

Brown and May, founded in the 1850s, specialised in portable steam engines, for which it gained an international reputation, but its inability to diversify led to failure just before the Great War.

The Fearless 7 HP Burrell General Purpose Traction Engine. Manufacturers of agricultural engines also made models with extravagant superstructure for the needs of showmen.

Mechanisation brought major efficiencies to farming but had devastating effects on the employment of farmworkers and caused much rural poverty.

While Marx was an acute social observer and historian, his prophecy for revolution and the overthrow of the bourgeois state did not come to pass in 19th-century Britain. Given the fraught conditions at the beginning of Victoria's reign in the late 1830s and early 1840s, historians have been puzzled as to why this was so, for rather than the collapse of society, confidence and a relative social harmony were the keynotes of the 1850s. This calm owed much to the economic prosperity of Britain and was reflected in the pride and excitement of the Great Exhibition and a new attitude to the monarchy. With Victoria's uncles, George IV and William IV, the monarchy had fallen into disrepute. Victoria herself had been disliked in the first years of her reign. While her youth and her clearly formed sense of duty were initial advantages, she courted unpopularity by revealing a stubborn streak in her personality that led her to interfere with politics. After her marriage her ever-increasing nursery and the Prince Consort's insistence on a high moral tone at court and a life of hard work increased her subjects' respect for the monarchy.

How can we account for this change in mood? Undoubtedly, the period 1815 to 1850, the era of the Napoleonic Wars to the Great Exhibition, was one of tension. Party strife was bitter, elections were tumultuous and corrupt, and both England and Ireland witnessed intermittent popular agitations. Apart from the fear of revolution, violence was never far from the surface of life. A Parliamentary Act of 1835 had placed on municipal corporations the obligation to establish police forces. Before this, consignments of troops or special constables were relied upon to protect property and maintain law and order. Even after 1835, many boroughs were slow to establish forces so that in the early part of Victoria's reign the police were an inefficient, impoverished organisation. Sir Robert Peel's reforms of the Criminal Code in the 1820s abolished capital punishment for a very large number of crimes, revised the scale of lesser punishments and improved the legal procedure and conditions of imprisonment. While this made the law less savage than in the 18th century, it still remained brutal. Transportation went on until 1846 and public hangings until 1868. The prison system was designed to be punitive, with little concern for the prisoners' rehabilitation. Young offenders were punished exactly the same as adults, for it was not until 1854 that a parliamentary act recognised juvenile delinquency.

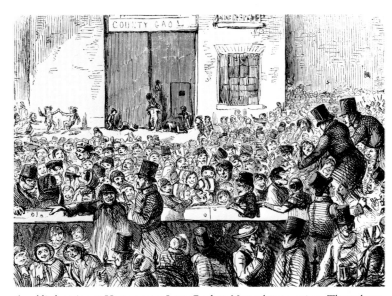

A public hanging at Horsemonger Lane Gaol on November 13, 1849. Throughout the 1800s the Criminal Law became less brutal and severe: in 1800 there were 224 capital offences, and by 1870 there were only two – murder and high treason. Hangings as public entertainment were ended with the 1868 Act.

RURAL INDUSTRIES

Until the mid 19th century the rural areas made an important contribution to the national economy. In pre-industrial and even early industrial Britain, the countryside was the domain not only of agriculture but of a host of processing and manufacturing trades; locally available raw materials were extracted and worked, clay was dug for pots, bricks and tiles, stone was quarried and dressed for building purposes, and in the upland areas of the north and west non-ferrous metal ores were mined and smelted.

Many trades were directly concerned with the processing of agricultural products. From livestock, wool was woven and spun as the raw material for cloth, hosiery and knitted garments, and hides were tanned to produce leather. From corn and the industrial crops came grain for milling and baking, malting and brewing, straw for the manufacture of hats and bonnets and hemp for rope making. Wood, in the form of timber planks and beams or as underwood, the product of deliberately cultivated coppice, was shaped into a multiplicity of manufactured products. Corn mills, fulling mills and paper mills lined the banks of fast running streams. The workshops of the carpenter, wheelwright, harness maker and blacksmith could be found in every community. The pattern of rural industries varied from region to region and even from parish to parish, and as old industries collapsed, new ones replaced them, perhaps employing the same water powered mills or a similar type of labour skill.

Rural manufacturing was commonly practised as a by-employment or part-time occupation with agriculture. Workers in pastoral districts were less heavily preoccupied with the daily routine of farming than in the common field arable areas, and such communities found a greater opportunity to follow other trades, for example metal working in the west midlands, lead mining and hand knitting in the Yorkshire Dales and, in many country districts, spinning, weaving, tanning, pottery and woodland work. Before the evolution of the large urban factory most of the stages of textile production were undertaken by rural outworkers in their cottages, supplied with raw materials by entrepreneurs who would also arrange for the finishing and marketing of the manufactured goods. The handloom weavers and framework knitters, as well as the cutlers, grinders and other metal workers, all tended to work within this domestic system.

The early stages of the Industrial Revolution saw tremendous expansion of many of these country-based industries: water-powered textile mills were established in remote Pennine dales and the upland mining settlements expanded as British output of non-ferrous metals reached its peak. The growth of cities and their industries stimulated the demand for rural commodities such as timber, underwood and basket willow and the goods produced from them. As agricultural production increased to meet the requirements of Britain's rapidly growing population so too did the particular trades which served it, including the manufacture and repair of agricultural tools and implements and of carts and wagons.

Subsequently, the industrial role of the rural districts diminished in importance against that of the cities. By mid-century many rural communities had reached and even passed their peak of inhabitants, and the numbers employed in agriculture also began to decline. The widespread use of steam power stimulated the growth of industries in towns by concentrating a high brake-horse power on a single site, usually on or near a coalfield, with easy access to water navigation or a railway; it became a positive disadvantage to an industry to be located in country areas where the cost of coal was high. As the rate of innovation quickened new materials were substituted for old ones, and iron and steel succeeded wood as the essential raw material. The demand for firewood decreased in favour of coal, and the rural charcoal iron furnaces were blown out, to be replaced by coke smelting. By 1900 the prices for underwood products had fallen and coppices became increasingly neglected. A precipitous collapse in the prices of non-ferrous metals had led to the closure of numerous mines in the previous 20 years. The national output of the clay-using industries was dominated by that of the Staffordshire potteries and the large brickworks of the east Midlands, and in the Sheffield area and west Midlands metal working had migrated from the outlying districts to the cities. The woollen industry of the West Country contracted sharply as the urban valley centres of the West Riding of Yorkshire became pre-eminent. In the south Midlands, the village pillow lace industry was supplanted by the Nottingham machine lace industry and the cottage plaiting industry died out in the face of competition from imported straw plait.

Other rural industries survived tenuously into the 20th century, including the remnants of the underwood trade and the small mills, maltings and breweries. The blacksmiths, wheelwrights and harness makers had a few more decades left to perform their essential supporting role for rural communities dependent on relatively unsophisticated implements and machines and upon the agricultural draught horse, but since the Second World War these trades too have declined almost to extinction. Rural industry had come to be regarded as an ailing sector of the economy requiring support and encouragement, like that provided after 1921 by the Rural Industries Bureau (now succeeded by the Council for Small Industries in Rural Areas).

Preparation of white willow in the basket makers' yard of the Beesley family, Oxford, 1900. On the left the osiers are peeled by drawing them between steel blades set into brakes. On the right completed eel and fish traps are displayed.

A thatcher working on a long straw roof, using undamaged straw from corn separately reaped and threshed. Longer lasting thatch required Devon or combed wheat straw or Norfolk reed.

Blacksmith's shop from Llawr-y-glyn, Powys, re-erected at the Welsh Folk Museum, and typical of the many smithies in rural Wales. The smith was an essential member of every village community, responsible for the making and fitting of horseshoes, the repair of farm tools and implements, the tyring of cart wheels and the production of a wide variety of wrought iron ware.

Edward Seymour and Sons, saddlers and harness makers of Minster Street, Reading. Several sets of cart harness, collars and hames are displayed. By 1900 town saddlers would have supplied the farming and transport needs of many local villages.

Shoeing smiths making horse shoes from hot bar iron with hammer and anvil. With the numbers of agricultural horses yet to reach their peak of 1,137,000 in 1910, it was still a time of prosperity for the village blacksmith.

Clog blocks stacked to dry before dispatch to clog sole makers of northern and midland towns. The blocks were roughly cut to shape by gangs of itinerant block-cutters, working the alder groves of Wales and the West Midlands.

Charcoal burners from the Furness district, west of Lake Windermere. They supplied the fuel for Backbarrow, the last charcoal iron furnace. The sod hut provided temporary shelter on site during the three days of firing.

Gate hurdle maker and temporary coppice shelter of cleft wood and bark peeling in southern England. Such hurdles, of oak, ash, chestnut and willow, were used as portable enclosures for sheep folding and lambing.

A hoop maker's workshop at Uckfield, Sussex. The bundles of 'smart' hazel wood hoops were supplied to the manufacturers of slack barrels for dry goods such as cement, sugar, fish, fruit and vegetables.

Strikes could be violent, needing troops to control them and trade unions often organised terrorist campaigns. While the atmosphere was charged with tension, excitement and vitality were also in the air. This was the time when the wealth of Britain was mounting and the empire was expanding.

Immense energy was the outstanding quality of the early Victorians, and the building of the railways was one of their characteristic achievements. Large scale construction began in the 1830s; by 1845, an estimated 5,000 miles of track had been laid down. With massive engineering works, such as embankments, tunnels, bridges and viaducts, the Victorians were not only changing the physical environment, but they were also beginning to alter the way society was organised by attacking the privileges of the aristocracy and the clergy. It

was a time of flamboyant opinions and dress, of great optimism regarding what had been accomplished and dark pessimism about what was yet to be achieved.

Improvements in the printing press meant that printed material was more readily available and a large public was eager to read the works of novelists such as Dickens and poets like Tennyson. Besides novels, there were travel books, works on religion and a growing number of periodical reviews to cater for different opinions. Through novels, and to a lesser extent plays, the reading public continued to be influenced by romantic ideals that placed emotion and imagination above reason.

While there was an atmosphere of tension, there was also excitement in the air that touched even religion. The effects of the great evangelical revival in the 18th century that had

THE FISHING TRADE

Now a traditional feature of the banqueting hall or important feast, until Victoria's reign and the advent of the railway, fresh fish was available only to those living near the coast; for people inland fish was usually preserved, and they had the unappetising choice between tasteless stock fish (air-dried cod) and the strong-flavoured red herring, salted and heavily smoked. Small wonder that fish was widely regarded as a Lenten penance.

However, observing that sole could tempt the appetite of the most delicate invalid recuperating at the seaside, while pilchards replaced meat for sturdy Cornish miners, doctors in particular began to look for means of getting this useful and abundant source of nourishment to the fast-expanding populations of the large inland towns. At the end of the 18th century the Royal Society of Arts offered money prizes for anyone who could devise a means of improving the supply of fish. This resulted in the development of special carriages that enabled fish to be brought inland swiftly with the minimum of bruising, and it also inspired imitation of the Dutch ships with their permitted large live fish, such as cod and flat fish, to be brought up river as far as Gravesend.

Both innovations improved the supply of fresh fish to the metropolitan wealthy, but another idea culled from successful Dutch fishery methods — salting gutted herrings packed in clean, airtight barrels — added fish to the diet of the poor and marked the beginning of fishing on an industrial scale.

Encouraged by a Royal bounty and

packed under the supervision of a Scottish Fisheries Board officer the soused herrings, that were first sold under the Crown brand during the Napoleonic Wars, found ready sale all over Europe. They provided work not only for fishermen, but for their womenfolk who gutted and barrelled the fish and for other shore-based workers, such as coopers and shipbuilders. More delicate in flavour than the red herring, fish for the new white herring trade had to be brought in as soon as they were caught, and the ships therefore moved southwards as the herring shoals appeared further down the coast, taking their catches to the nearest ports. Scottish ports, such as Wick and Dunbar and the new harbours at Fraserburgh, Cullen and Lybster, were not the only ones to benefit from the season that began in early summer off Scotland and ended in the Channel after Christmas; as the herring industry grew, black-sailed fifties and zulus (a type of boat invented at the time of the Zulu War) were joined by russet-sailed luggers from Yarmouth and Lowestoft, where the fishermen's wives let rooms to the Scottish lassies following their work and their menfolk south. This annual southerly migration of fishery workers continued right up to the 1930s. The Cornish pilchard (actually the sardine at its most northern limit) also received the gutting and salting treatment: an excellent way of dealing with a fish that appeared in huge shoals but, unlike the regular herring, turned up most erratically.

Herring, like pilchards and mackerel, are pelagic fish that swim near the

surface and can be caught in fine-meshed drift nets. These long nets are shot over the side of the ship and hang suspended like curtains from a series of floats while the ship drifts for a whole tide. The drifter fishermen exercised skill in sailing and placing their nets, and in judging where and when the highly mobile shoals would be found.

Until the middle of the 19th century, fish which live near the sea bottom, such as cod and other flat fish, were caught with baited hooks weighted to carry them to the bottom. When the railways reached the fishing ports the demand for these fish (which are available all year round) increased and a more effective way of catching them — trawling — was developed, in which a large, bag-shaped net is dragged along the sea bottom. However, as the best trawling grounds were further out in the North Sea the fish were not always in good condition when brought ashore. In fact, that great English delicacy — fish and chips — developed originally as a means of disguising the taste of stale fish (the chips joined it from France towards the end of the century). But to improve matters trawlers began to work in fleets with a fast, cutter-rigged ship that carried ice and was engaged solely in taking the catch back to port. Originally natural ice from the Norfolk Broads was used, stored from the winter in insulated ice wells, but towards the end of the century, with the development of refrigeration, manufactured ice became available.

The life of the drifter fisherman was rough and dangerous, but it offered even the miserable, seasick ship's boy

his chance of becoming a skipper if he survived and worked hard enough, and although work was continuous throughout the season, trips were short. The trawler fleets, on the other hand, stayed at sea in similar discomfort and danger for much longer periods. Their fishermen must have suffered also from the monotony of their job: work in which it gradually became less easy for them to achieve independence as ships became very much more expensive with the introduction of steam-powered trawlers in the 80s.

One result of this boredom actually added to the dangers of life at sea, for the 'copers' who sailed among the trawler fleets selling cheap tobacco also sold strong and poisonous spirits. This danger was tackled with typical late-Victorian 'muscular Christianity' by Ebenezer Mather who raised the money to send out the first missionary ship from Yarmouth in 1882. Jeered at as he sailed, Mather and later missionaries of the Royal National Mission to Deep Sea Fishermen showed a practicality likely to succeed: refused duty-free tobacco by the government he bought it in Ostende where the copers bought theirs, but undercut their prices to the fishermen. Despite preaching total abstinence his missionaries had considerable success with the fishermen who appreciated the books, scarves and sometimes the medical care offered by the mission ships: so successful were they, in fact, that in Yarmouth and Gorleston a number of pubs and two breweries went out of business!

Fish being gutted at Whitby. F. M. Sutcliffe was a pioneer photographer of the naturalistic school, although his people were often posed. The characters here are real enough and include auctioneer and fish merchant as well as fishermen.

Lifeboat being launched. The lifeboat service grew up alongside the fishing industry, the boats usually being crewed by fishermen. The Royal National Lifeboat Institution, still voluntarily manned and financed, was founded in 1824.

influenced people both within and outside the established church were still being felt. 'Evangelical' is the term used to describe those protestants who believe that the central message of the Bible is salvation by faith. Personal experience is central to evangelical beliefs, for the individual must realise his wickedness, acknowledge the saving power of Christ and then 'choose' the way of salvation. This dramatic choice is called conversion, and it was a deeply emotional experience that impressed upon the believer the fearful destiny of those who remained unconverted.

The evangelical movement gave religion a force and vitality that had been missing in the complacent 18th-century attitudes to the established church. By the 1830s it had influenced people in every walk of life and in every corner of England. Once converted, the individual lived a life of

Vast revivalist meetings suggest that the Victorians were deeply religious, but a 1851 survey showed that only about half the population attended church.

Mevagissey, Cornwall, long the heart of the pilchard industry; it is known that in the 18th century over 30 million were exported annually to Italy. Now a great variety of fish is caught locally, including turbot, plaice, crabs and congers.

Lifeboatman. His cumbersome life-jacket is made of cork. In action he would have worn oilskins over his guernsey.

Fishing boats in Scarborough harbour. The North Sea skippers' skill at navigation was remarkable.

Drifters crowded into Lowestoft harbour in the scramble to secure the best prices. Within hours the herrings will have been unloaded, auctioned, gutted, salted down in barrels and distributed all over the country by train.

GWR fish train being loaded. The boom in North Sea fishing was caused by the building of railways to the ports in the 1840s. For the first time fresh fish could be transported fast enough to reach inland towns in palatable condition.

Scarborough, 'the queen of watering places'. As well as stimulating the fishing industry the railway also made visits to the seaside accessible to all. For them the new Foreshore Road was built, with a fine view of the fishing fleet and pier.

Fishermen's huts at Hastings. These strange tall buildings made of tarred wood were built to store their equipment, the height enabling nets to be hung up. A fine example of architecture without architects.

seriousness. Hard work and keeping the Sabbath were important, as were abstinence from drink, gambling and sensual pleasures.

Evangelicalism was not only a religion, but also a moral code – a rigid system of distinguishing right from wrong – that was reflected in the lifestyle of the converted. Philanthropy became an essential part of this way of life. For the evangelicals, each person had a soul worth saving and the winning of others to their beliefs was of primary importance. Their social work was closely connected with their desire to convert the poor. Some believed that conversion should come before material help was given, because the newly serious attitude of the convert meant that he would make the most of any physical assistance. Others felt that the poor were so sunk in misery that the spiritual message would have little effect without some improvement in their physical condition. Numerous societies, charities and parliamentary pressure groups were founded by evangelicals to help the distressed. Lord Shaftesbury's parliamentary endeavours, especially in the 1840s, spurred the government into factory reform; he is one of the best-remembered of the evangelicals.

Both during Victoria's lifetime and thereafter, a great deal of criticism has been levelled against our great-grandfathers' insistence upon moral rectitude, reinforced by religious beliefs. These rigid standards have been blamed for making life dull and people inflexible. What is difficult for us to appreciate is the meaning which morality and religion had for our ancestors. Unquestionable standards of right and wrong, backed by established authority, gave many people the strength of purpose to go confidently about their own and the nation's business. For many, religion was an intensely real and personal experience. Exploring the depths of their souls or reading about and possibly venturing forth to convert the heathen at home or abroad fired the imaginations of many. In the early Victorian period particularly, anything seemed possible: society may have been torn apart but a better one could be built in its place; the physical environment would be tamed and the secrets of the heart and soul could be charted.

By mid-century, however, people were becoming more relaxed as feelings of tension and excitement were replaced by confidence. It was at this time that the Queen's subjects began calling themselves Victorians. They realised that they

ARCHITECTURE AND BUILDINGS

It was in the second half of the 19th century that Britain first became a nation of city-dwellers. One result was an increased demand for new types of building. Until the beginning of the 19th century the history of English architecture can be largely written in terms of housing and churches; now, as society became more complex and subdivided, there was a need for factories, commercial buildings, administrative buildings, schools, and for all the many buildings which catered for leisure, including hotels and theatres. These buildings were not only different in function from those on which earlier architects had exercised their ingenuity; they were also often much larger in scale. It became common for large tracts of slum housing to be cleared for just one new building, like the Law Courts in London, or the railway stations of the great cities. At the same time, city centres were transformed by a wholesale rebuilding of offices and shops, which pushed the average building height up several storeys (especially after the introduction of lifts in the 1860s). The great size of many Victorian buildings made the architect's task more difficult than it had been in earlier periods; a new building had to be adequately heated and lit and to have convenient internal communications as well as an impressive exterior. There were two other important considerations in any Victorian building: style and materials. The Industrial Revolution had brought into mass production materials like iron and steel, which could revolutionise traditional methods of

construction by dispensing with the load-bearing wall, and sometimes creating a completely new style which was not dependent on the architecture of the past. On the other hand, respect for older architecture was still very great, and despite continual pleas for a 'new style' most architects (as distinct from civil engineers) went no further than reinterpreting the styles of the past or mixing them together, often in a startlingly original way. The failure to adopt a new style based on functionalism did not come from perversity; it stemmed from a belief in the importance of ornament in architecture. Only through ornament, it was felt, could buildings be rescued from a lowest common denominator of bland mediocrity. Today's architects are now only beginning to re-learn this lesson.

The choice of a style depended to a great extent on what kind of message the patron and the architect wanted to convey; Sir Gilbert Scott, perhaps the most successful of all Victorian architects, wrote in 1857 that 'every building should tell a story'. Much depended on the function of the building; a town hall, for instance, would be expected to convey an image of civic pride and prosperity, and this message would often be enhanced by decorative carving and painting. It was generally accepted that some styles were more appropriate than others for certain types of building: Gothic, for instance, for churches, classical for banks and commercial buildings (though this was by no means always the case, and it became less so as time went on).

'Back to back' working class housing in Wortley, Leeds. An attempt to house the maximum amount of people possible, they were the result not only of greed but of the growth of industry outstripping the availability of land for building.

19th century Burnley, Lancashire. The growth of the industrial towns was sudden and rapid, and they were built to patterns rather than allowed to evolve around natural features. The gridiron street pattern shown here had not been seen since Plantagenet times.

Working class houses in Hammersmith, London, in a style used throughout England in the late 1800s and marking an improved lifestyle for many artisans.

Even here, however, there was little general agreement over which kind of Gothic – early or late, English or Continental – or which kind of classic – Greek, Roman, or Italian Renaissance. For most types of building there was no consensus as to which style was intrinsically best or most appropriate: how could there be for buildings like stations, hotels, workhouses and public baths that had few precedents in the past? Instead, architects and patrons, like the designers and purchasers of clothes, often followed whatever fashion was prevalent at the time. In the early years of Victoria's reign, classical styles still retained much of the prestige they had had ever since the 17th century, although their sway was beginning to be challenged by Gothic and Elizabethan. It was not until the 1860s, however, that Gothic came to be widely used for the larger secular buildings; it was never widely used for more mundane buildings like offices, and by the end of the 1870s it was being generally abandoned except in churches. Towards the end of the century many architects who had been trained in the Gothic style began designing in an eclectic manner often – misleadingly – called 'Queen Anne'. This style, which was often characterised by a widespread use of red brick, white-painted window frames and gabled roofs, lacked the solemn and ecclesiastical associations of Gothic, but, as one of its practitioners, J. J. Stevenson wrote: 'It is as pliable as Gothic, having inherited its freedom'. Meanwhile, however, classical architecture never died out, and began once again to be widely employed in public and commercial buildings in the early years of this century.

House design reflected these changes in fashion, although for the urban working classes and lower-middle classes, who by the end of this period were forming the vast majority of the population, 'style' meant no more than the provision of a little decorative ornament around doorways and windows. Most new houses were still terraced buildings two or three storeys high, their dimensions controlled by the end of the century by by-laws passed by socially-conscious local authorities. In the inner areas of the cities some of the worst slums were being replaced by barrack-like tenement blocks, often erected by philanthropic organisations. Meanwhile the middle classes were moving out of the inner cities to the suburbs in increasing numbers, as commuting became easier with the development of suburban rail services in the 1850s and 1860s. The more affluent outer suburbs resembled earlier estate villages in their seemingly haphazard arrangement of detached and semi-detached houses in leafy gardens. Architecturally, the houses took their cue from the country houses of this period. This meant at first a widespread use of Gothic, Italianate and Elizabethan models, but in the last third of the century domestic architects began to look back to the vernacular architecture of pre-industrial England, as if to recapture a vanished rural past. The 'domestic revival' greatly influenced the architecture of planned communities like Port Sunlight in Cheshire and of their successors, the early council estates; in a more pretentious form it created the 'stockbrokers' Tudor' of the outer suburbs and the large-scale speculative developments of the 1920s and '30s. In these respects it has profoundly influenced the physical environment in which many people in Britain live today.

Working class flats in Lever Street, London EC1. Tenement blocks of low-rental flats were built by philanthropic housing companies or trusts in an attempt to solve the slum problem, but rents were often still too high for the very poor.

Port Sunlight, Merseyside, was a completely new town begun in 1888 by the Sunlight Soap company, setting new standards of well planned workers' housing.

Middle class housing in West London dating from the third quarter of the 19th century. The attic room housed the single servant.

Upper middle class houses in St George's Square, Pimlico, London, built after 1850 with four storeys, basements and attics to house families with many servants.

CHURCHES AND CHAPELS

The years between 1820 and 1920 were a period of unparalleled churchbuilding throughout the British Isles. This was partly undertaken to meet the vast increase in population in the urban areas, and partly because there was strong dissatisfaction with the architecture and liturgical standards of the 18th century church. A great many individual churches, in a poor state of repair or in an unfashionable style, were demolished and rebuilt. Others were so heavily 'restored' as to be virtually unrecognisable afterwards.

The question of taste was fundamental in Victorian churchbuilding. Classical was denounced as vulgar and pagan; 'Gothick' was considered ridiculous; the only true style of Christian architecture was pure Gothic, preferably that of the 13th and 14th centuries. Perpendicular was considered debased though a few Victorian churches were built in this style. A few churches were also built in a neo-Norman style. The most influential architectural writer was A. W. N. Pugin, an Anglican convert to Roman Catholicism, who designed several Roman Catholic and a few Anglican churches in his own brand of high Gothic.

All denominations gradually accepted the Gothic Revival though some nonconformists were reluctant to do so. The contrast can be seen in Leeds between the splendid classicism of Brunswick Methodist Church, opened in 1825, and the equally splendid Gothicism of Mill Hill Unitarian Church, opened only 22 years later in 1847. Towards the end of the 19th century there developed some challenges to the Gothic style, with churches such as St. Barnabas', Oxford, and Westminster Cathedral designed in the Byzantine style, or alter furnishings in the exotic Baroque favoured by some avant-garde Anglican clergy.

Within the Church of England one of the greatest spurs to the Gothic Revival was the movement towards greater decency and ritual in church services. This had begun in the 1820s and 1830s among a small group of Oxford dons, and had at first been a purely theological affair aimed at restoring a greater sense of the historic church and its hierarchical ministry. But it was soon turned to practical advantage by some Cambridge undergraduates who established the Camden Society to campaign for the sort of church architecture that would provide a worthy setting for elaborate ritual. By the 1850s and 1860s there were Anglican churches in which the use of lighted candles, vestments and incense had been revived and the number of these was to grow rapidly through the rest of the century, especially in London and in fashionable seaside resorts like Brighton. At first the more Protestant Anglicans merely objected to these ritualistic tendencies. Later on, though they still objected, they were themselves active in promoting an improvement in the standards of public worship, though their churches smelled, not of incense, but of polished floors and woodwork.

In the later 19th century Yorkshire and Wales, both strongholds of nonconformity, produced magnificent chapels, often with elaborate Classical porticos and splendid galleried interiors. Roman Catholic churches appeared in all the major towns and some of these are buildings of considerable architectural merit. In Scotland a great many new Presbyterian churches were built, but they are on the whole not very exciting buildings. Probably the most impressive Victorian church is the Episcopal Cathedral of St Mary in Edinburgh.

Although so many churches were built throughout the British Isles for so many different religious groups in the 19th century, it must not be imagined that everybody went to church. The religious census of 1851 showed that only about half the population were regular churchgoers and that churchgoing was very much worse in the working-class districts of the large towns. It also showed that many of these newly built churches were far from full at the services held in them. Churches seem to have been built for potential rather than actual congregations, and this appears to have been as true of the various groups of nonconformists as it was for the established churches in England, Wales and Scotland.

St Mary's Episcopal Cathedral, Edinburgh. The finest of a group of cathedrals built for Anglicans in Scotland during the 19th century, it was designed by Sir G. G. Scott with three spires modelled on Lichfield and dominates the townscape.

Church of St Gastayn, Llangasty Talyllyn, Powys. An excellent example of a Gothic revival village church by J. L. Pearson in his typical lancet style, and with the usual 'high church' fittings.

Church of St Mary, Studley Royal, North Yorks (above). The interior is a riot of elaborate sculpture in a style which owes more to France than to England. It is one of only a few designed by William Burges, the most original of the major Victorian architects.

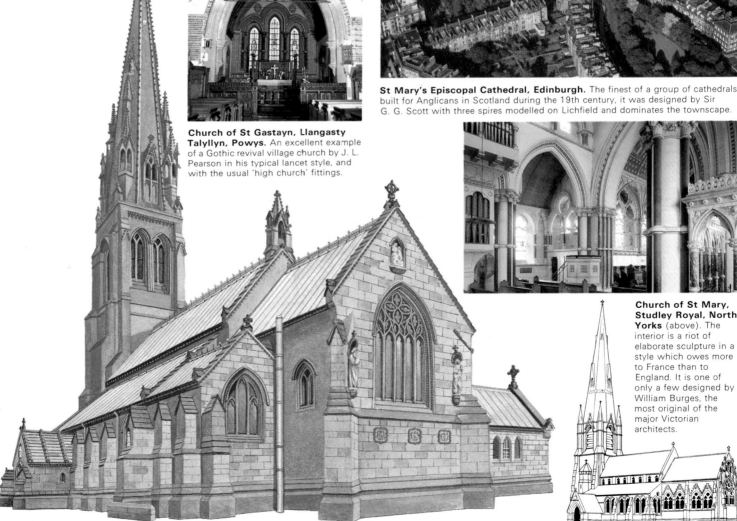

Church of St Giles, Cheadle, Staffs. This Roman Catholic church was built between 1841 and 1846, designed by A. W. N. Pugin and paid for by the Earl of Shrewsbury. Pugin, a convert from the Church of England to Catholicism, was the most influential architect of his day and St Giles is a remarkable example of the type of medievalism that he advocated.

Exterior of the Church of St Mary, Studley Royal. It was built between 1871 and 1878 and cost £50,000.

Church of St Mary and St Nicholas, Wilton, Wilts. This design in Italian Romanesque is a dramatic example of one alternative to the Gothic.

Church of the Holy Angels, Hoar Cross, Staffs (above and right), built by a grieving widow and intended to be a temple of extreme Anglo-Catholicism. The architect was G. F. Bodley, a 'high churchman' himself. The building was begun in 1872 and not completed until 1906. Inside, the screens, reredoses, font cover and the black and white marble flooring are all by Bodley. The style adopted is Decorated of the 14th century as is found in the grander churches of Somerset. The chancel, with its handsome stone vault, is particularly elaborate.

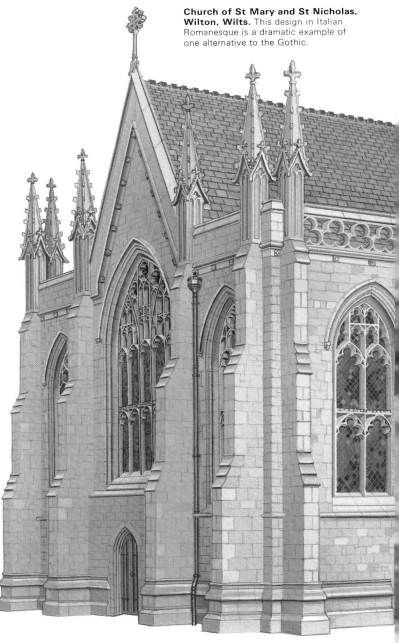

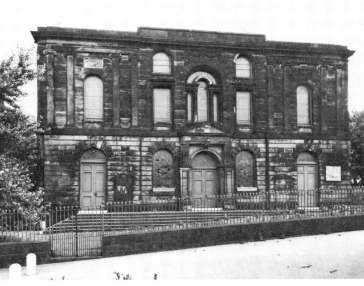

Brunswick Methodist Chapel, Leeds, West Yorks, now redundant and a candidate for demolition. In the Classical style which was favoured by many nonconformists until the late 19th century, it was built in 1824–5.

than winning their traffic. Cheap and efficient passenger travel, now available to all but the poorest, was the dominant factor in the profound social changes of the period. The main roads also ceased to be the chief means of communication in the country. The public mail coach gradually disappeared and with it went many posting inns, toll houses and other aids to long distance travel by road. Local roads as a means of 'getting to the station' were important but the great highways of the 18th century became deserted. Railway-owned towns, like Crewe and Swindon, sprung up on virgin land to service the railways' vast engineering undertakings and the busy junctions of important routes. Ashford (Kent), Bletchley and Rugby are other examples of railway towns and we should not overlook the fact that often where rail and river crossed, a new lease of life was given to decayed river ports such as Chester, Gloucester, Lincoln and Selby. Arrival of the railway stimulated urban growth everywhere, creating new classes of traveller — the commuter and the daytripper — by

enabling people to live away from their place of work and to take holidays away from home. The railways more than any other single factor were also responsible for the development of most 19th century seaside resorts. Places like St Ives, Falmouth and Newquay in Cornwall were revived with the arrival of the railway, whilst other towns such as Bournemouth, Blackpool, Clacton and Scarborough to name but a few were almost non-existent before the arrival of the rail-head. Almost every rail-head on the coast witnessed intense development around the terminus.

Not only did the railways promote the growth of holiday towns, railway towns and industrial towns but they were also instrumental in developing ports. Folkestone was the first railway developed port and this was followed by numerous others ranging from Barry (Cardiff) and Swansea in South Wales to Southampton, Grimsby, Middlesbrough and Fleetwood in England.

As well as seeing many hundreds of miles of new line and fabulous engineering works completed, the years

to 1900 were marked by widespread technical innovation as the steam locomotive was perfected, rolling stock design improved, safety standards and passenger comfort raised. The Midland Railway had run the first bogie coaches in 1874 — Pullman sleeping cars from the USA — and then set about equipping its long-distance trains with bogie stock long before its rivals. Introduction of side corridors led to provision of restaurant cars and lavatory facilities for all.

Higher speeds and the ability to haul heavier trains were the requirements pressed upon mechanical engineers by their general managers as the traffic growth continued unabated in the pre-motor age. Locomotive design gradually progressed, not without problems, towards the large-boilered 4-4-0 favoured as the standard express loco by the end of the century. But even this serviceable type was not sufficient to meet the needs of a new century; 4-4-2s were already at work, and 1900 brought the first 4-6-0 designed for express passenger work.

Clock from Gravesend Pier Station.
'Railway time' was standard and replaced local time, where for instance Oxford, 60 miles west of London, was 5 minutes behind.

...vay. All the GWR's loco and carriage ...nance, and by 1900 Swindon had ... people.

Classical magnificence at Huddersfield Station, designed by James Pritchett the elder and completed in 1850.

St Pancras Station is fronted by the Midland Grand Station Hotel, built 1868 by Sir Gilbert Scott.

RAILWAYS

The railways originated from experiments with the movement of coal from the pithead to the ports and to the industrial centres. The 1820s had seen much controversy as to the relative merits of iron rails or wooden rails combined with trucks drawn by horses, stationary engines and mobile engines or 'locomotives'. It was George Stephenson's locomotive of the Stockton and Darlington line, constructed for the carriage of coal, of 1825 which proved to be the most promising. The first passenger line was the Liverpool and Manchester of 1830, again constructed by George Stephenson.

Short lines laid down in the coal producing districts formed the basis in the 1830s and 1840s of what was to become a national system for the whole country, and there were two distinct periods of intense railway investment and speculation. The first was in 1836–37 and the second between 1844–48; the activity of the second period was so intense that it has become known as the 'railway mania', and during this time over 3,000 miles of railway lines were

added to the British landscape. This was nearly all pick and shovel work performed by Irish navvies, and the monumental nature of the task can be realised when we reflect that it has taken the present generation around 20 years to build 1,000 miles of motorway with all the paraphernalia of modern earthmoving equipment.

A completely new form of engineering had to be developed as cuttings, embankments, tunnels, bridges and viaducts were created to maintain smooth and even slopes for the permanent way. Extremely high standards of workmanship were insisted upon and the railway buildings which accompanied the line construction were also erected for posterity — some indeed have cathedral-like proportions. Despite the Beeching cuts of the 1960s, most individuals are acutely conscious of the place of the railways in our landscape. During Victoria's reign the national railway network grew steadily, a through route from London to Glasgow and Edinburgh being completed in 1848. This era of fevered progress produced

fine civil engineers, men like Thomas Brassey and Joseph Locke who, having made names and fortunes for themselves in Britain, went overseas to countries pressing for British engineering expertise.

One of the most colourful and far-sighted of these was Isambard Kingdom Brunel, who had chosen a gauge of 7 ft $0\frac{1}{4}$ in for his superbly-engineered Great Western Railway from London to Bristol. Spread of this broad gauge brought the GWR into conflict with other railways, all of which were to George Stephenson's standard gauge of 4 ft $8\frac{1}{2}$ in. The ensuing gauge war was won by the standard gauge, though Brunel's broad gauge lasted on the GWR until 1892.

Railway construction was promoted and funded largely by the fruits of the rapid industrialisation of Britain during the middle decades of the century. In their turn, the railways created new industries and new businesses, while they themselves grew to be powerful enterprises and often bitter rivals. The better-ordered phase of railway

construction up to the 1890s also saw many amalgamations of small lines, creating the great companies that were to dominate the scene until the grouping of 1923.

Mightiest of all was the 'Premier Line' — the London & North Western Railway — then the largest joint-stock corporation in the world, whose general manager Mark Huish rivalled Hudson for deviousness. In the steps of the visionary engineers had come powerful managers who fought to create monopolies for their railways, and who fuelled cut-throat competition on rival routes. Such conflict was not always to the benefit of the customer, though many improvements in passenger coach design and comfort, if not safety, can be attributed to healthy competition. Speed rivalry culminated in the 1895 races to Aberdeen between the East and West Coast factions, though the achievements were no more than one-off performances.

Goods traffic grew apace as industry expanded; strong canal resistance was killed off eventually, but by railways buying out the canal companies rather

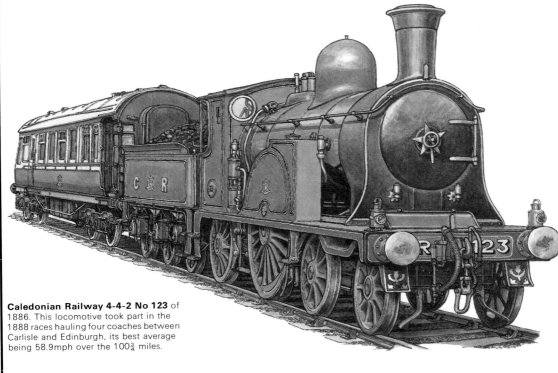

Caledonian Railway 4-4-2 No 123 of 1886. This locomotive took part in the 1888 races hauling four coaches between Carlisle and Edinburgh, its best average being 58.9mph over the $100\frac{3}{4}$ miles.

Swindon, Wiltshire, was created by the r building was concentrated here, as was mai grown from a mere village to a town of 40,0

Great Malvern station, Worcester-shire (below). This decorative expression of Gothic revival design was built at the Victorian spa town in 1863. The architect was E. W. Elmslie, one of the few to design both ecclesiastical and railway buildings. The pillars supporting the platform canopy have magnificently decorated cast iron capitals incorporating local flora (right). Even a relatively small country station such as this provided generous accommodation; there would have been separate waiting and refresh-ment rooms for first and third class, and probably a 'ladies only' waiting room as well. Sadly the tower no longer exists.

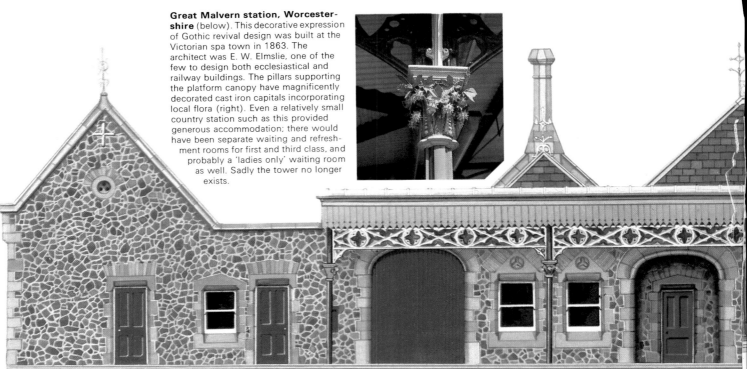

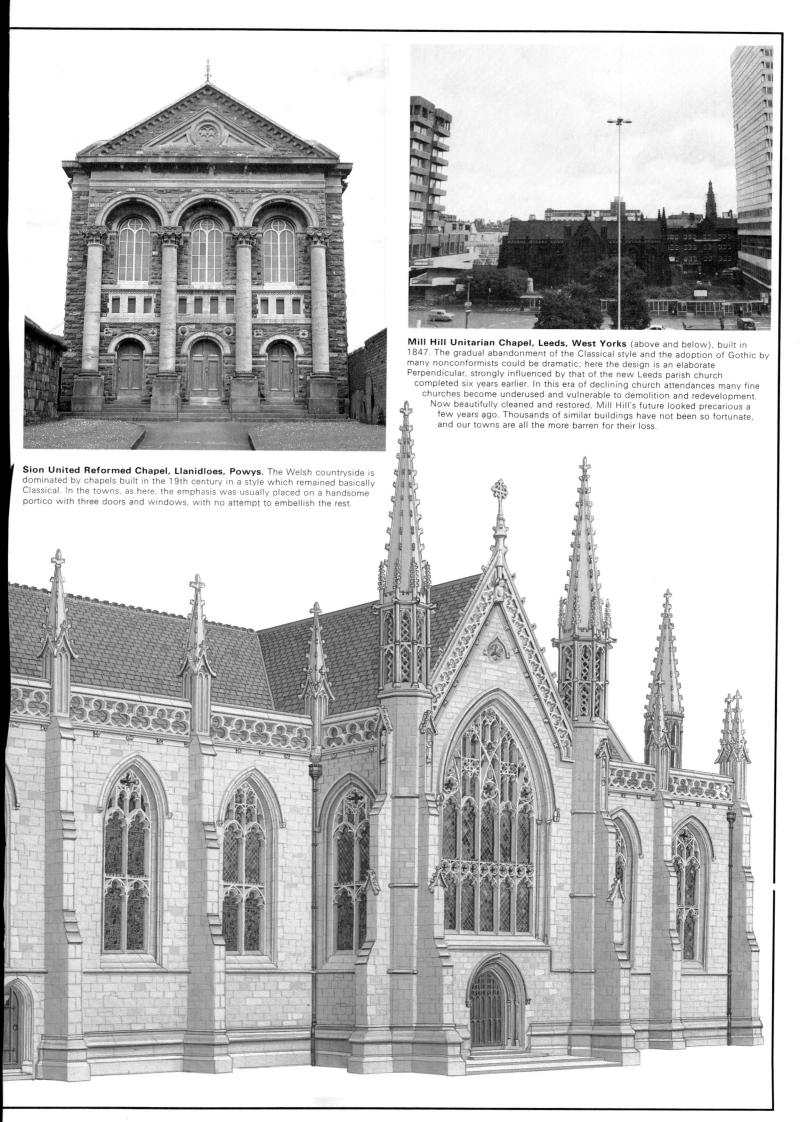

Mill Hill Unitarian Chapel, Leeds, West Yorks (above and below), built in 1847. The gradual abandonment of the Classical style and the adoption of Gothic by many nonconformists could be dramatic; here the design is an elaborate Perpendicular, strongly influenced by that of the new Leeds parish church completed six years earlier. In this era of declining church attendances many fine churches become underused and vulnerable to demolition and redevelopment. Now beautifully cleaned and restored, Mill Hill's future looked precarious a few years ago. Thousands of similar buildings have not been so fortunate, and our towns are all the more barren for their loss.

Sion United Reformed Chapel, Llanidloes, Powys. The Welsh countryside is dominated by chapels built in the 19th century in a style which remained basically Classical. In the towns, as here, the emphasis was usually placed on a handsome portico with three doors and windows, with no attempt to embellish the rest.

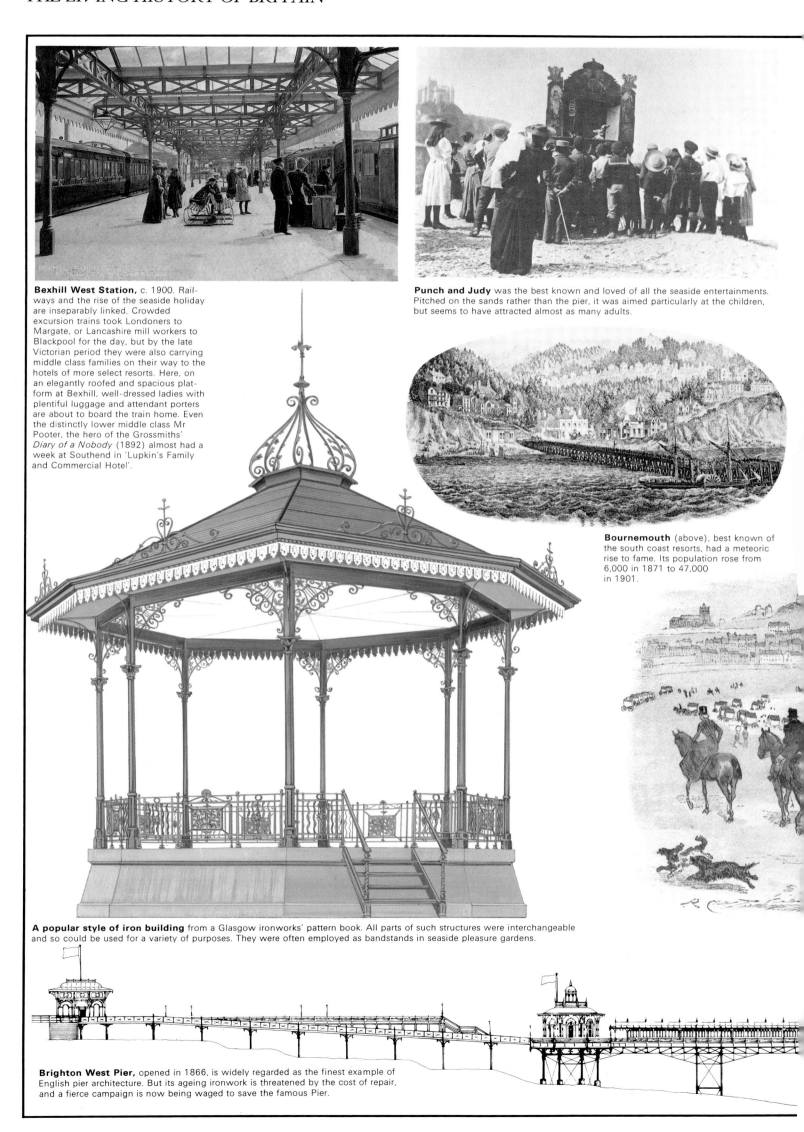

Bexhill West Station, c. 1900. Railways and the rise of the seaside holiday are inseparably linked. Crowded excursion trains took Londoners to Margate, or Lancashire mill workers to Blackpool for the day, but by the late Victorian period they were also carrying middle class families on their way to the hotels of more select resorts. Here, on an elegantly roofed and spacious platform at Bexhill, well-dressed ladies with plentiful luggage and attendant porters are about to board the train home. Even the distinctly lower middle class Mr Pooter, the hero of the Grossmiths' *Diary of a Nobody* (1892) almost had a week at Southend in 'Lupkin's Family and Commercial Hotel'.

Punch and Judy was the best known and loved of all the seaside entertainments. Pitched on the sands rather than the pier, it was aimed particularly at the children, but seems to have attracted almost as many adults.

Bournemouth (above), best known of the south coast resorts, had a meteoric rise to fame. Its population rose from 6,000 in 1871 to 47,000 in 1901.

A popular style of iron building from a Glasgow ironworks' pattern book. All parts of such structures were interchangeable and so could be used for a variety of purposes. They were often employed as bandstands in seaside pleasure gardens.

Brighton West Pier, opened in 1866, is widely regarded as the finest example of English pier architecture. But its ageing ironwork is threatened by the cost of repair, and a fierce campaign is now being waged to save the famous Pier.

'Seats for five persons'. The Duke of Wellington opposed railways 'because they would encourage the lower classes to move about'. Here they are doing so in the cramped and uncomfortable conditions of third class accommodation which prevailed until the 1870s, when the Midland Railway pioneered two-class travel.

First class comfort in 1854. The gentleman's silk hat is safely secured in a special rack. At this time railway carriage design was closely based on stage coaches, a succession of compartments with facing seats and no communication from one to another. Through-corridor trains were not introduced until 1892, by which time dining, Pullman and sleeping cars had made long journeys comfortable.

Spirit stove and kettle from the royal dining car shown above left. The royal trains are at the National Railway Museum, York.

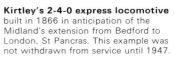

Kirtley's 2-4-0 express locomotive built in 1866 in anticipation of the Midland's extension from Bedford to London, St Pancras. This example was not withdrawn from service until 1947.

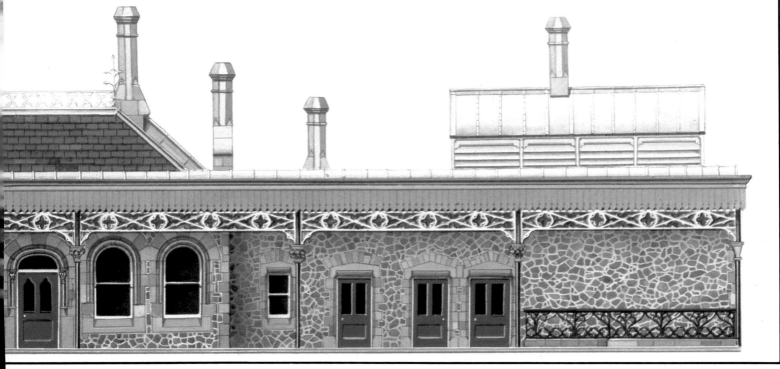

Paddington Station, the Great Western's London terminus (above). Isambard Kingdom Brunel created the GWR, known to its admirers as 'God's Wonderful Railway', and here he set out to build 'a station after my own fancy, that is, with engineering roofs'. These took the form of a central span 102ft wide flanked by two subsidiary aisles. Matthew Digby Wyatt was his assistant for the ornamental details and the interior colour scheme was the work of Owen Jones, who also designed the interior of the Crystal Palace.

LNWR First Class Dining Saloon No 76 (right), a prizewinner at the Paris Exhibition of 1901. It became part of the royal train in 1903 and was not withdrawn until 1956.

Queen Victoria's LNWR day saloon of 1869 appealed to her so much that she would not allow it and its adjoining night saloon to be replaced. In 1895 they were remounted on a single underframe.

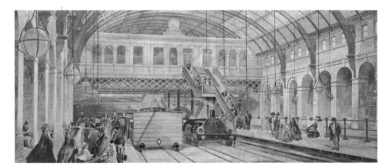

The world's first underground railway was the 3¾ mile Metropolitan Railway opened in 1863 between Paddington and Farringdon Street. Now part of the Circle Line, it was built just below ground level and used steam locos with condensers.

Dinting viaduct on the Sheffield, Ashton-under-Lyne & Manchester Railway. It was built in 1844 with arch spans of laminated timber, as shown here. These quickly deteriorated, however, and by 1860 had been replaced by iron plate girders.

Ramsgate sands, 1887. The Victorian working class enjoying a well earned break. The long pier, booths and stalls offered a variety of entertainment to the excursionists from London. The now ubiquitous deckchair had not then arrived, while hats and shades protected pale, delicate skins from the then unfashionable suntan.

Scarborough, Yorkshire's famous resort, where it is claimed sea bathing first took place before the end of the 17th century. The arrival of the railway in the 1840s brought holidaymakers in their thousands and provided an impetus for the expansion of the town's fishing industry.

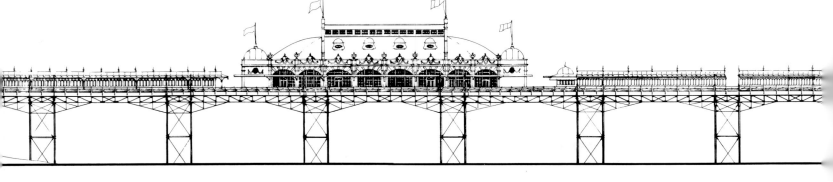

THE VICTORIAN SEASIDE

The first true resort towns were the inland spas — Bath, Buxton, Tunbridge Wells and others — where polite 18th-century society went to take the waters, enjoy a range of genteel amusements, conspicuously display the latest fashions and perhaps find suitable marriage partners for themselves or their progeny. The first seaside resorts initially publicised the health-restoring properties of dipping in the ocean and filling the lungs with the salt air; Scarborough, somewhere around the middle years of the 18th century, was the probable pioneer but the habit rapidly spread to the south. Little Brighthelmstone on the Sussex coast became the Prince Regent's Brighton; his father George III favoured Weymouth, and even Southampton before the building of the docks had its period as a fashionable place for sea-bathing.

Naturally social emulation ensured that the habit spread from the upper to the middle class, and there it might have stayed so long as long as expensive stage-coach journeys remained the only way to reach the coast and the ability to afford holidays without pay set a bottom limit. What changed things was the coming of the railway and the day excursion. Holidays away from home were beyond the reach of most but the day by the seaside became a Victorian institution. Temperance societies and Sunday School organisers were among the earliest to see the possibilities of the railway to take their groups away from the temptations of traditional working class wakes and holidays, but as the breezy proletarian resorts got fully into their noisy swing, many must have wondered whether the

cure was not worse than the disease. The day at the seaside developed among the workers in two areas: London and the industrial north, especially the cotton districts of Lancashire. Londoners quite far down the social scale had, even before the coming of the railway, known the delights of the boat-trips to Southend or Margate, but excursion trains began to take thousands for the day to Margate or Ramsgate. Before the Bank Holidays Act of 1871 the Saturday half-day was increasing but still far from general, and Sunday was a popular excursion day; the railway companies were also well enough acquainted with the working habits of many of the city's workers to put plenty of excursions on for summer Mondays: the traditional day for absenteeism.

In Lancashire two factors were important: the proximity of good beaches on the coast and in North Wales, and the fact that the cotton employers had long since recognised that their workers would keep their traditional Wakes Weeks. The most spectacular result was the rise of Blackpool, the first sizeable town devoted entirely to the holiday and excursion industry. Trippers arrived by means of every agency from the corner pub to Thomas Cook. By the end of the 1830s there were already more than a thousand visitors at the height of the season, but it was in the 1850s and 60s that the modern resort really emerged. The first pier was opened in 1863 and as rising real wages and lengthening holidays extended possibilities, the traditional amusements of the fairs and wakes began to appear at the seaside. At Blackpool, stalls, shooting galleries, quack doctors, wax works and

roundabouts spread along the shore. Blackpool was only the best known of the northern working-class resorts, but regular excursions took people to Scarborough, Redcar, Saltburn and Whitby as well as to North Wales where Aberystwyth, with 1500 visitors at the height of the season by the 1830s, was among the most rapidly growing of our seaside towns. On the east coast Yarmouth set the pace; the railway arrived here in 1844, presumably with the carriage of fish from one of England's most significant fishing ports as its main object. The six-mile seafront, however, enabled other profits to be netted — after the building of the pier and the coming of the donkeys, trains of unbelievable length brought firms on their annual outings.

What did the trippers expect from the seaside? Certainly they were not particularly attracted by swimming in the sea, and Victorian misses would certainly not have wanted their milk-white complexions tanned by over-exposure to the sun. The rest of their pale bodies was safely and decorously shrouded. They went for the healthy sea air, the amusements and the ritual paddle. They went to parade the 'prom' in their weekend clothes, to eat the seafood and to drink in the multiplying pubs. With their pennies they created a new demand for souvenirs — especially the well-known Staffordshire Crest-ware of china models, each bearing the name and coat of arms of the resort.

The most striking feature of the Victorian resort was the pier. The Brighton Chain Pier was opened in 1823 to unload the Dieppe packet, but it soon became a place of fashionable and

therapeutic promenade. From every major resort the coming of the railway was followed by the building of a pier, striking on its cast-iron legs out into the sea, to end in a pavilion. Behind the seafront were laid out the pleasure gardens invariably with a bandstand.

As resorts became increasingly the preserve of the common folk, those seeking peace and seclusion were enabled by the railway to move further away for their holidays — to the Isle of Wight (Ventnor, at the other side of the island, was preferable to Shanklin or Ryde which were so easy to reach from urban Portsmouth); to Eastbourne, Weymouth or Bournemouth; or further west to Lyme Regis, Torquay, Ilfracombe or Sidmouth. Cornwall was still largely unknown before 1900, although the bridging of the Tamar in 1859 had begun to permit the better off to visit the growing watering place of Newquay, the sub-tropical climate of Falmouth, or the picturesque old fishing villages of St Ives or Newlyn.

Working class holidays as opposed to trips had probably not reached far below the lower middle class before the 20th century, although there is evidence that the better-off skilled workers could afford a few days at Blackpool or Brighton by the 1860s. The TUC did not pass a resolution on holidays with pay before 1911, and the securing of that objective was a pre-condition for the growth of the modern resort with its hotels, boarding-houses, camping sites and caravans.

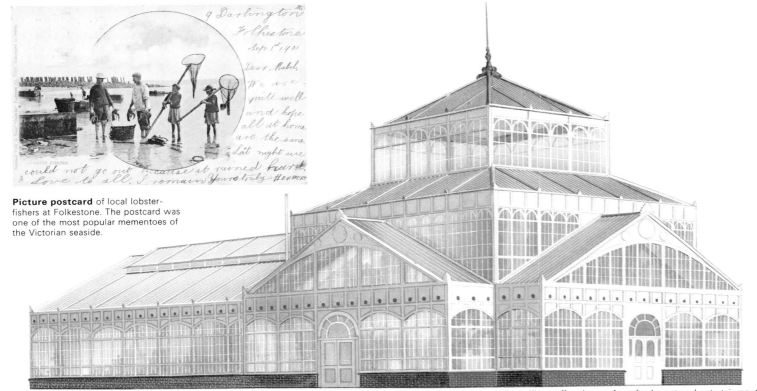

Picture postcard of local lobster-fishers at Folkestone. The postcard was one of the most popular mementoes of the Victorian seaside.

The Pavilion on Great Yarmouth's sea front, a fine example of seaside architecture. Often built at the pier end, pavilions offered room for refreshment and entertainment. Yarmouth, with six miles of sands, combined a successful career as a seaside resort with being one of Britain's leading fishing ports.

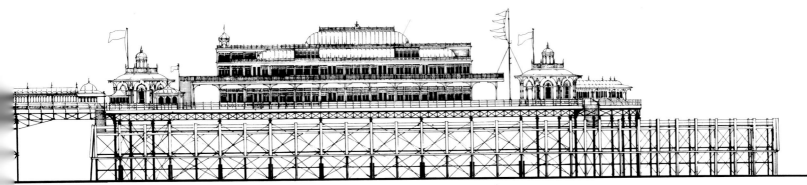

were passing through unusual times and that compared with that which had gone before, their achievements were tremendous. The Victorians, particularly the middle classes, never tired of reading about themselves, but during the 1850s and 1860s there was less concern in literature about stirring the conscience or broadening the mind. There was, however, a preference for amusement and interest. This concentration on themselves was also seen in their choice of painting. The vast canvases of W. P. Frith, depicting familiar scenes such as 'Derby Day', or 'Life at the Seaside', were immensely popular. They represented in meticulous detail Victorian everyday life. This emphasis on themselves reflected feelings of security in all classes and the atmosphere of relative social harmony that prevailed.

This change of mood owed much to improved living conditions. The fear that violence would erupt had passed. This was partly due to the increased efficiency of the police force and the availability of railways to transport the forces of law and order to areas of trouble more quickly. People also began to realise that difficult times had come and gone and yet revolution had been avoided. The aristocracy had lost very little of the real power it possessed when the electoral system was altered in 1832. The middle classes, however, felt that these changes gave them some political influence. They were content to share the governing of the country with the aristocracy whom they had always respected, and were glad to exclude the working classes from political power. The crime, poverty and drunkenness that had reached a peak in 1842 began to decline, and working people saw some improvement in their lives. Wages began

THE VICTORIAN PUBLIC HOUSE

The Victorians liked a drink. The average yearly consumption of beer per head in the years between 1895 and 1900 was 31.2 gallons, and of spirits 1.03 gallons, compared with the 1900–35 figures of 13.3 gallons of beer and 0.22 gallons of spirits. Mild ale had replaced porter as the main beverage of public bars by the turn of the century, but saloon and private bars continued to prefer bitter. Gin, so popular with the working classes in early Victorian times, lost its pre-eminence as successive rises in the spirit duty pushed up its price. Irish whiskey captured the spirit market in the 1860s followed by Scotch whisky in the 1870s.

While most of us drink to relax and be sociable, the Victorians, and particularly the working classes, consumed alcohol for a variety of other reasons. For them, it was a thirst quencher because water was unsafe and milk dangerous even when fresh. Intoxicants were believed to impart physical stamina and would provide energy in the same way as food, with the added advantage that the stimulating effects temporarily dulled fatigue. Any occasion requiring extra confidence called for a drink, as did times of pain or sickness: alcohol assisted dentists

and surgeons, quietened babies and helped women through the trials of childbirth.

The consumption of alcohol was made easier by the generous opening hours and the abundance of pubs, and excessive drinking was one of the major evils of city life. Opening hours were curtailed gradually between 1864 and 1874, but late Victorian pubs could still open between the hours of 5 a.m. and 12.30 a.m. on weekdays, and from 1–3 p.m. and 6–11 p.m. on Sundays.

There were pubs to suit everyone's taste: medical students, sportsmen, actors and prostitutes all had their favourite haunts. The most respectable drinking establishments were the inns, which accommodated travellers. Taverns were frequented by the casual social drinker. Below these establishments on the scale of respectability were the ale houses where beer but no spirits was sold, and on the bottom rung were gin shops supplying the needs of the urban poor. Inns and taverns had always been segregated by class but the division became more rigid as the century progressed.

The pub served a variety of functions in expanding urban communities.

It was first and foremost a recreational and social centre where many could enjoy the comforts of light, heat, furniture, newspapers and comradeship not available in their own homes. Before the establishment of large restaurants, pubs would often provide refreshments to workmen travelling to and from their jobs. Public meetings were frequently held there, and it was not until the mid century that pubs ceased to be the centre of political party organisation. Trade unions and benefit societies met in pubs, and workmen went to their 'local' to pick up jobs. They were also centres of sport and entertainment: the music hall developed from the musical entertainment given in pubs during the 1850s, and the association between music halls and drink long remained strong.

As the pub was an important social centre, the social prestige of the publican was high, and they were often the only literate and enfranchised individuals, aside from the clergy, in poor districts. Publicans usually held their property on long leases or freehold; brewers would sometimes provide the initial cash payment, but the majority of publicans had saved their own money by working previously

in other trades.

From domestic beginnings as extensions of people's homes, the 19th century saw impressive changes in the interior arrangements of pubs. Long bars were built and luxurious furnishings and fitments added. Coloured glass windows and decorative exterior lamps became popular, and the pub took on the look with which we are all familiar today.

Many people viewed pubs with a mixture of suspicion and dislike, claiming that men spent too much money on drink and that this prevented them from being hardworking, thrifty and respectable. As an inevitable reaction to excessive drinking habits the Temperance movement emerged; a very strong force during the Victorian era, its members aimed to improve themselves by taking the pledge not to drink, attending chapel and saving money. For them, music halls, racecourses and boxing rings were the haunts of the devil. For the majority, however, drinking, gambling and attending music halls were their only pleasures amid squalor and wretchedness.

The Barton Arms, Aston, near Birmingham, built at the end of Victoria's reign with a sombre exuberance expressing the self-confidence of the time.

The World's End, Chelsea, typical of the extravagant architecture of pubs, which tried to outdo each other in splendour.

to rise as food became cheaper and there was more time and money for leisure activities.

The decade 1833–43 also witnessed the beginning of government action towards social reform. In 1833 the Whig government introduced a bill that forbade the employment of children under nine years of age in factories and limited the employment of children aged nine to thirteen to an eight-hour day. This factory act was a turning point in the history of social policy, for it acknowledged the right of the state to intervene where there was a need to protect exploited members of society.

Public health was another area that began to receive attention at this time. The phenomenal population growth in the 19th century posed immense problems for urban communities. As migrants poured into the cities, places had

Children under ten were barred from employment in the mines after 1842, but it was not until the 1880s that the general employment of children declined.

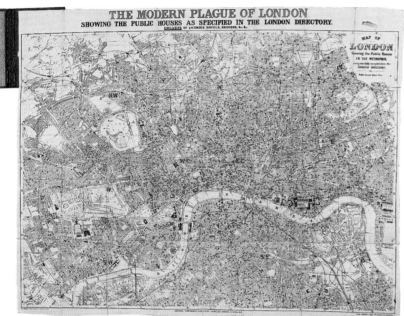

The many public houses in Victorian London disguise a surprising fact: the more crowded the housing conditions the lower the number of pubs. This was due to the large size of urban pubs and the licensing policy in the late Victorian slums.

Brakspear's Brewery, Henley. When men, women and children drank beer daily, every town and village had a brewery or a pub which brewed its own beer.

The rural beer houses were often cottages rather than public houses, and their owners were recruited from poorly paid workers whose wives supplemented the family income by running the bar while their husbands worked.

Hop picking was a summer employment for many London workers.

The Old Cork and Bottle, Leeds, a haven amid the city's crowded squalor.

Dray horses were an efficient means of transporting beer. Today a few local breweries like Samuel Smith's at Tadcaster use horses for transport and advertisement.

to be found for them to live. Cellars and attics were filled first, and then cheap houses of various kinds were erected: back to backs in Leeds, enclosed courtyards in Birmingham, tenements in Glasgow. Access to light and air was a problem in overcrowded conditions and 'jerry-built' houses, refuse accumulated in the streets, and cesspools were the normal sanitary arrangements. There were no local authorities to control building or provide essential services such as drainage, sewerage and clean water supplies. Under these conditions disease abounded. Typhus became almost exclusively a poor man's disease, as it was closely associated with cramped, insanitary housing conditions. Tuberculosis accounted for more deaths (perhaps as many as one-third of all deaths in the first half of the century) than any other disease as the smoky atmosphere, squalid houses and undernourished bodies provided a favourable environment for the spread of disease. Scarlet fever, diarrhoea and measles were also common killers, especially of children.

Before the devastating effects of these diseases could be checked, however, two serious problems had to be surmounted: the first was to understand what caused disease, and the second was to focus public opinion on the importance and urgency of the problem. The first difficulty was that early Victorian doctors believed in the miasmic theory that smells transmitted disease. Until the bacteriological causes of disease were understood in the late 19th century the connection between dirt and disease was not appreciated. However, the right actions could be taken for the wrong reasons; what was important to demonstrate was the connection between cesspools and illness.

This point was forcibly made in Edwin Chadwick's famous sanitary report of 1842. Chadwick was a great administrator and propagandist who became concerned with the question of public health while he was secretary of the Poor Law Commission. He realised that a large proportion of poor relief money was going to support the widows and orphans of men struck down by disease and he felt that this money could be saved if preventive measures were taken to improve the environment. In 1839 the House of Lords ordered an inquiry into the sanitary conditions of the labouring classes, and Chadwick was commissioned to undertake this survey, which was completed in 1842. Chadwick established conclusively, by the use of statistical

The Strand, London, in 1890. Traffic jams were common; all vehicles were horse-drawn — private carriages, delivery vans, hire vehicles and the new buses and trams — and although new streets were cut and others widened, the problem persisted.

THE DEVELOPMENT OF TOWNS

The Victorian period witnessed a dramatic change in the urban life of the country. A predominantly rural society at the beginning of the century was transformed into a predominantly urban society by the end; less than a quarter of the 10 million inhabitants of Britain in 1801 lived in towns, but by 1901 approaching 70 per cent of the 37 million inhabitants were urban dwellers. The transformation was largely related to the Industrial Revolution and the overwhelming increase in the working class population; towns doubled and then trebled in size within decades. Fastest of all grew the cotton towns of Lancashire, then the iron towns of the Midlands, the pottery towns of Staffordshire, and the woollen towns of Yorkshire. Surrounding them were the gaunt mining villages of the coalfields.

By the mid century the location of most towns had been determined and the second half of the century merely saw a continued growth of the industrial areas by outward expansion. The pattern of growth at first remained the same — individual factories surrounded by the workers' houses packed closely together as all had to walk to work. But a new factor was to change the scene; the emerging railway network of the mid 19th century increasingly permitted a zoning of work and residence, and before long 'suburbia' began to develop.

Before this stage was reached, however, the Victorians had first to learn by painful experience how to live in densely populated conditions. The cholera epidemics of the 1830s and 1840s revealed the need for adequate supplies of clean water and sanitation, but it was some time before the terrible conditions of the back to back houses,

the crammed courtyards and alleyways could be improved. The real transformation of working class living conditions did not come until the last quarter of the century when water was increasingly plumbed into houses. This permitted internal sanitation, hot and cold water and bathrooms. Gas lighting was also becoming general, but heat was still coal-derived. Gas cookers and heaters did not become generally available until after 1900 and electricity was still in the experimental stage.

The appalling conditions in some of the Victorian towns produced a reaction amongst the intelligentsia against the chaos which was being created in the industrial areas. As early as 1820 Robert Owen (1771–1858) had attempted to develop a model industrial town at Orbiston near Motherwell. In 1852 Sir Titus Salt (1803–1876) planned and built the model woollen town of Saltaire near Bradford, whilst in 1888 Lord Lever founded Port Sunlight for his soap workers and about the same time the Cadbury Brothers began to build the village of Bournville.

The second half of the century also saw the development of middle class housing in localities such as Didsbury (Manchester), Edgbaston (Birmingham), Ilkley (Bradford), north Oxford, Harrogate and Bournemouth. These developments of detached houses in their own grounds combined with the model town experiments provided the basis for the idea of the Garden City — marrying the best of town and country — which was set forth by Ebenezer Howard in his famous book *Tomorrow*, published in 1898. The foundations were being laid for the garden cities and garden suburbs of the early 20th century.

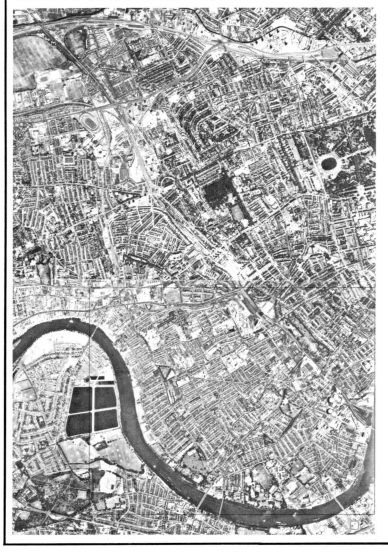

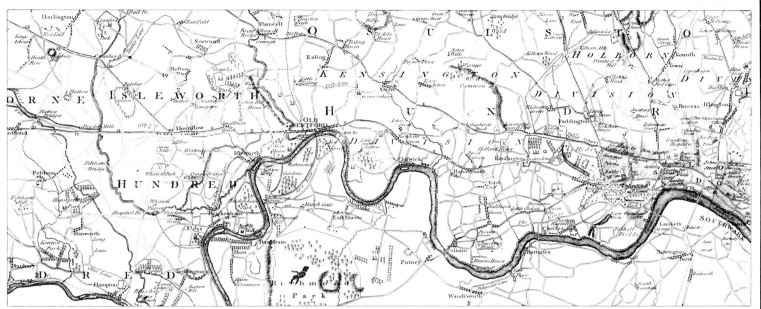

An aerial photograph of West London (below left) from Hyde Park in the east to Chiswick in the west. Virtually all this development (only about one eighth of the building activity that entirely encircled 18th century London) was Victorian and indicates the sudden rise in service industries, general trading and commerce.

A map of London and its environs (above) published at the beginning of the 19th century, shows the string of isolated villages along the ancient road to the west. By the end of the century, the area to Brentford had been engulfed by the metropolis. Forty more years saw its extension to Bedfont.

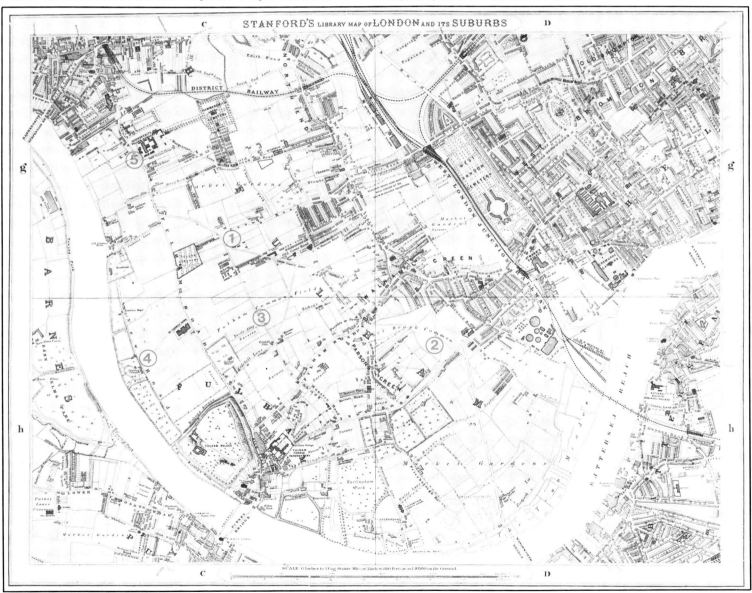

Stanford's map of Fulham in 1877 provides an interesting comparison to the photograph of West London (shown left) and forms a snapshot of a city in the making. Until 1860 Fulham was a rural community devoted to small scale market gardening. By 1880 it had been given a spur of the Metropolitan District Railway and urbanisation developed apace. Like most Victorian developments, the building of Fulham was undertaken piecemeal, following the pattern of existing lanes and roads. Individual fields were sold off for building and their boundaries dictated street layout. Such individual development is beautifully illustrated at Strode Street (1). Here a field has been sold and the builder has made a start on his street. Eel Brook Common (2), unenclosed and undrained grazing land, largely escaped development and remains to this day as a playing field and public green. Fulham Common Fields (3) were lost, becoming the site of almshouses, a new school and yet more street development. Craven Cottage (4) was destroyed by fire in 1888 and became the site of the newly formed Fulham Football Club. The village centres of Walham Green, Parsons Green and Fulham largely lost their identities, recognisable now only as a collection of minor shops around minor crossroads. The urban paraphernalia of railway lines, stations, goods and coal depots, gas works, hospitals (in the form of the workhouse (5) — now the site of the gigantic new Charing Cross hospital), cemeteries, some schools and pubs are already in place. Just 25 years later, the development of Fulham was complete; nothing of its rural past remained, save that of its enduring pattern.

evidence, the link between environment and disease. He did this by showing that where a person lived and his occupation greatly affected his chances of illness and early death. Chadwick discovered that the death rate in Manchester was 1 in 26 per annum, but in the outlying area of Cheetham it was 1 in 45; in central Leeds it was 1 in 28 but in the suburbs of Chapeltown it was 1 in 57. Not only was there a geographic variation in life expectancy, but life chances also differed between the classes of the community. In Rutland, a rural county, the average life expectancy of professional men was 52. It was not so high for those in trade, however, the average being 41. It was even less for labourers, whose life-span averaged 38 years. However, if an individual was unfortunate enough to live in Whitechapel, London, the average age of death was considerably reduced regardless of occupation. The averages were 45 for professional men, 27 for tradesmen and 22 for labourers. Figures such as these suggest that class differences in Victorian Britain could sharply affect not just the quality of life, but its length as well. By documenting these variations, Chadwick showed that there was a close correlation between insanitary housing, insufficient sewerage and water supply, and disease and death. While this appears logical to us and contemporary society considers environmental controls and public services essential, the early Victorians were not quite so sure.

Chadwick's report suggested what many doctors were beginning to notice in their own practices, but legislation on public health was slow in coming. Recognising the problem was only part of the solution; in addition, technical difficulties had to be surmounted. The sheer physical size of the job, first in supplying water to large cities and then, as the water closet came to be more widely used, in the disposal of liquid sewage, posed major engineering problems. Technical disagreements led to interminable disputes that hindered schemes, and there was always the problem of cost. Little money was available for social utilities, and civic improvement was as likely to mean building a new town hall as constructing a new town sewer. There was always the question of who was to pay. Wealthy people were less affected by the endemic diseases such as typhus, although epidemic diseases such as cholera, a waterborne disease, attacked all. The frightful cholera epidemics of 1831–32, 1848–49, 1854 and 1867 struck terror into the hearts of the prosperous classes, but their cries for public health measures

PUBLIC UTILITIES

As towns expanded the need for good street lighting, an adequate supply of pure water and an effective means of removing all kinds of waste products grew: in Victoria's long reign the means of providing these public services were established. The use of coal-derived gas was known before Victoria was born; in 1805 Murdock lit a mill in Manchester with coal gas, and two years later Pall Mall in London became the first public thoroughfare in the world to be illuminated by gas. By the 1840s London streets were lit by gas provided by a number of private companies; even quite small towns had their supplier by the 1850s, selling gas to the town for lighting as well as to private houses and shops.

Most of the early gas companies grew and amalgamated and by the end of the century many large companies were in operation, but by this time they had a rival: electricity. Although the basic means of producing and using electricity were discovered by Faraday as early as the 1830s and arc lights had been found effective for lighthouses and street lighting from the 1860s, they were expensive to run and too powerful for indoor use. By 1880 Joseph Swan in England with Thomas Edison in America had jointly devised the forerunner of the modern light bulb and the resultant demand for the fume-free and brighter light for indoors stimulated electrical engineers like de Ferranti to design equipment and set up companies to produce and distribute electrical power: the gradual replacement of gas lighting by electric had begun.

When Victoria came to the throne water was also supplied in towns by private companies, which often made large profits from selling a dangerously impure commodity: several London companies actually took water from the Thames and distributed it untreated. Attempts were made to control the purity of water supplied by private companies, but eventually most towns set up municipal water companies and cities like Liverpool and Manchester, which did not have a sufficient local supply, built large reservoirs and piped the water great distances. Manchester was a pioneer in piping water a long distance, building reservoirs in the Etherow Valley 15 miles away in the Pennines during the 1870s. A decade later even this supply proved insufficient and permission was obtained to take water from Thirlmere in the Lake District some 80 miles distant.

Liverpool created Lake Vyrnwy in North Wales between 1881 and 1892, forming at the time the largest artificial reservoir in Europe. This was 65 miles from Liverpool. Birmingham followed suit, constructing between 1893 and 1904 a series of four major reservoirs in the Elan Valley in central Wales, 73 miles away.

The removal of refuse and sewage was the responsibility of the local parish, but as cities grew it became impossible for parishes to deal with these problems individually: an overall system of drainage in particular was needed. The inadequacy of London's solution to the problem of drainage – using the Thames as a main sewer – was brought forcibly home to the country's legislators when they were driven from the new Houses of Parliament by the stench of the river in hot weather. The young engineer Joseph Bazalgette was authorised to go ahead with a major scheme for building two large trunk sewers to carry all the effluent from north and south London to discharge into the Thames well below the city, which was completed in 1865. But the battle was not yet won: publicity was again given to the state of the Thames when, in 1878, at the inquest on victims of an accident in which the paddle steamer *Princess Alice* had been cut in two by a collier, qualified medical witnesses claimed that many of the deaths were the result of the foul state of the River. It was then found that London's sewage, pumped into the river from Abbey Mills and Crossness, did not flow straight out to sea, but was actually carried back up to London by the tides. Once again money was found to build equipment, this time to treat the effluent before it was pumped into the river, and once again London set an example that was followed by many cities and towns, but is unfortunately not universal even in Britain today.

The King's Arms Yard, Drury Lane, London. When cholera struck in 1848, preventive measures such as washing, burning infected bedding and the immediate burial of the corpses was impossible for people living in conditions such as these. The epidemic eventually died out after causing thousands of deaths.

New electric lamps on the Thames Embankment in London replaced the dim gas lamps which had been there for half a century. Lighting was electricity's first success; soon everyone who could afford it was demanding it, and many private companies sprang up. They encouraged the development of new equipment which used electricity for cooking, heating and power.

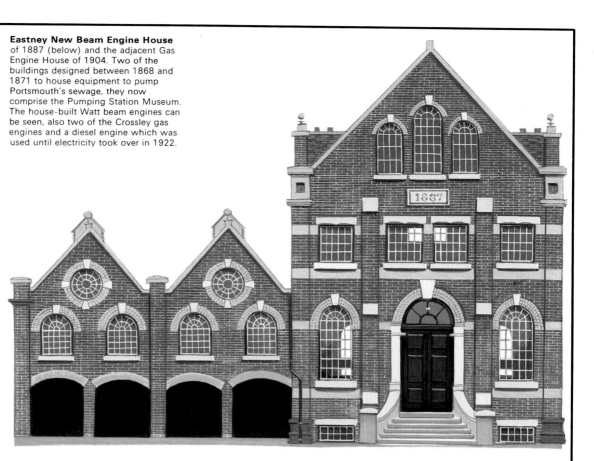

Eastney New Beam Engine House of 1887 (below) and the adjacent Gas Engine House of 1904. Two of the buildings designed between 1868 and 1871 to house equipment to pump Portsmouth's sewage, they now comprise the Pumping Station Museum. The house-built Watt beam engines can be seen, also two of the Crossley gas engines and a diesel engine which was used until electricity took over in 1922.

Abbey Mills Pumping Station (above). The ornate Moorish interior housed eight beam engines to pump north London's sewage. At Crossness, its south London counterpart, a Gothic building still contains its huge engines.

Main drainage at Wick Lane, Bow, London — the only sewers built above ground in the metropolis. Engineering bricks were used to construct the vast network throughout the country, and are only now beginning to show signs of wear.

A gas holder at Bethnal Green, built by the Imperial Gas Company. These immense and often finely crafted structures are usually the only surviving parts of the original coal gas works. Today natural gas is the main source of gas energy.

Beinn A'mheadhoin Dam, Scotland (above left) and Vyrnwy Dam, North Wales (above right). After taking over from the inefficient private companies, municipal water companies soon found themselves in difficulties as streams and wells in the urban areas proved contaminated or inadequate. After building reservoirs in the surrounding countryside, large cities had to look even further afield as domestic requirements (accelerated by population increases and new sewerage schemes) and burgeoning industrial needs increased the demand for water. Liverpool bought a Welsh valley in 1880 and created a reservoir with the Vyrnwy dam; in 1892 water from the new Lake Vyrnwy was available to the city.

ceased when the epidemics disappeared. These people usually provided for their own sanitary needs and they resented paying twice by being taxed to provide for the needs of others. In the large cities most in need of sanitary measures, the wealthy people were usually manufacturers and business-men who cherished the ideal of individual liberty. For these men, Chadwick was a busybody and building regulations were an infringement of their personal rights. Consequently, the line between economic self-interest and support for individual liberty was often blurred. These men were also against any extension of municipal jurisdiction, for enormous powers were given to authorities as they enlarged their functions.

Political squabbles over who should exercise power within the local community were overshadowed by the wider debate about centralisation. Many urban communities feared a situation where bureaucrats from London could impose costly legislation over which the local authorities had no control. Contentious issues such as technical factors, who should pay the bill and political squabbles not only delayed the passing of legislation but the acts that resulted were not as effective as they could have been. In 1848 a public health bill obliged local boards of health to undertake sanitary reforms if the death rate was higher than 23 per 1000. A General Board of Health was set up in London with Chadwick as its salaried Commissioner, but it was an advisory body rather than one which initiated action.

Today we are accustomed to government involvement in many aspects of our lives and it is hard to imagine a time when the state was reluctant even to request local authorities to take measures vital to the health of the nation. The assump-tion of government responsibility for medical, education and other welfare services did not follow a predetermined plan; rather, it was a haphazard process. Practical action was taken when situations became intolerable, but setting standards in areas such as working conditions or building regulations caused much discussion. Deciding precisely what were dangerous, unethical or unhealthy practices posed problems for the Victorians, as they had no guidelines on how to tackle the practical problems caused by in-dustrialisation.

Perhaps the one factor that really made it difficult for our great-grandparents to accept the idea that the state should be

Leeds Town Hall, opened by Queen Victoria in 1859, symbolised the pride and wealth of the cities and masked their uncertain response to the demand for public services caused by a growing population.

PUBLIC SERVICES

Victorian England's increasingly complex urban society demanded new means of control and communication, but the provision of these was neither smooth nor evenly distributed. There was an inevitable conflict between the demands of a society committed to unfettered individualism and the realisation that many problems could only be solved by the intervention of government.

Rising crime rates, popular disorder and fear of the impact of Chartism prompted a partial rethinking of the police services available in the later 1830s. On the one hand there was the legacy of the old rural society, with a parochial amateur constabulary, backed by justices of the peace and the assize judges and, on the other, the model of Sir Robert Peel's new Metropolitan Police, created in 1829; directly controlled by the Home Secretary, this provided a well-disciplined uniformed force.

Some towns used the permissive clauses of the 1835 Municipal Corporations Act to create new police forces, but implementation was very patchy; Leeds, for instance, created a force of 20 men. The real change came with the reform of the rural counties, on which a Royal Commission reported in 1839. The County Police Act which resulted was also permissive rather than mandatory, a sop to the considerable force of rural opinion, led by men such as the Duke of Richmond, who felt that central government would interfere unnecessarily with local autonomy and authority. It was not universally successful (only half of England's 56 counties adopted it) and many counties offered only a token gesture.

It was not until 1856 that all county and town authorities were obliged to create new police forces, supervised by government inspectors led by Major-General Cartwright. As a result, 208 borough and 56 county forces, all independent, came into being. There was still considerable variation: Rutland had two policemen (one the chief constable!) for its entire population of 11,491 people, whereas Liverpool had one 'copper' for every 393 of its inhabitants in 1860. The pattern lasted until it was modified by the 1888 Local Government Act, which reduced the number of forces to 183.

Led by officers drawn often from the army or the 'Met', the new police were heavily occupied; with small detective forces added as the century progressed, they faced a wide range of ordinary crimes and a few wider threats to order. On the whole, they had a deterrent as well as a punitive effect. Although they represented the dominant arm of the new industrial morality, the police enjoyed a relative independence and neutrality unmatched elsewhere in Europe. Open conflict with the public was rare – the most extreme case was 'Bloody Sunday', 13 November 1887, when 1,700 constables fought a pitched battle with political reformers in Trafalgar Square. That it was so unusual was no small measure of the success of the Victorian police forces.

Dealing with fire, a considerable risk in the new urban sprawl, did not attract the same sense of urgency as the fight against crime. Most large towns had long relied either on the haphazard provisions of the old corporations or the self-preserving benevolence of the insurance companies who provided their own brigades for their own clients. It was these brigades banded together in 1833, which formed the London Fire Engine Establishment, with 76 officers and men responsible

Most libraries began as private subscription institutions, but Parliament authorised free public ones in 1850. It was not until the 1890s, however, that many authorities responded and built libraries such as this one at Brentford.

Early libraries were cautious in allowing public access to books. Here the reader searched the index on the left and the book was found by the librarian.

for virtually the whole of London. Led by a Scot, James Braidwood, they concentrated primarily on saving property. Braidwood was killed in 1861 at the great fire of Tooley Street, to be replaced by an Irishman, Captain Shaw. It was partly his perseverance and partly the strain on private enterprise imposed by a growing metropolis that led to the formation in 1865 of the London Metropolitan Fire Board, whence the LFEE became the responsibility of the local authority.

Before he resigned in 1891, Shaw built up a service which was the best equipped and disciplined in the world; using steam pumps and specially trained horses, the men went into action following the maxims of Shaw's pioneer book, *Fire Protection* (1876). By the 1870s there were 500 firemen and 150 engines in 159 stations, coupled with an annual budget of £100,000.

On the whole it was effective, but the picture outside London was much more patchy. Some of the larger towns established brigades in imitation of the capital, but many relied either on the philanthropy of the rich, such as the private brigades of the Prince of Wales at Sandhurst or Lord Leconfield at Petworth, or the 'volunteer' brigades of local worthies, part-time soldiers happy to dress up in another glamorous uniform. Stricter by-laws made new town buildings less dangerous by the 1880s and industry responded with a wide range of new firefighting devices.

Communication grew in an odd mixture of technological innovation, commercial enterprise and government monopoly. The British postal service may be said to have started in 1635 when a system of packet posts was begun and farmed out at an annual rent. In 1657 the system became a government office under a Postmaster General,

and in 1710 a general office for the three kingdoms was set up. Mails were originally conveyed by post boys, then by mail coaches which were a prominent feature of the roads during the turnpike era. The railway was first used for the carriage of mails in 1830. The charges for this system were high, and increased with the distance the mail was carried.

Despite considerable opposition, a Warwickshire schoolmaster, Rowland Hill, persuaded Parliament to adopt a uniform letter rate of one penny in 1840. With the opportunities offered by the railways, growing literacy and the general population movements of Victorian England, postal use increased eventually some 24-fold to some 1,800 million letters and 400 million packets a year. Hill, Secretary to the Postmaster General and Post Office from 1846 until 1864, presided over other growths as well. In the 1860s the Post Office took over the electric telegraphy system pioneered by private enterprise; it also created a Savings Bank. Postal orders became available in 1881. The Office became the nerve centre of the Empire, employing 30,000 staff by 1880. The first transatlantic telegraph cable was laid in 1858 (it did not work properly until 1866) and it was possible for the government to interfere in the daily conduct of the Boer Wars, using the network which grew afterwards. In London, H. G. Wells and George Bernard Shaw could correspond by postcard five times in one day.

All these services created considerable job opportunities, especially in the countryside, with security, respectability and attraction of a uniform thrown in. But discipline was strict, turnover high, the hours long and the wages low; an experienced constable, fireman or postman earned about 30 shillings a week by the 1890s, less than a skilled craftsman.

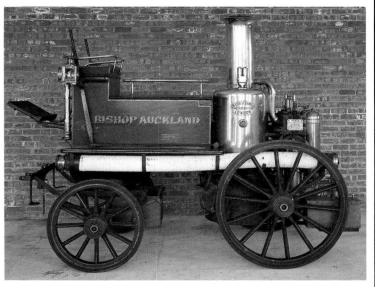

Victorian firefighting demanded new technology, most highly developed in steam pumps. This specimen was made by Shand Mason for the town of Bishop Auckland around 1890 and is now in the North of England Open Air Museum, Beamish.

One of Greenwich's horsedrawn steam pumps, manned by a crew in full dress. Heavy leather boots, serge jackets and brass helmets provided some protection, but this magnificence contrasted with the danger, long hours and low pay.

'Peelers' circa 1864. The uniforms and stance suggest military discipline and organisation in a war against urban crime. Note the new-style helmet on the right, a forerunner of modern headgear, more practical than the topper.

An urban post office in Leeds; note the uniformed staff. With its classical design, this was a solid shrine of Victorian achievement.

The Penny Black, the first and perhaps the most famous postage stamp ever issued, appeared on 6 May 1840. Rowland Hill was one of its five designers.

responsible for those who could not care for themselves was their cherished belief in 'self-help'. Essentially, this meant that every man should take responsibility for himself and that the common good was really the sum total of the self-interest of every member of society. If a man worked hard and saved carefully he could educate his own children, provide for himself and his family in times of unemployment and sickness, and put something aside for his old age. If a person did not do this, then he could blame only himself for his poverty.

For those who believed in self-help, the cause of poverty lay in morally flawed personalities, for to be virtuous was to be prosperous. This overlooked the fact that some people simply did not earn enough to support an independent, decent lifestyle. During the last two decades of the century,

Charles Booth surveyed the 900,000 inhabitants of London's East End. He discovered that 30 per cent of London's population were living below a poverty line defined as an income of between 18 s. and 21 s. per week for a moderate family. Seebohm Rowntree's study of York revealed the same figure of about one-third of the population sunk in poverty. Rowntree's survey also made allowances for variation in both general economic and family circumstances. By the use of statistics he documented the suggestion that an individual born into poverty could expect a period of prosperity when he left school and started work; this prosperity would decline when he married and had children, rise as his offspring began to earn, and finally worsen when his children left home and his strength began to fail with old age. Booth's study defined a life of poverty, while

MARKETS

One of the best ways to see a town and its people is to make a visit on market day: the goods on the market stalls may be modern, but you will be looking at a living tradition, for the majority of markets have Royal charters dating back to the Middle Ages and even these often indicate that they were a continuation of old-established practice. In view of the changes to Britain's retail and wholesale system that took place in the Victorian period it is somewhat surprising that so many of these old markets have survived: the rights to hold fairs, often covered by the same charters and once equally prized by towns as a boost to trade, are now very largely forgotten.

In small, pre-industrial towns the market was usually confined to one or two days a week and was a mixed one: all kinds of goods were bought and sold, both retail and wholesale. In the larger towns different streets or areas specialised in various commodities; old street names such as the Haymarket and the Shambles give an indication of the sites of these vanished markets. (A shambles was the place where butchers killed and sold meat, and the modern use of the word is an indication that they were not prized features of a locality.)

London, by far the largest town, developed three different types of market. As well as the retail street markets (e.g. Petticoat Lane, Berwick Market and Woolwich Market), large wholesale markets of two kinds emerged. These dealt with the main foodstuffs (e.g. meat at Smithfield, fish at Billingsgate, and fruit and vegetables at Covent Garden) where the commodities were brought to the capital for sale, or with bonded or warehoused goods (e.g. tea at Mincing Lane, diamonds at Hatton Garden, and grain at the Corn Exchange, Mark Lane) where samples formed the basis of trading.

Most of the urban commodity markets were either built or rebuilt during the Victorian era. Covent Garden fruit and vegetable market, which had grown up in the once-select Piazza, was rebuilt as a wholesale market in the 1830s before the coming of the railways and consequently suffered the major inconvenience of having all its supplies brought in by barrow and cart through narrow and busy streets. Billingsgate was another old-established market that, although ideally sited when fish was brought in by boat up the Thames, was not so convenient when the bulk of its supplies came from the east coast by train. In the 1850s the Great Northern Railway company built a wholesale potato market at Kings Cross, convenient for

crops from the newly tilled acres of East Anglia, which replaced the inconveniently sited potato market in Tooley Street on the southern approaches to London Bridge.

The most troublesome of London's wholesale markets, though, was undoubtedly Smithfield. When Victoria came to the throne, meat was driven to and from market 'on the hoof' and not only did the sights, sounds and smells upset Victorian sensibilities, but animals were driven through respectable districts on Sunday evening for Monday's market, and the drovers were infamous for their drunkenness, cruelty and bad language. After years of protests the City Corporation closed Smithfield in 1855 to be rebuilt as a dead meat market, and moved the livestock market to Copenhagen Fields — nearer to the railway termini where cattle were beginning to come in by rail from Scotland. This market — the Caledonian Market, or 'Cally' — became the most famous street market in London before the Second World War, selling a tremendous variety of secondhand goods on Tuesdays and Fridays, when the wholesale cattle market was not in operation.

The markets of London not only supplied much of the country, they also often determined commodity prices for the whole country; as a commercial

centre London was pre-eminent.

During the Victorian era retail markets were essential to working people who often could not afford food at shop prices. In the expanding industrial towns of the midlands and north, the civic pride of new town corporations could not tolerate their main thoroughfares cluttered with market stalls which would ruin the imposing effect of the new town hall. Therefore large market halls were built in which buyers and sellers had protection from the elements.

In London covered markets were not so popular; most of the London retail markets were in very poor areas and neither the customers nor the costermongers could afford the additional expense of a place inside. Mid-Victorian London had numerous daily street markets such as the Cut at Lambeth, Strutton Ground near Victoria and Leather Lane off Holborn — in fact, wherever the poor were congregated. But in the East End — the poorest quarter of all — the most famous street markets developed, and because many of the vendors were Jewish and most working men did not receive their wages until late Saturday night, these were at their busiest on Sunday: a tradition of Sunday trading that still survives.

Early morning in Billingsgate, London's wholesale fish market; by 10 a.m. the street would be deserted. Horse-drawn vehicles predominate, but a few early lorries are also bringing fish from the railway termini.

An open market at Whitby. Such markets (London had over 80) were vital to the poor as stallholders, with no overheads, could retail their goods at rock-bottom prices. The well-to-do, however, are also out in search of bargains.

Rowntree's work showed how incomes varied with an individual's age and capabilities. As one historian has said, Booth presented poverty as a snapshot while Rowntree showed it as a moving picture. Both men began their surveys on their own initiative, but they were not alone in their desire to understand why so many lived in poverty in spite of the wealth created by new industries.

Productivity had soared as machines replaced human labour; the result was an increase in national wealth. Even allowing for the growth in population, the gross national product increased four-fold in real terms during the 19th century. Fascinated by their ability to produce vast wealth, industrialists were proud and confident. However, other members of the middle class such as university dons, teachers in the better schools and other professional men who could

The Salvation Army, founded by Catherine and William Booth, was one of many Victorian evangelical missions that aimed to encourage the poor to lead respectable Christian lives. The Salvationists turned to social work in the 1890s.

Leadenhall, a market site for centuries, was by the 18th century a thriving poultry market. This hall was built in 1881 by the City Architect, Sir Horace Jones, but as the City's population declined the market's importance decreased.

Covent Garden early in the 19th century. The arches of the Piazza which originally attracted vendors to the square can be seen in the foreground, with the purpose-built market hall in the background. Many vegetable growers from erstwhile country areas — now part of London's suburbs — drove up regularly to sell their supplies; vegetables are displayed in the round baskets which the porters carried — 10 at a time — balanced on their heads.

Leeds Market slaughterhouse shows how unpleasant and unhygienic open butchers' shambles must have been. Municipal abattoirs were built in many Victorian towns, which at least removed such scenes from the market and usually provided better conditions.

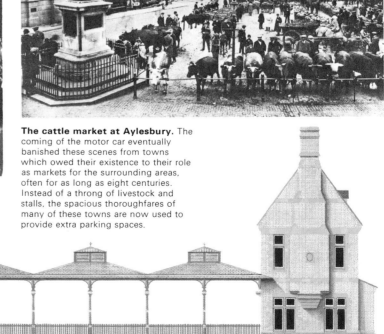

The cattle market at Aylesbury. The coming of the motor car eventually banished these scenes from towns which owed their existence to their role as markets for the surrounding areas, often for as long as eight centuries. Instead of a throng of livestock and stalls, the spacious thoroughfares of many of these towns are now used to provide extra parking spaces.

Darlington market hall, built in 1863, still houses a flourishing market today. The wide streets of Darlington proclaim its life as a market town in early times before the coming of the railway. This fine building replaces an earlier market Toll Booth and a subsequent Georgian town hall and shambles.

free themselves from the preoccupations of business began to worry about the price of this progress. Anxiety was expressed that material gains would outstrip spiritual progress and there was a realisation that greater wealth did not necessarily make men more Christian or moral. Many of these middle class men and women were eager to stir the consciences of contemporaries who were indifferent to the sufferings of the lower orders. They were attempting to come to an emotional understanding of the tremendous economic and social changes through which they were living.

Novelists, poets and philosophers played important parts in shaping people's attitudes to these changes. Romantic poets such as Blake, Shelley and Coleridge lamented the passing of the agrarian world, while Wordsworth criticised the railway as a symbol of the inhuman mechanisation of society. Tennyson, the one poet that most Victorians would have called their own, expressed concern with the intellectual assault on traditional Christianity in his poem 'In Memoriam'. Novelists such as Mrs Gaskell, Benjamin Disraeli and Charles Dickens criticised the degradation that they felt was destroying human potential, and philosophers like Thomas Carlyle and John Ruskin decried the new faith in material power.

This added to elements of bewilderment at work within the middle class itself. Doubt gathered force as time went on, so that uncertainty was as much a characteristic of the later Victorian period as confidence had been the hallmark of the 1850s and 1860s. Of course these doubts were even more troubling when contrasted with the calm and prosperity that preceded them. The economic supremacy of Britain began to be threatened by Germany and America in the 1870s, while British confidence was also challenged militarily by the bellicose gestures of Napoleon III of France at the end of the 1850s and German unification under Prussian leadership during the 1860s and 1870s. The 1870s also saw a depression in agriculture which resulted in the diminished importance of farming itself. In 1851, one-fifth of the working population had been employed in agriculture, an industry that was producing about one-fifth of the national income. By 1900, agriculture employed less than a tenth of the labour force and its share of the national income had fallen to less than one-fifteenth.

New ward for the casual poor at Marylebone workhouse. Able-bodied men were given relief only inside the workhouse, and conditions were harsh and unpleasant in order to create an incentive for paupers to find work.

HOSPITALS AND NURSING

The age of philanthropy in the 18th century resulted in the foundation of no less than 154 hospitals by voluntary means between 1700 and 1825. Accompanying this, a number of medical schools were also founded, mainly in London. The groundwork was being established for a surge of activity that was to extend throughout the urban areas of 19th century Britain. By the end of the century, over 1000 hospitals, most of them voluntary, had been built to meet the needs of the people.

The general hospitals of the 18th century continued to be built throughout the 19th century, especially in the form of the 'cottage' hospital (so-called because they were small and often housed in cottages) which first appeared at Cranleigh in Surrey in 1859. But the Victorian era also saw the development of a host of specialist hospitals in London, including the Royal Marsden Cancer Hospital, the Hospital for Sick Children and the Royal Dental Hospital.

Other specialist hospitals, including tuberculosis, isolation, military, maternity and mental hospitals were constructed, as well as general hospitals, in most large urban areas. Tuberculosis hospitals were a feature of the last two decades of the 19th century and were located in rural areas. With the eradication of the disease as a result of antibiotics, most of the tuberculosis hospitals now have other uses.

A quite different kind of hospital also developed during the Victorian period, and arose from the Poor Law Commission of 1834. These were municipal hospitals or workhouse infirmaries, which appeared as the sick poor were separated from the able-bodied poor.

Four individuals in particular are responsible for transforming conditions in Victorian hospitals: Sir James Simpson's use of chloroform in 1847 laid the foundation for the science of anaesthesia; Florence Nightingale from 1853 was largely responsible for reforming the nursing profession; Lord Joseph Lister in the 1860s promoted the theory of antiseptics; while Louis Pasteur's germ theory of the 1880s brought about the prophylactic treatment of diphtheria, tuberculosis, cholera, yellow fever and the plague.

The development of nursing might have taken a very different course had not a certain wealthy young woman become bored with the upper class social round and, in 1853, accepted the management of a nursing home for working women financed by a group of charitable ladies. Having embarked upon her career, Florence Nightingale took charge of nursing in the military hospital in Scutari during the Crimean War, for which she achieved the national prestige that enabled her, throughout the rest of her long life, to shape the nursing profession as we know it today.

At that time going into hospital was considered to be a social degradation, meaning either that you had no family or that they could not afford or did not want to nurse you at home. The upper classes never went into hospital: they were nursed at home by servants and relatives through all their illnesses, even those known to be infectious, such as scarlet fever and smallpox. The women had their babies at home and even surgical operations were carried out there, though performed by doctors and surgeons from the public hospitals. Florence Nightingale, however, considered that the patient in hospital usually received better care than the wealthy gentry who would be tended by ignorant servants, relatives or, even worse, by dreadful hired nurses, and it became her aim to institute organised hospital training for nurses.

She not only succeeded in establishing nursing as a profession, but also assisted rich Mr William Rathbone to set up the first training centre for district nurses in his home town of Liverpool. Florence Nightingale believed in providing cleanliness, fresh (but not cold) air, sunlight, and as stimulating a view as possible for the patient; these precepts she incorporated into plans for hospitals on which her advice had been sought, and most hospitals, even those being built today, bear some mark of her influence.

It was not until after the end of Victoria's reign, however, that hospital treatment became 'fashionable', and then a comic irony emerged: not in any of the respectable lying-in hospitals of London did Society ladies choose to produce their heirs, but in Queen Charlotte's hospital for unmarried mothers!

'Public disinfectors' were employed to take all bedding and linen from the sickroom of a patient ill with an infectious disease to be treated in a disinfecting oven. By the 1870s isolation was also commonly practised.

'**Awaiting Admission to the Casual Ward'**, by Sir Luke Fildes (1843–1927). Disease and ill health were rife among the poverty-stricken in the workhouse, and with the unwholesome conditions and harsh treatment there many died. The situation began to improve after the Poor Law Act of 1834, when workhouse infirmaries or municipal hospitals were set up especially to care for the sick poor.

Laundering in neat and hygienic surroundings in the workhouse infirmary. Under the influence of Nightingale-trained nurses, workhouses gradually became places of refuge rather than punishment for the sick poor.

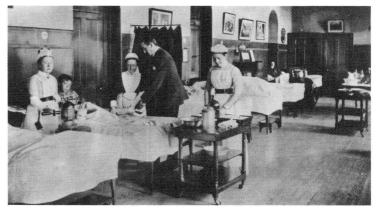

By the 1880s, Florence Nightingale's nursing precepts had been adopted in many hospitals. Staffed by teams of well-trained nurses, this ward at Aberdeen Royal Infirmary is cheerful, clean and homely.

Florence Nightingale is said to have disapproved of the suffragettes, but she fought hard to obtain her own independence. In achieving high standards of nursing practice she greatly improved the care of the sick.

The 1822 operating theatre (left) of the old St Thomas' Hospital near London Bridge. When the railway was extended in 1861, the hospital moved to Lambeth, but the theatre survived as a testimony to the early days of surgical practice.

Not only were overseas rivals to Britain's supremacy appearing, but alternatives were also being suggested for the ordering of British society and the traditional relationships within it. The very existence of God was questioned when the literal truth of the Bible was disputed in such works as Charles Darwin's *The Origin of Species* (1859). Feminist ideas also began to emerge at this time, decrying the limited educational and occupational opportunities for women and reacting against the idea that woman's sole function was to be a wife and mother. Socialism was another form of protest that attacked the way wealth was distributed and the relationship between workers and employers. While the full impact of these revolutionary ideas was not to be felt until our own time, their development during the last quarter of the 19th century undermined mid-Victorian feelings of confidence and security.

Criticism and doubt were therefore very much a part of the experience of educated and articulate Victorian men and women, but others in all social classes found emotional security by upholding common values and attitudes. The acceptance of similar ideas created a bond between different economic groups who might otherwise have felt resentment and hostility towards one another.

One of these beliefs was the widely accepted idea of deference, which was the acknowledgement that people in the classes above one were in some way innately superior and entitled to respect. Closely connected with the idea of deference was an emphasis on authority. Society was to be organised between groups who gave orders and those who obeyed: the poor were to obey the rich, wives their husbands, and children their parents. Even the political system worked along these lines, for while the second Reform Act of 1867 was designed to extend the franchise to the respectable working classes, MPs continued to be selected from the upper classes. This was partly because of the belief that social standing carried authority and therefore the upper classes were more suited to govern, and partly due to the fact that MPs received no salaries and therefore candidates needed to have an independent source of income.

The elements of respect and authority were also considered

Charles Darwin (1809–82). His theory of evolution based on natural selection was summarised by Herbert Spencer as 'the survival of the fittest'. By showing that man had evolved from the lower animals he upset the doctrine of man's immutability, thereby offending the church.

CRIME AND PUNISHMENT

The Victorian period witnessed a remarkable change in public attitudes to crime. At the beginning of the period hangings for murder were still commonplace, and the following extract from the Cornish *West Briton* newspaper for 17 April 1840 speaks for itself:

The execution of the brothers Lightfoot who murdered Mr. Nevill Norway took place at Bodmin on Monday last in front of the county gaol. . . . . the town of Bodmin on the Sunday evening presented the appearance of a fair. . . . thousands of persons traversed the high roads during the night . . . and by twelve o'clock, the hour of the execution, there could not have been less than twenty to twenty-five thousand persons present. The brothers were launched into eternity together and died almost immediately. After hanging for an hour the bodies were cut down and put into a couple of black coffins . . . they were then buried in a hole in the coal yard in front of the prison.

Public executions actually continued until 1868, by which time a new attitude was beginning to emerge; it owed much to the system of policing that had been initiated in London by Sir Robert Peel in 1829. The amazing thing is that society had held together for so long without the protection of a strong civic force trained to detect crime and control mob violence – it is perhaps a testimony to the honesty of the average citizen of the past when living in small inter-related communities. The expanding urban areas were however producing new problems.

Sir Robert Peel's great institution was a corps of civil police with truncheons, blue coats and top hats. London soon became fond of the good natured and effective 'Bobbies', and it was not long before other urban areas demanded their establishment. By 1856 every county and borough had to employ a police force. The days of the medieval Watchman were over, persons and property were looked after without any sacrifice of freedom and mobs were dealt with efficiently without having to call on an armed force as at Peterloo.

The Victorians believed in the existence of a 'criminal class', although they realised that this class included people of different types, united only in their reckless disregard for their fate. At the top of this social ladder were the well dressed, high-class pickpockets known as the 'swell-mob', and below them the skilled housebreakers such as Bill Sykes in Dickens' novel *Oliver Twist*. These professionals looked down on the 'shoplifters' and they in turn despised the beggars. Most of these criminals were recruited from the large number of juveniles who migrated to the cities

in search of work or, having been disowned by their families, were forced to work for themselves. Intelligent youngsters would be chosen by experienced thieves to be trained as experts, while less ambitious boys would survive by begging or pilfering small articles. Criminal groups were usually town-based, as urban areas offered greater opportunities for crime and easier escape routes. It was only in the large towns that distinctly criminal areas, known as rookeries, existed. From these rookeries criminals would venture out to do their work and retreat back into safety if pursued. Their meeting places, known as flash houses, were usually in the rookeries and stolen goods were handed over to receivers or fences, such as Dickens' immortal character Fagin, who was based on the real-life Isaac Solomons of Spitalfields, arrested for receiving in 1827.

While crime seems to have increased in the first half of the 19th century, it appears to have been less violent than 18th century criminal activity. However, between 1861 and 1864, there was an unexpected increase in street robberies, using the method of attack known as garotting. The boldness and brutality of these attacks caused great alarm but the introduction of the Garotting Act of 1863, which provided for the flogging of offenders and the increasing efficiency of the police, deterred the attackers. At the time people blamed the outbreaks on the changes in the penal system, particularly the stopping of transportation to Australia, but Victorian prisons still stressed punishment rather than rehabilitation. In 1853, when transportation for a term of less than 14 years was discontinued, it was reckoned that four years' penal servitude at home was equivalent to seven years' transportation.

The strict regimes in prisons sprang from the Victorian determination to reform what they thought to be a previously inefficient system: the haphazard arrangement in prisons had meant they were schools of crime, so the object of reform was to prevent criminals communicating freely inside jail. Solitary confinement, enforced silence and the wearing of masks so that nothing could be conveyed by the features aimed to prevent prisoners from communicating with each other. Constant occupation, such as shot drill or the treadmill not only sapped the energy of the inmates, but also undermined their mental and physical health. While the Victorian criminal class certainly terrified and preyed upon the prosperous and educated segments of society, the authorities could be equally harsh towards those unfortunate enough to be caught.

Convicts were imprisoned in the hulks of old naval ships, while awaiting transportation to penal colonies in America and Australia.

Severe penalties were used as deterrents against crime, as shown on this sign on a bridge near Blandford Forum, Dorset. But they lost effect because people were unwilling to prosecute and reasonable magistrates would not convict.

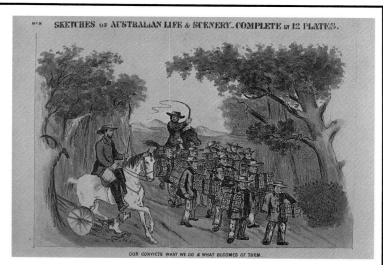

The colonies were seen as an ideal place to get rid of surplus population and convicted criminals. When America became independent, they were sent to Australia and Tasmania until protests by reformers ended transportation in 1867.

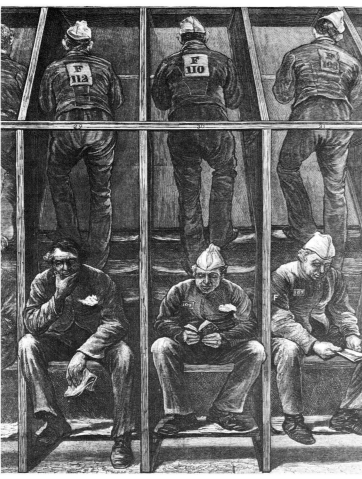

Men and women sentenced to hard labour spent hours on the treadmill. Victorians believed that work was the cure for criminal tendencies but had difficulty in finding labour harder than most of the jobs of the lower classes.

Pentonville prison in 1843. Part of the vision of people like Jeremy Bentham was the replacement of ancient dungeons with light, airy and easily managed prisons where it was possible to put ideas of prisoner reform into practice.

Oakum picking, the undoing of old tarred rope to make caulking for ships' timbers, was the work of prisoners not on hard labour. It often disabled their fingers.

Holloway's romantic exterior disguised the prison's notorious reputation for incarceration of ordinary criminals and ill-treatment of suffragettes.

essential to the smooth running of the family. The family was at the centre of Victorian life and its rituals were sacred: the gathering of the household for prayers, reading aloud in the evening, the annual seaside holiday. The central figure of the family was the father, who was to be obeyed out of respect to his superior knowledge and experience. To balance this, the Victorian mother was supposed to be a source of comfort and love. Many Victorians strove to fulfil these roles and indeed found them psychologically satisfying. Autobiographies of the time are filled with nostalgic longing for the security of the childhood home as a refuge from the inhuman commercial world. On the other hand, many intelligent and sincere people, such as the writer and critic Edmund Gosse, found this way of life empty and stifling, if not frustrating and repressive. A recent study of Victorian murderesses has shown how the strains of living up to the image of the perfect wife or daughter drove some women to see murder as the only way out of a dire personal dilemma. For instance, Madeleine Smith was the daughter of a respected Glasgow architect who murdered her shipping clerk lover in 1857. She was compelled to murder by the fear that her father would discover the affair and consequently know that she was not the sexually innocent daughter that all Victorian girls were supposed to be. While few individuals were actually driven to this extreme, the pressures to conform to accepted standards were immense.

If the Victorians were fascinated by class, they revered respectability. For them respectability meant a style of living which showed a proper respect for manners and morals and usually, but not always, involved church or chapel attendance. To be respectable you had to have some financial independence, as to be in debt or to take charity prohibited real respectability. This obsession to dress in a way that was tasteful but not gaudy, to be respectful to your 'betters' yet polite to those less fortunate, to speak without swearing and above all to live in an area or part of a street that had a good reputation was important to the Victorians because they believed that these outward signs of proper behaviour reflected inner personal virtues. This led to a great deal of hypocrisy, for if a man spoke and dressed correctly he could mask unsavoury if not downright criminal behaviour. Some Victorians were well aware of this contradiction and books and articles frequently appeared warning their readers that the display of fine houses, expensive carriages and lavish dinner parties did not suggest that their purveyors were more virtuous. However, the equation of outward appearances and inner virtue remained important; in fact, the lower down the social scale you descended, the more important respectability became, until you reached the level of the very poor where nothing except survival mattered. Many poor yet hardworking families scrimped and saved a few pennies each week against times of sickness and unemployment to avoid being forced to take charity. Working class women wore themselves out washing and scrubbing so that the family could sit in state in a spotless tiny front room for a few hours each Sunday evening. One wonders why this meant so much to people who had to work so hard for so few comforts, but it was important because it was the one way they had of maintaining their self-respect.

While the broad social developments of the 19th century, such as the increase in population, the industrialisation of the economy and the expansion of urban communities, are important to understand if we are to appreciate the experiences of our great-grandfathers, they form only a backdrop

VICTORIAN CHILDREN

The Victorian nursery ruled by nanny would seem to have been a separate world, far removed from the dark, satanic mills, the tensions of industrial unrest and the grinding poverty that was so much a part of Victorian city life. Many Victorians certainly felt this way and contemporary writings are filled with nostalgic longing for childhood as a time of peace, security and purity. Like so many other aspects of Victorian life, however, childhood experiences were being shaped by the tremendous changes that were transforming British society.

Today we recognise the individuality of each child and we see childhood as a time for playing and learning, with few responsibilities. The teenage years are frequently fraught with tension as parents are anxious that their children should begin to conform to adult standards of behaviour and to demonstrate the ability and willingness to assume responsibility. The Victorians did not see childhood and adolescence in this way. In fact, it was not until the last half of the 19th century that adolescence was acknowledged as a stage of development.

Victorian families were large, with five or more children the norm until the last quarter of the 19th century. It was during the 1870s that men and women in the middle classes began the practice of family limitation; it took a little longer for family planning to be usual in working class homes. Methods of family planning were crude and simple, with abortion probably at least as common as contraception. While throughout Victoria's reign individuals and groups existed that were anxious to spread birth control information, most women until the 1870s considered pregnancy to be inevitable after marriage.

There was also a high rate of infant mortality. Victorian parents would count on no more than nine of ten children surviving their first year of life; often only eight out of ten did so. Not many more than six out of ten lived until they were 20. Towards the end of the last century and the beginning of this there was a dramatic decline in infant mortality and the number of births; it would seem that married couples wished to limit the number of their children as more survived to adulthood. Historical trends and demographic patterns do not, however, always follow what would appear to be the logical explanation. Infant deaths only decreased after family planning began to be practised.

One of the reasons behind family limitation was the increased cost of child support. While today we face soaring inflation, the Victorian middle classes faced larger bills for other reasons. Actual retail prices increased only 5% between 1850 and 1870, but expectations of what was considered necessary to maintain a suitable living standard, altered greatly. Wives and daughters did less in the home, which meant that the employment of housekeepers, maids, cooks and nursemaids more than doubled. Families started travelling and the annual holiday away from home began to be considered a necessity.

Childcare was also affected by this attitude. Then, as now, parents felt it was their duty to help their children secure a position in life that was no lower, and if possible higher, than their own. For many this was only possible through education, but as professional work and industrial technology required men with a wider range of skills the education needed took longer and cost more money. The middle classes felt that public schools such as Eton, Harrow, Rugby and Winchester would provide the right education for their sons. Of course, not all parents could afford to send their children to these schools, so they either limited the number of their offspring or patronised inferior schools based on the model of the great public schools.

The public school system had a

Some of the amazing range of penny toys from the days when young children in well-to-do families usually had just that amount of pocket money each week.

A prayer sampler gave plenty of sewing practice and a reminder of godliness.

Elaborate toys, like this butcher's shop on view at the Museum of Childhood, Edinburgh, were hand made in every detail.

number of severe drawbacks. This type of education trained the boys to be Christian gentlemen with a high moral code and a developed sense of social responsibility, qualities that were not necessarily the best preparation for a life in industry and commerce. The discipline in these schools was harsh, with authority invested in the older students or prefects. Homosexuality was common, as were epidemics of fatal illnesses. Parents considered these risks to be insignificant in relation to the advantages of giving their sons the opportunity to mingle with the 'right sort of people' and to acquire the attributes of gentlemanly behaviour. The wish to provide one's children with correct accomplishments and polish was an important motive in girls' education as well. Daughters were either taught at home by their mothers and governesses, or attended schools that would train them in ladylike behaviour. It was not until the middle of the century that schools such as the North London Collegiate School (1850) and the Cheltenham Ladies College (1853) were founded with the aim of providing girls with the same intellectual training as their brothers.

A quite different set of conditions prevailed with the children of the working class and amongst the pauper and orphan children; in 1833 a working day of 14 hours was quite common even for six and seven year olds. It is not surprising that such conditions were also under attack in the period which led up to the abolition of slavery in 1833. In the same year there was an Act which forbade the employment of children in factories under the age of nine and which also prescribed maximum hours for those aged between nine and 18; factory inspectors were also appointed, and these paved the way for future reforms. Efforts were next directed to reducing hours for all employees and the Ten Hours Bill was eventually passed in 1847.

Until 1853 the Factory Acts were confined to textile factories but further

Acts in 1854, 1867 and 1878 brought all factories and workshops under some measure of control. Those most active in these reforms included Ashley Cooper (who became the 7th Earl of Shaftesbury in 1851), Lord Althorp and the factory owner Fielden.

Another problem area was the mining industry where both women and children were employed underground in appalling conditions, almost solely because of the cheapness of the labour. Ashley Cooper was again largely responsible for the Mines Act of 1842 which forbade the employment underground of females at any time and of male children under the age of 10. In 1850 a Mines Inspectorate was introduced.

In agriculture, women and children were employed on field work in gangs, under demoralising conditions, for long hours. This was especially so in the 1860s in areas of high unemployment. Lord Shaftesbury, as Cooper had now become, again spearheaded an attack on this system and in 1867 it was made illegal to employ any children under the age of eight in a gang, and no women and children could be employed in a gang in which men worked. A further advance came in 1873 when the employment of children was made contingent upon a record of school attendance. The latter had become possible as a result of the Education Act of 1870.

Throughout the whole of this period the abuse of the boy sweeps, forced to climb chimneys, continued despite much legislation. Charles Kingsley's *Water Babies* of 1863 stirred the public conscience and led to a further Act in 1864, but success in the abolition of the system was not achieved until Lord Shaftesbury's Act of 1875.

Rather strangely in this saga we do not see the emergence of Dr Barnardo's Homes for Orphans until 1870, nor that of the Society for the Prevention of Cruelty to Children until 1884.

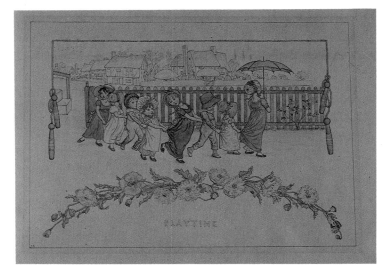

Kate Greenaway's drawings of idealised children in the easy clothes of the 18th century were popular with Victorian mothers and fathers.

The great age of the school uniform: the boys of the Amicable Society School, Yorks, with their Christ's Hospital collars, short Eton jackets and sailors' hats.

Dr Barnardo helped thousands of homeless children in Victorian cities. He set up a photographic studio to take 'before' and 'after' pictures of children admitted to his houses, to publicise his work and raise money.

'Bubbles', by J. E. Millais, an idealised view of Victorian childhood. The realities for most children were very different, and they were ill equipped for a tough future by an inadequate education system.

to the way people lived their lives. What was it like to be Victorian? How did they live and what did they experience? It is impossible, however, to describe one particular lifestyle and label it 'Victorian' for people in different economic groups or classes lived in different ways. Obviously the amount of money you earned affected the type of house in which you lived, the food you ate and the clothes you wore. In fact, it was not until after the First World War that a person's social position was not immediately identifiable by the type of clothes that he wore.

These differences in lifestyle could clearly be seen in the expanding urban areas, where different economic groups were settled in different sections of the city. In London, the poor were concentrated in the inner city areas such as Bethnal Green or Whitechapel, the scene of the 'Jack the

Ripper' murders in the 1880s. Most working men had to live near their work, and respectability, even snobbery, was determined by the street, even by the side of the street, on which people lived. In the fashionable West End, Mayfair and Belgravia were the most desirable addresses and much sought after by those coming to London for the Season. Kensington tended to be the home of professional men, politicians and businessmen. St John's Wood was favoured as the home for the mistresses of those living in Mayfair and Belgravia, and Bloomsbury had a literary flavour even before Virginia Woolf's time. For these people, the street that you lived on was important, but for the middle classes, it was the suburb where you lived that counted. In London, these might be Camden Town, Camberwell, Brixton or Islington. Not only did a person's economic position affect how he

VICTORIAN SCHOOLS

During the long reign of Victoria universal education gradually evolved in Britain not, as in other countries of the western world, in an integrated state system providing all the different grades of education, but in an enormous variety of private, denominational and, finally, state-provided schools. The haphazard way in which our educational system grew up is still evident today in regional variations in schooling and the names of schools: some still in use, some only remembered by being cut into foundation stones and over doorways.

When Victoria came to the throne the upper classes usually educated their daughters at home or at small private schools, while their sons had private tuition or went to one of the old public schools such as Eton or Winchester where the original founders' intention that they should provide education for poor children had usually lapsed. Public and grammar schools were widely criticised for their archaic syllabus and lack of discipline, both equally out of

harmony with Victorian requirements, but headmasters like Samuel Butler at Shrewsbury and Thomas Arnold at Rugby developed the type of education for which the public school is still famous and provided a model followed by many of the later grammar schools. The private schools that served the middle classes were extremely variable; some were undoubtedly good, and successful Victorians like Sir Titus Salt revered their schoolmasters all their lives, but with no form of inspection they could be very bad — even as bad as Dickens' Dotheboys Hall.

Charity schools provided for poor children by philanthropic landowners and the churches were also extremely variable, and in urban areas where there were the greatest numbers of poor children they were likely not even to exist, there being no wealthy landowner or congregation to provide them. The Quakers, who led the way with schools for their own children, also provided schools in some industrial areas, but

vast numbers of children received no education of any kind as parents were not legally obliged to have their children taught even to read and write.

The first state contribution to education was in the form of grants made to the churches for school buildings from 1833, but unfortunately schemes for universal education proposed at this time by clear-thinking men like Jeremy Bentham were submerged in the rivalry between the churches who were intolerant both of each other and of the idea of schools which gave no religious instruction.

In the middle of the 19th century, when the British generally were feeling particularly pleased with themselves, a few industrialists, scientists and the Prince Consort himself, who were aware of the educational systems being instituted in Holland, France, America and Germany, felt that by allowing most of the working classes to grow up illiterate and having no schools for scientific education the industrial future of the country was in grave danger. Unfortunately in the 1860s what

progress had been made in the provision of schools and the training of teachers was halted by cuts, and it was not until W. E. Forster, a Quaker with a real enthusiasm for education, became Vice President of the Education Department in 1868 that progress towards universal education was resumed with Forster's Act of 1870 which, while continuing state support for the church schools, set up Boards to provide elementary schools where none existed and offered free education to parents who could not afford to pay. By 1880 all children had to attend school between the ages of five and ten and by the end of the century the age of school leaving had been raised to 12. The State, however, was not yet involved in secondary education; in 1900 the Law Courts decided in the famous Cockerton case that ratepayers' money could not, under the terms of the 1870 Act, be spent on any form of higher education. This and other defects in the Act were remedied by the Balfour Education Act of 1902, which abolished the School Boards and gave responsibility for both primary and

Children at Daubenay Road school, Hackney, London on what looks like a special occasion. By this time new teacher training methods had brought a more relaxed atmosphere for young children.

Reconstruction at the Beamish museum of a 19th century schoolroom of the type that would have been found in the new compulsory schools.

School cookery class in Bradford, Yorks. Working mothers had no time to impart domestic skills to their children, hence this innovation.

lived, but it also influenced how he looked at life. Consequently, as the economy fluctuated throughout the century, the attitudes and activities of the various classes changed.

At the top of the social pyramid were the hereditary nobility and the country gentry. They had dominated the social hierarchy for centuries, but their privileged position was challenged during Victoria's lifetime, most particularly by wealthy, middle class businessmen and industrialists who resented the aristocracy's control of parliament. By the time of Victoria's death the aristocracy had surrendered some of its political power but still dominated the social scene. The hereditary nobility were not as numerous in the 19th century as they were to become later and it was this select group of titled men and their relations who formed the corps of the upper classes. They were the unquestioned leaders of

Typical housing of the urban poor in Leeds. Gruesome as it is, the continuous migration to the towns suggested that country conditions were often worse.

secondary education to the elected County and Borough Councils. Thus was determined the pattern of state education for the first half of the 20th century.

In retrospect, the 19th century and the Victorian era is important for the gradual assumption by the state of responsibility for mass education. Education was made universal and largely secular, and equally available for both sexes; and it included many new subjects which reflected scientific and industrial developments and world exploration. Elementary education was distinguished from secondary and technical, the universities were reformed and many new colleges, which were to grow into universities, were founded.

The total educational picture which resulted was a unique British compromise between tradition, privilege, class differences and new ideas which provided the basis for the educational systems of many emerging overseas countries.

Rugby School (above) was founded as a Free Grammar School in the Tudor period, and like many of its contemporaries was financed by a native of the town with money earned in London. It acquired its most famous headmaster, Thomas Arnold (right) in 1826. Not only did 19th century Rugby 'invent' the game that was to be played by public schoolboys in preference to common football, but Arnold introduced the ethics of 'playing the game' that were adopted by all public and grammar schools. *Tom Brown's Schooldays* was written by ex-pupil Thomas Hughes, and was probably the chief means by which Arnold's precepts spread.

Many 'National' schools, like this one at Tiverton of 1841, were built by the Church of England using government money allocated by Lord Althorp's Act of 1833. As a result, when compulsory education was introduced there was already a nucleus of good schools to build upon. This school is now a local museum.

Rhyl Street school, Kentish Town, London. When education became compulsory a great many schools like this were built, dominating the existing two-storey townscapes. Many of them have served for a century although they were designed to meet the educational needs of the 1880s.

society both in London and the country. The 'upper 1,000', to use a phrase of the time, consisted of an estimated 4,000 families who participated in the round of entertainment that came to a climax in the summer with the advent of the 'Season'. From late April until the end of July, members of society rode on horseback or in carriages down Rotten Row, attended numerous luncheons, dinners and balls, and participated in amateur theatricals and charity bazaars. The Marlborough House Ball at the end of July brought the festivities to a close. 'Society' then moved on, first to the Cowes week of yachting on the Isle of Wight, then to the grouse moors of Scotland, where shooting started on the 'glorious twelfth' of August. Later in the autumn, country house parties gathered for partridge shooting and hunting. The practice of spending a weekend at a country house became popular later in the century; this was made possible by the extension of rail travel.

London society was more cosmopolitan than its rural counterpart. It included professional men and the more dubious elements of the 'nouveau riche' as well as the aristocracy and gentry. In the country 'Society' was smaller but no less respected. Important county families were often related to the hereditary nobility and while they did not necessarily have a title themselves, their ancestry could often be traced far into the past.

Why were these people so important and powerful? Partly due to their wealth; but simply having money did not make one socially acceptable, the way that the money was acquired was also important. Primarily, the important families were landowners and as the demand for food products rose, agriculture remained profitable until the 1870s. Grain was protected from foreign competition by the Corn Laws until 1846, and for some time after that the majority of the population was still fed on British cereals. Unfortunately for landowners in the last quarter of the century, railways and steamships began to make food from other countries readily and cheaply available. Wheat from the American prairies was shipped across the Atlantic and the development of refrigeration meant that New Zealand lamb and Argentinian beef could be imported. This cut into the profits from agriculture and created financial problems for many aristocratic landowners. Under these circumstances the fate of the great landed estates was doomed, as government stock and mortgages became better investments than

Britain gave railways to the world; locomotives, rails and contractors such as Thomas Brassey were exported everywhere. From the 1870s onwards the emphasis changed, and Britain supplied capital to finance construction, especially in Latin America. The scene above is in Uganda.

VICTORIAN WOMEN

On the occasion of her Jubilee celebrations in 1887, Queen Victoria wore a 'springly white lace bonnet glittering with diamonds' instead of a crown. This simple gesture tells us that for the Queen her private life as a wife and mother was equal in importance to her public role as monarch and empress. Many of Victoria's subjects would have wholeheartedly agreed. For them, the fact that Victoria was a female monarch excused her faults, for women were considered to be weaker in body and mind than men. This idea that women were weak and therefore inferior had been held for generations, but the Victorians added to this the notion that women should be protected and not exploited. While the Victorians felt that women had few intellectual capabilities, they respected the 'fairer sex' for being pure and spiritual, virtues that gave women a special mission; they were to create a home atmosphere where their menfolk could escape from the corrupting, commercial world that prized material gains more than the moral values of compassion and love. The ultimate female mission was to be an 'Angel of the House', a term widely used by the Victorians and taken from the title of the famous poem by Coventry Patmore.

Prior to the 19th century, women, except those of the aristocratic and very wealthy classes, were expected to actively contribute to their families' maintenance. Before the Industrial Revolution people worked in small groups that were often centred in households. This made it possible for women to combine their responsibilities for caring for their families with helping to produce goods for sale or exchange. With the rise of factories, people were increasingly employed away from home, which meant that poor women had either to leave their families during the day or take the lowest paid jobs that could still be done at home.

The separation of home and work-place also affected women in those families whose prosperity placed them comfortably above the poverty line. Men from this group also began to work away from home, in trading and manufacturing, which meant that the women no longer were involved in the family business. As these families prospered, women were relieved of their housework and childcare responsibilities, as they could now afford servants to do the work for them. To have wives and daughters who did not need to work became a mark of a man's social standing. Consequently, the ideal of womanhood changed from that of 'The Perfect Wife' who participated in maintaining her family, to the image of the 'Perfect Lady' whose leisured lifestyle reflected her family's prestige. The 'Perfect Lady' was supposed to have no sexual desires, but to have strong family feelings and a desire for motherhood. Her education was to prepare her for the vocation of marriage, not by training her in household management but by helping her to acquire accomplishments such as painting, music and needlework. Daughters were warned against intellectual pursuits because helpless femininity and submissiveness to authority were the order of the day.

Above all, the perfect lady was to be sexually innocent so that she would be an inspiration to men without being a temptress. Sexuality to many Victorians represented the coarse, animal side of human nature that man had to learn to control if society itself was not to be threatened. For the Victorians, a good society was composed of good, moral individuals, and men were supposed to learn to be moral by exercising their free will in subduing their baser instincts. Women who were not pure, such as prostitutes or adulteresses, were feared and loathed because the passions they aroused appeared threatening; they

believed that family relationships and social unity would not last when individuals began thinking of their own pleasures before their duties to others.

The ideal of the perfect lady was fully accepted by the upper and middle classes, as they had the wealth to support and protect their women. For many, however, it was not possible to live up to this ideal. What happened to women who did not marry? Some commentators were cruel enough to suggest that there was no place in society for unmarried women. Others felt that their education in perfect ladyhood would fit them to be helpful aunts in their brothers' homes after their fathers could no longer care for them. Of course, many women did not have fathers and brothers to support them and without professional training they had limited job opportunities. They were forced to become governesses or seamstresses, gradually sinking below the social and economic level into which they had been born. Some were even forced into the ultimate debasement of prostitution; a few, but only the most courageous, emigrated.

For the working classes in steady employment, the family hearth was also an island of purity and peace and premarital chastity was important, for a 'bad' daughter could mean the loss of work for other members of the family. It was difficult for these girls to be innocent about sex, as they lived in cramped houses surrounded by the ravages of poverty. The ideal for them became knowledge without experience and a marriage centred on the home. The rising standard of living for these people after 1870 further encouraged their attitude that women should not work, as this meant that they neglected their families and undercut men's wages.

From the mid century onwards, the ideal of the perfect lady came under attack, as trying to live up to this model created hardships. The hysteria and fainting fits of Victorian women suggest how psychologically tiring it was always to be good and pure. Their superficial education encouraged a silly, trite attitude to life that made it difficult for women to support themselves if they had to. Even those women who wanted a more active life had few opportunities as the universities and professions were closed to them, they possessed few legal rights and did not have the vote.

Gradually, the courageous efforts of the early feminists began to effect change. They started campaigns for educational reform, entrance into the medical profession, and the fight for the vote. The invention of the telegraph service and the typewriter, along with the expansion of the teaching profession and the development of nursing, added to the range of women's opportunities and began to erode the prejudice against the idea of women taking work outside the home. By the end of the century a new view of women was appearing. She was appropriately called 'The New Woman'. Chastity was still considered the ideal but now it was equally important for men and women. Her sphere of activity was larger, she worked, sought education, and fought for political and legal rights. While changes in the attitude to women were slow, the development of an ideal that was easier to live up to and allowed women more freedom of action was a great step on the road to their emancipation.

Prostitution may have seemed the only solution for single women faced with a life of drudgery and poverty. Some became wealthy, but most trudged the streets all night in the hope of obtaining the price of a meal.

'The Governess' by Richard Redgrave, 1844. A position in a private household was often the only 'respectable' employment available to an educated but unmarried woman without means. The life was hard with few holidays and a pitiful salary.

Farmfield Reformatory, Horley. Women as well as men benefited from more liberal treatment.

A Victorian Valentine card, with a message reading 'Oh let your heart remember me'.

'Quilters at Work', by Ralph Hedley. While mill towns had plenty of work for women, in areas of heavy industry, particularly mining, there was little work for them outside the home. They contributed to the domestic economy by thrifty housekeeping: baking at home and making things from old materials, such as rag rugs and patchwork quilts.

By the end of the Victorian era schoolgirls were being taught gymnastics. With emancipation, activities previously practised by men became available to women.

Cloth checking, although tedious, was a welcome employment in an industry where most jobs involved standing all day tending noisy machines in an unhealthy atmosphere.

land. Country houses, often associated with the same families for generations, eventually began changing hands. The cost of maintaining such homes depended on cheap servant labour and when servants became more expensive and more scarce, the end was in sight. Old estates were bought by men with fortunes made in trade and industry, while other houses were converted into training establishments, schools, nursing homes, or simply left to decay. Fortunately for the Victorian aristocracy, the full impact of these economic changes would be experienced only by their children and grandchildren in the 20th century post-war generations. Some families were fortunate in that their entire fortunes were not tied up in land. Many landowners allowed railways to be built across their property in order to generate income, while for others the discovery of coal meant an addition to their income, especially for families in County Durham, Northumberland, South Yorkshire and Lancashire. Other noble families, such as the Dukes of Bedford, Portland, Norfolk and Westminster, owned land within cities and the increased revenue from these properties further contributed to their families' wealth. Some great noblemen sponsored developments in building, harbour construction, mining and industry as well as estate improvement, often at great financial risk to themselves. Business activity on the part of the aristocracy was not new in the 19th century, but the amount of activity increased and this was a different feature. Aristocratic names appeared on lists of company directors but business was not the only way to bolster a reduced estate income. The fortunes of American heiresses saved several well-known landed families from financial ruin.

There were of course degrees of wealth among the landed classes. The wealthiest, with incomes of tens of thousands of pounds per year, could afford to maintain a large country house and enjoy the attractions of the London season. Below these were the greater and lesser gentry and below them country gentlemen who lived on a few hundred pounds per year. Despite the differences of income, the great aristocrat was linked with the humble squire, for they both shared the same attitude as to how society ought to be governed – the owners of land should have power and influence. Gentry and aristocratic families were often inter-related, as younger sons and daughters of the aristocracy frequently married into the gentry. The sons of both families would be educated together at the same public schools and later at Oxford or Cambridge, where the emphasis on classical literature fostered a similarity of taste and outlook. They would also share the same pastimes, particularly hunting and shooting. Above all, they upheld the same code of behaviour, that of the 'gentleman'. A 'gentleman' would be admitted to the most select social circles, both in London and the country, even if he did not own land. There was no precise definition of 'gentlemanliness'; it was dependent upon an elusive combination of income, education, occupation and personal characteristics. You were only certain about your gentlemanly status when others treated you as a gentleman.

The aristocracy and gentry were powerful not only because they were a closeknit, wealthy group but also as a result of the positions of influence they held and the respect that society afforded them. The prestige of being an aristocrat was so great that even distant relations would exploit it for their own ends, and a peer would have to be very eccentric, even criminal, not to receive respectful treatment. The gentry were also highly respected because the ownership of land allowed them to pursue the leisured, independent lifestyle so admired by the Victorians. This respect added to

THE VICTORIAN HOME

Whilst the pattern of employment in 19th century Britain was being modernised by the pressures and demands of industrialisation, domestic service proved an exception to this trend as a traditional occupation which expanded and flourished under the impact of industrial prosperity. The gentry and above had always maintained large domestic staffs for their houses in the country and the town, but the new development was the wider diffusion of the practice of keeping servants. The advance of domestic service was mainly a reflection of the expansion of the upper middle class, covering occupations in business, administration and the professions, and reinforced by the growing confidence and prosperity of the era. So significant did service become in the middle class pattern of expenditure that servants were valued, and could be afforded, to a much greater extent than in countries abroad, even those rising in the league of industrial progress. Thus, in 1901 4.01 per cent of the British population were domestics, in contrast to 3.12 per cent in Germany, 2.45 per cent in France and only 1.98 per cent in the USA. The preoccupation with servants also bore witness to the influence on household organisation of the example of the gentry and to the belief in elaborate domestic displays as a means to solidify and express the progress of this newly-powerful class.

With the extension of domestic service, the duties of servants became more specialised: the inconvenience of high-Victorian houses, the rising expectations of cleanliness and the growing complexity of domestic arrangements, in respect of eating for example, only served to emphasise this.

By the same token, the worlds of upstairs and downstairs seemed to draw apart in social terms. This development was reflected in the plans of houses, where the green baize door became the symbol of the separation of servants from their masters. Indeed, the 19th century introduced the connotations of subservience into the term 'servant' where there had been none before, and the decline in the status of domestic service was epitomised by the widespread wearing of a distinctive servant uniform. The Victorian ideal of the leisured and protected female paralleled these changes and, whereas in the 18th century the lady of the house may have worked alongside her servants, in the 19th she usually preferred to supervise them at a distance.

Of course, the numbers and duties of servants, as well as the relationship between employers and employees, varied with the wealth and size of households. A family with an income of not less than £200 a year might just begin to afford a single 'living-in' servant; £1,000 would make possible a much larger establishment with a housemaid, nursemaid, cook, kitchenmaid, a valet perhaps doubling as a coachman, and a butler. Manservants became increasingly rare as the century progressed, declining between 1831 amd 1881 from 16 per cent to four per cent of the total. The great country houses might rise to 30 servants and more, constituting an independent community, far removed from the modest pretensions of suburban villas.

Domestic service was easily the largest form of employment for women. Apart from the special areas of the woollen and cotton industries in the

Sunday morning in a workman's home, 1875. Perhaps slightly idealised, this shows respectable family life being maintained in crowded circumstances at the city centre where it was necessary to live so as to be close to a place of work.

'Best' room of pitman's cottage in a row reconstructed at Beamish Museum, Co. Durham. The period is the 1890s, when this colliery was evidently prosperous. But the cottage is tiny, with just the kitchen next door and a small bedroom above.

north, the opportunities for women to find paid work outside the home remained limited despite the growth of new occupations associated with an industrial economy. The attraction of service, especially to country girls (the traditional source of supply) was that it provided a sheltered and secure route to the town, a means of leaving a crowded home at an early age and a way of acquiring domestic skills, invaluable later in contracting a respectable marriage. Moreover, good servants were in demand everywhere and the pay, allowing for board and lodging, was reasonable. The outcome was that the number of female servants increased at a faster rate than the growth in households, so that by 1871 a peak in provision was reached when servants amounted to 239 for every 1,000 families. The employment of indoor domestics continued to rise until 1891, although at a slower rate than the change in households, whereafter the decline in the ratio of servants to households was sharp and not reversed until the 1920s. One consequence of this mounting pressure in the provision of servants was that their pay increased twice as fast as for other female workers and so the falling-off in the supply of servants before the First World War was not to be explained in terms of poor remuneration. Rather, the supply of country girls had become exhausted with the decline of agricultural life, and the non-financial conditions of service, the long hours, the isolated existence and the servile status were beginning to prove unattractive to young women, who could now choose amongst an increasing range of occupations. As recruitment declined, the average age of servants began to rise, a further indication of the process of transition. Although middle class households were

subject to increased expense in other fields, including education and housing, the demand for servants continued unabated for a while. Only after the First World War did attitudes and tastes begin fundamentally to change when the rise in tax reduced the incomes and aspirations of the potential servant-employing class. The 'loyal retainer' now turned into the 'unwelcome stranger', as the presence of servants became inconsistent with the new intimacies and informality of domestic life.

In the mid Victorian period inventions and innovations, as applied to the fabric and equipment of the house, had concentrated on comfort and domestic ostentation. Only in the later decades of the 19th century did many inventions appear which seemed to contain labour-saving possibilities, such as the new devices powered by electricity, often originating in the USA. They were intended first for homes with servants, but in the 1920s, with the falling price of machines and power, they combined with new approaches to the planning of houses and original ideas about materials and cleaning to form the movement for the 'labour-saving home'. A copious literature on how to survive without servants appeared, of which the influential P. Randal Phillips' *The Servantless House* (1920) is a typical example, advising both those who could no longer afford servants and the younger households for whom servants were never an economic proposition. Despite this labour-saving campaign, the number of indoor domestics actually rose again between 1921 and 1931. It was not until the great social cleavage of the Second World War that domestic service finally declined to its current low levels.

Provision of servants in England and Wales 1861–1951

	Female indoor domestic servants	Households	Servants per 1,000 households
1861	963,000	4,492,000	214
1871	1,207,000	5,049,000	239
1881	1,230,000	5,633,000	218
1891	1,386,000	6,131,000	226
1901	1,194,000	7,037,000	170
1911	1,260,000	7,943,000	159
1921	964,000	8,739,000	110
1931	1,142,000	10,233,000	112
1941	no figures		
1951	359,000	13,118,000	27

Source: Census of England and Wales

Servants at Erddig, Wrexham, in the 1880s. The complexity of domestic management, especially on a self-sufficient country estate, required a wide array of servants, ranging in responsibility and status from butler to scullerymaid.

Victorian parlour in the Castle Museum, York. Lit by a gas chandelier and elaborately furnished, the front room was kept ostentatiously unused except on special occasions. Prosperity was increasing in the 1870s and is here shown off.

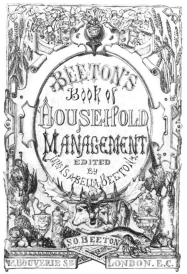

Mrs Beeton's popular manual on running a home, first published as a book in 1861.

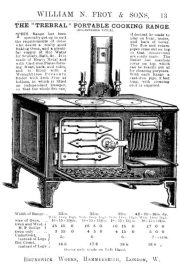

Cast iron cooking range. A technically advanced alternative to the open fire, it provided hotplates, oven and hot water.

The wash-down water closet was perfected in the 1870s and thereafter began to be incorporated in middle class houses. But most Victorians continued to depend on an outside privy, often shared, usually leaking and frequently unhealthy.

their influence; the gentry and aristocracy not only controlled most of the farming industry but they were also patrons of the church, benefactors of schools, and distributors of charity. Moreover, as justices of the peace they maintained law and dispensed justice by punishing petty crimes, licensing alehouses and regulating fairs and markets.

The life of the country gentleman was indeed a pleasant one. He would see the world as a young man, perhaps in the army or diplomatic service. When the time came to settle down and marry, he could choose his bride from one of the young ladies doing the London season, or more probably from a neighbouring county family. Unless he became a member of parliament, he would spend the rest of his life concerned with estate and county affairs. He would be involved in the administration of justice and local government by being a JP or member of the quarter sessions, but most of his time would be spent hunting, shooting and entertaining relations and friends at his country home. So admired was this way of life that even by the end of the century when the majority of people lived in cities and earned their living in industry, trade and commerce, the gentry and their stately homes were still considered to be the 'best' of England.

At the bottom of the social scale were the workers, but it is not possible to talk about them as 'the working class'. Their attitudes and lifestyle differed depending on the type of work they did. Basically there were three groups: manual labourers, artisans or skilled craftsmen, and 'uniformed' workers. This last group consisted of those who wore some form of uniform to work, such as servants, policemen and railway workers.

Life was most difficult for the labourer, because he did not have the security of employment and the promise of a pension that the uniformed worker possessed, nor the respect and better wages that the skilled craftsman could command. The vast increase in population resulted in too many unskilled workers chasing the few jobs that were available; men actually fought one another for the right to work. For example, the foreman of a gang of labourers would place a spade for each job he was offering at the gate of the work site and the man who could win the fight for the spade would get the job. Factory workers were not secure in their employment either, as thousands could be laid off if the economy took a downward swing. Other jobs were seasonal so that workers moved into the cities in winter to be chimney-sweeps or street-lampers, and moved out to the country in summer to pick hops and fruit or do general harvest work.

Obtaining work did not necessarily mean the end of poverty, however, as wages remained comparatively low. While Britain's economic expansion would not have been possible without the ceaseless toil of countless men, women and children, the workers did not share in these profits. Large amounts of the great capital gains were reinvested at home and abroad and it could be argued that this ultimately benefited the workers. But much of this money was also wasted and a lot went towards supporting employers in lavish lifestyles. However, real wages – how much the workers' pay packets could actually buy – did improve throughout Victoria's reign. From the 1860s onwards the trend was upwards until 1900; between 1860 and 1891 the rise in real wages averaged about 60 per cent. In spite of this many workers lived in terrible poverty because their lifestyles and spending patterns meant that they were unable to make the most of their limited means. Irregular earnings meant that accommodation was rented at the price of the

SHIPBUILDING AND SHIPPING

Britain's industrial and agricultural revolutions were gradual, starting in the mid 18th century but gaining momentum in the 19th. This was a century of shattering change in every field, not least in the maritime. Whereas in previous centuries a ship built in the first decade of a century would not look wildly out of place in the last, during the 19th century this was no longer the case. The changes came about for all sorts of reasons. There were many new markets for our merchants: India and the Far East (after the end of the East India Company's monopolies), South America after the collapse of the Spanish Empire, and Australasia when the settlers had built up farms and started to exploit the mineral wealth of the country. No serious wars came to distract trade, and technological advances gave ships of greatly improved design and capabilities to builders and owners alike. Because of increased competition speed became vital to success, and the search for fast ships, both sail and power, produced some sensational vessels.

Timber was becoming too expensive to use for building ships, except in North America, where many sailing vessels were built for sale to British owners. Moreover there was a limit to the size one could build a wooden ship. The only solution was to use a new material – iron. An iron barge had been built on the Severn in 1787 and further iron craft, mostly for river and estuary work, were built in the early 19th century. It was the use of steam as a means of propulsion, however, that was eventually to revolutionise water transport and a series of experiments in

the early part of the century laid the foundations for the next major advance.

Sailing vessels, however, were to maintain their supremacy for several more decades, and until well into the century steamships were really combined sailing and steam vessels as the steam engines were not yet efficient. Paradoxically, therefore, the steamboat preceded the steam train largely because there was no 'bed-running' problem, but the steamboat age comes later than the steam train because of the inefficiency of the engines.

Iron won through as a hull material when allied with the steam engine, achieved in the 1840s by the construction of the passenger ship *Great Britain*, now preserved at Bristol. This remarkable vessel demonstrated the the possibilities not only of a large iron hull, but of the screw propeller as a means of efficient propulsion. Iron, and later steel, created ships of immense capacity for cargo and passengers: the 32,000 tons displacement *Great Eastern*, completed in 1858, showed what could be achieved. Iron was equally successful with sailing ships, passing first through the interesting composite stage of iron frames and wooden planking. This was so that sailing ships could retain their copper sheathing, effective in the discouragement of marine growth to which iron bottoms were very prone. Not until anti-fouling paints were introduced in the 1870s was the coppered composite hull abandoned.

Iron and steam power created a shipbuilding revolution. More capital was needed to set up an iron shipyard which needed space and expensive machinery to succeed. Nearness to

The frigate HMS Warrior, now under full restoration, was the first ironclad in the Royal Navy. Built at Blackwall in 1860, her armour was 6½ inches of iron backed by 18 inches of teak, and she carried 32 guns of various calibres.

Alexander Hall (1760–1849) of Aberdeen founded his yard in 1790 and in 1839 built the first of a new style of fast sailing ship, later called the clipper. Many more followed; two are seen behind this group of shipyard personnel.

ironworks was an advantage, so the new shipbuilding centres grew up with an industrial hinterland, on the Clyde, the Tyne, Wear, Mersey, and Tees. Barrow-in-Furness was out on a limb, save that it had its own large ironworks. For a while the Thames area was a major producer of iron ships, but the last yard closed in the 1900s. Belfast was exceptional, with no industrial backcloth but with the advantage of deep water and easy sea access to the Clyde for supplies. Many other industrial centres remote from the sea benefited from the shipbuilding revolution, notably the Black Country where forges shaped anchors and chains and brass foundries made fittings like port lights, cleats, gauges and so on. Wooden shipbuilding still had a long innings, small wooden sailing ships having an assured future in the coastal trade until killed by the 20th century motor lorry. They continued to be built in West Country estuaries and up Essex creeks and Yorkshire rivers.

Parallel with the shipyards, the ports grew on an unprecedented scale, totally unrecognisable by 1900. All the major centres embarked on a massive dock building programme, an achievement almost equal to the creation of the country's railways. London, Liverpool, Glasgow, Hull, Cardiff and Avonmouth became the great ports. Southampton was a late-comer, a medieval port revived by the London & South Western Railway. Here no enclosed docks were found necessary because the four high tides a day enabled big ships to lie at open quays.

Sailing ships survived in large numbers to the end of the 19th century. They were able to compete successfully with steam on the longer trade routes because it took decades for steam to become at all economical. Very early steamships had to carry so much coal that there was only room for high-

return freight, mail, parcels and passengers. But when the first extravagant engines were superseded in the 1860s by the compound and in the 1880s by the triple expansion, the reduced fuel consumption enabled steamers to go further and carry more. At first expensive cargoes like tea and packaged goods for export were transported, and later bulk grain, coal, rails and timbers.

One important decision which was to influence the development of steamship routes was the abandonment by the government of the Admiralty Packet system for the conveyance of mails. Control, however, was still retained by a system of contracts with subsidy, and the securing of mail contracts made the P&O (Peninsula and Oriental) line, the Cunard line and the Royal Mail Steam Packet Company into household names.

There was a parallel revolution in the Royal Navy. The Admiralty were quick to see the advantages of steam for handling sailing men-of-war so they ordered steam tugs. But paddle steamers were vulnerable in action and only small patrol vessels were built with engines, retaining, as did merchant ships, a full complement of sails to eke out coal and use in the event of breakdown. Introduction of the screw propeller in the 1840s placed the steam warship at an advantage: the engines, and naturally the screw, would be kept below the water line. Screw propelled wooden battleships and frigates were built, but iron offered new possibilities — armour to protect a wooden hull — and in 1860 a hull was constructed entirely of iron, portions of which were protected by thicker plating. This was the steam frigate *Warrior*, Britain's first ironclad, still with sails. But in 1871 the *Devastation* was built, the first large warship without sails, and indeed the first warship with a silhouette which could be called modern.

The clipper Cutty Sark was built in 1869 for the China Tea run, but soon transferred to the Australian wool trade.

Isambard Kingdom Brunel (1806–59) in front of one of the checking drums of the Great Eastern before its 1857 launch.

The Cutty Sark, now preserved in a dry dock at Greenwich, looks towards the Thames, her home river.

Launch of the battleship HMS Albion at Blackwall on the Thames in 1898. Of 12,950 tons displacement, she carried four 12-inch guns and 12 six-inch, plus many smaller weapons. She fought in the Dardanelles and was scrapped in 1919.

The Great Eastern laid up on the gridiron at Milford Haven after her successful career as a cable layer. She was however far from successful as a passenger ship, and never sailed in the Far East trade as had been intended.

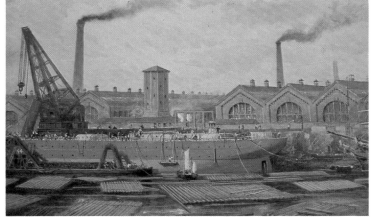

An early view of the Barrow Shipbuilding Company in a watercolour by W. H. Andrews. Founded in 1871, it became part of the major shipbuilding centre of Barrow-in-Furness and was taken over by Vickers in 1896.

The steam launch Dolly, claimed as the oldest mechanically propelled boat in the world, was built about 1850. She sank on Ullswater in the great frost of 1895. Raised in 1962, she is an operable member of the Windermere Steamboat Museum.

workers' lowest rather than average earnings – in times of distress, therefore, the rent could still be paid.

Food and drink were the largest items in the workers' budget. Food was bought in small quantities which was the least economical way of purchasing. Adulteration of such foods as bread (plaster of Paris was baked into it), pepper (into which red lead was injected) and coffee (mahogany sawdust was mixed with the ground beans) also diminished spending power as well as posing a health hazard. There were, however, changes over time as a basic diet of bread and cheese eventually came to include tea, cocoa, sugar and fruits. As real incomes rose, the proportion of money spent on food decreased and there was more available for clothing, fuel and light.

Other practices also prevented the labourer from making the most of his income. The father would often take what he wanted from his pay packet and leave his wife to manage as best she could on what was left. Early marriages and lack of experience and example meant that the labourer's wife was not particularly skilled in budgeting or housekeeping. When the wife worked the results could be even more disastrous, since the little extra money that she earned did not compensate for the lack of properly cooked food, washing, and cleaning for which she no longer had time. A tired, overworked wife, a dirty tenement and crying, hungry children drove many men to the pub where they could easily find comfort and recreation. For these people the accepted Victorian values of thrift and self-help meant nothing because they were so poor that they could only live from day to day. Conventional religious belief was also of little im-

DOCKLAND

In Britain, rivers have long functioned as highways to the sea, and were important arteries for old-established towns. Even in the Victorian period the recently created industrial towns and cities on inland coalfields were connected to estuarine ports, first by canals and improved navigations, and later by railways. Accordingly docks and harbours became more highly developed and more numerous in Britain than almost any other country during the 19th century. Through the docks passed the manufactured goods that accounted for less than ten per cent of British imports, but more than 90 per cent of British exports by mid-century. To the usually unco-ordinated construction of docks, warehouses, railways, dockers' lodgings and houses, dock-related industries and trades, is given the name 'dockland'. The growing number and size of dockland areas thus becomes the physical expression of Britain's status by the end of the Victorian period as the world's dominant manufacturing, maritime trading, and shipbuilding nation.

Any city's dockland was originally found around the riverside quays that formed the nucleus of a port, as in London's Dowgate and Queenhithe, or Newcastle's Key and Sandgate Key. But between the 1780s and 1820s Hull, Liverpool, Bristol and London all undertook the construction of enclosed wet docks of varying proportions, usually on unoccupied downstream marshlands. The wet dock proved advantageous wherever tidal ranges exceeded about 15 ft (4.6 m). It eased loading and unloading, for vessels no longer lay on the river bottom at low tide. It reduced fire risk, and it especially reduced pilfering from vessels, which in one author's view had reached the level of 'pillage'. Whereas before the 19th century vessels simply became more numerous rather than larger, during the century the size of vessels increased dramatically. The largest vessel afloat in 1838, the *British Queen*, was 2,016 tons gross; the *Celtic* in 1900 was 20,904 tons, although a more modest 7,500 tons was then quite typical for a cargo steamer.

Wet docks and their entrance locks thus increased in size as the century progressed – and as construction enclosed new sites further downstream. Some early wet docks, such as St Katherine's in London (1828) were hewn out of densely populated areas – 12,000 people were displaced – and never connected to the railway system. Later docks were connected to railways, indeed often built by railway companies, as in the case of Barrow, Cardiff, Grimsby, Hull and Southampton. In Southampton's case its significant growth as a passenger port followed the London & South Western Railway Company's acquisition of docking facilities in the 1890s. Extensive linear quays fringed first with cranes, then lined by warehouses and transit sheds overlooking railways, came to typify the late Victorian docks. Glasgow by 1900 had 11 miles (7 km) of quayage and an enclosed water area of 240 acres (100 ha); London's docks enclosed 750 acres (310 ha) by 1908, and the Royal Albert Dock of 1880 exceeded 1½ miles (2.5 km) in length.

Ships brought sailors, hence seamen's hostels, and all manner of services from ship repair and chandlers to victualling depots, and cargoes, hence railways and horse drawn carts to take goods away. But outside the high security walls so typical of the Liverpool and London docklands, riverside quays also lifted cargoes from ships and barges into food processing factories, chemical works, local gas works and electricity power stations. Many of these industries, gas production especially, showed marked seasonal fluctuations in demand, so casual labour was recruited. The docks themselves displayed even more variable demand for labour according to tides and wind (for the steam tonnage on the British register only overtook sail in the 1880s). In London the 'calling foremen' would appear at 7.30 a.m. to recruit dock labourers seeking a day's work. Many lived in the lodging houses crammed into adjacent courts and alleys. Henry Mayhew described the motley dockers in his mid-century observations of *London Labour and the London Poor*:

. . . a striking instance of mere brute force with brute appetites . . . as unskilled as the power of a hurricane. Mere muscle is all that is needed; hence every human locomotive is capable of working there . . . decayed and bankrupt master butchers . . . grocers . . . old soldiers . . . Polish refugees . . . pensioners, servants, thieves – indeed, every one who wants a loaf, and is willing to work for it.

Remarkably, it was not until 1967 that 'decasualisation' came to London's dockland, so that 'blue-eyes' no longer had to catch a foreman's attention with its many possible abuses through nepotism, bribery, and cultural and ethnic preference. Not surprisingly such dangerous and unstable labour conditions proved conducive to militant trades unionism, most notably in the 1889 strike for the 'docker's tanner'. In recent decades of course containerisation has hastened the contraction of dock workforces; vessels are turned round quickly, and the seamen's hostels, even dockland pubs and clubs have emptied.

For whatever reasons the flow of people across the gangways of Victorian dockland is less commemorated by artists than the press at railway stations or on omnibuses. Of the 5½ million emigrants departing Britain between 1860 and 1900, 4¾ million sailed from Liverpool, mainly to the new world which until the southern Europeans caught up in the 1890s had been peopled mainly by settlers from the British Isles and from Germany. Immigrants to Britain likewise passed through the docks. Often ships' crews brought undesirable cargoes – cholera and other diseases from the tropics fanned out to smaller British ports along the coastwise shipping lanes – and the 19th century witnessed increasingly stringent regulations for port health. It also witnessed booms and slumps in the fortunes of dock companies, and often ownership changed hands from municipal authorities and private companies into public trusts.

In the 20th century dock investment has continued to migrate towards estuary mouths, leaving behind derelict dockland on such a scale that in 1979 the government announced the creation of urban development corporations to oversee the rebuilding of the London Docklands and Merseyside Dock Area. Industrial archaeologists will doubtless urge the retention of many docks and warehouses. Few people would now share J. A. Picton's 1875 description of Liverpool's Albert Dock as 'a hideous pile of naked brickwork'. Already St Katherine's Dock adjacent to London's Tower Bridge, closed in 1967 after 140 years in operation, offers an 850-room hotel, restaurants, business apartments, council flats, a yachting marina, and a historic vessels collection including Captain Scott's *Discovery*. The lure of the waterfront and the symbolism of docks as gateways to foreign places remains potent for tourists, while the docker sees in the growth of air cargo and passenger traffic the spectre of further unemployment.

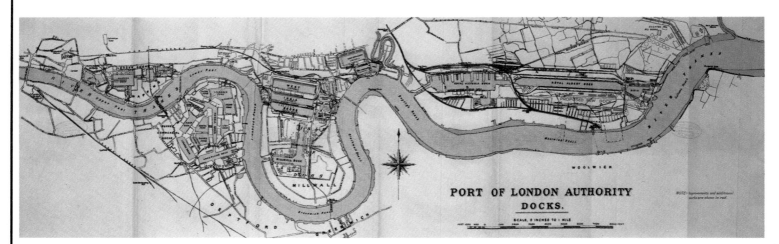

PORT OF LONDON AUTHORITY
DOCKS.

London's docks. Larger ships required ever larger berths and dock entrances, so during the 19th century private dock builders sought larger tracts of land for expansion. Mean dockers' housing, food processing, cable manufacturing businesses and shipbuilding and repair yards surrounded the wharves. Now the upstream docks lie derelict. Many have been filled in and reduced to anonymous real estate.

portance except among the Irish Roman Catholics and the Jews. Moral codes such as feminine sexual purity made little sense to people sleeping six to a room. The poor were suspicious of those classes above them, and they keenly realised that their own kind were the friends to help them through their numerous times of need.

Life could be quite different for the skilled artisan. Dudley Baxter in his book on *National Incomes* estimated that about one in seven workers was highly skilled. The mechanics of Birmingham, the potters of Staffordshire, the engineers of Manchester – workers such as these in apprenticed trades formed an elite group, an aristocracy of labour, within the working class. They enjoyed higher wages and a more stable income than other workers. For example, a skilled man could earn between £60 and £73 per annum and semi-skilled

workers between £46 and £52, while labourers averaged a yearly income of £20 to £41. Skilled tradesmen maintained these advantages by limiting the number of men entering their trades and by effectively organising themselves in trade unions. Towards the end of the century, the secure position of the artisan was undermined, as the division between skilled and unskilled workers became blurred as a result of the rise of the semi-skilled machine operator. Unions tried to ensure that the introduction of machines did not result in a flood of semi-skilled rivals and a consequent reduction in wages did not occur. However, there was no question of industrial unionism or the collection in one union of all those workers engaged in a single industry.

The artisan was distinguished from the rest of the working classes not only by occupation and income, but also by

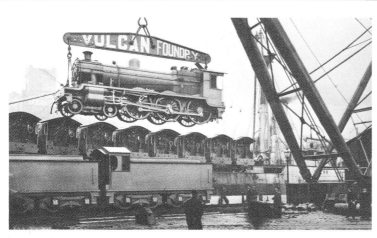

Locomotives being exported through Liverpool docks. Until the building of the Manchester Ship Canal in 1894 Liverpool was the exporting centre of the industrial north, handling goods to the ever growing Empire market.

A Liverpool dockside scene, with the customary paraphernalia of hoists, hooks and pulleys used to raise the various cargoes, and the casual labourers whose muscle power operated – and indeed built – the docks.

The Liver Building, along with the Mersey Docks & Harbour Board and Cunard offices, dominates Liverpool's Pier Head, reflecting the port's prominence. Dock Road separates the city from the adjacent Princes Dock along the Mersey.

'C' Warehouse, St Katherine's Dock, London. Until the late 18th century dockland simply meant congested riverfronts. Thereafter, enclosed docks were built downstream behind lock gates and protective dock walls. St Katherine's, built 1825–8 by Thomas Telford and Philip Hardwick, offered sheds, vaults and warehouses for over 100,000 tons, but over 11,000 residents were displaced by its construction. 'C' warehouse now faces imminent destruction at the hands of developers.

values and lifestyle. For these men and their families self-respect originated in the dignity and confidence of possessing a skill, and from being self-supporting, hard-working and thrifty. They felt that this behaviour distinguished them from the common labourer, with his fatalistic attitude and self-indulgent habits of drunkenness and sexual immorality. Many craftsmen delayed marriage, not only because earnings were better when apprenticeships were completed, but also because the chance to save might mean obtaining a home away from the slums. There was little council housing, but in the last part of Victoria's reign, private contractors built thousands of row houses in London and the industrial cities of the north. Often dreary and cramped, these homes did at least have water, gas and proper drainage.

The working week was reduced by as much as a fifth throughout the period, so that the artisan, along with other workers, had more time for leisure. The Saturday half-holiday became an established practice. After 1871 there were also four statutory bank holidays a year. From the mid-century onwards, organised games which later developed into professional sports became popular, replacing the earlier and less civilised pastimes of bull and bear-baiting and cock-fighting.

While the artisan often shared the same views on hard work and thrift that were cherished by the middle classes, he was also proud of his independence in much the same way as were the aristocracy. His skills made him dependent on no one, and his attitude to life stressed individualism. In politics

The corner shop, perhaps the most important social institution of a rural or urban working class village. Poorly stocked with meagre home-made and manufactured items, they were often started in the front room by the mother of the family, desperate for the extra income her trade might bring. Before the advent of cheap travel to town centres, the shop provided the basic essentials of life — scanty provisions, medical attention in the form of 'advice' and patent medicines, help with forms and letters, gossip, and that most important of commodities — credit.

THE GREAT EXHIBITION OF 1851

The Great Exhibition of 1851 was by no means the first large exhibition, but for a number of reasons it overshadows any other in British history. It took place when the Industrial Revolution – which was not so much a revolution as a slow evolution – had been in progress for about a century, at a time when Britain's industry and trade were greater than that of any other nation. It was also a time of great national confidence when, despite the vociferous (if not very intelligent) protests of Colonel Sibthorp who led the anti-exhibition lobby in Parliament, it was thought that Britain could 'show the world' and had nothing to fear from allowing potential rivals like France and Germany to exhibit their manufactures in London.

Credit for the whole thing is often given to Queen Victoria's husband Prince Albert, but although it might not have succeeded without the Prince's intelligent patronage it would probably not have taken place at all without civil servant Henry Cole's original idea and organising ability, and not in its magnificent setting without former garden boy Joseph Paxton's Crystal Palace.

Henry Cole was a leading member of the Society for the Encouragement of Arts, Manufactures & Commerce (now known as the Royal Society of Arts, but still occupying the same building in Adelphi, just below the Strand). A society of gentlemen and professional men formed mainly to promote invention and design in industry, this society had, under Cole, organised successful exhibitions of machinery and industrial produce in 1848 and 1849, when it was decided that the 1851 exhibition should be on a much larger international scale. There was a competition for the design of a temporary building to stand in Hyde Park, but despite 245 entries no suitable design had been found when Paxton sketched the Crystal Palace – almost as it was finally built – on a blotter at a railway committee meeting. It was altogether a remarkable building; completely designed in a week, with a light iron frame of a new pattern that Paxton had devised for the Duke of Devonshire's hothouses, it was prefabricated and constructed so that it could be taken down when the exhibition was over. Larger than St Paul's Cathedral, it was erected in 22 weeks and finished in a further 15. So quickly did all this take place that there was never time to overload the Palace with Gothic detail. In fact it was uniquely plain among Victorian buildings and, unlike its elaborate contemporary

the new Houses of Parliament, functioned perfectly, the glass roofs being entirely waterproof and the ventilating and shading so effective that even Victoria, who hated the heat, never found it too warm on her many visits that summer.

If the building was plain the exhibits certainly were not. Design was at a very low ebb: even utilitarian items had every inch covered with pattern and little thought was given to the overall form of the object. The young designer William Morris was appalled by what he saw there and concluded that the machine was to blame. But machine production cannot be blamed for the heavy sentimentality of most of the decorative art: like the over-exuberant decoration, it was a characteristic of the mid-Victorian period.

Pessimists predicted every calamity for the exhibition from financial failure to revolution and, although all over Europe there had recently been uprisings, the English working man simply saved up his pennies to take his family to the Great Exhibition on the days when tickets were only a shilling. It was the first social event that all classes could share: from the Royal Family and their visitors who went to the exhibition frequently, to parties of ordinary people who came to London, many for the first time in their lives, on the special excursions organised by the railway companies.

At the suggestion that some of the profits from the exhibition should be used to erect a statue of the Prince Consort on the site of the Crystal Palace, the Prince said that it would spoil his rides in Rotten Row and (with great perspicacity) that if it were 'an artistic monstrosity, like most of our monuments' he did not wish to be perpetually ridiculed in effigy. He also suggested that the money should go to build a museum of art and science and this was done; nearly all the museums and institutions in South Kensington owe their existence to the Great Exhibition in the Crystal Palace in nearby Hyde Park.

After a successful 141 days Londoners were reluctant to lose the Crystal Palace, but the prudent Joseph Paxton – a financial genius as well as a brilliant designer – formed a company to buy the building and re-erect it on a beautiful site at Sydenham where it was the Londoners' favourite resort for every sort of entertainment for the next forty years. It was still regarded with affection by the people when it burnt down in December 1936.

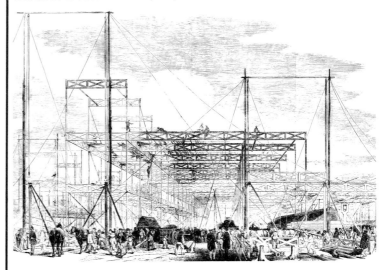

The Crystal Palace, designed by Joseph Paxton and shown during construction, was a unique building made from huge prefabricated parts supplied by Britain's growing iron and glass industries. There was one strike – the glaziers demanded higher rates, but the matter was settled in typical 19th century fashion by sacking the leaders, whereupon the men returned to work for the old rates.

The opening ceremony in May 1851 which Queen Victoria found very moving; she was proud of her well behaved subjects and even more proud of her husband's part in organising the exhibition.

The main transept during the Great Exhibition, where the madly ingenious and hopelessly overdecorated exhibits were not so thick on the ground. Oslers' 4-ton crystal fountain was a favourite meeting place.

Poor visitors to the Great Exhibition; a special dispensation was made for the Colonisation Loan Society's Emigrants, victims of the Highland clearances, to see the exhibition for only 1/- in the first week as they were about to sail for Australia (the normal price would have been £1). It was reported at the time that many people were surprised at the civilised appearance and behaviour of the 'lower orders'.

The Crystal Palace in its new position at Sydenham, where it was rebuilt in 1854. Although it had been designed as a temporary building, people had become so fond of it that Paxton had no trouble raising the money to finance the move. It was considerably enlarged and became a favourite place for Victorian family outings with its gardens, fountains and exhibitions of art, natural history — and fireworks.

The end of the Crystal Palace during a fire in December 1936. The big building was expensive to maintain and had become dowdy and unfashionable, but still had a place in the hearts of the people. In both Crystal Palace and its north London counterpart, Alexandra Palace, early work had been done in television, the medium that was largely to replace family outings as a source of entertainment.

his views were often radical. For the casual labourer, respectability meant little when survival was a daily struggle and he was dependent on others for the right to work. For the uniformed worker, however, dependence and respectability were both important parts of his job. These workers were the ones who most frequently came into contact with the prosperous classes; in fact, the largest group of uniformed workers were domestic servants. Their employers demanded not only that they should work hard but also that they should behave in a respectable way. Women in domestic service were often forbidden to have callers, and any suggestion of promiscuity would result in instant dismissal. Employees of large companies, such as railway workers, were expected not to drink or swear, both on and off the job. Failure to comply with this strict code of discipline would result in demotion or loss of good conduct increments.

Working hours were longer for uniformed workers in comparison with other jobs. Railway employees were working an 80 hour week even in the 1890s, and servants were on call 24 hours a day. The pay was lower than that of the artisan and sometimes less than many labourers earned. Policemen were paid about 16 shillings a week in the 1850s and at the end of the century servants were earning only an average of £15 to £25 a year, with 30 guineas, including lodging and food, as the maximum salary. Recruitment for these jobs usually ran in the family, with a son following in his father's footsteps or an aunt in the city finding a place for her niece. The patronage of wealthy people was also important in securing employment; for example, MPs were responsible for selecting the local postmen until the 1870s and the reference or testimonial of character of a local dignitary or previous employer was always required. To be dismissed without a 'character' made it extremely difficult to find another job.

There were, however, some attractive features about these positions that made them eagerly sought after as jobs. The uniformed workers were the only members of the working class who were sure of regular, year-round employment. Unlike the labourer, whose capacity to work declined with his strength, the uniformed worker could stay in the same job for a lifetime. In fact, the longer he stayed with the same employer, the more security he had. While employers expected to dictate on matters of dress and behaviour, giving the impression that the worker almost belonged to them, they were also more likely to care for them in other ways. Living accommodation would be provided, such as servant

A bakery workers' manifesto, 1872. After a century of industrial reform there was room for improvement. Many workers suffered unhygienic and even dangerous conditions, but as today there was resistance to the introduction of machinery.

GAMES AND SPORTS

The growth of the industrial economy transformed the leisure habits of the nation. In the past, as long as most people were employed on the land, everyday life had followed the pattern of the seasons. Periods of hard work – ploughing, sowing, lambing, sheep-shearing and harvest – were followed by slacker intervals when recreation was possible. But in the new factories idle men and machines meant loss of productivity and loss of profit. The number of official holidays (those recognised by the Bank of England) dropped dramatically. In 1808 there were 44; by 1834 only four remained – Christmas Day, Good Friday, 1st May and 1st November. Similarly the working week had been extended almost to the limits of endurance. Opportunities for leisure were scant and in the crowded working class ghettoes the space needed for the older rural sports was severely limited. In these circumstances it was only to be expected that many traditional forms of recreation should disappear and be replaced by new ones.

Football is one example of a game which altered greatly in the 19th century. In pre-industrial times it was a popular pastime played by any number of people on a pitch of any size and without any nationally agreed rules. But by 1780 the game had declined in rural areas as more and more land was enclosed by improving landlords. Surprisingly it survived within the public schools, and the mid-century saw the gradual codification of rules and the split between football and rugby. Football won the support of the urban working classes, however, only in the second half of the century. Its attractions lay in its cheapness (it required little equipment), the fact that

it could be played on factory premises and its easy adaptation to factory hours. With the institution of the FA cup in 1872 the basis was also laid for the expansion of football as a spectator sport, providing cheap entertainment on that hard won concession from employers – the Saturday afternoon off.

Cricket was akin to football in that it thrived largely as an amateur pursuit in the 18th century and attracted a mass following only from the middle of the 19th. The development of the professional game owed much to the 'wandering circuses' of players who toured the counties in early Victorian years; foremost among them was William Clarke's all England XI, formed in 1846. Further landmarks were the publication of *Wisden's Almanack* in 1864, the first tours of Australia in the 1860s and the inauguration of the county championships in 1873.

Many sporting initiatives were undertaken primarily as business ventures at this time. The origins of tennis, for instance, like football and cricket, lay far in the past, but the modern version was invented by Major W. C. Wingfield who patented the rules and equipment in 1874. It was taken up quickly because it could be played on the private lawns of country houses and suburban villas, although several defects in the game were remedied and a revised set of rules issued by the Marylebone Cricket Club the following year. The decision to introduce a tennis championship at Wimbledon in 1877 was also taken for financial reasons by the All England Croquet Club, in the hope that its spectator appeal would provide income to offset the expenditure of developing the site. The Club's expectations were

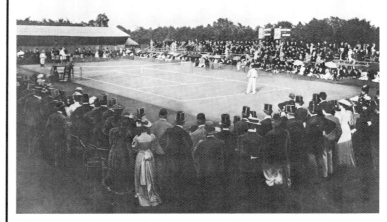

A final of the all-comers' singles contest at Wimbledon, between E. W. Lewis and J. Pim.

A ladies' croquet championship at Wimbledon. Croquet was probably imported from France in the 1850s.

W. G. Grace (b.1848), became a national figure – the most famous member of a cricketing family.

more than realised, although one consequence was that the rise of tennis contributed directly to the decline of croquet.

By the end of the century various sports had sprung into prominence and attained their modern forms, including golf, arena athletics, cycling and swimming (in the new municipal pools). The pattern of development was similar in each: key stages were the formulation of accepted rules and standards, the growth of professionalism, the establishment of a bureaucratic structure, the staging of competitive events and the emergence of a commercial approach. By 1900 sport had become a major industry, reflecting the fact that playing or watching others play had become an important activity — a carefully timetabled part of the working week — for millions of men and, increasingly, women.

Yet while organised sports were still in their infancy, traditional pastimes were under vigorous attack in the countryside. Besides the direct pressure afforded by enclosure, the moral protests against 'cruel' sports gathered strength in the early 19th century. The attack was mounted by the more 'cultured' among the gentry in particular and by nonconformists in general. The harsher human endeavours — prize fighting, Cornish wrestling and clog fighting declined after 1850, and animal baiting too became less widespread. Bull-baiting was declared illegal in 1835 and cockfighting in 1849, thereafter lingering only in the remoter districts. One blood sport, however, which increased rather than diminished in popularity was fox hunting: it was the characteristic pursuit of the aristocracy and gentry, although the thrill of the chase appealed to all sections of rural society. The expense of keeping a pack

of hounds preserved it as a rich man's sport until the mid-century, when the growth of subscription packs enabled farmers and the professional middle classes to ride to hounds. But participation remained beyond the means of the agricultural labourer, who had to be content to be a foot follower or to cheer as the hunt crossed the line of his working plough.

The decline of traditional recreation reflected the more general breakdown of the rural community. Many people born before 1850 were not attracted to the new pursuits, preferring the prize-fight to boxing, 'rough and tumble' sports to the vicarage organised event, folk song and dance to brass bands and the temperance movement. Often these men and women retreated to the pub to drink and remember the past — or to play such ancient games as cards and dice. Yet inn games themselves were subject to constant adaptation; shovelboard became the more restricted game of shove-ha'penny, while comparatively new games, such as darts, dominoes and billiards, gained greatly in popularity in the Victorian period. Even here, however, the trend was towards greater uniformity. By the end of the century the many regional varieties of skittles had been reduced to the two principal forms and other localised games, for example 'ring and bull' and 'devil among the tailors', were found in only a few areas. The passing of familiar pastimes was accounted loss by the older generation, but was little mourned by the younger. From the 1870s the rural labourer was better paid, better educated and more mobile. Increasingly he looked to the towns for some part of his entertainment and in this manner assisted the process whereby urban industrial culture slowly surplanted the older rural culture.

GEORGE WILSON.
The Blackheath Pedestrian.

Walking contests used to be called pedestrianism. One of the greatest performances was by Captain Allardice, who covered 1,000 miles in 1,000 consecutive hours on Newmarket Heath in 1809.

Ladies' golf course, Minchinhampton Common. By the late 19th century, many felt that sport should be played by all. Women soon made their mark.

Prize fights, such as that between Broome and Hannon in 1841, attracted thousands. The battering ended when the more humane Queensberry Rules were introduced in 1867.

Football match, 1899. The Football League was founded in 1888 and the powerful sides of the Midlands and North with their attacking play provided regular excitement on Saturday afternoons for thousands of working class supporters.

Staghounds at Hunters Inn, Barnstable, Devon, c. 1900. The destruction of woodland cover over a long period led to the decline in staghunting. After the Restoration hunting wild red deer survived only in the west of England.

quarters in country houses, barracks for soldiers and cottages for estate workers. The uniform itself would be smart, clean and durable and while providing good clothes for the worker it also could be a source of pride and self-respect. In fact, many 'uniformed' workers gained a great deal of personal satisfaction from giving a family or a company a lifetime of loyal service.

The Middle Classes

Sandwiched between the aristocracy and gentry above them and the workers below them, were the middle classes. Like other social classes, this group included a variety of occupations, attitudes and lifestyles. The top ranks of the middle class were associated with the aristocracy and gentry. The daughters of wealthy tradesmen married into the upper classes where their substantial dowries were welcomed by impoverished landed families. The system of primogeniture whereby the eldest son alone inherited the family fortune meant that the younger sons of the aristocracy and gentry were forced to make their own ways in the world. Many entered professions which strengthened the link between the upper and middle classes.

To be middle class, or to aspire to be middle class, was not solely a matter of income. Some artisans earned as much if not more than clerks, but the latter group definitely considered themselves above the man who worked with his hands. The expanding army of government and business workers, together with school teachers, the emergent managerial class and the 'lesser' professions of accountancy, pharmacy and various branches of engineering formed what became known as the lower middle class. A regular salary meant that these families wished to live in a genteel manner, copying as many habits of the aristocracy as they could afford. Employing at least one servant was considered essential if one aspired to middle class status, but for some members of the lower middle class even this modest lifestyle was difficult to maintain. Marriage and the birth of children could cause severe financial strain for middle class workers who earned less than £200 per year. Because many of these families felt that they were so close to the line that divided the respectable from the unrespectable in terms of lifestyle, they placed great emphasis on the symbols of their status. They insisted on being called 'Mr' or 'Miss' at work, rather than by their surnames, as was the custom with domestic servants and factory hands. This rather conventional, stuffy attitude to life, epitomised by Mr Pooter, the clerk in *The Diary of a Nobody* (1892), would appear to many now as being typical of the Victorian middle class, but this group had not always been considered so staid.

During the period 1815 to 1885 it was possible, as never before, for individual men with imagination and initiative to organise the work force and harness the power of nature to create vast wealth. Prior to 1815 the technical knowledge to accomplish these feats had not been available and after 1885 the individual was less able to act alone due to the development of joint-stock undertakings and a trend towards government intervention. This placed the businessman in a unique position, for as industry grew so did business opportunities.

Naturally these middle class men wanted the expansion of industry and commerce to continue, but they feared they would be thwarted in this by the aristocracy who maintained their dominance in society by a system of privilege. The cornerstone of these privileges was patronage. When an aristocrat wished to make an appointment for a job, he

ENTERTAINMENTS AND THEATRES

Despite its successes, the campaign against popular recreations and cruel sports, disruptive 'holydays' and idleness which had accompanied the Industrial Revolution by no means created a cheerless world of unremitting work. Indeed, the Victorian age inherited a varied range of entertainments from which a vigorous commercial expansion of leisure took place, as impressive in its way as the material achievements of the age. In turn, many of the plays and entertainments that delighted Victorian audiences are with us today, notably Gilbert and Sullivan operas and the plays of leading dramatists such as George Bernard Shaw (*Mrs Warren's Profession, Candida*) and Oscar Wilde (*Lady Windermere's Fan, The Importance Of Being Earnest*).

Travelling troupes of players, who took shows to the minor locations — the market towns and suburbs of expanding London — remained basic providers of entertainment until late in the 19th century. They offered variety, pantomime and circus; the latter had been devised only in the 1760s, and entered the Victorian era in a particularly healthy state with a spate of permanent circus buildings erected in provincial towns during the 1830s and 40s. On the other hand, the 18th century playhouse tradition was degenerating in the early 19th century. The patent theatres, which held a monopoly over straight drama, were challenged by the growth of popular audiences for melodrama; numerous minor theatres appeared catering for this cheaper taste, whilst the established theatres lost their previous, wealthy patrons when they adapted their fare to the new clients. From the 1830s to the 60s, typically the Theatre Royal, Brighton went over to melodramatic attractions — *The Wife of Seven Husbands* and *Agnes or the Bleeding Nun of Lindberg*, for example — the more sensational the better.

The conflict which this popularisation of the theatre created was partly dispelled by the Theatres Regulation Act of 1843 which abolished the patent monopoly. This Act also had an important effect on the various precursors of the music hall — the concerts, or 'free and easies', held at the larger public houses, the song and supper rooms, the saloon theatres for poor audiences and the even cheaper 'penny gaffs'. All offered a combination of spoken and sung entertainment with alcoholic refreshment, but the 1843 Act forced them to specialise either in straight drama without drink or in music hall, which might be accompanied by alcoholic refreshment but must exclude dramatic presentation.

As the industrial pattern of work came to replace the natural rhythm of an earlier age and the availability of regular leisure time increased, the Victorians began to emphasise the firm moral purpose that was needed for the building of a new industrial nation. Some feared that commercial enterprise as applied to entertainment might undermine the working classes, and the flourishing public houses, with their pervasive influence over many aspects of recreation in addition to the demon drink, seemed a particular danger in this respect. Yet, as the idea of 'rational' or 'improving' recreation began to take hold, propagated by voluntary associations and other agencies of reform, commercial entertainment could not escape its influence, and by the late 19th century it had made itself seem safe and harmless in the eyes of the reformers. Even the music halls acquired an air of respectability; as the fully-professional music hall developed, the link with the public house was severed and the amateur acts of the early days were replaced by professionals who were paid in money rather than

with alcoholic drink.

Rougher forms of entertainment persisted, however, and pubs with singing licences continued to provide seedy amusements, but they did so under the watchful eyes of increasingly-careful regulatory magistrates. Despite the fact that many music halls tended to become the resort of prostitutes, most contemporary accounts emphasised the orderly character of these relatively innocuous places of entertainment.

The life of the proto-music hall quickened in the 1840s, culminating in the erection of Charles Morton's celebrated Canterbury Hall, Lambeth (1851), but the numbers of professional performers recorded in the 1851 census remained quite small at 2175. Indeed, no new theatres were built in London between 1840 and 1868; it was not until the late 1850s that the combination of rising wages, improved transport and an enlarged urban population with regular leisure time on its hands made possible a rapid development in the provision of entertainment.

The resurrection of theatre building in London in the late 1850s slightly anticipated this expansion in employment, with Wilton's (1856) and Weston's (1857) Music Halls and the Adelphi Theatre (1858). The provision of music :halls accelerated in the 1860s and, after a lull in the 70s, a network of halls was extended to cover the whole country, concentrated into rival chains owned by leading impresarios, such as Stoll and Moss. In the process the parlour concert was transmuted into the glittering variety show.

By the same token, the number of legitimate theatres expanded greatly with the result that in 1899 London had 61 — 38 in the West End and 23 in the suburbs — to add to its 39 major music halls. During the 1880s alone 10 new theatres were opened in London. New theatres were also created throughout the provinces on such a scale that, by the end of the century, as many as 206 towns possessed at least one playhouse and several had many more — Liverpool had 12, for example, and Newcastle and Manchester eight each. In place of the stock companies of the early Victorian period the theatres were served largely by London touring companies, and theatrical standards greatly raised as a result. This expansion in 'serious' drama was fostered by a marked return of respectable audiences to the theatre: as one commentator remarked in the 1890s, 'Modern civilisation is rapidly multiplying the class to which the theatre is both school and church'. The rise of matinee audiences in the 1880s reinforced this improving trend.

Between the straight theatre and the palace of varieties there existed the 'minor mixtures', the lavish spectacles, circuses and pantomimes, musical shows and popular opera to vary the entertainment diet at the end of the 19th century. The Victorian age also saw the rise of other forms of popular entertainment: the mass spectator sports, religious and popular concerts and technological treats — the big wheels and thrilling rides of the new seaside and suburban pleasure parks.

Technical developments also occurred in the theatre, and were applied to increasing both safety and delight; for example electric light, which was introduced at the Savoy Theatre, London in 1881. Of course the culmination of this trend was the invention of the moving picture in the 1890s, first displayed at variety shows. The 1890s also saw the invention of the gramophone and of radio transmission, both of which were eventually to place new emphasis on the home, rather than the theatre, as a place of entertainment in the 20th century.

Grand Theatre, Blackpool, 1894. A sparkling design by Frank Matcham, the leading late Victorian theatre architect.

A portrait by Walter Lambert of more than 231 of the principal artistes of the music hall, including Marie Lloyd (right of the policeman), Little Tich (bowler hatted in centre foreground) and Vesta Tilley (in male attire in right foreground). Lambert himself performed as a female impersonator under the name Lydia Dreams, and has used this signature on the painting.

Haymarket Theatre, London, one of the first to be built without a pit.

Richmond Theatre, 1899, offered serious drama to 'respectable' audiences, though the pit was still there for the poor.

would cast about for a suitable candidate from amongst his 'friends'. The term 'friend' included his nearest relatives, members of his household and their relations, as well as tenants, villagers and political helpers. Positions awarded on this personal basis ranged from the highest court and government offices, to bishoprics and church livings; in addition, jobs as salaried borough and parish officials, estate agents, secretaries and tutors were distributed this way. While army officers were not appointed in this exclusively personal manner, commissions were obtained by purchase, which meant that to become a general one needed to be a wealthy gentleman rather than a competent soldier. The middle class businessman resented this system, for he came to believe that free competition and the self-made man were the ideals for which to strive. These ideas were not new, but what was different about the 19th century was that they began to be widely accepted.

The next stage then was to change society so as to allow the maximum room for individual initiative and this required the destruction of aristocratic privileges. The Victorian middle class undertook this task as never before because they felt a greater assurance about their own importance. Prior to the 19th century, middle class men had been lawyers, shopkeepers and tradesmen, all of which were jobs that catered primarily to the needs of the aristocracy and gentry. They had little to do with manufacturing, for that was the concern of craftsmen. With the development of an industrialised economy, middle class men became entrepreneurs,

MUSEUMS AND COLLECTING

Museums have emerged from the deeply rooted human passion for collecting curios and related *objets d'art*. Collecting seems to be a feature of all societies and periods, but the Victorian era has given us the museum as an educational tool for teaching and research and as a means of conserving the past. There are now over 800 museums in Britain ranging from the general to the special and covering almost every aspect of knowledge.

The origin of the modern museum is to be found in the intellectual fervour of the 17th century epitomised by the establishment of the Royal Society in 1645 and the great interest in matters scientific. Collecting itself became scientific and the Tradescant family was one of the most prolific. Their collection was inherited by Elias Ashmole in 1662; he presented it to Oxford University in 1679, where it formed the basis of the Ashmolean Museum of 1683.

The next century was to see the emergence of the British Museum and Library in 1753 following Hans Sloane's bequest to the nation. To his library was added the Cotton collection of 1700 and the Royal Library of George II of 1757.

The pattern was thus laid for the great flood of museums which were a by-product of the wealth and leisure created by the Industrial Revolution combined with the world explorations of the 19th century. Private collections were followed by Society collections, and eventually municipal pride produced public museums. Collections at first followed the Ashmolean pattern, being general and covering all aspects of knowledge: some examples include the Hancock Museum of Newcastle (1822), The Castle Museum at Norwich (1825), the Leicester Museum (1835) and the Belfast Museum (1832).

However, numerous literary, philosophical and natural history societies began to appear in the 1820s and specialist private collections

naturally followed. The Ashmolean again showed the way by forming separate museums for aspects such as Geology (1831), Zoology (1860) and later Ethnology (the famous Pitt-Rivers, 1886). Similar moves were being made in the public sector; for example, the Geological Survey and Museum originated in 1835 as a branch of the Ordnance Survey.

The museum movement received a major boost from the Great Exhibition of 1851 and the work of Prince Albert. Out of this venture emerged the idea of making South Kensington a national museum centre. The existing Victoria and Albert Museum replaces an earlier building in Exhibition Road and dates from 1899 when Queen Victoria directed that the Museum should be known as the Victoria and Albert. The Science Museum was created on the opposite side of Exhibition Road, the Natural History section of the British Museum moved to the site in 1880 and more recently the Geological Museum transferred from Jermyn Street. A Scottish counterpart to this activity is to be found in the Royal Scottish Museum of Edinburgh.

Along with Museums are the art collections, which as public galleries are largely Victorian in development. Originally associated with the great country houses and in private hands, the collections gradually became public with a wave of 19th century benefactions leading to the establishment of national centres such as the National Gallery (1824), the Tate Gallery (for British works of art, 1841) and the National Portrait Gallery (1857).

Provincial cities followed with their own art galleries, soon to be plentifully supplied with pictures from private collections which were being decimated by progressive taxation. Some notable examples include Glasgow (1856), Edinburgh (1859), Birmingham (1867), Liverpool (the Walker, 1877), Manchester (1882) and Leeds (1888).

Beecham's Pill manufactory. As Beecham's life was a typical Victorian rags-to-riches story, so this advertisement illustrates the premises of a successful manufacturer at the end of that period: impressive offices, efficient steam-powered machinery, even a private power plant for lighting.

The Royal Scottish Museum dated from 1812, but the major development came after the Great Exhibition of 1851 which led to a Parliamentary Grant for a site and building in Edinburgh. The Main Hall was based on Paxton's Crystal Palace.

The British Museum (Natural History). The area to the south of the Great Exhibition site in Hyde Park was open country in 1851 and ideally situated for development as a national museum centre; the natural history section of the British Museum moved there from Bloomsbury in 1880. With its annexe at Tring it has thousands of specimens forming collections of world wide importance, including the great collections of Sir Hans Sloane and Lord Rothschild.

Lionel Walter, Lord Rothschild, founded the Zoological Museum at Tring, Herts in the late 1800s. He had been passionately fond of natural history all his life and had the largest collection of specimens ever amassed by one man.

Potters Museum of Curiosity, Arundel, West Sussex. Walter Potter (1835–1918) amassed a large collection of anthropomorphic groups of animals which he had stuffed himself. This one is called the Rats' Club.

THE RSPB STORY

The wearing of bird plumage as part of women's fashionable attire led to a huge trade in feathers and skins. Many, particularly egret plumes, were collected during the breeding season so that many species suffered serious population decline. The Society for the Protection of Birds was founded in 1889 to campaign against this slaughter, and its 'Royal' status was granted in 1904. Birds such as the great crested grebe, tern and kittiwake, once seriously threatened, are now flourishing, and some like the avocet and osprey which had ceased to breed in Britain now do so again, thanks largely to the RSPB.

The Great Auk, which became extinct in 1844, from one of John Gould's magnificent hand-coloured bird books.

The Avocet once again breeds in Britain, under protection by the RSPB, and now forms the Society's emblem.

that is, the organisers of capital and labour. The entrepreneur was considered to be the creative force behind the economic cycle because the worker, while indispensable, took no part in the planning of production. Taking initiatives in business often involved great risk and it is not surprising that contemporaries at the mid-century began describing business enterprises in Darwinian terms, whereby the fittest were selected and the less fit rejected.

Men who did succeed in business felt that it was due to individual effort and an austere lifestyle. The popular belief was that any man who followed this example would succeed in this world and be saved in the next. This was a highly radical doctrine for it attacked the traditional social system in which every man was to know his place and keep to it. Under the impact of these new beliefs the old ways were altered. In the late 1860s and early 1870s the army was reformed and all its officers were required to undergo formal military training at either Sandhurst or Woolwich. At the same time the civil service was thrown open to entry by competitive examination in order to combat the incompetency that was part of the patronage system.

While the middle classes were anxious to change the social system, they did not want to overthrow it, for they had a great respect for the established order and wished to be a part of it. They shared with the aristocracy and gentry a fear of the working classes and despised democracy as much as they resented traditional aristocratic privilege. As the economy became specialised and the demands of Victorian life became more sophisticated, there was a greater need for middle class technical and professional expertise. As commercial activity expanded clerks, commercial travellers and technicians were required. New professions came into being, such as mechanical and civil engineering to equip the factories and build the railways; accountants were needed to handle the complex business finances. Lawyers and doctors prospered as more people could afford professional advice in their private affairs. These men and their families became more concerned with maintaining their social status than with altering the social system; hence they were more conventional than the earlier radical middle class manufacturers.

The Professions

The professions became organised during Victoria's reign. The medical profession set the example of qualification by examination, a legally based right to practise and the right of a profession to internal self-government. The aim of professionalisation was not only to raise standards but also to achieve a higher social status for its practitioners. Some professions were more prestigious than others; for example,

The Viceroy, Lord Curzon, visits an Indian prince. On the whole the British governed India with dedication and integrity. Curzon said, 'Remember that the Almighty has placed in your hands the greatest of His ploughs'.

THE BRITISH EMPIRE

In 1837 Britain ruled not so much an empire as a chain of colonies scattered haphazardly around the world, acquired after wars with France and exploration. It included parts of Canada, India and Australia. Sixty years later, the British Empire comprised almost a third of the world's land surface: Canada, India and Australia had been consolidated and much of Africa had been added; in India alone, a fifth of the world's population were British subjects. It was still not a unity and local practices and responsibilities varied greatly, especially between white and non-white subject populations. Canada became a self-governing 'dominion' in 1867, while Australia remained a loose federation of powerful states; with Queen Victoria as their head, they ran their own affairs, leaving only foreign policy to Whitehall. By contrast, India, the 'jewel of the Empire', epitome of the British *Raj*, remained under direct British control with an uneasy relationship between local princes and the quasi-divine Viceroy. Less majestic, but equally subject, was the tiny Atlantic possession of Ascension Island with its 380 inhabitants. Despite its size and prestige, the Empire ran with relatively few white officials; there were only 1,000 white civilians to manage all of India in the 1890s, albeit with the help of 70,000 troops.

The main driving force behind British expansion was economic, the search for profits in raw materials and markets; ivory and gold prompted the exploration of Africa, fear of competition from German industrialism led to its seizure.

As the 19th century progressed, economic individualism was supported, and sometimes camouflaged by more altruistic motives. Victorian imperialism developed as a complex mixture of greed, fervour to spread the Christian gospel, an urge to offer the benefits of industrial urban civilisation to the less fortunate, a desire to conquer the inferior and a passionate seeking after individual adventure and the lure of wild places. At its peak, between 1876 (when Victoria was proclaimed Empress of India) and 1901, it seized the popular imagination and often drove reluctant politicians such as Gladstone to militant actions they wished to avoid. At times of crisis, such as the defeat of the Zulus at Rorke's Drift in 1879 or the death of General Gordon at Khartoum in 1885, this feeling became frenetic; by the 1890s 'jingoism' had become endemic, prompted by a growing sense of international insecurity.

There were a number of setbacks to imperial growth, not least the Indian mutiny of 1857, the defeats by the Zulu army at Isandhlwana in 1879 and by the white Boers at Majuba in 1881. In time, even these became part of the pervasive imperial dream, in which real events were interwoven with imagined ones; a whole range of virtues such as 'grit', courage and heroism unto death in the face of overwhelming odds combined to produce a potent myth of indefatigable British superiority. It was diffused through a range of media — the poems of Rudyard Kipling (1865–1936), the stories of G. A. Henty (1832–1902) and H. Rider Haggard (1832–1902), the

At Isandhlwana on 22 January 1879, 20,000 Zulus of King Cetewayo annihilated an army sent by Sir Bartle Frere, governor of Cape Province, to suppress them. This legendary 'last stand' was redeemed when the Zulus were defeated by a handful of troops at Rorke's Drift on the following day.

Where possible, the British built railways, to move both goods and troops. This temporary viaduct on the Uganda Railway, photographed around 1900, used local materials and labour but British-made equipment.

pages of *Boys' Own* (first published in 1864), the epic paintings of Lady Elizabeth Butler (1844–1933), and their many imitators. It represented a potent interchange of cultures: the British exported arrogance, whisky, railways and the piano and in return they received curry and the bungalow.

In theory, the great imperial benefit was the *Pax Britannica* (British Peace), the imposition on much of the world of a universal authority backed by armed might. On the whole, it was a fallacy since there were at least 230 'savage wars of peace' (Rudyard Kipling) during Victoria's reign. With the exception of the Crimean War (1854–1856) and the Boer Wars (1881, 1899–1902), these were fought against native insurgents or the unruly neighbours of imperial possessions. The key was the army which, unlike those of Britain's European rivals, was composed of volunteers. It was essentially two forces, the home and the Indian, the latter formed after the disastrous failures of the old East India Company's troops during the Mutiny. It was never very large; by the 1890s the total British regular forces comprised 230,000, of whom 120,000 were divided between India, Egypt and the colonies. All the troops had much in common; fierce regimental pride, elaborate uniforms, a rigorous ritual drill system, rigid discipline and considerable combat experience. But there were also many differences. The home-based soldiers were less 'professional' than their overseas counterparts, their officers in particular tending to come from the landed gentry for whom service was often a pleasant recreation. The ordinary troops tended to be recruited from the poor, for whom even the hard life of enlistment was an escape. Repeated attempts at reform had only partial success and there were repeated set-backs; it took defeat by the Boers for scarlet uniforms to be replaced by 'khaki' in battle. The growing insecurity of the second half of Victoria's reign was reflected in the growth of the home-based Volunteer forces, which emerged, as a response to French threats, in 1859. With their elaborate uniforms, parades and bands, these groups of small trades-men and artisans could be found in every small town in Britain, a focus for national and county patriotism.

If the army kept an uncertain peace around the globe, playing the 'Great Game' with the Russians in Afghanistan, it was the navy which maintained the tenuous links of empire. There were dramatic changes as the old 'three-deckers' gave way to steam-powered ships of the line and heavy breech-loading guns replaced the muzzle-loading cannon. The key to this was the building in 1860 of *HMS Warrior*, the first 'ironclad', covered in armour. By the Spithead Review of 1897 the navy had 92,000 sailors in 330 ships. Yet, with the exception of a few engage-ments, ferrying troops and 'gunboat diplomacy' (such as the bombardment of Alexandria in 1882 or facing the French at Fashoda in 1898) the rôle of Victoria's navy as 'ruler of the seas' was a glorious exercise in a bluff which was never called. It created a chain of coaling stations which made sense of the siting of many imperial possessions. It also gave to the empire a sense of security and unity which it did not entirely deserve.

The Diamond Jubilee issue of the Illustrated London News, 1897; a panorama of 'heroic' British achievements, with defeats turned into victory. The 'wooden wall' and 'thin red line' stretched a great way around the world to keep the *Pax Britannica.*

Infantry camp at Sebastopol prior to the Charge of the Light Brigade. The apparent order of the tents hides the chaos and inefficiency which characterised the Crimean War.

British officers of the Indian cavalry — only two are wearing 'western' dress.

Infantry officers, School of Musketry, Hythe, about 1860.

Practice for war: the Hussars on manoeuvres in India, 1895 — cavalry with elephant backup.

For many British officers, the chief justification of the Raj was its magnificent hunting.

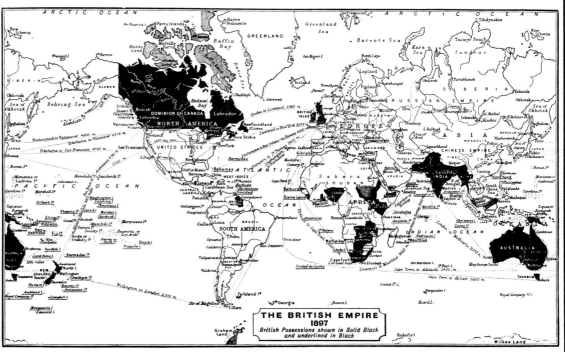

THE BRITISH EMPIRE 1897
British Possessions shown in Solid Black and underlined in Black

Victoria's Empire at its peak, the Diamond Jubilee. The solid blocks of India and the Dominions contrast sharply with the isolated coaling stations and the piecemeal annexation of Africa, territory disputed with the natives, the Boers and other ambitious European powers.

barristers ranked socially higher than solicitors, and the direct handling of goods and money was downgraded. It is ironic that the middle classes, based as they were on trade and manufacturing, came to despise these occupations, all the while aspiring to be ladies and gentlemen of leisure. This did not prevent them, however, from making money. While incomes varied according to individual ability, £5000 per year for a top man was not unknown and an income of around £1000 was the average for moderate professional success.

In spite of their feelings of growing social importance, many middle class Victorians felt unsure about matters of conduct, or did not know how to cope with their rising social positions. The middle classes were not only defining for themselves a more dynamic role in society, but there were also more middle class people than at any time previously. Seventeen professional occupations in England and Wales increased their membership more than two-fold between 1841 and 1881, compared with only a 66 per cent rise in total population. For the first time in any society there were now a large number of people who had to turn their attention to the problem of disposing of income. Many of these people had no experience in budgeting and had no guidelines to determine exactly what was needed to make life pleasant and comfortable.

Suburban society

Without examples the middle classes attempted to copy the fashions of the aristocracy, often with disastrous results. What was suitable for the aristocratic country house was not always best for a suburban villa. Range of choice became limited as factory production rather than individual craftsmanship came to dominate furniture manufacturing. As the factories developed, articles were designed to conform to the needs of machines, and shape often became static due to the cost of retooling. Many newly prosperous families, anxious to consolidate their social position, purchased frantically and filled their houses with massive pieces of furniture, numerous ornaments, photographs and potted plants. Concern about correctness of dress became important to a larger proportion of society than ever before, and swings of fashion caused untold anxiety, especially among women.

The fear of appearing common or vulgar gripped the middle classes and hundreds of books and pamphlets

EVENTS AND PERSONALITIES

1837 **Queen Victoria** succeeds William IV
1838 The Infant Custody Bill is passed, allowing women of unblemished character who have separated from their husbands right of access to their children
  The Anti-Corn Law League is formed
1839 The only attempt at armed rebellion in Victoria's reign, the Newport uprising, occurs
  A Royal Commission recommends extension of the Police Force to the country around London
1840 Queen Victoria marries the minor German Prince, Albert of Saxe-Coburg-Gotha
1842 Britain annexes Hong Kong
  The Mines Act is introduced by Lord Ashley (later Lord Shaftesbury), prohibiting the employment of women and boys under ten years of age to work in the mines underground
1844 The Bank Act is passed, aiming to centralise the issuing of notes in relation to the country's gold supply under the jurisdiction of the Bank of England
  Gladstone introduces the Railway Act, requiring the running of at least one train per day which offered covered third-class accommodation at a maximum fare of a penny a mile
1845 John Henry Newman, a leading figure in the Church of England, causes a furore by becoming a Roman Catholic
1846 The failure of the Irish potato crop forces Prime Minister Robert Peel to revoke the Corn Laws, thereby ending agricultural protection and initiating an age of free trade
1847 The first of the Factory Acts limits the working day of women and children to ten hours
  Charlotte Brontë publishes *Jane Eyre* and her sister Emily publishes *Wuthering Heights*
  Chloroform is used for the first time
  Liverpool appoints the first medical officer of health
1848 The Chartist movement, which demanded the democratisation of the constitution, assembles its great petition but many of the signatures turn out to be forgeries
  The Public Health Act, inspired by Edwin Chadwick, creates local boards of health in certain areas, with a General Board of Health at the centre of the network in London
1849 Charles Dickens publishes *David Copperfield*
1850 Alfred, Lord Tennyson publishes his first acclaimed book of poetry *In Memoriam* and succeeds Wordsworth as Poet Laureate
  The Don Pacifico debate in which Lord Palmerston asserts the right of Britain to protect her citizens throughout the world

1851 The Great Exhibition, designed to display the products of industrialisation, becomes a symbol to the Victorians of their material prosperity and international prestige
1852 Death of the national hero, the Duke of Wellington, Commander in Chief at the Battle of Waterloo
1854 Establishment of the Working Men's College for Adult Education, the first institution of its kind
  October 18, the brave but ill-fated charge of the Light Brigade at the Battle of Balaclava
  The Battle of Inkerman is fought on November 5
  Defeats in the Crimean War lead to the rise to power of Lord Palmerston's central moderate coalition
1855 Limited Liability Act is passed, allowing for the formation of joint stock companies under a committee of directors which can appeal to the public for money, while limiting the directors' financial responsibility to the value of their subscribed shares
  The Civil Service Commission is created as a step towards the structural unification of the service, and some qualifying examinations for nominees are introduced
  Sebastopol is captured
1856 Russia accepts defeat in the Crimean War
  The Peace of Paris is signed with Britain and France
1857 The Indian Mutiny breaks out over fears that the British are attacking the Hindu religion
  The Marriage and Divorce Act is passed, providing protection for the earnings of a wife deserted by her husband and enabling her to inherit and bequeath wealth in the same way as a single woman
1858 A permanent orchestra is founded at Manchester by Sir Charles Hallé
  The Sovereignty of India is transferred to the Crown
1859 John Stuart Mill publishes his classic work on liberal doctrine, entitled *On Liberty*
  Charles Darwin publishes *The Origin of Species*, in which he demonstrates the case for evolution and suggests a method by which this had occurred — natural selection on the basis of chance variation
  Sir Edwin Landseer's sculptured lions are placed in Trafalgar Square
  Samuel Smiles publishes *Self Help*, which expresses the cherished middle class belief that true progress in business and in the nation is expected to result from individual initiative and self-help
1860 The Adulteration of Foods Act is passed, the first but not successful attempt to legislate against the adulteration of food

COINS

The young Victoria's accession to the throne was celebrated by the issue of an extremely rare gold £5 piece. The reverse shows Una and the Lion, characters from Spenser's poem *The Faerie Queen*, who were used to symbolise the young queen and her mighty nation.

The Queen's two jubilees were celebrated on the coinage. Unfortunately the first jubilee issue was most unpopular with Victoria herself; she disliked the rather silly little crown — but it was soon replaced by the 1893 issue.

Many medals were struck in celebration of the Great Exhibition. They were intended to express the Victorians' pride in their engineering skill and in their growing empire and influence in the world at large.

The reverse of the £5 piece issued to celebrate Victoria's accession, showing 'Una and the Lion'.

The 1893 £5 piece. It replaced the original 1887 crown, which Victoria disliked.

The Charge of the Light Brigade, a gallant but useless episode in the Crimean War, which was fought to stop Russia controlling Constantinople as the Turkish Empire declined. The British Army and its supply system proved to be hopelessly disorganised and ill-equipped, the result of too much economy in 40 years of peace.

The Albert Memorial in London's Kensington Gardens was started in 1864 as a monument to Prince Albert and took 12 years to build. The architect was Sir Gilbert Scott and the total cost was £120,000.

British soldiers in the Boer War beside an armoured train at Modder River Station in 1900. That same year the Relief of Mafeking was the turning point.

1882 W. T. Stead of the *Pall Mall Gazette* causes a sensation by employing women journalists and paying them the same rate as men
1883 Robert Louis Stevenson publishes *Treasure Island*
1884 Gladstone and Salisbury work out a compromise arrangement over the Third Reform Bill which satisfies both parties
The Fabian Society, precursor of the Labour Party, is founded
1885 As a result of the newspaper campaign of the *Pall Mall Gazette*, the Criminal Law Amendment Act is passed, raising the age of consent from 13 to 16
Gilbert and Sullivan produce their most successful operetta *The Mikado*
1886 Gladstone takes up home rule for Ireland, thereby splitting the Liberal Party
1887 Queen Victoria celebrates her Golden Jubilee
1888 The County Councils for local government are created
1889 A lengthy London dock strike ends in victory for the dockers, who win a standard wage of 6d per hour, one of the first trade union victories
1890 The Irish nationalist leader, Charles Stewart Parnell, falls from power after a divorce scandal
1891 Free elementary education is introduced
1892 Keir Hardie, first Labour member

of Parliament, is elected
1893 The first woman factory inspector is employed
1894 Liberal Chancellor Harcourt introduces a new form of taxation — death duties
Gladstone retires from the Premiership, ostensibly over naval armament but in fact due to his failure to carry the Cabinet on his Irish policy
1895 The Jameson Raid fails to resolve the South African Boer problem by force
The National Trust is founded by Octavia Hill
1896 The *Daily Mail* is created, the first newspaper aimed at a mass popular reading public
1897 The Workmen's Compensation Act gives automatic compensation for accidents at work, although certain industries and certain accidents were still excluded
Queen Victoria celebrates her Diamond Jubilee
1898 William Ewart Gladstone, four times Prime Minister in the reign of Queen Victoria, dies
1899 Elgar produces his first major work, the Enigma Variations
1900 The Relief of Mafeking, the turning point in the Boer War, follows the 'Black Week' of British defeats in South Africa
1901 Queen Victoria dies

1862 The Peabody Trust is founded by the banker George Peabody, who gave £500,000 for the building of model dwellings for the poor in London
1864 The Contagious Diseases Act is passed, aiming to prevent the spread of venereal disease among the armed forces by registering prostitutes in garrison towns
1865 Sewage Utilisation Act is passed, creating sewage authorities and the first public health legislation to reach into rural areas, as well as being the first to apply to the whole of the United Kingdom
Cambridge Local Examinations are opened to women
The death of the Prime Minister, Lord Palmerston, opens the way to Parliamentary reform
Elizabeth Garrett Anderson becomes the first woman to qualify as a medical doctor in Britain
1867 Disraeli's and Derby's Conservative government pass a large measure of Parliamentary reform in order to thwart Gladstone
1868 Gladstone becomes Premier, and initiates a wide range of reform measures
The Artisans' and Labourers' Dwelling Act is passed, widening the permissive powers of local authorities to order the renovation or demolition of property unfit for human habitation
1869 Foundation of Girton College for women, which in 1872 became part of Cambridge University
1870 The Married Women's Property Act gives women the right to own property after marriage
Forster's Education Act sets up the basis of a national system of elementary education
1871 A prolonged but successful strike by Tyneside engineers leads the way to a nine-hour working day
The Local Government Act brings together in one department the functions of Local Government Act Office, the

Registrar-General's Office, the Medical Department of the Privy Council and the Poor Law Board
Religious tests in universities are abolished
The system of purchasing commissions in the army is abolished by the Secretary of State for War, Cardwell
1872 Slade School of Art and the Pharmaceutical Society are opened to women
The secret ballot is introduced to eliminate corrupt voting practices at elections
George Eliot publishes *Middlemarch*
1873 The Remington typewriter is invented
1874 Winston Churchill is born, son of rising young politician Lord Randolph Churchill
1875 Gladstone retires after the disunity of the Liberals leads to defeat in the 1874 general election
1876 Queen Victoria is proclaimed Empress of India
Gladstone returns to public life with the Bulgarian agitation, a vigorous campaign against Disraeli's policy on the Eastern Question
The Zulu War involves Britain in the defence of the expanding South African colony
1880 Election of the atheist Charles Bradlaugh to the House of Commons provokes a long religious controversy over whether he should swear the oath
Consecration of Truro Cathedral, the only cathedral built during Victoria's reign
Gladstone is triumphant in the general election after the first modern open-air campaign in his constituency of Midlothian
1881 Formation of the Social Democratic Federation, Britain's first Marxist party, by H. M. Hyndman
Death of Disraeli, Queen Victoria's favourite Prime Minister, leaving the party divided and in opposition

Queen Victoria (1837–1901). Unpopular early in her reign, she became one of the best-loved monarchs ever. Her husband Prince Albert was a valuable consort and her reign saw the continuing industrialisation and prosperity of Britain and the establishment of its role as a world-dominating imperial power.

appeared offering advice on how to 'keep up appearances'. Mrs Beeton's *Book of Household Management* (1861) was perhaps one of the most famous of these works, but while the middle classes had money to spend, they still had much to learn about comfort and hygiene. For example, Mrs Beeton suggested menus that were abundant in meat, fish and solid foods but deficient in fresh fruits, vegetables and salads. Concern for personal cleanliness was not highly developed in the early part of the 19th century even among the prosperous classes. The daily bath, imported from India by the Duke of Wellington, was adopted slowly. By the mid 1860s the wealthy bathed daily, while the middle classes took only a weekly bath and washed daily. While it was possible to wash the person, personal linen and woollen clothes could only be cleaned by brushing and spot removal;

ironing was confined to linen and clothes about to leave the tailors.

The task fell to the Victorian middle classes of developing a lifestyle that was based primarily on salaried or earned income as opposed to inherited wealth. They had a certain amount of income available for luxuries beyond the basic necessities of life. Much of this was spent on enhancing their social status rather than on improving the quality of personal life. For many of these men and women, conforming to rigid standards of personal conduct was a source of great satisfaction. The middle class ideal was a solid suburban house with a semi-circular drive, a carriage of their own, several servants and an annual seaside holiday. Towards the end of the century life became more relaxed, with time spent pleasantly with the new amusements of croquet, lawn

QUEEN VICTORIA'S JUBILEE AND DEATH

The last decades of the 19th century were marked in some respects by growing domestic uncertainties and a sense of international insecurity. In this, Victoria emerged as a focus for national hopes and sentiment as the nation attempted to reassure itself of its greatness in a rediscovery of the Queen.

Between Prince Albert's death in 1862 and the 50th anniversary of her accession in 1887, the Queen was a virtual recluse, 'The Widow at Windsor'. Before the Golden Jubilee, *The Times* wrote:

To many of her people she is a name rather than a living reality: A generation has grown to manhood since the happy days in the Queen's reign when her appearance and that of Prince Albert enlivened all State ceremonies and public entertainments. We cherish the hope that the celebration of Her Majesty's jubilee may mark the beginning of a new and brighter period, both in her own existence and in the social annals of the country.

Their hopes were fulfilled beyond everyone's dreams. On 21 June, 1887 a Service of Thanksgiving was held in Westminster Abbey. The Queen's procession from Buckingham Palace included 47 carriages, Indian and European royalty and their attendants, and was followed by her numerous sons, grandsons and nephews splendidly uniformed and mounted on horseback. It took a long route via Piccadilly and Pall Mall so that as many people as possible could see her pass.

At the Abbey a choir of 300 voices sang music by Prince Albert, and the congregation included England's leading poets, bishops, dons and that redoubtable pair of female educationists, Miss Beale and Miss Buss. In the midst of the magnificence, the tiny Victoria perched on the Coronation Chair whilst the Archbishop of Canterbury thanked God for her reign and beseeched him to 'stay the growth of iniquity'. The Queen returned through crowds of ecstatic foreigners and Cockneys: 'Here she is; I have seen her; she is alive!' roared a sturdy patriot from the East End.

In the country generally there was an effervescence of decently ordered rejoicing. 10,000 gas lights illuminated the Bank of England, 120 electric lamps (of 20 candle power each) the Drapers' Hall. Across the landscape 1,000 bonfires were lit, like Armada beacons, started by one above Malvern at 10 p.m. In Swindon, a procession of mounted yeomanry led the celebrations; in Barnsley there was a dinner for the poor in the workhouse, and in Wigan 15,000 schoolchildren and 1,300 old people were fêted, whilst in Grimsby an ox was roasted whole. For a while the dimmer recesses of industrial England were lit up.

Ten years later, her Diamond Jubilee brought even more rejoicing; she had defeated expectation by living so long and there were darker clouds on the horizon. The poet laureate, Alfred Austin, composed 30 stanzas, ending in a celebration of this belated spring of feeling:

And ever when mid-June's musk-roses blow,

Our race will celebrate Victoria's name,
And even England's greatness gain a blow,
From her pure fame.

On 22 June, 1897 the Queen rode in procession through the City of London to a Thanksgiving on the steps of St Paul's Cathedral (she was felt to be too infirm to enter the building). Tickets on the route sold for 2 guineas each, often with champagne included. Troops from the British and Imperial regiments marched before her, with a guard of honour provided by 22 Indian cavalry officers. Forty-two English and foreign princes rode in threes in the procession, which was led by the tallest man in the army, the mounted 6 feet 8 inches of Captain Ames of the 2nd Life Guards. In the midst of all this magnificence sat the plainly dressed little figure of Victoria, not just the Queen and Empress but 'The Mother of the People'. After a *Te Deum* and a few simple prayers, the Archbishop of Canterbury broke with all protocol and shouted for three cheers for the Queen.

It was a profound explosion of nostalgia and sentiment. The Bank of England carried the illuminated message, 'She wrought her people lasting good'. There was rejoicing all over the Empire and there were many attempts to erect permanent monuments. Newcastle-upon-Tyne raised £100,000 for a new infirmary, the little town of South Molton built a cottage hospital, and many towns, as in 1887, provided even more public clocks to mark the passing of an age. Lincoln Cathedral was lit up

with lights of 84,000 candle power and in Manchester 11,000 children from the poorest schools marched through the city to a treat. At Spithead, the greatest naval review ever held reminded 'inferior' nations, not least Germany, who really ruled the waves. Salesmen of Jubilee souvenirs and catering contractors made small fortunes.

From then on it was a matter of waiting for the end of a century and an era, as Victoria aged and weakened. She died at Osborne on 22 January, 1901, surrounded by her family, including even her renegade grandson, Kaiser Wilhelm. 5,000 people went spontaneously to a service in St Paul's Cathedral; the Royal Artillery fired 81 minute guns, one for every year of her life. After lying in state for 10 days, she was taken to London and then to Windsor to be buried. It was, at her wish, the simplest of state occasions — a plain military funeral, but white since she felt it should not be an occasion of gloom. In accordance with her known views, London was hung with purple and white, not with black. At Windsor, there was an unexpected hitch which has given a model for state funerals ever since; the traces of the artillery horses broke and Prince Louis of Battenberg ordered the guard of sailors to drag the cortège, using the communication cord taken quickly from the royal train. Victoria lay in St George's Chapel until 4 February when she was taken to be buried alongside Albert in a quiet family service at the mausoleum at Frogmore.

Victoria's Diamond Jubilee, 22 June 1897. The Queen's carriage halted at Temple Bar, entrance to the City of London, to receive the homage of the Corporation. The Prince of Wales, later Edward VII, rides on horseback behind the Queen.

The Diamond Jubilee – the Queen in the City. Grooms and outriders in state livery precede the carriage, which is followed by royal princes on horseback and a sovereign's escort of the Household Cavalry.

tennis, rollerskating, and cycling. Maintaining the conventions of religion was still important but a life of hard work and abstinence from drink, dancing and theatre-going was not so universally accepted. Such a life was described by Carola Oman, daughter of Charles Oman the historian, who grew up in Oxford at the turn of the century. For people such as these and for many members of the aristocracy and gentry the reign of Queen Victoria was indeed a pleasurable time to live, but for those whose social position was not so secure, or for the working poor, the 19th century was a time of great trial and hardship.

It is perhaps in the words of Charles Dickens, the Victorian novelist, that we can find a fitting epitaph for the experience of our great-grandparents. For them it was both 'The Best of Times and the Worst of Times'.

A Sunday School procession in Stockport. In the mid 1800s the schools provided the only opportunity for many poor children to learn to read and write.

A slap-up meal for the people of Chipping Norton held in the market place, through which the main road still passes. A diamond jubilee had never occurred before, and the whole country celebrated with bonfires, binges and good works. The Empire was just as enthusiastic – the Cape Colony gave Her Majesty a battleship.

Victoria's funeral in London – the visible end of the 19th century. A great occasion but one of simple mourning, the white and purple hangings from balconies counterpointing the state dress of the troops.

Another view of the funeral, with closed carriages for royal women and the civilian members of the Queen's household. Male members of the European royalty rode behind the funeral carriage on horseback.

193

Edward VII and the New Century

*Britain's wealth and power seemed invincible,
but rivals were catching up. The instruments of mass communication – telegraph,
telephone, radio, moving pictures and the popular press – began
to influence a society whose bases were being questioned; imperialism,
trades unions, the class system, women's suffrage and the Irish question were the
issues of the day. Then the Great War came and the lights went out.*

Despite the relative brevity of his reign from 1901 to 1910, Edward VII will in all probability be the last British monarch to lend his name to an era. That this should be so is a tribute less to his constitutional role than to the impact of his personality, reinforced in the public consciousness by the coincidence of the first new reign for 65 years with the dawn of a new century.

The style imparted to the monarchy by Edward's outgoing nature was in marked contrast with Queen Victoria's withdrawal from the public gaze for so much of the latter part of her reign. This change was apparent within a few weeks of the old queen's death with the revival of the royal attendance at the state opening of Parliament for the first time since 1861. Edward's coronation, however, proved something of an anti-climax, having to be postponed at the last moment while the king underwent an urgent operation for appendicitis.

Already 59 years old at his accession, Edward had served a long apprenticeship. Since the death of Prince Albert he had in effect been the public figurehead of the monarchy, yet rarely during his mother's lifetime had he been permitted to play more than a symbolic role. This combination of public onus without real responsibility or influence for so much of his life perhaps helps to explain the controversial and occasionally scandalous image of Edward as a playboy Prince of Wales (he had been called as a witness in a much publicised court case concerning cheating at cards, and had been cited in divorce proceedings). The limitation of his early experience also sheds light on the role Edward was subsequently to play as king.

For Edward's supreme achievement, with the assistance of the complementary personality of his consort, the Danish Queen Alexandra, was to popularise the monarchy. At home, amongst upper and lower classes alike, his easy charm and love of ceremonial won public acclaim and affection. Abroad he reinforced the inter-relationships of birth and

marriage with the ruling houses of Europe by wide and frequent travels, during which he proved a roving ambassador of no mean ability, while his preference for France and dislike of his nephew the Kaiser facilitated, but did not dictate, his government's entry into a French alliance during this period.

At his accession Edward declared his intention to pursue the path of constitutional monarchy. Here his experience, or rather the lack of it, as Prince of Wales fortuitously coincided with the realities of the early 20th century political scene. Though ironically the nature of constitutional monarchy was to be put to a severe test in the controversy over the powers of the House of Lords between 1909 and 1911, Edward VII and the less extrovert George V accomplished a significant shift in the style and function of British royalty. Between them they inaugurated and established a conception of the monarchy as the symbol of national unity at home and as ambassador-in-chief for Britain overseas, combined with a closely circumscribed constitutional role above and

The Cunard White Star liner 'Mauretania', which regained the Blue Riband for the fastest crossing of the Atlantic from Germany. The luxury passenger liner of the Edwardian era was no less than a floating hotel, and like a hotel provided every comfort and attention for those who could afford it. Before the Great War the contrast between rich and poor reached its peak.

Oxford Street, London. The new century brought with it a substantial increase in the transport network based on cars, buses, trams and delivery vans. These cheap and multifarious means of transport were quickly introduced throughout the country, and broke down the barriers between towns and villages, making possible the creation of the suburbs.

beyond the politics of party. In this way traditional institutions were reconciled with, and in some respects even enhanced by, 20th century attitudes.

An age of ambivalence

In some respects the Edwardian age signified, in more than chronological terms, the birth of the 20th century. In other, arguably more fundamental, ways the years 1901–14 formed an epilogue to the Victorian era. Though the British economy reached new heights based on the 19th century pillars of industry, exports to all corners of the world and substantial overseas investments, doubts as to the soundness of the foundations of her economic prosperity, born in the 'Great Depression' of the 1870s and 1880s, still lingered. While the class system achieved its most subtle and extreme forms of

expression during this period, its stability was threatened by the realisation from the 1880s onwards of the extent of poverty in the midst of plenty. The comfortable division of the spoils of party politics between the Liberal and Conservative representatives of the upper and middle classes was imperilled by the arrival in the Parliamentary arena of the movement for the direct representation of labour which had taken root in the 1890s.

During this period the fundamental concepts underlying the framework of post-industrial Britain were brought under scrutiny. The Boer War shook Britain's belief in the invincibility of her armed forces, and provoked the questioning of the economic, political and ethical bases of imperialism. Through Joseph Chamberlain's conversion to protectionism, the defence of the imperial idea was linked to an

THE NEW AGE OF TRANSPORT

The 'Age of the Automobile' arrived in Britain with the new century. A series of motoring events in the spring of 1900, called the Thousand Miles Trial, transformed popular attitudes to the car. Alfred Harmsworth, proprietor of the *Daily Mail*, was a keen enthusiast of the motor car and ensured that the Trials received extensive publicity. The public was persuaded that the horseless carriage worked, and was inspired by its potential.

Vehicle registration statistics reflect the rapid progress of private motor transport in the early years of the 20th century. Private car registration was introduced in 1904 – the number-plate A1 was given to Earl Russell's Napier. There were 8,000 private cars in Britain in 1904; 10 years later there were 132,000 and car ownership was spreading from the upper class to the more affluent members of the middle class such as doctors. The motor cycle was the poor man's motor vehicle – by 1914 there were 124,000 on British roads.

Public transport converted wholesale from horse to combustion engine, and by the outbreak of war the horse bus and Hackney carriage were fast disappearing. Motor buses and taxis increased from 5,000 in 1904 to 51,000 in 1914. Deliveries were made increasingly by motor vans and lorries. The rate of growth of motorised goods vehicles was fastest of all – their number rose from 4,000 to 82,000 in the same period.

Germans and Frenchmen took the lead in the development of the motor car and commenced production in the 1880s, while the first British car firm was not formed until 1896. Altogether 393 British firms began motor manufacturing prior to the war, but it was a risky and highly competitive business; by 1914 only 113 firms were still trading, the others having succumbed either to bankruptcy or to takeover by more successful rivals.

British car firms in 1914 each had a small share of the 34,000 output, making expensive cars for a luxury market. The Rolls Royce Silver Ghost of 1906 was the supreme achievement of striving for technical sophistication and elegant styling. In the US, by contrast, car makers were aiming for mass production for a large market and were deliberately sacrificing quality and performance, where necessary, to reduce production cost and hence price, and to improve reliability by not overstraining engines. By 1912 US output was already 500,000 vehicles – a figure not reached in Britain until the 1920s.

The slow start of motor production in Britain has often been attributed to restrictive legislation which, so it is alleged, discouraged experiment. An Act of 1865, passed with heavy agricultural traction engines in mind, limited the speed of a motor vehicle on a public highway to four m.p.h. and required it to be preceded by a man on foot carrying a red flag. The restrictions

were relaxed by an Act of 1896 which abolished the flags and raised the speed limit to 12 m.p.h. In celebration the Motor Car Club organised an 'Emancipation Run' from London to Brighton, an event now re-enacted every November. The original publicity stunt sadly misfired; to the glee of a rather hostile press and public only 10 out of 36 starters completed the run and rumours were rife that some of the finishers had arrived by train. The Motor Car Act of 1903 raised the legal limit on public roads to 20 m.p.h., the speed which remained in force until 1930.

Motoring in Edwardian Britain was a far from comfortable activity. Protective clothing was vital to guard the driver, and passengers too, from wind, rain and particularly from dust. The widespread adoption of the pneumatic tyre just after the turn of the century made for a less bumpy ride than the old solid rubber tyres, but wear and tear on poorly made up roads — only the most major roads were metalled — made tyres one of the principal costs of motoring. Alfred Harmsworth claimed that he spent £500 on tyres in 1901, probably rather more than the cost of his car.

Motoring was not merely uncomfortable, it was also dangerous. Roads in towns were frequently made up of wooden blocks which became slippery and highly dangerous in wet weather; braking systems were still far from satisfactory and the technology of stopping lagged behind the advances in

ability to go faster.

The rapidly increasing power of vehicles led to common violations of the slow statutory speed limits. The policeman with stop watch hiding in ditch or behind hedge for the unsuspecting 'scorcher' became a stock figure of fun. The Automobile Association was created by drivers in response to this hazard. All too often, however, the motorist's problem was not an excess of speed but the refusal of his machine to move at all — though the reliability of cars increased substantially during the Edwardian age, both fuel and mechanics were still in short supply in many rural areas and the car at the end of a horse's tow rope with a caption about horsepower became a cartoonist's cliché.

Motor bus services and motorised taxi services began in towns around the turn of the century. The horse population of Britain reached a peak in 1905, but by 1913 the 2,500 motor buses in service in London had all but driven the horse bus off the streets, although the horse was still used for many heavy delivery duties, such as coal.

The advent of motorised urban transport ensured that alarmist predictions of city streets choked with horse manure, based on the assumption of an ever increasing horse population, were never realised.

Rolls Royce Silver Ghost, 1912. Designed in 1906 by Henry Royce, the car set new standards of reliability, comfort and elegance. It was manufactured for 18 years.

Medina 4 h.p. steam traction engine. From the 1860s until the 1930s traction engines were used to haul heavy loads short distances on roads.

assault on another late 19th century article of faith, free trade. The rejection of Chamberlain's programme in the 1906 election temporarily drove these issues beneath the political surface, yet neither imperialism nor free trade emerged from the Edwardian period without serious cracks in their foundations.

If the early Edwardian years were a time of questioning, the latter half of the period was one of conflict. The years leading up to the outbreak of war were marred by acute industrial strife. Constitutional stability was threatened by the crisis over the powers of the House of Lords, and by the militant campaign of the suffragettes.

Irish Home Rule reopened a running sore in the body politic. Hovering above these domestic conflicts was an escalation in tension within Europe destined to bring the

period, and with it many features of Edwardian society, to a traumatic close. All these issues had their roots in or before the last quarter of the 19th century. All attained sharper focus, presenting an intensified threat to the established order, during the Edwardian years.

Rich and poor

Edwardian society was diverse, hierarchical and, above all, unequal. Though only about eight per cent of the population of 37 millions in 1901 drew their living from agriculture, urban and rural society were sharply differentiated. London, with over seven million inhabitants, was unique. Scotland, Wales, Ireland and the English regions still exhibited distinctive cultures despite the increasingly pervasive influence of national communications. Inequality was

Gateshead electric tramcar. Trams provided the first cheap urban transport, permitting workers to live in new suburbs.

A trailer car in the rush hour, 1913. The London County Council took over London's tramways during the 1900s.

Motor vans, like motor buses, replaced horse-drawn vans for local distribution of goods in the 1900s. Long distance freight was moved by rail.

The starting line of the 1908 Paris–London race. Motor racing began in France in 1895 and soon became a popular sport.

Bayswater omnibus. During the Edwardian era motorised public transport largely replaced the horse-drawn buses of the late 1800s. The first motor buses went into regular service in 1899; the last horse-drawn bus was withdrawn from service in 1915.

Middlesbrough's first car (left) **1896.** Mr George Scoby-Smith in his 1½ h.p. Benz, a popular car of the 1890s. In 1896 the British speed limit was raised to 12 m.p.h.

Whitechapel hay market, 1914. Typically, market streets were wide and well supplied with tramways. The open roads remain, but the markets have gone.

Electrification of tramways at the junction of Old Street and Goswell Road, London, 1906. Early trams were horse drawn; electrification began in the 1890s.

intrinsic not only within these diversities but between young and old, men and women, as well as being fundamental to the class system.

A mere one per cent of the adult population controlled two thirds of the nation's capital. With income tax at the end of the Boer War at 1/3d (6¼ new pence) in the pound on incomes over £160 per annum paid by only a seventh of all earners and yielding a revenue only just in excess of that gained from indirect taxation, the distribution of incomes was only a little less unequal than that of capital. While the higher professions such as law or medicine might command salaries up to £5000 a year, many agricultural labourers, casually employed men and most women even in regular employment earned as little as £30–40 a year.

Inequalities of income were reinforced by distinctions in life style. For the wealthy, status was in part defined by the ostentatious display of conspicuous consumption. At the other end of the social scale were those for whom the maintenance of 'mere physical efficiency' (the standard set by Seebohm Rowntree in his study of poverty in York) necessitated not merely scrupulous avoidance of waste on their own part but dependence, whether through charity or scavenging, on the surplus of their superiors.

Among the well-to-do, meticulous attention to the appropriate dress for every activity in accordance with time of day, season and status contrasted with working-class school absenteeism for want of shoes. Diet was another prominent sign of inequality. It was not exceptional for the cost of a dinner party to exceed the annual income of the servant at table. Not only were malnutrition, disease and ill health endemic among the lower working classes but their mortality was almost twice as high as at the top of the social hierarchy. Class was almost as apparent from such physical characteristics as the weight and height of children as from accent and dress. In the First World War the nation was shocked to find that only a third of all adult male recruits was in good health.

Deficiencies in health were compounded by housing conditions. At one extreme was the country house or town mansion with an array of guest and reception rooms. Even the substantial middle class home had its servants' quarters in addition to several living rooms, while in the working-class tenement occupational density was frequently as high as two per room. At the very bottom came those among the poor and aged whose destitution led them to the doors of the workhouse, or to sleeping rough.

While all the waking hours and energies of many of the working classes were consumed in the pursuit of bare subsistence, those at the opposite end of the spectrum devoted as much time and not much less energy to the pursuits of leisure. The seasons dominated alike the working rhythm of those employed in agriculture or building, and the living cycle of 'society', with Ascot, Cowes and Henley, the grouse season and the hunt all fixtures in the social calendar.

For the working class the conviviality of the public house was the nearest equivalent to the weekend house party. Only those with incomes at or above the average of £80–100 a year could regularly afford to attend the music hall or the novelty of the cinema (the first moving picture show in London opened in 1896) as their superiors did the opera or legitimate theatre, though football was already becoming a mass spectator sport.

The tensions inherent in the contrast of extremes were, however, only one aspect of Edwardian society. Equally fundamental was the stabilising effect of the subtle gradations

SHIPBUILDING AND SHIPPING

Up to 1914 the shipping industry continued to expand and develop. Merchant ships became bigger, the passenger liners in particular achieving their zenith of opulence for the first class, that is; the steerage passengers were herded into bleak crowded quarters right aft above the vibrating propellers, hence the name 'steerage'. Sailing ships, save in the coastal trade, were dwindling fast; a further reason for this, apart from improved steamships, was the increased capacity of shipyards to produce steamers. A potent reason for sail power continuing had, in the 19th century, been the lack of yards to produce engines and boilers – a situation now eased, with the bigger shipyards having their own engine and boiler works, and the smaller able to turn to large marine engine specialists.

One very notable advance in marine propulsion was made at the turn of the century: the introduction and rapid adoption of the steam turbine. Sir Charles Parsons had demonstrated this in his launch *Turbinia* in the 1897 Diamond Jubilee naval review. Within a very few years his works at Newcastle was receiving orders for turbines to power destroyers and excursion and cross channel steamers, and by 1907 the new Cunarders *Mauretania* and *Lusitania*. At about the same time a very new type of marine engine was making a cautious appearance: the diesel. Much of the pioneer work here was left to Continental shipyards and shipowners; the British, with abundant coal and abundant labour, did not feel any economic need to abandon their steamers, nor even, save in the Navy, to go over to oil fired boilers.

Oil as a boiler fuel had obvious advantages: ease of refuelling, precise control of fuel injection, and a vast reduction in the number of stokehold personnel; a large coal burning battleship employed 200 stokers, but an oil burner needed only 50. There were other astonishing developments in the Edwardian period. By 1900 the Royal Navy had given up sail – this had only been an auxiliary source of propulsion since the 1860s and had gradually been dispensed with altogether in the larger ships, although retained in sloops and gunboats where they still had some practical use. Ironclads had quickly replaced wooden walls and guns had increased in calibre. The trouble was that there were few 19th-century naval engagements in which the new capital ships could try out their armaments. Some very weird and impractical designs had appeared toward the end of Victoria's reign, but the mounting threat of German sea power caused a revolution in British naval planning. A new all big-gun warship, the *Dreadnought*, was launched in 1906 which made every other battleship obsolete. Unfortunately Germany had only to build a dreadnought as well to come on equal terms, so naval rivalry turned into a desperate race.

More sinister than the dreadnought was the Holland submarine, the first of which was completed for the Royal Navy in 1901. There had been many experimental submarines in previous decades, but now the underwater vessel, diesel powered on the surface and electric when submerged, was a practical weapon of war. Barrow-in-Furness became a leading port for building submarines, a lead which was retained, but here again the British found intense German competition which was to achieve a near victory over British sea power in the 1914–18 War.

Royal Naval vessels after the Great War. Naval power had largely been a competition between battleships, but inventions such as the aeroplane and the torpedo-firing submarine gave rise to many other types of vessel.

The Thames spritsail barge Cambria was built at Greenhithe by Everard's for their own fleet. For many years her skipper was the well known Bob Roberts. She is now preserved by the Maritime Trust in St Katherine's Dock, London.

Last of the paddle excursion steamers, the Waverley, was built on the Clyde for the London & North Eastern Railway. During her long career she ran on most of the Clyde Services and can still be seen travelling around our coasts.

The White Star liner Titanic left Southampton on 10 April 1912 on her maiden voyage to New York, with 1,316 passengers and 885 crew. On the night of 14 April she struck an iceberg, and because of a lack of lifeboats and no apparent sense of urgency, 1,589 passengers and crew were drowned.

Liverpool landing stage at its busiest just before the First World War; in the foreground is one of the Birkenhead vehicular ferries or 'luggage' boats, while the four-funnelled liner is the Cunard's *Aquitania*, launched in 1913.

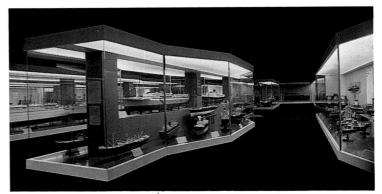

The new display of model ships at the Glasgow Museum of Transport is comprehensive, from liners and battleships to dredgers and ferries. This view shows models of ships from the Firth of Clyde.

The Royal Navy's first submarine entered the water on 2 October 1901. Submarine construction had begun in 1886, but success came only when a licence was granted to Vickers to build submarines of the American Holland design, shown above.

The battle-cruiser Tiger was built by John Brown at Clydebank and launched in 1913. Although they carried the same armament as the Dreadnoughts, the battle-cruisers' lighter weight allowed greater speed and the chance of escape from confrontation.

of hierarchy in which the middle and artisan classes supplied a crucial cement. Between the extremes of luxury and penury lay a broad range of social groups living in various degrees of comfort, from the foremen and craftsmen of the skilled working classes, through lower middle class salesmen and clerks, shopkeepers and the lesser professions, to the manufacturers, merchants, doctors and lawyers of the upper middle classes.

Comfort for these middle ranks typically meant an urban or suburban house and one or more servants – perhaps the most significant of all the divisions in Edwardian society was that between those who employed and those who were, or whose equals were, servants. For some among the comfortable classes modern technology was already relieving the burden of domestic chores, through the electric light, the gas cooker and multipoint water heater, the vacuum sweeper and electric iron. Business and leisure alike were being transformed by the telephone and the gramophone, the motor vehicle and the bicycle. The middle classes, as the patrons of a retailing revolution marked by the advent of the chain and department store, formed the basis for a new mass consumer society, dependent on advertising and integrally linked to the growth of a popular press. If the extremes of poverty and privilege were a legacy of Victorian Britain, the Edwardian years saw the coming of age of the middle classes.

The rise of Labour

These years also witnessed the first stage of an attack on hierarchy and inequality which was in due course to transform British society. In the 1880s the recognition of the extent of poverty, combined with the reinforcement of the British radical tradition by Continental political philosophies, had prompted the formation of a number of socialist societies including the Social Democratic Federation and the Fabian Society. Though the founding of the Independent Labour Party in 1893 provided a new forum for the political aspirations of the working classes, as yet such agitation was too factional and on too small a scale to act as more than an irritant to the established order.

More propitious conditions came with the new century. In the context of stiffening resistance by employers to the militancy of the New Union movement which had from the late 1880s been fostering unionism among the unskilled, a series of legal decisions, culminating in the award of substantial damages to the Taff Vale Railway Company for losses incurred through strike action, undermined the hitherto accepted rights of trade unions, finally convincing the Trades Union Congress of the desirability of forming a political party directly representative of the interests of labour. The collaboration of the TUC with the socialist societies in the creation in 1900 of the Labour Representation Committee, with Ramsay MacDonald as its first secretary, gave the necessary focus and finance to the political wing of the labour movement. In 1906 the new body, now renamed the Labour Party, held 53 parliamentary seats either in their own right or on a joint 'Lib-Lab' ticket. In the long term the advent of Labour as a serious political force was to prove far more significant than the extent of the Liberal majority over the Conservatives.

In the short term, although Labour was influential in securing the passage of several important measures, including in the 1906 Trades Disputes Act the restoration of trade union immunity from damages arising out of strikes, it was the Liberals' programme of social reform which captured the public imagination. The infant Labour party suffered a debilitating blow when in the Osborne judgement the House of Lords declared illegal the financial support of MPs from trade union funds.

With momentum checked on the parliamentary front, working class discontent was temporarily diverted to the industrial arena. Here radical trade unionists could point to the stagnation of wages while prices and profits rose in the pre-war boom. A sharp deterioration in industrial relations was evident in major strikes in 1911–12 in the coal industry, the docks and on the railways. The formation in 1913 of a Triple Alliance between the miners, railwaymen and transport workers for the simultaneous termination of contracts as a prelude to concerted pressure on employers through the government indicated the collision course on which industrial relations were headed, and from which they were temporarily diverted only by the outbreak of war.

The recognition of political and industrial discontent at home, combined with a growing awareness of the pressures of imperial responsibility and German economic competition, promoted a reconsideration of the balance of responsibilities between the state and the individual for social welfare. From the 1880s social investigators such as Charles Booth and Seebohm Rowntree had focussed attention on the crushing poverty in which nearly a third of the population of Britain's cities lived. By the turn of the century it was widely accepted that poverty was closely associated, as both cause and effect, with old age, sickness and unemployment. It was also increasingly evident, as both the majority and minority reports of the Royal Commission on the Poor Laws testified in 1909, that the social and economic system itself was at least as potent a cause of distress as more traditional attributions to such personal failings as drink or idleness.

The Conservatives took some tentative steps towards greater state involvement in welfare. The 1902 Education Act transferred to the county and county borough councils the administration of elementary schools, which were to be supplemented by the first state aided secondary schools. The Unemployed Workmen's Act of 1905, though extremely limited in its practical impact, was the first major legislation since the 1834 Poor Law Amendment Act to grapple with the problem of the able-bodied poor.

With the rejection of the Conservative panacea of protection in 1906, and faced through the rise of the Labour party with the threat of a socialist future, the Liberals initiated a substantial programme of welfare legislation. Local authorities were given powers to provide meals and medical inspection for school children. The 'Children's Charter' of 1908 consolidated much previous child welfare legislation, while a new system of juvenile courts and borstal institutions aimed at reform rather than retribution, detaching the young offender from the adult criminal world. By the first open intervention of the state in the working hours of adult males, an eight hour day was granted to the miners. Through Trade Boards empowered to fix minimum wages, protection was also attempted for the low income groups exploited in such 'sweated' trades as the clothing industry. In 1909 Winston Churchill introduced the labour exchange system, based on the belief of William Beveridge that unemployment was essentially a problem of the organisation of the labour market.

The pension of five shillings a week for those over 70 with a weekly income of less than ten shillings provided by the act of 1908 was long overdue. It nonetheless created the first personal social service in Britain, at the same time freeing many elderly people from the fear and stigma of the poor

COMMUNICATIONS

When Edward VII came to the throne in 1901, 19th century forms of communication between places and people were at their zenith. Railways were the basis of Victorian communications: in addition to facilitating direct contact by enabling people of all classes to travel, they allowed newspapers and periodicals to establish countrywide circulations and provided the means for a swift and reliable postal service. They had also encouraged the development of the electric telegraph: in the 1830s Cooke and Wheatstone had difficulty in selling their invention until the Great Western Railway adopted it as a means of signalling the movement of trains; telegraph wires soon accompanied all railway lines and by the second half of the century the telegram had become an accepted part of business and social communication. Furthermore, the advent of undersea cables enabled messages, also in the code devised by American Samuel Morse, to provide links between continents and contribute substantially to the successful operation of the British Empire. In 1876 Alexander Graham Bell, a Scot who had emigrated to America, patented the first practical telephone. The following year Bell visited Britain, where the telephone proved as popular as in America, and by 1879 the first telephone exchange was in service. By the end of the century telephone engineering had advanced to the stage of making possible direct speech communication with Europe via a cable on the bed of the Channel, and cables were being laid across similar sea barriers elsewhere. (For various economic and technical reasons a telephone cable was not laid to America until 1958, half a century later and nearly a century after the first transatlantic telegraph cable came into use!) With such comprehensive systems in operation it is perhaps surprising that the Edwardian period saw the beginnings of new means of communication that were to revolutionise life in the 20th century.

As the century opened travel was increasing among all classes of people. The 'safety' bicycle, introduced by Rover in 1885, was rapidly superseding the inconvenient 'penny farthing', enabling women as well as men to use this cheap means of transport for work or recreation. It has been said also that the bicycle abolished the 'village idiot' by breaking down the isolation and inbreeding of villages. Among the rich the car was providing greater mobility, while the practical engineering experience gained in the making and servicing of both motor cars and bicycles provided the skill to push the development of the aeroplane forward rapidly in America and France after the Wright brothers' historic flight at the end of 1903. Sea travel, particularly across the Atlantic, also affected large numbers of people: the poor usually crossed once only in the hope of finding in the West the new life and opportunity lacking in Europe; the rich often travelled on the same liners but in accommodation offering the height of luxury and sophistication. One thing all passengers shared, however, was the complete isolation of even the biggest ship once out of sight of land and other vessels.

In 1896 a young Irish Italian arrived in England with an invention that was to end this isolation and change the whole concept of communications. The young man was Guglielmo Marconi who, unable to interest the Italian government, had come to England to sell his system of 'wireless' telegraphy. After patenting his invention, Marconi gave demonstrations to the Post Office (which had just acquired the monopoly of telephone and telegraphic communication in Britain), the Army and the Navy; a public demonstration that captured the interest of the press was given at Toynbee Hall and Marconi became famous overnight. He was able to establish a manufacturing company at Chelmsford and supply equipment to naval and commercial vessels, which not only enabled them to call for

assistance and warn each other of danger, but also established communication on a less serious level allowing Cunard to publish a newspaper on its liners and intership games of chess to be played. When the coronation was postponed because of Edward VII's sudden illness, Cunard was able to cancel celebrations on its liners. In 1901 Marconi managed to transmit the morse code letter 'S' from Poldhu in Cornwall to Newfoundland. Another major advance came in 1904 when Professor Sir Ambrose Fleming invented the thermionic valve which accelerated the development of wireless telegraphy. These advances posed a threat to the established telegraphic cable companies, but one whose effect was not really felt until after the Second World War. Wireless telegraphy received a great public boost in 1910 when the murderer Crippen was caught trying to escape to America; his arrest as he landed was arranged entirely by wireless.

In 1877 the American inventor, Thomas Alva Edison, devised, as a spin-off from his work in telegraphy and telephony, the forerunner of the gramophone. As a talking machine, a novelty for the parlour, it was an immediate success, but although Edison predicted for it a wide range of uses, from speaking books for the blind to recording telephones, he turned his attention to solving the problems of the electric light bulb and designing America's first power station. As a result little progress was made in improving the gramophone's performance until the turn of the century when, in America and Europe, various forms of record and player were designed capable of reproducing sounds with sufficient fidelity to communicate music. In 1905 the famous HMV gramophone appeared. The first serious music to go on record was opera – Caruso, in particular, had the type of voice that reproduced especially well on the equipment available – but because of the brief playing time at first only short songs could be recorded. With Edwardian equipment (the singers had to sing directly into a horn) it was not easy to

record a whole orchestra, but by the end of the period orchestral recording was beginning to develop.

Some of the leading names in the Edwardian gramophone world, such as the Pathé brothers, were also pioneers in motion pictures, which like the gramophone were beginning to develop from a novelty into a form of communication at this time. The first moving pictures in London had been seen in 1896, and proved so popular that the famous Empire Theatre introduced them into its variety bill shortly afterwards.

An early form of communication at a distance was also expanded during the Edwardian period when newspapers began to reach a far larger audience. In 1896 Alfred Harmsworth (later to become Lord Northcliffe) launched a halfpenny morning paper. Northcliffe used all the experience he had acquired as a magazine proprietor to sell his *Daily Mail* because, even then, a halfpenny would not cover the production costs of a daily paper. However, Northcliffe intended the paper to be paid for by advertising, but in order to attract advertisers he needed a very high circulation. He knew he would not find this circulation among existing newspaper readers so he aimed to attract new people to the newspaper-buying habit by providing a lighter approach to the news in contrast to the heavy political theorising of *The Times*. His paper provided news of personalities, short, easily read articles that could be assimilated on commuter trains and trams, and a serial suitable for family reading, for the *Daily Mail* was aimed at women as well as men. The paper was an immediate success, but imitators such as the *Daily Express* (started in 1900) and Northcliffe's own *Daily Mirror* did not really get established until after the First World War. In 1906 *John Bull* was published for the first time at the price of one penny, and in 1913 the price of *The Times* was reduced to twopence.

Fleet Street. Northcliffe created the popular press; papers 'written by office-boys for office-boys'. In 1901 his Daily Mail sold 800,000, The Times 40,000.

Marconi with the spark apparatus he invented to send messages without wires ('wireless' telegraphy). The first transatlantic message was sent in 1901.

The popular press exploited the new working class literacy and greatly reinforced it. Unlike the elitist papers news was presented as short illustrated articles.

law. However, the central achievement of these years was Lloyd George's National Insurance Act of 1911. In return for a weekly contribution from the employee, supplemented by the employer and the state, a degree of protection was given to most working people (though not their dependants) against ill health and, for an experimental few, against unemployment. Though borrowed in principle, like much else in the Liberal programme, from Bismarck's Germany, the national insurance system in practice was a brilliant and very British compromise, linking the support of the state to the continuing encouragement of self-help, and disarming the opposition of such influential pressure groups as the insurance societies, the British Medical Association, the trade unions and employers.

Financing these schemes inevitably created budgetary problems, all the more acute for the simultaneous demand of the Admiralty for an increase in the construction of 'Dreadnoughts' in the face of German naval expansion. The solution proposed by Asquith as Chancellor of the Exchequer and carried through by his successor Lloyd George was the 'People's Budget' of 1909, incorporating substantial increases in income tax and promising a tax on increments in land values. These proposals provoked a veto from the massive Conservative majority in the House of Lords, unprecedented in recent history in relation to a finance bill. The ensuing constitutional crisis, into which the royal prerogative was drawn as Edward VII and then George V were requested to create the peers necessary to give a Liberal majority in the second chamber, dominated the two general elections of 1910. Only after the return of a Liberal

OFF TO WAR

Britain entered the First World War on a bank holiday; without newspapers and with radio in the very early stages of development the dramatic news did not have countrywide impact. Nevertheless, in a London unusually crowded for August with wealthy holidaymakers hurriedly returned from European resorts and Americans on their way to the liners that would take them home, excited crowds waited in Whitehall for Germany's reply to the British ultimatum. Young upper class men, both professional soldiers and those who had trained in school OTCs, were elated at the prospect of putting into practice their military training and gaining promotion.

The response was overwhelming. 'Kitchener's Army' followed the 'contemptible little army' of regulars to the front. Fighting with modern weapons but with less advanced defensive equipment (steel helmets were not issued until later in the war and advancing troops had no cover until the tank was introduced in September 1916) casualties were appalling and reinforcements were soon needed. Although enlistment was voluntary until 1916, from the beginning the government spent money to promote the idea that it was every man's duty to offer himself

for service. Women were also exhorted to join the Voluntary Aid Detachment and to become ambulance drivers, and to release men for the front by taking over essential work in munitions factories, on the land and in the new women's sections of the armed forces.

Most of the suffragettes flung themselves enthusiastically into war work – here was the opportunity they had sought to work alongside men but a few, notably Sylvia Pankhurst, held the socialist view that the war was caused by capitalist ambition; she could see at first hand from work in the East End of London that the absence or loss of the men, combined with a rising cost of living, was bringing great hardship to the women and children.

The Great War was the first for centuries in which British civilians were directly involved. Soon after war started, coastal towns, notably Scarborough, were shelled by German battleships and throughout the war the German air force had access to London and eastern England from bases in Belgium. Britain, on the other hand, was unable to bomb Berlin because of its distance from any allied held territory. Although they were relatively rare, Zeppelin raids loom large among civilian memories of the First World War, because many people rushed

outside to watch. For this reason, and because no protection had been devised for civilians, casualties were high.

As the war that was supposed to be 'over by Christmas' (1914) dragged on into 1917, with great battles for tiny strips of devastated land and horrifying casualties for both sides, the crusading spirit in which Rupert Brooke and some of its early victims went to the front was lost, and the newly conscripted soldiers went off to war with a grim idea of reality; and to the more perceptive the logic of pacifists, whose voices had been lost in the earlier jingoist uproar, began to appeal. Such attitudes were a danger to the continuance of the war, and conscientious objectors and those advocating a negotiated peace received severe treatment. Meanwhile newspapers and periodicals like the *Daily Mail* and Horatio Bottomley's *John Bull* renewed their hysterical demands for reprisals even against naturalised Germans in Britain that had originally encouraged destruction and looting of German-owned shops early in the war.

War weariness pervaded all the combatants, and at home, as the cost of food rose and wages became inadequate to maintain even the low pre-war standard of living, unofficial strikes broke out. These grievances were

swiftly removed with wage increases and supplements by a government that could not afford a breakdown in the supply of ammunition and equipment to its long front lines. Even so, many skilled workers were uneasy as their hard-won privileges were whittled away by the 'dilution' of non-union women and war wounded taking over skilled work.

In April 1917 America entered the war, giving the Allies the advantage of fresh troops who came voluntarily to fight with the same enthusiasm with which our first volunteers had hurled themselves into the fray in 1914. 1918 began with military setbacks – the Germans had learnt new fighting techniques – but at last in November, the Armistice was signed and the troops returned to look for their promised 'land fit for heroes'. Instead they found a country that no longer had work for the able-bodied, let alone for the thousands of war disabled men, and where the 'gallant munitionettes' were turned off without even a week's notice. Back in a world where everyone was fighting for a job, the comradeship of the trenches was remembered strongly, while memories of the boredom, the misery, even the horror of the war, tended to diminish.

A long column of volunteers marches off to war in 1914, ambitious to emulate the smart regulars who march alongside them. A shockingly large number of working class volunteers did not pass their medical: a fact that was to benefit future generations in the form of free school milk and other allocations to poor schoolchildren after the War. Those that did get in found that the war lasted longer than they had been led to expect, while their wives, who had often urged them to join up, suffered unexpected hardships even if they were not widowed. After the recruitment of the adventurous and the unemployed, it became difficult to enlist large numbers like this.

A recruitment poster of the First World War. After the initial excitement, the government had to remind men of their duty, often, as here, implying that those who did not enlist would find themselves in a shameful minority.

government in both these elections, albeit now dependent on the minority parties, did the House of Lords, threatened with the creation of 500 Liberal peers, capitulate. Under the 1911 Parliament Act the Lords were limited to a two year delaying power on all measures other than finance bills.

Through a timely dose of social reform the Liberals succeeded in preserving the essential characteristics of individualism and free enterprise. They contained, without being able to avert, industrial unrest, and they emerged from the constitutional crisis with a qualified victory. They coped less successfully with another challenge to the existing order – the suffragettes.

The status of women had been advanced by the 1882 Married Women's Property Act and the reform of the divorce laws, and by the widening of educational oppor-

tunities and employment prospects. There were signs of a change in attitudes, especially amongst the upper classes, towards the place of women in society. Yet women, particularly middle and working class women, remained one of the principal victims of inequality; wages and working conditions for women were generally deplorable, while the personality and dignity of women below the highest strata of society were stifled by double standards of morality, the assumptive role of the male head of household, and the enduring belief that 'a woman's place is in the home'.

For the generally educated middle class women who sought it, the vote was both a symbol of equality and the means to an end. Lack of progress through the constitutional methods of the National Union of Women's Suffrage Societies led in 1903 to the formation of the Women's

'Gassed', by John Singer Sargent. Germany's use of gas was one of the greatest shocks of the war; other forms of killing had become acceptable to the military mind, but poison gas was regarded as unethical.

The Soldier

If I should die, think only this of me:
That there's some corner of a foreign field
That is for ever England. There shall be
In that rich earth a richer dust concealed;
A dust whom England bore, shaped, made aware,
Gave once her flowers to live, her ways to roam,
A body of England's breathing English air,
Washed by the rivers, blest by suns of home.

And think this heart, all evil shed away,
A pulse in the eternal mind, no less
Gives somewhere back the thoughts by England given;
Her sights and sounds; dreams happy as her day;
And laughter, learnt of friends, and gentleness,
In hearts at peace, under an English heaven.

Rupert Brooke

In marked contrast to the jaunty recruits of 1914, *Return to the Front,* painted by Jack in 1918, reflects the dull misery of soldiers and their womenfolk in the latter part of the war.

Memorials in towns and villages are almost the only reminders of the war. Most, like this one in Hemel Hempstead, are in the form of a cross; in other places village halls were built or recreation grounds laid out.

Social and Political Union which, under Mrs Emmeline Pankhurst and her daughters Christabel and Sylvia, declared open warfare on male privilege. Their willingness to court arrest and accept a prison sentence rather than a fine, and then to go on hunger strike, and the decision of the authorities first to attempt forced feeding and then to apply the 'Cat and Mouse' Act whereby prisoners could be temporarily released on grounds of health only to be subsequently rearrested, attracted much sympathy to the women's cause. Less favourable responses were aroused by the stoning of Parliament and West End shop windows, slashing a famous painting depicting a female subject, arson and the bombing of Ministers' homes. In 1913 Emily Davison presented the cause with a martyr by throwing herself under the King's horse on Derby day.

For the vast majority of women as well as men the outbreak of the First World War drove votes for women from the headlines, and the WSPU dissolved into factions over pacifism. When in 1918 the vote was finally conferred on women over 30 (they did not achieve equality with men until 1928) it was in recognition rather of the vital contribution of women to the war effort than of their pre-war militancy. The expanded employment opportunities during the war for women in offices and transport, munitions factories and auxiliary armed services, combined with the increasing availability of birth control in the inter-war years, for middle class women at least, gave credence at last to talk of an age of the 'new woman', first aired in the 1890s.

Home Rule and Ulster

The threat to order presented by the suffragettes was magnified many times over in the resurrection of the Irish problem. Gladstone's unsuccessful Home Rule Bill of 1886 had served not to pacify the Irish but to divide the Liberal party. Having laboriously climbed back to office the Liberals ironically found themselves after the two elections of 1910 perilously dependent on the support of the 82 Irish Nationalist MPs. Their price was a new Home Rule Bill, a measure bound to raise fierce opposition in Commons, Lords and the country.

Though by mid 1913 the bill awaited only the royal signature, the virulent opposition of the Ulster Protestants and their Conservative allies at Westminster led by Sir Edward Carson, the formation of an Ulster Provisional Government and Volunteer Force to resist enforcement and dissent in the armed forces obliged Asquith to propose the exclusion of Ulster from Home Rule for an initial six years. The rejection of this compromise by the Unionists, fortified by gun-running and the near farcical Curragh 'mutiny'

A peaceful suffragette demonstration, 1912. Frustration drove the movement to window-breaking and arson, which lost them much support. Women over 30 were enfranchised in 1918 in recognition of their sterling performance in the war.

SHOPS AND BRANDS

In the brief reign of Edward VII shopping was beginning to change from the leisured occupation of the rich to a part of the way of life of all classes. The famous department stores were at their peak, not only in London where the most flamboyant of them all – Selfridges – was opened in 1909, but in towns of all sizes from Kendall Milne in Manchester to Medhursts in Bromley (in a shop on the site of which H. G. Wells had been born), from John Barnes, the newest suburban one, to Bainbridges, long established in Newcastle.

Until The Great War carried away all the young men, department stores large and small were a world of Mr Kips. The customer alighting from her carriage would be met by the principal shop walker, asked which department she required, then escorted by a lowlier shop walker to the department and offered a chair; then summoned would be female if the object of her shopping were intimate – corsets or underwear. Male or female, the assistants were usually treated very like servants in a large house: they worked long hours (especially Saturdays) and lived over the shop under the care and supervision of a housekeeper. Gordon Selfridge from the Marshall Field Store in Chicago was appalled by all this deference, and when he opened his 130-department Oxford Street store the emphasis was on attracting the ordinary woman by means of good window display, then allowing her to look around freely (his slogan was 'Why not spend a day at Selfridges').

It must have been even more daunting to buy clothes at a 'Court' dressmakers, but one of them, 'Lucille' (appropriately the sister of Elinor Glyn) claims to have introduced the first light and filmy underwear which ultimately replaced the formidable garments still worn at the beginning of the century. Another 20th-century fashion, for knitted outer clothes, arose when the Jersey Lily (Lily Langtry) discovered the flattery of 'jersey'. One of the first chains of clothing shops – the Scotch Wool & Hosiery Stores – came into being as a result of this fashion; starting in Greenock in 1881 selling knitting wool, their shops by 1910 totalled 200. The firm of William Hollis claims the first fabric to be sold under a registered name, with 'Viyella', a mixture of short staple wool and cotton, first made in 1894.

Shoe manufacture in the later 19th century benefited from the introduction of a heavy variant of the sewing machine, but there was still a wide gap between the quality of the made-to-measure shoes of the upper classes and the factory-made boots of the poor. This gap narrowed as shoe shop chains began to grow, bringing working class customers of shops like Freeman, Hardy & Willis and Tyler Brothers the benefits of competition in the form of reduced prices and better quality. But the area where the 'multiples' and mass production gave the greatest all round benefit was food. In the mid 19th century a society whose aims were to solve social problems by scientific and technological means was concentrating its efforts upon improving the food of

Selfridges' imposing shop front must have been even more impressive in 1909 when Oxford Street comprised little shops like the one next door.

Edwardian Marks & Spencers were just beginning their rise to fame, but still showed evidence of their penny bazaar origins and were sited in the poorer parts of towns.

the poor. The Food Committee of The Society for the Encouragement of Arts, Commerce & Manufactures found that many workers were only able to buy their food in squalid shops and street markets where it was usually stale, dirty and often poisonously adulterated. Co-ops helped combat the problem where workers were drawn together in one industry, but in other heavily populated areas a new type of working class food shop, selling very limited ranges at low prices by means of bulk buying and production, began to succeed and branch out. The Home & Colonial Stores originally specialised in tea, and Maypole Dairies in butter (and later margarine), while Tommy Lipton had made a fortune by the turn of the century selling cheap bacon and ham. (The Kaiser, who referred sarcastically to Lipton when he spoke of his Uncle King Edward going sailing with his grocer, was not even accurate, for Liptons were grocers to the working man, not to Royalty who were supplied by firms like Jacksons or Fortnum & Mason). By the Edwardian period most urban areas had their representative of one or more of the 'multiples'. With hundreds of branches and money invested in bacon processing plants and creameries these firms could not afford bad publicity so their goods, although cheap, tended to be of high purity. Packaged food was only just coming in and one of the features of these shops was the advertising provided by having assistants (like the department stores, predominantly male) weighing up tea or 'knocking up' butter in the window. Another feature of shops that many people can remember was the Lamson

cash system: 'cable-cars' that carried money to the cashier esconced in a lofty desk, which would come whizzing back with receipt and change, to the delight of any child, or the pneumatic tube brought out by the same company in 1900.

In the Edwardian period, just as today, manufacturers produced goods to be sold under their own brand names and under the names of department stores and chains, but in advertising earlier in the century greater stress was laid upon the purity of the product and the social and hygienic conditions under which it was manufactured: pictures of Bournville and Port Sunlight naturally impressed a public used to products manufactured in squalor by an ill-housed workforce.

Dairies, like department stores, reached a high point in Edward's reign, but unlike them are now almost a memory. The London dairies where the cows were kept almost in the shop had been outlawed after an epidemic of Rinderpest in the 1860s, and thereafter the townsman's milk came from cows living in fields as much as a 200 mile train journey away. A dairy now was a clean, inviting marble and tile palace advertising its presence by its cool dairy smell and the china cows and dairymaids posing coyly in the window; not only could you buy a glass of milk for a penny, but under the blue banner of the Express Dairy or the orange of the 'UD' you could have a piece of cake or a light snack with it. These two companies originated with George Barham (later Sir George), whose father grazed cows where the Ritz Hotel now stands.

Dairy windows were decorated with china dairymaids, cows, storks or swans, while blocks of butter and pails of milk stood on marble slabs in the cool interior.

The chemist's shop from Stockton-on-Tees, reconstructed at Beamish Museum, Durham, illustrates the image of solid reliability desired by all types of shops at the turn of the century, with glowing mahogany counters, gleaming brass scales and bottles.

Dairy cows were kept in London parks and children were bought a glass of milk straight from the cow as a treat. It must have been quite a feat to milk a cow into a bottle like this.

The Christmas display of a prosperous butcher in Godalming. Butcher's shops had large sash windows to allow good air circulation.

Dairy companies had show farms in the countryside around London although some of their dairy produce came from further afield. This big shop had a tea room where respectable ladies could eat unescorted as well as a smoking room where men and women could take tea. The roundsmen did not deliver bottled milk, but poured it into the customer's jug from a tap at the bottom of the churn.

when British officers in the province announced their willingness to resign rather than put down a rebellion, precipitated a crisis. Though the conciliation of George V secured a conference of all interested parties in the summer of 1914, this was frustrated by the outbreak of the First World War.

By this time the Nationalists were equipping themselves with arms in imitation of the Volunteers. The abortive Dublin rising of 1916 and its uncompromising suppression by the British not only encouraged German hopes of dividing the United Kingdom from within but bequeathed the Irish problem to the post-war period in a yet more embittered form, which the creation of the Irish Free State in 1921 could hardly resolve.

Britain at war

The war that Britain entered on 4 August 1914 was, despite a naive declaration of 'business as usual' at the outset, the first to require the virtually total commitment of the nation's resources to the war effort. In the process most of the features making for change in Edwardian Britain were sharply accelerated. The first mechanised war made new demands on science and technology. The conscription of one in three adult males, and the absorption of many, including women, into the civilian war effort, transformed the labour market. The creation of a war economy necessitated unprecedented state intervention in the management of that economy, with the active assistance of the trade unions.

Rationing, the licensing of alcohol and the advent of the queue changed life styles, while increased taxes on incomes and profits altered the relations between social classes, albeit largely by a process of levelling down. Trade was disrupted, industrial production distorted and investments liquidated. The Versailles settlement redrew not only the political but also the economic map of Europe.

Three quarters of a million Britons died on active service; over one and a half million were wounded. By the Armistice on 11 November 1918 the securities and certainties of Victorian Britain, which though weakened by doubt and questioning largely survived the Edwardian period, had been transformed into the uncertainties and insecurities of the 20th century. Paradoxically the Edwardian years were to be seen, through a hindsight coloured by the cataclysm of war and the trauma of depression, as a golden age of peace and harmony.

The Easter rebellion, Dublin, 1916. British soldiers confront the Irish rebels across a barricade. 450 rebels and 103 soldiers died, and some of the finest streets of Dublin were destroyed.

EVENTS AND PERSONALITIES

Edward VII (1901-1910) did not come to the throne until the age of 59. He had not been on the best of terms with his mother — who believed that her husband's death had been caused in part by worry over Edward's riotous living — and had received little training from her in constitutional matters. He proved a competent and respected king, however, and was mourned on his death in May 1910.

1901   Edward VII ascends to the throne

The Australian Commonwealth is inaugurated

In South Africa Kitchener introduces a 'scorched earth' policy, blockhouses and concentration camps

Under the Taff Vale court decision trade unions are held liable for financial losses incurred as a result of strikes

Marconi transmits the first transatlantic wireless message from Cornwall

1902   Arthur Balfour succeeds Lord Salisbury as Conservative Prime Minister

The Education Act replaces local school boards with county administration and extends state aid to secondary education for the first time

The Peace of Vereeniging brings the Boer War to an end

An Anglo-Japanese defence alliance is signed, ending Britain's 'splendid isolation'

1903   Joseph Chamberlain resigns from the Cabinet to advocate tariff reform and imperial preference

The Women's Social and Political Union is founded by Emmeline Pankhurst to intensify the campaign for women's suffrage

The Irish Land Purchase Act gives state aids for tenants to purchase land

There is controversy over importation of Chinese coolie 'slave' labour into the Rand mines in South Africa

The first motor taxi appears in London

1904   The Licensing Act introduces a levy to establish a compensation fund for the withdrawal of licences

The Workers' Education Authority is established. Franco-British colonial agreements launch *Entente Cordiale*

1905   The partition of Bengal leads to a nationalist terrorist campaign until partition is revoked in 1911

The Unemployed Workmen's Act requires the establishment of Distress Committees in substantial towns

The Aliens Act attempts regulation of immigration (predominantly Jewish from Eastern Europe)

In the December election Liberals win 377 seats to Conservatives 132, Irish Nationalists 83, Labour Representation Committee (soon renamed as the Labour Party) 53 and Liberal Unionists 25

Sir Henry Campbell-Bannerman becomes Prime Minister

John Burns is the first working man to enter the Cabinet

1906   The Trade Disputes Act reverses the Taff Vale decision, leaving trade unions immune from prosecution for damages

The Merchant Shipping Act regulates conditions of service and imposes British pilots and standards on foreign ships using British ports

George V (1910-36). He had received a good grounding in state matters from his father Edward VII, but nevertheless had a difficult first year on the throne as a result of the Parliamentary dispute between the Lords and the Commons. He became a well-loved king, and the enthusiastic Jubilee celebrations of 1935 caused him to remark, 'I had no idea I was so popular'.

The school meals service is introduced

The first Census of Production is taken

Baden Powell's 'Scouting for Boys' is published

Colonial self-government is granted to South Africa

HMS Dreadnought is launched as part of a naval building drive

1907 The Triple Entente is completed by Anglo-Russian Convention

School medical inspection is introduced

1908 Herbert Asquith succeeds Campbell-Bannerman as Liberal Prime Minister

The Children's Act codifies previous legislation, and Borstals and juvenile courts are established

A non-contributory Old Age Pension of 5/- a week is introduced for the over 70s

1909 The Trade Boards Act legislates for minimum wages in 'sweated' trades

An eight hour day is introduced by law for miners

A national system of Labour Exchanges is established

A House of Lords judgement in the Osborne case declares trade unions' financial support for MPs illegal

Suffragettes embark on a hunger strike

The Royal Commission on the Poor Laws produces Majority and Minority Reports

Lloyd George introduces the 'People's Budget' with provision for supertax and the promise of duties on land values. This is rejected by the House of Lords, provoking a constitutional crisis

1910 George V ascends to the throne

Bonar Law succeeds Balfour as Conservative leader

In the January election the Liberals retain office with 275 seats, against 273 Conservative Unionists, 82 Irish Nationalists and 40 Labour. In the December election, following constitutional deadlock, Liberals and Unionists both secure 272 seats, the Liberals retaining office with the support of Labour and Irish Nationalists

Troops fire on Welsh coal strikers at Tonypandy

Selfridge's department store opens in London

1911 Under threat of the creation of large numbers of Liberal peers, the House of Lords accepts the Parliament Bill depriving Lords of their powers of veto over finance bills, limiting them to two years' delay in other matters, and providing for five-yearly Parliaments

The payment of MPs is introduced at the rate of £400 a year

The National Insurance Act provides for insurance of workers against sickness and of selected trades against unemployment, through contributions from employees, employers and the state

The Shops Act regulates working hours in retailing

There are strikes by seamen, firemen, dockers and railwaymen

The anarchist 'Peter the Painter' is involved in the siege of Sidney Street

Britain prepares for war during the Agadir crisis between France and Germany

1912 Liberals introduce the third Irish Home Rule Bill (passed twice in the Commons and rejected twice in the Lords before being put into abeyance in 1914 on the outbreak of war)

Sir Edward Carson founds the Ulster Volunteers to resist Home Rule by force if necessary

The miners and London's dockers strike

1500 lives are lost when the Titanic sinks after collision with an iceberg

Captain Scott is beaten to the South Pole by the Norwegian Amundsen

1913 The 'Cat and Mouse' Act is passed to out-manoeuvre suffragette hunger strikers. Emily Davison throws herself under the King's horse at the Derby

1914 Miners, railwaymen and transport workers form a Triple Alliance for supportive action in future disputes

The Church in Wales is disestablished

British officers at the Curragh 'mutiny' by declaring their unwillingness to enforce a Home Rule settlement in Ireland

Germany invades Belgium and on August 4 Britain declares war. Though the Defence of the Realm Act grants the government wide powers, Liberals express faith in 'business as usual'. A British Expeditionary Force is despatched to the Continent. British forces retreat from Mons, but German advance is checked at the Marne, followed by the first battle of Ypres

1915 Government and the trade unions reach agreement over dilution of labour, embodied in the Munitions of War Act, which also provides for compulsory arbitration of disputes, government control of private munitions firms and the construction of state munitions factories

The McKenna Duties impose tariffs on non-essential imports

Licensing hours are introduced

There are scandals over shortages of sandbags and shells

Conservative and Labour leaders take office in a coalition government under Asquith, but Ramsay MacDonald remains in opposition to the war

Lloyd George is appointed Minister of Munitions

The Dardanelles campaign is launched with landings at Gallipoli and the *Lusitania* is sunk by German submarines

Gas is used by the Germans at the second battle of Ypres.

General Haig replaces Sir John French as British Commander

1916 Conscription is introduced to supplement voluntary enlistment. Excess Profits Duty is imposed as the first tax on business, to counter profiteering

The Clyde Workers' Committee of shop stewards co-ordinates disputes in Glasgow

There is an indecisive naval battle at Jutland. The Germans attack Verdun and the British attack on the Somme in a 4½ month 'war of attrition' in which 400,000 British soldiers die. The Secretary for War, Lord Kitchener, is lost at sea

The Easter Rising in Dublin proclaims a republic before being overwhelmed by British forces and the ringleaders shot

In December Lloyd George, with Conservative support, ousts Asquith as Prime Minister, forming a streamlined War Cabinet and Ministries of Labour, Food, Shipping, Information and Reconstruction, and bringing leading businessmen into government

1917 A Coal Controller is appointed to take charge of the coal industry. Convoy system is instituted to combat submarine warfare. Rationing is introduced. Imperial War Cabinet of Dominion Prime Ministers is formed. British stage offensives at Ypres and Passchendaele. United States enters the war. Russian Revolution. Foreign Secretary Balfour declares Britain's support for the creation of a Jewish homeland in Palestine. George V responds to anti-German feeling by adopting the surname Windsor

1918 The Germans attack at Arras but are forced to retreat after the British counter-attack with tanks. The second battle of the Marne takes place. The Armistice comes into force on November 11

Fisher's Education Act makes education compulsory to 14, with part-time provision to 18. The Labour Party adopts a new constitution including commitment to public ownership. There are strikes by police, munitions workers and railwaymen. The Representation of the People Act extends the franchise to all men over 21 except peers, lunatics and felons and to women over 30

The 'Coupon' election returns Lloyd George's Coalition

A poster satirising the 'Cat & Mouse' Act, which was passed in 1913 with the ostensibly well-meant intention of freeing suffragettes from prison when they were near death as a result of hunger strike and re-arresting them when they had recovered — or when it was convenient to do so.

The Inter-War Years

The First World War left Britain with problems.
A prolonged slump preceded the General Strike of 1926, and by 1930
nearly three million were out of work. The traditional
industries of the north declined, but for others there was prosperity. Mass production
reduced the price of motor cars and ownership increased dramatically;
holiday resorts flourished, and the cinema and radio became part of
everyday life. But hopes of perpetual world peace foundered
with the rise of the European dictators in the 1930s and the prospect
of war loomed once more on the horizon.

The uneasy peace between the two world wars was for Britain a period of paradox. It was ironic that victory in the Great War should be followed by the first stages in the fragmentation of empire, with the creation of the Irish Free State in 1922 and the first steps towards Indian independence in 1935; ironic too that the prelude to Britain's 'finest hour' should witness her failure to make a stand against international aggression, culminating in the appeasement of Hitler's ambitions in central Europe by the Munich agreement.

In a Europe increasingly polarised between extremes of Right and Left, Britain was notable for the failure of either to establish a significant hold, despite the formation of the Communist Party of Great Britain in 1920 and of the British Union of Fascists in 1932. (It was wryly appropriate that the leader of the latter, Sir Oswald Mosley, should be a baronet and former Conservative who had reached Cabinet rank in the Labour party.) The vacuum left by the decline of the Liberal Party, which never regained office after the fall of Lloyd George's coalition in 1922, was filled by the alternation of the Conservatives, in power in their own name for most of the 1920s and as the dominant partner in the National government in the 1930s, and Labour governments in 1924 and 1929–31 whose minority status prohibited the implementation of the commitment to public ownership in the party's 1918 constitution.

There was irony too in that it was the Conservative leader, Stanley Baldwin, who despite his image as the representative of national unity had to preside over the General Strike and the abdication of Edward VIII, while the pioneer Labour leader, Ramsay MacDonald, was disowned by his party for his acceptance of the premiership in the National government of 1931 (an administration which, incidentally, belied its name by the exclusion of the two indisputably greatest national leaders of the early 20th century, Lloyd George and

Winston Churchill). Paradoxically Labour's Philip Snowden proved the most orthodox Chancellor of the Exchequer of the period, while it was left to the National government to dispense with the pillars of orthodoxy, the gold standard and free trade.

However, the most profound paradox of these years lay in the coexistence of what historian A.J.P. Taylor has described as a million more cars alongside a million more unemployed. On the one hand there was the Britain of depression and slump, of declining exports and the collapse of those industries on which her industrial revolution had been so triumphantly based, the Britain of mass unemployment and hunger marches. On the other hand was a Britain of rising living standards and improved rates of economic growth, of new industries and the spread of luxuries and semi-luxuries beyond the narrow confines of the rich. In

A 1937 Alvis, a sports car catering for a quality market. The growth of the car industry reflected many of the positive aspects of inter-war Britain, from new technology and mass production methods to increased flexibility in transport and communication; it epitomised middle class affluence and new fashions, and symbolised the shift of industry towards the more prosperous south and Midlands.

The Odeon, Leicester Square: a typical temple of the great new medium of the masses, the cinema. The 'talkies' provided a diversion which even those on the dole could afford, and unlike football they were enjoyed equally by men and women. With Saturday morning shows for children, the whole family was for the first time provided with entertainment, both escapist and educational.

place of the extreme divisions of social class in Edwardian society came the geographical distinction between the distressed areas of the north of England and South Wales and the growth areas of the Midlands and the south of England; in short, a new version of Disraeli's 'two nations'.

An uneasy peace

Despite the uncertainties of the period from the armistice on 11 November 1918 until and beyond the signing of the peace seven months later, the dismantling of the machinery of war proceeded rapidly, even precipitately. Four million men were demobilised in less than a year. The statutory powers of the war government expired in 1919, rationing and price controls were abolished by the end of 1920. War surplus and national factories were sold and the coal industry and railways returned to private ownership. By 1921 most

wartime ministries and committees had been disbanded. Thus little time was lost in initiating the restoration of pre-war conditions seen by many as the key to prosperity.

However, there were early signs that the war had both exacerbated some of the less stable features of Edwardian Britain and brought about irreversible changes. During demobilisation there were demonstrations and even riots among the armed forces. In 1919 there were strikes or the threat of strikes from miners, railwaymen and even the police, while the streets of Glasgow saw tanks and baton charges. In May 1920 the threat of a general strike against the sending of arms to opponents of the revolutionary regime in Russia indicated the link between industrial and political discontent.

Lloyd George's coalition triumphed at the 'Coupon' election of 1918 under the twin slogans of 'squeezing the

OLD AND NEW INDUSTRY

Even before the turn of the century the industries on which Britain's status as 'workshop of the world' had been built in the mid 19th century – coal, cotton textiles, iron and steel, engineering and shipbuilding – were experiencing slowing growth, declining productivity and lagging technology in the face of increasing international competition. During the Great War, though the productive capacity of the heavy industries was expanded to meet the demand for munitions, their labour forces were diluted as a result of the enlistment of skilled men, out-of-date equipment was retained rather than replaced, export markets were severely restricted, and costs and prices inflated.

Optimism inspired by replacement demand in the post-war boom was dashed when, with the onset of a recession in 1920, the staple industries were exposed harshly and abruptly to the full implications of the loss of their traditional markets to Japanese and American competition, to the growing self-sufficiency of countries as diverse as India in textiles and the Dominions in metal goods, and to the advent of increasingly effective substitutes such as electricity, oil and artificial fibres. In the early 1920s these problems were compounded by the general sluggishness of world trade, and from 1925 by the over-pricing of British products as a result of the overvaluation of the pound on Britain's return to the gold standard. In some of Britain's basic industries output and exports in the 1920s failed to regain 1913 levels. In industries where pre-war production was exceeded it still fell well short of capacity, as in steel where actual output in 1929 at 10 million tons contrasted with a potential of 12 million.

From 1929–32 the export industries bore the brunt of the slump triggered by the Wall Street Crash, and of the rash of tariffs by which each nation in turn

sought to isolate itself from depression and unemployment transmitted through the world economy. Between 1924–30 the output of cotton piece goods fell by 75 per cent. In 1931 Britain's steel production dropped to five million tons, while in 1933 the shipbuilding industry launched a mere seven per cent of its 1913 tonnage. Because of their traditional location near the coalfields, the heavy unemployment experienced by the depressed export industries was regionally concentrated in Scotland, the north of England and South Wales.

It was in this context that the impossibility of reviving the pre-war strength of the staple industries was reluctantly and belatedly recognised by government and industries alike through a programme of rationalisation by which the excess capacity and labour represented by the less efficient units of production was curtailed. During the 1930s National Shipbuilder's Security Ltd was responsible for scrapping a million tons of shipbuilding capacity, while the Lancashire Cotton Corporation similarly eliminated a large number of spindles. In many industries the remaining market was shared out amongst surviving producers, with varying degrees of success, through defensive mergers and combinations. In the coal industry cartels and quotas established by legislation in 1930, later reinforced by selling agencies, a Coal Commission with powers to facilitate mergers, and the long-advocated nationalisation of mineral royalties. The iron and steel industry, sheltered by a 50 per cent tariff on imports, was able to negotiate entry into the powerful European Steel Cartel. Shipbuilding received government subsidies for the *Queen Mary* and for tramp shipping. However, it was not until the commencement of substantial rearmament in 1936 that any general relief was brought to the basic industries and distressed areas

or to their unemployed workers.

Before the First World War Britain was slow in developing industries based on new technology. In the production of motor vehicles the United States and France took the lead, while Germany dominated the European market in electrical engineering and industrial chemicals. After 1914 the military significance of these industries resulted in their promotion, along with aircraft and radio, new materials such as aluminium, plastics and rubber, and new processes from welding to electrolysis and electro-plating. Government support continued in the 1920s with the extension of wartime import duties to protect stategic new products. In 1926 the government underwrote the merger of three chemical companies with armaments interests to form ICI. Imperial Airways, established in 1921, received a state subsidy, while the creation of the Central Electricity Generating Board in 1926 provided an administrative model for subsequent acts of nationalisation.

Though comparing favourably with the stagnation or decline of the staples, the growth of new industries in the 1920s was restrained by high interest rates imposed to support the pound on the gold standard, while commitment to the export sector discouraged substantial transfers of resources away from established industries. However, by the end of the decade many new industries, and especially large-scale firms such as ICI in chemicals or Courtaulds in artificial fibres, were poised on the brink of a breakthrough into mass production.

Unlike the staples, the new industries were in general more dependent on consumer than capital demand, and on the home market rather than exports. As a result they were less affected by the depression of the international economy after 1929, and more responsive to the buoyancy of real incomes in the domestic economy as prices, especially

of foodstuffs and raw materials fell. Demand for many new products, such as rayon clothing and electrical appliances, benefited from their very novelty, while their command of the home market was reinforced by a general tariff from 1932 and by the spread of hire purchase. The new industries were able to reinvest the profits of the past decade in expanded production at falling costs through flow-production techniques; between 1930–4, for instance, the price of a vacuum cleaner fell from £14 to £8 as output multiplied tenfold. The average ex-factory value of a car dropped from £259 in 1924 to £130 in 1935 as Austin, Morris and Ford came to dominate the market.

Thus for the new industries recession was brief and mild and recovery early and pronounced. Because of the inter-dependence of their technology an advance in one industry had innovative effects on others. In particular the new industries were linked by their dependence on electricity, the output of which expanded sevenfold and the number of consumers tenfold between 1920–38 while the price per unit was halved, largely consequent on the construction of 4,000 miles of National Grid transmission lines.

Freed of dependence on coal, the new industries gravitated away from the depressed areas to concentrate on the more prosperous markets of London, the south east and the south Midlands, where their growth reinforced and was reinforced by the building boom and the expansion of the service sector in the 1930s. Thus the new industries made a major contribution to raising Britain's rate of economic growth between the wars; their geographical concentration and their capital rather than labour-intensive nature, however, limited their impact on the unemployment problem, and only after 1945 did they make a substantial contribution to exports.

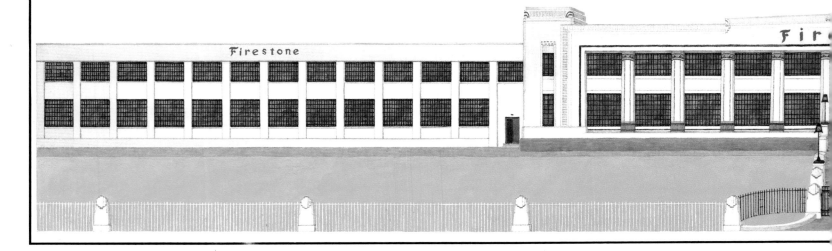

German lemon until the pips squeaked' and the creation of 'a fit country for heroes to live in'. The former was embodied in the massive reparations exacted from Germany at the Versailles settlement, with disastrous effect on the future stability of the European economic system as predicted by the young economist John Maynard Keynes. A guarded beginning was also made to the fulfilment of the latter pledge. In recognition of the war effort the vote was extended for the first time to all adult males and to women over 30 (they had to wait ten years for equality with men). The 1918 Education Act laid the foundations for the reorganisation of elementary and secondary education, increased the number of free secondary school places and abolished exemption from school-leaving before 14 (though the promise of an early increase to 15 was not redeemed until 1944). The 1919 Housing Act introduced for the first time a

" WHAT'S THE DISTURBANCE IN THE MARKET-PLACE?"
"IT'S A MASS MEETING OF THE WOMEN WHO'VE CHANGED THEIR MINDS SINCE THIS MORNING AND WANT TO ALTER THEIR VOTING-PAPERS."

Punch, ever famous for its satirical and often bitter comment on current political scenes, had a field day with the women's suffrage movement.

Coming from the Mill, by the Salford artist L. S. Lowry, 1930. He depicts the drab realities of life in the Lancashire cotton towns whose 19th century buildings and technology were unaffected by the 'brave new world' of the '30s.

Slough was the site for one of the earliest trading estates. It attracted light engineering and new industries freed from the coalfields by the coming of electricity and road transport to the markets of the south.

1938 Panther with Watsonian sidecar: relative comfort and cheaper than a car.

1936 Austin Ruby. Austin became the second largest of British car-makers.

Anglia and Prefect production at Ford's Dagenham plant in 1939, incorporating Anglo-American capital and technology in Britain's largest car factory.

The Firestone factory complex on the Great West Road, London. Built in 1928 and decorated with 'Egyptian' ceramic motifs, it expressed the proud spirit of modern industry. Tragically, it was destroyed in 1980 only days before it was to receive national protection.

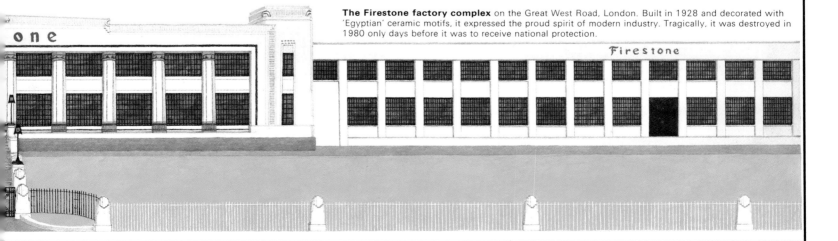

Firestone

state subsidy for local authority housebuilding. Out-of-Work Donations were provided to ease the lot of both ex-servicemen and civilians through any transitional unemployment. The Ministries of Labour and Pensions had both survived the dismantling of the war economy, and to these were added the Ministries of Health and Transport.

Until mid 1920 an ordered transition from war to peace was aided by a restocking boom, which kept demand and employment high (albeit at the cost of continuing the inflation which had doubled prices during the war) and further expansion of the heavy industries, already swollen by the artificial requirements of munitions production well beyond any realistic assessment of normal peacetime demand. In April 1920 the satisfaction of pent-up demand, the inherent instability of the economies of central Europe, and the determination of the British government to bring inflation under control by the restriction of money and credit brought about a sharp swing from boom to slump. Prices and wages fell, output and exports declined, investment contracted, industrial relations deteriorated and unemployment leapt to over two million. The government responded in the conventional manner, cutting expenditure, especially on defence and welfare, in its determination to balance the budget.

Henceforth, with increasing evidence that fundamental aspects of economy and society had been changed for ever, the war ceased to be regarded as an unfortunate interruption to the continuance of progress on pre-war lines and became, with an equally dangerous oversimplification of the realities of world change, the scapegoat for all the ills of the nation, from economic impoverishment through lost exports to political impoverishment through a 'lost generation' of leaders.

Coal and Gold

The war had an ambivalent effect on industrial relations. Though the great majority of trade union leaders agreed to suspend such peacetime practices as job demarcations

David Lloyd George, the 'Welsh wizard', inspiring a Scottish audience in 1925. He became Prime Minister in 1916 by splitting the Liberal party, thus incidentally causing its decline. In office until 1922, he was 'the man who won the War' and created the system of cabinet and departmental ministries. He was the last Liberal Prime Minister; after some years in the wilderness he led them from 1926 to 1931, without success.

AGRICULTURE 1900–1939

One aspect of the British economy that derived benefit from the Great War was agriculture. Farmers were protected against imports by the efficiency of the German submarine campaign while, after 1917, home production was encouraged by price incentives offered by the State. Government support of agriculture was a welcome novelty and many urged the retention of the policy in peacetime.

By 1921, however, the post-war boom had collapsed and world prices fell sharply. The government, fearful that the cost of support would become an increasing liability, revoked its wartime legislation. Once again the agricultural industry stood isolated and had to face the renewed challenge posed by Britain's traditional commitment to free trade. The volume of imports grew rapidly in the 1920s, reflecting a rise in world wheat production, the development of chilling – enabling Argentina to export good quality meat which undercut the High Street butcher – the expansion of New Zealand's trade in mutton and dairy produce and Denmark's trade in bacon and dairy produce. Yet, in spite of what virtually amounted to dumping of surplus produce, successive governments held fast to the philosophy that buying in the cheapest market was of the greatest advantage to the economy.

The problem of survival in a truly free market might have been less daunting had many farmers not been crippled by high debts. Before 1914 an increasing number of landowners, embittered by the imposition of death duties and other land taxes, had started to sell all or part of their estates. This process accelerated between 1918 and 1921, during which period the *Estates Gazette* estimated that as much as a quarter of England changed hands. Farmers, in particular, seized the opportunity to buy out their tenancies at a time when agricultural prospects were bright. But after 1921 falling prices and higher labour costs made mortgage repayments difficult and by the end of the decade a substantial number of farms had passed into bank ownership.

The obvious response to foreign imports was to switch production into commodities – milk, eggs, fresh fruit and vegetables – which enjoyed a naturally sheltered market. Those who could invested in more intensive methods of production, and the late 1920s saw the beginnings of factory farming with the introduction of fattening houses for pigs ('pig palaces') and battery henhouses. For farmers with less foresight, however, or whose borrowing capacity was stretched to its limit, the only alternative seemed to be to cut costs, the outcome of which in the 1920s was undercapitalisation and lowered standards of cultivation. As confidence in the future of the industry waned, more and more workers left the land. But this, instead of encouraging an advance in mechanisation as might have been expected, led to an increasing proportion of the arable acreage being returned to grass, which could be grazed rather than harvested by machine. Indeed this decade was one of the bleakest for the agricultural engineering industry.

Yet worse was to come: in 1929 the collapse of the US stock market precipitated world-wide economic recession. Prices fell dramatically: in 1931 world wheat prices stood at half their 1929 level – a situation created not merely by the financial crisis but also by the more alarming long-term trend for grain production to pull ahead of consumption. Most European countries reacted to this by becoming highly protectionist and when this proved insufficient by inducing new and sweeping measures of State control. Even Britain was forced to introduce a general tariff in 1932, although certain important food-stuffs were exempted.

Deciding the policy on Empire goods, the majority of which were agricultural, was a major problem; the course adopted was to admit these goods free of duty and to impose duties on agricultural products imported from other countries. This change of policy led to a fundamental shift in the pattern of world trade. But it did little to help farmers, since the quantity of imports actually increased slightly over the course of the decade. Such was the plight of British agriculture that from 1931 the government brought in legislation specifically to assist the industry. This involved the introduction of subsidies, various import restrictions, and the setting up of Marketing Boards. Boards were established for milk, pigs, potatoes and hops, but their development was somewhat diverse. The most important were the Milk Marketing Boards, especially those established for England and Wales. The Boards acted as sole buyer and seller of milk and prevented the price of milk sold for butter and cheese from undercutting the price of milk sold liquid. A method of equalisation between producers was also introduced and this, along with the certainty of a market and a regular monthly cheque, encouraged a considerable increase in dairying: so much so that between 1933 and 1938 the volume of milk sold increased by 30 per cent.

The National Mark Scheme that had been started in 1928 was a more direct attempt to combat foreign competition. British goods frequently sold at a disadvantage because they were unpacked and ungraded and often of varying quality, whereas imported foods were packed to suit the requirements of wholesalers and graded to uniform standards, thus meeting the growing consumer preference for better quality, packaged and branded foods. The government response was to give the Ministry of Agriculture power to assign quality grades for British produce and to licence sellers to use the National Mark on graded commodities.

The legislation of the 1920s and 1930s did not constitute a carefully thought out policy for British agriculture; it was a response to crisis. Nonetheless the 1930s saw the beginnings of State control that was extended during and after the Second World War. The measures did help farmers through the worst times, although by 1935 the world economy was reviving and much of the subsequent improvement in the fortunes of the industry can be attributed to the general price recovery. Yet deep-seated problems remained – not least those posed by our special relationship with the Empire – and these were to provide a teasing legacy for the future.

One disturbing feature which affected farming during the inter-war years came to be realised towards the end of the period, largely as a result of the pioneer work of Professor Sir Dudley L. Stamp who organised the First Land Utilisation Survey of Great Britain during the 1930s. This pointed out the large amount of good agricultural and market gardening land which was being lost each year as a result of housing and industrial development of green field sites. In the 1930s this was running at a rate of 20–25,000 hectares each year. Great areas of land disappeared under the red tide of suburbia, especially to the north west of London and south of Manchester. The sum total of the agricultural land consumed by the four and a half million garden city houses and the thousands of single storey model factories of the inter-war period inevitably reduced the potential output of home produced food by a substantial amount.

Sheep-washing in the river Teify at Cenarth, Carmarthenshire, 1933. Once the first sheep crosses the river, guided by the men in the coracles, the others follow. The coracles were otherwise used for salmon fishing. In an age where mechanisation was technically feasible, undercapitalisation meant a shaky outlook for agriculture and a great deal of arable land was given over to grazing, which at least meant stability for communities such as this.

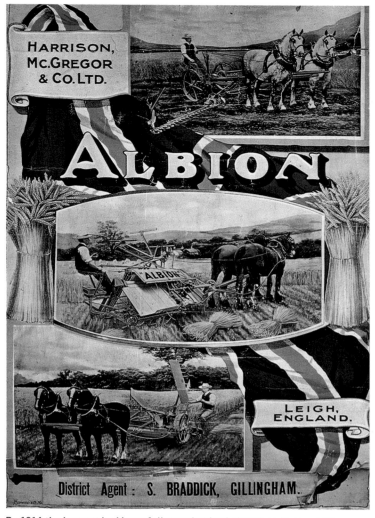

By 1914 the harvest had been fully mechanised, though no single machine was used. The 'combine', already generally adopted for cutting corn in North America, was not introduced until 1926 and as late as 1939 less than 100 were in operation.

Steam tractors were used for pulling felled trees and logs. The First World War saw massive fellings of mature and semi-mature trees on private estates. The Forestry Commission was established in 1919 to undertake the task of replanting.

Haymaking at Swanley, Kent. The employment of women in agriculture declined after 1870 as better paid prospects opened up elsewhere. But harvest piecework continued to provide families with a welcome supplement to their income.

The three-wheel drive was an attempt to overcome the difficulty of working hillsides. But technical defects and high costs limited their uptake before the mid 1930s.

The blacksmith provided a valuable service in repairing implements and utensils, but could not long survive the decline of the horse in rural areas.

and official strike action, discontent at rising prices and profiteering led to the growth of the shop steward's movement as a focus for unofficial strikes in engineering and the coal industry.

Though the militancy of 1919 was blunted by boom conditions and government diplomacy, attempts to cut wages in the post-war slump brought renewed tension, focussed on the coal industry, its history of militancy and poor productivity compounded by the uncertainties of post-war export demand and the rise of alternative energy sources. When in 1921 the miners struck to preserve wage rates, the failure of their action was ensured by the decision (on 'Black Friday') of their allies in the pre-war Triple Alliance to back away from conflict.

The problems of the coal industry, and of Britain's export industries in general, were deepened by the govern-

ment's economic priorities. In the hope of restoring a sound basis for the world monetary system, and with it the conditions for the recovery of Britain's financial prestige and exports, the government and the Bank of England were determined to restore the convertibility of sterling into gold, suspended after the war owing to inflationary pressures. To this end the government began in mid 1920 a policy of deflation to encourage the appreciation of the value of the pound. In his 1925 budget Winston Churchill announced Britain's return to the gold standard at the pre-war equivalence of one pound to four dollars 86 cents. Unfortunately, as Keynes pointed out, the true purchasing power of the pound was still 10 per cent less compared to the dollar than it had been in 1913. The result was to impose in effect a 10 per cent surcharge on British exports. The resulting balance of payments difficulties necessitated the maintenance of high interest

LONDON'S PASSENGER TRANSPORT

London's public transport system has evolved from multiple beginnings. Its Underground railway system, among the finest in the world, is an amalgamation of traditional tube railways, surface railways and extensions, as well as completely new lines such as the Victoria Line, giving a modern network to serve the everyday needs of Londoners and their visitors.

The world's first underground railway was the Metropolitan Railway, which was built by 'cut-and-cover' methods that tended to follow the line of the existing streets. The first trains ran in 1863, and linked the City of London with the Victorian suburbs around Paddington, and the Great Western Railway's terminus. People at first were afraid of 'smoke damp' and suffocation, and great care was taken to provide some escape for the smuts and fumes from the steam locomotives. The exhaust steam from their boilers was condensed in a clever system of pipes, and at first fresh water was taken on and dirty water discharged after each underground journey. By 1884 London's Inner Circle Line, formed by the Metropolitan and District Railways, was completed.

First experiences of travelling under the London streets were a terrifying undertaking. Only a dull light from gas condensed in india-rubber bags stored in the carriage roofs pierced the murk. It was a great relief to travellers when the new electric traction was developed during the first years of the century so that steam engines could be retired to the outer parts of the railway system around London, and fast powerful electric locomotives could haul trains out to the suburbs. And London was expanding rapidly at this time. The Metropolitan Railway which saw itself as a main line railway linking London with Oxford, was also a go-ahead concern which developed new housing estates upon its surplus lands and vigorously promoted the idea of commuting from these places in the country by fast electric train.

This was 'Metro-land' a clever advertising term that quickly caught the imagination of the London public, and was promoted by posters and literature. 'Live in "Metro-land"' the public was urged. The advantages of buying a house for little more than £550, a fast electric train service and very low rates in these country areas were too good to

resist, and those who could afford to do so flocked out into the new estates. Country walking (or 'hiking' as it was called in the 1930s) was popular and the Chiltern Hills of Metro-land were alive with walkers on Sundays. Between the two World Wars Metro-land became to the public the image of clean air, health, relaxation and country joys at a time when tuberculosis, diphtheria and scarlet fever still swept the London streets. This double-flow idea of electric train travel was London's first successful travel advertising, and from it arose a new commuter society (although the term was unknown at the time).

Lord Ashfield, who had managed the 'Underground group' of Tube Railways in the 1920s, became the first Chairman of the London Passenger Transport Board, set up in 1933 to co-ordinate all London's public transport – both trains and buses. Over 170 separate bus, railway, coach and trolleybus undertakings were placed under monopoly control. The Board's first policy was to avoid wasteful competition, standardise design, and to serve London as it rapidly expanded in all directions. Underground railways reached out to Cockfosters, High Barnet, and into the

Essex countryside at Epping. The housing estates continued to roll over the fields, orchards and hills of London's nearby countryside, creating more traffic but new problems as the lines lengthened; it became harder to provide an efficient and adequate service as the years went by. Plans to expand the Underground as far as Aldenham were killed by the Second World War.

All this extra passenger traffic meant new trains and new buses. Trolleybuses replaced trams and were themselves to be replaced by buses. Under Ashfield's able assistant, Frank Pick, a new renaissance in design emerged as Pick brought in new designers, artists and craftsmen to carry out his policy of linking design with efficiency; skilfully building upon the old 'Metro-land' advertising with a new generation of posters, literature and graphic art, and backing it with new stations and the modernisation of old ones that balanced practical design and modern taste in a way that placed London Transport high in goodwill with the travelling public. Posters, street furniture and station architecture developed a standardised, considered, sense.

The Metropolitan Railway, the first railway to run underground in any city, started in 1863 so that new housing developments around the Paddington area, as well as the terminus of the Great Western Railway, could be linked to the City of London. Early carriages held 10 people, and were lit with two flares of gas fed from india-rubber bags. Smuts from the steam locomotive pervaded everywhere. This borrowed Great Western locomotive runs on broad gauge; some mixed gauge rails at Praed Street Junction, shown in this lithograph, were never installed.

London Transport's world-renowned 'roundel' device may be traced back to the LGOC's 'winged wheel' (above left). By the 1930s, the 'bullseye' (above right), an interplay of the circle of motion with horizontal vision, was widely used.

The Piccadilly Line was extended to Uxbridge from South Harrow soon after the Metropolitan Railway was merged into London Transport, to cater for the rapidly-growing housing estates in West London. The larger, Metropolitan Line train carried first class accommodation. The positive electric rail for the Metropolitan train is located nearest the platform – a dangerous feature from the early days.

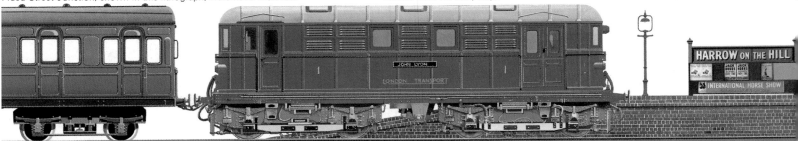

rates which discouraged new investment, while manufacturers in vulnerable export industries resorted to wage cuts to maintain profits.

No industry was worse hit than coal. In the artificially prosperous conditions created by the Ruhr strike, miners' wages had been increased in 1924. By June 1925, with the industry registering heavy losses, the owners once again gave notice of their intention to cut wages and increase hours. The TUC, determined to avoid a repetition of the fiasco of 'Black Friday', promised support for the miners. This threat of a general strike was sufficient on 'Red Friday' to prompt a new inquiry into the problems of the industry backed by a temporary government subsidy to enable the maintenance of existing wages. Though the commission made a number of sensible, if modest, proposals for the long term it saw no alternative in the short term to wage

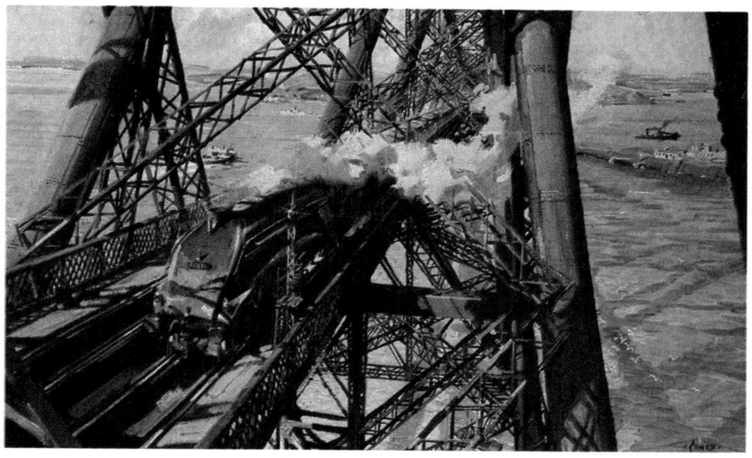

An LNER express crossing the Forth Bridge. Over long distances the train ruled supreme between the wars, but it had lost its monopoly position to road transport – for shorter journeys the lorry, bus and car grew in popularity.

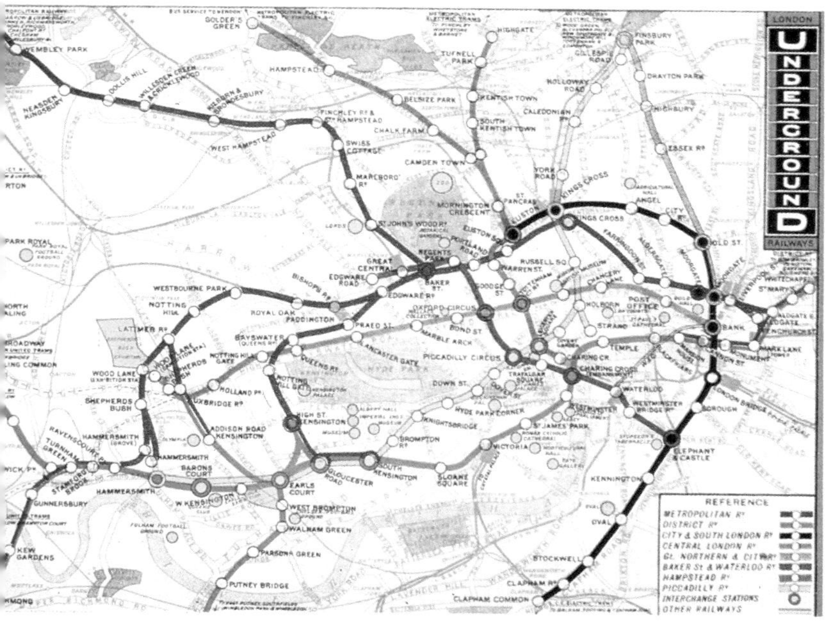
LONDON
UNDERGROUND
RAILWAYS

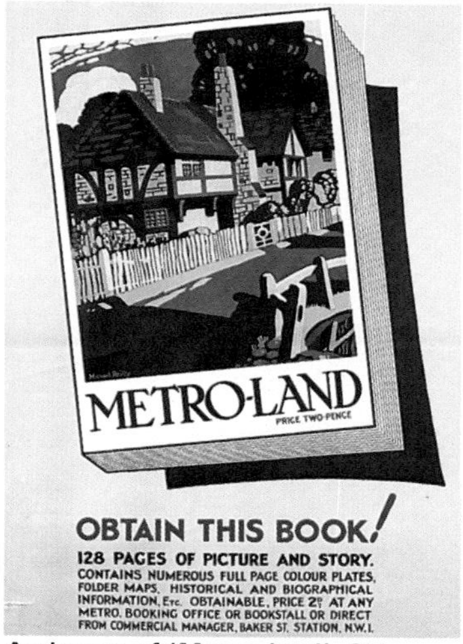
METRO-LAND
PRICE TWO-PENCE
OBTAIN THIS BOOK!
128 PAGES OF PICTURE AND STORY.
CONTAINS NUMEROUS FULL PAGE COLOUR PLATES, FOLDER MAPS, HISTORICAL AND BIOGRAPHICAL INFORMATION, Etc. OBTAINABLE, PRICE 2d AT ANY METRO. BOOKING OFFICE OR BOOKSTALL OR DIRECT FROM COMMERCIAL MANAGER, BAKER ST. STATION, N.W.1.

An image of 'Metro-land'. Old cottages, leafy lanes and wild flowers were used by the Metropolitan Railway's publicity to entice Londoners to live or relax in the countryside served by its trains. Houses often cost under £600, and the air was free of London's fogs.

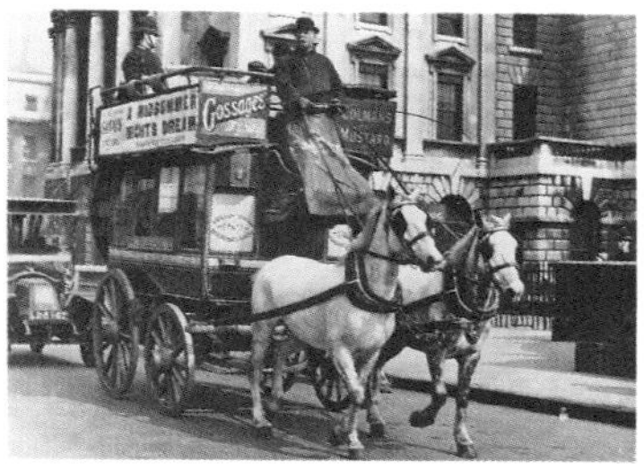

One of London's last horse buses, operated by Fred Newman, crosses Waterloo Bridge in 1914.

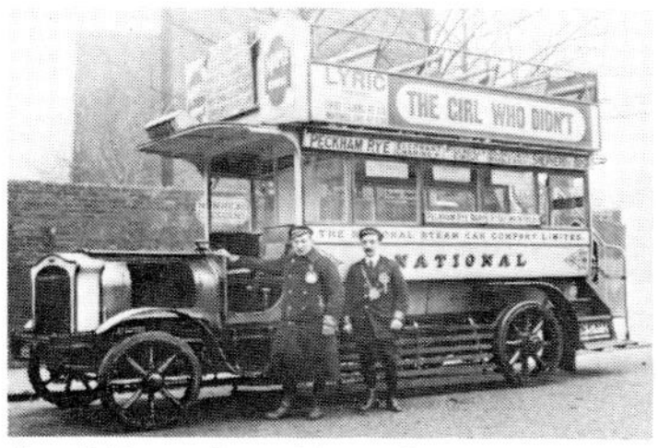
THE GIRL WHO DIDN'T
NATIONAL

A white-painted bus. Steam, battery and petrol/electric propulsion were tried before the petrol bus became standard.

Early Underground maps were geographical but used colour to identify the various lines. Beck's diagrammatic map (below) overcame the problems of extra lines and more stations by clever planning and use of angles. It is interesting to look out for stations which have been closed down.

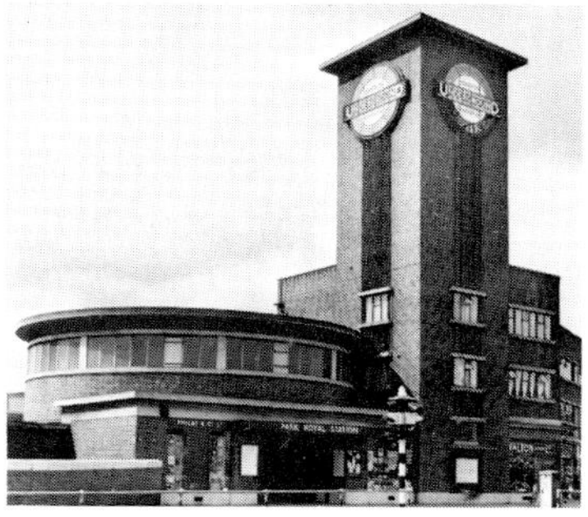

Park Royal Station, 1935–6, a complex group with circular ticket hall, tall tower and curving arcade of shops.

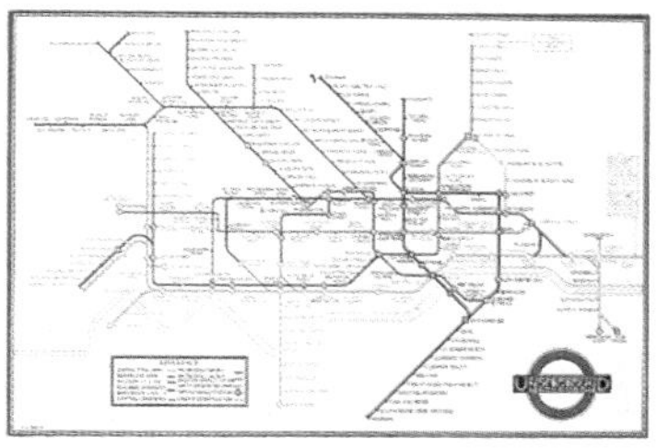

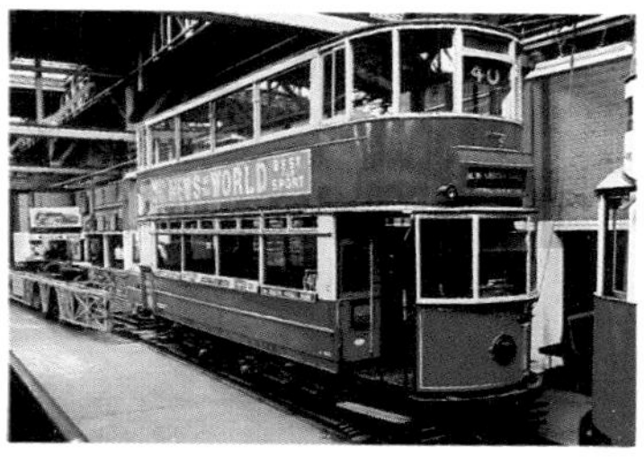

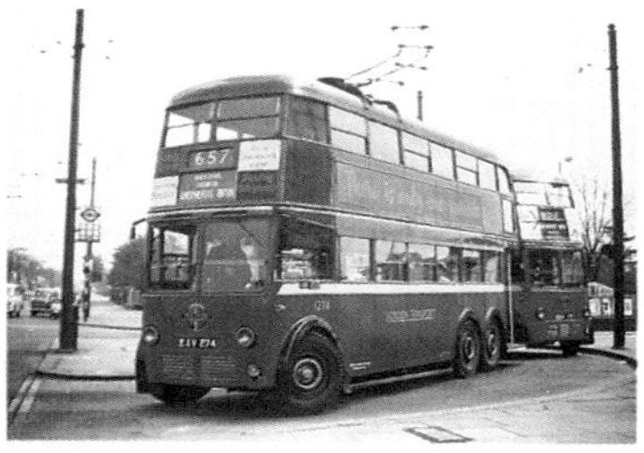

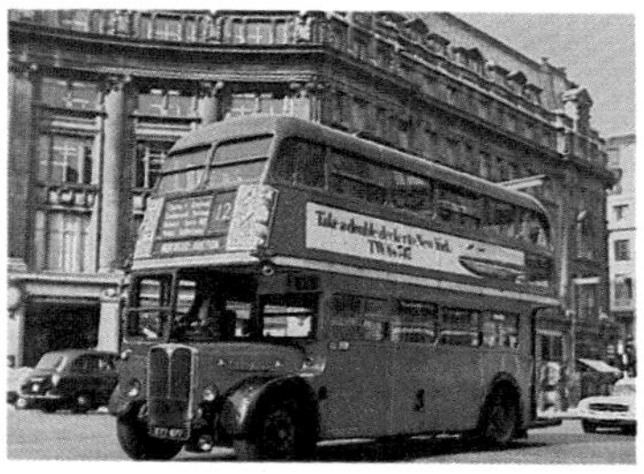

Three landmarks of London's transport. The tram was a cheap mode of transport, but was restricted by its rails to the centre of streets. The trolleybus replaced the tram and was quick and flexible, bringing passengers to the pavements, but was restricted by its overhead wires. The oil-engined 'RT' bus, first introduced in 1939, was so successful that it ran for almost 40 years and became one of London's landmarks.

Harrow-on-the-Hill Station. Metropolitan Railway. Harrow was an important junction between the main line to Pinner and Amersham, and the Uxbridge branch. The railway reached Harrow in 1880 when houses were already spreading northwards over rich farming land. From 1908 until 1925 Harrow-on-the-Hill was the locomotive change point; electric locomotives which had hauled trains from Baker Street were replaced by steam locomotives for the journey into the country districts of 'Metro-land'. Electric traction brought speed and reliability to London's expanding suburbs.

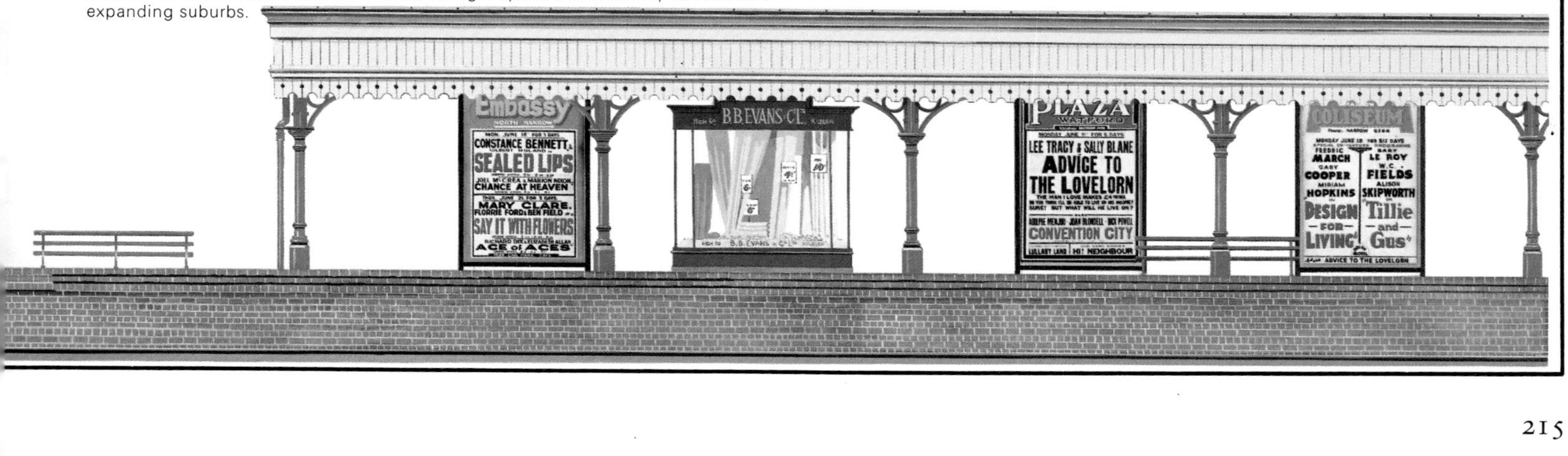
Embassy
CONSTANCE BENNETT
SEALED LIPS
CHANCE AT HEAVEN
MARY CLARE
SAY IT WITH FLOWERS
ACE OF ACES
B.B. EVANS & Cº
PLAZA
LEE TRACY & SALLY BLANE
ADVICE TO THE LOVELORN
CONVENTION CITY
COLISEUM
MARCH
LE ROY
COOPER
FIELDS
HOPKINS
SKIPWORTH
DESIGN FOR LIVING
Tillie and Gus

reductions. On 30 April 1926 the miners ceased work on the slogan 'Not a penny off the pay, not a minute on the day'. The early days of May were occupied in urgent consultations between the government and the TUC. Then, on the night of 3 May, the government broke off negotiations amidst a web of misunderstanding. The TUC, obliged to go through with its threat, called out the 'front line' industries while the government declared a state of emergency.

Despite solid support amongst trade unionists called out, the General Strike lasted a mere nine days. On 13 May the leaders of the TUC informed the government of their decision to call off the strike, with only the flimsiest pretext. In part their surrender reflected recognition of the government's ability to maintain essential services with the aid of middle class volunteers and troops. The TUC also shied away from the constitutional implications of the strike, on which government propaganda dwelt. Though so far a spirit of tolerance had been more evident than the occasional bout of violence, there was also the fear that the longer the strike lasted the more likely it was to get out of control.

The miners, betrayed as they saw it by the wider movement, struggled on alone until the end of the year before being compelled to submit to the owners' terms. Baldwin, who by comparison to some cabinet colleagues had so far set a conciliatory tone, now threw away much of the fruits of victory; under the Trades Disputes Act of 1927 sympathetic strikes were declared illegal and the right of trade unionists to opt out of the political levy to the Labour Party converted to the necessity of opting in. Though after the General Strike there was a sharp decline in the number of days lost annually through strikes and an initial decline in Trade Union membership, the government's apparently

Ribbon development along an early dual carriageway, the newly-built Great West Road, in 1931. Transport was, as ever, the key to development and the new suburbs followed the paths of commuter railways and roads. Once the skeleton was established, further speculative housing estates would infill the fields behind. Purpose-built shopping parades would often be sited at important crossroads, and together with an imposing pub a new 'village' would soon be in existence.

THE DEVELOPMENT OF SUBURBIA

The 19th century architectural 'Battle of the Styles' – between Classical and Gothic – was repeated in the 1920s and 1930s, except that the opposing styles were 'Tudor', 'Georgian' and 'Modern'. Looking back to the Tudor period was not new – the Victorians had a liking for mock Tudor – and nor was Georgian, a style in which leading architects such as Lutyens had been producing dignified public buildings and private houses since before the turn of the century; only the modern movement was, appropriately, quite new, being an underivative style based upon the use of new materials such as glass, steel and reinforced concrete in the way most appropriate to the function of the building, that emerged in Europe after the War. The three styles competed in all fields: private houses, blocks of flats, cinemas, petrol stations, shops, council offices.

At the end of the 1920s prices fell and many people with steady jobs were able to buy a house of their own for the first time. Cheaper urban transport provided by electric trams, trolleybuses and trains, and motor bus services, meant that the ordinary clerk as well as the man who was 'something in the city', could achieve a step towards that national ideal – a home in the country – by moving to the suburbs. The house he bought was probably semi-detached. At around £600 it was cheaper than a detached house (usually over £1,000) and was considered superior to a dark, old fashioned terraced house. The plan of the inter-war 'semi' varied little: two bedrooms, a bathroom and boxroom that could be used as a child's bedroom upstairs, two rooms and a small kitchen and hall downstairs. The kitchen could be small because there would be no servants and little equipment to house apart from a cooker, sink and wash boiler.

With little choice in actual accommodation the house buyer of the 1920s and 1930s had, however, every opportunity to select one that fitted his image of home. At the one extreme he could opt for fake Tudor with blackened beams inside and out and fill it with toby jugs, leather bellows, brass candlesticks, copper warming pans and reproduction Jacobean furniture, and decorate it with pictures of convivial monks and embroidered crinoline ladies. The whole effect was warm, cosy and rather like the sets for historical romances seen at the local picture palace. In complete contrast there was the 'Moderne' semi, which was the

speculative builder's version of continental Modern Movement houses, but with features which suggest it came to Britain via Hollywood. It had a flat roof, was smooth cement rendered and painted white inside and out. It was the setting for a Women's-League-of-Health-and-Beauty-type of wife, who would furnish it with chromium and glass and adorn it – sparingly – with figures of lissom women holding mirrors or lamps. Between these two extremes a great variety of houses were built and suburbs grew rapidly, especially around the more prosperous Southern towns.

Class distinctions were often evident in the style and layout of these suburbs: the developer wishing to sell houses in the upper price range had to build at low densities, preferably in woodland, for clients who liked to think they were living in a village and resist any features associated with urban building. All suburban house buyers wanted their house to be distinctive – not similar to its neighbours like the houses on the new Council estates – which resulted in the rather fidgety mixture, described so aptly by Osbert Lancaster as 'By-Pass Variegated'. Nevertheless the suburban 'semi' has provided a satisfactory home for more than one generation of small families and few of them have been demolished as unsuitable or obsolete.

The layout and structure of suburbia was very much influenced by the concept of the Garden City, which had been proposed by Ebenezer Howard in his book *Tomorrow*, published in 1898. Drawing upon the trend of the upper middle merchant class of the late 19th century for separate dwellings in a rural situation (well exemplified by Didsbury near Manchester, Edgbaston near Birmingham, Ilkley near Bradford and many other localities), the idea of marrying town and country emerged as the ideal for the future.

Within a short time of the publication of *Tomorrow* the first Garden City was springing up among the meadows of Hertfordshire at Letchworth (1903), and a Garden Suburb was building at Hampstead (1907). Welwyn Garden City (1920) was to follow later. These early experiments in the planning of layouts, streets, closes, cul-de-sacs and crescents with detached and semi-detached houses were copied wholesale by architects, builders and developers in the growth of inter-war suburbs, and have produced distinctive patterns not only on the ground but also on the Ordnance Survey large and medium scale maps.

Peacehaven, Sussex. This large housing estate sprung up haphazardly on the cliff tops, a product of individualism, escapism and the rising living standards which created the suburban and retirement communities of inter-war Britain.

Detached house in Tudor style, c. 1920, Chislehurst, Kent. The outer suburbs had more individually-styled middle class developments where mass production had little part to play. Many miles of the English home counties are given over to these elegant homes.

Mass-produced metal windows were an important innovation in the construction of houses in the '30s. With reinforced concrete lintels to carry the load, they could be of unlimited width, giving a new horizontal emphasis.

Ossulton estate is typical of the well-built, Georgian-style housing that was the pride of the LCC in the '30s. Many were demolished in the '60s in favour of tower blocks.

The Odeon, Rayners Lane, Middlesex, one of the new types of building which helped alter the face of Britain between the wars. Cinemas were built in every imaginable style; here, in one of the new suburbs of Metro-land, the cinema-goer was drawn through a modernistic facade with its wide expanses of concrete and glass into the warm, dark interior where illusions were conjured up and satisfied.

Typical house advertisement, 1929. As usual, the selling pitch stresses the property's rural seclusion combined with its proximity to the station. Building society mortgages meant that lack of capital was no longer a bar to ownership.

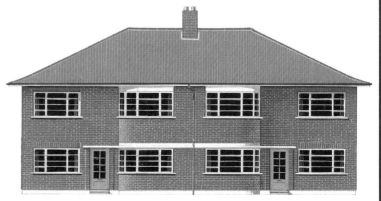

The semi-detached house became almost universal in the 1930s. They were a bit cheaper to build than detached houses and the land cost was much less since 12 went to the acre, the density for which nearly all building land was zoned.

vindictive action created a climate favourable to the renewed growth of the unions and of the Labour Party. However, the economic and social cost of the General Strike now supplemented the Great War as an all too simple scapegoat for the nation's ills.

Economic and political crises

Principal amongst the nation's ills was unemployment of unprecedented extent and duration. Between 1920 and 1929 the numbers unemployed rarely fell below a million, or 10 per cent of the insured workforce. In the key export industries – coal, iron and steel, heavy engineering, shipbuilding and cotton – and in the geographical regions in which those industries were concentrated – Clydeside, the north east, the north west, Northern Ireland and South Wales –

the levels of unemployment were far higher.

The chief response of government was to press on with deflation and economy measures in the hope of restoring Britain's competitive efficiency in the long run while giving partial protection to the victims of unemployment through the extension of unemployment insurance. In 1920 the scheme was expanded to cover the majority of the workforce, and in 1921 dependants' allowances and additional periods of 'uncovenanted' benefits were grafted on. For those who failed to qualify or who had exhausted their entitlement to insurance benefits, the poor law provided a last resort.

In 1929 Britain's deep-seated economic difficulties were worsened by the world slump which followed the collapse of the American stock exchange in the Wall Street crash. Britain's exports fell from £839 million in 1929 (still 20 per

RAILWAYS 1900–1939

Conclusion of the Victorian era saw the railways at their apogee. Outside the great conurbations, where electric trams had begun to eat into suburban traffic, the railway monopoly was unchallenged. Yet despite the many competing companies there was considerable public dissatisfaction with the standard of service and the rates charged, particularly for goods. Parliament had stepped in to fix goods rates, effectively pegging them to the 1892 level; later, with coal and labour costs rising, this regulation was causing financial problems.

The early years of the century were also a testing time for labour relations. After a long period during which railway staff had been treated harshly by their employers, a national strike in 1911 forced the government to intervene. Earlier, in 1893, parliament had legislated to reduce the working hours of railwaymen – long a matter of great public concern. Now the employers were compelled to negotiate with the trades unions they had so strongly resisted.

Barely had rate regulation been abolished in 1913 than the prospect of stability was dashed by the outbreak of the Great War. Though badly affected by loss of skilled staff to the trenches, turnover of their workshops to war production, and an increasing shortage of locomotives, the railways made a magnificent contribution to the war effort.

Competition was set aside; the entire network came under the control of a committee comprising the general managers of nine of the leading companies. In this way, the resources of the larger railways were made available to assist the smaller ones, on which the mammoth war transport task fell disproportionately. The gallant little Highland Railway, largely single track, shouldered the burden of hauling coal, supplies and personnel to the fleet based at Scapa Flow, while the lines serving the Channel ports were also severely taxed.

At the start of the war, the government had guaranteed railway income in return for free carriage of wartime traffic, but settlement of the debt afterwards was a lengthy and acrimonious business. There was also concern in the post war period that the benefits of having the railways under central control should not be foregone. Nationalisation was proposed, but the government favoured a scheme of amalgamations. The Railways Act of 1921 grouped a total of 120 companies into four large undertakings. From January 1, 1923 the public had to accustom themselves to three new company names – the London Midland & Scottish, the London & North Eastern, and the Southern. The fourth member of the 'big four', the Great Western, was the only railway to retain largely intact its pre-grouping identity as well as its name.

As formerly jealous competitors, it was natural that some of the constituents of the 'big four' were uneasy partners. Bitter rivalry persisted between the Midland and the London & North

Western members of the LMS. But at least the railways were now united against a new common enemy – motor transport. Very early on in the development of commercial motoring, the GWR had started the first railway feeder bus to avoid costly extension of the Helston branch to the Lizard. Road competition began for real after the First World War, and very quickly the 'big four' found themselves pressed on all sides by a challenger that could not be bought off. Buses were helping the electric trams to steal suburban passengers; lorries were running away with high-value general goods; and motor coaches began to provide a cheap alternative to rail over long distances. Most sinister, though, was the threat of mass motoring, for the 1920s saw the price of cars fall dramatically. Rail's monopoly was at an end.

Competition from electric trams gave the impetus to the first railway electrification schemes. Those in Newcastle and Liverpool were followed closely by the London Brighton & South Coast's South London line in 1909. After the grouping, the LBSCR's AC overhead system was superseded by the 660 volts DC third rail system of the London & South Western Railway. Under its general manager Sir Herbert Walker, the new Southern Railway pressed ahead with an electrification programme which eventually extended to much of southern England.

Suburban electrification did much to hold competition at bay, and was to be a valuable insurance against even more testing times to come. In goods

transport, on the other hand, the railways remained handicapped even after licensing of road hauliers was introduced in 1929. High-value traffic drained away, leaving the railways with their common carrier obligation to transport the residue at low-value rates.

While the railways looked around for ways to economise in the face of growing road competition – developing steam and later diesel railcars, the push-pull train, and opening unstaffed stations to promote traffic – this was also the era in which steam traction reached its zenith. In 1929 the GWR held the world speed record of 66.3 m.p.h. average between Swindon and London with the *Cheltenham Flyer*, and the 1930s saw renewed competition on the Anglo-Scottish routes with the great stream-lined trains of the LMS and LNER.

It was one of the LNER's Class A4 streamlined Pacifics *Mallard* that achieved the world speed record for a steam loco, touching 126 m.p.h. on July 3, 1938. Improved speed and comfort standards gradually reached down from the prestige trains to those patronised by lesser mortals. The early 1930s brought widespread accelerations which were not to be bettered for over 30 years.

When war again caused the railways to be placed under central control, the transport task was significantly increased by the threat of air attack. Evacuation of the big urban areas produced statistics unsurpassed in railway lore when 1.3 million people were moved in over 3,800 trains between September 1 and 4, 1939.

The Railways Act of 1921 amalgamated 120 companies into just four groups, the London Midland & Scottish, London & North Eastern, Southern, and Great Western. Swept away too were their colourful heraldic crests widely used in locomotive and passenger liveries. Only the Great Western retained its name and thus its crest (top left), which combines the arms of the cities of London and Bristol.

The Midland Railway's Toton yard was at the hub of its network. It sprawls across the border between Derby and Nottingham and dominates the town of Long Eaton.

cent below their 1913 level) to £461 million in 1931. By December 1930 unemployment had risen to nearly three million, or 22.5 per cent of the insured workforce. In some industries such as shipbuilding and some towns like Jarrow it was 60 per cent or more.

The storm had broken over a minority Labour government ill-equipped to generate the international confidence necessary to withstand the financial crisis which by mid 1931 had arisen from the deterioration of Britain's balance of payments, the drain on her gold reserves and the threatened massive budget deficit due to rising expenditure on unemployment benefits. To balance the budget and to secure the foreign loans necessary to preserve the gold standard the government was forced to consider stringent economy measures. The inability of the Cabinet to agree on, and the refusal of the

The Jarrow Crusade, 1936. The liquidation of Palmer's shipyards had put two-thirds of the town's employees out of work. Over four weeks, 200 men marched to London to petition Parliament, acquiring much popular sympathy but no action.

Hagley Hall, one of a large class of GWR 4-6-0s, which saw service almost to the final days of steam, and is now preserved at Bridgnorth, Severn Valley Railway.

The Great Eastern Hotel in London, typical of the majestic hotels built by the railway companies in a constant battle to attract custom.

William Stanier's Class 5, workhorse of the LMS, hauls a Manchester-bound parcel train on the Chester to Warrington line as the sun sets on the steam era in the mid 1960s. Introduced in 1934, a total of 842 of these mixed-traffic 4-6-0s were built.

Open saloons were the style in the 630 volts d.c. multiple-units for the London & North Western's electrification from Broad Street to Richmond, which was inaugurated in 1916.

Proud station staff at Romsey, Hampshire, a typical postcard portrait. The railways provided solid, respectable and secure employment in return for loyalty to a strict regime.

Margate station was completed in 1926 on the site of the former Margate West. At this time the lines in this area were reorganised when a new connection from Broadstairs to Ramsgate allowed closure of the old South Eastern Railway direct line from Margate to Ramsgate.

TUC to accept, a 10 per cent reduction in unemployment benefits demanded by international financiers led on 23 August to the resignation of the Labour government. To the dismay of the bulk of the Labour movement, however, Ramsay MacDonald accepted the King's request to stay on as Prime Minister, taking a handful of colleagues with him into a Conservative-dominated National Government.

The National Government implemented the economy measures, including the application of a highly controversial household means test to some unemployment benefits. However, despite securing substantial overseas loans, the Bank of England was unable to stem the run on the pound and on 21 September the government was forced to abandon the gold standard, for which so high a price had been paid, allowing the pound to devalue. Having secured a sweeping Parliamentary majority at the polls – 556 seats against Labour's 55 – the National Government next introduced a general tariff on a wide range of manufactured imports, negotiating a series of preferential agreements with the Dominions, to protect the home market for domestic products. Now that the maintenance of the exchange rates no longer dictated otherwise the government was also able to reduce interest rates.

Thus the slump prompted a significant change in policies, as a result of which the British economy received some temporary alleviation, until in 1933 the dollar too was devalued. Yet the National Government, like its Labour predecessor, stopped short of adopting the radical remedies proposed by John Maynard Keynes. Keynes claimed that unemployment was caused by insufficient demand for goods, and that the remedy lay not in the reduction of government expenditure but in the state's 'priming the pump' of the economic system through public investment, financed if necessary by borrowing and deficit budgets. By creating work and wages, Keynes argued, such investment would increase demand, creating further employment in a multiplying progression. Though governments indulged in the

Unemployed cotton workers at the Oldham labour exchange, 1931. They are smiling for the camera, but had nothing else to be cheerful about; in that year unemployment benefit was cut by 10 per cent and the means test was introduced.

THE FIRST AIRPORTS

Although aviation engendered some of the most potent images of progress and modernity in the inter-war years, its real contribution to public transport services remained somewhat nugatory. This is not to deny that civil aviation underwent an important, pioneering evolution, of which the belated provision of an extensive network of airports formed a valuable part, but, in comparison to the developments in Germany in the 1920s and the USA in the 1930s, commercial passenger aviation in Britain mounted only a modest challenge to its surface rivals.

Civil passenger flying began in a serious sense in 1919. Before 1914 commercial flying had been confined largely to stunts, of which the experimental air mail service from Hendon aerodrome to a field in Windsor in September 1911 was a notable example. Although Hendon, adopted by the RAF during the War and the headquarters of Aircraft Transport and Travel Ltd (ATT), was prominent in the efforts to re-establish civilian flying in 1919, the first scheduled flight organised by ATT – to Paris on 25 August 1919 – actually departed from Hounslow Heath. The aerodrome there was on loan from the RAF to the newly created Department of Civil Aviation (DCA), and at that time had customs facilities. The RAF, aware of Hounslow's climatic advantages for aviation, was unwilling to release this aerodrome on a permanent basis and so another RAF field at Waddon, Croydon was taken over in 1920 as the London Terminal Port. It remained under the direct control of the DCA throughout the inter-war years, and was easily the most important British airport and virtually the only one handling international traffic.

ATT was joined by several other companies in the attempt to provide regular services to Europe but, under the impact of subsidised competition from the French airlines, they soon ceased operations. In order to preserve British commercial aviation, the government was then forced to intervene, first with subsidies and in 1924 by the creation of Imperial Airways, a subsidised monopoly operating company. Imperial Airways had its successes in establishing international services, although in the 1930s it was criticised for increasingly concentrating on the Empire routes at the expense of other directions, especially Europe. In 1935, therefore, the government nominated a second company, British Airways, to develop the European routes. As for internal services, little happened in the 1920s, but encouraged by the technical progress of aircraft and the example of countries abroad, a spate of companies came into existence in the early 1930s to experiment with services, although they did so without the help of subsidies. It proved a risky business and the government was again planning intervention to regulate and subsidise the development when war broke out in 1939. By that time the industry had expanded into providing for 170,000 passengers on international flights and for 150,000 on internal ones.

The fact that the busiest internal traffic routes were those over water, connecting with the islands or across estuaries, tended to confirm the view that internal air services within Britain were not really viable. On the other hand, the absence of suitable aerodromes had often been cited as a reason for the slow progress of civil aviation. In 1919 the DCA had conceived of a scheme to utilise some of the surplus RAF fields by constructing a network of 'key aerodromes' which would serve the great cities. Supplementing the government's firm undertaking to provide navigational and meteorological

Aircraft had proven a popular and fascinating innovation to the ordinary public, and they seldom missed an opportunity to see them. Hendon was the centre for air displays of circus-like character and the Underground laid on day trips.

services to aviation, this would have created a sound infrastructure on which passenger traffic might have expanded, but the scheme was quashed by a government and a treasury committed to reducing all forms of public expenditure. Croydon was the only permanent legacy, although for a brief time a network covering Manchester, Birmingham and Glasgow also existed.

The DCA found its strongest ally in the Manchester City Corporation, which came close to acquiring an aerodrome in 1923. By the same token, in the late 1920s, several ambitious municipalities began to show interest in creating airports as marks of civic progress and a means of economic development. The allure of airports was sustained by the civil aviation industry, which saw little hope of appropriate funds coming from central government. The Controller General of Civil Aviation from 1923, Sefton Brancker, and Alan Cobham, an aviation pioneer and airport consultant, were especially active in animating the municipal airport movement. The first results of the campaign were seen in 1929 when municipal airports were opened at Nottingham in July, Blackpool in August and Hull in October. Manchester, always very air-minded and frustrated by the delays to its main scheme at Barton, won a technical victory in the race to be first by opening a temporary aerodrome at Wythenshawe in May 1929. By 1939 a total of 38 municipal airports were in operation in England and Wales, with a further three in Scotland and one each in Belfast and Jersey.

The pattern of provision, as it developed in the 1930s, was the relatively haphazard consequence of successful local initiatives, modified by the influence of central government, but with no national plan. The Maybury Committee of 1937 did suggest a plan whereby a national network of key routes would be centred on a 'junction aerodrome' near Manchester and Liverpool, but the scheme was not implemented because of opposition from the airlines. Nevertheless, with the exception of Edinburgh and Sheffield, all the major cities built airports, including the most important projects at Birmingham Elmdon (1939), Manchester's second airport at Ringway (1938) and Liverpool Speke (1933–9). Progressive seaside resorts, such as Blackpool, and seaports also made a vigorous contribution to the development of airports, with their particular interest in advanced communication, especially over water.

In addition to the municipal airports (several of which were in fact managed by private companies) there also existed numerous privately owned aerodromes, 20 of which were licensed in 1938 for general public use. These included several flying clubs and two airport companies of some significance: Airwork Ltd, which created the most successful of the private enterprise airports, Heston in London, eventually bought by the state in 1937; and Airports Ltd, which owned and operated airports at Gravesend and Gatwick, commissioning for the latter the most imaginative terminal building of the the inter-war period.

Many of the municipal airports equipped themselves with forward-looking terminals but from a technical point of view British airports often lagged behind European ones. By 1939 there was still no paved, civilian runway, and night flying and blind landing facilities were not generally available. The first airports, like the airlines, were not profitable operations and so perhaps, for once, the city fathers could be accused of being too visionary for their times; however, of the 38 municipal aerodromes in England and Wales in 1939, 21 are still operating airports today.

A pageant of modern air transport celebrated in a publication of the time. The inter-war years had seen important developments in the industry for Britain, and it was to play a vital role in the war only four years hence.

Amy Johnson in her Puss Moth 'Jason' was the first person to make a solo flight to Australia, in 1930.

Alcock and Brown achieved the first non-stop flight across the Atlantic in June 1919.

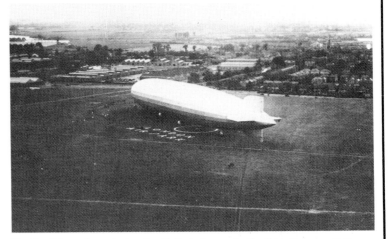

The Graf Zeppelin at the London Air Park, Hanworth. The Zeppelin successfully carried passengers on regular services from Friedrichshafen, including the South Atlantic route, until repeated accidents terminated the development of the airship.

Imperial Airways landing stage at Southampton docks brought passengers to within 100 yards of the flying boats. In 1937 Southampton Water replaced Croydon as the point of departure for Empire air services.

Croydon Airport (now an industrial estate) was London's main airport from 1920 to 1939, and Imperial Airways operated a London-Paris service throughout the period. Air travel was then the preserve of the wealthy and of the businessman.

1920s in limited grant aid for local authority relief works, and in the 1930s in limited regional policies to take work to unemployed labour and vice versa, Keynes' proposals had to await the Second World War for their acceptance. The overwhelming response to the slump was the orthodox, and counter-effective, one of cutting expenditure and thus demand to match government revenue.

Despite a degree of economic recovery in Britain from 1933, unemployment persisted at around a million and a half throughout the 1930s. Notwithstanding the elimination of excess capacity in the basic industries and the impact of rearmament from 1936, unemployment remained concentrated in the 'distressed areas', the emergence of a hard core of long term unemployed adding intensified social and psychological strains to material pressures.

The new society

The distressed areas were only one aspect of inter-war Britain. Equally significant was another Britain – a Britain of new industries, rising living standards and new social patterns. For the 75 per cent of the population in work even during the depths of the slump, falling prices, especially that of imported foodstuffs, more than compensated for any reduction in wage levels, while the redistributive effect of taxation and welfare benefits cushioned the worst material effects of economic depression. Between 1924 and 1937 real income per head rose by nearly a quarter. When Seebohm Rowntree undertook a second study of poverty in York in 1936, he found working class poverty less than half as prevalent as in 1899.

Some of the nation's increased purchasing power was spent on a diversified diet. The growth of leisure activities reflected both escapism for the poor and the rising incomes of the better-off. In the 1930s up to 40 per cent of the population visited the cinema weekly (the 'talkies' had arrived in the late 1920s). Spectator sports continued to thrive, and gambling on horses, greyhound racing and on the football pools became an industry in itself. The BBC was given a monopoly of broadcasting in 1922 and by 1939 there were nine million radio licences. Nearly 13 million people were now entitled to holidays with pay, reflected in the growth of resorts and holiday camps. The motor bus, through the excursion, created a new relationship between town and country.

Some of the increased purchasing power, aided by hire purchase, was devoted to a growing range of new products. The electrical revolution came of age in the inter-war period. Such pre-war innovations as the electric fire, iron, vacuum cleaner and cooker became available to the better-off working class home, while the middle classes began to benefit from such labour-saving devices as the washing machine, refrigerator and immersion heater. The family car became a status symbol for many middle class families (their numbers grew from 200,000 in 1920 to over two million in 1938) while the motor cycle brought some of the same benefits to the upper working classes. Plastics and artificial fibres revolutionised many household products as well as the clothing industry.

New products meant new materials, from rayon to aluminium, and new sources of energy, especially electricity, which were in turn the bases of important new industries.

The flexibility brought by electricity and the motor vehicle led to the location of these new, consumer-orientated industries not in the traditional industrial areas determined by the coalfields, but near the more prosperous markets of London, the south east and the south Midlands. In the south,

LEISURE BETWEEN THE WARS

The late 1920s and early 1930s are always associated with the Depression and the dole queue but, while it is true that for many families in the northern industrial areas this was a decade of frustration and poverty, for those who had secure jobs, such as in the expanding service industries, goods were cheap and leisure was increasing with regulated working hours and paid holidays becoming the rule.

Most children in the 1930s had been to the seaside. Ones from poor families would have been 'for the day' while lucky ones spent a week or more there every summer. Wealthy families rented cabins right on the beach for the day, which avoided their children bringing shoes full of sand into the smart hotels on the sea front where they stayed. These cabins may have inspired Billy Butlin who opened his first holiday camp and changed the whole holiday idea in 1936 at Skegness. But most families stayed in boarding houses at the back of the town. Entertainments were simple and traditional: donkey rides, Punch & Judy, and concert parties on the pier at which you might be able to *see* well-known radio characters such as Arthur Askey or Uncle Mac, or film stars like Gracie Fields or George Formby. Hastings had its special character: the old man in a tub, who paddled up and down the beaches clowning to the delight of young and old. In the 1920s and 1930s the seaside was a lively place of young people and children where an increasing interest was being taken in swimming rather than simple bathing as a recreational activity. This and the sunbathing cult which grew from 1931 onwards led to a progressive emancipation in beach attire. Whereas the period began with full skirted and trousered costumes, it passed via the beach pyjamas of 1930 and the functional close fitting single piece costume to the forerunner of the bikini at the end of the period.

Many working class people had houses with small gardens for the first time and the long summer evenings and shorter working hours found many people growing flowers and lawns, constructing rustic rose arches or sitting in deck chairs enjoying the fruits of these labours of love. Tennis clubs were popular if less fashionable than they had been and now the novice could learn the game on public courts in the parks. Tournaments were organised by tennis clubs and local authorities and tennis as as a spectator sport emerged, with Wimbledon becoming the Mecca of all serious players and spectators. Another sport which originated among the well-to-do in the 19th century was also enjoying the peak of its popularity: with an abundance of metalled roads and few cars, cycling could be enjoyed as never before or since and cycling clubs went out every weekend in the summer; some members took longer holidays, staying the nights at inexpensive bed and breakfast accommodation displaying the enamel badges of the Cyclists Touring Club or the Cyclists Union.

Those who could not afford even the modest outlay for a 'bike' went hiking, and this included some of the unemployed in the northern counties. Hikers were not universally popular and the decade was a time of great battles to re-establish old rights of way and to establish a right to walk over the grouse moors of the gentry, including the Pennine Way. Hikers had their own accommodation in the Youth Hostels which offered only bunks and simple food or cooking facilities, but a great atmosphere of comradeship.

Another plebian sport that increased its audience in the 1920s and 1930s was the football match. Unlike Rugby football played at the public schools, soccer was a working man's game and the stars of the local clubs and even Internationals were almost invariably men from working class backgrounds. The game received a considerable publicity boost with the completion of the Wembley Stadium in 1923, which enabled the Football Association Cup Final to be staged before an audience of nearly 100,000.

During the summer months cricket replaced football, and the County championships and the Test Matches with Australia attracted large crowds and much public interest.

Ballroom dancing developed from an activity indulged in by people with their own ballrooms to a paying industry. Ballrooms with resilient 'sprung' floors were often included in the design of large cinemas and the huge suburban pubs, but dancing, especially the Tea Dance (as the afternoon session was called) was made quite respectable by leading exponents such as Victor Sylvester.

Entertainment by the theatre, music hall and the cinema also played an important part in the leisure industry of the inter-war years. The theatre and music hall continued actively from the base established in the Victorian period. The 1920s and 1930s were the great age of Ivor Novello and Noel Coward, and in most years the London theatres were staging up to 20 new first class plays, comedies and musicals, many of which subsequently went on tour around the provinces. Some notable examples included *Chu Chin Chow* (which established a record of 2,238 performances), *Lilac Time*, *Rookery Nook*, *The Desert Song* and *The White Horse Inn*.

The inter-war period also saw the gradual development of a network of cinemas across the country. Beginning with the silents, the industry received a great boost in 1928 when Al Jolson's *Singing Fool* ('Sonny Boy') ushered in the age of the talkies. By the end of the decade the cinema was dominating the entertainment world. From the luxury cinemas of the West End of London to the local fleapit, all classes had their cinema and a twice weekly visit was common for many. The unemployed were criticised for spending their dole on cinema seats, but who can blame them for escaping from grim reality into a fantasy world of glamour and happy endings?

The popularity of the cinema was beginning to affect theatre attendances towards the end of the second decade, but both came increasingly under attack from another quarter – the rise of radio. The British Broadcasting Company had started as long ago as 1921 and had become the British Broadcasting Corporation in 1926. Radio increased in strength and popularity steadily throughout the period and more especially when the crystal set began to give way to the valve. Radio licences soon passed the million mark and climbed steadily to over three million by 1930 and over nine million by 1939.

Successful attempts at televising pictures had been demonstrated by a Scotsman, John Logie Baird, as early as 1925 but the system was based on mechanical methods involving scanning by means of a rotating disc; definition was poor as pictures could only be transmitted on 30 lines. Television only became a commercial proposition in the 1930s when the mechanical system was abandoned in favour of an electronic system, and transmissions on 405 lines were introduced. By 1939 a regular service was beginning to emerge, but TV receivers were still very expensive and little more than 12,000 licences had been issued before all development was brought to a halt by the outbreak of the Second World War in 1939.

Hiking and cycling gained popularity once transport had been established to take townspeople to the countryside.

News cinema, Piccadilly Circus. With the coming of the talkies, the 'pictures' became the nation's entertainment, many enjoying the escape from reality twice a week. Before television the events of the day were dramatically presented in newsreels, which appeared before each main feature, as well as in specialist cinemas like this one.

Derby Day at Epsom, 1939. Horseracing was an enthusiasm shared by all classes, as was gambling on the results. Open coaches provided a good view in fine weather.

Wembley Stadium was opened in 1923 and immediately became a venue for major footballing (and other) fixtures, with its 100,000 capacity. Football was a regular Saturday afternoon viewing pastime for the working class.

Seaside resorts continued to flourish between the wars. Places like Southend, easily accessibly by rail because of surrounding flat terrain and close to a large city, were favourites for a day trip.

prosperity bred prosperity just as in the north depression bred depression.

The late 1920s and 1930s also experienced a boom in housebuilding. Four and a half million new houses were built in Britain between the wars, many in the 1920s with the assistance of subsidies and more in the 1930s by private enterprise, stimulated by cheap mortgages and falling building costs. In 1939 a third of all houses had been built since the end of the First World War. New houses embodied new housing standards, reinforced in the 1930s by a slum clearance campaign. Three bedrooms, parlour, kitchen, bathroom and indoor lavatory were common to many of the new estates, whether council or private, which mushroomed on the outskirts of towns and cities, especially in the south. New estates were served by new forms of transport, and commuting became a feature of life for many. The conjunction of the housing boom with the growth of new industries based on domestic consumer demand was largely responsible for the fact that in Britain the slump was milder and recovery more pronounced than elsewhere.

Shifts in industrial structure were complemented by changing social patterns. At least in the more prosperous areas of the south, mass production and mass consumption began to break down traditional indicators of social class such as material possessions, mobility and leisure, creating an increasingly uniform regional culture. The BBC, the cinema and the national press fostered the growth of an informed society with standardised values and images. As a substitute for domestic service, convenience foods and labour saving devices contributed to the diminution of one of the most striking demarcations of class and, in association with the spread of effective methods of contraception, brought new dimensions to the emancipation of women. (The decade which saw the publication of Marie Stopes' *Married Love* and the 'flapper' also saw the first woman cabinet minister.) Of course distinctions of class and sex remained, especially in the less prosperous regions. Still, in social relations as well as in the sciences, in inter-war Britain relativity was beginning to replace what had formerly seemed absolute and certain.

'I've got it.' Neville Chamberlain returns to Heston with the Munich agreement, 30 September 1938. At the cost of sacrificing the Sudeten territories of Czechoslovakia, Chamberlain acquired Hitler's signature on a statement of mutual non-aggression. Of this he said, 'I believe it is peace for our time'. He was wrong; less than a year later was was declared.

EVENTS AND PERSONALITIES

King George V and Queen Mary riding in the traditional carriage procession from Windsor to the Royal Ascot race meeting in 1932.

1919   The Treaty of Versailles is signed and demobilisation begins.

There is industrial unrest on Clydeside and strikes of police and railwaymen.

The Ministries of Health and Transport are established.

Lady Astor becomes the first woman to enter Parliament.

Addison's Housing Act introduces a state subsidy for local authority housing and the Town and Country Planning Act is passed.

A self-constituted Irish Parliament declares an independent republic: the Irish Republican Army commences fighting.

379 Indians are massacred at Amritsar.

Alcock and Brown fly the Atlantic and the first commercial air service, from London to Paris, begins

1920   London dockers strike in protest at the loading of the 'Jolly George' with government aid for Poland against Russia.

The Communist Party of Great Britain is founded.

The Government of Ireland Act partitions the island.

The League of Nations allots the Palestine mandate to Britain.

Rationing and price controls are abolished.

Unemployment insurance is extended

to cover the majority of the workforce.

200 state university scholarships are instituted.

The Emergency Powers Act is passed to deal with the threatened national coal strike.

Women are admitted to degrees at Oxford (but rejected by Cambridge).

The Marconi Company makes first commercial wireless broadcast

1921   In Ireland the truce leads to creation of the Irish Free State with Dominion status.

The post-war boom turns to a slump.

Abandoned by their partners in the Triple Alliance on 'Black Friday', the miners are forced to accept reduced wages on a district basis.

Railways are rationalised into four major regional groupings

1922   The 'Geddes Axe' imposes expenditure cuts on army, navy and education.

There are wage reductions in private industry.

Prompted by opposition to government handling of the Chanak crisis between Greece and Turkey, Conservatives withdraw from the Coalition, winning in the subsequent General Election 357 seats to Labour's 142 (with Lloyd George Liberals 60 and Asquith Liberals 57).

Bonar Law becomes Prime Minister,

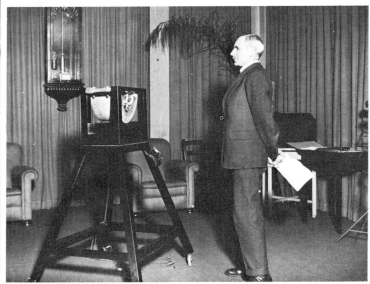

A broadcasting studio at Savoy Hill, 1923. The object on the trolley is the microphone. Formality ruled under Reith: announcers wore dinner jackets to read the nine o'clock news. By 1924 over 1,100,000 receiving licences had been issued.

Soldiers guarding buses during the General Strike, 1926. The strike was remarkable for its spontaneity, solidity and lack of violence. It failed to achieve its object, which was a compromise between coal miners and pit owners. The miners continued alone for a further five months, without success.

The Duke and Duchess of Windsor at their wedding in 1937. The Prime Minister and others believed that the country would not tolerate the marriage of Edward VIII to Wallis Simpson, who had been married twice before. He abdicated to do so.

and Ramsay MacDonald leader of the opposition.

There is civil war in the Irish Free State between the Provisional Government, supporting a treaty with Britain, and the republican Irregulars.

Ulster provinces elect to remain in the United Kingdom. In India Gandhi is imprisoned for a civil disobedience campaign against British rule

1923 Stanley Baldwin succeeds Bonar Law as Prime Minister.

In the December election on the issue of tariff reform the Conservatives win 258 seats, Labour 191 and reunited Liberals 159.

There is an Irish ceasefire.

Southern Rhodesia becomes a self-governing colony

1924 Ramsay MacDonald takes office as Prime Minister of a minority Labour government with Liberal support.

Unemployment insurance is liberalised, state scholarships for secondary education are introduced and the Wheatley Housing Act extends state subsidies for municipal housing.

The Soviet government is recognised.

Labour lose a vote of confidence over their failure to prosecute Communist journalist J. R. Campbell.

In an election dominated by the publication of a (probably forged) letter from Zinoviev, President of the Russian Praesidium, Conservatives win 415 seats to Labour's 142 and Liberal 42

1925 Churchill, as Chancellor of the Exchequer, returns Britain to the Gold Standard at the over-valued pre-war parity of $4.86 to the pound.

The Widows, Orphans and Old Age Contributory Pensions Act reduces pensionable age to 65

1926 The General Strike, in support of resistance to wage cuts for miners, is called off after nine days. Miners stay out for five months before submitting to wage reductions and increased hours.

The Central Electricity Board is established to supervise construction of a national supply grid

1927 The Trade Disputes Act outlaws sympathetic strikes and requires unionists to 'opt in' to payment of the political levy to the Labour Party.

Parliament rejects the 'Revised' Prayer Book

1928 The Industrial Transference scheme for movement of the unemployed, especially miners, to areas of greater employment opportunity.

Women are granted equal franchise with men

1929 The Local Government Act introduces block grants, derating of agricultural land and partial derating of industrial premises, and public assistance in place of poor relief.

In the General Election Labour win 287 seats to Conservative 261 and Liberal 59. Ramsay MacDonald becomes Prime Minister for the second time.

State-aided relief works are extended and unemployment insurance liberalised.

Press barons Beaverbrook and

Rothermere launch the Empire Free Trade campaign.

The Wall Street crash in American share values triggers a world recession

1930 The Housing Act emphasises slum clearance.

The Coal Mines Act reduces hours to $7\frac{1}{2}$ a day and encourages cartellisation.

In India Gandhi begins a second campaign of civil disobedience

1931 The report of the May Committee advocating severe economy measures exacerbates financial crisis.

In August Cabinet divisions over a proposed reduction in unemployment insurance benefits provoke resignation of the Labour government and formation of a National government with Ramsay MacDonald at its head.

The Economy Act cuts unemployment insurance benefits by ten per cent.

Sailors 'mutiny' at Invergordon against cuts in pay.

The Gold Standard is abandoned in September.

The October General Election gives the National Government a majority of 497 and George Lansbury becomes leader of Labour's rump of 46 MPs.

The Agricultural Marketing Act provides for the creation of marketing boards for agricultural products.

The Statute of Westminster defines the autonomy of the Dominions as 'freely associating as members of the British Commonwealth of Nations'.

Churchill resigns in opposition to the possibility of future independence for India

1932 Unemployment reaches three millions.

The Import Duties Act imposes a general tariff.

Imperial preferences are negotiated at the Ottawa Conference. The Anglo-Irish tariff war begins and lasts until 1938.

Former Labour minister Sir Oswald Mosley forms the British Union of Fascists.

Cambridge scientists split the atom.

George V delivers the first royal Christmas Day broadcast

1933 In the year in which Hitler becomes German Chancellor Labour votes against a United Front with Communists, and the Oxford Union Society 'will in no circumstance fight for its King and Country'.

Economic recovery begins

1934 Commissioners are appointed under the Special Areas Act to aid economic recovery of depressed regions.

1931 cuts in unemployment insurance are restored and the Unemployment Assistance Board is established to take national responsibility for the uninsured unemployed

1935 Protests at Unemployment Assistance Board relief scales force the government to introduce the Standstill Order.

Baldwin succeeds Ramsay MacDonald as Prime Minister of the National government, returned in the

General Election with a majority of 247.

Clement Atlee replaces Lansbury as Labour leader after a debate on pacifism.

The Government of India Act provides for native provincial governments.

The Anglo-German Naval Treaty limits size of fleets.

George V's Silver Jubilee is celebrated

1936 Edward VIII succeeds George V but subsequently abdicates in order to marry the American divorcee Wallis Simpson. The Crown passes to **George VI**

J. M. Keynes publishes his *General Theory of Employment, Interest and Money*, attributing unemployment to inadequate demand and advocating state expenditure on public works during a depression. The Tyneside unemployed stage a hunger march from Jarrow to London.

The Public Order Act bans political uniforms, gives police authority to prohibit processions and extends the offence of 'insulting behaviour'.

British and French Foreign Ministers formulate the Hoare-Laval plan acquiescing in Mussolini's invasion of Abyssinia.

Rearmament commenced.

Television broadcasts begin

1937 Coronation of George VI.

Neville Chamberlain succeeds Baldwin as Prime Minister.

The Matrimonial Causes Act adds desertion and insanity to adultery as grounds for divorce.

The Air Raid Precautions Act is passed

1938 Chamberlain's appeasement of Hitler's aggression against Czechoslovakia takes him to Munich and an agreement promising 'peace in our time'

Coronation of the Duke of York as King George VI, 1937; the Royal Family appear on the balcony of Buckingham Palace after the ceremony. As second son, the role was unexpected, but as Queen Mary said, 'the Yorks will do it very well'.

The Second World War

*Hitler invaded Poland in September 1939 and Britain declared war.
Fighting alone in 1940, she was saved from invasion by triumph in the
Battle of Britain. Many city centres were destroyed by the bombing which followed.
America joined the war after the attack on Pearl Harbor by the Japanese.
The global conflict came to an end in 1945.*

This was not a war that was greeted, as was the First World War, with enthusiasm. Already the British people had been issued with warnings about air raids, young men had been called up as early as June, and there was a general expectation that the war would not be easily won.

It was not; for it was to last longer than the First World War and was to be fought over a much greater area of the globe. In truth it was not just one war, but several. At first Britain and France were allied against Nazi Germany, then quickly a war developed between Finland and the Soviet Union. In June 1940 as France surrendered, Italy entered. A year later Germany attacked Russia and a few months later Japan attacked both Britain and the United States, so that by early 1942 it was truly a World War. On the Allied side only the British fought for the whole length of the war, and so it should come as no surprise that Britain exhausted herself in the process.

Yet the people of Britain were to be more united than in any other war of the 20th century. Partly it was because the civilian population were as endangered as the fighting forces, for whilst 264,000 servicemen were killed so were 60,000 civilians, over two thirds of them during the Blitz and many of the others by 'doodlebugs' later in the war.

The war was to impose hardships; homes were destroyed, children evacuated and strict rationing imposed, but it was also a war that gave a new purpose to the idea of a more socially just society. Change came also in other directions. By late 1942, besides Frenchmen, Poles, Dutchmen, Belgians, Norwegians and Danes in exile in Britain, there were thousands of men from the colonies and Dominions and also over 170,000 American servicemen. They were to bring, especially the Americans, new words into the language and new habits and dress into society.

Socially the Second World War was a catalyst, bringing together many unlikely strands and producing a society which by 1945 was looking for a new world, not a reversion to the old.

The outbreak of war

When war was declared in September 1939 one of the first surprises was that other countries failed to join in. After the defeat of Poland, Britain and France faced Germany alone,

for no other European power was involved.

In Britain gas masks were issued, a blackout imposed and over one and a half million people evacuated: mainly children, but also mothers with children under five. Many wealthy people also moved to the country. Evacuation often caused considerable hardship, for the children were the responsibility of the local authority from which they came and some areas, like Croydon, had their charges dispersed over 110 different areas, which made it almost impossible to keep effective control. The children who remained were in many instances worse off, for schools in large cities, including London, remained closed until November. This caused more hardship than just loss of education for many of the children also relied upon the school for free milk and meals. Gradually many of the evacuees returned, so that by early 1940 only about one-third remained in the countryside.

In other spheres the government had prepared plans but was reluctant to act. Ration books had been printed, but it was not until January 1940 that butter, cheese and bacon were rationed. What did soon become a common sight was the queue, especially for goods in short supply but on 'points' in a ration book. Yet the queue also represented much of British attitudes during the war in that it showed patience and a desire for fair shares.

At the outbreak of war, the government took wide-

Of the many thousands built, only a handful remain of the RAF's most prized aircraft from the Second World War. These Spitfires and the Hurricane of the Battle of Britain memorial flight are often seen at air shows.

St Paul's Cathedral in the Blitz, 1940. This image symbolised the spirit of London and other cities during the bombing with which Hitler hoped to break the morale of the civilian population. If anything it achieved the opposite effect.

ranging powers through the Emergency Powers Act, and this allowed the Home Secretary almost unlimited judicial powers – which remained hardly used. The war seemed 'phoney' in other ways: there was no fighting in France, little air activity and only at sea did there seem to be any combat. The U-boats were soon active, sinking the aircraft carrier HMS *Courageous* in September 1939 and the battleship HMS *Royal Oak* at Scapa Flow in October. Coupled with magnetic mines, the U-boats began to inflict considerable damage (despite the convoy system) on merchant shipping, with 800,000 tons lost by May 1940. The Royal Navy gained some revenge when the cruisers *Ajax*, *Achilles* and *Exeter* forced the pocket battleship *Graf Spee* to take refuge in Montevideo harbour and then scuttle itself.

The government itself changed little. No Labour or Liberal was invited to join the government, although Winston Churchill, long regarded as a Tory rebel, was made First Sea Lord of the Admiralty.

The war suddenly began to turn sour in April 1940 when Germany struck at Denmark and Norway, both of which were quickly overrun. The real calamity, however, started on 10 May 1940 when a blitzkrieg was launched through the Ardennes into France and Belgium. On the same day that the Germans struck, Chamberlain was replaced by Churchill as Prime Minister, mainly through the support of the Labour Party which announced it would vote for Churchill but not the alternative candidate, Lord Halifax.

Events in France soon worsened and by early June, with Holland and Belgium overrun and with the Germans having reached the Channel coast, the British evacuated what forces they could from Dunkirk (Operation Dynamo). It was the greatest military defeat in British history, yet it saved enough of the army to allow Britain to fight on and the 'Dunkirk Spirit' was to become the embodiment of the British nation's determination not to give up.

The odds were soon to be even more unfavourable, for on 22 June France surrendered and by this time Italy had joined the war on the Axis side. Britain was alone.

At last Britain moved on to a true war footing. Ernest Bevin (the General Secretary of the Transport and General Workers' Union) was made Minister of Labour, with power to direct labour and conscript women. Direction was little used, but through the work of trade unionists like Bevin the union movement was soon seen to be a key part of the economy and a respected partner of government.

Britain was now vulnerable to attack both by air and sea,

The King and Queen made a great contribution to war-time morale. They refused to send their daughters to America for safety and constantly visited the worst-hit areas.

but the first priority was to increase dramatically the number of fighters available. This was done by the dynamism of Lord Beaverbrook, the Minister of Aircraft Production, with his demand for 'Action this Day'. Part of Beaverbrook's dynamism lay in his ability to appeal to the public, which he did with his appeal for scrap metal. Aluminium pots became a rarity and many iron railings were lost, never to be replaced. Churchill also appealed to the nation when on 18 June he warned that a German invasion was imminent and ended his speech with 'Let us therefore brace ourselves to our duties and so bear ourselves that, if the British Empire and Commonwealth live for a thousand years, man will still say, "This was their finest hour"'.

Fear of invasion led to orders for the removal of signs from railway stations and road signs. Over 1700 British subjects (including Oswald Mosley, who was released in 1943) were interned in case they were part of the 'Fifth Column'. Posters warned people that 'Walls have Ears!'

The Local Defence Volunteers were renamed The Home Guard and had soon recruited over one million men into 'Dad's Army'. Large parts of the south and east coast became 'Defence Areas' which a person needed a permit to visit.

It was from the air, however, and not the sea that the main attack came. In July the Germans attacked convoys in the Channel and stopped allied shipping. On 13 August the 'Blitz' began on south east England, mainly attacking the fighter bases in Kent, but in late August the attack was switched to cities with London as the main target. The 'Battle of Britain' lasted until 15 September, by which time the RAF had lost over 900 fighters – but the Luftwaffe had lost over 1700. The Blitz itself was not over, however, and during the winter of 1940–41 heavy night bombing raids were made on cities like Coventry, where the cathedral was destroyed, Southampton, Bristol, Birmingham and the East End of London. Over three and a half million houses were damaged or destroyed, and over 43,000 people killed. Morale did not crack despite the fact that by 18 October London had been attacked on 41 consecutive nights.

Although with 'Operation Sea Lion' Hitler was poised ready for the invasion of Britain, the defeat of the Luftwaffe in the Battle of Britain meant that the command of the English Channel could not be assured. With both the Royal Air Force and the Royal Navy to contend with along with the survivors of Dunkirk a 'blitzkrieg' on England looked very unpromising, and Hitler decided to postpone the invasion plans and bring forward the secret intention of moving east against the USSR. After overrunning the Balkans the German attack on the USSR was launched on 22 June 1941. In the event this proved to be Hitler's undoing, for it gave Britain a much-needed breathing space to rebuild its forces and rally the Allies in preparation for the

Children were evacuated from the major cities at the beginning of the war. In the south east there was a second official evacuation towards the end to take children out of range of the flying bombs.

second front and a return to the continent of Europe.

Before this event, however, other disasters were to follow although in retrospect many of these were to prove favourable to the Allied cause. The collapse of France in June 1940 produced a vacuum in French Indo-China, and this proved too much of a temptation for the militarist expansionists of Japan. But the strategy of any advance southwards involved a two-pronged and simultaneous attack on the Indo-Pacific peninsula and the Philippine Islands; the latter of course were possessions of the United States. Hence the opportunist Japanese strike against the American Navy at Pearl Harbor on 7 December 1941. This one stroke turned the European conflict overnight into a global war. Although Japan was to overrun south east Asia in the early part of 1942 and it was to take the Allies three years to recover the lost territories, full scale American participation in the war was now assured and in Europe full scale realistic plans for a second front and a return to the continent were now possible.

One problem brought about by the Blitz was that people injured were not always covered by medical insurance, but after some hesitation the government ordered that such people should be given free medical treatment.

Other signs of social change towards a fairer society were also beginning. In 1940 a graduated purchase tax was introduced, a Rent Restrictions Act froze rents at their 1939 rate and the publication of reports like Barlow (Royal Commission on the Distribution of the Industrial Population) and Uthwatt (Committee on Compensation and Betterment) were seen as expressions of a desire for a better post-war world. The report with the greatest impact of all, however, was the Beveridge Report: in February 1941 the TUC asked the government to examine the inadequacy of health insurance provision, with the result that in June Arthur Greenwood, Minister without Portfolio, set up a committee under Sir William Beveridge which in December 1942 published the 'Report on Social Insurance and Allied Services', an instant seller with over 600,000 copies sold.

Beveridge argued that 'Social insurance, fully developed, may provide income security; it is an attack upon Want. But Want is only one of five giants on the road of reconstruction and in some ways the easiest to attack. The others are Disease, Ignorance, Squalor and Idleness'. He proposed that a flat rate insurance contribution should in future cover unemployment pay, death grants, sickness benefit, child benefit, maternity benefit, old age pensions and also that 'Medical treatment covering all requirements will be provided for all citizens by a National Health Service'. Yet it envisaged no more than a minimum, for the scheme

The assembly line for Lancaster bombers at the A. V. Roe factory at Woodford, Cheshire. Evidence of wartime industry can still be seen in the fading camouflage adorning many older factories.

'should leave room and encouragement for voluntary action by each individual to provide more than that minimum for himself and his family'. Despite this the *Daily Telegraph* saw it as 'Half Way to Moscow', but it was to become the basis for the post-war welfare state.

The Beveridge Report was a badly needed tonic in raising morale, for 1941 and most of 1942 were grim years. Reverses in North Africa were followed by disasters in Greece and Crete. After the entry of Japan into the war in December 1941 there were also disasters in the Far East with Hong Kong, Singapore, Malaya and Burma all lost. The war at sea, particularly the Battle of the Atlantic, went badly with over 1.7 million tons of merchant shipping lost. Food became very short, despite over four million acres of marginal land having been ploughed up by the end of 1941. Lord Woolton, the Minister of Food, urged people to 'Dig for Victory'. He also took care that rations contained sufficient vitamins. White bread disappeared from the shops but chocolate and sweets were still available on 'personal points' in ration books, although only eight ounces was allowed for a four week period. In March 1942 the private petrol ration was stopped completely.

Despite the reversals of war there was a major revival of the arts. CEMA (the Council for the Encouragement of Music and the Arts) had been established by the government at the end of 1940 and led to such events as the old Vic Company touring Wales and Lancashire and to the free lunchtime concerts run by Dame Myra Hess at the National Gallery. Many people came in contact for the first time with serious theatre and classical music. Many more listened to popular entertainment on the BBC, epitomised best by *ITMA (It's That Man Again)* starring Tommy Handley. The characters in the show – Colonel Chinstrap, Mrs Mopp and Mona Lot – became part of British folklore. As popular as *ITMA* was *The Brains Trust*, started as an experimental programme in 1941 with questions answered by a trio, usually consisting of Commander Campbell, CEM, Professor Joad the philosopher, and scientist Julian Huxley. The programme became a major means of popular education.

By 1943 the war had begun to turn in favour of the allies. General Montgomery had won the Battle of El Alamein in north Africa, whilst on the west coast an Anglo-American force had landed (Operation Torch). In the USSR the Russians had smashed the German Seventh Army at Stalingrad. The 'Second Front' became increasingly talked of, and in preparation for it thousands of American soldiers and sailors were stationed in Britain. The GIs (Government Issue), referred to as 'oversexed, overpaid and over here', brought

The incredible ring of devastation around the almost undamaged St Paul's Cathedral. Blitzed Londoners must have been encouraged to see St Paul's each morning, still serenely dominating the City.

with them their own radio programmes, to which many people tuned as an alternative to the BBC. It was radio which brought American jazz and popular music, especially the big band sound of Duke Ellington, Tommy Dorsey and Glen Miller, into British homes. Britain however kept its own 'forces sweetheart' in Vera Lynn, yet ironically arguably one of the most popular tunes of the war was a German one, *Lili Marlene*.

By the end of 1943 Italy had been invaded and had surrendered, whilst a massive bombing programme (Operation Point Blank) had begun against Germany. 1944 was to see the Allies cross the channel in the greatest amphibious operation in history. At home the government and people sensed victory, yet there was to be one more ordeal. On 13 June the first VI weapon fell on London. The second Blitz had started. The pilotless bombers were aimed mainly at the capital, and over 6000 people were killed. The second Blitz was mercifully shorter than the first, and by August fighters and anti-aircraft guns had destroyed over four fifths of the 'buzz bombs' in the air.

By the autumn of 1944 much of Europe was liberated, with France and Belgium again free and the Allies poised for the last thrust against Germany. In the east the Russians were moving steadily westwards following upon the decisive victory of the Red Army at Stalingrad (Volvograd) in 1943. Bulgaria, Romania, eastern Hungary and eastern Poland had all fallen into Russian hands by 1944. Nazi Germany now found itself squeezed between the Allied and Soviet Armies and soon collapsed; on 8 May 1945 the common enemy made the required unconditional surrender. Meanwhile Hitler had committed suicide in the ruins of Berlin. Thus ended the war in Europe.

The war in the Far East also came to a sudden dramatic end. On 16 July 1945 a combined team of British, American and refugee research scientists exploded the world's first atomic bomb on the Alamogordo Desert bombing range in the south west USA. Three weeks later replica atomic bombs were dropped on Hiroshima and Nagasaki with casualties of over 100,000 lives apiece. The decision to drop the bombs was made on the calculation that an invasion of Japan might cost anything up to two million lives. The ruling military junta recognised that they had no answer to the atomic bomb, and immediately sued for peace.

It was on this dramatic note that the military action of the Second World War ended. Total casualties were even more horrific than those of the First World War, which had resulted in eight million dead; in the Second World War total casualties amounted to 56 million dead. The world was also suddenly brought face to face with the fact that any future struggle between nuclear powers might mean not only the prospect of widespread devastation, but also the possibility of 500 million casualties.

In 1945 people in Britain began to think of a better life in the post-war world, particularly in areas such as education; the outbreak of war had stopped the proposed raising of the school leaving age to 15 but there were other factors leading to an increased demand for educational opportunity. Conscription and evacuation both revealed widespread illiteracy; war work for women created a demand for nursery school places of which over 2,000 were created. In the Army itself the AEC (Army Education Corps) was asked to fulfil a widespread demand for education and in 1943 alone ran 3,750 courses and gave in addition over 62,000 lectures.

This vast increase in the desire for educational opportunity led after the war to the Butler Act of 1944. Few Acts of Parliament are known by the name of the Minister rather than the Act itself, yet 'Rab' Butler deserved the honour because of his skill in getting this major piece of legislation through Parliament on a bi-partisan basis. The Act raised the school leaving age to 15 and declared that it should be raised to 16 as soon as possible. All children were to have secondary as opposed to 'extended elementary' education with the dividing line between primary and secondary education set at 11, the children then moving to Grammar, Modern or Technical schools. Fees were abolished and provision was made for both nursery and further education. For the first time compulsory religious education was added to the syllabus and the day was to begin with 'collective worship on the part of all pupils in attendance'. The Butler Act set the pattern of English education for the next two decades.

By 1944 the country was moving towards the left politically. The Labour Party drew up a new programme of nationalisation; Keynesian economics had also become influential, and with it the government's determination to maintain full employment in the post-war world. The Beveridge Report began to be implemented in February 1945 when family allowances (5/- per week for the second and subsequent child) were introduced.

The coalition government was finally dissolved on 23 May and a caretaker government under Churchill took over until the General Election, called in July. Many people voted against a return to Conservative pre-war domestic policy; many blamed the Conservatives for the failure of foreign policy in the 1930s and many believed that only the Labour Party was committed to full employment and the welfare state. The comedian Tommy Trinder, for instance, was to campaign for the Labour Party because of its promise to bring in a free National Health Service. The Conservatives had a great asset in Churchill but he made the mistake of suggesting that Labour, if elected, would set up a Gestapo; this offended many people in what was essentially a serious-minded electorate. When the votes were counted the Labour Party had won a landslide victory with 393 MPs to the Conservative Party's 213.

To many it now appeared that the 'People's War' was going to produce a radical new world, yet in retrospect it now seems, as Dr Angus Calder has written, that 'the war was not to sweep society on to a new course, but to hasten its progress along the old grooves'.

The Royal Family and Churchill on VE-Day, 8 May 1945, when victory in Europe was announced and celebrated. The Germans had surrendered unconditionally the day before. The British people rejoiced in the traditional way. Church bells rang too; they had been silent during the war, to give warning in case of invasion.

THE RELICS OF WAR

Considering the fact that a considerable quantity of physical damage was sustained by Britain between 1940 and 1945, and that the country formed the springboard from which the Allied powers launched their invasion of north west Europe in 1944, there is surprisingly little concrete evidence left of the United Kingdom's participation in the Second World War. The majority of what does survive is a legacy of the air war, for which Britain was rightly considered an 'unsinkable aircraft-carrier' from which the Allies launched their ever more destructive strategic bombing campaigns against Germany's war-making potential and cities.

The dual aspect of the air war led to the evolution of two types of airfield, in different parts of the country. Located along the south and east coasts were relatively small grass strip airfields for the short range defensive fighters. The pre-war fields were strategically located to control defensive sectors, and during the early part of the war many of them were allocated satellite airfields built up from pre-war civil facilities or in other suitable locations: for example, Middle Wallop had Warmwell, Biggin Hill had Gravesend and Manston, and North Weald had Martlesham Heath. Most of the sector airfields remained in RAF hands after the war, and are recognisable by the disposition of their runways (now fully paved) and by their 1930s buildings. Most satellite airfields returned to their erstwhile owners after the war, and some such as Lympne in Kent are still in use as civil airfields; some satellites returned to agricultural use; and still others fell into decay. Typical of this last is Warmwell in Dorset, where the visitor may still make out the remains of earthwork dispersal pens, temporary buildings, slit trenches for local defence, and more martial relics such as drop tanks.

Associated with the fighter defence was a chain of radar stations disposed mainly along the vulnerable south and east coasts in places with evocative names such as Worth Matravers, Stoke Holy Cross and Ottercops Moss. At many of these sites, built both before and during the Second World War, there still remain the pylon masts (mostly built of wood) surmounted by their rectangular antennae.

The Allies' strategic bombing effort, launched as a major effort in 1942, was centred on East Anglia, the east Midlands and southern Yorkshire. Some 240 airfields were built for the US 8th Air Force, mostly in East Anglia, and these airfields generally covered some 500 acres, complete with a triangular arrangement of paved main runways, together with their associated dispersal points, slipways, perimeter track, hangars and accommodation/ administrative buildings. Most of these have now returned to agricultural use, but many may be located by their runway remnants and hangars, now used for agricultural purposes.

Apart from a large quantity of building to accommodate and administrate the vast number of conscripts taken up by the Royal Navy and British Army during the war, there remains relatively little evidence of the UK's vast naval and military effort. Such as does still exist tends to reflect the country's preoccupation with the threat of invasion: on East Anglian estuaries and beaches there are still to be seen the tangled remnants of the wire nets which hung from kapok-filled canvas tubes across rivers, and the scaffolding obstacles (hung with mines during the war) that were designed to prevent vehicles from getting off the beaches onto the shore proper.

Also visible as tangled and rusted relics are portions of the more elaborate booms used to protect harboured ships from the depredations of submarines and torpedo boats. Such boom defences were altogether more substantial, with heavy-gauge netting suspended from massive booms, with tug-operated gates to allow the movement of shipping and naval vessels. Perhaps the largest and most comprehensive relic of the naval effort is the fleet anchorage at Scapa Flow in the Orkney Islands.

HMS Belfast is the largest surviving warship of the Second World War in the British Isles, and is preserved as a museum on the Thames near Tower Bridge.

The massive fortifications on Jersey. Typical of other mainland emplacements — except that they face England, bearing witness to their German occupation.

This magnificent example of the Avro Lancaster I, the RAF's most important heavy bomber of the Second World War, is preserved at Hendon. Together with the Imperial War Museum collection housed at Duxford in Cambridgeshire, Hendon is the most important air museum for military aircraft in the UK, although the Shuttleworth Collection at Old Warden in Bedfordshire and the Fleet Air Arm museum at Yeovilton also house important collections.

Towards a Post-Industrial Britain

*Peace in 1945 was followed by a great wave of
social, political and economic change. The Welfare State was established
and new towns, housing estates, factories, roads, schools and
universities were built. The Empire was transformed into the free association of the
Commonwealth. Britain came closer to Europe, and after some
hesitation joined the European Economic Community. Living standards rose as never
before, albeit slower than in the rest of Europe. The
unexpected bonanza of North Sea oil and gas proved a mixed blessing and
economic stability remained sadly elusive.*

In certain respects Britain has exhibited in the last two centuries a remarkable ability to adjust peacefully to changing circumstances. This ability was to be subject to its greatest test after the Second World War; although victorious, the struggle had cost the country a quarter of its wealth, a third of its capital and two thirds of its exports. The economy was basically weak, and could no longer support the massive armed forces needed to sustain the concept of the largest Empire the world had ever seen. Moreover, independence movements had been emerging in nearly all colonial territories in the wake of Ghandi's activities in India and the Japanese wartime 'liberation' of European possessions in south east Asia.

The inevitability of change and the need to allow change to take place by evolution rather than revolution was recognised by British politicians with views as diverse as those of Attlee and Macmillan. The result was a relatively peaceful transformation of the British Empire into a British Commonwealth and eventually a freely associating Commonwealth of Nations, based on the British Crown and/or British links. Few parts of the old Empire elected to remain outside the Commonwealth, as the benefits of membership of the 'club' are considerable even in a time when the founder member is as much interested in Europe as in the Commonwealth. Adjustment internationally has also been achieved by membership of the United Nations and the North Atlantic Treaty Organisation.

American aid to Britain under the 1947 Marshall Plan paved the way towards post-war economic recovery, but adjustment internally has yet to be achieved as two major problems have bedevilled the domestic scene for much of the post-war period. British domestic politics have been dominated since the return to peace by the twin spectres of inflation and unemployment. Changing technology, archaic trade unionism, conflicting economic theories and overseas competition have further confounded the politicians, and the complexity of the situation largely accounts for the oscillations of the political pendulum over the last 30 years. The age old problem of Ireland has also reared its head yet again and seems as intractable as ever.

The political pendulum

In 1945 the Labour Party under Clement Atlee confounded expectations by winning its first overall majority and the claim to a mandate for socialism. The electorate had distinguished between Churchill the war leader and the needs of a nation at peace. While the Conservatives were still associated with the unemployment and appeasement of the 1930s, Labour seemed in 1945 to embody a new spirit of national unity and a wholehearted commitment to social betterment.

However, after five years of Labour austerity, Conservative emphasis on individual economic freedom and private enterprise, now mitigated by acceptance of the welfare

Harold Macmillan, Prime Minister from 1957 to 1963. He presided over the growth of Britain's affluence, coining the phrase 'You've never had it so good'. He also perceived the 'wind of change' in Africa; many colonies acquired independence.

A North Sea oil rig, symbol of Britain's new wealth and, some would say, problems. Whilst providing vital oil and revenue for the nation it has propelled us into the upper strata of 'rich' nations and has overpriced and destroyed the older, traditional industries, causing millions to suffer the misery of the dole queue. Are we to become a leisured oil state or remain an industrialised nation in the future?

state, had a renewed appeal. Though Labour retained a narrow majority in 1950 her leaders were either tired or ill, and in 1951, despite Churchill's age and ill health, the Conservatives secured an overall majority of 17 (though winning a smaller share of the popular vote than Labour). A year later the accession of the young Elizabeth II reinforced the impression of a new age. Paradoxically it was the Conservatives, benefiting from a fall in import costs, who were able to win three successive elections, under Winston Churchill, Anthony Eden and Harold Macmillan respectively. Despite the Suez fiasco of 1956, sufficient electors agreed in 1959 with Macmillan's claim that 'you've never had it so good' to give the Conservatives a 100 seat majority over a Labour Party internally divided on defence policy and public ownership.

But by 1964 triumph had turned to demoralisation: the economy was stagnating, foreign policy was in disarray after France's Common Market veto, and the Vassall and Profumo scandals (together with Macmillan's abrupt dismissal of one third of his cabinet) called the government's competence in question. Both parties fought the 1964 election under new leaders, Sir Alec Douglas-Home's 'grouse moor' image contrasting unfavourably with Harold Wilson's stress on 'the white heat of the scientific revolution'.

The early 1960s saw a turning point in British politics, reflecting growing economic and social volatility. In the next two decades there was a succession of single-term governments (Labour's second victory in 1966 being the logical result of her narrow win in 1964). Some majorities, especially Labour's in 1964 and 1974, were very small, and massive by-election swings occurred; in 1977 and 1978 Labour retained power only through a pact with the Liberals. The Welsh Nationalists won their first parliamentary seat in 1966, the Scottish Nationalists following suit a year later (though their influence waned with the rejection of devolution proposals by referendum in 1979).

AGRICULTURE AND FORESTRY

The last war saw the emergence of a new, closer relationship between farmers and the national government. The 1947 Agriculture Act gave substance to this partnership by extending the guarantees made in wartime to agriculture in time of peace. The basic principles of the Act were to affirm the State's responsibility for securing an adequate supply of food at reasonable prices and for ensuring that farmers were properly remunerated for their labours. The possibility that these aims might conflict was scarcely considered, but the significant feature for farmers was that agricultural support in the future was to be permanent.

In the late 1940s the government's priority was to stimulate agricultural production in order to make good food shortages and to rebuild scarce reserves of foreign currency. The State continued to buy all home-produced grains, potatoes, sugar-beet and fatstock, and later acquired a monopoly in wool; it also maintained strict controls over food imports. This policy was unashamedly expansionist and undoubtedly contributed to rapid post-war recovery: between 1947 and 1951–52 net agricultural output grew by no less than 20 per cent.

The defeat of Labour in 1951 and the return of a Conservative government led to a change in the *methods* of State support for agriculture but not in its underlying aims. The new administration restored the freedom of the market to farmers and importers and, much to the rejoicing of the British housewife, ended rationing. Farmers were to be protected against sudden price falls, however, by a system of deficiency payments, negotiated annually, which made up the difference between the market price and the assured commodity prices. At the same time the distribution of produce was to be improved by the re-establishment of the pre-war Marketing Boards and the setting up of new ones.

While the achievements of British agriculture in the first post-war decade owed something to the State subsidies and marketing aids, the industry also benefited from the relative cheapness of key inputs – particularly agricultural machinery and chemical fertilisers – as the production of these increased and became more efficient. Additionally, the relaxation of import controls provided a cheap supply of foreign feeding stuffs and stimulated competition among British and American machinery manufacturers.

By the end of the 1950s, however, the continued expansion of the industry was causing problems. Liquid milk was in such supply that large quantities had to be sold cheaply for processing into

milk products, eggs and pigs were in surplus and the country was rapidly becoming self-sufficient in barley. The situation was aggravated by increasing food imports, which caused market prices to fall and the cost of government support correspondingly to rise.

In 1957 the government had opted for a policy of selective expansion only and the 1960s was to prove a decade of further retrenchment. Successive governments sought to prevent any increase in the subsidy bill and to limit the production of those commodities which lacked a profitable market outlet. In 1964 the Conservatives introduced a system of standard quantities for wheat and barley (milk was already covered), whereby production in excess of that quantity was penalised by a progressive reduction of the deficiency payment. In an attempt to curtail the dumping of foreign foodstuffs, agreement was reached with the principal supplying countries on minimum import prices for cereals and import quotas for cereals and other commodities. When it came to power in 1964 the Labour Party maintained these arrangements and no further significant modifications of agricultural policy were made by any administration until Britain's entry into the European Economic Community in 1973.

In the decade or so before joining the EEC, Britain's farmers faced increasing difficulties. At bottom, national economic policy favoured consumers rather than producers. Despite support for farm prices, these increased much more slowly than the average retail price and the gap between farmers' incomes and comparable industrial incomes widened.

Yet, whatever its troubles, British agriculture remained fairly healthy and competitive in this period. It was the weakness of the British economy overall and a growing feeling of political isolation that finally dictated alignment with Europe. The date of entry was 1 January 1973, but there was a five year transitional period to 1978 in order to provide for a smooth change from the old system of guaranteed prices and deficiency payments to the full adoption of the Common Agricultural Policy.

The basic principles of CAP involve common prices, protection against cheap food imports from outside Europe and priority for internal production. This policy is achieved through the concepts of threshold prices and intervention prices. Threshold prices are the basis for assessing levies on imports to ensure that they do not enter the community at prices below agreed levels. Intervention prices are those which national and other agencies are required to pay for the supplies they take.

The landscape effect of joining the EEC will not be fully apparent until CAP has been in operation for some time, but we are already witnessing some changes. For example, the balance between arable and livestock is altering. It has become more expensive to feed cereals to livestock and hence a more efficient grassland management will be necessary. At the same time there is pressure to grow cereals rather than grass because of the higher prices that cereals command, and so cereal production (especially barley) has grown at the expense of livestock. Hedge boundaries have been removed (especially in East Anglia) in order to adjust to high levels of mechanisation. Marginal upland areas in highland Britain formerly used for pasture have gone out of production. Market gardening and fruit farming in less favoured areas have suffered from cheaper mass production (for example, France's Golden Delicious apples) in the better climatic conditions of Europe.

The centuries-old trend of deforestation in Britain was finally arrested in the 20th century and a major landscape change has taken place as a result of a national policy of afforestation. The United Kingdom had by the end of the First World War achieved the unenviable position of having the smallest proportion of forest area as well as the smallest forest area

per capita of all the major countries of Europe. Even today Britain imports 92% of its annual timber requirements at a cost of £2,400 million per annum.

The Forestry Commission was created in 1919 to remedy this situation and to work towards a strategic three years' supply of timber. The acquisition of suitable land and the planting of the forests and woodlands has proceeded steadily since, and now over five million acres or some eight per cent of the land surface of Britain carries useful forest and woodland.

It is the post-war period that has witnessed the most dramatic changes as the inter-war plantings have matured and new forests have been laid down. Whilst the distribution is inevitably patchy, some notable major new forest areas have been created in Scotland (Glen Tool, Speymouth), Wales (Coed Morgannwg) and England (Thetford in East Anglia and Kielder in Northumberland). Much of the planting has been in relatively quick-growing conifers with a cut-over rotation of 60–80 years, but there are also mixed and hardwood forests with cut-over rotations of 120 and 150 years respectively. With crop intervals of this magnitude there has been a steady decline in the private ownership of forest and woodland and a corresponding increase in State ownership and concern for afforestation.

After 1940 scarcer, dearer labour stimulated mechanisation in the form of imported combine harvesters. But with them came massive reductions in the rural workforce and the amalgamation of many small farms into semi-industrial units, resulting in the decline of many small communities.

Though neither the National Front nor parties of the extreme Left achieved electoral success in the 1970s, their influence was apparent.

In Northern Ireland the divisions inherent in the partition of 1920 were reinforced by high unemployment and the dissatisfaction of the Catholic minority with the pace of reform at the hands of a Unionist government in which the Protestants had a monopoly of political power. In 1969 British troops were sent to the province to protect the Catholic community from the Protestant backlash aroused by the civil rights campaign. The situation worsened when the breakaway Provisional Irish Republican Army launched a campaign of terrorism against the British Army and the Protestant establishment in the name of Irish unification.

After the death of 13 civilian rioters at the hands of the British Army on 'Bloody Sunday' in 1972, the Northern Irish Parliament at Stormont was suspended and direct rule from Westminster imposed. Though this was unpopular

During the late 1960s the Catholics of Northern Ireland had become incensed by the inequalities of the Province, and civil disturbance ran riot. The British Army was sent to keep the peace, but the situation polarised into a cruel and bloody battle rekindling the fire of independence and the resurgence of the IRA.

Battery hens. Previously a source of pin money for women, hen-keeping had become a specialised branch of farming in the 1920s. By the '50s, battery production brought unlimited cheap eggs (and chickens) onto the market.

Kielder Forest, Northumberland. By 1939 Forestry Commission plantings were a controversial feature of the English landscape. Here, a huge forest of softwoods – the largest artificial forest in Europe – grew up on formerly treeless hills. It became part of The Border Park, opened in 1955.

Bulk milk transport (above) developed rapidly in the early 1960s following successful research encouraged by the Milk Marketing Board. By 1973 over 50 per cent of the nation's milk was collected daily from farms in tankers.

A recently deserted croft, South Uist, Hebrides (right). The drift from the land continues among rural communities, the consequence not so much of poverty but of the draw of better prospects in the towns.

Pigs were once the pets of rural families or favourite members of the mixed farmyard. Now they are mass produced by intensive rearing with highly artificial foodstuffs. But cheap pork has become a basic family requirement.

with both Protestants and Catholics, the attempt to restore self-government through a power-sharing executive that included politicians from both camps collapsed in 1974 after the fragmentation of the Loyalists at the polls and a political general strike by the Protestant Ulster Workers' Council. Violence escalated, overflowing outside Northern Ireland in a campaign of bombings which included the murders of Lord Mountbatten and Airey Neave, Conservative spokesman on Northern Ireland. Despite the efforts of the Peace People (who received the Nobel Peace Prize for their endeavours), there seems no sign of a solution.

At Westminster, the governments of the 1970s were increasingly obliged to recognise the influence of the trade unions. Having, in 1969, forced Labour to abandon its proposals for the reform of industrial relations, the TUC rendered the Conservative's 1971 Industrial Relations Act unworkable. A miners' strike against pay policy brought down the Heath government in 1974 giving credence to the view that in contrast to their status in the 1920s the unions were now a fourth estate as powerful as the other three combined. A 'Social Contract' with the unions was Labour's trump card in its 1974 election victory; the collapse of that contract in the 1979 'winter of discontent' was their undoing.

In the 1950s the substantial area of agreement between the major parties was dubbed 'Butskellism' (after the Conservative R. A. Butler and the Labour leader Hugh Gaitskell). By the late 1970s that consensus had substantially broken down under the pressure of economic and electoral volatility. While the Left demanded a more aggressive socialism from a future Labour government, Mrs Thatcher's Conservative administration expressed a more thorough-going allegiance to *laisser-faire* than any of its post-war predecessors.

The economics of instability

Post-war British politics have been dominated by the economy. The war cost Britain much of her wealth and capital, an enormous two-thirds of her exports, raised the national debt to £250 billion, halved the value of the pound and distorted industry. In some respects peace only intensified the problems: the United States' abrupt ending of lend-lease necessitated a £1,500 million loan, repayable over 50 years but conditional on an early restoration of the international convertibility of sterling, and thereby provoked a sterling crisis in 1947. Despite Marshall Aid, the pound was devalued in 1949 by a massive 30 per cent, and although by 1950 exports were 75 per cent above their pre-war levels, rising prices occasioned by the Korean War led to balance of payments difficulties.

A subsequent fall in import costs helped the balance in the 1950s, but periodic Conservative attempts to stimulate domestic growth led, as a result of increased imports reinforced by heavy overseas expenditure (mostly on defence), to a pattern of 'stop-go' with balance of payments deficits and sagging confidence in sterling, which necessitated the restriction of credit and consumption at home. During the 1960s and 70s external crises became both more frequent and more severe as Britain faced an increasingly volatile international economy, until in 1967 Labour belatedly again devalued the pound. In 1972 the Conservatives, with a record balance of payments deficit and a new sterling crisis, allowed the value of the pound to float. The quadrupling of Britain's oil import bill in 1973 and the continuing depreciation of the pound were weathered only by recourse to a massive loan from the International Monetary Fund that was conditional on heavy cuts in public expenditure.

ARCHITECTURE AND BUILDINGS

Britain has undergone as great a rebuilding in the last 30 years as in any period in her history. Prosperity increased steadily in the post-war years, and the material standards of living of the mass of the people reached unprecedented heights. With more money to spend, and higher expectations, people demanded better housing, and private developers and local authorities endeavoured (with varying degrees of success) to give it to them. The rehousing of inner-city dwellers was seen as a particularly important social priority, and large areas of what was considered to be sub-standard, usually 19th century, housing were totally cleared. The Swiss architect, le Corbusier, had written about the 'radiant city', clean, light and efficient, which would replace the crowded, unplanned city of the past; this ideal of a city made up of blocks of flats surrounded by open spaces was shared by many British architects and planners. The rebuilt city allowed great scope for 'social engineering'; the urban working-class, shattered by the loss of its familiar streets, shops and meeting-places, was to be rehoused in the new blocks with their 'vertical streets' or 'streets in the air' leading to flats with modern gadgets and services which the old terraced houses lacked. Meanwhile, however, in the expanding suburbs, and in the dormitory towns and villages near the big cities, private developers continued to build at a low density in a more or less traditional manner. As the populations of the inner cities declined, more and more people came to live in these essentially suburban communities.

The housing boom, which began in the 1950s, coincided with a spate of city-centre rebuilding as the economy became more buoyant and restrictions on building were removed. Commercial interests, which wanted more office space, worked closely with local authorities who were eager to push up rateable value and to give the cities a new 'image'. At the same time the vast extension of car ownership was putting a great strain on existing road systems. 'Comprehensive redevelopment' could solve traffic problems by widening streets, demolishing decaying old buildings, and segregating vehicles from pedestrians; at the same time new offices could be built both for private companies and public authorities, together with the covered shopping centres and leisure centres the consumer society was thought to demand.

Architects responded eagerly to the challenge. Many of the leaders of the profession after the war had been won over by the gospel of modernism which had been preached for a long time on the Continent, but which had remained largely unheeded by the pre-war establishment in Britain. Modernism meant abandoning the styles of the past in favour of a functionalist approach. Decoration, inseparably connected with architecture since the earliest times, was now taboo; buildings were to be machines, relying externally on the materials furnished by industrial mass production – steel, concrete, glass – and providing a controlled environment inside, with artificial lighting, heating and ventilation on an unprecedented scale. Technological advances made it possible for buildings to be pre-fabricated and to soar upwards to new heights; the National Westminster Bank tower in the City of London is taller than the cross of St Paul's Cathedral. Modernism was attractive not only because it appeared to be a rational, efficient style in an age which valued technology and its works very highly; it also marked a clean break with the past and offered a tough and uncompromising alternative to the supposedly weak-minded dependence on earlier styles which, it was felt, had held back British architecture in earlier years. Hence some architects took a delight in emphasising relatively new materials like concrete, and drawing attention externally to features like lift-shafts and ventilation ducts.

The new architecture, especially in its more 'brutalist' manifestations, began to be widely criticised at the end of the 1960s when the economic success which had underpinned it had already begun to falter. Attention focused first on high-rise flats, which were felt by many to be unsuitable on social and even (especially after the well-publicised collapse of a block in east London in 1968) on structural grounds. Some architects had already begun to build low-rise high-density estates which were felt to be less impersonal than the earlier schemes; during the 1970s, however, an increasing number of people became convinced that it was better, and often cheaper, to rehabilitate older housing in the cities rather than clearing and replacing it. The idea of 'comprehensive redevelopment' also came under attack; schemes prepared in the early 1970s to virtually rebuild Piccadilly Circus and Covent Garden in central London were abandoned after a great deal of public protest. One of the most interesting developments of the 1970s was the great growth of support for conservation, which led to the designation of conservation areas, and the refurbishing of the older parts of many towns and cities. This growing interest in the past led some commentators to look nostalgically even at the semi-detached suburban houses of the 1930s, which had been long reviled (except perhaps by those who lived in them). Whether or not this change of heart will lead to the evolution of a new and perhaps more popular architectural style, still remains to be seen.

Prefabricated houses in Homerton, east London. 'Prefabs' were run up in great numbers after the Second World War to provide temporary accommodation for the homeless. Their appearance and methods of construction were purely functional.

The headquarters of the National Westminster Bank in Bishopsgate, London, is the highest building in Britain. The architect, Richard Seifert, designed many of the huge commercial buildings which transformed the skyline of London in the office boom of the 1960s and '70s.

The Metropolitan Cathedral of the Roman Catholic archdiocese of Liverpool (irreverently known as 'Paddy's Wigwam') was built to the designs of Sir Frederick Gibberd in 1960–7. Following modern liturgical practice, it is centrally planned, with the main altar underneath the lantern, which dominates the building from outside and provides much of the light for the interior. Sixteen concrete struts support the roof.

The new working environment: the headquarters of Willis, Faber and Dumas in Ipswich, Suffolk (above and top). Designed by Foster Associates in 1975, it was the world's largest toughened glass assembly. By day its envelope of 930 panes of anti-sun armour plate glass presents a stark, forbidding appearance, but by night the building is transformed into a transparent structure of light and space. Four storeys high, it has a roof garden and swimming pool.

These new houses at Basingstoke, Hampshire, are typical of many built in the expanding towns of post-war Britain. Though monotonous and unimaginative externally, they represent a widespread improvement in the owners' living standards.

This detached house, with its neo-Georgian details, mass-produced materials and pitched roof, represents to some the 'ideal home' of the early 1980s.

A post-war bungalow. First built in large numbers in the inter-war period, their appearance marked a minor revolution in living conditions, being especially suitable for older and retired people. After the Second World War they continued to be popular and form large estates in many parts of the country.

Though by the end of the decade North Sea oil had eased the import bill, its effect in raising confidence in sterling was ironically to the detriment of exports.

To their traditional responsibility for the external accounts, post-war governments have added such novel policy objectives as full employment, the Welfare State and stable prices, all of which require increased industrial productivity. In 1945 Labour, with its enthusiasm for planning and controls, seemed best placed to attempt these objectives. The cornerstone of Labour's industrial strategy was nationalisation of the transport, power, communications and iron and steel industries. However, these undertakings proved to be uneconomic social services rather than keys to 'the commanding heights of the economy', and despite the denationalisation and renationalisation of the steel industry, in the 1950s and 60s both parties accepted a mixed economy in which private enterprise had the lion's share. Attempts to promote economic growth through 'planning', whether by the Conservatives' National Economic Development Council in 1962 or Labour's National Plan in 1965, were frustrated by external constraints. From the mid 1960s growth averaged around two per cent a year, and throughout the 1970s British industry lost ground to international competitors. A new polarisation in industrial policies was betokened in 1975 by Labour's National Enterprise Board, when the extension of state funds was exchanged for public finance to ailing industries; while the Conservatives proposed in 1979 the sale of profitable segments of the nationalised industries.

Despite these difficulties, until the late 1960s unemployment remained, with the brief exception of the severe winter of 1947 to 48, well below the three per cent defined by Beveridge as 'full employment'. Yet the high priority given to full employment inevitably imposed limits on the attainment of other objectives, especially checking inflation. As early as 1948 Stafford Cripps recognised the dangers inherent in full employment combined with scarce resources, by suggesting a voluntary restraint policy which operated

TRANSPORT

Exhausted by their superhuman war effort, 1945 found the railways practically bankrupt, but salvation of a sort was at hand in the form of nationalisation by the incoming Labour government. Although strenuously resisted by the 'big four', a united British Railways came into being on 1 January 1948.

The first task of the Railway Executive of the new British Transport Commission was to get the railways back on their feet, but as little cash was available for investment, recovery was slow. After flirting with the idea of building an entirely new fleet of steam locomotives, the deteriorating financial situation in the early 1950s forced the decision, under the modernisation plan of 1955, to abandon steam altogether in favour of electric and diesel traction. But even at this time, with rail traffic reeling from unfettered road competition, no attempt was made to reorientate the network and its ancient operating methods.

Escalating deficits finally forced the government to act with the 1962 appointment of industrialist Dr Richard Beeching as head of the new British Railways Board. Beeching proposed and largely implemented the closure of 5,000 miles of route and 2,000 stations and cut BR's rolling stock fleet by half.

By the late 1960s modernisation was beginning to pay dividends as the inter-city concept of fast-interval passenger services spread, on the strength of which BR developed the 125 m.p.h. diesel High Speed Train and the 150 m.p.h. electric Advanced Passenger Train.

Although the overall tonnage carried by the railways declined throughout the 1970s, and costs were still far too high to allow penetration of the lucrative general merchandise market, passenger traffic continued to grow and 1979 saw passenger-miles at their highest level since 1961.

One of the major threats to the railway system came with the increasing development of the motorway, the first of which — the Preston bypass (now part of the M6) — was opened in 1958. Expansion was rapid: by 1968 there were 563 miles of motorway and by 1978, 1,501 miles.

Travel by private road transport has increased enormously since the last war and, unlike the railways, new road construction and improvements to existing roads have kept pace with the increased demand. By 1970 the government's aim of road building was the creation of a 'strategic network' of high quality roads to motorway or near motorway standard, linking the country's major towns and ports. However, the imposition by successive governments of expenditure cuts has modified this aim, and much of the concept has been abandoned.

Although the broad impact of motorways has been investigated less than it might have been, comparisons have been made between estimated traffic levels before construction and actual patterns of use. It is certain that many cities, notably Birmingham, Bristol, Glasgow, Manchester and Newcastle upon Tyne, are easier for the motorist and lorry driver to approach and circumnavigate; while the construction of modern, purpose-built roads often allows local councils to ban through journeys by heavy lorries, so relieving residential neighbourhoods.

Despite the sensitive landscaping and juxtaposition of curves, embankments, cuttings and tunnels, motorway users will often feel more divorced from their surroundings than do rail travellers. With similar standards in design and construction, even broadly similar service area cafes and petrol stations, common signposting and, since 1965, a common maximum speed limit of 70 m.p.h., motorways add to the suspension of the traveller's sense of place.

This notion of time standing still applies particularly to the air traveller. During the 1950s, the decade of the fast growth in traffic, the aeroplane came to dominate the long-distance routes, on which it could best exploit its increasing advantage of speed.

From 1970 to 1979 British international air traffic increased by almost 100 per cent, from 21 million passengers in 1970 to 41 million in 1979. Although internal air traffic expanded during the 1950s and 60s, in the early 70s it experienced strong competition from the improved rail system and faster trains; latterly, however, with decreasing costs of fares, it has come to account for over a quarter of all Britain's air passengers.

The explanation of this rapid growth in air travel lies in the combination of rising real incomes — which in themselves expanded the demand for leisure travel — the considerable technical progress of the passenger aeroplane and the increased efficiency of the airline industry. The introduction of the jet in the late 1950s also brought significant reductions in direct operating costs as well as a great increase in available seat-capacity on routes.

As the nationalised corporations (BEA and BOAC) had a monopoly over scheduled services, only charter and trooping were left to the independent companies. But the latter turned this arrangement to great advantage by developing charters and inclusive tours aimed at lower income groups. In the 1960s Laker Airways and Britannia Airways in particular were responsible for the advent of the package tour, with its cheap, all-inclusive holiday to the sun-drenched beaches of the Mediterranean.

The public response to such bargains was enormous and the scheduled airlines replied to the challenge of the independent charters by introducing a wider variety of lower fares on scheduled services. When, in 1977, Freddie Laker won his seven-year battle to start a simple, walk-on service across the Atlantic — the so-called Skytrain — his low fares were matched by the other airlines, and the 'price war' had begun.

While the contribution of improved air services to business communication was obviously important, a survey of British passengers in 1972 revealed that over four-fifths were travelling for leisure rather than work. The principal effect of the increase in air travel was therefore on the structure of tourism: just as the excitement of flying and the native pleasures of the Mediterranean resorts were extended to the popular market, so those who wished to avoid the crowds were able to fly virtually anywhere within the space of a day.

In addition to these great practical changes, it seems probable that the accelerated speed of air travel has fundamentally altered people's perception of the world. Yet while distances and times have certainly changed, the purposes of travel, even by air, have remained very much the same.

British Rail's Advanced Passenger Train, with its top speed of 150 m.p.h. and special coach tilting system that permits very fast but comfortable cornering, has the ability to knock at least one hour off the London to Glasgow rail travelling time. Being electric powered it is also cheaper to run than the High Speed Train.

The Newcastle Metro, Britain's first new underground system of the 20th century. Opened in August 1980, its 34 miles of track link the expanse of Newcastle and Gateshead, serving new housing, industrial and commercial developments along the river Tyne. Eventually there will be 41 stations, seven of which will be underground.

until 1950 with the co-operation of a Trades Union Congress grateful for the repeal of the penalties imposed on unions after the General Strike.

Despite being accelerated by the Korean war and the 'go' phases of Conservative economic policy, inflation remained manageable during the 1950s at three per cent a year. But in the 1960s, with rising international prices compounded by wage settlements in excess of the growth of productivity, the adverse effects of inflation on sterling, the balance of payments, unemployment and the extent and distribution of purchasing-power at home came to be seen as the major obstacles to economic growth and political stability. As a result a succession of experiments in income restraint by both voluntary and compulsory means was inconsistently and erratically applied.

The combination of a statutory wage freeze and cuts in public expenditure imposed by Labour in 1966 and the Conservatives in 1972 provoked strong opposition from the unions. Then the determination of the miners for a wage

settlement outside the limits of Conservative pay policy led to a state of emergency, a three-day working week for industry and finally, in February 1974, an election on the basis of 'who governs the country?', which the Conservatives lost. Labour's counter-inflation strategy was based on a 'Social Contract' with the TUC, which offered social policies to keep down the cost of living in return for voluntary wage restraint. This fragile agreement, together with expenditure cuts and rising unemployment, helped to reduce inflation from 24 per cent in 1974 and 1975 to single figures in 1977. Thereafter renewed external pressures, growing trade union demands for a return to free collective bargaining, bankruptcies and unemployment produced by expenditure cuts combined to erode the credibility of both Social Contract and government. The 1979 election then returned a Conservative administration committed to combating inflation through monetarism and market forces rather than incomes policy.

In 1980, with zero growth, inflation again in double

Gatwick Airport, Sussex, now London's second airport, was wholly rebuilt in the 1950s and expanded throughout the 1970s to keep up with increasing air traffic. It is being developed towards an eventual annual capacity of 25 million passengers.

Gravelly Hill interchange, Birmingham, links the M5 and M6 motorways, providing a through route for the fast national movement of goods. Ironically, huge cracks in its superstructure have led to road closures and considerable traffic congestion.

Tilbury Docks, Essex, cover a 56-acre site on the Thames Estuary opposite Gravesend. Constructed in the 1880s, Tilbury has survived a succession of problems to become one of the most important docks in Europe. After modernisation, in the 1970s Tilbury handled more than 150,000 containers a year and served 30 overseas ports.

The Severn Bridge, which carries the M4 motorway from Bristol to South Wales, was opened in September 1966. One of the longest suspension bridges in the world, it spans 3,240 feet, and its suspension cables contain 18,000 miles of steel bridgewire. Its opening resulted in an immediate commercial boom for Bristol.

figures, unemployment over two million, sterling over-valued, the balance of payments unstable, the social services suffering cuts and industry burdened with record interest rates, post-war economic objectives have apparently proved mutually contradictory. While consensus has been replaced by polarisation, government policy has increasingly been dictated by, rather than directing, the performance of the economy.

The Welfare State

For all the economic constraints, the greatest achievement of the post-war era has been the implementation of the Welfare State. During 1944 the coalition government issued a series of White Papers outlining its commitment to an attack on the 'five giants' – disease, idleness, ignorance, squalor and want – described by Beveridge in his 1942 Report. However, it fell to Labour to usher in the Welfare State.

The essence of Labour's programme was the replacement of the selective, means-tested benefits of the 1930s with universal entitlements. The 1946 National Insurance Act was comprehensive both in the 25 million people covered and the range of benefits provided, from unemployment, sickness, maternity and death to pensions (though finance prevented the implementation of Beveridge's national minimum at subsistence level). National Insurance was supplemented by an Industrial Injuries Act and by family allowances which tackled the problem of large families on low wages by making the first welfare benefit payable direct to the housewife. Unfortunately, the limitations of these provisions were all too evident, even in their first year, in the million claimants for National Assistance, which had replaced the discredited Poor Law with more generous but still means-tested supplementary benefits.

The apparent affluence of the 1950s and early 1960s placed emphasis on relative rather than primary poverty with the introduction of graduated or earnings-related schemes for pensions, redundancy payments, unemployment and sickness benefits, and through a substantial recasting of the system in the mid 1970s. At the same time rising costs, exacerbated by inflation, revived selectivity in the provision of free school meals and milk, and the introduction in 1971 of a Family Income Supplement in recognition of the extent of child poverty that remained despite the Welfare State. By 1975 there were 2.8 million claimants of supplementary benefits and pensions and perhaps a million more entitled non-claimants.

The second pillar in Labour's welfare programme was the provision of the National Health Service, which gave patients free access to doctors, hospitals, medicines and other services. That 95 per cent of doctors agreed to participate at the scheme's inception in 1948 was a reflection of popular enthusiasm and Aneurin Bevan's skill as a negotiator (he was prepared to concede the continuance of private practice alongside health-service work, pay-beds in hospitals and complex administrative arrangements to overcome the resistance of the British Medical Association). The high level of demand experienced by the Health Service created major financial difficulties within a very few years, and the introduction of prescription charges in 1951 provoked the resignation of Bevan and Harold Wilson. By the 1970s despite, or because of rapidly escalating expenditure and an unprecedented advance in medical technology, the financing of the Health Service from nurses' and doctors' salaries to pay-beds and expenditure cuts, had become a bone of political contention.

TOWN AND COUNTRY

After the war the rebuilding of 'blitzed' cities, from London to Coventry, Plymouth and Southampton, was one of the first priorities. The war also provided, through the success of policies for the direction of industry, the basis for a new approach to urban and regional development to counter the regionalised depression of the 1930s, and to fulfil pledges of new programmes for housing and education through planning the use of land and other resources. The 1947 Town and Country Planning Act charged county and county borough councils, with the aid of enhanced powers of compulsory purchase and planning permission, with responsibility for the promotion of plans for the residential, industrial and recreational needs of their communities. Loans and grants were offered as incentives to the location of industry in development areas. To regulate the speculative profits which could be made from land required for development, a Central Land Board was established with powers to levy development charges. (Though the Board was abolished on the Conservatives' return to office, the Labour Party made subsequent efforts with the Land Commission in 1968 and the 1975 Community Land Act. By the early 1970s, however, building land was valued at 20 times the price of agricultural land.) Following criticism of planning delays and the subordination of social to purely physical considerations, procedures were revised in the 1968 Town and Country Planning Act, though the complexity of the system remained a source of dissatisfaction.

The most striking achievement of town planning was the establishment of 28 new towns to accommodate the overspill populations of London, Lancashire, the Clyde Valley and South Wales and to check the urban sprawl that had disfigured the suburbs. The 1946 New Towns Act provided, through development corporations, for the establishment of communities of 30–50,000 inhabitants to meet both residential and employment needs. Although the early efforts were often criticised for their lack of social amenities, in the 1950s Cumbernauld was the recipient of architectural prizes. The 1952 Towns Development Act applied similar principles to the expansion of existing communities, and in the 1960s new town projects, such as Milton Keynes in Buckinghamshire, were approved on a scale far larger than their predecessors. By the 1970s, however, the escalating costs of new town development combined with concern over the decay of old city centres and slow progress in slum clearance brought to a halt the promotion of any further new towns.

In the 1950s much concern had been expressed at the speculative profits to be made from the development of inner city land for the building of offices that often remained unlet. However, during the 1960s the tendency for employment to be concentrated in city centres, with housing at the periphery, experienced a reversal as high-density tower blocks maximised the profitability of scarce and expensive land. But their failure to meet the needs of substantial sections of the population, especially the elderly and families with young children, was only gradually appreciated. In addition, the spread of vandalism was widely attributed to the dehumanising effects of high-rise living. In London and the west Midlands especially the early 1960s' influx of immigrants urgently seeking accommodation at low rents threatened the conversion of areas of older housing into quasi-ghettos. In 1967 a national survey reported that of the 15.5 million houses in England and Wales 1.8 million were unfit for habitation and a further 4 million lacked at least one major amenity. The result was the upgrading of improvement grants and the designation of urban action areas entitled to special funds.

An increase in the number of road vehicles from 4.5 million in 1950 to 18 million in 1978, together with the growth, especially in the south east, of commuting, brought problems of congestion, noise, smell and pollution. Few towns had been laid down in the age of the internal combustion engine. The 1963 Buchanan Report on *Traffic in Towns* recommended the creation of environmental areas distinct from and defined by primary road networks. There followed the promotion of motorways and by-passes, one-way systems and pedestrian precincts, and the regulation of urban traffic through zones and parking meters. Yet in the 1970s towns and villages suffered the invasion of the juggernaut as a consequence of Britain's membership of the Common Market.

Environmental considerations were evident in the application of controls to such areas as mineral workings (highlighted by the Aberfan coal tip disaster of 1966) and industrial effluence. The great London 'smog' of 1952, which was responsible for 4,000 deaths, led to the promulgation of the Clean Air Act of 1956 and the creation of smokeless zones. A new problem, endangering fishing, wildlife and tourism was oil spillage from the increasing number of tankers in British waters; disasters such as the *Torrey Canyon* in 1967 to the *Amoco Cadiz* in 1979 were frequent. Electricity pylons in Devon, a nuclear power station in Snowdonia, defence establishments on the Yorkshire Moors, the discovery of uranium in the Orkneys, the building of an oil terminal in the Shetland Isles and oil refineries on estuaries from Milford Haven and Avonmouth to Fawley, all brought economics into conflict with environmental considerations.

The creation of the Nature Conservancy Council in 1948 introduced the public to ideas of conservation, and under the 1949 National Parks Act the Lake and Peak Districts, Snowdonia and Brecon, the Yorkshire Moors and Dales, Northumberland, Dartmoor and Exmoor were designated areas for the preservation and enhancement of natural beauty. The invasion of the countryside by ribbon development was checked by the green belt. Operation Neptune has done much to protect Britain's unique coastline, while bodies such as the National Trust, and the popularity of archaeology have helped to preserve the nation's heritage from the developers. By the 1970s the National Parks Commission had become the Countryside Commission, tourism had become a vital earner of foreign currency, while paid holidays, a shorter working week and rising living standards contributed to a growing demand for urban and rural leisure facilities through such bodies as the Tourist Board and Sports Council. However, even this pursuit of leisure might prove too much of a good thing, as illustrated by the need to protect Stonehenge from the public and English holiday cottages in Wales from hostile nationalists.

Many once-massive tracts of natural landscape have been reduced to pocket-sized relics, maintained by the Nature Conservancy Council and other bodies.

Basildon New Town in Essex envisaged as part of a plan for London's overspill population. Around the town centre, planned industrial and residential zones are interspersed with open spaces and linked by a communications network.

St Paul's Cathedral stands isolated in a sea of post-war reconstruction following the devastation of central London in the blitz. The economics of inner city land values is reflected in the many tower blocks.

Graffiti on the Anglesey Estate, south east London, emphasises the problems and realities of new housing estates — a stark contrast to the dreams of post-war planners.

Shopping precincts like this one in Birmingham have helped to maintain the vitality of city centres, but they tend to favour national retailing chains rather than small shops.

Pedestrian precinct, Winchester. Traffic has become a major threat to the fabric and spirit of many town centres, and its expulsion has proved a rewarding policy.

Three generations of urban housing on Everton Heights, Liverpool: in the background 19th century tenements and 20th century terraces, and in the foreground the 'Piggeries', a recent high-rise scheme now declared uninhabitable.

The Roehampton Estate was started in the 1950s by the then London County Council. It was a pioneering prize-winning high-rise development. But whilst it was a success, many of its followers were definitely not.

Though Labour had built a million new houses by 1951, including temporary 'pre-fabs', demand still outran supply, as evidenced by the squatter. In contrast to Labour's aim Harold Macmillan's 'national crusade', which reached the target of 300,000 houses in 1954, concentrated on the private sector in pursuance of Eden's belief in a property owning democracy. More controversial was the release from state control of many private rents in 1957, which was attacked for facilitating exploitation. In the 1960s and 70s both political parties encouraged the provision of improvement grants for older properties, but the private rented sector continued to decline; slum clearance proceeded more slowly than before the war; and in the 1970s the Conservatives advocated the sale of council houses. Throughout the period rising house prices reflected the excess of demand over supply.

A new system of education

The foundations of the post-war education system were laid by R. A. Butler, a Conservative minister in the wartime coalition. The 1944 Act provided free secondary education for all to the age of 15 (extended in 1972 to 16) through grammar, secondary modern and, rarely, technical schools, according to ability. By the 1960s selection by examination at the age of 11 was the subject of much criticism, and in 1965 Labour required all local authorities to submit plans for a non-selective comprehensive system. Against Labour's support for equality of opportunity the Conservatives defended the academic quality of grammar and direct-grant schools. In 1974, with Labour again in power, the 11-plus examination was abolished and the comprehensive programme accelerated. The school curriculum also underwent controversial changes, with increasing emphasis on the development of personality and self-expression at the expense, some believed, of more traditional skills.

In the 1960s higher education underwent unprecedented expansion, with the creation of seven new universities and the elevation of several Colleges of Advanced Technology

INDUSTRY

During the war industries such as coal and the railways suffered a run down of plant and capital; some, like food processing and clothing, were constrained by rationing and utility specifications; others, from steel and shipbuilding to aircraft and electronics, underwent rapid expansion. Though factories were damaged or destroyed by bombing, the war also stimulated new technology in radar, the jet engine, petrochemicals, nuclear fission, synthetics and antibiotics.

In 1945 the Labour government was determined to apply the lessons of the war economy to peacetime problems, both in encouraging investment and research and through the nationalisation of key industries. The Bank of England, cables and wireless, post and telephones, civil aviation, electricity and gas were relatively uncontroversial, being already substantially under public control. It was also widely accepted that nationalisation was essential to the modernisation of coal and the railways. But as the most profitable sectors remained in private hands, while some of those taken into public ownership were almost inevitably uneconomic in commercial terms, Labour's package, which covered 20 per cent of the economy by output, did not give effective control over the economy as a whole. The public corporation produced no significant changes in management or industrial relations, nor did governments of either party succeed in reconciling subsidies to national services with commercial dictates. With investment and pricing subject to political interference, the public sector merely sharpened the difficulties, particularly of balancing employment against efficiency, inherent in a mixed economy.

Not that Labour's industrial policies were without success: industrial output expanded by 8 per cent a year, and exports had increased by 1950 to 175 per cent of their pre-war level, despite shortages of capital, fuel and raw materials, reduced hours of labour, high taxes and restrictive controls. In 1947 Britain's industrial production was 5 per cent above that in 1937. In the decade to 1958 it rose by half, and by 1968 it had doubled, but thereafter grew more modestly as foreign competitors invaded all areas of the domestic market, with products ranging from ships and aircraft to cars and electrical goods. An average growth rate of 2.8 per cent until the 1970s, while an improvement on the inter-war years, was however well behind that of other industrial nations.

In part this reflected the benefits to competitors of the continuing transfer of resources from agriculture to industry, or

of a fresh start after war damage, as well as the return of Germany and Japan to international markets in the mid 1950s. But some of British industry's failings must be attributed to low productivity and high prices caused by inappropriate or inconsistent government policies, trade union resistance to technical change and weak management.

There were, of course, notable achievements: by the late 1960s the vehicle and components industries contributed one-tenth of Britain's industrial output and 17 per cent of her exports. Yet, despite flow production techniques and the merging of the major British companies into British Leyland, economies of scale were less than those achieved by Japanese and continental competitors, industrial relations were turbulent and by 1979 car imports equalled the sales of British cars on the home market.

The aircraft industry expanded rapidly under the impetus of rearmament from 1950 to 1954, followed by successes in civil aviation (especially the first jet airliner, the Comet) as well as with aero-engines and the hovercraft. However, the industry's heavy reliance on the government as both customer and financier for research and development could, as with the cancellation of the TSR2, prove highly demoralising. By the end of the 1960s imports from the USA outweighed exports, and contraction continued despite the formation by merger of the British Aircraft Corporation, nationalisation in 1977 and co-operative projects with continental manufacturers (of which Concorde was the most spectacular but the least commercially successful).

The electronics industry embraced radar, radio and television, missiles and computers. Though Britain produced its first commercial computer in 1951, International Computers Limited, formed in 1968, faced increasing difficulty in competing with the scale of the American industry. The advent in the late 1970s of microelectronics brought predictions of both significant cost reductions and mass technological unemployment.

Until the late 1950s demand at home and abroad outran the capacity of the British steel industry. With the decline of such heavy users as the railways and shipbuilding, more economical techniques and materials, and the revival of Japanese and continental competition, the 1960s saw a new emphasis on productivity, but despite significant improvements the British industry, suffering in addition from poor location and political uncertainty, did not match competitors' efficiency. To meet massive investment costs from falling profits the industry became increasingly dependent on government,

before and after renationalisation in 1967. In a world of surplus steel capacity, redundancies and closures in the late 1970s affected South Wales, the Midlands and the north east.

In 1949 Britain built nearly half the world's shipping tonnage. Though buoyant international trade and the demand for oil tankers cushioned the industry in the 1950s, the return of Japan to the market, foreign subsidies, the high prices and poor delivery record of British shipbuilders led to a reduction in her share of the market to a mere five per cent by 1968. Nationalisation in 1977 could do little to check redundancies and closure of yards on Clydeside and Tyneside.

The building in the post-war period of many oil refineries in key estuarine sites was followed by a rapid expansion of the petrochemical industry in areas such as Billingham and Port Talbot and this in turn led to the emergence of a flourishing artificial fibres industry at Wilton (Teesside) and Kilroot and Coleraine (Northern Ireland). The rise of the artificial fibres industry combined with cheap imports, however, had adverse effects on the textile industry of Lancashire (which by 1980 was almost extinct) and the woollen industry of Yorkshire (which was also in serious trouble by 1980).

The chemical industry in its many guises, ranging from salt and soap production to glass, pharmaceuticals, fertilisers, dyes and explosives, generally prospered as it drew upon research advances and the expanding petrochemical industry. Many other industries such as paper, printing, furniture, ceramics, leather, footwear, rubber etc have been subject to fluctuating trade cycles and changes of fashion which have produced an ever-changing pattern of productivity.

While government welcomed mergers

to achieve the economies of scale essential to international competition, they attacked the price-fixing potential of monopolies. The 1948 Monopolies Act established a Restrictive Practices Commission which, in 1956, became a Court, and in 1964 the Conservatives abolished Retail Price Maintenance. By the mid 1970s, however, industry was as much in need of protection as the consumer from inflation and recession. In 1972 the Heath government was reluctantly obliged to rescue Rolls Royce aero-engines and Upper Clyde Shipbuilders from bankruptcy by nationalisation. In 1975 Labour's Industrial Reorganisation Corporation was empowered to exchange financial assistance for such companies as British Leyland for a degree of state control, as well as taking a 51 per cent share in the British National Oil Corporation. The Conservative administration elected in 1979, like its predecessor in 1970, found its reluctance to protect 'lame ducks' in conflict with its commitment to major employers, including British Leyland and British Steel.

Industrial Britain in the 1980s finds itself at a crossroads; the traditional industrial revolution base of cotton textiles, shipbuilding and coal has gone whilst the secondary base of heavy engineering, aircraft production, cars and cycles is under serious attack both at home and overseas by competitors. There has even been talk of the de-industrialisation of Britain and this is a possibility if trade unions pitch their standard of living aspirations too high. Meanwhile North Sea oil and gas, petro-chemicals, light engineering, nuclear engineering, micro-electronics, telecommunications, food processing and traditional British ingenuity offer hope of a new industrial pattern for the future.

The Ford Fiesta production line at Dagenham, Essex. Multinational, highly automated, mass production car manufacture has reduced several hundred makers to just four companies in the space of two generations.

to university status. The foundation of the Open University in 1969, which relies on the modern media rather than the lecture hall, transformed the opportunities for further education available to mature students and housewives among others.

Lifestyles and living standards

In post-war Britain, while rationing continued on many items, and was even introduced for the first time on bread, the 'black market' and the 'spiv' flourished and the queue became a way of life. By 1950 Britain had made progress along the road of reconstruction: the rationing of bread, potatoes, clothing and petrol had ended; earnings, if not levels, were rising ahead of a cost of living kept down by food subsidies; and the working week had been reduced to 45 hours. Emergence from austerity was symbolised in 1951 by the Festival of Britain with its accent on modernity and in its lasting legacies such as the Festival Hall.

With falling import prices, the end of rationing in 1954 and Conservative tax cuts, the living standards of the average wage earner rose by nearly 30 per cent in the 1950s. Much of this increase was spent on items, especially electrical goods, which had hitherto distinguished upper from middle and working class lifestyles. By 1960 there were eight million television licences, and four million cars on the roads. Supermarkets appeared in almost every high street, advertising flourished and commercial television, founded in 1955, was described as 'a licence to print money'. However, with pre-tax unskilled wages averaging £800 a year, working-class affluence rested heavily on full employment, welfare benefits, second incomes as more women went to work and especially the easy availability of hire purchase. Many remained too poor to partake of the fruits of affluence at all.

The late 1950s were marked by doubts and disillusion over the direction taken by post-war society: 1956, the year of Suez, was also the year of 'the angry young men', John Osborne's *Look Back in Anger* expressing dissatisfaction with the state of the nation and especially its continuing

Steel production has dominated the landscape of Consett in Co. Durham since 1850. Faced with a glut in world steel output, the British Steel Corporation announced the closure of the Consett works in August 1980 as part of a programme to reduce the industry's labour force by a third. The closure resulted in the loss of 3,700 jobs and threatened to raise unemployment in the area to 40 per cent. What is to become of such towns in a future of automated industry?

Treforest industrial estate was established in 1937 in South Wales, at the time a distressed area of high unemployment, with the assistance of government agencies under the Special Areas Act as a result of a visit by the Prince of Wales. After the war it expanded in the range of light industry and diversified the economy of a region previously almost exclusively dependent on the declining staple industries of coal and steel, becoming the forerunner of many similar estates throughout the land.

Skelmersdale, Lancs, begun in 1962 for Liverpool's overspill, but by 1980 unemployment was at 20 per cent.

Aggressive mass picketing at Grunwick's dispute in 1977 focused attention on deteriorating industrial relations.

Despite job-creation schemes, rising unemployment in the 1970s severely affected school leavers.

The computer has changed the face of modern industry, but will its effect on employment outweigh its advantages?

permeation of class consciousness; the campaign for Nuclear Disarmament questioned the values of the nuclear age; opponents of 'pornography' were aghast at the acquittal in 1960 of an unabridged edition of D. H. Lawrence's *Lady Chatterley's Lover*; prostitution was concealed rather than controlled by the 1959 Street Offences Act; gambling was given a cloak of respectability by state premium bonds in 1955 and licensed betting shops in 1960; juvenile delinquency and illegitimacy were on the increase; the Vassall and Profumo scandals of 1963 were seen as products of a 'permissive society'. However, the 'swinging sixties' had their more positive aspects: Mary Quant's mini-skirt revolutionised the fashion scene; the Beatles received the OBE for breaking American dominance of popular music; theatrical censorship was abolished; tourism flourished. And more important, capital punishment was repealed, the laws on homosexuality and abortion were liberalised and 'irretrievable breakdown of marriage' became the only grounds for divorce. For many these were signs of a new humanitarianism; for others, spearheaded by Mrs Mary Whitehouse, they were, along with student unrest and a sub-culture based on drugs such as LSD and cannabis, evidence of national decadence. In the 1970s an increase in crimes of violence, especially 'mugging', and in vandalism and hooliganism bore witness to a decline in authority which had its most extreme manifestation in the brief but horrifying campaign of urban terrorism by the Angry Brigade. On the other side of the coin was the strength in that decade of such movements as Voluntary Service Overseas and the various forms of community service.

During the 1960s and 70s three groups attracted particular attention: the young, women and blacks. In the 1950s full employment and the ending of conscription brought a combination of affluence and leisure to the teenager, which was displayed in fashion – first as the 'teddy boy' and then over the next two decades as 'mods and rockers', 'hippies' and 'punks' – and by the importation from America of 'rock and roll' music. Youth culture reflected values in conflict with those of their elders, as well as the belief that above all the post-war world was one of opportunity for the young. In 1967 the age of majority was lowered to 18 years. But by the late 1970s rising unemployment amongst school leavers threatened bleaker prospects for British youth.

For women too the 1950s offered some widening of horizons, as a modest expansion of nursery education combined with full employment to attract more married women into employment. By the 1960s the contraceptive pill gave women an equality of sexual freedom for the first time. The women's liberation movement emphasised a woman's right to control over her own body and freedom from the sole responsibility for child rearing; it supported abortion law reform, the rights of the single-parent family, paid maternity leave, creches and nursery schools. For some the campaign for battered wives was of more immediate importance than the case for multiple orgasm. The Equal Pay Act of 1970 and the Sex Discrimination Act of 1975 endorsed the demand for sexual equality, though their practical effects were felt only slowly. In 1980 though Britain had in Mrs Thatcher its first woman prime minister, there were still disproportionately few women in top posts and very many in the poorest paid jobs.

The same was true of Britain's black community. Coloured immigrants began to arrive from the West Indies, India and Pakistan in the 1950s; in 1958 the Notting Hill riots highlighted the difficulties of assimilation. With the

POWER AND ENERGY

When the National Coal Board sign was erected outside Britain's collieries in 1947 coal had a virtual monopoly on Britain's fuel supplies (other than for motor vehicles) either by direct use or in the generation of electricity and gas. In that same year the dangers inherent in this dependence were brought to the fore by a major fuel crisis during the severest winter since 1880. In the first decade after nationalisation output was expanded from 187 million tons to 224 million (still below the 1937 level), more rapid growth being constrained by declining manpower as a modest increase in wages, in line with the government's reluctance to charge an economic price for coal, fell short of that necessary to attract labour at a time of full employment. Shortage of coal supplies led to the virtual cessation of exports in the late 1950s, while imports were necessary to supplement domestic production.

From the late 1950s competition from oil, and later natural gas, intensified. The coal industry responded with improved productivity, output per man-shift rising from 1.25 tons in 1957 to 2.24 in 1978, and by opening the world's first fully automatic, remote-controlled colliery at Bevercotes in 1967. However, by 1968 output had declined to 156 million tons as the labour force contracted from 704,000 in 1957 to 350,000 in 1968 and the number of collieries under production fell from 980 in 1948 to 420.

By 1968 oil was supplying nearly 40 per cent of the nation's energy requirements, not only as fuel for road vehicles and domestic heating but in electricity power stations, gas works (until the discovery of natural gas beneath the North Sea in 1967), and in steelworks and on the railways. The oil-processing industry expanded as refineries sprang up on estuaries such as the Severn and Solent, bringing with them an expansion of the petrochemical industries, especially the production of plastics and synthetics. Yet the dominance of oil may be short-lived.

The late 1960s and 1970s saw the formation and increasingly effective operation of the Organisation of Petroleum Exporting Countries with the raising of the international price of oil as its principal objective. But in 1974 the cost of Britain's oil imports quadrupled, with disastrous consequences for the balance of payments as well as domestic prices. Moreover, a series of wars and political crises in the Middle East were reminders of the insecure nature of this increasingly vital commodity. Britain's own discovery of North Sea oil, struck in 1969 and first brought ashore in 1975, promised self-sufficiency by the end of the decade, and even export potential. The North Sea oil boom also had important economic, political and environmental implications for Scotland, with pipelines to Aberdeen and the Orkneys, rig-building on Clydeside and a major terminal in the Shetlands. However, it was evident that North Sea oil was a finite resource, providing at best a breathing space. In fact proven world oil resources might, in the opinion of some experts, last a mere 30 years at

At Dounreay in Caithness, the UK Atomic Energy Authority's prototype fast-breeder reactor began generating electricity in 1975, though high costs and safety factors have inhibited the adoption of a substantial country-wide programme.

Drax coal-fired power station with its giant cooling towers dominates the surrounding Yorkshire landscape. Despite the advent of the nuclear age, British electricity is still cheaper to produce from coal.

1975 consumption levels.

In the short term the solution was seen in a reversal of the contraction of the coal industry, though the advantage of a domestic resource was to some extent countered by the increased economic and political leverage given to the miners in seeking wage increases well beyond productivity improvements or the rate of inflation. Nonetheless, despite the continued fall in output to 122 million tons and employment to 235,000 by 1979, the industry now seemed, contrary to the predictions of only a decade earlier, to have a future stretching at least to the end of the century.

For the longer term the oil crisis brought renewed support for atomic energy. Britain had opened the world's first commercial nuclear power station at Calder Hall in 1946, producing electricity through the fission process. Britain's electricity consumption grew rapidly from 23.1 million kW in 1937 to 55.6 million in 1950, 120.5 million in 1960 and 204.4 million in 1968, as the pylons of the Central Electricity Generating Board (before 1948 the British Electricity Authority) marched across the countryside. Initially output was derived overwhelmingly from coal, with a minor addition from hydroelectric sources. With the escalation of oil prices, atomic energy became an increasingly attractive alternative to fossil fuels. In 1977, whereas electricity generated from oil cost 1.27 pence per kW and from coal 1.07 pence, that from nuclear power cost only 0.69 pence. Further-

more, the fast breeder reactor promised the creation of more fuel than it consumed. However, despite the very high safety record of the British Atomic Energy Authority, the initiation of a major nuclear energy programme was held back by public fear of the risk of explosion or radiation leakage, the dangers of terrorism and the environmental hazards in the disposal of nuclear waste. In 1979 only 34.8 million out of a total of 279.8 million kW electricity were generated by atomic power stations.

While politicians debated the pros and cons of nuclear power, and the world's oil resources diminished in life-expectancy and escalated in price, other voices were heard extolling the merits, both economic and environmental, of 'alternative technology' – the harnessing of the power of the sun, wind, waves and tide, of geothermal sources such as geysers and of vegetable matter – while there were appeals from all quarters for conservation and economy in the use of fossil fuels. Though, as yet, few of these proposals have reached more than an experimental stage it is probable that, irrespective of the resolution of the nuclear debate, the price of oil or the politics of coal, they will prove of increasing significance in the coming decades. Meanwhile Britain's immediate post-war coal fired economy has passed via a coal and oil phase into a four fuel economy based on oil, natural gas, coal and nuclear power.

Lee Hall colliery, Staffordshire, with the coal-fired Rugely power station in the background. The rising cost of oil in the 1970s gave coal a new lease of life.

Grangemouth on the Firth of Forth has been a base for crude oil imports since the 1930s, and subsequently the location of a BP refinery. In 1951 it was linked to the west coast by a 57 mile pipeline in response to increased tanker size.

Canvey Island in the Thames estuary was selected in 1959 for the import of liquefied natural gas. In the late 1960s, with the construction of an oil refinery, the site became a centre of growth for the petrochemical industry.

BP's Forties Alpha production platform in the North Sea Forties field. Situated 110 miles to the east north east of Aberdeen, it is one of four BP platforms in the field and with them produces 500,000 barrels a day.

pace of immigration accelerating in response to labour shortages (especially in transport and the health service), and concentrated in London and the west Midlands, the Conservatives stemmed the flow in 1962 with the first immigration act, which was tightened up by Labour in 1968. Meanwhile government tackled race relations: in 1965 discrimination in public places was outlawed and in 1968 the law was extended to discrimination in housing and employment for Britain's one million coloured citizens. Though the example set by the law and the Community Relations Council has been generally beneficial and racial violence has been rare, racial tension has been kept in the public eye by Enoch Powell and by the National Front.

The position of the immigrant emphasises the enduring extent of poverty and inequality in post-war Britain. Peter Townsend has claimed that there are five million in poverty, due especially to old age and large families on low wages. Despite capital gains tax, introduced in 1965, just under two million people, or five per cent of the population, still own nearly half the nation's wealth. Between the underprivileged poor and the propertied wealthy lies a wide band, from the traditional middle classes to the skilled working classes, which is living increasingly, like the nation at large, beyond its own and the economy's current means.

In the closing decades of the 20th century, the present and future lifestyles of the British people depend, as they have since the dawn of civilised society, on the exploitation of our natural resources – in agriculture, fishing and manufacture or in the extraction of energy from timber and coal, gas and oil fields – by the ingenuity and efforts of the people themselves, as expressed in the political, social and economic institutions of the nation.

COINS

The old 'f.s.d.' coinage.

Decimal coinage, introduced 1971.

The cost of the two World Wars had its impact also on the British coinage. After the first war the silver content of the 'silver' coinage was reduced from sterling standard to 50 per cent (1920). After the second war silver was replaced altogether as a coinage metal by a copper-nickel alloy (1947).

Only the Queen's Maundy money is now issued in sterling silver, and it is only as Maundy money that the famous silver threepenny piece – essential ingredient of so many Christmas puddings – survives. The Queen distributes sets of these coins, 4d, 3d, 2d and 1d, to a group of pensioners on Maundy Thursday each year.

The Sovereign is the only English coin in production today. The first coin of that name was issued by Henry VII in 1489, but the George and Dragon design on the modern coin goes back to

that used on the later sovereigns of George III designed by Pistrucci.

Nowadays the crown is a denomination used only for special issues, but the first silver crown was issued by Edward VI and it continued in regular production into this century. An outstanding 19th century example was struck for William IV, while an example of a modern celebration crown is provided by the Queen's Silver Jubilee issue.

Our own generation has seen the most dramatic development in the history of the coinage for centuries. The introduction of a decimal coinage in 1971, with one hundred new pennies in the pound, has replaced the old f.s.d. system which dates from eighth century Carolingian times. In those days there were no pound or shilling coins, only pennies.

EVENTS AND PERSONALITIES

1945 After the end of the Second World War the Labour Party under Clement Attlee wins an absolute Parliamentary majority of 154 seats.
Family Allowances are introduced
1946 The National Insurance and National Health Service Acts lay the foundations of the Welfare State.
The Trade Disputes Act repeals penalties imposed on trade unions in 1927.
Bread rationing is introduced.
At Fulton, Missouri, Churchill declares 'an iron curtain has descended across Europe'
1947 India Independence Act is passed and Pakistan is created by partition.
The National Service Act introduces eighteen months' 'call-up'.
Restoration of sterling convertibility provokes an exchange crisis.
Under Marshall Aid Britain receives £681 million from the United States by 1951.
The coal industry is nationalised
1948 Railways, road haulage and electricity are nationalised.
National Assistance replaces the Poor Law and Sir Stafford Cripps introduces wage restraint.
Following a Jewish terrorist campaign Britain surrenders the Palestine mandate.
A twelve year counter-insurgency campaign against communists begins in Malaya.
Britain assists in the airlift of supplies to Berlin, blockaded by Russia.
Independence for Burma and Ceylon
1949 The North Atlantic Treaty establishes a defence alliance between the United States and Western Europe. The Commonwealth Prime Ministers' Conference designates the King 'the symbol of the free association of its independent member states'. The pound is devalued from $4.03 to $2.80.
The Parliament Act reduces House of Lords' delaying power to one year.
The Representation of the People Act abolishes business premises' vote and university constituencies, redefines boundaries and introduces postal voting
1950 Labour's overall majority is reduced to five in the General Election.
Britain enters the Korean War under United Nations auspices until 1953. Rearmament is commenced
1951 Foreign Office spies Burgess and Maclean defect to Moscow.
Principal companies in the iron and steel industry are nationalised.
Prescription charges are introduced, provoking the resignation of Bevan and Wilson.
In the General Election the Conservatives win an overall majority of 17.
The Festival of Britain takes place
1952 **Elizabeth II** succeeds George VI.
Britain tests the atomic bomb. Mau Mau rebellion in Kenya, in support of increased African representation, lasts until 1958

1953 The coronation of Elizabeth II coincides with the Commonwealth expedition's ascent of Mount Everest.
Iron and steel are denationalised
1954 Rationing ends.
The South East Asia Treaty Organisation is set up
1955 The Central Treaty Organisation is established
Eden succeeds Churchill as Prime Minister and Hugh Gaitskell becomes leader of the Labour Party.
Conservatives increase their overall majority to 56
1956 Russian leaders Bulganin and Kruschev visit Britain.
Following the nationalisation of the Suez Canal by Colonel Nasser, France and Britain occupy the Canal Zone, subsequently withdrawing under United Nations' censure
1957 Eden resigns through ill health and Harold Macmillan becomes Prime Minister. Britain tests the hydrogen bomb. A Defence White Paper recommends the ending of conscription by 1960 and reliance on nuclear deterrence. Opposition to nuclear weapons is mobilised by the Campaign for Nuclear Disarmament.
Britain declines to sign the Treaty of Rome founding the European Economic Community.
The Gold Coast becomes the first African colony to gain independence (as Ghana)
1958 Independence is granted to the West Indian Federation.
There are race riots in Notting Hill, London.
Life peerages supplement hereditary membership of the House of Lords
1959 The Conservative majority is increased to 100 seats.
Cyprus is granted independence after culmination of EOKA campaign of violence.
The European Free Trade Area is formed under British initiative
1960 Macmillan delivers his 'wind of change' speech on apartheid in South Africa.
Nigeria is granted independence
1961 The Republic of South Africa withdraws from the Commonwealth.
Britain requires a loan from the International Monetary Fund. 'Pay Pause' is introduced
1962 The National Economic Development Council is established with membership from industry, trade unions and government.
The Nassau Agreement is negotiated with the United States for supply of 'Polaris' submarine-borne nuclear missiles.
Independence is granted to Uganda.
The Commonwealth Immigration Act restricts immigration through vouchers.
Macmillan sacks a third of his Cabinet in the 'night of the long knives'. The Vassal Admiralty spy scandal is uncovered
1963 John Profumo (Minister for War) is involved in a scandal with call girl Christine Keeler.

The coronation of Queen Elizabeth II took place on 2 June 1953, and revived Britain's flagging post-war spirits with hopes of a new age of prosperity.

The future King of the United Kingdom, of Great Britain and North Ireland and of other realms, head of the Commonwealth and Defender of the Faith, with Lady Diana Spencer at the announcement of their engagement in February 1981. They were married on July 29th 1981.

Macmillan retires through ill health, to be succeeded by Lord Home who renounces his peerage.

On the death of Gaitskell, Harold Wilson becomes leader of the Labour Party.

Britain signs the Nuclear Test Ban Treaty.

Kenya becomes independent.

General de Gaulle vetoes Britain's application to join the Common Market

1964 Zambia, Malawi and Malta are granted independence.

The General Election gives Labour an overall majority of four.

An import surcharge is imposed to remedy the inherited balance of payments deficit of £8,000 million.

1965 'Circular 10/65' urges local authorities to draw up schemes for comprehensive schooling.

The Race Relations Act bans discrimination in public places and establishes the Race Relations Board.

The death penalty is abolished.

The Trade Disputes Act gives unions legal indemnity against breach of contract.

Capital gains tax is introduced.

Natural gas deposits are discovered offshore.

The Commonwealth Secretariat is established.

Ian Smith's white minority government in Rhodesia issues a Unilateral Declaration of Independence and Britain imposes economic sanctions.

John Lennon, 1940–80. Perhaps the most notable and admired member of the cultural renaissance that marked the '60s, his presence extended beyond his media and had a radical philosophical effect on the thoughts of his (then) youthful audience.

Edward Heath becomes the first elected leader of the Conservative Party

1966 Labour's overall majority is increased to 96.

Supplementary benefits replace National Assistance.

In the wake of a seamen's strike and the Arab-Israeli Six Day War, the Prices and Incomes Act imposes a six months' 'wages freeze' to be followed by a period of 'severe restraint'

1967 The pound is devalued from $2.80 to $2.40, and three billion dollars' worth of international credits are negotiated, conditional on expenditure cuts.

Unemployment passes half a million.

The iron and steel industries are renationalised.

The Parliamentary Commissioner for Administration (Ombudsman) is appointed

1968 The race relations law is extended to outlaw discrimination in housing and employment, and the Community Relations Commission is established.

Expulsion of the Asian community from Kenya leads to tighter immigration controls.

Withdrawal from Aden initiates Britain's commitment to terminate her presence 'East of Suez' by 1971.

De Gaulle vetoes Britain's second application to join the Common Market.

Northern Irish Civil Rights Association agitation on behalf of the Catholic minority leads to rioting in Londonderry

1969 British troops are sent to Northern Ireland. The Provisional Irish Republican Army begins a campaign of terrorism.

Trade union opposition obliges Barbara Castle to withdraw her proposed legislation for the reform of industrial relations

1970 In the General Election the Conservatives obtain an overall majority of 30.

Oil is struck in the North Sea

1971 The pound is allowed to 'float' free of fixed parity with other currencies.

The Industrial Relations Act attempts to make collective bargains enforceable at law, leading, in conjunction with restraints on wage bargaining, to industrial unrest.

The Immigration Act revises Commonwealth citizens' preferential status and creates the offence of illegal entry.

Internment without trial is introduced in Northern Ireland

1972 'Direct rule' from London is imposed over Northern Ireland. Thirteen die in clash between the British Army and civil rights demonstrators in Londonderry on 'Bloody Sunday'.

The Pearce Commission declares that the proposed settlement over Rhodesia

is unacceptable to the African population.

Britain and Communist China exchange ambassadors.

Miners secure a substantial wage increase after a strike and arbitration.

Statutory prices and a pay standstill are introduced

1973 Britain joins the Common Market on January 1.

The 'Yom Kippur' War in the Middle East leads to a rapid rise in oil prices.

There are strikes by gas workers and civil servants, followed by overtime bans and work-to-rule by electrical power workers, railwaymen and miners, leading to declaration of a state of emergency

1974 The three day working week is introduced in response to the miners' work-to-rule. A ballot in favour of a coal strike leads to the February General Election. Labour, with a majority of four over Conservatives but without overall majority, form a government. Wilson settles with miners and in an October election gains an overall majority of three.

The 'Social Contract' is introduced between the government and the Trades Union Congress for wage restraint.

Under Local Government reform, country borough powers are reallocated between district councils and county councils with revised boundaries.

In Northern Ireland a new Executive in which power is shared between representatives of both Protestant and Catholic communities is brought down by the Protestant Ulster Workers Council's general strike, and direct rule is restored

1975 Unemployment passes one million.

The National Enterprise Board is established with power to develop state involvement in the management of private industries in return for public investment.

The Sex Discrimination Act is passed.

Following 'renegotiation' of the terms of Britain's membership, a referendum declares by a two to one majority in favour of Britain remaining in the Common Market.

Margaret Thatcher defeats Edward Heath in the Conservative leadership election

1976 Harold Wilson retires from premiership, succeeded by James Callaghan.

As the pound slides to a new low, a four billion dollar International Monetary Fund loan is negotiated.

The Peace People's movement is launched in Northern Ireland

1977 Queen Elizabeth II's Silver Jubilee is celebrated.

The aircraft and shipbuilding industries are nationalised.

Labour government, its majority reduced to one by by-election losses, enters a four month pact with the Liberals.

Britain's first official fireman's strike takes place

1978 The European Court of Human Rights clears Britain of torture in Northern Ireland but finds her guilty of 'inhuman and degrading treatment' of prisoners.

Britain refuses to recognise 'internal settlement' in Rhodesia

1979 Scotland and Wales reject devolution of political authority in a referendum.

There is a winter of industrial discontent.

In the General Election Margaret Thatcher becomes Britain's first woman Prime Minister, with a Conservative majority of 43.

The first direct elections to the European Parliament take place. Airey Neave (Conservative spokesman on Northern Ireland) and Lord Mountbatten are killed by IRA bombs.

The Lancaster House Conference reaches constitutional settlement for Rhodesia, leading to ceasefire in the guerilla war

1980 Robert Mugabe is elected as Prime Minister of Zimbabwe (formerly Rhodesia) and independence is granted.

There are continuing economic difficulties and unemployment passes the two million mark, but inflation falls.

James Callaghan resigns as leader of the Labour Party and is replaced by Michael Foot.

1977 was the year of the Silver Jubilee of Queen Elizabeth II. Celebrations took place throughout the country and especially in London; Pall Mall is shown above.

Britain, past, present & future

Britain in the mid 20th century is a synthesis of the work of Nature and Man. It was a historian of the 19th century, F. W. Maitland, who first drew attention to the palimpsest character of our landscape, a theme which has been explored in the 20th century by historians and geographers such as W. G. Hoskins and H. C. Darby.

Our survey, necessarily superficial in places, nevertheless amply demonstrates the richness of our landscape heritage and the ease with which much of our history can be read as we move about our towns and countryside. Prehistoric monuments, Roman roads and towns, Anglo-Saxon villages, majestic Norman castles and cathedrals, sturdy medieval churches, ruined monasteries, beautiful Elizabethan manor houses, Georgian country towns, dark satanic mills and Victorian railways jostle with the intricate pattern of our medieval lanes, 20th century motorways, picturesque fishing ports, the gleaming towers of modern city centres and many other landscape features.

But no landscape is static, and even as we examine and understand what it has become it is in the process of becoming something different. The only constant factor in the landscape is that of change. We are spectators of a transient scene and the process is never-ending with or without Man, though Man will often accelerate the rate of change or, conversely, slow down the process with conservation measures.

We have seen that the human factors which bring about change are many and varied, ranging from demographic, economic and social forces to strategic, religious, racial, cultural and political movements. Can we detect any pattern in the past that might enable us to peer into the future?

According to the American psychologist McClelland there are three basic types of human motivation; achievement, affiliation (friendship) and power, which successively mark the rising, peaking and declining phases of all civilisations. At each phase the overall national motivation is regarded as the mass outcome of millions of individual motivations. Britain is seen by McClelland to have been an achieving society in the Elizabethan period with triumphs as diverse as global exploration, Shakespearian drama and the defeat of the Spanish Armada, but with the Civil War of the 17th century and the decadence of the 18th century it became power oriented. A new cycle of achievement began with the great scientific and engineering advances of the Industrial Revolution and the accretion of Empire by individual actions. By the 20th century, however, the affiliation phase had again set in, marked by the social awareness of the welfare state, the encouragement of colonial independence, the giving of foreign aid, the ceding of world leadership and the growth of the permissive society.

Currently there is much talk of decline and de-industrialisation, which raises the possibility of continuing downhill into the power phase with its threat of dictatorship. Can Britain find some way of renewing its former motivation towards achievement? The economic and cultural resources of the country and its people are by no means exhausted, but future success does seem to depend upon developing more positive attitudes.

Whatever the outcome, the landscape of Britain will continue to change, but its appearance in the 21st century could be dramatically affected by whichever path is eventually followed.

Bibliography & Suggested further reading

Picture Acknowledgements

Index

BIBLIOGRAPHY AND SUGGESTED FURTHER READING

The Publishers would like to acknowledge their indebtedness to those of the following books which were consulted for reference.
For ease of reference, we have listed books under a number of headings: Britain, England, Scotland, Wales and Ireland, followed by the 12 section headings and several subject headings.

Britain
THE HISTORY OF BRITISH CIVILIZATION, E. Wingfield-Stratford, Routledge & Kegan Paul
BRITISH HISTORY, Ramsay Muir, George Philip & Sons Ltd
A NATURAL HISTORY OF MAN IN BRITAIN, H. J. Fleure, New Naturalist Series, Collins 1951
THE BRITISH ISLES, L. Dudley Stamp and S. H. Beaver, Longmans 1971 (6th ed)
BRITAIN IN THE CENTURY OF TOTAL WAR, PEACE AND SOCIAL CHANGE 1900–1962, A. Marwick, Bodley Head 1968
A COMPLETE ATLAS OF THE BRITISH ISLES, Readers' Digest 1965
THE LAND OF BRITAIN: ITS USE AND MISUSE, L. D. Stamp, Longmans 1962 (3rd ed)

England
THE OXFORD HISTORY OF ENGLAND, ed. G. N. Clark, Oxford UP (15 vols, 1936–65)
A HISTORY OF THE ENGLISH PEOPLE, R. J. Mitchell and M. D. R. Leys, Longmans
AN ILLUSTRATED HISTORY OF ENGLAND, G. M. Trevelyan, Longmans 1973
A HISTORY OF ENGLAND FROM THE COMING OF THE ENGLISH TO 1918, K. G. Feiling, Macmillan 1973
THE PELICAN HISTORY OF ENGLAND (8 vols, 1955–65)
AN ILLUSTRATED HISTORY OF ENGLAND, John Burke, Collins 1974
EMPIRE TO WELFARE STATE: ENGLISH HISTORY 1906–1976, T. O. Lloyd, Oxford UP 1979 (2nd ed)
A HISTORICAL GEOGRAPHY OF ENGLAND BEFORE 1800, H. C. Darby, Cambridge UP 1936
THE MAKING OF THE ENGLISH LANDSCAPE, W. G. Hoskins, Hodder & Stoughton 1955
ENGLISH SOCIAL HISTORY, G. M. Trevelyan, Longmans 1944
THE MAKING OF THE ENGLISH WORKING CLASS, E. P. Thompson, Penguin 1968
A SOCIAL HISTORY OF HOUSING, J. Burnett, David & Charles 1978
THE PAST AT WORK, Anthony Burton, BBC/Andre Deutsche 1980
ONE MAN'S ENGLAND, W. G. Hoskins, BBC 1978
LIFE IN THE ENGLISH COUNTRY HOUSE, M. Girouard, Yale UP 1978
LONDON: THE BIOGRAPHY OF A CITY, Christopher Hibbert, Allen Lane 1977
A HISTORY OF LONDON, Robert Gray, Hutchinson 1978
A NEW HISTORICAL GEOGRAPHY OF ENGLAND BEFORE 1600, ed. H. C. Darby, Cambridge UP 1978
A NEW HISTORICAL GEOGRAPHY OF ENGLAND AFTER 1600, ed. H. C. Darby, Cambridge UP 1978
THE COMMON LANDS OF ENGLAND AND WALES, W. G. Hoskins and L. D. Stamp, New Naturalist Series, Collins 1963

Scotland
A HISTORY OF SCOTLAND, J. D. Mackie, Penguin 1964
THE KINGDOM OF THE SCOTS, G. W. S. Barrow, Arnold 1973

Wales
WALES THROUGH THE AGES, A. J. Roderick, C. Davies 1974 (2 vols)
A HISTORY OF WALES TO THE EDWARDIAN CONQUEST, Sir John E. Lloyd, 1939 (3rd ed)
A HISTORY OF WALES FROM 1485–1939, D. Williams, 1950
WALES, F. V. Emery, Longmans 1969
WALES: A PHYSICAL, HISTORICAL AND REGIONAL GEOGRAPHY, ed. E. G. Bowen, Methuen 1957

Ireland
A SHORT HISTORY OF IRELAND, J. C. Beckett, Hutchinson 1952
IRELAND: A HISTORY, Robert Kee, BBC 1981
IRELAND, T. W. Freeman, Methuen 1969 (4th ed)
EARLY CHRISTIAN IRELAND: INTRODUCTION TO THE SOURCE, K. Hughes, Cambridge UP 1972

The Birth of Britain
THE STRUCTURE OF THE BRITISH ISLES, J. G. C. Anderson and T. R. Owen, Pergamon 1968
BRITAIN'S STRUCTURE AND SCENERY, L. Dudley Stamp, New Naturalist Series, Collins 1946
A GUIDE TO THE BRITISH LANDSCAPE, J. W. R. Cheatle, Collins 1976
THE COASTLINE OF BRITAIN, J. A. Steers, Cambridge UP, 1946
GEOLOGY AND SCENERY IN ENGLAND AND WALES, A. E. Trueman, revised by Whittow and Hardy, Penguin 1971
GEOLOGY AND SCENERY IN IRELAND, J. B. Whittow, Penguin 1975
GEOLOGY AND SCENERY IN SCOTLAND, J. B. Whittow, Penguin 1977

The First Settlers
THE ENVIRONMENT OF EARLY MAN IN THE BRITISH ISLES, J. G. Evans, Elek 1975
THE PREHISTORIC SETTLEMENT OF BRITAIN, R. Bradley, Routledge & Kegan Paul 1978
EARLY MAN IN BRITAIN AND IRELAND, A. Morrison, Croom Helm 1980
INTRODUCTION TO BRITISH PREHISTORY, J. V. S. Megan and D. D. A. Simpson, Leicester UP 1979
THE AGE OF STONEHENGE, C. Burgess, Dent 1980
IRON AGE COMMUNITIES IN BRITAIN, B. W. Cunliffe, Routledge & Kegan Paul 1978 (2nd ed)
THE PERSONALITY OF BRITAIN, Cyril Fox, National Museum of Wales 1932 (4th ed 1950)

Roman Britain
A COMPANION TO ROMAN BRITAIN, ed. Peter Clayton, Phaidon 1980
INVASION AND RESPONSE, ed. B. Burnham and H. Johnson, British Archaeological Reports 1979
THE END OF ROMAN BRITAIN, ed. P. J. Casey, British Archaeological Reports 1979
ROMAN POTTERY STUDIES, ed. J. Dore and K. Greene, British Archaeological Reports 1977
SILCHESTER, G. C. Boon, David & Charles 1974
THE ARCHAEOLOGY OF ROMAN BRITAIN, R. G. Collingwood and I. A. Richmond, Methuen 1969
ROMAN BRITAIN, Ordnance Survey 1979 (4th ed)
HADRIAN'S WALL, Ordnance Survey
THE ANTONINE WALL, Ordnance Survey

The Dark Ages
THE NORTHERN WORLD, ed. D. M. Wilson, Thames & Hudson 1980
THE ANGLO-SAXONS, D. M. Wilson, Pelican 1981
ANGLO-SAXON ENGLAND, D. Brown, Batsford 1978
ARCHAEOLOGY OF ANGLO-SAXON ENGLAND, ed. D. M. Wilson, Methuen 1976

LIFE IN ANGLO-SAXON ENGLAND, R. I. Page, Batsford 1970
AN INTRODUCTION TO ANGLO-SAXON ENGLAND, P. Hunter Blair, Cambridge UP 1977 (2nd ed)
THE BEGINNINGS OF ENGLISH SOCIETY, D. Whitelock, Pelican 1952
THE VIKING WORLD, J. Simpson, Batsford 1980
FROM ROMAN BRITAIN TO NORMAN ENGLAND, P. H. Sawyer, Methuen 1978
BRITAIN IN THE DARK AGES, Ordnance Survey
BRITAIN BEFORE THE NORMAN CONQUEST, Ordnance Survey

The Later Middle Ages
THE DOMESDAY GEOGRAPHY OF ENGLAND, H. C. Darby, Cambridge UP (5 vols)
THE MEDIEVAL ENGLISH ECONOMY 1150–1500, J. L. Bolton, London UP 1980
NEW TOWNS OF THE MIDDLE AGES, M. Beresford, London UP 1967
PLAGUE, POPULATION AND THE ENGLISH ECONOMY 1348–1530, J. Hatcher, London UP 1977
ENGLISH CASTLES, R. A. Brown, London UP 1976
THE MEDIEVAL FENLAND, H. C. Darby, Cambridge UP 1940
THE ENGLISH WOOL TRADE IN THE MIDDLE AGES, T. H. Lloyd, Cambridge UP UP 1977
ENGLISH RURAL SOCIETY 1200–1350, J. Z. Titow, London UP 1969
THE LOST VILLAGES OF ENGLAND, M. Beresford, Lutterworth 1965
MONASTIC BRITAIN, Ordnance Survey 1968 (3rd ed)

The Tudors and Stuarts
THE ENGLISH CIVIL WARS: CONSERVATION AND REVOLUTION 1603–49, R. Ashton, Weidenfeld & Nicolson 1978
THE ECONOMY OF ENGLAND 1450–1750, D. C. Coleman, Oxford UP 1977
THE STUART AGE: A HISTORY OF ENGLAND 1603–1714, Barry Coward, Longmans 1980
CHURCH AND PEOPLE 1450–1660, Claire Cross, Fontana 1976
REFORM AND REFORMATION: ENGLAND 1509–1558, G. R. Elton, Edward Arnold 1977
COUNTRY AND COURT: ENGLAND 1658–1714, J. R. Jones, Edward Arnold 1978
GOVERNMENT AND COMMUNITY: ENGLAND 1450–1509, Edward Arnold 1980
THE CRISIS OF PARLIAMENTS: ENGLISH HISTORY 1509–1660, Conrad Russell, Oxford UP 1971
JOHN LELAND'S ITINERARY, ed. Thomas Hearne 1768; also THE ITINERARY OF JOHN LELAND IN OR ABOUT THE YEARS 1535–1543, ed. L. T. Smith 1906–1910 (5 vols)
WILLIAM CAMDEN'S BRITANNIA 1607, ed. G. J. Copley, Hutchinson 1977 (2 vols)
LATE TUDOR AND EARLY STUART GEOGRAPHY, E. G. R. Taylor 1933
THE DRAINING OF THE FENS, H. C. Darby, Cambridge UP 1956 (2nd ed)

The Industrial Revolution
THE FIRST INDUSTRIAL REVOLUTION, Phyllis Deane, Cambridge UP 1980
THE TOWN LABOURER, J. L. and Barbara Hammond, ed. J. Lovell, Longmans 1979
THE VILLAGE LABOURER, J. L. and Barbara Hammond, ed. G. E. Mingay, Longmans 1979
THE SKILLED LABOURER, J. L. and Barbara Hammond, ed. J. G. Rule, Longmans 1979
THE FIRST INDUSTRIAL NATION, Peter Mathias, Methuen 1969
LIFE AND LABOUR IN ENGLAND 1700–1880, R. W. Malcolmson, Hutchinson 1981
EIGHTEENTH CENTURY ENGLAND 1714–1784, Dorothy Marshall, Longmans 1975
THE AGE OF IMPROVEMENT 1783–1867, Asa Briggs, Longmans 1959
THE FIRST FOUR GEORGES, J. H. Plumb, Fontana 1966
ENGLISH PEOPLE IN THE EIGHTEENTH CENTURY, Dorothy George, Longmans 1956
HANOVERIAN LONDON 1714–1808, George Rude, Secker & Warburg 1971
GEORGIAN LONDON, J. Summerson, Barrie & Jenkins 1978
THE JOURNEYS OF CELIA FIENNES (1685–1703), ed. Christopher Morris, Gresset Press 1947
A TOUR THROUGH THE WHOLE OF GREAT BRITAIN C. 1707, Daniel Defoe, Dent (Everyman Edition) 1962
QUAKERS IN SCIENCE AND INDUSTRY, Arthur Raistrick, David & Charles 1968
INDUSTRIAL ARCHAEOLOGY IN BRITAIN, Angus Buchanan, Penguin 1972
THE BP BOOK OF INDUSTRIAL ARCHAEOLOGY, Neil Cossons, David & Charles 1975

The Victorian Era
VICTORIAN ENGLAND: PORTRAIT OF AN AGE, G. M. Young, Oxford UP 1953
DRINK AND THE VICTORIANS: THE TEMPERANCE QUESTION IN ENGLAND 1815–1872, Brian Harrison, Faber & Faber 1971
SUFFER AND BE STILL: WOMEN IN THE VICTORIAN AGE, ed. Martha Vicinus, Indiana UP 1973
OUTCAST LONDON: A STUDY IN THE RELATIONSHIP BETWEEN THE CLASSES IN VICTORIAN LONDON, Gareth Stedman Jones, Clarendon Press 1971
THE VICTORIAN CITY: IMAGES AND REALITIES, H. J. Dyos, Routledge & Kegan Paul 1973
THE VICTORIAN COUNTRY HOUSE, M. Girouard, Yale UP 1979
ENGLISH LANDED SOCIETY IN THE 19TH CENTURY, F. M. L. Thompson, Routledge & Kegan Paul 1963
VICTORIA R.I., Elizabeth Longford, Weidenfeld & Nicolson 1964
VICTORIAN CITIES, Asa Briggs, Pelican (various)
PAX BRITANNICA, James Morris, Faber & Faber 1968

Edward VII and the New Century
THE EDWARDIANS, J. B. Priestley, Heinemann 1970
EDWARDIAN ENGLAND 1901–1915, D. Read, Harrap 1972

The Inter-War Years
BRITAIN BETWEEN THE WARS 1918–1940, C. L. Mowat, Methuen 1955
THE LONG WEEKEND: A SOCIAL HISTORY OF GREAT BRITAIN 1918–1939, R. Graves and A. Hodge, Faber & Faber 1941

The Second World War
LIVING THROUGH THE BLITZ, Tom Harrison, Penguin 1978
HISTORY OF THE SECOND WORLD WAR, Winston Churchill, Cassell
THE PEOPLE'S WAR: BRITAIN 1939–1945, A. Calder, Cape 1969

PICTURE ACKNOWLEDGEMENTS

The Publishers would like to thank all those who provided photographs for this book.

All colour and line drawings were commissioned by and are the copyright of Midsummer Books Limited unless stated below. The outlines of the British Isles maps were prepared by the Ordnance Survey and are Crown Copyright but the additional artwork is the copyright of Midsummer Books Limited unless stated below. Maps and drawings are not included in the page-by-page credits.

Photographs credited to Midsummer Books were commissioned by and are the copyright of Midsummer Books Limited.

We are grateful to the British Museum (Natural History) for their permission to use as artist's reference drawings from their publications DINOSAURS AND THEIR LIVING RELATIVES and BRITISH PALAEOZOIC FOSSILS.

The geological map on page 15 is based on the map appearing in BRITAIN BEFORE MAN, a publication of the Geological Museum (Institute of Geological Sciences), who kindly allowed us to use it as artist's reference.

The line drawings of St Pancras Church on page 116 and the Great Eastern Hotel on page 147 are the copyright of Doreen Yarwood, under licence to Batsford & Co Ltd, and are taken from the book ARCHITECTURE IN BRITAIN by Doreen Yarwood, Batsford & Co 1979.

Photographs credited to the following organisations are Crown Copyright: Department of the Environment, Institute of Geological Sciences, National Monuments Record, National Railway Museum, Ordnance Survey, Public Records Office, Science Museum, Scottish Development Department.

Photographs credited to the British Museum appear by permission of the Trustees of the British Museum.

Photographs credited to the British Library appear by permission of the Trustees of the British Library.

Photographs have been credited by page number, from top to bottom and from left to right. Some abbreviations have been made as follows:

British Museum: BM
Department of the Environment: DOE
Institute of Agricultural History and Museum of English Rural Life, University of Reading: MERL
Institute of Geological Sciences: IGS
National Railway Museum: NRM

Page 10: IGS. **11:** IGS. **12:** IGS (all pictures). **13:** IGS (all pictures). **14:** IGS/IGS. **15:** IGS (all pictures). **16:** Aerofilms/Aerofilms/Cambridge Committee for Aerial Photography. **17:** Aerofilms/John Bethell/Heather Angel/Aerofilms/Heather Angel/Cambridge Committee for Aerial Photograph/Aerofilms/Aerofilms. **18:** Aerofilms. **19:** BM. **20:** Aerofilms. **21:** British Tourist Authority/Scottish Development Dept/BM/BM/DOE/DOE/DOE/BM/DOE/Salisbury & South Wilts Museum/BM/DOE. **22:** British Tourist Authority. **23:** Grosvenor Museum, Chester: Pictorial Colour Slides/BM/Grosvenor Museum, Chester: Pictorial Colour Slides/National Museum of Wales/BM/BM/BM. **24:** Aerofilms. **25:** Scottish Development Dept/Scctish Development Dept/BM/BM/BM/BM. **26:** Aerofilms. **27:** BM. **28:** National Monuments Record. **29:** Leicester Museum: Pictorial Colour Slides/Museum of London/Pictorial Colour Slides/Aerofilms/Unichrome: Bath Museum/British Tourist Authority. **30:** Cambridge Committee for Aerial Photography. **31:** DOE/DOE/Irish Tourist Board/IGS/North Yorkshire County Library. **32:** Ashmolean Museum/Ashmolean Museum/Verulamium Museum. **33:** BM/Verulamium Museum/BM/BM/BM/BM/BM/BM/BM/BM. **34:** Aerofilms. **35:** BM. **37:** Peter Jones. **38:** National Museum of Antiquities of Scotland/Midsummer/A. F. Kersting/Midsummer/Midsummer. **39:** A. F. Kersting/A. F. Kersting/Midsummer/Midsummer/Midsummer. **40:** Ashmolean Museum (all pictures). **41:** British Library/Ashmolean Museum/Ancient Art & Architecture Collection/British Library. **42:** Ashmolean Museum/Ashmolean Museum/Museum of London/British Library. **43:** Ancient Art & Architecture Collection/National Museum of Antiquities of Scotland/Scottish Development Dept/Museum of London/BM. **44:** Aerofilms. **45:** British Library. **46:** John Bethell/John Bethell. **47:** Public Record Office/Ancient Art & Architecture Collection. **48:** John Bethell. **49:** Aerofilms/John Bethell. **50:** The Dean and Chapter of Durham Cathedral/Midsummer/Woodmansterne (Clive Friend)/BTA. **51:** A. F. Kersting/BTA/Midsummer/A. F. Kersting/A. F. Kersting. **52:** John Bethell/John Bethell. **53:** Aerofilms. **54:** Victoria and Albert Museum/Bodleian Library. **55:** John Bethell/Aerofilms/John Bethell. **56:** Cooper Bridgeman Library, reproduced by courtesy of the Guildhall Library, London/Bodleian Library/Heather Angel. **57:** Heather Angel/Victoria and Albert Museum/John Bethell/British Library. **58:** Pitkin Pictorials Ltd. **59:** Aerofilms. **60:** Ashmolean Museum/British Library/Fotomas Index. **61:** British Library (all pictures). **62:** John Bethell. **63:** BM. **64:** MERL. **65:** Aerofilms/Bodleian Library. **66:** National Army Museum/Heather Angel. **67:** Aerofilms/John Bethell/John Bethell/Peter Jones. **68:** National Trust. **69:** National Trust/Pat Morris/John Bethell/John Bethell/John Bethell/John Bethell. **70:** Mansell Collection/John Bethell. **71:** Aerofilms/John Bethell. **72:** Aerofilms/A. F. Kersting/Pitkin Pictorials Ltd. **73:** Peter Mackenzie, Martin Johnston Ltd/Midsummer/Midsummer/Peter Mackenzie, Martin Johnston Ltd/Midsummer/Midsummer/Aerofilms/Midsummer/A. F. Kersting. **74:** Museum of London. **75:** National Trust/Woodmansterne Ltd/Woodmansterne Ltd. **76:** The Mansell Collection/The Mansell Collection. **77:** Woman's Realm/Castle Museum, York/John Bethell. **78:** National Maritime Museum/National Maritime Museum. **79:** BBC Hulton Picture Library/Pepys Library/Pepys Library (both by permission of the Master and Fellows of Magdalene College, Cambridge)/City of Kingston upon Hull Art Galleries. **80:** Museum of London. **81:** British Library/British Library/The Golden Hinde. **82:** Ashmolean Museum/Ashmolean Museum/National Portrait Gallery/National Portrait Gallery. **83:** National Portrait Gallery (all pictures. **84:** Derek Pratt. **85:** Science Museum. **86:** MERL/MERL. **87:** MERL/Pat Morris. **88:** MERL. **89:** MERL/MERL/Cambridge Committee for Aerial Photography/Aerofilms. **90:** Clive Coote. **91:** Styal Museum, Cheshire/Science Museum/Rod Teasdale. **92:** Furness Museum. **93:** North of England Open Air Museum, Beamish/North of England Open Air Museum, Beamish/Aerofilms/Pat Morris. **94:** Science Museum. **95:** Roger Worsley/Roger Worsley/The Thursford Collection/Brighton Engineerium/Roger Worsley. **96:** Ironbridge Gorge Museum Trust–Brian Bracegirdle. **97:** Ironbridge Gorge Museum Trust/British Tourist Authority/Ironbridge Gorge Museum Trust/The Furness Museum/Ironbridge Gorge Museum Trust–Brian Bracegirdle. **98:** Royal Institution of Cornwall. **99:** Royal Institution of Cornwall/IGS/Pat Morris/Aerofilms/Royal Institution of Cornwall/Royal Institution of Cornwall. **101:** Leeds City Libraries/Colne Valley Museum, Golcar, Huddersfield/City of Manchester Art Galleries/Illustrated London News. **102:** Aerofilms/Wedgwood Museum/Wedgwood Museum (both reproduced by permission of the Trustees of the Wedgwood Museum, Barlaston, Staffs). **103:** Fitzwilliam Museum; reproduced by permission of the Syndics of the Fitzwilliam Museum, Cambridge/Aerofilms/Mr E. P. Stanham/Ironbridge Gorge Museum Trust/British Tourist Authority. **104:** Scottish Labour History Society. **105:** Birmingham Public Library/MERL/Aerofilms/The Mansell Collection. **106:** John Bethell/Museum of London. **107:** John Bethell/Cooper Bridgeman Library/Science Museum/Castle Museum, York/British Tourist Authority. **108:** Cooper Bridgeman Library/British Waterways Board/British Waterways Board/British Waterways Board/British Waterways Board. **109:** Derek Pratt (all pictures). **110:** NRM. **111:** NRM/NRM/Humberside County Council/NRM/NRM/NRM. **112:** National Maritime Museum. **113:** Beamish

Towards a Post-Industrial Britain
THE BRITISH EXPERIENCE 1945–1975, P. Calvocoressi, Pelican 1979
THE SEVENTIES, Christopher Booker, Allen Lane 1980
FOOD, CLOTHING AND SHELTER: TWENTIETH CENTURY INDUSTRIAL ARCHAEOLOGY, Kenneth Hudson, Baker 1978
THE WELFARE STATE, Pauline Gregg, Harrap 1967
THE 1945 REVOLUTION, W. Harrington and P. Young, Davies Poynter 1978
THE PENDULUM YEARS – BRITAIN IN THE 1960s, Bernard Levin, Cape 1971

Architecture
ARCHITECTURE IN BRITAIN 1530–1830, J. Summerson, Penguin 1970
THE PATTERN OF ENGLISH BUILDING, A. Clifton-Taylor, Faber & Faber 1972
THE ILLUSTRATED HANDBOOK OF VERNACULAR ARCHITECTURE, R. W. Brunskill, Faber & Faber 1971
THE ARCHITECTURE OF BRITAIN, Doreen Yarwood, Batsford 1976
VICTORIAN ARCHITECTURE, R. Dixon and S. Muthesius, Thames & Hudson 1978
THE BUILDINGS OF ENGLAND, WALES, SCOTLAND AND IRELAND, ed. N. Pevsner, Penguin (49 vols to date)
GUIDE TO PARISH CHURCHES OF ENGLAND AND WALES, ed. John Betjeman, Collins 1980 (4th ed)
THE ARCHITECTURAL SETTING OF ANGLICAN WORSHIP, G. W. O. Addleshaw and F. Etchells, Faber & Faber 1948
CATHOLIC CHURCHES SINCE 1623, B. Little, Robert Hale 1966
CHURCH BUILDERS OF THE NINETEENTH CENTURY, B. F. L. Clarke, David & Charles 1969 (2nd ed)
FASHIONS IN CHURCH BUILDING, P. F. Anson, Faith Press 1965 (2nd ed)

Agriculture, Forestry and Rural Crafts
THE AGRARIAN HISTORY OF ENGLAND AND WALES, Cambridge UP (3 vols)
THE FARMER'S TOOLS 1500–1900, G. E. Fussell, Orbis 1981 (2nd ed)
A HISTORY OF FARM BUILDINGS IN ENGLAND AND WALES, N. Harvey, David & Charles 1970
THE INDUSTRIAL ARCHAEOLOGY OF FARMING IN ENGLAND AND WALES, N. Harvey, Batsford 1980
THE ENGLISH FARM WAGON, J. G. Jenkins, David & Charles 1971 (2nd ed)
HISTORY OF ENGLISH AGRICULTURE 1846–1914, C. Orwin and E. H. Whetham, David & Charles 1971 (2nd ed)
ANCIENT WOODLAND: ITS HISTORY AND VEGETATION AND USES IN ENGLAND, O. Rackham, Edward Arnold 1980
THE EVOLUTION OF THE ENGLISH FARM, M. E. Seebohm, Allen & Unwin 1976 (2nd ed)
FIELDS IN THE ENGLISH LANDSCAPE, C. Taylor, Dent 1975
RURAL CRAFTS OF ENGLAND, K. S. Woods, Educational Press 1975
COMMON FIELDS AND ENCLOSURES IN ENGLAND 1450–1850, J. A. Yelling, Macmillan 1977
WOODLAND CRAFTS IN BRITAIN, H. L. Edlin, David & Charles 1974
TREES AND WOODLAND IN THE BRITISH LANDSCAPE, O. Rackham, Dent 1976
SICKLE TO COMBINE, E. J. T. Collins, University of Reading 1969

STUDIES OF FIELD SYSTEMS IN THE BRITISH ISLES, ed. A. R. H. Baker and R. A. Butlin, Cambridge UP 1973
ENGLISH FARMHOUSE AND COTTAGE, M. W. Barley, Routledge & Kegan Paul 1961

Transport
BRITISH CANALS: AN ILLUSTRATED HISTORY, Charles Hadfield, Phoenix House 1959
BRITISH TRANSPORT: AN ECONOMIC SURVEY FROM THE 17TH CENTURY TO THE 20TH, H. J. Dyos and D. H. Aldcroft, Leicester University Press 1969
EARLY DAYS ON THE ROAD, Lord Montagu of Beaulieu and G. N. Georgano, Michael Joseph 1974
A HISTORY OF LONDON TRANSPORT, T. C. Barker and M. Robbins, Allen & Unwin (3 vols)
BRITISH TRANSPORT SINCE 1914, D. H. Aldcroft, David & Charles 1975
EARLY BRITISH RAILWAYS, H. G. Lewin, Locomotive Publishing Co 1926
THE RAILWAY MANIA AND ITS AFTERMATH, H. G. Lewin, David & Charles 1968
RAILWAYS IN THE VICTORIAN ECONOMY, Reed, David & Charles 1969
THE BRITISH STEAM RAILWAY LOCOMOTIVE, Ahrons, Ian Allan 1966
THE ILLUSTRATED HISTORY OF RAILWAYS IN BRITAIN, Allen, Marshall Cavendish 1979
LONDON'S TRAMS AND TROLLEYBUSES, John Day, London Transport 1977
TUBE TRAINS UNDER LONDON, J. Graeme Bruce, London Transport 1972
THE STORY OF LONDON'S UNDERGROUND, John Day, London Transport 1979
THE ROMANCE OF METROLAND, Ron Pigram and Denis Edwards, Micas 1979
THE DOCKERS: CLASS AND TRADITION IN LONDON, Stephen Hill, Heinemann 1976
LONDON'S DOCKS, John Pudney, Thames & Hudson 1975
THE MAJOR SEA PORTS OF THE UNITED KINGDOM, J. H. Bird, Hutchinson 1963
MOTORWAYS, James Drake with H. L. Yeadon and D. I. Evans, Faber & Faber 1969

Numismatics
ENGLISH COINS FROM THE 7TH CENTURY TO THE PRESENT DAY, G. C. Brooke, Methuen 1950 (3rd ed)
ENGLISH COINAGE 600–1900, C. H. U. Sutherland, Batsford 1972
THE MINT: A HISTORY OF THE LONDON MINT FROM AD 287 TO 1948, Sir John Craig, Cambridge UP 1953
THE COINAGE OF ANCIENT BRITAIN, R. P. Mark, Spink & Seaby 1975
COINAGE AND CURRENCY IN ROMAN BRITAIN, C. H. U. Sutherland, Oxford UP 1937

Leisure
TIME TO SPARE IN VICTORIAN ENGLAND, J. Lowerson and John Myerscough, Harvester Press 1977
LEISURE IN THE INDUSTRIAL REVOLUTION, H. Cunningham, Croom Helm 1980
POPULAR RECREATION IN ENGLISH SOCIETY 1700–1850, R. W. Malcolmson, Cambridge UP 1973
LEISURE AND SOCIETY 1830–1950, J. Walvin, Longmans 1978
THE LIFE AND SPORT OF THE INN, M. Brander, Gentry Books 1973

INDEX

Page numbers in ordinary type denote a mention in the main narrative text, numbers in *italics* denote box text and numbers in **bold** denote a picture.

Apart from significant British royalty and politicians, the text of the 'Events and Personalities' boxes has not been indexed as it is not the function of this book to cover constitutional and international events in detail. Please refer to these boxes if the name you require does not appear here.